The Art of
Ballets Russes

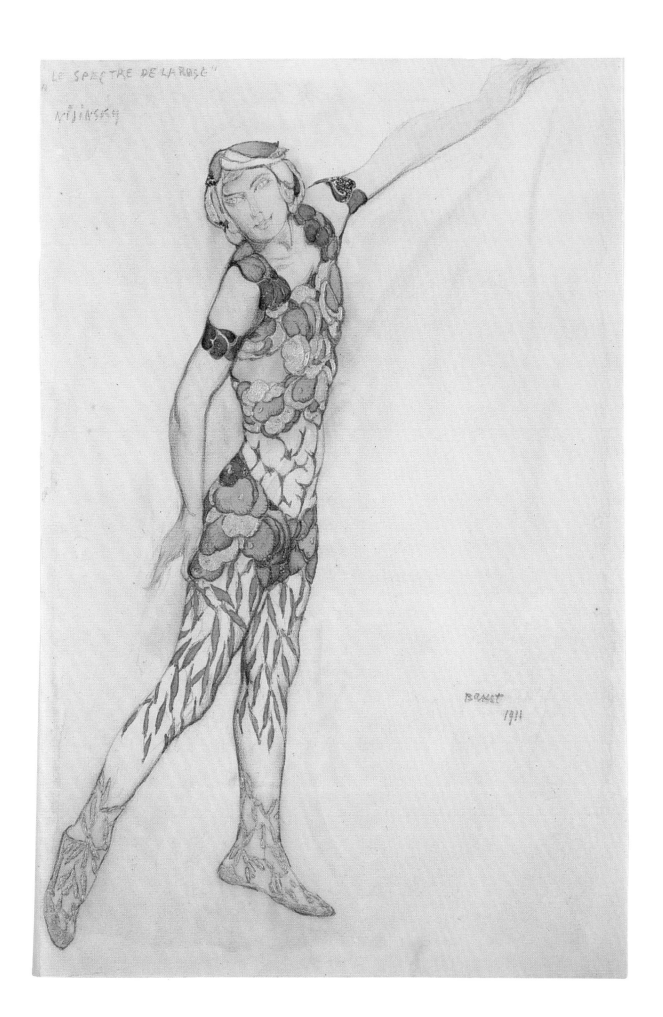

LE SPECTRE DE LA ROSE"

NIJINSKY

BAKST
1911

The Art of Ballets Russes

The Serge Lifar Collection of Theater Designs, Costumes,
and Paintings at the Wadsworth Atheneum,
Hartford, Connecticut

ALEXANDER SCHOUVALOFF

YALE UNIVERSITY PRESS

NEW HAVEN AND LONDON

IN ASSOCIATION WITH THE WADSWORTH ATHENEUM

This catalogue is published in conjunction with the exhibition *Design, Dance and Music of the Ballets Russes 1909–1929*, organized by the Wadsworth Atheneum.

Distributed by Yale University Press, New Haven and London, for the Wadsworth Atheneum.

The exhibition and the catalogue were made possible by generous grants from the following sources:

The National Endowment for the Arts
United Technologies Corporation
The John G. Martin Foundation.

Additional support was provided by The Robert Wood Johnson 1962 Charitable Trust; The Edward C. and Ann T. Roberts Foundation; The Silas Chapman, Jr. Fund for Conservation; The Costume and Textile Society of the Wadsworth Atheneum; The Katherine S. Hoffman and Dr. Anthony S. Krausen Fund; The European Fine Arts and Decorative Arts Fund; The Bari Lipp Foundation.

Exhibition dates
Wadsworth Atheneum, Hartford, CT
7 September 1997–4 January 1998

Sezon Museum of Art, Tokyo, Japan
13 June–3 August 1998

Shiga Museum, Shiga, Japan
22 August–11 October 1998

Frontispiece: Léon Bakst, Costume design for Vaslav Nijinsky as the Rose in *Le Spectre de la Rose*, 1911 (see page 68).

Editing, design and production: Jane Havell

Typeset in Palatino and Frutiger
Printed in Italy by Conti Tipocolor

Library of Congress Cataloging-in-Publication Data

Schouvaloff, Alexander.
    The Art of Ballets Russes : the Serge Lifar Collection of Theater Designs, Costumes, and Paintings at the Wadsworth Atheneum, Hartford, Connecticut/Alexander Schouvaloff.
       p.   cm.
    Includes bibliographical references (p.   ) and index.
    ISBN 0-300-07484-0 (hardback)
    1 Ballet—Costume—Exhibitions. 2. Ballet—Stage-setting and scenery—Exhibitions. 3. Ballets Russes—Exhibitions. 4. Lifar, Serge, 1905–
I. Wadsworth Atheneum. II. Title.
GV1789.2. S36 1997
792.8'0947—dc21   97–42146
                                                    CIP

Contents

Preface and Acknowledgments

The scene is an office in London's Theatre Museum late one afternoon in 1979. Enter a young secretary announcing, "A Mr Serge Lifar to see you." A sparkling, lithe, dark figure in a black overcoat springs into the room. I greet him, astonished by his visit and rather overawed. He is unmistakable, and I quickly convince myself that I remember years ago seeing him dance, like a panther; yes, I am sure I saw him dance. We talk in Russian long into the evening; well, he talks and I listen, enthralled. Here is Diaghilev's last great dancer, remembering. Lifar is touching and modest in his devotion to his mentor. 1979 is fifty years after Diaghilev's death, and commemorative exhibitions are planned. Seventy years earlier, Diaghilev and the Ballets Russes had reinvented the art of ballet and, after 1929, surviving members of his company had ensured that the art would continue and prosper: George Balanchine in the United States with what became the New York City Ballet; Ninette de Valois in England with what became The Royal Ballet, and Serge Lifar in France with the ballet of the Paris Opéra.

It was Lifar, most of all, who had kept the memory of Diaghilev and his work alive while continuing with his own distinguished career. He wrote a forthright but loving biography of Diaghilev's life and work using the extensive and invaluable archive he had inherited; gave lectures; organised and lent works to exhibitions, and, as an ultimate distinction, arranged to have the square behind the Opéra in Paris renamed in Diaghilev's honor. He already had a significant collection of designs when Diaghilev died in 1929, and he continued to enlarge it. Lifar arranged the first great retrospective Diaghilev exhibitions in Paris in 1930 and 1939; between these two events, he was forced to sell a major part of his collection, of which this is the catalogue. The Wadsworth Atheneum cleverly snapped it up, and it must have been galling for Lifar to have to borrow most of it back for the 1939 show. In fact, no exhibition on the Ballets Russes can now be seriously contemplated without relying heavily on this collection. Richard Buckle would certainly not have been able to redefine the word "exhibition" with his startlingly brilliant and now legendary Diaghilev exhibition in 1954 without the Wadsworth Atheneum's extensive loan. Indeed, the museum has been very, perhaps even too, generous in its willingness to lend. But the generosity is justified: when one sees the collection, comprised of designs by the greatest artists of the twentieth century, one realises what an amazingly creative period was masterminded by that unique artistic director who was Diaghilev, and what an enormous and lasting contribution his Ballets Russes made to the cultural life of Europe and America.

The muster-roll of the artists, composers, conductors, directors, singers, choreographers, and dancers who appeared with the Ballets Russes during its twenty-year history, and who are recorded in this catalogue, is a magic list of famous names compiled by Diaghilev, the chief magician. Some of the ballets described here have disappeared, some are revived from time to time as museum pieces or in new versions, but a surprising number have remained in the repertory of the major ballet companies throughout the world and are revived with regular frequency to delight new audiences. I have fortunately been able to see several of them while working on this catalogue. Some were ostensibly genuine revivals—such as *Schéhérazade* performed in its original 1914 scenery, dis-

10

covered in 1992 in a store in Stockholm—others, such as *Petrushka*, were recreations. They were thrilling to see. I began to have an inkling of what they must all have been like when they were first performed, but I could also tell somehow that what I was seeing was no longer the authentic thing. Time had blurred the details, carelessness had intervened. No one now remembers seeing the early ballets, very few are left who remember seeing the later ones. No one could tell me what was right—and memory, in any case, is usually imperfect, as perhaps was my memory of Lifar dancing. Richard Buckle remembered a conversation he had had with Tamara Karsavina. He said that Lydia Sokolova had told him that she had taught her the part of the Miller's wife in *Le Tricorne*. Karsavina, rolling her eyes, had replied, "Lydia has very good memory, but she tends to rely upon it too much." In writing this catalogue I have had to rely on many memories, mostly written, but people tend to remember only what they want others to know. The truth is a different matter: even critics, who have all seen the same thing, reach different conclusions about what they saw. There is, however, one certainty: it was defined by Cyril W. Beaumont, an honest writer who saw all the productions from 1912 to 1929, when he wrote that the hours he had spent seeing the Russian ballet were "never-to-be-forgotten hours whose aesthetic joys still remain unmatched." Although the Ballets Russes no longer exist, their influence is still all-pervasive. The most damning criticism I ever heard of a ballet made after 1929 is: "It's as if Diaghilev had never existed."

This collection, however, is not exclusively devoted to items relating to the Ballets Russes; other productions are included, and other drawings and paintings, including several portraits of Serge Lifar. The Wadsworth Atheneum was lucky in acquiring it as a collection when it did, in 1933. Although Lifar did not relinquish everything then, what was left was mostly finally dispersed at auction in 1984, two years before he died. This collection therefore remains his best memorial.

✳

Many people have very kindly helped me during the preparation of this catalogue. I should like to express my grateful thanks to Asya Chorley and Geraldine Morris for their frequent pertinent advice; to Elena Gaginskaya, Maria Polkanova and Vladimir Gvozdev for providing me with details about productions in Russia; to Mme Françoise Renault Bauchant for telling me about her uncle André Bauchant; to Marina Bowater and John Mollo for telling me about his father Eugene Mollo; to Bettina McNulty and Jane England of England & Co for telling me about Sir Francis Rose; to Janis Ekdahl, Acting Director of the Library, The Museum of Modern Art, New York, for information about Pavel Tchelitchew; to M Daniel Aubry of the Société des Bains de Mer, Monte Carlo, for giving me information about performances in Monte Carlo and for sending me photographs; to Lisbet Grandjean of the Teatermuseet, Copenhagen, for sending me details about the production of *Petrushka* in Copenhagen; to Frances Pritchard of the Whitworth Art Gallery, Manchester, for advising me about Natalia Gontcharova's costumes for *Les Noces*; to Madeleine Nichols of the Dance Collection, New York Public Library, New York; to Pierre Vidal of the Bibliothèque-Musée of the Opéra, Paris; to Sarah Woodcock, Leela Meinertas, and Andrew Kerr of the Theatre Museum, London, for their unstinting help whenever I visited their collections and archives.

Most especially I should like to thank Cynthia Roman, Curatorial Assistant at the Wadsworth Atheneum, for her detailed and painstaking help in compiling the list of exhibitions. During the preparation of this catalogue the museum added to its collection by acquiring a number of original costumes from Diaghilev's Ballets Russes. I am exceedingly grateful to Carol Dean Krute, Curator of Costume and Textiles, for providing the detailed descriptions.

I owe particular thanks to Laura Phillips for so generously letting me read and quote from the unpublished diaries of her grandmother, Florence E. Grenfell, a devoted admirer and generous patron of Diaghilev's Ballets Russes.

I also owe a huge debt of gratitude to Jane Havell, who edited this book with such patient efficiency and designed it with great sensitivity.

And I thank Jean Cadogan, who was the Charles and Eleanor Lamont Cunningham Curator of European Art at the Wadsworth Atheneum, for giving me the opportunity to discover the Lifar Collection, and my wife, Daria, for sharing that discovery with me.

ALEXANDER SCHOUVALOFF
LONDON 1997

The Lifar Collection in the Wadsworth Atheneum

Jean K. Cadogan

A. Everett Austin, Jr., 1936, photographed by George Platt Lynes.

When the Wadsworth Atheneum acquired from Serge Lifar his collection of set and costume designs for the Ballets Russes in 1933, it was in the midst of one of the most extraordinary renaissances in modern museum history. Only a few years before, in 1927, a new director had been appointed, A. Everett "Chick" Austin, then twenty-six years old and fresh from Harvard and international study. His arrival preceded by only two months the bequest of Frank Chester Sumner, which came to the museum after the death of Mary Catlin Sumner on 11 August 1927. Sumner's bequest, at the time just over one million dollars, was to be used as an endowment for the purchase of paintings, to be known as the Ella Gallup Sumner and Mary Catlin Sumner Collection.[1]

A man of myriad interests, Austin, at the advent of the Sumner bequest, threw himself into the task of forging "a small but distinguished collection" in the Atheneum, whose offerings at the time were a decidedly mixed bag. Austin at first proceeded predictably, given his schooling in the history of art at Harvard and his surveillance by Edward Forbes, then director of the Fogg Museum at Harvard and honorary director of the Atheneum. His first acquisitions reflect the Fogg taste for old master pictures, especially of the Italian Renaissance. In early 1928 he bought, in conjunction with Forbes, a painting by the Venetian master Tintoretto, *Hercules and Antaeus*, and a panel fragment by the Florentine Fra Angelico, *Head of an Angel*.[2] His intentions, articulated in the local press on the occasion of his first exhibition, *Distinguished Works of Art*, in January, 1928, were to seek out objects of great quality, regardless of century or national school, and to concentrate his financial resources, purchasing only one picture per year.[3]

In spite of his professed acquisition policy devoted to the highest quality objects, Austin's own omnivorous tastes soon led him to acquisitions seemingly in direct opposition to his stated goals. In particular, the notion of buying one great object per year seems to have gone immediately by the board. The list of acquisitions for the late 1920s and early 1930s is not only long but has an almost dizzying variety, ranging from an anonymous fifteenth-century French *Pietà* to Blackburn's *Portrait of Sir Francis Bernard, Governor of Massachusetts*. At the same time, the Sumner Bequest's stipulation that the funds be used for the purchase of paintings seems to have been broadly interpreted; Edward Hopper's watercolor of *Captain Strout's House, Portland*, was the second Sumner purchase in 1928, immediately following the Tintoretto. Clearly, in Austin's mind, watercolors on paper were paintings, too; but there was another reason for his frequent drawing acquisitions. In a letter to the editor of the Hartford *Times* in 1929, Austin responded to a critic of his policies: "In the investment of funds in pictures, it is the wisest course always for the Museum to place its income in works of certain and recognized value rather than to run the risk of buying expensive paintings by modern artists, the value of which may be considerably lowered by the criticism of the next generation. However, the policy of buying water-colors in a sound one, as in this way much smaller amounts are involved."[4]

This was the rationale behind the acquisition of many beautiful "modern" drawings at this time: a *Still life* by Charles Demuth, the *Mountebanks Changing Place* by Daumier, Hopper's *Rockland Harbor, Maine*, and Cezanne's *Bather*, all bought with Sumner funds.

Austin's acquisitions with the Sumner bequest came to an abrupt halt in 1932, with the purchase of a mythological painting by the Florentine early Renaissance artist Piero di Cosimo, *The Finding of Vulcan on Lemnos*.[5] Austin purchased the picture from the dealer Duveen, for the then considerable sum of $100,000—more than twice what he had paid for any picture to date. While hailed as a masterpiece—which it undoubtedly is—it nonetheless soaked up acquisition funds for the better part of two years. When the money came back on stream again in late 1933, there was a perceptible change in Austin's acquisitions. In practice, the notion of buying one great picture a year did not appeal to his acquisitive yearnings. Moreover, he became increasingly convinced of the incongruity of price and quality in the art market. With confidence in his eye and judgment, honed over the first five years of his directorship, he embarked on a more intuitive and personal acquisition strategy.

It was at just this moment that the Lifar collection became available through the art dealer Julien Levy, under circumstances outlined by Alexander Schouvaloff in his introductory essay (see pp 21–23). The Lifar collection brought together aspects of Austin's taste that had been evident singly in acquisitions and exhibitions up to this time. Foremost was his interest in modern art which—under the tutelage of his Harvard colleague Henry Russell Hitchcock, then teaching at Wesleyan University in nearby Middletown, his friend James Thrall Soby, a collector and scholar who became curator of paintings and sculpture at the Museum of Modern Art in New York, and Levy himself— had broadened to embrace truly contemporary ideas of abstraction and formalism as well as newer movements such as surrealism and neo-romanticism. In a 1930 lecture, Austin had adhered to the party line of modern art, first articulated by the artists of the late nineteenth century, that celebrated the purely visual design elements of art: "All great paintings can be enjoyed in fragments, if the quality is good enough. The appeal is through design, color, surface texture and not through literary ideas, which have no place in painting . . . . A painting must not tell a story."[6]

By 1933, his views had changed to embrace subject matter and figuration as legitimate components of modern art, as proposed by some contemporary artists in opposition to formalism. The exhibition *Literature and Poetry in Painting* in 1933 was a strikingly novel exposition of this enriched view of contemporary art. In this show Austin exhibited nineteenth- and early twentieth-century pictures in pairs, in order to demonstrate the literary content of contemporary art: Picasso hung next to Puvis, Gerome to Dali, and Monet to de Chirico. Russell Hitchcock, writing in the introduction to the catalogue, stated the motivating idea forcefully: "The antithesis between form and content, between technical matters and poetry, rather generally accepted by the modern mind, is based on a misinterpretation. Perhaps only the Impressionists at their purest, and the Cubists, really established a way of painting in which the subject matter was not only of little interest to the lay mind, but relatively unimportant in the aesthetic whole."[7]

The broadening of Austin's view of modern art is traceable as well in other exhibitions he undertook in the early 1930s, many of them the first of their kind, including the first exhibition of photography at the Atheneum from the collection of the Harvard Society for Contemporary Art (from 7–19 December 1930); Modern German art (19 May–2 June 1930); the surrealist painter Giorgio de

Julien Levy, c. 1931–39, photographed by Jan Leyda.

Chirico (1930); "Newer Super-Realism" (15 November–6 December 1931); the first exhibition of the surrealists in America; the neo-Romantics Tchelitchew, Berman, Leonid, and Bérard (15 April–16 May 1931); and Picasso (6 February–1 March 1934), on the occasion of the Avery Memorial's inauguration.

Austin's interest in contemporary art was more than just a response to the contemporary scene; it affected his activities in the old master field as well. He was increasingly convinced of the relevance of contemporary art to the art of the past; some years later he wrote: "contemporary art has always a double importance. Besides its own intrinsic interest, it is perpetually leading us into some new part of the past which has been forgotten."[8] The exhibitions of earlier art that he staged during the 1930s, highlighting themes of landscape, still life, portraiture, and baroque painting, unfailingly treat their subjects as historical antecedents to contemporary movements. In the exhibition *The Painters of Still Life* of 1938, Austin rejected the notion of still life painting as an exercise in formalism and celebrated the integrity of objects. In the introduction to the catalogue Austin (and co-author Hitchcock) emphasized, in an analogy with surrealist paintings, the thematic potency of objects illusionistically rendered and suggestively juxtaposed. Included were paintings by Dali, Matisse, Braque, and Miró, as well as a Cornell box, "a composition of real objects." The exhibition *Forty-three Portraits* of 1937 included a portrait by Salvador Dali, in reference to which Austin noted in his introduction, "Only within the last five years, with the various forms of reaction against abstract art, has the portrait . . . entered upon a revival."[9]

Austin's acquisitions of old master paintings were also infused with a sense of the continuity of past and present. His acquisition in 1934 of a major landscape by Salvator Rosa, *Landscape with Tobias and the Angel*, a perfect example of proto-romantic sensibility in the seventeenth century, followed closely on the exhibition of the neo-Romantics Tchelitchew, Berman, Leonid and Bérard.[10] *The Finding of Vulcan* by Piero di Cosimo, the artist claimed by surrealist theorist André Breton as the spiritual ancestor of the modern surrealists, was bought within a year of the exhibition "Newer Super-Realism." The Dali *Apparition of a Face and Fruit Dish on a Beach*, a celebrated example of the Surrealist double image, was bought in 1939, the same year as the Archimboldesque pair *Spring* and *Summer*; in which reclining allegorical figures are composed of fruits and flowers.[11] Valdés Leal's *Vanitas* was purchased in 1939, almost contemporary with the purchase of its modern equivalent, Balthus's *Still Life in Violence*.[12]

If Austin's broadening interest in contemporary art led him to jump at the purchase of Lifar's collection, so too his longstanding interest in theater fired his enthusiasm. Not only was he a devotee of theater and ballet, but also he was a performer, notably as Hamlet in the 1941 performance in Hartford, which he also directed, but also as "The Great Osram" in memorable magic shows. T. H. Parker described Austin as a magician: "In magic, Mr. Austin preferred the illusions to the simple tricks. The illusions were again a union of the arts, for he produced them in wondrous settings often accompanied by music and ballet, and he performed and presided over them with a patter of wit, sophistication and suavity that made his acts unrivaled in the world of presto-change-o."[13]

The search for the unity of the arts that Parker notes in Austin's own performances was undoubtedly fueled by his appreciation of Diaghilev's Ballets Russes when he first encountered them in London in June 1923. The ideal of the *Gesamtkunstwerk*, first embodied by nineteenth-century opera, found its twentieth-century equivalent in Diaghilev's sumptuous productions. But Austin was characteristically interested in antecedents: he had already staged an exhibition of the history of baroque theater in 1929.[14] Moreover, the fascination with illusion—and reality, its counterpart—evident in his magic shows also found its outlet in Austin's interest in Baroque painting. He emphasized the essential theatrical nature of the baroque in an essay he wrote for the *Art News*: "Today the adverse critics of the Baroque find it over-theatrical and pretentious. They merely fail to comprehend its true greatness. Theatrical it may be . . . . The world itself had become a vast and exciting stage."[15] Indeed, his interest in Baroque painting had evolved through the 1930s to concentrate on its realism and its drama. Caravaggesque illusionism, with its precisely described surfaces and dramatic light effects, had come to dominate his acquisitions. The list of seventeenth-century realist pictures acquired through the 1930s ranges from Le Nain's *Peasants in a Landscape*, Poussin's *Crucifixion*, Melendez's *Still Life with Pigeon*, Sweerts's *Head of a Boy* and *Burying the Dead*, and Cavallino's *Flight into Egypt* to Caravaggio's *St Francis* and many others. Austin's Old Master exhibitions also reflect his fascination with theater; the startlingly novel exhibition *Night Scenes* of 1940 again focussed on an aspect of baroque painting, its dramatic light effects, and illustrated the theme in art from the sixteenth through the twentieth centuries.[16] In the exhibition, no fewer than fifteen paintings in the Atheneum's collection, all acquired by Austin, were shown, including Leandro Bassano's *Flagellation of Christ*, van Orley's and Poussin's *Crucifixion*s, and the Caravaggio *St Francis*, acquired in 1943.

The link between the theatrical in history and in the present was made by Austin himself in his characterization of Diaghilev as "the last of the great Baroque princes . . . who knit together the arts of painting, music, literature, acting and choreography into a brilliant pattern . . ."[17] Certainly Austin saw himself in this light, as did others. T. H. Parker stresses the theatrical nature of his personality: "The peculiar attribute of Mr. Austin's genius was a flair for the dramatic . . . . His spirit, at least, was primarily of the theater. The other worlds were part of his stage . . . . But viewed from the grander point, and certainly that was the vantage from which Mr. Austin looked upon things, life and theater were interchangeable experiences to him."[18]

The last—but not least—of the themes that drove Austin to secure Lifar's collection was his passion for ballet. Indeed, in a remarkable scheme in 1933, he was instrumental, along with Lincoln Kirstein, James Thrall Soby, Paul Cooley, and Edward Warburg, in sponsoring the emigration to America of George Balanchine, Diaghilev's principal choreographer in his later career. The oft-told tale of Austin's efforts to organize a ballet company and school in the Wadsworth Atheneum headed by Balanchine led to an ignominious conclusion: Balanchine, after barely a week, returned to New York, where he eventually founded the School of American Ballet and established classic dance in America. As Kirstein wrote years later: "That the whole notion of the founding of a ballet school and a ballet company in Hartford was mad is self-evident. However, it all but happened, and without the chance that it might have happened, who can say whether or not Balanchine would ever have come to New York, rather than pursuing a logical European career as was certainly indicated?"[19]

The motivating force behind this unlikely scheme was something greater than ballet. As Kirstein perceptively noted, "It was Chick's constant conviction that a museum is alive, that art is only active when breathed upon by the lively muses." His attempt to bring performances into the museum that would, in Kirstein's words, equal "in intrinsic interest and excellence the important objects of a museum's permanent historic collection" is perhaps Austin's most individual and most lasting legacy, not just to the Wadsworth Atheneum but to all

The $10,000 check paid to Julien Levy in 1933 for the Serge Lifar Collection.

American museums.[20] When the Avery Memorial opened in 1934, it was the first modern museum with a theater; now they are standard equipment. The lively variety of programs Austin brought to Hartford, including films, lectures, concerts, and balls, is equally widespread. His vision of the museum—unique in the 1930s—as not just a repository for old art, but as a lively center where past and present come together, is today pervasive.[21]

In his purchase of the Lifar collection, Austin in one fell swoop secured for the museum the visual documentation for the emergence of modernism not only in the theater but in western art generally. Productions represented every year of Diaghilev's activity and chart the history of the Ballets Russes, from the eighteenth-century revival style of *Le Pavillon d'Armide*, one of Diaghilev's first Paris productions, to the exoticism of *Schéhérazade*, to the daring musical and choreographic innovations of Stravinsky and Nijinsky in *Le Sacre du Printemps*, to the first choreographic efforts of the young Balanchine in *Jack-in-the-Box*, *La Chatte*, *Le Bal*, and *Le Fils Prodigue*. The artists represented in the collection embraced all the major movements of modern art, from the Russians Bakst and Benois, to major figures of the school of Paris—Picasso, Matisse, Derain, Léger, Rouault, Cocteau—to the surrealists Ernst, Miró and de Chirico, and the neo-Romantics Tchelitchew and Bérard.

Though he failed in his attempt to establish a ballet school in Hartford, Austin's acquisition of the Lifar collection helped salve the wound. Lincoln Kirstein, his partner in the ill-fated scheme, described his reaction to the collapse of their plans: "I was whipped and sullen, disappointed and ignorant as to where to put the blame. . . . I smouldered; I obviously could never see Chick again." Yet Kirstein was back in Hartford six months later, lecturing on Russian ballet and Balanchine, with reference to the Lifar collection. Kirstein goes on to a succinct, but apt, assessment: "To acquire the Lifar Collection for Hartford was a master stroke. . . . It is fair to say that there was not another museum director in the country who realized the significance of this collection. It has been loaned all over the world and reproduced widely. It is one of the most influential and useful bodies of practical historic materials that exists. It is the inspiration of theatrical designers everywhere."[22]

Austin had succeeded in another of his objectives, penned in Edward Forbes's hand at the very beginning of his directorship, to "make Hartford a place of pilgrimage."[23] "These pictures," he wrote of the Lifar collection, "will be a Mecca for art and ballet lovers," and so they are today.[24]

Notes

1 See A. Galonska, "The Sumner Collection: The First Fifty Years," 1977, typescript in Wadsworth Atheneum curatorial file; E. R. Gaddis, ed, *Avery Memorial, Wadsworth Atheneum: The First Modern Museum*, 1984; J. Cadogan, "Introduction: the formation of 'a small but distinguished collection,'" in J. Cadogan, ed, *Wadsworth Atheneum Paintings II: Italy and Spain, Fourteenth through Nineteenth Centuries*, Hartford, 1991, pp 11–21.

2 See Cadogan, ed, 1991, pp 42–44, 247–48.

3 "Atheneum Buys a Noted Tintoretto," Hartford *Times*, 25 January 1928.

4 A. E. Austin, 19 February 1929, curatorial file.

5 Cadogan, ed, 1991, pp 122–26.

6 "Austin Speaks on Abstract Art," Hartford *Times*, 21 November 1930.

7 Hartford, Wadsworth Atheneum, *Literature and Poetry in Painting since 1850*, 24 January– 14 February 1933, p 5.

8 Hartford, Wadsworth Atheneum, *The Painters of Still Life*, 25 January–15 February 1938.

9 Hartford, Wadsworth Atheneum, *Forty-three Portraits*, 26 January–10 February 1937, n.p.

10 Austin had acquired the small *Night Scene with Two Figures*, then attributed to Rosa, in 1930; it is now considered a later work in Rosa's style; see Cadogan, ed, 1991, p 218; the large *Landscape with Tobias and the Angel* was acquired in 1934; see Cadogan, ed, 1991, pp 212–13. The neo-Romantics were first exhibited in America as *Five Young French Painters*, 15 April–16 May 1931.

11 For this pair of paintings by an unknown North Italian artist of the seventeenth century, see Cadogan, ed, 1991, pp 268–70.

12 For the *Vanitas* by Valdés Leal, see Cadogan, ed, 1991, pp 325–27.

13 T. H. Parker, "A. Everett Austin, Jr. and the Theatre," in *A. Everett Austin, Jr.: A Director's Taste and Achievement*, Wadsworth Atheneum, Hartford, 1958, p 57.

14 H.-R. Hitchcock, "The Baroque Theatre," *Wadsworth Atheneum Bulletin*, VIII, no 1, January 1930, pp 12–14.

15 A. Everett Austin, Jr, "The Baroque," *Art News Annual*, II, November 1949, p 12.

16 Hartford, Wadsworth Atheneum, *Night Scenes*, 15 February–7 March 1940.

17 A. Everett Austin, Jr., "The Lifar Collection," *Wadsworth Atheneum Report for 1933 and Bulletin*, XII, no. 2, October–December 1934, p 30.

18 Parker, *op cit*, 1958, p 53.

19 L. Kirstein, "The Ballet in Hartford," in Hartford, Wadsworth Atheneum, *A. Everett Austin, Jr.: A Director's Taste and Achievement*, 1958, p 67.

20 Kirstein, *op cit*, p 65.

21 Further information is provided in the "Foreword" by Henry-Russell Hitchcock and "'The New Athens': Moments from an Era," by Eugene R. Gaddis, in Gaddis, ed, 1984, pp 13–14, 33–58.

22 Kirstein, *op cit*, p 69.

23 Austin papers, box 35, Wadsworth Atheneum Archives.

24 Hartford *Times*, 2 December 1933.

The Serge Lifar Collection

Serge Lifar, photographed by Peter North.

This is a collection of 188 works, paintings, and drawings, of which the great majority were specifically made as set or costume designs for the theater. Most of these were for Serge Diaghilev's Ballets Russes: thirty-seven productions are represented from the first, *Le Pavillon d'Armide* in 1909 (see pp 108–16), to the last, *Le Fils Prodigue* in 1929 (see pp 300–5). Other designs in the collection are for ballets produced by Serge Lifar at the Paris Opéra after Diaghilev's death, and several other productions with which Lifar was not concerned.[1] The collection also contains portraits and some other works unrelated to the theater.

In 1933 "Chick" Austin, then Director of the Wadsworth Atheneum, described the collection when he acquired it as "an unique pictorial record of the greatest artistic movement of the first three decades of the twentieth century. It represents the work of many artists who created the ever novel visual aspects of the ballet from its earlier years when first, in 1909, fresh from Russia, it fell like some great flaming comet at the feet of the enchanted audiences in the Théâtre du Châtelet in Paris, to the last period, when internationalised, the ballet chose for its decorators the, at the time, often unknown younger painters of the school of Paris . . . The Wadsworth Atheneum is indeed fortunate to possess this unique collection."[2] He had every reason to blow his own trumpet. It was an acquisition of extraordinary foresight and brilliance although, at the time, it seemed somewhat rash to most of the trustees. In 1933 the names of Picasso, Matisse, Rouault, Braque and the others did not resound as they do now. The purchase price of $10,000 was considered then to be extravagant; now, the collection is not only priceless, but could not even be formed.

One criticism made of the original collection at the time of its acquisition was that it lacked examples of designs from the early ballets. This was understandable since Lifar had only joined the company in 1923, after it had already been in existence for fourteen years, and he therefore presumably found it more difficult to assemble designs of the earlier ballets than of the later ones, in most of which he himself appeared. This criticism, however, is no longer valid. The additions to the collection by both gift and purchase since 1933 have been made with the deliberate intention of filling the obvious gaps. The Serge Lifar collection now is not only the most comprehensive of its kind relating to Diaghilev's Russian Ballet but also, and crucially, because of its quality, the most significant and revealing. The Ballets Russes continue to live through this collection.

Serge Lifar was Diaghilev's last great protégé dancer. He was born in Kiev in 1905. In 1921, realizing that his vocation was to be a dancer, he joined Bronislava Nijinska who had started a dance studio. "I had," he wrote, "already become a dancer, but I did not know how to dance. I didn't know anything about technique but I knew that I would master it one day, and that no obstacle would stand in my new found way."[3] He was not a good student. In 1922, when Diaghilev, short of trained dancers for his company, telegraphed Nijinska in Kiev to send him her "five best pupils," Lifar was not included. At the last moment, one of the five dropped out and Lifar, realizing his opportunity, took his place. He arrived in Paris on 13 January 1923. Lifar himself described his first interview, when Diaghilev said to the five students, "'And now to work. It's a matter of surprising Europe. What can you do?' . . . His velvety look rests on me: I am going to lose my composure. 'And you, young man? Madame Nijinska hasn't told me anything about you.' I feel small, weak, my lips suck the air; all I can do is weep when my friends come to my rescue. 'Oh, him, he can do everything.'"[4] Diaghilev was not convinced, but the five joined the company in Monte Carlo to continue their training with Nijinska. Later, after sitting in on a class and furious at the apparent lack of improvement in the new recruits, Diaghilev remonstrated with Nijinska; Lifar, nevertheless, overheard him acknowledge to her that "He will be a dancer."[5] Whether Lifar really overheard this remark or imagined it is now immaterial because from then on he ensured that he caught Diaghilev's eye. Beginning with small parts in the standard repertory, the Telescope demonstrator in *Petrushka* and a Warrior in *The Polovtsian Dances*,[6] he quickly progressed up the cast list.

Diaghilev then sent Lifar to Italy for further study under the great teacher Maestro Cecchetti, who was already over seventy. Lifar, aware of his shortcomings but determined to overcome them, learnt rapidly and improved his technique through painful and intensive hard work. Diaghilev cast him in his first major role as Boréas in *Zéphire et Flore* (see pp 150–52) in 1925. In spite of dancing, with great courage, on the first night with two dislocated ankles, he came through the test and was triumphant—a word of which Lifar became very fond when referring to his own performances.

The homosexual Diaghilev undoubtedly found Lifar physically attractive, as everyone did. Lifar was well aware of his own beauty and used it to his advantage in furthering his relationship with the impresario, who was thirty-three years older. But the pedagogue in Diaghilev found the innocence and ignorance in Lifar even more attractive; he began to educate him in the arts by giving him books, guiding him round museums and art galleries, and buying him pictures. Diaghilev particularly enjoyed educating his favorites, and starting them on collecting pictures. Lifar has stated how his collection began. After Diaghilev had

Serge Lifar and Serge Diaghilev at the Lido, Venice, 1928.

sent him and Boris Kochno, his secretary since 1921, to look at an exhibition of the work of the surrealists Max Ernst and Joan Miró in 1926, Lifar reported back to him, "I didn't like Ernst and Miró, and I didn't understand surrealism at all, but you'd perhaps better go and see for yourself."[7] The next thing he knew was that when Diaghilev arrived in Monte Carlo a few days later, "In gratitude for my advice to go and see the surrealists for himself, Diaghilev had brought from Paris some paintings by both Miró and Ernst which had particularly taken his fancy, and these he presented to me, thus laying the foundation of my collection."[8] Some of these paintings were used in the production of *Romeo and Juliet* (see pp 193–99, 262–65). Boris Kochno mentions that at about the same time Diaghilev also gave Lifar Derain's designs for *Jack-in-the-Box* (see pp 185–90).[9]

After only a short time, therefore, Lifar, with Diaghilev's financial help and artistic guidance, had a collection important enough to be exhibited in London at the Chenil Galleries[10] in 1926 during the visit of the Ballets Russes. This was the nucleus of the collection, which was enlarged during the next few years and after Diaghilev's death in 1929. Boris Kochno had also acquired a collection by this time, mostly given to him by Diaghilev, and he wrote: "At the time of Diaghilev's death, the Lifar collection was stored in Paris, in an apartment on the Boulevard Garibaldi leased in Diaghilev's name and mine. As co-tenant, I had free access to the apartment, which made it possible for me to return to Lifar his collection, which was in danger of being dispersed at public auction, as were all Diaghilev's possessions."[11]

Lifar's collection was next exhibited in Paris at the Galerie Vignon in 1929 as a memorial exhibition to Diaghilev.[12] The catalogue includes introductory articles by Jean Cocteau, Waldemar George, Serge Schoukine, and Boris Kochno, most of them written in a typically grandiloquent French style, high-falutin' and high-minded, but when translated into English reduced for the most part to pretentious rubbish. However, Kochno perceptively and amusingly wrote: "We are used to travelling. We travel with useful objects and we know how heavy these indispensable objects will be along the way. Lifar travels with a picture under his arm."[13]

There was undoubtedly some division of the spoils between Kochno and Lifar immediately after Diaghilev's death merely to avoid tax but, contrary to malicious rumours which persist even still, Lifar acquired the pictures, designs, and books that were in Diaghilev's possession when he died quite legally by purchase from his heirs. Letters and documents proving this were among the Kochno archives sold at auction by Sotheby's in 1991.[14]

The Lifar collection was again shown in London in 1930 at the Arthur Tooth Gallery.[15] It is therefore logical to assume that most of the additions to the collection for this exhibition originally belonged to Diaghilev. Lifar continued to collect, mostly designs for ballets which he choreographed and in which he now danced for the Paris Opéra where he became the resident ballet master. The meaning of the term *maître de ballet* has changed over the years, so that the importance of the position has diminished; in Lifar's day it meant that he was in charge of all the ballet activities of the Paris Opéra, a position of great responsibility, under the general director of the Opéra, Jacques Rouché. In 1933 Lifar formed his own company in order to extend his renown first to England[16] and then to America where he traveled with the major part of his collection. In the United States it was first shown at the Julien Levy Gallery in New York. The exhibition was held for the benefit of the Architects' Emergency Committee. Among the grand sponsors, apart from H.I.H. Grand Duchess Marie of Russia, were Julien C. Levy himself, as Chairman of the Architects' Emergency Committee; Mr and Mrs A. Everett Austin; Lincoln Kirstein, who was to play such an important part in the development of ballet in America; Prince and Princess Alexis Obolensky; the Marquise de Polignac and Mrs and Mrs James Thrall Soby. In his foreword to the 1933 catalogue Lifar explained how and why he had started his collection: "It was ten years ago that I first came to Paris. Haunted by the great fame of Diaghilew [sic] I had left Russia with but one idea, to meet him and to join his celebrated *Ballets Russes*. My dream came true. Suddenly I found myself in the midst of the intense artistic activity of Europe, and the beginning of my career as a dancer coincided with my introduction to a knowledge of art. The great Italian paintings were revealed to me during my prolonged visits to Italy. Other European museums helped my study of old masters. But it is to Picasso, Matisse, Braque, Derain, Rouault, who, with many others, revolved about Diaghilew, that I owe my most vivid artistic emotions. From that time on modern painting became a passion with me. I was not satisfied to see it at the *Ballets Russes*, in exhibitions, or in the studios of artists: I was soon taken with the desire to have constantly around me, under my eyes, the things I loved. This is how I decided to form a collection of my own."[17] It is curious but characteristic that Lifar does not in any way acknowledge Diaghilev's educative influence or generosity in the acquisition of his collection. The exhibition was seen very much as Lifar's own collection, made by his own choice. The Ballets Russes had not performed in the United States since 1917, so Lifar's visit with his small company and the exhibition rekindled in some the memory of a forgotten glory. The critic Edward Alden Jewell described the exhibition: "This fascinating display tells a story of romance; a story whose elements have already begun to take on the serene and far-away glamour of legend. The famous Ballets Russes has become history . . . The exhibition at the Julien Levy Gallery has to do with the growth and strange bright flowering of an institution that belongs to an earlier generation and that lives on in memory as a kind of hearthstone of modern art in Paris."[18]

Lifar should perhaps have realized that after the devastatingly poor notices which he and his company had received in London he might not succeed in America[19] unless he changed or improved his program. But, not lacking in confidence, he was billed as the "Sensational Young Russian Dancer, Legitimate Successor of Nijinsky." Unfortunately, as John Martin pointed out, "His name was far greater than his single-handed accomplishment could justify,"[20] and the tour was an artistic catastrophe. He had to replace the obviously appalling *Prometheus* (see pp 306–10) after one performance with a *Divertissement*, but the damage had been done by the critics. Audiences stayed away. To be fair, however, audiences in America were also not yet ready for the kind of ballet Lifar was presenting. Poor audiences also meant that the tour was a financial failure. This should not have mattered, as Barbara Hutton had promised in Paris to sponsor his tour, but by the time Lifar had arrived in America she had forgotten her promise and had eloped with her first husband, Prince Mdivani. Lifar, recalling his predicament later in his autobiography, was not bitter and even rather generous: "My dear friend Barbara Hutton, who had sponsored my journey . . . let me down. So I had been obliged to hire an orchestra at my own expense and pay the salaries of all the dancers. To meet these expenses I had to sell to the Hartford Museum a whole collection of modern pictures that I had obtained with the Diaghilev estate and which were at that moment on exhibition in New York."[21]

Julien Levy had agreed to show the exhibition: "Because of the many drawings by certain artists I was particularly interested in—major painters in the

Surrealist movement who were then almost unknown in America: Max Ernst, Miró, de Chirico."[22] Levy does not describe the terms under which he showed the exhibition, but it was certainly not for sale when he agreed to show it. *Force majeure* made Lifar sell his collection: he had to get himself and his company back to France. Levy was a friend of Chick Austin as well as a dealer who sold contemporary art to Austin. He therefore knew not only his taste but also the museum's financial position. He admired Austin as a museum director for showing "that flavour that could compensate for limitations in size and financial endowment . . . the quality that renders quantity unimportant."[23]

It therefore seemed obvious to Levy when he discovered Lifar's predicament that the collection could be a perfect acquisition for the Wadsworth Atheneum. As he described: "Since his museum provided meagre funds for the acquisition of a large modern collection, it made sense to me for Chick to find one theme for a small contemporary and specialised display. The ballet was close to his fancy. Then the miracle happened. The Serge Lifar collection of designs for the ballet came to my attention, and Serge was willing to sell for a nominal price. Among the numerous sketches for costumes, backdrops, and curtains there were some half a dozen important paintings by artists soon to become very well known. I pointed out to Chick, making a prophecy, that the value of these alone would soon soar so high it would justify the entire purchase, a bold guess that very soon proved true."[24] Austin required no convincing. He knew the importance and significance of the collection and the extraordinary opportunity he was being offered by Levy. The ballet was more than "close to his fancy," it was a passion. Since 1923 he had regularly visited Europe, his itinerary always including visits to the Russian Ballet "when every year I went to London for two or three weeks of ballet, every season brought to me the joy of experiencing new artistic forms. Of all the memories of the last ten years these remain the most intense."[25] His enthusiasm obviously convinced the trustees, and they indeed got a bargain. The collection was bought with funds from the endowment to the museum known as the Ella Gallup Sumner and Mary Catlin Sumner Collection.[26]

Lifar, too, was overjoyed for he could now return to Europe with his company. (I do not think that he ever intended to settle in the United States or to supplant Balanchine. He was, after all, quite secure in his position at the Paris Opéra.) When Lifar received the check he wanted to cash it immediately in order "to feel the dollars." So he asked Levy to introduce him to the Central Hanover bank. Levy described the occasion: "We entered the bank. Lifar took an appraising look at the bank counters. With a joyous shout he executed a double entrechat and a leap—the famous leap in which he seemed suspended in air, magically evoking the great Nijinsky. Then he was over the counter, landing on an overturned drawer of hard coins, to the consternation of tellers and the two armed guards, who somehow saw fit not to shoot. 'The most famous leap of Lifar,' he said as he calmly cashed his check. 'If only Nijinsky had seen.'"[27]

The Serge Lifar collection immediately became the major public testament of Diaghilev's Ballets Russes, and remains so still. Its unique importance is that it covers the whole twenty-year period of that company from 1909 to 1929, as well as the first few productions when Lifar was on his own at the Paris Opéra beginning his impressive career, a period that brought the artist of the theater to the fore. Since it was acquired, the collection has been shown extensively in Europe and America, as the full list of exhibitions testifies. Many items have been illustrated with increasing frequency as the literature devoted to this unique period of ballet expands. No serious exhibition about the art of theater can be contemplated without recourse to the Lifar collection, nor can any book on the subject be adequately illustrated without including examples from it.

Lifar naturally regretted having to sell his collection and selling it for so little. He even made a tentative inquiry about it in 1967 in the vague hope of perhaps being able to show that it had not been acquired legally and so having it returned. The museum courteously sent him copies of the legal transaction and that was the end of the matter. This collection, complete and comprehensive as it is, never represented his entire holding. It was always a selection, albeit a selection of the best works specifically and almost entirely related to the theater. As Lifar wrote in his foreword: "The theatre is my universe, and it is this universe, seen through the eyes of the artists, that I submit to the American public."[28] Lifar kept the rest of his collection and added considerably to it over the years. It included many paintings by artists of the School of Paris as well as other designs, sketches, drawings, and papers relating to Diaghilev's Ballets Russes and his own subsequent distinguished and prolific career. In the early 1970s, some time after he had retired from the Paris Opéra, he himself began to paint, always in acrylic, mostly imaginative portraits of Diaghilev, Nijinsky, Stravinsky, Massine, Picasso, and others, but also crucial moments in some of his ballets. A selection of these designs and paintings was offered at auction in Paris in 1974, but many lots remained unsold.[29] A larger selection, including the unsold lots from Paris and an important and extensive archive, was then sold at auction by Sotheby's in 1984 in London two years before he died.[30] Sotheby's publicity and panache ensured a successful sale and most of the remainder of Lifar's collection was then dispersed among private collectors and public museums and libraries.[31] The Wadsworth Atheneum's horde of so long ago, however, is the true and unrepeatable treasure chest.

Notes

1 For a full chronological list of productions represented in the collection see Appendix A.

2 A. E. A. jr [Austin Everett Austin], *Wadsworth Atheneum Report for 1933 and Bulletin*, Vol XII No 2 October–December 1934, p 30.

3 Serge Lifar, *Du temps que j'avais faim* [*When I was hungry*], pp 237–8.

4 Serge Lifar, *ibid*, pp 237–8.

5 Serge Lifar, *ibid*, p 241.

6 Lifar's first performance was on 13 June 1923, when he was also one of the characters in *Les Noces*, at the Théâtre Gaité-Lyrique, Paris.

7 Serge Lifar, *Diaghilev*, p 433.

8 Serge Lifar, *ibid*, p 434.

9 Boris Kochno, *Diaghilev and the Ballets Russes*, p 243.

10 See Appendix B for complete list of works exhibited.

11 Boris Kochno, *op cit*, p 243.

12 See Appendix B for complete list of works exhibited.

13 Boris Kochno, *Galerie Vignon* catalogue, p 23.

14 *Collection Boris Kochno*, Sotheby's, Monaco, 11–12 October 1991.

15 See Appendix B for complete list of works exhibited.

16 Lifar's company alternated with *Les Ballets 1933* sponsored by Edward James for which George Balanchine choreographed several ballets. This prompted Lincoln Kirstein, who saw them, to invite Balanchine to America with the original suggestion that the new company should be based at the Wadsworth Atheneum. See also Schervashidze, pp 306–10.

17 Serge Lifar, "Foreword" in *Twenty-Five Years of Russian Ballet from the Collection of Serge Lifar*, catalogue of Julien Levy Gallery, p 2.

18 Edward Alden Jewell, "Art in Review" in *The New York Times*, 2 November 1933.

19 He was booked to appear in New York, Providence, Buffalo, Toronto, Chicago, and Montreal.

20 John Martin, "The Dance: Lifar's Debut" in *The New York Sunday Times*, 12 November 1933.

21 Serge Lifar, *Ma Vie: from Kiev to Kiev*, p 147.

22 Julien Levy, *Memoir of an art gallery*, p 15.

23 Julien Levy, *ibid*, p 140.

24 Julien Levy, *ibid*, p 140.

25 A. Everett Austin Jr in a letter to the *Hartford Courant*, 21 November 1934.

26 See Jean K. Cadogan's note on this endowment in General Note to the catalogue, p 54.

27 Julien Levy, *op cit*, p 15.

28 Serge Lifar "Foreword", *op cit*.

29 *Collection Serge Lifar Les Ballets Russes* (104 lots) sold by Ader, Picard, Tajan at Hotel George V, Paris, 20 June 1974.

30 *Ballet Material and Manuscripts from the Serge Lifar Collection* (228 lots) sold by Sotheby's, London, 9 May 1984.

31 Lifar had also acquired from the Diaghilev estate his collection of rare Russian books. After having been unable to sell the books as a collection to a single institution he was persuaded to sell them at auction by Sotheby's who inaugurated their sales in Monaco with the *Diaghilev–Lifar Library* (826 lots) on 28 November–1 December 1975.

Design for the Theater

There is a distinction between the art of the theater and theater art. The first is performance, what the spectator sees on stage, the living picture peopled by actors or dancers or singers in costume, bringing the scene to life in a total setting. It is a synthesis of several different arts working together for a common purpose. It is imaginary but real, true but ephemeral. It is four-dimensional, because the art of the theater only begins to exist in front of an audience and over a period of time when a fragile pact is made between performers and spectators. The audience knows full well when it goes to the theater that it is entering a world of make-believe, but it sends a silent message across the footlights: "Make me believe." The performer is aware of the tension that message creates. Whether the audience is transported or not, whether it is convinced or not, is often a matter of luck. The theater requires more than the flow of a gentle current—it needs sparks to fly. When they do there is no other art so powerful.

Theater art, on the other hand, is set and costume design. It is imagined but permanent. A design is a unique document, often the only surviving visual record of a performance. As such it is, of course, inadequate because a single drawing cannot replace the effect of a whole performance. A drawing for the theater is a statement of an intention; it is primarily an instruction to a craftsman, and therefore is not necessarily conceived as a work of art although it may often finish up by being one. The objective of a design for the theater is not the same as the objective of a painting, which is to be complete in itself.

The invention of photography has not lessened the lasting value of a drawing for the theater, any more than it has affected the intrinsic value of any work of art. Nor, to my mind, has color photography, film, or video replaced the experience of performance. The ballets and operas represented in this catalogue were all performed during the first three decades of the twentieth century, and while there exist many photographs of the performers (some of which are reproduced in this book), they are in black-and-white and were often taken in the studios of the photographers. Film was not fast enough then to catch Nijinsky's leap in mid-air, so we can only believe in the accuracy of the verbal descriptions. Historically, we have to accept a lot on trust, but uncertainty is necessary for the establishment of legends. It is curious that Diaghilev, who was so interested in novel techniques in the theater, was never seduced by the possibilities of film. Perhaps, after all, he was more interested in preserving legends.

The theater is a cooperative art. The designer works as one of a group, but often in solitude. Ralph Koltai (b. 1924), a distinguished British designer, calls him "a lonely animal."[1] Any number of ideas may flow from the group, but the designer has to crystallize them into a concrete and acceptable form. Koltai explains that the designer is alone because "in the final analysis the decisions are his. It is entirely a matter of decisions; the quality and appropriateness of the design is dependent on these. Therein lies the difficulty—to recognise the right decision."[2] But there is no one right way to design a production, and the designer always has to make a great many decisions. A production also requires the designer to make a great many drawings, at least one for each costume and set, which may mean several hundred altogether. Some designers make only drawings, some (especially nowadays) make only models, some make both. Models get damaged or broken in the scenic workshops; drawings too easily disappear.

The success or failure of the designer's work depends ultimately upon its interpretation by others: the craftsmen or women who make and paint the sets and props, cut and sew the costumes. For this reason the designer's work is always subject to compromise. Rarely does a designer paint his own set, or make his own costume. Norman Bel Geddes (1893–1958) reminded his listeners in a lecture: "Remember at all times you are a designer, not a carpenter, painter, interior decorator or office boy."[3] On the other hand, as Herman Rosse (1887–1965) put it: "In order to do his best work as an artist, the designer should dominate and control the scene, yet, actually, he does his best work as an *an artist of the theatre* when he is able to compromise and to cooperate with his fellow workers."[4] These two statements, both by designers, are not necessarily contradictory, but they express the designer's dichotomy: he works alone, but as others make up his work he tries to ensure that the compromise is minimal. In order to achieve this he needs to have the right temperament, toughness balanced with sensibility. Léon Bakst (see pp 59–101), for example, found his true vocation as an artist only when he began to work in the theater. Although he complained endlessly about the number of drawings he had to do, the deadlines, and the frenzy of production, they provided him with the adrenalin he needed for his creative work. Matisse (see pp 257–61), on the other hand, could not stand the hurly-burly and the fact that, however hard he tried, he could not be in complete control. Dame Alicia Markova told me that when, as a young girl, she appeared in Stravinsky's *Le Chant du Rossignol (The Song of the Nightingale)* Matisse himself painted the designs on her costume while she was wearing it. He felt so frustrated by working in the theater that he declined all Diaghilev's subsequent invitations to design for the ballet again.

Lee Simonson (1888–1967), for many years the principal designer of the New York Theatre Guild, vividly and succinctly described the wide compass of a designer's responsibilities: "The scene-designer remains what he has always been: one of a member of a group of interpreters. As such he must, usually in four weeks' time, construct a home or a palace, costume princes or paupers, transport any corner of the five continents or any one of a number of Arcadias to the theatre, provide any object that the actors must touch or handle, whether a throne or a kitchen chair, a dead sea-gull or the Sphinx, and out of paint, glue, canvas, gauze, wood and papier mâché create a world real enough to house the conflicts of human beings."[5] A designer therefore needs to have an encyclopaedic knowledge of art, architecture, social and military history, fashion, and dress; but a designer who merely reproduces accurately what is correct will fail. Of course, he needs to know how a set is built, how a costume is made, how a stage is lit; but he needs to distort reality with his imagination. Reality in the theater has to reflect life as it is inwardly felt, not as it is outwardly lived. Robert Edmond Jones (1887–1954)[6] defined a good stage setting as "not necessarily a 'stage picture,' not a pictorial background against which players move. It is a shell of light and color, so arranged as to express and intensify the playwright's vision."[7] Simonson and Jones were primarily concerned with the straight theater, whereas designing sets and costumes for ballet poses additional spatial problems. The choreographer Sir Peter Wright explained the particular enigma with ballet: "Dancers 'eat' space and it is the designer's job to create an interesting stage and at the same time provide as large an area as possible to reveal the choreography and allow the artists to extend and express themselves without too much visual distraction, remembering always that they cannot use their voices to attract attention and the body must be sufficiently exposed to use its limited powers of expression."[8] He wrote this in 1995; while dancers have always "eaten" space, design for ballet has progressed (or, some would say regressed) into a sparseness which would not have been acceptable to Diaghilev.

By the end of the nineteenth century, in Russia as elsewhere, design in the theater, from its inventive freshness during the Romantic period, had been reduced to a craft with craftsmen merely supplying a background for the action. A stage director ordered a sky, a forest, or a castle. Scene painters, paid by the square meter, would provide whatever was desired; sky was cheaper than architecture, but for the sake of economy the same sky, the same forest, the same castle would be used again and again. Settings became stylized, as did costumes. Indeed, performers traveled from theater to theater with their own trunks of costumes and other paraphernalia. As they had to pay for what they wore, they ignored any specific design intentions, and wore what they liked. This insensitive indifference to theater design was changed in Russia by the highly influential visit of the Duke of Meiningen's company to Moscow. Georg II von Meiningen (1826–1914) was a private patron and impresario who also had extraordinary talent and originality as a designer. He revived both the art of the theater and theater art. Having studied painting under Kaulbach (1805–74), he formed his own theater company which, from 1874, toured extensively throughout Europe including Russia. Constantin Stanislavsky (1865–1938), the founder with Vladimir Nemirovitch-Danchenko (1859–1943) of the Moscow Art Theater, devoted a whole chapter of his autobiography *My Life in Art* to the Duke's company. He wrote: "During Lent, Moscow was visited by the famous ducal players of Meiningen, headed by the stage director Kronek. Their performances showed Moscow for the first time productions that were historically true, with well-directed mob scenes, fine outer form and amazing discipline. I did not miss a single one of their performances, I came not only to look but to study as well."[9] Stanislavsky followed the Duke's example of meticulous preparation and intensive periods of rehearsal at his Moscow Art Theater. He was also profoundly impressed by the Meiningen company's innovation in the matter of stage decoration: that, however "historically true," it should not provide only a background, a mere illustration, but provide an appropriate setting for the action, and that the actor should not be considered separately or in isolation, but that there should be a meaningful unity between them. Georg II's own drawings almost always show groups of figures at some point in the action; while his sets are realistic, they are also symbolic, because he only includes such architectural or decorative elements as are necessary to place the performer. These principles of design are commonplace now, but then they were new and made everyone who was seriously interested in the art of the theater think afresh. Stanislavsky, total man of the theater that he was, later also became intrigued and influenced by the completely opposite theories of minimalist theater design and innovations in lighting which were developed and practised by Adolphe Appia (1862–1928) and Edward Gordon Craig (1872–1966). Indeed, Craig designed a stylized, experimental *Hamlet* for the Moscow Art Theater in 1911.

While Stanislavsky put the lessons he had learnt from seeing the Meiningen company into practical effect in his own theater, his cousin, Savva Mamontov (1841–1918), also learning from the Duke, did more than anyone else in Russia to reinvigorate theater design. A fabulously rich member of the merchant class[10] who, like Vanderbilt, also built railways, Mamontov was equally interested in all the arts: painting, ceramics, sculpture, and architecture, as well as the theater. In 1870 he acquired the estate of Abramtsevo[11] near Moscow, which he developed into a colony for Russian artists. It became a center where Mamontov could realize his dream: the renaissance of Russian art. As on almost any estate in Russia at the time there was a private, amateur theater, with the difference that Mamontov took the art of theater more seriously than usual. He was directly responsible for bringing artists to work for his Private Opera company and was critical of the work at the Imperial Theaters. He commissioned easel painters who had previously worked on portraits and landscapes to design stage sets and costumes: among them Constantin Korovine (1861–1939; see pp 223–29) and Valentin Serov (see p 64). Korovine went on to work for the Imperial Theaters where attitiudes also changed in time. The influence of these artists was decisive, particularly on the remarkable group of people who gathered round Alexandre Benois (1870–1960; see pp 108–37), devoted to art in various ways and multi-disciplined, who became known collectively as *Mir Iskusstva (The World of Art)*.

The formation and progress of the Ballets Russes is described in the final section of this introduction, but Benois put his finger on it when he wrote: "It was no accident that what was afterwards known as the *Ballets Russes* was originally conceived not by the professionals of the dance, but by a circle of artists, linked together by the idea of Art as an entity. Everything followed from the common desire of several painters and musicians to see the fulfilment of the theatrical dreams which haunt them; but I emphasise again that there was nothing *specific* or *professional* in their dreams. On the contrary, there was a burning craving for Art in general."[12] Their "dreams," though, led quite soon specifically toward the art of the theater as defined (or confined) by ballet, and the "circle" quickly became a group of such highly skilled professionals that they changed the definition of ballet until it was no longer confined by traditional rules and techniques but had leapt into a new domain.

Ballet was seen by the circle to be the most perfect expression of the idea of a total work of art (or Wagner's *Gesamtkunstwerk*). Diaghilev made very few public statements but, interviewed when he went with his company to America, he explained exactly what he and his collaborators were trying to achieve—or, rather, what in fact they were achieving: "In our modern ballet, the union of the line and rhythm of the dancer's body, of his gestures and facial expressions, and the music, is intended to be as intimate as the union of text and music dreamed of, if not always achieved, by Richard Wagner. In fact, I sometimes think that we have at our command a more perfect medium for the arts of the theatre than any composer of opera, however gifted, or fortunate in his libretto, can find. With the elimination of speech, with the emphasis on the factor of design, which must remain an inherent principle of the most fantastical ballet, in place of the clumsy literalisms which threaten the composer of music-drama, we have an opportunity for combining music and other arts more perfectly, in all probability, than he can ever combine them. The poignant musical expression of the modern composer, accompanying symbolical interpretation by the dancers, can express moods as well as represent events with unsurpassable intensity, dispensing with everything that is trite and commonplace in opera. The composer is freer to express himself. The word, which is anti-lyrical, is no longer, at times, his deadliest enemy, as at other times it may prove to be his inspiring angel. Then the introduction of color as a dramatic art, as an element in itself can convey the most potent suggestion, and stir the imagination, by means of the eye, fully as much as music by means of the ear—all this, to me, represents the most significant of recent developments in the theatre."[13] Although Diaghilev believed that a perfect fusion of all the arts takes place when all the artists (composer, choreographer, dancer, designer) participate equally in its creation, he nevertheless accorded a certain precedence in that equality to the designer.

The correct atmosphere for a production is created the moment the curtain goes up on a stage, and Diaghilev knew that the first visual impact of the set and costumes is crucial. Because ballet is not a literal but a symbolic art, the designer of ballets can have great freedom of expression. Following the practise set by Mamontov, the designers for the Ballets Russes were for the most part trained as painters not as craftsmen, and brought their personal interpretative vision to bear on each production. The ballets produced before the First World War were designed by Russian painters with the work generally being allocated by mutual agreement according to the appropriate individual talent of the painter. Ballets in a classical or romantic mood were given to Alexandre Benois and Mstislav Dobujinsky (see pp 191–92). The exotic oriental, the fantastic, the anthropomorphic, and the Biedemeier romantic were the moods for which Léon Bakst excelled. The barbaric Russian and the peasant Russian were the specialities respectively of Nikolai Roerich (see pp 291–95), and Nathalie Gontcharova (see pp 208–16) or Michel Larionov (see pp 230–41). A writer in the *Boston Transcript* understood precisely the role of, and the contribution made by, the Russian designers when he wrote: "they take thought for the drama—its motives and moods, its developments and subtleties—more than the old scene designers ever did. Their great principle in the application of their art is that the stage picture should reveal the inner purpose and meaning of the drama. The inner purpose—because they hold that nature can never be accurately represented on the stage, however great the skill used, and that even if it were accurately represented, it would be of no use. Why should we go to the trouble to reproduce nature, they ask, when anyone can step out of doors and see the original? Art and especially stage art, must add some artificial element. Especially it must add the one thing that nature never gives—human purpose and human emotion . . . So the inner qualities, emotion and mood, are what the Russian school seeks chiefly to show on its stage. And this, strangely enough, is com-

Léon Bakst's designs for *Schéhérazade*: the scene on stage at the Opéra, Paris, 1910.

passed by the most abstract means. Line, mass, color—these reveal the human soul, as trees and mountains cannot. Just what it is that establishes the connection between the most abstract of means and the most personal of facts (the emotions) is hard to say. Certain it is that a design in pure line, or a 'symphony' in pure color, can bring to a spectator the sense of intimate and revealing emotion as nothing else in the world can, save possibly music. So when the Russians, throwing overboard verisimilitude, show us stage pictures which are primarily designs in line and color they are not withdrawing from life but penetrating deeper into it."[14] This point of view applies to all designers for the theater, whether Russian or not, who approach their art with the painter's eye, seeking the "inner qualities" of the piece to be performed.

This proven and successful aesthetic continued unchanged after the war and the Revolution of 1917, when Diaghilev became marooned in the West never to return to Russia. The artists, however, did change along with the style. Although he still occasionally used Gontcharova and Larionov, Bakst and Benois, Diaghilev now turned with new-found enthusiasm to painters of the School of Paris. He was guided by Jean Cocteau (see p 176) to the Cubist Pablo Picasso (see pp 272–78) and later to other Cubists, Georges Braque (see pp 147–54), Juan Gris (see pp 217–22) and Léopold Survage (see pp 318–22, incidentally another Russian. The French painter André Derain (see pp 188–90) provided a coherent transition between the Russian and French styles. Other French artists who designed ballets included Henri Matisse (see pp 257–61), Marie Laurencin (see

Juan Gris's designs for *Les Tentations de la Bergère*: the scene on stage with the two heralds on either side.

pp 242–46), Maurice Utrillo, Georges Rouault (see pp 300–5), and the primitive painter André Bauchant (see pp 102–7). Picasso recommended the Spanish painter Pedro Pruna (see pp 279–88) to Diaghilev, while another Spaniard, José-Maria Sert (see pp 311–14), was a friend. Giorgio de Chirico (see pp 155–75), and the surrealists Max Ernst (see pp 193–99) and Joán Miró (see pp 262–65) were discovered by Diaghilev during his wanderings around the Parisian galleries. His search for the new and the avant garde also made him turn to the Russians Naum Gabo (see pp 204–7), Antoine Pevsner, Georgi Yakoulov and Pavel Tchelitchew (see pp 323–31). This amazing list of artists who designed for the Ballets Russes during the first three decades of the twentieth century reads like a roll-call of the most famous painters of the period. Perhaps this is why, in spite of all the legends that have grown up connected with the Ballets Russes, the strongest element in the artistic collaboration during the creation of any of the ballets now appears to have been the design. The original performances have disappeared, and revivals, though attempted, are never the same as the first productions, especially when the artists who created them are no longer concerned. Legends thrive on the ephemeral, but the designs, as can be seen from this unique collection, remain as the only permanent and treasured evidence.

Serge Lifar, after Diaghilev's death, rightly decided that the Ballets Russes could no longer continue exactly as before,[15] but at the same time he stated that he wanted "to perpetuate, in my own way, the aesthetic tradition of the *Ballets Russes*."[16] He therefore paid as much heed as Diaghilev had done to choosing for his ballets designers who were painters. Some, such as Giorgio de Chirico and Michel Larionov had been used by Diaghilev, and Lifar knew their work. Others, such as Christian Bérard (see pp 142–46) and Paul Colin (see pp 178–81) were new to ballet but their work successfully maintained the tradition of theater art set by the Ballets Russes.

Notes

1 Ralph Koltai, "Theatre Design—the exploration of space" in *The Royal Society of Arts Journal*, No 5368 Vol CXXXV, London, March 1987, p 302.

2 Ralph Koltai, *ibid*, pp 302-3.

3 Norman Bel Geddes, from *Miracle in the Evening* quoted in Orville K. Larson, *Scene Design in the American Theatre from 1915–1960*, p 171.

4 Herman Rosse, "The Stage Designer" in *Theatre Arts Monthly*, New York, May 1924.

5 Lee Simonson, *The Stage is Set*.

6 Robert Edmond Jones was the American designer of Vaslav Nijinsky's ballet *Til Eulenspiegel*, first produced at the Manhattan Opera House, New York, on 23 October 1916 during the second tour of the United States by the Ballets Russes.

7 Robert Edmond Jones, quoted in Orville K. Larson, *op cit*, p 161 .

8 Sir Peter Wright, "Introduction" to exhibition catalogue *The Designers: Pushing the Boundaries—Advancing the Dance*, p 5.

9 Constantin Stanislavsky, *My Life in Art*.

10 In class-conscious Russia of the last quarter of the nineteenth century merchants had a peculiar standing. Although they were very rich and lived in an opulent style, they were not considered to be part of "society." Their wealth, however, commanded a certain hesitant respect, and they occasionally found themselves on the fringes of the nobility.

11 Now a museum.

12 Alexandre Benois, *Reminiscences of the Russian Ballet*, p 371.

13 Serge Diaghilev, quoted by Olin Downes in *The Boston Post*, Boston, ?23 January 1916.

14 Anon, "Bakst and Benois Clothe the Russian Dancers in Rich and Radiant Plumage," in *The Boston Transcript*, Boston, 29 January 1916 .

15 See Appendix C.

16 Serge Lifar, *Ma Vie*, p 111.

The Costumes

Costumes were not part of the original Lifar collection acquired by the Wadsworth Atheneum in 1933. They were acquired much later. When Diaghilev died in August 1929 his company, the Ballets Russes, died with him. Serge Lifar and Boris Kochno were briefly tempted to carry on but then sensibly decided that the company, without Diaghilev, had indeed succumbed to a timely death and should not be revived. They issued a joint statement of "abdication,"[1] and went their separate ways, leaving everyone to sink or swim. Other attempts at reviving the Ballets Russes at that time also failed.

The stock-in-trade of the company—costumes, cloths, properties and musical scores, stored in a warehouse on the outskirts of Paris—had to be sold to pay off debts. Leonide Massine acquired the stock with the help of Diaghilev's attorney, Maître Aaron, when E. Ray Goetz, a Broadway theatrical producer, wanted to back Massine in an American revival of the Ballets Russes in 1930. However, the effects of the Wall Street crash scotched the plan, because it proved impossible to raise funds to sponsor the company. Goetz had abandoned his idea by 1931. As Massine wrote: "My contract was cancelled, and I found myself the owner of all the Diaghilev material, stored far away in Paris, with no means of using it."[2] At the end of 1932 Massine joined the Ballets Russes de Monte-Carlo.[3] This company, which had been formed at the beginning of that year—with Col. Wassily de Basil[4] as administrative director, René Blum as artistic director, Boris Kochno as artistic adviser, George Balanchine[5] as ballet master, and a number of dancers who had been with Diaghilev—was the true successor company to Diaghilev's Ballets Russes. In 1934 the London Committee of Friends of the Ballet, organized by Bruce Ottley, raised the funds to buy the costumes and cloths from Massine. There is now no means of knowing exactly either what he had bought or what he sold. Although Massine wrote that he had "managed to buy everything belonging to fifty-five ballets—backcloths, front curtains, costumes, properties, and all scenic accessories,"[6] he was being either careless or boastful because it seems an unlikely large number.

This acquisition of costumes and scenery immediately allowed de Basil's company to revive several of Diaghilev's ballets, notably *La Boutique Fantasque*, *The Firebird*, *Le Tricorne*, and *Contes Russes*. Other revivals in the original costumes, such as *Le Bal*, would follow. But some revivals, such as *Schéhérazade*, had to be danced in remade costumes as the originals had worn out.[7] Some ballets, such as *Les Tentations de la Bergère*, were never revived even though the original costumes existed.

Although the costumes were used by de Basil, they did not belong to him but to a foundation which was formed in 1932 under the name of Educational Ballets Ltd. Anthony Diamantidi, a long-standing friend of de Basil who eventually controlled the costumes, stated in a letter: "From the beginning its Memorandum and Articles strictly maintained that it was to be a non profit making Company for the purpose of preservation and development of Classical Ballets as well as for the purpose of assisting to the extent of its liquid funds, ballet dancers, choreographers and other participants of the Diaghilev and de Basil Ballets, whenever such assistance was required."[8] In 1939 the name of the foundation was changed to Russian Ballet Development Company Ltd. De Basil was never a director of either company. The senior director was Tom Bischoff, a partner in the firm of lawyers Bischoff Coxe & Co. By a strange coincidence de Basil and Bischoff died on the same day, 27 July 1951, one in Paris, the other in London. In consequence the lawyers resigned, and Anthony Diamantidi, with the cooperation of another firm of lawyers, Fink Proudfoot & Waters, gained control of the foundation. According to Kathrine Sorley Walker, a co-director of the foundation was Olga Morosova, the dancer who lived with de Basil but "who did not understand business matters."[9] De Basil had assured Morosova, who was twenty-five years younger than him, that Diamantidi would look after her when he died. Another director of the foundation at one time was Nubar Gulbenkian. Diamantidi described, not with total truth, that by 1951, "There was nobody left of the old supporters and the Foundation remained with only two of the old Moicans—old Mr GULBENKIAN and myself. GULBENKIAN, although having the possibility of immense funds was not a great Balletomane and therefore not a great donor, and so we came to the decision that we had no other way, but to put all our decors, costumes, etc. into warehouses where they have been kept until 1967. One of the warehouses was in PARIS, and another in LONDON and yet another in MONTREAL; the latter came into being when during the War LONDON came under German bombardment and it was decided to evacuate the greatest part of our Ballets from the London depot to a large warehouse in MONTREAL; this was done after one or two bombs hit the London warehouse which resulted in the loss of some very fine property. Unluckily in the Montreal depot a fire occurred in December 1958 which has irreparably damaged some 40 Ballets and costumes, decors, etc. including creations by BRAQUE, PICASSO, DERAIN, BERARD, MIRO, JUAN GRIS, etc. etc."[10] At first, Diamantidi tried to find the necessary financial backing to start a company, with possibly either Massine or Lifar, but admitted that "unfortunately all my personal attempts, as well as some attempts of friends failed, with the result that we had to come to a decision of doing something, for this immense property necessitated more than £10,000 a year in warehousing, insurance, etc. which was provided entirely by myself."[11] Next, he tried unsuccessfully to interest the Lincoln Center in New York and the Kennedy Center in Washington in acquiring the collection for a museum. Diamantidi does not mention, in his otherwise revealing letter, that in 1964 he had tabled a special resolution to supplement the objects of the foundation which, as Kathrine Sorley Walker states, "allowed Diamantidi not only to 'acquire, own, maintain or preserve' every kind of item relevant to 'the artistic heritage of the production of ballet in classical Russian style directed or projected' by the companies of Diaghilev and de Basil but 'to buy, sell, hire out, exhibit, dispose of or otherwise deal with any of the said articles upon any terms.' It therefore constituted a *carte blanche* to cover himself in the eventual dealings with Sotheby's."[12] Noticing that Sotheby's had conducted a successful sale of Diaghilev material in June 1967 which, as Richard Buckle later wrote, "proved that anything connected with the Diaghilev Ballet held an interest for the public and possessed a market value,"[13] Diamantidi offered them the collection for sale by auction. By the time Diamantidi approached Sotheby's the name of the foundation had been changed to the Diaghilev and de Basil Ballet Foundation.

Richard Buckle, highly regarded as an expert on the Diaghilev period and famous as the organizer of the Diaghilev Exhibition in 1954, was asked by Sotheby's to advise them whether it would be worth their while to undertake the sale or not. He described his first visit to see the collection: "So, September of last year [1967] found Thilo von Watzdorf, David Ellis-Jones [from Sotheby's] and myself in a warehouse at Montrouge in the southern suburbs of Paris, unpacking trunks and baskets, unfolding curtains, coughing and blinking from

the clouds of dust. We could hardly believe our eyes as lid after lid was thrown open and treasure after treasure was identified; we were seized with a curiosity which was akin to greed. Huge wired and beaded skirts by Bakst from 'Le Dieu Bleu'; Chirico's strange architectural costumes for 'Le Bal'; Gontcharova's dazzling dresses from 'Coq d'Or'; the white satin ball-dress worn by Karsavina in 'Le Spectre de la Rose', with her name-tape inside; fantastic Chinese robes from 'Le Chant du Rossignol', hand-painted by Matisse . . . Pulling out a gorgeously embroidered eighteenth-century coat, immediately identified as a creation by Bakst for 'The Sleeping Princess', that most lavish of all spectacles, given at the Alhambra in 1921, we assumed, because of its splendour, that it was worn by the King or Prince Charming—but no, there were five more like it: it was just one of the courtiers in the background . . . Among the most exquisite costumes in this first sale are those for Wilzak as the King and the two Heralds in 'Les Tentations de la Bergère'. The mauves and ochres devised by Juan Gris for the pseudo-Roman costumes have the subtlety of genius."[14] Richard Buckle convinced Sotheby's to take the risk. They asked him to write the detailed catalogues. He was helped by Julian Barran of Sotheby's. Initially it was decided that there was enough material for two sales. Sotheby's agreed with Richard Buckle that they should not hold them in their auction rooms in New Bond Street, where the curtains could not be shown and the costumes would look drab and lifeless, but in a theater with lighting and music and, unthinkable now, with the costumes worn by students of the Royal Ballet School posing in positions rehearsed by Lydia Sokolova who had been in Diaghilev's company since 1913.

The first sale was at the Scala Theatre, London (now demolished), on 18 July 1968 at 8 p.m.[15] The second sale was at the Theatre Royal, Drury Lane, London, on 19 December 1969 at 2.30 p.m.[16] In his preface to both catalogues Léonide Massine, without acknowledging that he ever owned any of the collection, wrote: "By being worn and shown to a public, not only of balletomanes but also of art lovers in general, even without the choreographies in which they have been used, these remarkable costumes will create a vivid impression of the many masterpieces initiated by Serge Diaghilev."[17] The sales also became glittering social occasions, not forgotten by anyone who was there whether they bought anything or not. There was a third and final sale at the Chenil Galleries, King's Road, Chelsea, on 3 March 1973 at 2.30 p.m.[18]

At these sales the Wadsworth Atheneum only considered bidding for the costumes relating directly to their designs in the Lifar Collection, which they did successfully. The main buyers at all the sales were other museums: the Theatre Museum in Amsterdam, the Theatre Museum in London, the Dansmuseet in Stockholm, the National Museum in Canberra. One of the other main buyers was Mr George Howard, as he then was, for his Gallery at Castle Howard in Yorkshire. It is his collection which was sold at Sotheby's on 14 December 1995 when the Wadsworth Atheneum successfully enlarged its own collection and acquired costumes which did not necessarily relate to designs in the existing Lifar Collection. This happily fulfills the desire which Richard Buckle described at the end of his introduction: "And what a happy conclusion it would be if whole groups of costumes could find their way to museums, where, displayed on models, flattered by theatrical lighting, standing before their appropriate scenery, they could bear witness for a few more centuries to the genius of Diaghilev and incite further ceaseless revolutions in the world of art!"[19]

Giorgio de Chirico, *Le Bal*: Alexandra Danilova as the Woman and Serge Lifar in scene 2.

1   See Appendix C.

2   Leonide Massine, *My Life in Ballet*, p 178.

3   Kathrine Sorley Walker in *De Basil's Ballets Russes* rightly states that there is much confusion about and many inaccuracies over the title of this company during the long period of its existence. It is outside the scope of these pages to describe the history of that company. For a detailed list of the names by which it was known at various times and the names of other companies based on Russian dancers, see Walker's *De Basil's Ballets Russes*, pp x–xiii. In 1934 in London the company was described as "Ballets Russes du Col W. de Basil, director general W. de Basil, artistic director René Blum, maître de ballet and artistic collaborator Leonide Massine".

4   Real name Vassili Grigorievitch Voskressensky, born in Kovno in 1888. Vassili is the Russian form of Basil.

5   Kochno and Balanchine left in 1933 for "Les Ballets 1933."

6   Leonide Massine, *op cit*, p 178.

7   The Diaghilev ballets revived by de Basil were: *L'Après-midi d'un faune* (Alhambra, London, 2 October 1933); *Le Bal* (Auditorium, Chicago, 8 March 1935); *Les Biches* (Monte Carlo, 14 January 1934); *La Boutique Fantasque* (Covent Garden, 16 July 1934); *Carnaval* (Alhambra, 14 September 1933); *Cimarosiana* (Metropolitan,

4 November 1936); *Cléopâtre* (Academy of Music, Philadelphia, 10 November 1936); *Contes Russes* (Covent Garden, 7 August 1934); *Le Coq d'Or* (Covent Garden, 23 September 1937); *The Gods Go A-Begging* (Covent Garden, 17 September 1937); *Les Femmes de Bonne Humeur* (Academy of Music, 16 February 1935); *Le Fils Prodigue* (Theatre Royal, Sydney, 30 December 1938); *Le Mariage d'Aurore* (Academy of Music, 12 November 1934); *Les Matelots* (Monte Carlo, 22 April 1933); *Les Noces* (Metropolitan, 20 April 1936); *L'Oiseau de Feu* (Monte Carlo, 28 April 1934); *Les Papillons* (Auditorium, 27 December 1936); *Petrouchka* (Monte Carlo, 19 April 1932); *Polovtsian Dances* from *Prince Igor* (Monte Carlo, 11 February 1932); *Schéhérazade* (Academy of Music, 16 February 1935); *Le Soleil de Nuit* (Academy of Music, 15 February 1935); *Le Spectre de la Rose* (Covent Garden, 28 August 1935); *Les Sylphides* (Monte Carlo, 12 April 1932); *Thamar* (Covent Garden, 16 August 1935), and *Le Tricorne* (Auditorium, 20 February 1934).

8   Anthony N. Diamantidi in unpublished letter, dated Vevey, 21 January 1970, to M. Morton.

9   Kathrine Sorley Walker, *op cit*, p 163.

10 Anthony N. Diamantidi, *op cit*.

11 Anthony N. Diamantidi, *op cit*.

12 Kathrine Sorley Walker, *op cit*, p 164. She is quoting from the special resolutions of the Russian Ballet Development Company Ltd,

dated 20 November 1964, in the Companies House, London file.

13 Richard Buckle, "Introduction" in *Costumes and Curtains from the Diaghilev and de Basil Ballets*, 1972, p xiii.

14 Richard Buckle, *ibid*, p v.

15 The productions included in this sale were *Le Dieu Bleu*, *Le Spectre de la Rose*, *La Tragédie de Salomé*, *Schéhérazade* (cloth only), *Le Coq d'Or*, *Sadko*, *La Boutique Fantasque*, *Cléopâtre* (cloth only), *Le Chant du Rossignol*, *Les Tentations de la Bergère*, *Le Bal*, *Le Train Bleu* (cloth only), *Zéphire et Flore*, and *The Sleeping Princess*.

16 The productions included in this sale were *The Polovtsian Dances*, *Giselle*, *Schéhérazade*, *Petrushka*, *L'Oiseau de Feu*, *Narcisse*, *Daphnis et Chloë*, *Le Sacre du Printemps*, *Cléopâtre* (cloth only), *Chout*, *Le Médecin malgré lui*, *Les Biches*, *Le Train Bleu* (cloth only), and *Barabau*.

17 Léonide Massine, "Preface" in *Costumes and Curtains from the Diaghilev and de Basil Ballets*, 1968, 1969, p iii.

18 The code name for this sale was, appropriately, "Goodbye," and the lots were mostly comprised of bits and pieces from many ballets (including many produced by de Basil) rather than whole, identifiable costumes as in the previous two sales.

19 Richard Buckle, *op cit* 1968, p vi.

Diaghilev's Ballets Russes

This chapter is a short introduction to the general background and history of the Ballets Russes. The background to the first performance of each of the productions represented in the collection is described in greater detail after each title in the main catalogue.

When the eighteen-year-old Serge Diaghilev (1872–1929) arrived in St Petersburg in 1890 as an "apple-cheeked young country bumpkin"[1] he was lucky to be introduced by his cousin Dimitri (Dima) Philosophoff[2] (1872–1940) into an artistic circle led by Alexandre Benois (1870–1960), the painter and deeply cultured art historian, which included Evgeny Lanceray (1875–1946), Constantin Somov (1869–1939) and Walter Nouvel (1871–1949). In the same year the circle was also joined by the painters Léon Bakst (1866–1924) and Nikolai Roerich (1874–1947). At first, this was merely an informal and somewhat boisterous group of young men; but they took themselves, and art, seriously.

Diaghilev alone had the vision to realize that he could exploit and develop the talents of the artists among whom he found himself in a more structured way so that all might benefit. He let nothing stand in his way, and soon became their catalyst and leader, forming them into a team with defined objectives. The luxurious magazine called *Mir Iskusstva* (*The World of Art*), which they published under Diaghilev's editorship from 1898 to 1904, gave the group its justifiably ostentatious name. They also organized exhibitions under the same banner. In 1901, with Diaghilev as producer, they undertook an abortive production of Delibes' ballet *Sylvia* commissioned by the director[3] of the Imperial Theaters for the Mariinsky Theater, St Petersburg, while Diaghilev, as an assistant director, was editor of the yearbook. Planned as a cooperative effort by the World of Art group, the hodge-podge production never took place because halfway through Diaghilev was dismissed[4] for refusing to accept that he could not be solely responsible. Ultimately it was a fortunate dismissal, for had Diaghilev stayed in the employment of the Imperial Theaters there might well have been no Ballets Russes. After the demise of the *World of Art* magazine Diaghilev set his sights on a more ambitious goal: showing Russian art to the West. Paris was chosen as the "shop window," because then, as now, it was the cultural center of Europe. The first Russian season presented by Diaghilev was an exhibition of paintings in 1906, followed by a series of concerts of Russian music in 1907, and the first productions of Russian operas and ballets in 1908 and 1909. Finally, in 1910, Diaghilev produced his first complete program of ballets, and the World of Art became Diaghilev's Ballets Russes.

During the second half of the nineteenth century the art of ballet had declined so much in the West that it had all but disappeared, whereas in Russia it continued to thrive in the Imperial Theaters, supported exclusively by the patronage of successive Emperors and under the tutelage of the great choreographer and teacher Marius Petipa (1822–1910), who worked in St Petersburg from 1847 until his death. He was largely responsible for creating Russian dancers with the impeccable technique for which they became, and still are, famous. But, by thriving on its very success, ballet became trapped in outmoded convention. Diaghilev would change that.

Alexandre Benois first enthused Diaghilev about ballet when he took him to a performance of his *Le Pavillon d'Armide* (see pp 108–16) at the Mariinsky

Theater in Şt Petersburg in 1907, after which Diaghilev said to him: "This must be shown to Europe."[5] His sympathies were instinctively directed more toward opera, but he recognized from Benois's example that there was greater potential in ballet for creating the complete work of art. In a letter written in 1928, Diaghilev described his conversion to ballet while preparing for the 1909 season in Paris: "From Opera to Ballet is but a step. At that time there were more than 400 ballet dancers on the roster of the Imperial Theaters. They all had a remarkably good training, and they danced the traditional classical ballets . . . I could not help observing, however, that among the younger members of the St Petersburg ballet, a sort of reaction to the classical tradition, which Petipa so jealously preserved, was beginning to make itself felt. From that moment, I began wondering whether it would not be possible to create a number of short new ballets, which besides being of artistic value, would link the three main factors, music, decorative design, and choreography far more closely than ever before."[6]

Much has been written about Diaghilev's not being a creative artist, but this is grossly to underestimate his stature and influence. Diaghilev first of all created the climate and the conditions in which the artists around him could work. His chosen medium, the theater, is probably the most fickle because, by its very nature involving so many people in a single enterprise, it is constantly subject to compromise. The art of the theater depends upon the skill of the impresario in minimizing the compromise, and Diaghilev was an impresario of genius. To my mind, impresarios of genius, whose taste, overall supervision, and minute attention to detail effectively control and determine the result on stage, are equal in creativity to the other artists who are individually concerned in any given production. Diaghilev was not the *deus ex machina* he is sometimes labeled,[7] for he did not appear providentially in the nick of time to save a situation; on the contrary, he was always at the forefront arranging, urging, persuading, criticizing. He was the master (often infuriating and intractable) who manipulated the strands of theater into a new form. Diaghilev himself defined his artistic innovation: "We gave the public something new, and we were frankly opposed to everything obsolete and to whatever was too much hampered by tradition. Our programmes were nothing short of revolutions in art."[8] The art of the theater, however, also depends very much upon luck, and Diaghilev was lucky in the group of people gathered round him.

Diaghilev always began with the composer. He had himself trained as a musician and, while neither his voice, his playing, nor his composing ability showed much discernible talent, his critical faculty was sharp and sensitive and his knowledge encyclopaedic. Russian music was flourishing as never before. Nikolai Rimsky-Korsakov (1844–1908) had been his teacher for a time; Alexander Glazunov (1865–1936), Nicholas Tcherepnin (1873–1945), Anton Arensky (1861–1906) were contemporaries; Mikhail Glinka (1804–1857), Alexander Borodin (1833–1887), Piotr Tchaikovsky (1840–1893) were idols. From the music followed the choreographer. It was Alexandre Benois who introduced Michel Fokine (1880–1942) to the group when they were considering which ballets to take to Paris. Benois, while accustomed and attached to Petipa's ideals of ballet, had been affected by Fokine, his young choreographer of *Le Pavillon d'Armide* who, believing those ideals to be old-fashioned, sought to modernize ballet by liberating it from the constraints of its rigid rules of mime and movement. As a revolutionary young student at the Imperial School, Fokine had submitted to the Director of the Imperial Theaters in 1904 a libretto for a ballet based on Longus's *Daphnis and Chloe*, together with a plan setting out in detail his rules for the reform of ballet of which the following are the most pertinent: "In the ballet the whole meaning of the story can be expressed by the dance . . . The ballet must no longer be made up of 'numbers,' 'entries' and so forth. It must show artistic unity of conception . . . the ballet must have complete unity of expression, a unity which is made up of a harmonious blending of the three elements—music, painting, and plastic art."[9] Fokine had reached the same conclusion as Diaghilev, only earlier. But *Daphnis and Chloe* was thrown into a cupboard along with the notes. Fokine, undeterred, began to experiment with his ideas using fellow students. It was ballet's good fortune that among the students were a number of young dancers of incomparable talent who were in sympathy with his ideas: Anna Pavlova (1881–1931), Tamara Karsavina (1885–1978), Vaslav Nijinsky (1889–1950), and Adolph Bolm (1884–1951) among them. The male dancer was beginning to be equal, if not even superior, in importance to the ballerina.

With a choreographer who shared Diaghilev's artistic aspirations, with such talent available among dancers, with Russian composers providing suitable music, and with painters such as Alexandre Benois and Léon Bakst, the designer of *The Fairy Doll* (see pp 59–61) in 1903 (already experienced in working for the theater), it was natural to include ballet as well as opera in the second Russian program for Paris in 1909. Besides, ballet was cheaper, and logistically easier, than opera. Diaghilev hoped that his program would again be subsidized by the Emperor. He therefore thought it prudent to include in his company Mathilde Kshessinska (1872–1971), *prima ballerina assoluta*[10] of the old school, ex-mistress of the Tsar, married to Grand Duke Andrei Vladimirovitch, and extremely influential. But when she discovered that she was only to dance one role, Armida, she refused to accept the engagement and used her influence at Court to have any intended subsidy withdrawn.[11] By witholding the subsidy from Diaghilev, Grand Duke Serge Mikhailovitch spitefully hoped that the Emperor "would send the ballet company of the Imperial Theaters to Paris with Kshessinska at the head,"[12] thus thwarting Diaghilev's plans. A more crucial factor, however, in the Emperor's sudden withdrawl of vital subsidy was the death, in February 1909, of Grand Duke Vladimir Alexandrovitch who had for some time been Diaghilev's loyal supporter. Diaghilev sensibly ignored all the Court intrigues, and hastily approached his French impresario Gabriel Astruc (1864–1938) for financial help in order to salvage the season. Without Astruc the whole enterprise would have collapsed before it had even started. Primarily a concert promoter, he nevertheless saw the artistic potential in Diaghilev's ideas. His whole life was inspired, as Robert Brussel wrote in an obituary, "by the true ideals of journalism: to spread new ideas capable of creating a change of opinion quickly, clearly, precisely, and truthfully."[13] Astruc wholeheartedly backed Diaghilev's ideas, and therefore quickly arranged, with the help of the Russian Embassy in Paris, adequate financial guarantees. The project could continue.

In establishing the program for the first season, Diaghilev relied for the most part on a repertory of ballets, choreographed by Fokine, which had already been tried out in St Petersburg. *Le Pavillon d'Armide* opened the first evening on 18 May 1909,[14] a gala occasion which Astruc ensured, with his flair for publicity, that no member of Parisian society could afford to miss. He even arranged pretty girls alternately blonde and brunette to fill the front row of the dress circle, called the *corbeille* (basket), a name still used today. The expectation was eager. Richard Buckle wrote of the *pas de trois* in the second scene: "The conquest of Europe by Russian dancing and the reign of Diaghilev as Director of the Ballets Russes can be said to begin at the moment Nijinsky takes the stage with his two partners."[15] The response to *Le Pavillon d'Armide* was nothing compared to that given to the second ballet, the *Polovtsian Dances* from Alexander Borodin's opera *Prince Igor* (see pp 225–29). The passionate frenzy of Borodin's music and its interpretation by equally energetic and barbaric dancing, startled the Parisian audience. They hadn't expected anything like it but, having thought about it, they admired it for what they thought it was: essentially Russian. Diaghilev, thereafter, could hardly afford to leave it out of his programs. Another Fokine ballet from the first season which Diaghilev had to revive almost every year in response to public demand was *Les Sylphides* (see pp 153–54). Deliberately recalling the famous Romantic ballet of the 1830s *La Sylphide*, Diaghilev gave this title to a ballet originally performed in 1907 using Chopin's music orchestrated by Glazunov. *Cléopâtre* was Diaghilev's new title for *Egyptian Nights*, first performed in 1908, which he agreed to include provided the score was strengthened. With his unerring sense of what was right (or wrong), he had pinpointed the two weaknesses of the ballet: the title and the music. Although it remained something of a *pot-pourri* musically, *Cléopâtre* was another sensation with its startlingly exotic and blazingly colorful scenery and costumes by Léon Bakst, and the dancing of Anna Pavlova, Fokine himself, and Ida Rubinstein[16] (1885–1960), introduced in the title role. The last item was a suite of dances from operas and ballets already familiar to the dancers presented under the general title, *Le Festin*, scrambled together because a new, purely Russian, work had not materialized. Diaghilev had also cheekily wanted to present the French *Giselle* but this also had to be postponed (see p 132).

The 1909 season was an artistic triumph but a financial failure, a pattern that was repeated more or less every year. Since box office receipts were never enough to cover costs, Diaghilev would skip lightly from financial crisis to financial crisis and, using his charm, would beguile rich, usually titled, ladies of Paris and London to subscribe to boxes for the season and part with the necessary cheques. He never cared about money for himself, he only really cared about money for his productions. Among his most faithful supporters were Princesse Edmond de Polignac (née Winnaretta Singer), Comtesse Greffulhe, Lady Cunard, and Lady Ripon. A friend who was always ready to help with a desperately needed cheque was Misia Edwards.[17] Diaghilev's relationship with her was as with a sister. According to Jacques-Emile Blanche, the painter of flamboyant portraits of both Nijinsky and Karsavina, "it was her taste that decided whatever Diaghileff undertook, and he never embarked on a production without her sanction."[18] He is certainly crediting her with too much artistic authority, but there is no doubt that she was very influential in keeping Diaghilev financially afloat.

The first program set the pattern in many ways for the choice of ballets in the subsequent pre-War seasons, which expanded from Paris to include Berlin in 1910; Monte Carlo, Rome, and London in 1911; Dresden, Vienna, and Budapest in 1912, and ever further afield until, in 1913, the company visited South America. Throughout its existence, however, the Ballets Russes, as a company, never performed in Russia, although its renown abroad was well documented and appreciated in the Russian press. Once, in 1912, Diaghilev did try to present his company in Russia. He described this attempt during an interview a month before he died: "On one occasion before the war we were asked to appear in Russia. Prince Oldenburg, who sympathised with the Czar's views, built a large institution called the 'People's Building' containing a beautiful theatre, and we were invited to attend the opening ceremonies and give a performance. We started off happily with our big trunks and other luggage and reached the

Léon Bakst, *Le Spectre de la Rose*: the setting.

Russian frontier, where we received a telegram informing us that the 'People's Building' was burnt down and the theatre with it. There would be no inaugural ceremony and no ballet, and our services were no longer required. Accordingly, we returned to the place from which we came. We could not show our art in our own country."[19]

The exotic, spectacular, and "oriental" (that is, east of Suez rather than east of Calcutta) style set by Fokine and Bakst with *Cléopâtre* was continued by them with *Schéhérazade* (see pp 62–66) and *Les Orientales* in 1910, *Le Dieu Bleu* (see pp 71–73) and *Thamar* in 1912. The Romantic style of *Les Sylphides* (see pp 153–54) was followed by *Le Carnaval* in 1910, *Le Spectre de la Rose* (see pp 67–70) in 1911, and *Papillons* (see pp 191–92) in 1914. An innovation in 1911 was Bakst's Greek style with *Narcisse*, followed by Nijinsky's *L'Après-midi d'un faune* (see pp 74–78) and Fokine's *Daphnis and Chloë* (see pp 79–81) in 1912.

Schéhérazade has always been considered to be the epitome of the Ballets Russes. The first night on 4 June 1910 at the Opéra in Paris was an occasion of the utmost artistic importance because *Schéhérazade* changed the way people considered the art of ballet. Nothing like it had ever been seen before. It was not just the dancing that was astounding, it was the whole production, music, decor, costumes, lighting, all combined into forty minutes of pure and overwhelming sensation that made it so memorable. Good taste kept a fine balance between the exotic and the erotic, and preserved its oriental Russianness from degenerating into kitsch. So instantly popular was this ballet that, with its repercussions in fashion and interior design, Diaghilev could have kept his company going profitably for years by always including *Schéhérazade* in his programme. But he chose not to. That was not his style. Diaghilev was never interested in profit, he was interested in art.

The promised "purely Russian work" also had to wait for the second season in 1910, when only ballets were presented. Diaghilev now made his greatest musical discovery. After hearing his *Scherzo Fantastique* at a concert, he commis-

Alexandre Benois, *Petrushka*: Enrico Cecchetti as the Showman, Tamara Karsavina as the Ballerina, and Vaslav Nijinsky as Petrushka in the puppets' booth, scene 1.

sioned the young Igor Stravinsky (1882–1971) to compose a ballet on the theme of the Russian folk tale *The Firebird* (see pp 212–16). Stravinsky followed the Slav magic of *The Firebird* with the Russian pantomime of *Petrushka* (see pp 117–27) in 1911, the story of the puppet with human feelings. Fokine created a choreography in which dance is not used as an end in itself but as a means of psychological expression. It succeeded primarily because Nijinsky was able to interpret Stravinsky's and Fokine's intentions convincingly.

Nijinsky was a dancer whose art appears to be inexplicable. No description among the volumes of praise seems adequate. His own alleged famous response about his elevation—"I jump, I stay up there for a while, and then I come down"—does not explain his art. Yet, if one considers carefully the contemporary comments that not only was his technique so perfect as to be unnoticeable, but also that he could by turns transform himself, and not by make-up alone, into the essence of a rose in *Le Spectre de la Rose*, or a faun in *L'Après-midi d'un faune*, or a straw puppet with a heart in *Petrushka*, then one has to believe that indeed there was never another dancer like Nijinsky.

Diaghilev long wanted to promote Nijinsky, his lover and favorite, as a choreographer as well as a dancer. He therefore encouraged him, with Bakst's help, to arrange the choreography for *L'Après-midi d'un faune* to an existing score by Claude Debussy (1862–1918). He thus hoped that Nijinsky would replace Fokine, who was becoming tiresome and too demanding. It was not an easy transition. Nijinsky, not very articulate although musical, needed more than a hundred rehearsals over a period of nearly two years for this twelve-minute work. Although his ideas for movements based on profiles on Greek friezes and vase paintings were revolutionary, the dancers found them almost impossible to execute. At the first night, the audience was scandalized by the final moment of the ballet, when Nijinsky as the Faun made love to a scarf discarded by one of the nymphs. Diaghilev, revelling in the scandal, mischievously mistook the boos for cheers and ordered the ballet to be repeated immediately. He was always supremely masterful at manipulating public relations to his advantage.

Although Diaghilev had used the score by the non-Russian Debussy for *L'Après-midi d'un faune*, the first work he commissioned from a non-Russian composer was *Daphnis and Chloë* by Maurice Ravel (1875–1937). This ballet, which took much longer to compose than originally intended, was finally produced only reluctantly by Diaghilev. Fokine, suffering many frustrations, was so exasperated by the treatment he received that he resigned immediately after the first performance, something else that Diaghilev had successfully manipulated.

Nijinsky's other two ballets *Jeux*, and especially *Le Sacre du Printemps* (see pp 291–95) created even greater difficulties for the dancers. The first performance of *Le Sacre du Printemps* on 29 May 1913 created a riot in the audience, caused in fact more by Stravinsky's music than Nijinsky's choreography. This original version (now irretrievable) was performed only eight times, but it is now recognized that Nijinsky was a genius choreographer, too. As Karsavina pointed out, "in these two works of his, Niiinsky declared his feud against Romanticism and bid adieu to the 'beautiful.'"[20] However, Diaghilev's hopes for Nijinsky as his choreographer were quickly dashed. Instead of permanently replacing Fokine, he was dismissed by an enraged Diaghilev when he suddenly and astonishingly got married on 10 September 1913, soon after the company's arrival in Buenos Aires, to a Hungarian girl, Romola Pulszky. Diaghilev's jealous rages were often spontaneous and took no account of the consequences: this was perhaps the only serious flaw in his character, but it never had a lasting deleterious effect.

The 1914 season had to be saved. Diaghilev, swallowing his pride—or, rather, his rage—recalled Fokine to choreograph the new ballet by Richard Strauss, *La Légende de Joseph*, in which the young Leonide Massine (1895–1979) made his first appearance as Joseph. Fokine, taking advantage of Diaghilev's weak position, was able to impose severe conditions: he would dance all the major parts, but he would not do all the choreography. In addition to *La Légende de Joseph*, Fokine agreed to choreograph *Midas* and *Papillons*, and Rimsky-Korsakov's opera *The Golden Cockerel*, but not Stravinsky's latest work, his opera *Le Rossignol* (see pp 128–31). After 1914 Fokine did not work for Diaghilev again, although his ballets continued to be performed.

Nikolai Roerich, *Le Sacre du Printemps*: one of the Young Men (left) and one of the Elders.

As early as 1895, Diaghilev had announced that he had found his vocation. He wrote to his adored stepmother, Elena Panaev-Diaghilev (1851–1919):

> I am
> First, a charlatan, but full of dash;
> Secondly, a great charmer;
> Thirdly, cheeky;
> Fourthly, a very reasonable man with few scruples;
> Fifthly, someone afflicted, it seems, with a complete absence of talent. And yet I think I have found my true vocation: to be a patron of the arts. For that I have everything I need except money, but that will come.[21]

Up to 1914 Diaghilev was essentially a patron of Russian art and Russian artists.[22] Usually through sensible discussion and civilized argument, though sometimes through violent tantrums and bitter quarrels, the *impossibiliste*[23] Diaghilev nurtured the talents of his Russian colleagues. Together they reinvented the art of ballet. From this period, many of the ballets in their original form are still in the repertory of major dance companies throughout the world.

Thus much for his patronage. As for money, Diaghilev never changed his attitude toward it. Capitalizing on his dash, his cheek, and not a little deceit, he continued to extort cheques from those rich ladies of Paris and London who remained under his spell. He was an accurate assessor of his own character.

When the company gave its last performance of the season on 25 July 1914 in London, Diaghilev's intention was that it should reassemble in Berlin after the summer vacation in October. This was not to be. The First World War, which began in August 1914, put a stop to all future plans of performances by the Ballets Russes as most of the members of the company returned to Russia. Diaghilev was left alone with Massine, his new protégé. It is not clear why Diaghilev did not return to Russia as well at this time; perhaps, like many others, he thought that the war would not last longer than a few months, or perhaps he foresaw further disaster. Whatever the reason, he stayed instead in Switzerland where he was lent the Villa Belle Rive in Lausanne. According to Lydia Sokolova, who joined him there a little later: "Of all the years we travelled with Diaghilev, those six months in Switzerland were the happiest, and I believe if he had been asked later he would have said the same."[24]

Happy he may have been but he had no work, no engagements and no immediate prospects. Undaunted as ever, Diaghilev gathered some of his old friends round him: Nathalie Gontcharova, Michel Larionov, Léon Bakst among them. Stravinsky was living not far away. Massine would now replace Fokine as the company's main choreographer and start the second era of the Ballets Russes. His tentative beginnings were with *Liturgie*, a ballet based on the life of Christ, which was rehearsed but finally abandoned because of the difficulty of getting the right music sent from Russia. Massine's first completed and successful ballet was *Soleil de Nuit* (see pp 230–32). Because of the war, however, it was performed only twice at that time, in Geneva and Paris, at charity performances in aid of the Red Cross.

As tours of Europe were no longer possible, Diaghilev had to find other engagements and was fortunate in signing a contract with Otto Kahn, Chairman of the Metropolitan Opera Company, for a tour of the United States in 1916. This contract not only saved the company's precarious position but also ensured its future. In signing it, however, Diaghilev characteristically took a fearsome gamble. The contract stipulated the appearances of both Nijinsky and Karsavina. Karsavina was in Russia expecting a baby, and Nijinsky was interned in

Hungary. A long tour was planned beginning at the Century Theatre in New York on 17 January 1916, visiting sixteen cities, and ending back in New York at the Metropolitan Opera House on 29 April.[25] Diaghilev sailed with his company but, because of his fear of the sea, stayed terrified in his cabin throughout the crossing. Karsavina never arrived. Nijinsky, after protracted diplomatic negotiations, reached America only on April 4. The repertoire included all the favorite and most successful ballets which had been performed regularly in Europe: *Le Pavillon d'Armide, La Princesse Enchantée,*[26] the *Polovtsian Dances* from *Prince Igor, Cléopâtre, Les Sylphides, Le Spectre de la Rose, Thamar, Narcisse, Carnaval, The Firebird*, as well as Massine's new ballet *Soleil de Nuit*. The delay in Nijinsky's arrival meant that Massine also had to learn his parts in *Schéhérazade, Petrushka* and *L'Après-midi d'un faune*. The programs of the performances always consisted of four ballets. Although Massine admitted to being delighted by this unexpected thrust into stardom, he was also "not a little frightened at having to take over from the most distinguished dancer of our day."[27] Learning the ballets and watching all the rehearsals, however, was for him like a crash course in choreography. It taught him to admire Fokine but, as he later wrote, "it was while working on *L'Après-midi d'un Faune* that I discovered how much Nijinsky's choreography surpassed Fokine's."[28]

While no such ballet as Diaghilev's Ballets Russes had previously performed in the United States, its reputation preceded its arrival, nurtured by a knowledgeable press and sustained by enthusiastic critics. Bookings were encouraging. The report in the Boston *Herald* of the first night of the tour was typical: "The premier of the ballet in New York last Monday evening, at the Century Theatre, was one of the most brilliant functions that that city has seen. All succumbed to the magic of Serge de Diaghileff, who has welded together the sister arts of decoration, music and dance, and approached more nearly to the ideal that Wagner sought in his drama than even Wagner himself was able to do."[29] It was the total artistic experience which impressed the public and critics alike, an impression summarized by Oliver Sayler after he saw *Les Sylphides, L'Après-midi d'un faune, The Polovtsian Dances* and *Schéhérazade*: "It is difficult if not impossible to conceive of a more effective combination and succession of the arts of the ballet, a more irresistible stimulus to the human imagination. Here was perfection, indeed—not only the mechanical perfection of the precision and preparation by which these Russians shame our slipshod stage, but the perfection born of long experiment and flowering in the calm assurance of a completely finished work of art."[30] All the critics praised the dancing and especially the sets and costumes of Bakst but, as W. B. Chase wrote: "Everybody in the polite stalls had long since given up all attempts at the jawbreaking names. The house simply warmed to the performers themselves, while as for the scenery, one man said it set his neighbors 'baksterical.'"[31] The company had a similar ecstatic reception in all the cities it visited, except Chicago: there, it was a surprising and financially catastrophic failure for its backers, partly no doubt because it spent too long there, and partly because of indifferent audiences and hostile critics. Percy Hammond seemed to conduct a deliberately antagonistic campaign in the Chicago *Daily* and *Sunday Tribune*. After a week he wrote: "It appears that we are repaying with but scant contributions of money the disinterested benevolence of the solvent New Yorkers who have sent hither the Ballet Russe [sic]. That is to say that the present carnival of dancing at the Auditorium theater is proceeding to no accompaniment of substantial gratitude, and that the visitors from Muscovy are lavishing their art with futile magnanimity, while we in large numbers stay away. Other American communities have not been indifferent to

Léon Bakst, *Le Spectre de la Rose*:
Tamara Karsavina as the Young Girl, and
Vaslav Nijinsky as the Rose

the beauty of these performances and to the munificence of those who make them possible; so why, it is asked, does this center regard their ministrations with a stubborn apathy like that of Caliban to the practices of Ariel? . . . The experience of the Ballet Russe in Chicago seem to prove that sometimes, even in a center of grace and manners, may so imponderable an art fall upon evil days."[32] Percy Hammond also complained about the absence of the promised Nijinsky and Karsavina, but admitted that this was not the reason for the poor audiences.

Nijinsky finally made his American debut at the Metropolitan Opera House at the Wednesday matinée on 12 April, when he danced in *Le Spectre de la Rose* with Lopokova and in *Petrushka*. The critic of the *New York Times*, under the headline "Nijinski Puts Life in Ballet Russe," continued in a slightly reserved manner, matched in general by other critics: "Mr Nijinski's debut was a success, though he scarcely provided the sensational features that the public had been led to expect of him. This was to some extent due to the roles in which he appeared, which are limited in their possibilities in one sense because they are 'character roles.' The guise in which he presented himself yesterday was rather that of a highly accomplished dancer whose work put new life into those appearing with him than as one especially remarkable in himself. The public will probably have to wait for his appearance in ballets of the purely classical style to get more knowledge of the technical wonders that have been so liberally promised and that were indeed foreshadowed yesterday."[33] By arriving late Nijinsky had done himself, and the company, a disservice. As Grigoriev, the company manager, put it, "the public had seen his parts taken by other dancers; and not being particularly knowledgeable, liked those dancers in them just as much. Moreover, after a two years' interval he was out of practice and his dancing was by no means what it had been, though it improved as time went on."[34] Although American audiences did not see Nijinsky at his best, and although he proved to be a suspicious and unfriendly member of the company, he was good for the box office. Therefore, Otto Kahn, in spite of constant bickering and arguments with Diaghilev, wanted to conclude a further contract with him for another tour in the autumn, but this time on condition that Nijinsky would head the company and that Diaghilev himself would not return. Diaghilev agreed, delighted that he could keep his company employed while things were still difficult in Europe, and even more delighted that he would never have to endure crossing the Atlantic again after returning to Europe.

Before the end of their season at the Metropolitan Opera House, Diaghilev had accepted an invitation from Alfonso, King of Spain, for the Ballets Russes to perform in Madrid between the two American tours. When the *Dante Alighieri* set sail for Europe on May 6 with its cargo of "ammunition, horses, and the Russian Ballet,"[35] Nijinsky stayed behind to work on the choreography of *Til Eulenspiegel* before the company returned in October. This second tour would last from 16 October 1916 until 24 February 1917, starting at the Manhattan Opera House in New York and visiting this time an astonishing fifty-two cities coast-to-coast.[36] The repertoire was almost the same as for the first tour. The only new ballet was *Til Eulenspiegel* by Richard Strauss, designed by the American Robert Edmond Jones, first performed on 23 October which, after a disastrous dress rehearsal, according to Lydia Sokolova "was the only time in ballet history when the dancers more or less improvised nearly half a ballet on its opening night."[37] Perhaps it was just as well that it was the only ballet performed by his company which Diaghilev never saw. In general, however, the performances were well received by the critics, although a noticeable irritation was frequently expressed. The *Boston Evening Transcript*, in common with many newspapers, began its notice with praise by stating: "The Russian Ballet—and its audiences—have profited by its first American experiences of last winter. Returning to the Opera House yesterday, it proffered a more diversified and interesting bill than it was sometimes wont to do last February; the ensemble was smoother and more alert; the secondary dancers and mimes of clearer individual ability; and the whole performance of more exactitude and animation," but then continued: "The prudent will cast their eyes each morning over the programme then announced for the evening rather than trust to earlier lists, 'subject to change'; while only the patient will sit resignedly under the length of the intermissions, even though the orchestra mitigate one by the performance of a piece of Russian symphonic music. As everyone knows, few of the ballets or mimodramas are long in themselves. Some evening a mathematical and misanthropic person will cast up the time that actual representation and recurring intermissions relatively consume, confide it to the public and touch it, perhaps, in that exceedingly sensitive spot, 'the pocket nerve.'"[38] The word must have got round, for in fact audiences in many of the cities stayed away and the tour was cut short because the box office receipts fell far below expectation. The backers lost half a million dollars, but the dancers had a worse time, often not having enough money to eat properly. It had again been a case of art triumphing over money, but this time at the cost of a lot of disgruntled artists.

During the second tour, Diaghilev and Massine remained in Spain, planning future productions together. While there, Massine spent his free evenings watching *flamenco* dancers and "was fascinated by their instinctive sense of rhythm, their natural elegance, and the intensity of their movements."[39] At the same time he studied the works of earlier choreographers, in particular Carlo Blasis (1797–1878) who, as Massine recognized, "realized that all choreography must strive for an emotional and visual harmony."[40] Massine now developed his own theories of choreography by inventing new movements for the body which he demonstrated through his "Spanish" ballet *Las Meninas*[41] and, balancing it with a Russian ballet, continued through *Kikimora* (see pp 233–34) which was expanded later into *Les Contes Russes*. Although Larionov, the designer of *Kikimora*, still exerted some influence on Massine as a choreographer, it was Diaghilev who guided him and led him by suggesting the subjects and choosing the music for his ballets. Diaghilev next decided on an adaptation of Goldoni's play for *The Good-Humored Ladies* (see pp 82–84) with music by Scarlatti, a reworking of *The Fairy Doll* as *La Boutique Fantasque* (see pp 182–84), and Stravinsky's opera *Le Rossignol* as a ballet *Le Chant du Rossignol* (see pp 257–61). In 1920 Massine also restaged *Le Sacre du Printemps*. He had the modesty to say that he thought people preferred Nijinsky's version, but Lydia Sokolova, who danced in both, said that Nijinsky's "was a vague work, far less complicated and accurate than Massine's."[42] The only person from outside the company who seemed to have some influence with Diaghilev was Jean Cocteau. An early devotee of the Ballets Russes, he insinuated himself into Diaghilev's coterie and, after being asked to "astonish" him, persuaded him to produce his Cubist ballet called *Parade* with a circus background.[43] Diaghilev accepted Cocteau as a kind of court jester whom he nevertheless took seriously. *Parade*, with a commissioned score by the eccentric and revolutionary Erik Satie (1866–1925), was also Pablo Picasso's first work for the theater. Picasso's next work was for Manuel de Falla's *Le Tricorne* (see pp 273–78), in which Massine perfected a "fusion of native (Spanish) folk-dances and classic choreographic techniques."[44]

Léon Bakst, *Les Femmes de Bonne Humeur*: Leonide Massine as Leonardo, 1917.

Although the war had effectively put a stop to the activities of the Ballets Russes in Europe, and although the Russian Revolution meant that Diaghilev and most of his dancers became uprooted for ever, the company paradoxically found solace in a long season in London and Manchester from 5 September 1918 until 19 April 1919. Grigoriev wrote: "We began living the orderly and peaceful existence for which we had been longing throughout the turmoils and anxieties of the preceding years."[45]

Permanent severance from Russia led Diaghilev into a change of artistic policy. While Massine was still responsible for the choreography, Diaghilev now began to commission artists who were not Russian to design sets and costumes. As well as Picasso, who also designed *Pulcinella*[46] and *Cuadro Flamenco*,[47] he commissioned Matisse for *Le Chant du Rossignol* (see pp 257–61, André Derain for *La Boutique Fantasque* (see pp 182–84) after one of his periodic but this time more destructive rows with Bakst who had been promised the production, and José-Maria Sert for *Le Astuzie Femminili* (see pp 311–14).[48]

This period of relative stability came to an end suddenly in 1921 when Diaghilev, jealous as ever and quarrelsome, dismissed Massine for noticeably spending too much time with the English dancer Vera Savina.[49] Diaghilev was now without a choreographer, but he had to fulfill a contract at the Gaité-Lyrique theater with new productions which Paris insisted upon. *Cuadro Flamenco*, traditional Spanish dances to the accompaniment of guitar, castanets, and voice in a setting devised by Picasso, was a production such as had not been seen in Paris before and proved to be most popular, while Diaghilev himself said of the Russian *Chout*, with music by Prokofiev, designed by Larionov, and choreographed by Larionov and the dancer Thadée Slavinsky, that "the best part is the music. The next best is the décor, and the worst is the choreography." So Diaghilev, without a choreographer, back-tracked from innovation and decided that the best way out of his artistic and financial difficulty would be to produce one of the great classic Russian ballets to run for at least six months, preferably in London because the audiences there were more loyal than elsewhere. He settled on creating a revival of Tchaikovsky's and Petipa's *The Sleeping Beauty* which he renamed *The Sleeping Princess* (see pp 87–101) in order not to confuse it in the audience's mind with a traditional English Christmas pantomime. He found the necessary backers in London to provide the investment capital. He returned to Bakst for the design, knowing that he, of all designers, would bring a uniquely spectacular sumptuousness to the production. He engaged all the dancers. He invited Bronislava Nijinska (Nijinsky's sister), who had been a dancer in his company until 1914 and who happened to be in London, to arrange some new dances. The production, following a familiar but this time unexpected and definitely undesired pattern, was again an artistic triumph but a commercial failure.

An unforeseen bonus, however, was that Diaghilev had found his new choreographer. Bronislava Nijinska made such an impression on him that he avowed: "If I had a daughter, I would like one with such gifts."[51] When the run of *The Sleeping Princess* was cut short in London in February 1922 the scenery and costumes were sequestered, and Diaghilev could not take the whole production to Paris as he had been contracted to do. He devised instead a one-act selection of excerpts, which he called *Le Mariage de la Belle au Bois Dormant* or *Aurora's Wedding*, with the set and costumes which he still had from *Le Pavillon d'Armide* and some new costumes designed by Gontcharova. He asked Nijinska to arrange the choreography. He also asked her to make the choreography for Stravinsky's new ballets *Renard* (see pp 235–38) and *Les Noces* (see pp 208–11), as well as direct his opera *Mavra* (see pp 318–22). *Mavra* was the cause of Diaghilev's final and irreconcilable break with Bakst, his oldest friend and staunchest collaborator. Bakst had agreed to design *The Sleeping Princess* on condition that he would also design *Mavra*, but when the time came Diaghilev reneged and gave the production to Leopold Survage. This time Bakst never forgave him. They never spoke to each other again, but Diaghilev wept when he heard in December 1924 that Bakst had died.

In other ways matters improved. The final phase of the Ballets Russes was the only one during which the company had reasonable financial security: at the end of 1922 Diaghilev had come to an agreement with the Société des Bains de Mer at Monte Carlo that the company would be based there during the winter months in order to rehearse and try out new productions. Prince Lieven wrote: "Diaghileff heaved a sigh of relief. At last, after many years of trouble and uncertainty, he felt firm ground beneath his feet. A definite income for the ballet was assured, and some sort of refuge which they could consider their own provided for the homeless wanderers of the Ballets Russes."[52] This security also gave an incentive to the company to be adventurous artistically. Several experimental strands are evident during the last few years which contradict the generally accepted view that Diaghilev was losing interest in his search for the new, that he was tired and bored, irritated by having to go on being an impresario, and that his only enthusiasm was for collecting rare Russian books and manuscripts. It is thought that once he was settled in Monte Carlo Diaghilev became merely a courtier or "Minister of Fine Arts at the Court of Monaco."[53] This view is sustained because it is also believed that Boris Kochno, a young man of seventeen who had appeared on the scene in February 1921 and was instantly engaged by Diaghilev as a secretary, had a much greater influence on the affairs of the company than in actual fact he did—a view, incidentally, subsequently greatly encouraged by Kochno himself. Diaghilev's lack of interest is not substantiated by the personal memoirs of several of the participants in the productions during the last seven years. While it is true that Kochno wrote the libretto of many of the ballets and of Stravinsky's opera *Mavra*, and while it is also undoubtedly true that Diaghilev allowed—even encouraged—his young collaborators to have a free hand during the preparation of a new ballet, it is perfectly clear not only that he tightly controlled the program, by deciding which ballet to produce, which composer, designer and choreographer to commission, and which dancer to cast in which role, but also that he minutely supervised the final rehearsals, often saving a new production from impending disaster. Lighting was often the unifying technical factor of a successful production, and no one understood better than Diaghilev the importance of getting it right for the sake of the whole show. Anton Dolin, the leading dancer for several years, observed that: "To light one scene Diaghileff would spend hours. l have known him sit in a theatre from ten o'clock in the morning until two-thirty in the afternoon and even then not finish lighting it to that perfection which was his fetish—never tired, always watching, watching, watching!"[54] Diaghilev remained the same Diaghilev to the end.

If he had really lost interest in the art of ballet. he might have been tempted to relax and merely repeat his past successes with his young company of new dancers. While it is true that he relied on some favorites as the core of his annual programs—*Petrushka, Polovtsian Dances, Les Sylphides, L'Après-midi d'un faune*, and from 1926 a revival of *The Firebird* (see pp 212–16)—the 1920s found him just as adventurous as before. As an impresario he understood that in order to maintain the support and interest of an enthusiastic audience he had to provide them with some new ballets each year, and being the man he was he would have gone out of his mind with boredom if he hadn't.

One example of Diaghilev's innovation was the idea of a French festival. As so often with Diaghilev, this was musically based and devised in two parts: new ballets by young French contemporary composers, and the revival of some neglected operas by Charles Gounod (1818–1893).[55] Only the opera "Festival" came off according to plan. The ballets, largely because the composers did not deliver on time, were produced over several years. They were *Les Biches* (see pp 242–46) by Francis Poulenc (1899–1963); *Les Fâcheux* (see pp 147–49), *Les Matelots* (see pp 279–85), and *La Pastorale* (see pp 286–88) by Georges Auric (1899–1983); *Le Train Bleu*[56] by Darius Milhaud, and *La Chatte* (see pp 204–7) by Henri Sauguet (1901–89). *Jack-in the-Box* (see pp 185–90) and *Mercure*[57] by Erik Satie were produced in his honor after his death. Parallel to commissioning these scores, Diaghilev also commissioned scores from the English composers Constant Lambert (1905–51) with *Romeo and Juliet* (see pp 193–99, 262–65), and Lord Berners (1883–1950) with *The Triumph of Neptune*,[58] and the Italian Vittorio Rieti (1898–1994) with *Barabau*[59] and *Le Bal* (see pp 155–71).

In spite of these musical excursions, Diaghilev also remained faithful to his early discovery, Igor Stravinsky. He produced not only his latest ballets *Renard, Les Noces* and *Apollon Musagète* (see pp 103–7), but also his operas *Oedipus Rex*[60] as well as *Mavra*. He was very hurt when his fidelity was repaid by Stravinsky giving the rights to *Le Baiser de la Fée* (*The Fairy's Kiss*) in 1928 to Ida Rubinstein. However, Diaghilev continued to discover and promote young Russian composers. Serge Prokofiev (1891–1953) had already established a certain reputation with *Chout*, which Diaghilev had produced in 1921. He now followed this with *Le Pas d'Acier*—so called, according to Massine, because "it would suggest the metallic atmosphere of modern industrial progress"[61] at a time when Diaghilev flirted briefly with Communist ideas and even considered returning to Russia after receiving an invitation to be a kind of Minister of Culture—and *The*

Marie Laurencin, *Les Biches*: the scene on stage (right); Leon Woizikovsky as one of the Athletes and Vera Nemtchinova as the Girl in Blue (below).

Prodigal Son (see pp 300–305), the last new ballet produced by the Ballets Russes. Before that, Diaghilev had encouraged Vladimir Dukelsky (1903–69) by producing his ballet *Zéphire et Flore* (see pp 150–52) in 1925, and Nicolas Nabokov (1903–78) with his ballet-oratorio *Ode* (see pp 323–31) in 1928. Dukelsky later became an American citizen, called himself Vernon Duke, wrote musical comedies and *April in Paris*, his most famous song. In his amusing and racy autobiography, *Passport to Paris*, he describes Diaghilev more evocatively than anyone else: "Sergei Pavlovitch Diaghilev was a big man—slightly over six feet tall—broad and big-limbed, but not corpulent; his head was enormous, and the face—a world in itself; you hardly noticed the rest of his body. The still-abundant graying hair was parted meticulously on the side and displayed the oft-described silver-white patch in the middle—no crafty coiffeur's trick but, from all accounts, something of a birthmark. When I first gazed at Diaghilev's face, I thought instantly of a decadent Roman emperor—Caligula, perhaps—although Diaghilev was allergic to horses among other things, then the Tartar in him—possibly Genghis Khan—or even a barbarous Scythian, became visible—and lastly what he really was: a Russian *grand seigneur* of Alexander III vintage. The eyes had a piercing, mocking intensity about them, softened by unusually heavy eyelids, and he was fond of closing them slowly, as if persuaded by some unseen Morpheus, but only for a moment: they were soon peering at you again, not missing a thing. The mouth was cruel and soft at the same time, the mustache even more close-clipped than Valithcka's (Nouvel), the smile irresistible and oddly feminine. Sergei Pavlovitch carried monocles in all his pockets and had a habit of dropping one into his left hand, producing another with the right and screwing it into his eye languidly, making a lazy chewing motion with his mouth the while, as if munching spinach. He was well, although not conspicuously well, dressed and wore his Davis dinner jacket as if it were a dressing gown. His voice seemed monstrously affected at first—the Imperial Page's voice of aristocratic St Petersburg—but you soon knew that he must have, too, been born with it. Diaghilev spoke French superbly, and English adequately."[62]

To decorate the new ballets, Diaghilev continued with his policy of commissioning artists from the school of Paris; in doing so, he demonstrated that he was as ever keenly interested in the latest developments. He stayed in touch with what was going on by visiting the avant-garde art galleries in Paris. This is how he chose Max Ernst and Joan Miró for *Romeo and Juliet*, and André Bauchant for *Apollon Musagète*. He preferred to choose easel painters rather than professional theater designers, believing that the artist is necessarily superior to the craftsman. (He also believed that an artist should be quite happy living in a garret without any money.) The other contemporary painters he singled out for his ballets were Marie Laurençin for *Les Biches*, Georges Braque for *Les Fâcheux* and *Zéphire et Flore*, Juan Gris for *Les Tentations de la Bergère* (see pp 217–22), André Derain for *Jack-in-the-Box*, Georges Rouault for *Le Fils Prodigue*, Maurice Utrillo for *Barabau*, and Giorgio de Chirico for *Le Bal*. On Picasso's recommendation he asked another young Spanish painter, Pedro Pruna, to design *Les Matelots* and *La Pastorale*, probably the silliest ballet Diaghilev produced. At the same time he also remained faithful to his particularly close Russian colleagues Nathalie Gontcharova and Michel Larionov, who were responsible for designing the two Stravinsky revivals: she redesigned *The Firebird* in 1926, he his own *Renard* in 1929. Diaghilev also had a flirtation with Russian constructivism, with Naum Gabo and Antoine Pevsner designing *La Chatte*, and Georgi Yakulov designing *Le Pas d'Acier*. All in all, Diaghilev had an unerring sense of choosing the right painter to design a given ballet, and maintained the reputation of the Ballets

Georges Rouault: *Le Fils Prodigue*. Anton Dolin and Leon Woizikovsky as the Confidants, and Serge Lifar as the Prodigal Son.

Russes for being at the forefront of avant-garde art. This reputation, however, was secured by Diaghilev being fortunate in having at his disposal two scene painters who were supreme masters of their craft: Vladimir Polunin and Prince Alexander Schervashidze (see pp 306–10). They were brilliantly able to interpret the painters' designs into a suitable form for the stage, although they were not always able to avoid the criticism that many of the sets were merely enlargements of paintings. Diaghilev even encouraged this quality by insisting on his painters designing front cloths for their ballets. One such cloth, an enlargement by Schervashidze of a gouache by Picasso for *Le Train Bleu*,[63] was so monumental and spectacular that it was then regularly used as a front cloth before all performances of the Ballets Russes.

During the 1920s the Ballets Russes, in the personification of Diaghilev, became like a magnet, attracting not only wandering émigré dancers from Russia but eager novices from England. The company's reputation was such that if you wanted to be a dancer then you had to work for Diaghilev. On the other hand, among all those he employed, Diaghilev did not hold his dancers in the highest regard—indeed, he often treated them with a disdain amounting to cruelty. Anton Dolin made this comment about Diaghilev's attitude: "It always seemed to me that the last thing he ever thought about was the dancers. Somehow he never appeared to pay so much attention to them as he did to the lighting and to the orchestra. I often wondered if they were less important or if he had more faith in them."[64] Diaghilev had good reason not to worry about his dancers. Throughout the whole period of the Ballets Russes there was one vital stabilizing factor that guaranteed its unfailing and much admired standard of technical excellence: the daily classes conducted according to traditional techniques by Enrico Cecchetti (1850–1928), the company's principal teacher from 1910 to 1923 who taught all Diaghilev's major dancers. He also created the parts of the Chief Eunuch in *Schéhérazade*, The Showman in *Petrushka*, and Luca in *Les Femmes de Bonne Humeur*, as well as celebrating fifty years on the stage on 5 January 1922 by performing Carabosse in *The Sleeping Princess*, a role he had created thirty-two years earlier.

Diaghilev liked to nurture his choreographers from among his dancers. After Massine left the company, Bronislava Nijinska stayed to create the choreography of some of the most and the least successful ballets of the final years. Lydia Sokolova, who danced in her ballets, wrote: "She was brilliantly clever and inventive. No music seemed to present any difficulties for her, but her style of movement was even more pronounced and idiosyncratic than that of Massine, and she was not an easy person to work for in class or at rehearsal, because of her extreme mannerisms."[65] *Les Noces* was instantly recognized as a supreme work, and established Nijinska as a major choreographer; but although it was much admired, it was not universally liked. This was followed in quick succession by a hit, *Les Biches*, two misses, *Les Tentations de la Bergère* and *Les Fâcheux*, and another hit, *Le Train Bleu*. In the end, Nijinska was too traditional for Diaghilev. She herself later described her dilemma when she wrote: "A choreographer who worked for Diaghilev was required above all to abjure the old school but nevertheless to expand the artistic possibilities of the classical dance."[66]

It was never easy working for Diaghilev. He had a tendency to be secretive and go behind his colleagues' backs, and the irritations he caused often led to serious rifts. So it was with Fokine when Diaghilev wanted to promote Nijinsky as a choreographer; now it was the same with Nijinska when he wanted to promote Serge Lifar, who had joined the company as an incompetent tiro in 1923.

Lifar rapidly improved as a dancer through sheer hard work under Cecchetti's tutelage, but he failed his first test as a choreographer with *Zéphire et Flore*. Diaghilev's rifts did not last long, and he now recalled Massine who also stayed for *Les Matelots* and returned for *Ode*. Nijinska also returned for *Romeo and Juliet*. These were makeshift appointments, for Diaghilev again found himself without a regular choreographer. But then he struck gold: four young Russian émigré dancers—Alexandra Danilova, Tamara Gevergeva, Nicolas Efimov, and George Balanchivadze—joined his company in 1924 while touring Europe. The last, with the simplified name Balanchine, became Diaghilev's final great choreographer. He began by arranging the dances for some operas in Monte Carlo, and then devised a new choreography for the revival of Stravinsky's *Le Chant du Rossignol*. His first original ballet for Diaghilev was *Barabau*.[67] After some slight, modish works, the absurd *La Pastorale*, the clever *Jack-in-the-Box*, and the modernistic *La Chatte*, Balanchine, by his own admission, reached the "turning point" in his life with Stravinsky's *Apollon Musagète*. At a rehearsal, Nicolas Nabokov overheard Diaghilev say to Derain: "What he is doing is magnificent. It is pure classicism, such as we have not seen since Petipa's."[68] Diaghilev may have reinvented ballet, but Balanchine reinvented classicism. In his last works for Diaghilev, *Le Bal* and *Le Fils Prodigue*, Balanchine stretched his classical definitions of movement into new dimensions.

Joan Miró, *Romeo and Juliet*: Tamara Karsavina as Juliet and Serge Lifar as Romeo.

Chided for having apparently approved the new choreography, Diaghilev stated his case publicly and disingenuously in a letter to *The Times* just before the first night of the revival of *Renard*, the first choreographic work by Serge Lifar, of which the following, in its original peculiar translation, is an extract: "For 25 years I have endeavoured to find a new 'Mouvement' in the theatre. Society will have to recognize that my experiments, which appear dangerous today, become indispensable tomorrow. The misfortune of art is that everybody thinks he is entitled to his own judgment. When a scientist invents an electrical machine it is only experts who assume the right to be competent to criticize, but when I invent my artistic machine, everybody, without ceremony, puts his finger into the most delicate parts of the engine and likes to run it his own way. But let us come to the events of to-day! The new appreciation of my 'Spectacles' of to-day is a series of exclamations: What an 'Etrange,' 'Extravagant,' 'Repellent' show, and the new definitions of the choreography are 'Athletics' and 'Acrobatics.' The show, before anything must be 'Etrange.' I can picture to myself the bewilderment of the people who saw the first electric lamp, who heard the first word on the telephone. My first electric bell for the British public was the presentation of the Polovtsian dances of *Prince Igor*. The small audience could not then tolerate this eccentric and acrobatic savagery, and they fled. And this only happened in 1911, at Covent Garden. At the very same theatre in 1929 the critics announced that my dancers had transformed themselves into 'athletes' and my choreographic parts were 'pure acrobatics.' . . . The coarsest acrobatic tricks are the toe-dancing, the 'Double tours en l'air,' next to the classical 'Pirouettes en dehors,' and the hateful 32 'Fouettés,' that is where acrobatics should be attacked. In the plastic efforts of Balanchine, in *The Prodigal Son*, there are far less acrobatics than in the final classical *Pas de deux* of *Aurora's Wedding*. Monday next I am presenting to the public two new items. Lifar is, for the first time, in charge of the dances; he is the inventor of the choreography of the *Renard*, and it is there where really one has the first opportunity to talk of acrobatic ballet. It is not all Lifar's principle, but just because he could not see any other form to express the acrobatic music of Stravinsky."[69] Diaghilev, with characteristic modesty, did not mention in his letter that the "acrobatics" in *Renard*, in which true acrobats doubled the parts with the dancers, were his idea. The ballet was only reasonably successful, but Lifar the choreographer (or "chore-author" as he always preferred to be called) was safely launched, albeit with considerable help. Diaghilev, however, was now moving on in his attachments, and was much more keen to promote his new discovery, the sixteen-year-old composer Igor Markevitch and his piano concerto, the other "new" item mentioned in his letter. Sadly, his enthusiasm was premature because the piano concerto was a complete failure. His disappointment was so intense that his health, which had lately been poor, now rapidly deteriorated. Perhaps Diaghilev, the avuncular pedagogue, expected to be reinvigorated by taking his new protégé on a cultural tour, but after guiding Markevitch round Munich and Salzburg, he went on alone for his usual summer vacation in Venice in a state of total exhaustion. He was joined there by Lifar. He later summoned Kochno and Misia Sert, his beloved friend, to Venice too. Instead of finding relief, he never recovered his strength. Surrounded by this faithful band, Diaghilev died on 19 August 1929. The Ballets Russes died with him.

Léon Bakst, who in his time probably knew Diaghilev better than anyone, inadvertently gave him the best and most accurate epitaph during an interview before the Company's first tour of the United States in 1916: "It doesn't matter who the principal stars are, if Diaghilev is with the troupe. When Diaghilev is on the ground he is the bright particular star—although the public never sees him and he avoids all personal publicity. Rather he is the central star, for everything in the organization revolves round Diaghilev. He is its maker, its soul and its spirit. No such ballet existed before Sergei Diaghilev brought it into being, and knowing the genius as I, who have been his friend for over twenty years, know it, I cannot conceive of him having a successor."[70] How right he was.

Léon Bakst, *The Sleeping Princess*: the arrival of the Wicked Fairy in the first scene.

Notes

1   Arnold Haskell, *Diaghileff, his artistic and private life*, p 45. This book was written in collaboration with Walter Nouvel, Diaghilev's trusted friend and confidant, and one of the group gathered round Alexandre Benois. This descriptive phrase is no doubt his. Diaghilev's home town was Perm in Siberia, and anyone coming from Siberia was considered to be beyond the pale. The snobbery of those living in a capital city often persists unjustifiably.

2   I prefer this spelling to the now more common "Filosofov" because it acknowledges the classical derivation of the name. Furthermore, I remember my uncle's fob watch on which the

hours were marked by the 12 Roman letters PHILOSOPHOFF.

3   Prince Sergei Mikhailovitch Volkonsky (1860–1937) was appointed Director on 22 July 1899, but resigned in July 1901.

4   Under Paragraph 3 of Article 838 of the "Rules of State Service." This meant "dismissal without pardon" and "dismissal without reason given and without appeal." Anyone dismissed according to Paragraph 3 could never be employed by the state again.

5   Quoted in Alexandre Benois, *Reminiscences of the Russian Ballet*, p 266.

6   Quoted in Serge Lifar, *Serge Diaghilev*, p 176–7. Lifar did not say to whom this letter was addressed.

7   By Jacques-Emile Blanche, among others, in *La Revue de Paris*, 1 December 1913.

8   Serge Diaghilev, "About the Russian Ballet" in *The Graphic*, London, 20 July 1929, p 133.

9   Cyril W. Beaumont, *Michel Fokine & his ballets*, p 23.

10 The only dancer, apart from Pierina Legnani (1863–1923), ever to be given the title.

11 Kshessinska later made it up with Diaghilev and danced in the company's first season in London in 1911.

12 Vladimir Telyakovsky, *Vospominaniya* (*Memoirs*), p 63.

13 Robert Brussel, "Gabriel Astruc: mars 1864– juillet 1938" in *Revue Musicale*, Paris, Sept–Nov 1938, No 186, p 113.

14 Called the "Répétition générale publique" or "Public Dress Rehearsal," often a grander occasion than the official first night which, in this case was on 19 May.

15 Richard Buckle. *Diaghilev*, p 141.

16 Both Pavlova and Rubinstein left Diaghilev after 1910 to start their own companies.

17 Polish by birth, her maiden name was Godebska. She married a succession of rich husbands, first Thadée Natanson, founder and editor of *La Revue Blanche*, then Alfred Edwards, the multi-millionaire owner of *Le Matin*. She then married the Spanish painter José-Maria Sert, who would design the sets for *Le Légende de Joseph* in 1914, costumes for *Las Meninas* in 1916, and both sets and cotumes for *Le Astuzie Femminili* in 1920.

18 Jacques-Emile Blanche, *Portraits of a Lifetime*, p 262.

19 Serge Diaghilev, quoted in "About the Russian Ballet," *The Graphic*, London, 20 July 1929.

20 Tamara Karsavina, *Theatre Street*, p 236.

21 Also quoted in Arnold Haskell, *op cit*, p 87, in a different translation.

22 Diaghilev had, however, commissioned the contemporary French composer Reynaldo Hahn (*Le Dieu Bleu*) as well as Maurice Ravel (*Daphnis and Chloë*), used a score by Claude Debussy (*L'Après-midi d'un faune*) and commissioned him to compose another (*Jeux*). Another commission for 1912, *La Péri* by Paul Dukas, failed to materialize because of difficulties over his mistress, the leading ballerina Tamara Trouhanova.

23 A sobriquet invented by Alexandre Benois.

24 Lydia Sokolova, *Dancing for Diaghilev*, p 69.

25 The itinerary was as follows: New York City, 17–29 January; Boston, 31 January–9 February; Albany, 10 February; Detroit, 11–12 February; Chicago, 14–26 February; Milwaukee, 28 February; St Paul, 29 February–1 March;

Minneapolis,2–3 March ; Kansas City, 4 March; St Louis, 6–8 March; Indianapolis, 9–11 March; Cincinnati, 13–15 March; Cleveland, 16–18 March; Pittsburgh, 20–22 March; Washington D.C., 23–25 March; Philadelphia, 27 March–1 April; Atlantic City, 31 March; New York City, 3–29 April.

26 A *pas de deux* from Tchaikovsky's *The Sleeping Beauty*.

27 Leonide Massine, *My Life in Ballet*, p 80.

28 Leonide Massine, *ibid*, p 84.

29 Anon, "Beautiful and Graceful Women and Men Who Are Not Effeminate Compose the Troupe" in *The Boston Herald*, Boston, 23 January 1916.

30 Oliver M. Sayler, "'The Faun" and "Scheherazade" Escape the Censorial Eye— Diaghileff Ballet Reaches New Hights" in *Indianapolis News*, Indianapolis, 11 March 1916.

31 W. B. Chase "Bravo, Russian Ballet" in *The Sun*, New York, 18 January 1916.

32 Percy Hammond, "Are the Russians Naughty or Nice?" in the *Chicago Sunday Tribune*, Chicago, 20 February 1916.

33 Anon, *New York Times*, New York, 13 April 1916.

34 Serge Grigoriev, *The Diaghilev Ballet*, p 120.

35 Serge Grigoriev, *ibid*, p 122.

36 The itinerary was as follows: New York City, 16–28 October 1916, with the tour from 30 October 1916–24 February 1917 visiting Providence, New Haven, Brooklyn, Springfield, Boston, Worcester, Hartford, Bridgeport, Atlantic City, Baltimore, Washington D.C., Philadelphia, Richmond, Columbia, Atlanta, New Orleans, Houston, Austin, Fort Worth, Dallas, Tulsa, Wichita, Kansas City, Des Moines, Omaha, Denver, Salt Lake City, Los Angeles, San Francisco, Buffalo, Portland, Vancouver (Canada), Seattle, Tacoma, Oakland, Spokane, St Paul, Minneapolis, Milwaukee, Indianapolis, St Louis, Nashville, Cincinnati, Dayton, Detroit, Toledo, Grand Rapids, Chicago, Cleveland, Pittsburgh, Syracuse, Albany.

37 Lydia Sokolova, *Dancing for Diaghilev*, p 91.

38 H. T. P., "The Russians in Full Glory" in the *Boston Evening Transcript*, Boston, 7 November 1916.

39 Leonide Massine, *op cit*, p 89.

40 Leonide Massine, *ibid*, pp 93–4.

41 *Las Meninas*, composed by Gabriel Fauré, with set by Socrate and costumes by José-Maria Sert, was first performed at the Teatro Eugenia-Victoria, San Sebastian on 25 August 1916.

42 Lydia Sokolova, *op cit*, p 162.

43 *Parade* was first performed at the Châtelet Theatre, Paris on 18 May 1917.

44 Leonide Massine, *op cit*, p 119.

45 Serge Grigoriev, *op cit*, p 150.

46 *Pulcinella* by Igor Stravinsky after Pergolesi was first performed at the Opéra, Paris on 15 May 1920.

47 *Cuadro Flamenco* to traditional Spanish music was first performed at the Gaité-Lyrique, Paris on 17 May 1921.

48 Robert Delaunay had also been commissioned to redesign the set for *Cléopâtre* in 1918, the original having been destroyed by fire.

49 Née Vera Clark. She and Massine were married in London on 26 April 1921.

50 Quoted by Serge Grigoriev, *op cit*, p 173.

51 Arnold Haskell, *op cit*, p 69.

52 Prince Peter Lieven, *The Birth of Ballets-Russes*, pp 229–30.

53 Prince Peter Lieven, *ibid*, p 230.

54 Anton Dolin, *Divertissement*, p 197.

55 The operas by Gounod were: *La Colombe*, first performed on 1 January 1924; *Le Médecin malgré lui*, first performed on 5 January 1924, and *Philémon et Baucis*, first performed on 10 January 1924. In addition, Diaghilev produced *Une Education Manquée* by Emmanuel Chabrier on 17 January 1924. All the operas were performed at Monte Carlo.

56 *Le Train Bleu* was first performed at the Théâtre des Champs-Elysées, Paris on 20 June 1924.

57 *Mercure* was first performed at the Théâtre Sarah-Bernhardt, Paris on 2 June 1927.

58 *The Triumph of Neptune* was first performed at the Lyceum Theatre, London on 3 December 1926.

59 *Barabau* was first performed at the Coliseum Theatre, London on 11 December 1925.

60 *Oedipus Rex*, really an opera-oratorio, with a libretto by Jean Cocteau translated into Latin, was first performed as a fifty-fifth birthday present to Diaghiley at the Théâtre Sarah-Bernhardt, Paris on 30 May 1927.

61 Leonide Massine, *op cit*, p 172. *Le Pas d'Acier* was first performed at the Théâtre Sarah-Bernhardt, Paris on 7 June 1927.

62 Vernon Duke, *Passport to Paris*, p 113.

63 The original gouache on wood is called "The Race" (32.5 x 41.5 cm) and remained in the artist's collection (illustrated in Douglas Cooper, *Picasso Theatre*, pp 349–50). The front cloth measures 10 x 11 meters; it is in the collections of the Theatre Museum, London.

64 Anton Dolin, *Divertissement*, p 198.

65 Lydia Sokolova, *op cit*. p 203.

66 Bronislava Nijinska, "On Movement and the School of Movement," quoted in exhibition catalogue *Bronislava Nijinska: A dancer's legacy*, p 86.

67 *Barabau*, with music by Vittorlo Rieti, sets and costumes by Maurice Utrillo, was first performed at the London Coliseum theater on 11 December 1925.

68 Nicolas Nabokov, *Old Friends and New Music*.

69 Serge Diaghileff [sic], "The Russian Ballet. Acrobatics and Dancing," letter to *The Times*, London, 13 July 1929. The text of the letter was originally dictated in Russian to Pavel Koribut-Kubitovitch and Serge Lifar, and probably translated into English by the former. The Russian text, dated 9 July, is published in Zilberstein and Samkov, *Sergei Diaghilev i Russkoe iskusstvo*, Vol 1, pp 256–8, and is discussed by Lifar in his *Serge Diaghilev*, pp 329–35, with extracts in a better translation. For example, the first sentence quoted from *The Times* above is translated: "For twenty-five years now I have sought to find new movements in the theatre, and Society should therefore accept once and for all these experiments of mine which today seem so dangerous to it, but which tomorrow will form part and parcel of its life."

70 Quoted by William J. Guard, "Sergei Diaghilev, Slavic Sorcerer, and His Magical Russian Dancers," in the *Boston Evening Transcript*, Boston, 8 January 1916, Part Two p 8.

General note

The catalogue is arranged in alphabetical order of artist, and then in chronological order of work. The costumes have been integrated with the works on paper or canvas, either immediately following the design if one exists or, if not, at the end of the relevant production. A catalogue number followed by * indicates a work acquired after the main purchase of the collection from Serge Lifar in 1933.

All the works, except those given, have been acquired through the fund known as the Ella Gallup Sumner and Mary Catlin Sumner Collection. Jean K. Cadogan has described how this fund came into being: "The Sumner bequest, created through the generosity of Frank Chester Sumner (1850–1924), came to the Atheneum following the death of his wife, Mary Catlin Sumner, on 11 August 1927. Frank Sumner, a prominent local figure and president of the Hartford, Connecticut Trust Company from 1919, was not a collector and indeed had little interest in art. He had inherited the estate of his brother George Sumner (1841–1906), who was, however, interested in the museum, and who had stipulated in his will that if Frank predeceased him, the estate should go to the museum to form a collection of paintings in memory of his wife, Ella Gallup Sumner. Frank outlived George Sumner by eighteen years, but when he died in 1924, he followed George's example and bequeathed his estate to the Wadsworth Atheneum, providing his wife, Mary, with the use of it during her lifetime. Upon her death, the funds, then just over one million dollars, came to the museum to be used as an endowment for the purchase of paintings to be known as the Ella Gallup Sumner and Mary Catlin Sumner Collection."[1] The costumes added to the collection in 1996 were acquired through the J. Herbert Callister Fund, the Florence Paull Berger Fund, and the Costume and Textile Purchase Fund. (See also "Credit lines," below.)

French productions, as well as Diaghilev's Ballets Russes productions, are called by their original French titles—e.g. *Le Spectre de la Rose* rather than *The Spirit (or Phantom) of the Rose*—unless the English title has become better known. Original Russian titles have been translated into English.

Each production is listed with the main credits of the first performance relevant to the particular work or works. They are followed by a synopsis, and a detailed note on the background to the original production, its creation and reception. Contemporary opinion has been gleaned wherever possible from the memoirs of the participants which are not, of course, necessarily reliable, and critics of the day, who were not necessarily objective. Since these descriptive background notes appear within the alphabetical order of artist, a chronological list of all the productions represented in the collection is given at Appendix A, p 332. There is a further note on individual works when additional information or explanation is required. Notes, giving the source of quotations, refer to the Select Bibliography.

Russian names have been transliterated into their generally accepted and usual anglicized form, or according to the person's known preference, except in direct quotations when the original spelling has been retained. All translations from Russian and French, unless otherwise acknowledged, have been made by the author. Russian dates are given in the old (Julian calendar) style, followed by the new (Gregorian calendar) style in brackets. The difference in the calendars increases by one day every century. From 1 March 1901 the difference has been thirteen days. (The Julian calendar is now used only by the Russian Orthodox church.)

Works on paper or canvas

When there is no given title, then the title is the description and/or the purpose of the work. This is followed by the medium. The designation of tempera has been used for pigment in a water-soluble binder; depending on consistency, it can be opaque or translucent. Since visual analysis is inconclusive, many drawings are described as "tempera and/or watercolor."

Measurements, height before width, are given in both inches and centimeters. Signatures, dates, and inscriptions are by the artist unless otherwise stated.

The museum number shows the year of acquisition followed by the unique number identifying the object.

Costumes

The descriptions have been made by Carol Dean Krute, Curator of Costume and Textiles.

Credit lines

The credit line for all designs is "The Ella Gallup Sumner and Mary Catlin Sumner Collection Fund" unless indicated otherwise.

The credit line for all costumes is "The Herbert Callister Fund, the Florence Paull Berger Fund, and the Costume and Textile Purchase Fund" unless indicated otherwise.

Provenance

Unless otherwise stated the provenance of all the works is by purchase from Serge Lifar.

Many of the works listed in the exhibition catalogues of the New Chenil Galleries, London (1926), and the Galerie Vignon, Paris (1929) were originally bought by Serge Diaghilev and given to Serge Lifar. The additional works listed in the catalogue of Arthur Tooth, London (1930), specifically relating to Ballets Russes productions, presumably belonged to Diaghilev and were acquired, after his death, by Lifar. See Appendix B for the lists of works in these exhibitions.

The costumes sold by Sotheby's on 14 December 1995 were incorrectly described in the catalogue as being "The property of the Executors of the late Lord Howard of Henderscelfe: Castle Howard." This statement was corrected by Simon Howard in the *Art Newspaper* Vol VII No 55, London January 1996, p 3, and the true provenance is given with each costume.

Exhibitions

The lists are shown in abbreviated form. The full list with titles and dates is given in Exhibitions on pp 336 ff. The exhibition entitled *Design, Dance and Music of the Ballets Russes 1909–1929* at the Wadsworth Atheneum, Hartford, CT, 5 September–4 January 1988 has not been included.

Illustrations

The lists, which are not comprehensive, show in abbreviated form the publications in which the works have been illustrated. The full title and details are given in the Select Bibliography.

Note

1 Jean K. Cadogan, *Wadsworth Atheneum Paintings II, Italy and Spain, Fourteenth through Nineteenth Centuries*, Hartford 1991, p 11.

Boris Anisfeldt

Russian
born 1879 Beltsey, Bessarabia
died 1974 Waterford, Connecticut

Snegourotchka (The Snow Maiden)

Opera in 4 acts and a prologue by Nikolai Rimsky-
    Korsakov after the play by Alexander Ostrovsky,
    translated into French by Mme P. Halperne and
    P. Lalo
Composer: Nikolai Rimsky-Korsakov
Conductor: Artur Bodanzky
Designer (sets and costumes): Boris Anisfeldt[1]
Principal singers:
    Snegourotchka: Lucrezia Bori
    Lel, a shepherd: Raymonde Delaunois
    Koupava: Yvonne D'Arle
    Fairy Spring: Marion Telva
    Bobylicka: Kathleen Howard
    The Faun: Giordano Paltrinieri
    A Page: Grace Anthony
    The Tsar: Orville Harold
    Mizguir: Mario Laurenti
    King Winter: Leon Rothier
    Bobyl: Angelo Bada
    Bermiate: Louis D'Angelo
    Carnival: George Meader
    First Court Jester: Pietro Audisio
    Second Court Jester: Vincenzo Reschiglian
Company: Metropolitan Opera Company
First Performance: 23 January 1922, Metropolitan
    Opera House, New York City

Synopsis

The action takes place in the fabulous Land of the
Berendeys, in prehistoric days.

Prologue: the "Red Hill" near the castle of
Berendey, the Tsar's capital. The birds are beginning
to arrive from the south carrying with them Fairy
Spring. Many years ago, Fairy Spring made the
mistake of wooing ice-cold King Winter and,
although their love is now dead, they continue to
have a bond in the child born of their love,
Snegourotchka, or the Snow Maiden. She is now
sixteen years old and as she can no longer be kept
hidden they are afraid for her, because if the sun-
god Yarilo sees her she will die. Spring and Winter
entrust her to the Spirit of the Forest (The Faun)
who promises to protect her from any calamity. As
Spring and Winter leave, a carnival begins.
Snegourotchka takes part and her beauty
impresses Bobyl and Bobylicka who adopt her.

Act 1: in the village of Berendeyevka.
Snegourotchka begs Lel, a young shepherd, to sing
for her. He sings two songs, but he does not fall
for her and goes off with other girls. Snego-
rotchka has learned the pangs of unrequited love.
Mizguir, a rich young man, comes to marry
Koupava, but on seeing Snegourotchka falls in love
with her, and refuses to go through with the
marriage. Snegourotchka ignores Mizguir, but
Koupava is desolate and only saved from suicide by
the warm-hearted Lel.

Act 2: in the Palace of the Tsar. Koupava seeks
redress for the indignity she has suffered from
Mizguir. The Tsar convenes a court of justice and
requires the presence of Mizguir and
Snegourotchka. The Tsar, much taken by Snegourotchka's beauty, asks her who her lover is.
When she replies that she has none the Tsar says

that not to be in love is a sin against the sun-god,
Yarilo, and ends the trial by promising to reward
anyone who wins the love of Snegourotchka.

Act 3: in the Sacred Forest. During festivities in
the Sacred Forest the Tsar sings a *cavatina*, and
there is a dance of acrobats during which, at the
Tsar's command, Lel sings a pretty song. As a
reward Lel is allowed to kiss any girl he chooses.
He passes by Snegourotchka and chooses Koupava.
Snegourotchka is broken-hearted. Mizguir
professes his love for her, but Snegourotchka
refuses to listen and vanishes into the Forest. The
faithful Spirit of the Forest prevents Mizguir from
following her.

Act 4: in the Valley of Yarilo, the sun-god.
Snegourotchka is in despair and appeals to her
mother Fairy Spring: she wishes to love and be
loved. Fairy Spring grants her wish, and when
Mizguir returns she greets him lovingly. The Tsar
greets all the couples waiting to be married,
Mizguir and Snegourotchka among them. But the
sun-god has warmed Snegourotchka's heart with a
ray of sunshine, and her destiny must be fulfilled.
Snegourotchka must die. As the mist rises she
melts away. Mizguir drowns himself in sorrow. The
Tsar interprets their deaths as a blessing, saying
that henceforth Yarilo will pour his bounty upon
the earth. A youth appears carrying a sheaf of corn
and the opera ends with a hymn to Yarilo led by Lel.

Snegourotchka,[2] based on a popular Russian fairy tale, was composed in 1880–1,
and first performed in St Petersburg in 1882.

Giulio Gatti-Casazza (1869–1940), from
being the director of La Scala, Milan since
1898, went to New York to direct the Metropolitan Opera in 1908. He stayed until 1935
during which time he staged more than
5,000 performances of 177 works, many of
them new to the city.

There were only two new productions
during the 1921–2 season, both operas new
to New York: *Snegourotchka* and, somewhat
surprisingly at such a relatively late date,
Mozart's *Così fan tutte*. Gatti-Casazza recognized that unknown Russian operas provided a rich musical seam worth exploring;
although his productions were often sung
neither in Russian nor by Russian singers,
they generally proved popular attractions
with audiences. As Irving Kolodin, historian
of the Metropolitan Opera, noted: "The
interest in their freshness, and the worth of
the music placed them among the most
admirable of his various endeavours."[3]

Although *Snegourotchka* was new to
American audiences, some of the music was

familiar through its use in the ballet *Soleil de
Nuit* (see pp 230–32) and, even in its hybrid
form, was a *succès d'estime* rather than a
smash hit. Gilbert Gabriel summed up the
season: "But the two loveliest novelties of
the season were conceived in a far more
idyllic spirit, sung in more lyric fashion. For
that reason, possibly 'Snegourotchka' and
'Cosi Fan Tutte' have drawn more ecstasy
from the newsprint than they have money
to the box office. Yet they have lifted the
season's list to distinction and have plucked
it out of lugubrious revival into great
delight."[4] Of all the singers, Lucrezia Bori as
Snegourotchka was well praised for her
charm as well as her voice. As W. J. Hender-
son noted: "Charm is the factor most
needed in the impersonation of Rimsky-
Korsakov's legendary character. But of
course a prima donna has to sing. The first
air of the little snow maiden is wholly
operatic and in some phrases reveals the
fine hand of the composer of the hymn to
the sun in 'Coq d'Or.' Miss Bori sang this
difficult air admirably and throughout the
opera gave pleasure with the beautiful tones
of her voice." Otherwise, as the same critic
noted, a common factor with many Russian
operas is the emphasis on the chorus: "In
'Snegourotchka' the voice of Russia is heard
as soon as the chorus becomes audible. The
music of the people animates much of the
score, and as usual in Russian operas keeps
the chorus effectively occupied. Mr Letti's
well trained singers discharged their duties
very well indeed."[5]

There was some doubt about whether
Snegourotchka should be revived or not, but
the original production had been expensive
and the Metropolitan had to amortize some
of the initial capital costs. The management
was sufficiently encouraged to repeat the
opera in the 1922–3 season with almost
entirely the same cast, and even restored the
cuts in the score which had nervously been
made for the first season. Although musically proficient rather than sensational,
much of the production's effectiveness was
acknowledged to be due to the designs by
Anisfeldt which were universally praised.

Boris Anisfeldt had first been brought to
the attention of Diaghilev as an easel
painter by Igor Grabar, himself a painter,

critic, and art historian. Diaghilev was sufficiently impressed to invite Anisfeldt to exhibit six paintings at the exhibition of Russian art which he organized in 1906 at the Salon d'Automne in Paris. In the same year Anisfeldt designed his first work for the theater, *The Marriage of Zobeinde* by Hugo von Hofmannsthal at the Vera F. Kommisarjevskaya Theater in St Petersburg. He then became an important member of Diaghilev's production team as a scene painter. In 1908 he painted some of the sets designed by Alexander Golovine for *Boris Godunov* with Fedor Chaliapine in the title role.[6] In the following year, when Diaghilev presented ballets for the first time, Anisfeldt painted the scenery for the *Polovtsian Dances* from *Prince Igor*[7] from the design by Nikolai Roerich, and for *Cléopâtre*[8] from the design by Léon Bakst. In 1910 he painted the set for *Carnaval*[9] and some of the set for *Schéhérazade* (see pp 62–68), both designed by Bakst. In 1911 he painted the sets for *Petrushka* designed by Benois (see pp 117–27). He also designed the set and some of the costumes for a ballet derived from the opera *Sadko* (Scene 6: The kingdom under the sea) instead of Roerich;[10] this was his only production for Diaghilev as designer.

After the October revolution in 1917 Anisfeldt left Russia with his wife, young daughter, and as many paintings as he could carry by going east to Vladivostok, and from there to Japan, Canada, and the United States. In 1918 the Brooklyn Museum organized an exhibition of his paintings which toured twenty cities throughout the United States. His first designs for the Metropolitan Opera were for *La Reine Fiamette* and the world premiere of *L'Oiseau Bleu* by Maeterlinck and Albert Wolff in 1919, about which one critic wrote: "It was the artist rather than the composer who was the star of the evening. Boris Anisfeld is the alchemist in color who provided these magnificent settings."[11] These were followed by *Mefistofele* in 1920. In 1921 Anisfeldt went to Chicago to design the first production of Prokofiev's *The Love for Three Oranges*, and in 1922 returned to New York for *Snegourotchka*.

Anisfeldt maintained his reputation with the revival of *Snegourotchka*. One critic noticed: "The scenery was fantastic, rustic, colorful, the costumes also were faithful to the setting, the ballet was rich in color and bizarre in action, while the singing was creditable."[12] It was his contribution in particular which persuaded the management to arrange a special children's mati-

nee, as "there is ever so much for them to see, including dances not only of men and maidens, but of huge crows and other birds, and fantastic fairy scenes aplenty by Boris Anisfeld."[13] Only one critic, while joining in the praise for Anisfeldt, was more forthright: "Boris Anisfeld painted scenery that is Russian and gorgeous for the Metropolitan's production of 'The Snow Maiden.' I was continually remembering that fact with gratitude while yesterday I sat through as dull an evening of opera as I can recall. Within the last two years New York has learned enough of the authentic Russian art of the theatre, from Feodor Chaliapin to Stanislavsky's Moscow Company, to refrain from getting unduly excited over a translated and denatured performance of a Russian work like Mussorgsky's [sic] 'Snow Maiden.' But taking the Metropolitan offering for just what it is, French version and all (does it occur to the Metropolitan rulers that if an opera must of necessity be translated for us, it might be translated into English) one is sure the manner of presentation could be a little more vivid, a trifle less persistently sedative . . . Miss Bori as the Snow Maiden and Mrs Delaunois as the shepherd Lel sang well enough but without achieving in either case anything like a strongly marked impersonation."[14] Clearly, he was not seduced by the charm of either the singers or the Russian fairy tale, but then he was also ignorant as he seems not to have known who the composer was.

1* Costume design for three Berendeyevki girls in act 1

Graphite, tempera, and crayon with surface coating on illustration board
11 x 14¹³⁄₁₆ in: 28 x 37.5 cm
Signed, inscribed, and dated bottom right: "Boris Anisfeld, New York, 1921"
Inscribed in Russian bottom right: "Снегурочка" (Snegourotchka)
Inscribed above girls' heads: "4"
Gift of Nikita D. Lobanov
1967.21

In his costume designs, Anisfeldt preserved the essential Russianness of the fairy tale by using and adapting authentic Russian folk art patterns. Although he allowed himself greater liberties than, for example, Roerich who, with his more scholarly attitude, was more ethnographically correct, Anisfeldt's costumes are bright, colorful, theatrically effective, and, for a foreign audience, unmistakably Russian.

Notes

1 The use of a final "t" in the English spelling of the name is in accordance with the artist's known preference after he had definitely settled in the United States.
2 The opera was known by its transliterated Russian title, which was followed in the program by the title in English in brackets.
3 Irving Kolodin, *The Metropolitan Opera 1883–1935*, p 295.
4 Gilbert W. Gabriel in unidentified press cutting.
5 W. J. Hendesron, "'The Snow Maiden' with Bori in the title role, revived" in *The New York Herald*, New York, 6 April 1923.
6 Gala performances at the Théâtre de l'Opéra, Paris on 19, 21, 24, 26, 31 May, and 2, 4 June 1908, the so-called "3rd Season."
7 First performed (public dress rehearsal) on 18 May 1909 at the Théâtre du Châtelet, Paris.
8 First performed on 2 June 1909 at the Théâtre du Châtelet, Paris.
9 First performed on 20 May 1910 at the Theater des Westens, Berlin.
10 *Sadko*, composed by Nikolai Rimsky-Korsakov, conducted by Nicholas Tcherepnine, with choreography by Michel Fokine and principal dancers Lubov Tchernicheva, Vera Nemtchinova, Léon Woizikovsky, was first performed on 6 June 1911 at the Théâtre du Châtelet, Paris.
11 "The Blue Bird in Music and Picture" in *Arts and Decoration*, New York, January 1920, p 187, quoted in Janet Altic Flint, *Boris Anisfeldt*, p 14.
12 F. D. Perkins, "'Snow Maiden' is Repeated at Metropolitan" in *New York Tribune*, New York, 6 April 1923.
13 Henry T. Fink, "Bori Enchants as the Snow Maiden" in *New York Evening Post*, New York [April 1923].
14 Pitts Sanborn, "'The Snow Maiden' Presented at the Metropolitan—Other Music" in unidentified newspaper, New York, 6 April 1923.

Léon Bakst

Russian
born 1866 Grodno, Beloruss
died 1924 Paris

Feya Kukol (Puppenfee, The Fairy Doll or La Fée des Poupées)

Ballet in 1 act, 2 scenes by Hassreiter and Gaul
Composer: Josef Bayer, with additional items
   "March of the Dolls" by Peter Ilyitch
   Tchaikovsky; *pas de trois* and dance of the
   French Doll by Riccardo Drigo; dance of Baby
   by Anatole Liadov; Russian dance by Anton
   Rubinstein, and dance of the Two Negroes by
   Louis Moreau Gottschalk
Conductor: Riccardo Drigo
Choreographers: Nicolas and Serge Legat
Designer (set and costumes): Léon Bakst
Principal dancers:
   Fairy Doll: Mathilde Kshessinska
   The Manager: Stanislaus Gillert
   Chief Assistant: Pavel Gerdt
   Baby: Olga Preobrazhenskaya
   French Doll: O. Tchoumakova
   Japanese Doll: Vera Trefilova
   Chinese Doll: Agrippina Vaganova
   Tyrolean Doll: Makarova
   Spanish Doll: Anna Pavlova
   Two Negroes: Alfred Bekeffi, Alexander
      Schiraiev
   Two Pierrots: Serge Legat, Nicolas Legat
First Performance: 7 (20) February 1903, Hermitage
   Theater, St Petersburg. Transferred on
   16 February (1 March) 1903 to Mariinsky
   Theater, St Petersburg

Synopsis

While the manager of a toy shop checks the accounts, his assistants tidy a cupboard full of dolls. A postman enters with packets and registered letters. A messenger delivers a large box, the manager tells his assistant to tip him. The messenger, dissatisfied, asks for more. As the manager begins to open the letters a young girl enters with a broken doll; the manager, promising to mend it, begins to flirt with her. She leaves in a hurry. A merchant, his wife, and daughter enter the shop and begin to look at the dolls. The daughter goes from doll to doll but stops in front of "Baby" and asks her mother to buy it for her. Meanwhile, the merchant has stopped to look at a soldier. It springs into life when the merchant's wife accidentally bumps into it. Terrified, she tries to rush out of the shop with her daughter, but in her rush trips over a box from which springs a little devil which terrifies her even more, so that she hides in a corner with her daughter. The merchant tells the assistant that he has come to choose a doll for his daughter. The assistant shows him round but the merchant, finding the prices high, tries to bargain. Then a rich English family arrives. The manager greets them and begins to show them his dolls. He first shows them the Chinese doll, but the clockwork mechanism is broken and he cannot mend it. Disappointed, the English family want to leave. The manager stops them from going and shows them the Tyrolean doll, a doll that says "Mama" and "Papa," and various other dolls. The English like what they have seen, but the manager tells them that they have not yet seen the best which he keeps hidden behind a curtain, the Fairy Doll. They are delighted with this toy and want to buy it whatever the cost. The manager asks an incredible price. The English wife, also thrilled with the doll, does not believe it is a mechanical toy. While the assistant tries to persuade her that it is, her husband agrees a price, pays the manager, and asks to have the doll delivered to his hotel. Both families leave the shop. It is closing time. The assistants turn out the lights and leave with the manager. Twelve o'clock strikes. On the final stroke, the Fairy Doll appears from behind her curtain, and with a sign brings all the toys in the shop to life. Lit by a magic light, they all begin to dance. The lights dim again and the dolls return to their places. The manager and his assistants, having heard a noise in the shop, run in, but seeing that all is quiet and tidy they begin to leave. As they go the dolls tear themselves away from their places and, with the Fairy Doll in command, form a picturesque group round the manager and his assistants.

The original performance of this extremely popular ballet was on 4 October 1888 at the Court Opera theater in Vienna where it remained in the regular repertoire for many years. In 1903 a new production was commissioned by the Tsar for a single performance during the closed season at his private Hermitage theater. The Director of the Imperial Theaters, Vladimir Arkadievitch Teliakovsky[1] (1861–1924), invited the brothers Serge and Nicolas Legat[2] to stage the ballet. The invitation came as rather a surprise because they had not until then choreographed a whole ballet and "naturally expected that only Petipa[3] would be asked."[4] However, the brothers got over their initial modest reluctance and accepted. As it was generally agreed that the music by Bayer was only mediocre, several extra numbers were introduced to improve the overall score and liven up the entertainment. "My brother and I, dancing the two pierrots with the doll Mathilde Kshesinskaya,[5] set the ballet together, doing alternately eight bars at a time,"[6] which seems a rather haphazard way of arranging a ballet. This method, however, was vindicated because the choreography was broadly thought to be successful, an opinion confirmed by Tamara Karsavina when she wrote that "the choreography all through had a naivety redolent of childhood joys and a keen wit. The main item, a *pas de trois* of the fairy doll with two pierrots, had

many daring technical feats brought into relief by the seeming clumsiness and superb burlesque of the two Legats."[7]

Léon Bakst was pleased to be commissioned to design the sets and costumes and frenetically set to work. According to Alexandre Benois, "his enthusiasm and love for our native city, St Petersburg, and personal recollections of his childhood, gave Bakst the happy idea of transferring the action to the St Petersburg Arcade,[8] known to every St Petersburg child because of the toy-shops that were concentrated there . . . These memories formed the foundation of the scenario as adapted by Bakst, and luckily he found the friendliest support for the idea in his two ballet-masters, the brothers Legat."[9] Bakst's set for the first scene was therefore an accurate representation of the interior of a large, nineteenth-century toy shop. The sides were lined with showcases of dolls and shelves for other toys with a large clock on the wall above; center stage were red plush-covered chairs and a rocking horse. At the back of the set were two large windows in the arcade overlooking the street through which the audience could see passers-by coming and going. The difference between the first and second scene was a most effective theatrical trick: Bakst changed the scale. Instead of the normal human scale of the first scene, he enlarged everything to be in scale with the dolls. Karsavina again, remembering the scenic effect: "In his display of toys, Bakst had been inspired by Benois' collection of hand-made Russian peasants' toys often carved in wood. These primitive, unsophisticated, vividly coloured toys had a fascinating, bizarre quality which was sensitively interpreted by the two ballet masters."[10] In his enchanting costume designs Bakst also made a clear distinction between the humans, who look real, and the dolls, wide-eyed and delicate as if made of porcelain, which are perched on stands.

The performance at the Hermitage was reported in *Novoe Vremya*[11] but more attention was given to listing the members of the Imperial family who attended the performance than to commenting on the entertainment. It reported that their Highnesses appeared at 9 o'clock in the evening and that the Empress, dressed in black, was attired in diamonds and emeralds, that His Majesty the Emperor, in naval uniform, sat in the middle of the front row with Her Majesty the Empress beside him, and that to her right sat His Majesty the Heir to the Throne. The report then listed the other members of the Imperial family and the court who were present. The ballet followed the performance of a one-act comedy *Permettez, madame!* (*Allow me, madam!*) by Labiche and Delacour. According to *Novoe Vremya*, dinner was served at midnight after the performance, and dancing, in which the Emperor and Empress participated with true Imperial stamina, went on until half-past two in the morning. It was quite different, however, for the artists; Nicolas Legat recalled: "After the performance a special supper was served for the artists, but when we arrived after concluding the programme, we found that the operatic and dramatic artists had supped before us and consumed the best of the viands. Serge and I were furious at such treatment of our companions who had given the principal part of the evening's performance, and I got up and publicly announced that 'such hospitality did not meet with my approval,' and I invited the entire ballet troupe to be my guests at a well-known restaurant, where I would see that everyone had his favourite dish."[12] This snub of Imperial hospitality was forgiven after Kshessinska successfully interceded on behalf of the brothers.

They were perhaps forgiven more readily because the performance was acknowledged to have been a great success and to have pleased their Imperial Majesties; so much so, indeed, that the ballet was revived almost immediately at the Mariinsky Theater on 16 February (1 March) 1903. In an evening of ballet, *The Fairy Doll* was the first item, followed by *The Magic Flute* in one act with Anna Pavlova, and *Paquita* in three acts. The critic of *Novosti i Birzhevaya Gazeta* (*The News and Stock Exchange Gazette*) began his notice by drawing attention to the musical inadequacies of the ballet: "there is nothing original in this music, but it is not lacking in melody and is good for dancing. Indeed, as a divertissement before an opera a ballet such *The Fairy Doll* could be quite successful on foreign stages but here, where we expect something completely different from choreography, where, after all, we already have ballets like *The Nutcracker* with wonderful music by Tchaikovsky, a production of *The Fairy Doll* seems to be rather superfluous."[13] But he went on to add: "the

administrators of our ballet obviously realised this which is why they made some significant changes and additions." Even though this critic thought that the whole production was rather pointless he had nothing but the highest praise for the dancing, especially the "extra" classic *pas de trois* by Riccardo Drigo which was danced by Kshessinska, Serge Legat, and Michel Fokine "with great brilliance and virtuosity." Fokine had replaced Nicolas Legat as the latter had had an accident which left him "on crutches for three months."[14] The critic of the *Journal de St Pétersbourg* was altogether more generous in his praise, saying that the brothers' new creation "reveals a very individual artistic sense in these two young men, a great originality of conception, a constant desire to stay off the beaten track, to open up new paths, and to innovate."[15]

In this production, as in others of the Imperial Theaters, the *corps de ballet* was made up of students from the Imperial Ballet School, and two of the students were Vaslav Nijinsky and his sister, Bronislava, then thirteen and twelve years old. She later remembered taking part and especially "the enchanted memory of the costume. It was our first contact with the painter, Lev Samoilovitch Bakst, watching him create his designs. Before this I had worn only stock costumes from the wardrobe, but for *The Fairy Doll* each costume was individually designed and we were all specially measured."[16] Nijinska also remembered that Bakst was meticulous about their make-up and applied it himself in order to be sure to create the complete look that he wanted in each of his characters.

Bakst was also praised in the *Journal de St Pétersbourg*: "the sets and costumes from designs by M. Bakst are exquisite in their veracity and charm. The change of scale which he effects between the first and second scenes is of particular interest, and makes us want to see this young painter's work more often in the theatre because he seems to have a real talent for it."[17] This production was Bakst's first complete ballet after having found his true artistic vocation at the age of thirty-five. The critic, flattering about Bakst's age, was also astute about his talent.

2   Costume design for Evgenia Eduardova as a lady's maid

Graphite, tempera and/or watercolor on paper
14⅛ x 7⅛ in: 36 x 18 cm
Signed in pencil lower left: "Bakst" over a previous
  signature in pencil in Russian "Л. Бакст"
1933.390

Exhibitions: New York 1933, No 2;[18] Chicago 1933,
  No 2;[18] Northampton 1934, No 2;[18] Hartford
  1934b; New Haven 1935; San Francisco
  1935–6; Williamsburg 1940; Cambridge 1942;
  Richmond 1959; Hartford 1964; New York
  1965–6, No 1 (illustrated p 14); New York
  1966–7; Amherst 1974; Columbus 1989;
  Worcester 1989
Illustration: Postcard for the Russian Red Cross,
  1904 (color)

The Fairy Doll was Bakst's third production but, ignoring *Sylvia* which was not produced, his first ballet. The first two productions, both in 1902, were the plays *Le Coeur de la Marquise* (*The Heart of the Marchioness*) in the Directoire style of the 1790s, and *Hippolytus*, the first of many set in ancient Greece. Bakst learnt his craft very fast, for by the time he came to design *The Fairy Doll* he had not only mastered most of the techniques but had developed his individual style which, quite new to theater design, applied especially to the design of costumes. He interpreted on paper the character of the relevant part by drawing it at some precise moment in the action. His designs try to catch the atmosphere of the production and are also often portraits.

This drawing, although still somewhat in the manner of mere illustration, charmingly conveys the character of the young girl by the delicacy of its execution and muted coloring. At the same time the detailed instructions to the costumier are clear from the design: the white cuffs, the tasseling round the waist and shoulders, the cross round the neck, the earring, and the little white bonnet.

The existing signature has been written later, in about 1910, over an erased but still legible signature in Russian. Bakst also later strengthened the lines of the arms and torso of the doll. While the drawing still had a signature in Russian, Bakst had the unusual distinction of having a set of twelve postcards made from his designs for this production in 1904 for the benefit of the Red Cross. This design was reproduced as No 9.[19]

Notes

61

1 The last Director of the Imperial Theaters from 1901 to 1917.

2 Serge Legat (1875–1905) and Nicolas Legat (1869–1937), also known for their caricatures of Russian ballet personalities.

3 Marius Petipa (1819–1910) made his debut in St Petersburg in 1847 and then spent the next 56 years working for the Russian ballet establishing the art of choreography, until his contract was not renewed in September 1903.

4 Nicolas Legat, *Ballet Russe*, p 31.

5 At one time the mistress of Tsar Nicholas II. married morganatically Grand Duke André, became *prima ballerina assoluta* in 1895.

6 Nicolas Legat, *op cit*, p 31.

7 Tamara Karsavina, *Dancing Times*, London, August 1964, p 573.

8 Known as the Gostinny Dvor on Nevsky Prospekt.

9 Alexandre Benois, *Reminiscences of the Russian Ballet*, p 229.

10 Tamara Karsavina, *op cit*, p 573.

11 Anon, "Spectacl i Bal v Ermitazhe" ("Performance and Ball in the Hermitage") in *Novoe Vremya* (*New Times*), St Petersburg, 9 (22) February 1903.

12 Nicolas Legat, *op cit*, p 39.

13 Y. K-v., "Balet" ("Ballet") in *Novosti i Birzhevaya Gazeta* (*The News and Stock Exchange Gazette*), St Petersburg, 18 February (3 March) 1903.

14 Nicolas Legat, *op cit*, p 31.

15 M., "Théâtre-Marie" in *Journal de St Pétersbourg*, St Petersburg, 18 February (3 March) 1903, the French language daily newspaper.

16 Bronislava Nijinska, *Early Memoirs*, p 118.

17 M., *op cit*.

18 In the catalogues of these exhibitions, this design is incorrectly ascribed to *Schéhérazade*.

19 The others were: 1 The Fairy Doll, 2 The English Woman, 3 Her daughter, 4 The Spanish Doll, 5 The Chinese Doll, 6 The Japanese Doll, 7 The French Doll, 8 One of the porcelain dolls, 10 A *corps de ballet* costume, 11 The Postman, 12 The Batman.

Schéhérazade

Choreographic drama in 1 act by Michel Fokine and
    Léon Bakst (actually Alexandre Benois[1])
Composer: Nikolai Rimsky-Korsakov
Conductor: Nicholas Tcherepnine
Choreographer: Michel Fokine
Designer (set and costumes): Léon Bakst
Front Cloth (1911): Valentin Serov
Principal dancers:
    Shahriar, King of India and China: Alexis
        Boulgakov
    Shah Zeman, his brother: Vasili Kissilev
    Zobeida: Ida Rubinstein
    Zobeida's Favourite Slave: Vaslav Nijinsky
    Grand Eunuch: Enrico Cecchetti
Company: Diaghilev's Ballets Russes
First Performance: 4 June 1910, Théâtre national de
    l'Opéra, Paris

Synopsis

The ballet is based on the prologue to *The Thousand and One Nights*.

Shahriar, in his harem surrounded by his concubines, is making love to his favorite Zobeida. The Chief Eunuch suggests an entertainment and Odalisques dance provocatively. Shah Zeman, Shahriar's brother and jealous of Zobeida, tells him that he suspects his concubines of infidelity. Shahriar reluctantly agrees to a test. They both pretend to go hunting and, as soon as they have gone, the concubines cajole the Grand Eunuch into opening first a bronze door through which enter Negroes dressed in copper, then a silver door through which enter other Negroes dressed in silver. He refuses to open the third, gold door until a large bribe persuades him, and a Negro dressed in gold leaps forth. This is Zobeida's favorite Negro. An orgy begins, and when the dancing is at its frenzied height, Shahriar returns. He is so angered by the bacchanale he sees that he signals his guards to massacre all the dancers. Shahriar hesitates over the fate of Zobeida but she, realizing that all is lost, snatches a dagger from one of the guards, stabs herself and dies at the feet of her master. As the curtain falls Shahriar laments the death of his beloved.

Schéhérazade burst on the Paris scene in 1910 like un uncontrollable fireball. It was performed only five times in the first year and so relatively few people saw it. But its effect spread quickly throughout Paris. All fashionable ladies, whether in society or not, had to have their "Schéhérazade" dresses, whether designed by Bakst or not, in which to be seen at an ever more lavish succession of "Schéhérazade" parties. It was the catalyst for an emerging fashion, and became a sort of Russian trademark. After the Revolution, Russian émigrés in Paris in the 1920s danced the nights through at a nightclub called *Schéhérazade*. The club is still there, and now the new Russian émigrés are dancing there.

Schéhérazade was the first completely original ballet to be presented in Paris by Diaghilev during the so-called "fifth" season. The "first" season had been in 1906 when Diaghilev mounted an exhibition of Russian art at the Grand Palais in a winter-garden setting designed by Léon Bakst; the second season in 1907 was a series of concerts of Russian music. In 1908 Diaghilev presented Chaliapine for the first time in the West in Moussorgsky's opera *Boris Godunov*. In 1909 there was both opera and ballet: Rimsky-Korsakov's opera *The Maid of Pskov*, again with Chaliapine, and the ballets *Le Pavillon d'Armide* (see pp 108–16) and *Les Sylphides* (see pp 153–54), designed by Alexandre Benois; the *Polovtsian Dances* from *Prince Igor* (see pp 225–29) and *Le Festin*, with costumes by Bakst and Benois, and *Cléopâtre* designed by Bakst. For financial reasons Diaghilev could not include opera in his 1910 season, so for the first time he risked presenting only ballets. As well as *Schéhérazade*, performed on the first night of the season, the new productions were *Giselle* (see pp 132–41) designed by Benois; *Les Orientales* and *The Firebird* (see pp 212–16) with three costumes designed by Bakst, and *Le Carnaval* designed by Bakst. This program of ballets only was a considerable risk; although the colorful and flamboyant *Cléopâtre* had been the talk of the town the year before, the sophisticated Parisian audience, skeptical and blasé, stood back and waited to see what those Russian "country bumpkins" would do. The Russian critic, N. Kostilev, wrote: "Merely repeating the previous year's success would not be enough because, however well disposed the public might be towards us, it is not easy to recognise another nation's excellence especially in a theater like the Grand Opéra where we presented our productions. There, hundreds of pairs of eyes, among the subscribers and among the resident artists, are only too ready to say 'it's just the same after all' and 'they can't do anything else.'"[2]

Schéhérazade was not the same as anything else. It was entirely new, and proved to the Parisians that the Russians could not only do something else, but do something which no one had thought of doing before.

Although Bakst is credited with the libretto it was actually Alexandre Benois who had the idea of using Rimsky-Korsakov's music for a ballet. Benois also changed the story from Sinbad the Sailor to another one in the Arabian Nights. According to Fokine, the only contribution Bakst made to the libretto was the ludicrous and impractical suggestion that when the Shah returns to discover his wives in the arms of their lovers he "orders them to be sewn in sacks and cast into the sea."[3] Benois was therefore amazed to discover, when he saw the printed program, that his name had been omitted. He complained angrily to Diaghilev, who retorted: "Que veux-tu? [What do you want?] Bakst had to be given something. You have *Pavillon d'Armide* and he will have *Schéhérazade*."[4] The choreography is Fokine's alone. In staging the ballet he applied his own new principles of describing action through the movements and positions of the body and not through the complicated and often incomprehensible sign language of the hands. "Only those gestures were used which clearly expressed the action. *Schéhérazade* contained love and passion, guilt, treachery, and anger, grief and desperation, and there were no hand gesticulations."[5] The apparently abandoned erotic dancing, especially of Ida Rubinstein and Vaslav Nijinsky, was sensational.

Schéhérazade was seen to be the achievement of Diaghilev's ideal of a *gesamtkunstwerk* as originally described by Wagner—a work of art in which all the elements of music, design, choreography, and dancing fused into a perfect whole. The entire production was a hitherto unseen harmony of colors, sounds, and movements. As W. A. Propert wrote: "We saw the ballet for the first time breaking away from all traditions and expressing itself firmly and fully in a language entirely of its own invention."[6] It overwhelmed the French, as J. Tugendhold reported: "It was as if some electric shock had suddenly informed the whole of France of the feverish excitement which the word 'theater' had meant for us Russians during these last few years, and Paris began somehow to wake up from its theatrical drowsiness."[7] Above all, the ballet established Bakst as "the most famous painter in the world," a distinction for which he had immodestly craved for some time. He already had had a foretaste of his success when he wrote to his wife on 18 (31) May: "we have done the fit-up for *Schéhérazade* and it's a great success with the artists (Vuillard, Bonnard, Seurat, Blanche and others). Seriozha [Diaghilev] hugged and kissed me in front of everyone, and the whole company exploded in a thunder of applause and then rocked me on stage. I could hardly escape, and after the dress rehearsal they threatened to rock me again.

I must admit I was not expecting such a deafening success."[8] After the public dress rehearsal Bakst wrote to his wife again: "The fantastic success of *Schéhérazade* (the whole of Paris now dresses in 'oriental' clothes) has forced Diaghilev to repeat it in the second program."[9] Indeed, everyone began talking about Bakst and the Orient. At the time, everything east of Suez was called "oriental," but *Schéhérazade* was not the real Orient. It was a Russian idea of an Orient as seen by the French, and they were taken in by it because they had not seen anything like it on stage before. There was, after all, nothing new about the Orient as such—it had been more or less in fashion since the time of Delacroix—but everything was new about *Schéhérazade*. Rimsky-Korsakov's music, firmly based on Russian folk music, was unlike any music for ballet that the French were used to. The choreography by Fokine demonstrated the strength and virtuosity of both Russian male dancers and the ensemble, but it was not "oriental." Fokine himself wrote: "I realised that Orientals do not live or dance in such a manner. After the composition of this ballet, I undertook the study of authentic Oriental dances. But nothing would have induced me to stage my ballet in the authentic Oriental style, for such an undertaking would have required a genuine Oriental orchestra. The symphonic music of Rimsky-Korsakov would be completely unsuited. The Orient, based on authentic Arabian, Persian, and Hindu movements, was still the Orient of the imagination. Dancers with bare feet, performing mostly with their arms and torsos, constituted a concept far removed from the Oriental ballet of the time."[10]

The stage picture was described in detail by the critic Pierre Lalo, who stressed Bakst's amazingly original color scheme: "On stage, a set of extreme simplicity, reduced to its bare essentials showing the interior of the Shah's harem: a sort of enormous tent of the most intense and magnificent bright green, a green which is dazzling yet constant, a green both violent and astonishingly sumptuous. No other color, or practically none: a touch, on the immense green surface, of two or three large Persian designs, in black and orange red. The floor is covered with a carpet of orange red in a paler shade. At the back, doors of blue almost black. Most of the costumes for the men and women are in colors which complement the set: subtle tones of red and few greens. Against this general color scheme the gold and silver on the costumes of the amorous negroes discreetly glint and sparkle. Here and there darker touches of color as in the costume of the Shah in which blues and deep violets predominate and which recall the most beautiful Persian miniatures. It all combines to produce an effect of power and miraculous harmony. It is spell-binding and a constant thrill for the eye. M. Bakst, the Russian painter, who created this wonderful picture with his colors for both the set and the costumes, is a truly great artist."[11] Lalo was both right and wrong in this estimation. While it was an apparently complex piece of design—with Bakst playing with diagonal perspective and two vanishing points to create an illusion of space on an essentially cramped stage—its execution was simple in the extreme and consisted only of a back cloth, borders, wings, and a floor cloth. By continuing the color scheme to the floor, as Lalo noted, the stifling atmosphere of the harem was completed. Vladimir Polunin, who was asked by Diaghilev to repaint the worn-out scenery in about 1918, recalled that "although the painting of the back-cloth was technically rather easy, the drapery . . . offered considerable difficulty. The rendering of folds is always difficult, but when these are decorated with intricate patterns, it requires much time, skill and patience to ensure that the tones shall be in their respective places and blend with the folds."[12] Polunin worked from a new design made in 1915, as the original had been bought by the Musée des Arts Décoratifs, Paris, during Bakst's highly successful first one-man show in the West.[13]

In view of the severe slight that Benois had received, his appraisal of the production, after a preliminary rap on the knuckles, was remarkably generous: "*Schéhérazade* has for some reason been described as a ballet by Bakst, while the entire libretto with every detail was composed by another person, whose name Diaghilev has found it not necessary to mention. But it is to Bakst that belongs the honour of having created the success of *Schéhérazade* as a spectacle, a production that is really amazing. When the curtain rises over the grandiose green alcove, one seems at once to enter into a world of strange and peculiar sensations— the sensations that are awakened by reading the *Arabian Nights* . . . Spicy, sensuous aromas seem to be wafted from the stage, but the soul is filled with foreboding . . . It is difficult to imagine an exposition of drama more sympathetic, more to the point than Bakst's décor. And what of Bakst the colourist? Here indeed he has found his real vocation. We see in *Schéhérazade* that Bakst can produce pictures that are truly great . . . Bakst becomes simple and free on the stage, and acquires *range*—that most valuable artistic quality. His décor is executed (in collaboration with Anisfeld)[14] with a simple and broad virtuosity in the most telling colours; the performers, too, who move against this background in Fokine's amazingly clever combinations, are Bakst's creation, and are in complete harmony with the décor. I don't think I exaggerate when I say I have *never* seen such absolute harmony of colour on the stage."[15] While Benois' view reflected the general opinion of the production, a few critics were less convinced and perhaps saw through the ballet's essential thinness. However, these critics tended to be English with a puritan streak who disapproved of entertainment for entertainment's sake. Geoffrey Whitworth, writing only in 1913, already has a faintly critical misgiving: "Seen for the first time, *Schéhérazade* is one of the most startling of the ballets. The effect of the decoration, the costumes, the music, is intensely moving, while the dancing is only another instance of that wonderful flexibility of style which renders the Russian ballet so perfect an instrument for the expression of almost every phase of feeling. But on a second visit, or a third, this fine effect seems hardly maintained."[16] This was, in fact, a perceptive comment: by the 1920s Diaghilev himself began to laugh at the absurdity of *Schéhérazade*, but allowed it to be performed occasionally[17] as it remained popular with audiences, in spite of the fact that it had become, according to Cyril Beaumont, a travesty of its former self. After Diaghilev's death in 1929, however, it became the most performed ballet of Colonel de Basil's Ballet Russe de Monte-Carlo, although the original frenetic and erotic power had vanished.

*

A serious criticism to do with *Schéhérazade* was Diaghilev's use of Rimsky-Korsakov's music. Rimsky-Korsakov had died in 1908 and was revered like a national monument. Diaghilev was castigated by many people in both Russia and France, first for using the music for a ballet at all, then for a ballet on a theme which had nothing to do with the music, then for cutting the score, and, final insult, for using it without permission. The composer's widow complained publicly in a letter to the influential St Petersburg newspaper, *Rech*, with the conclusion: "Not being able to sue Mr Diaghilev . . . I will not cease to protest with the loudest voice that I can muster against such wilful and inartistic actions on the part of Mr Diaghilev."[18] *Rech* gave Diaghilev the right to reply, a dangerous thing to do. He began: "Here, in Russia, people are divided into two categories— those who are for ever protesting 'with the loudest voice' and those who are for ever silent. Both are equally useless because they leave out a third category—those who are 'doers.' . . . In general there are very few events of any artistic merit and people are not sued for them, particularly by those who have neither seen them, nor even taken the trouble to see how and what they have created."[19] Game, set, and match to Mr Diaghilev.

✱

In 1911 Diaghilev commissioned a front cloth for *Schéhérazade* from the painter Valentin Serov (1865–1911). Based on the theme of a Persian hunting scene, Serov painted it from the end of May to the beginning of June 1911 in Matisse's old studio-workshop which Bakst had arranged to hire for him. The cloth was first shown in Paris on 13 June 1911 on the same night as the first performance of *Petrushka* (see pp 117–27). The cloth continued to be shown until 1914, when Diaghilev deemed it too valuable to continue its use as scenery.

✱

In 1992 the Royal Opera in Stockholm discovered the original scenery for *Schéhérazade* which had been used for a production staged by Fokine in 1914, and had been in store ever since. It was found to be in perfect condition, so the Royal Opera decided to restage the ballet using this scenery. I was in the audience on the first night on 29 April 1993; when the curtain went up on the set we all burst into spontaneous applause. I suddenly understood a little of what it must have been like to have been at the Opéra in Paris on 4 June 1910.

3 **Costume design for an aide-de-camp to Shahriar**

Graphite, watercolor and/or tempera, gold and
 silver paint on paper
13¾ x 8½ in: 35 x 21.5 cm
Signed and dated, right in pencil: "L. Bakst / 1910"
Inscribed upper right in pencil: "Schéhèrasade" [sic]
1933.389

Exhibitions: New York 1933, No 1; Chicago 1933,
 No 1; Northampton 1934, No 1; Hartford
 1934b; New Haven 1935; San Francisco
 1935–6; Boston 1938; Paris 1939, No 12
 (described as "Schariar"); Williamsburg 1940;
 Edinburgh 1954, No 72; London 1954–5, No 82
 (described as "Shah Schariar"); East Lansing
 1975; Indianapolis 1959, No 12; Houston 1965;
 New York 1965–6, No 2 (illustrated p 14); New
 York 1966–7; Princeton 1968; Strasbourg 1969,
 No 60; Blommenholm 1971; Hartford 1974;
 Houston 1976; Hartford 1979; New York 1980;
 Columbus 1989; Worcester 1989.
Illustrations: *Comoedia Illustré*, supplement to 15
 June 1910 "Les Ballets Russes," p 13 (color);
 de Mille, p 140 (color); Souvenir Program "Les
 Ballets Russes," 1915 (color).

This costume design is not for a dancer; the cumbersome headdress alone would make it impossible to dance in such a costume. It is a design for one of the French extras who were hired for the last scene when Shahriar returns unexpectedly and, seeing the orgy, orders the killing of the concubines. The extras had to rush on with their scimitars and take part in the slaughter. The only problem, according to Bronislava Nijinska, was that they "did not understand Fokine, and would not follow his directions. They appeared ridiculous among the dancers, and Fokine became furious and often lost his temper."[20]

In the souvenir program for 1911 there is a photograph of a M. Gaboret wearing the costume for which this is a design; however, he is not wearing the same trousers. The caption to both the reproduction of the design and the photograph is "aide du camp du Schah." M. Gaboret was never listed as a member of the Ballets Russes company, and I have been unable to discover if he was in the production in 1910. Although the design is for an extra, Bakst has treated his drawing with the same meticulous care and delicacy as if it were for one of the major characters.

The costume designs for *Schéhérazade* have been likened to Persian miniatures, and there is no doubt that Bakst was to some extent inspired by them. He was a diligent researcher and would have looked at books and been to museums, but in his designs he did not slavishly copy or imitate

anything he had seen. His designs are more complex, more intricate, and more colorful than most Persian painting. The originality of Bakst is not that he interpreted the "Orient" or any particular style of painting, but that he introduced into the theater a palette of colors hitherto unseen on stage. Robert Brussel from *Le Figaro* was at the first night: "Everything in this performance blends into a prodigious orgy of gleaming colors, rhythms and contrasting movements; and everything also dissolves into a harmonious beauty. M Léon Bakst's décor is in itself a masterpiece, and every single one of his costumes is another; they would be enough to evoke what in other respects is evoked by the music and the rhythm of the movements and the groupings."[21] Although the Ballets Russes never performed in Russia, their activities and productions were frequently reported and discussed at great length. The Russian critic, Tugendhold, sent regular in-depth reports back from Paris. Although he was almost unique in disliking the set of *Schéhérazade*, saying that he much preferred Gauguin, he was flattering about the costumes: "On the other hand, the costumes, designed by Bakst, are truly masterpieces; it is not just their detail, but their beauty, a special kind of beauty, refined, heady, sensual, such as we only find in Bakst."[22]

In his costume designs for *Schéhérazade*, Bakst also perfected his method of creating both a detailed indication to the costumier as well as the precise character of the role to the dancer. In this case, the balanced stance, the rings on the fingers, the heavy camouflaging beard, and the watchful but malign glint in the eyes define the character exactly.

✻

Schéhérazade was first revived by de Basil's Ballets Russes on 16 February 1935 at the Academy of Music in Philadelphia during the company's seven-month American tour, which began in October 1934. This was followed by a revival on 19 June 1935 at the Royal Opera House, Covent Garden, with Lubov Tchernicheva recreating her Zobeida, a role she had performed with Diaghilev's Ballets Russes. As the *Daily Telegraph* reported: "She is thus the link between the past and present. She alone can pass on the traditions of the rôles she has played so superbly."[23] While Tchernicheva dazzled, the *corps de ballet* displayed a disappointing lack of precision. The choreography for this revival was credited in the program as being only "after Michel Fokine." His

absence was only too apparent. However, Fokine joined the company in June 1937. Under his strict tutelage the performance of *Schéhérazade* improved immeasurably, and the famous ballet then remained steadily in the repertory. But the production still suffered from a dilution in the set and costumes. Although acknowledged to be by Léon Bakst, the set, in its reconstructed form, lost its magnificence. "The great ornate hanging lamps have disappeared, and a lot of fussy detail has appeared on the left of the stage. It is difficult to describe all the many minor changes that have taken place, but the total effect gives one the impression that 'making do' has been rather too much the order of the day."[24] The costumes did not suffer so much, being remade quite accurately from Bakst's existing designs.

The costume design for the youths was accessible, as it had been reproduced in Arsène Alexandre's *Decorative Art of Léon Bakst*. The description of the costumes overleaf matches the design except that the latter also included a tall blue hat with peacock feathers. Both the costumes reproduced here, made up from parts of different costumes, are late remakes dating from the post-war period.

4*   Costume for a Youth

Bright yellow satin jacket, painted green foliage
and pink bud motif, bright blue faux lapel
outline. Peach crepe undersleeves match the
chemisette insert at the front opening. Red
satin Turkish trousers with painted gold moons
are caught at intervals by blue moiré ribbons
and gathered into a gold lamé ankle band.
1996.7.1a-b

The labels inside the jacket "[Vladimir] Arapov" and
"Chaurand" show that this costume was worn
by these two dancers between 1947–9.

5*   Costume for a Youth

Not illustrated. For description see Plate 4. This
costume, however, also has a blue taffeta belt.
1996.7.2a-c

The label inside the jacket "[Anatole] Joukovsky"
and "Vas[iliev]" show that this was worn on
the Spanish tour in 1948. The trousers labeled
"[Pierre] Klimoff" show that they were worn in
1947. The belt labeled "[Vladimir] Irm[an]" is
earlier, as Irman was a member of the company
from 1939–43.

Provenance of both costumes: Diaghilev and de
Basil's Ballets Foundation Ltd. Sotheby's
London, lot 48, 3 March 1973. Castle Howard
Estate Ltd. Sotheby's London, lot 5,
14 December 1995.

Notes

1 See below and note 4.
2 N. Kostilev, "Nash balet v Parizhe" ("Our Ballet
   in Paris") in *Apollon*, No 9, St Petersburg 1910,
   p 25.
3 Michel Fokine, *Memoirs of a Ballet Master*, p 151.
4 Alexandre Benois, *Reminiscences of the Russian
   Ballet*, p 311. After not getting a passport in time,
   Benois, in a fury, put his fist through a window
   and severely injured his hand. His departure
   from Russia was therefore delayed. He then
   went first to Montagnola (near Lugano, Switzerland) to convalesce, before deciding to go to
   Paris. He missed the first performances of
   Schéhérazade, and saw only the last on 16 June,
   as he was still in Montagnola on 14 June. When
   he returned to Montagnola he wrote to
   Diaghilev saying that he never wanted to work
   for him again, but it was not a long-lasting wish.
   The very next year he produced his masterpiece,
   Petrushka, for him (see pp 117–27).
5 Michel Fokine, *op cit*, p 154.
6 W. A. Propert, *The Russian Ballet in Western
   Europe*, p 17.
7 J. Tugendhold, "Russkii sezon v Parizhe" ("The
   Russian Season in Paris") in *Apollon*, No 10, St
   Petersburg 1910, p 7.
8 Quoted in Irina Pruzhan, *Lev Samoilovitch Bakst*.
9 Quoted in Irina Pruzhan, *ibid*.
10 Michel Fokine, *op cit*, pp 154–5.
11 Pierre Lalo, from *Le Temps*, quoted by Valerian
   Svetlov in *Le ballet contemporain*, p 117.

12 Vladimir Polunin, *The Continental Method of
   Scene Painting*, p 44.
13 6 July–15 October 1911 at the Musée des Arts
   Décoratifs, Pavillon de Parsan, Paris.
14 See also pp 56–8.
15 Alexandre Benois in *Rech* (Speech), St Petersburg
   12 (25) July 1910, p 2, quoted in Alexandre
   Benois, *op cit*, p 315.
16 Geoffrey Whitworth, *The Art of Nijinsky*, p 58.
17 But it was not performed in London after 1921,
   nor in Paris after 1922 .
18 *Rech*, 25 July (7 August) 1910.
19 *Rech*, 10 (23) September 1910.
20 Bronislava Nijinska, *Early Memoirs*, p 294.
21 Robert Brussel, "La Saison Russe à l'Opéra" in
   Le Figaro, Paris 6 June 1910, p 6.

22 Y. Tugendhold, "Russkii balet v Parizhe" ("The
   Russian Ballet in Paris") in *Apollon*, No 8, St
   Petersburg May–June 1910.
23 Anon, "Tchernicheva returns" in the *Daily
   Telegraph*, London, 19 June 1935.
24 *The Dancing Times*, London, July 1935.

Le Spectre de la rose (The Spirit of the rose)

Ballet in 1 scene by Jean-Louis Vaudoyer[1] from a poem by Théophile Gautier
Composer: Carl-Maria von Weber (*Invitation to the Waltz*), orchestrated by Hector Berlioz
Conductor: Nicholas Tcherepnine
Choreographer: Michel Fokine
Designer (set and costumes): Léon Bakst
Dancers:
    The Young Girl: Tamara Karsavina
    The Rose: Vaslav Nijinsky
Company: Diaghilev's Ballets Russes
First Performance: 19 April 1911, Théâtre de Monte-Carlo

Synopsis

From the program: "When the curtain rises, a young girl returning from a ball, overcome with fatigue, goes to sleep in a chair. In her dream the rose which she holds in her hand becomes a genie, who kisses her and disappears at daybreak."

The inspiration for the ballet comes from the first four lines of the romantic poem by Théophile Gautier (1811–72):

Soulève ta paupière close
Qu'effleure un songe virginal;
Je suis le spectre d'une rose[2]
Que tu portais hier au bal.

Raise your eyelid closed
Caressing a maiden's dream;
I am the spirit of a rose
You wore at the ball last night.

Jean-Louis Vaudoyer, the poet and critic, had on impulse put the last two lines of this verse at the head of a piece he had written about the Ballets Russes production of *Carnaval* in 1910, and then suggested to Bakst the idea of a ballet using Weber's piano piece *L'Invitation à la Valse* orchestrated by Berlioz. His letter was not acknowledged: "summer, autumn, winter passed, but no reply was forthcoming. We were no longer thinking of *Le Spectre* when, in May, we received a note from Diaghilev requesting us to appear without delay in Monte Carlo, there to witness the final rehearsals of this trifling divertissement."[3]

Diaghilev had hoped to present *L'Après-midi d'un faune* (see pp 74–78) during the 1911 season, but when it became apparent that it would not be ready in time, an alternative had to be found. Bakst remembered the suggestion of *Le Spectre de la rose*, and everyone agreed that it would make a suitable replacement.

It is one of the shortest of ballets, only eleven minutes long, and yet one of the most memorable and popular. It was pro-duced very quickly by Fokine: "I rehearsed . . . and choreographed it very rapidly, for it was almost an improvisation . . . While I utilized all the resources of the classic ballet, I still considered the work as belonging in the classification of 'new ballet.' It contained no dances to display technique . . . and the dances were expressive at all times."[4] The achievement of a great work of art does not necessarily require ponderous and lengthy preparation. Prince Lieven states that the ballet was produced in "three or four rehearsals," and makes the comment that "perhaps the very speed with which the work was done gave it that character of extraordinary freshness and unity."[5] Fokine always worked fast—usually, as a true genius, relying on his initial inspiration.

Le Spectre de la rose is a *pas de deux* in which the subject, the music, the choreography, the décor, and the costumes were all perfectly matched in a poetical synthesis. The scene is set in the 1830s. Many of the published synopses of this short ballet vary considerably in detail, but Cyril Beaumont usually recorded accurately what he saw. The impression made on him by this ballet is clear from his description: "I can still see Karsavina as the Young Girl, wearing her demure bonnet and cloak, as she walked slowly from the garden into the room, to draw off her cloak, revealing her simple white crinoline, and then settle down in her friendly armchair. She looked affectionately at her lover's gift, a red rose, and pressed it to her lips as though recalling those deli-cious moments when she had danced with him . . . As she pondered, her eye-lids drooped and she fell asleep. The rose slipped through her limp fingers and stained the floor. Suddenly the tempo changed to an infectious whirl of rhythm, and Nijinsky, in rose-coloured tights and a cap and tunic of rose petals, flashed through the window high in the air, then floated down with the lightness and slow descent of a falling leaf, to descend by the sleeping girl. He spun slowly round, and then, pass-ing his hands over the maiden's head, with an exquisite gesture drew her from her chair as though by magnetic force, and guided her, still sleeping, to dance to the ever-quickening rhythm of the waltz . . . At the end, he returned the maiden to her chair, glided across the floor to the opposite side of the room, and, rising into the air, disap-peared through the open window and into the night whence he had come."[6]

Bakst designed a classically simple set for the girl's bedroom, redolent of flowers with two french windows opening on a floral background, decorated and furnished in Biedermeier style with a blue-gray floral wallpaper, white woodwork, a curtained-off bed, a sofa and chair, a draped table with a large urn of flowers, a harp, an embroidery frame, and a birdcage which caused endless trouble. Karsavina remembered how Bakst fussed on the first night: "Bakst moved about helpless, agitated, carrying a canary cage. The cage was a feature of the scenery from his point of view, a nuisance from everybody else's. He had installed the canary over a window from where it had been banished; Nijinsky had to appear through it, and the other window was to be free for Nijinsky's famous leap."[7]

That "leap" has become legendary, and like so many legends has been so exagger-ated in people's minds, whether they saw it or not, as to defy all reason. Nijinsky's wife, Romola, was responsible for nurturing the exaggeration: "Nijinsky's famous last leap in *Spectre*, in which he crossed the whole stage, from front to back, in a single bound, was an astonishing tour de force."[8] Fokine, in his *Memoirs*, brought Nijinsky back to earth: "Nijinsky would kiss the girl sleeping in a chair on stage left, then slowly turn to face the window, and find himself nearly in the middle of the stage. He would then run five steps and, with the sixth, leap out of the window . . . no one has ever jumped from the spot without a running start."[9] There were several technical reasons why the leap became the stuff of legend. First, the skirt-ing board of the french windows, as designed by Bakst, was low enough to make any leap through the window appear to be higher than it really was and, sec-ondly, Nijinsky was caught in mid air by four men, so that no one in the audience saw him actually land on the ground—two technical tricks to help create the illusion. Jean Cocteau described it: "He [Nijinsky] had noticed that half of the leap which ends *Le Spectre de la rose* was invisible from the house. He invented a double leap by which he curled himself up in the air backstage and fell perpendicularly. They caught him like a boxer, with warm towels, slaps, and water which his servant Dimitri threw in his face."[10] Another reason was the music. Pierre Monteux, who replaced Tcherepnine as conductor for the 1911 season in Paris, explained his trick: "I have always smiled over the stories of Vaslav Nijinsky's famous elevation, and his leap through the window at the very end of *Le Spectre de la rose*. The truth is (and this does not detract from the fact that this great dancer was superb in this lovely ballet) he was nobly assisted by Monteux in the pit, who played the chord before the last with a slight *point d'orgue*, thereby creating the illusion of a prolonged elevation of the dancer."[11] However, as Monteux understood, the most important reason for the illusion was quite simply Nijinsky's genius, as explained by Fokine: "the thunderous applause which followed the 'flight' of Nijinsky out of the window was not due to the height of that leap—not at all—but to its being the termination of a most ethereal, light, and poetic dance, immensely difficult to perform, which Nijinsky danced magnificently."[12] In all great artists who master their craft, the technique is subjugated so that no strain is evident in the accomplishment of their performance. Beaumont again: "Fokine made use of Nijinsky's wonderful *élévation* in such a manner that his leaps and bounds seemed the embodiment of grace and ease, the natural attributes of an ethereal being, and not the products of an extraordinary *élévation*."[13] From all accounts, Nijinsky's artistry also lay in his ability to transform himself entirely into the character he was portraying—in this case not even a person,

but a rose. The effect was accurately described by Geoffrey Whitworth: "He truly shows us the very heart of a red rose. For so quiet and tender is his dancing, so exquisitely adapted to the theme, that he becomes the very being he would portray, a spirit rather than a man, a fairy thing and as light as a waft of perfume."[14]

6   Preliminary costume design for Tamara Karsavina as the Young Girl

Graphite, tempera and/or watercolor with brown ink notations on paper (newspaper mounted to laid paper)
10⅞ x 8⅛ in: 27.7 x 20.8 cm (overall)
Signed, lower right of small sheet in pencil: "Bakst"
Inscribed by Bakst upper right of large sheet: "Le Spectre de la Rose / 'Mme Karsavine' [sic] / Robe de chambre"
Inscribed by Karsavina at bottom of large sheet in ink in Russian: "Милому Сергею Лифарю / [illegible] я всегда / танцовала Spectre de la Rose [sic] / 5 июля 1926 / Тамара Карсавина (To dear Serge Lifar [illegible] I always danced Spectre de la Rose, 5 July 1926, Tamara Karsavina)"
1933.391

Provenance: Tamara Karsavina
Exhibitions: New York 1933, No 3; Chicago 1933, No 3; Northampton 1934, No 3; Hartford 1934b; New Haven 1935; San Francsico 1935–6; Paris 1939, No 20; Williamsburg 1940; Cambridge 1942; Edinburgh 1954, No 76; London 1954–5, No 88; Indianapolis 1959, No 13; Hartford 1965, No 2; New York 1965–6, No 7 (illustrated p 16); Princeton 1968; Strasbourg 1969, No 107; Blommenholm 1971; Amherst 1974; Hempstead 1974, No 21; Chicago 1975; Columbus 1989; Worcester 1989.

Illustrations: Beaumont 1946, p 107; *Dance and Dancers* April 1963, p 27; de Mille, p. 140 (color); Palmer, p 22; Pozharskaya and Volodina, p 75.

The page from the sketchbook was not large enough to complete the drawing, so Bakst attached it to a larger sheet with tape and finished it in pencil on the tape. As Bakst inscribed the drawing in the top right hand corner of the larger sheet, he clearly thought that he had done enough for the costumiers to provide the gown. Indeed he had, judging from the photographs of Karsavina wearing it, except that the actual cuffs were much smaller. The fact that the drawing is impossible, with the gown falling completely off the shoulders, is somehow irrelevant. And the face is not that of an innocent young girl. The design for the young girl's dress, which remained in Karsavina's possession,[15] is much more detailed and delicately drawn.

From the date of the inscription, Tamara Karsavina gave this drawing to Serge Lifar after she had danced with him in *Romeo and Juliet*. Frequent and prolonged exposure has faded part of the inscription into illegibility. It is tempting to decipher what is illegible as being some reference to her having danced with Lifar in *Spectre*, but this cannot be so, for Lifar did not dance in the ballet until 1931. It is more likely that she compared Lifar, flatteringly, with Nijinsky.

7   Costume design for Vaslav Nijinsky as the Rose

Graphite, watercolor and/or tempera, silver paint and purple glaze on paper
15½ x 10³⁄₁₆ in: 39.5 x 25.8 cm
Signed and dated in pencil lower right: "Bakst / 1911"
Inscribed upper left in pencil: "'Le Spectre de la Rose' / Nijinsky"
1933.394

Exhibitions: Paris 1911, No 33; New York 1933, No 4; Chicago 1933, No 6; Northampton 1934, No 6; Hartford 1934b; New Haven 1935; San Francisco 1935–6; Boston 1938; Paris 1939, No 21; Williamsburg 1940; Baltimore 1941, No 3; New York 1944; Edinburgh 1954, No 76; London 1954-5, No 90; Elmira 1958, No 40; Indianapolis 1959, No 14; Storrs 1963; Hartford 1964; Hartford 1965, No 4; Houston 1965; New York 1965–6, No 8 (illustrated p 16); New York 1966–7; Princeton 1968; Strasbourg 1969, No 106; Blommenholm 1971; Washington D.C. 1971, No 179; Hartford 1973; Hartford 1974; Hempstead 1974, No 20 (illustrated); Storrs 1975; Chicago 1975; Hartford 1979; Coral Gables 1982; Frankfurt-am-Main 1986, No 131 (illustrated in color, p 213); Hartford 1988; Worcester 1989.

Below: Tamara Karsavina as the Young Girl wearing the gown, and Vaslav Nijinsky as the Rose.

Illustrations: A. E. A., Jr, cover; Beaumont 1946, p 107; Buckle 1955, p 17 No 13; Lister 1954, Palmer, p 23; Percival, p 124; Pozharskaya and Volodina, p 75; Schouvaloff 1991, p 106 (color).

bound his biceps. This jersey was stitched with rose-leaves, which Bakst would colour as they were needed. Some were ragged, as from a dying flower; others were stiff and firm; while still others curled even from his thighs. And after every performance Maria Stepanovna[18] would refresh them with her curling-iron. On his head he wore a close-fitting helmet of rose leaves, and the whole effect was an extremely close blending of different reds, rose-violets, pink, and purple, shading one into another, which is the essential indefinable tint of the rose."[19]

During performances Nijinsky inevitably used to shed some rose petals and the story goes that his Russian valet, Vasili, sold them as souvenirs to admirers. Quite soon he was able to build himself a large house on the proceeds, which became known as the Château du Spectre de la Rose.

Bakst was very particular about the make-up, seeing it as an integral part of his costume design. This fastidiousness was shared by Nijinsky, who always spent a long time preparing for a performance and who began truly to enter a part as he applied his make-up. Romola Nijinsky likened his face in *Spectre* to "a celestial insect, his eyebrows suggesting some beautiful beetle which one might expect to find closest to the heart of a rose, and his mouth was like rose petals."[20]

A simple comparison between the design and the photographs of Nijinsky in the costume still shows many differences between the two and, furthermore, the design is not a drawing of either Nijinsky's face or his body. The color of the costume was changed, because all the references to it are to a violet-pink color rather than blue as in the watercolor, and there was never any silver in the costume. Bakst has cleverly used the edges of the paper to contain his drawing, a trick he often used, which paradoxically creates a sense of movement. He was also often careless about hands and feet. While this is a most evocative design, it is rather a lazy drawing.

*

This famous drawing has been called a "portrait" of Vaslav Nijinsky, as if it was made after the costume. This is not so, as both Benois[16] and Prince Lieven[17] draw attention to the fact that when Nijinsky appeared in his costume before the dress rehearsal Diaghilev was furious because it was not according to Bakst's design. The costume was then altered, not "created" as Romola Nijinsky states, while Nijinsky was wearing it. She does, however, give an accurate description of the costume: "It consisted of a close-fitting, fine silk elastic jersey, into which Nijinsky was sewn covering his entire body, except part of his breast and arms, where bracelets of silk rose petals

Bakst suggested to Gabriel Astruc that Jean Cocteau, who had already shown himself to be a gifted young man, should be asked to design the poster for the 1911 season of the Ballets Russes. "He draws very well and will do you a stunning Nijinsky, for he has often sketched him."[21] Astruc and Diaghilev agreed, and Cocteau designed two posters, one showing Karsavina (but more a self-portrait than of her), the other Nijinsky, in their costumes for *Le Spectre de la rose*.

closely to the description by Romola Nijinsky quoted above, with the predominance of "rose, rose lavender, dark reds and various pinks."[22]

Gustave, the name inside the skull cap, was a well-known theatrical wig maker in London. As the company moved from 87 to 10 Long Acre in 1919, the skull cap must have been made after that date. In the Sotheby's catalogue for 1968 Richard Buckle described this costume as being "possibly that of Idzikowsky." This seems more than possible: Stanislas Idzikowski,[23] who joined the Ballets Russes company in 1915, first danced the part of the Rose when the ballet was revived in Paris in 1922. His costume would have been ordered during the run of *The Sleeping Princess* in London during the winter of 1921–2.

Le Spectre de la rose was revived by de Basil's Ballets Russes on 23 August 1935 at the Royal Opera House, Covent Garden, with Irina Baronova as the Young Girl and Paul Petrov as the Rose.

Notes

1 Vaudoyer is not credited in the Monte Carlo program of the first performance.
2 This line is usually misquoted as being the title of the ballet.
3 Jean-Louis Vaudoyer, quoted in Serge Lifar, *Serge Diaghilev*, pp 252–3.
4 Michel Fokine, *Memoirs of a Ballet Master*, pp 180, 182.
5 Prince Peter Lieven, *The Birth of Ballets-Russes*, p 158.
6 Cyril W. Beaumont, *The Diaghilev Ballet in London*, pp 26–7. John Percival, correcting Beaumont, has stated that Nijinsky "did not flash through the window high in the air, but stepped on to the window ledge and then 'floated down'."
7 Tamara Karsavina, *Theatre Street*, p 240.
8 Romola Nijinsky, *Nijinsky*, p 135.
9 Michel Fokine, *op cit*, p 181.
10 Jean Cocteau, *La Difficulté d'être*, p 69. The valet's name was really Vasili.
11 Doris G. Monteux, *It's all in the music*, p 77.
12 Michel Fokine, *op cit*, p 180–1.
13 Cyril W. Beaumont, *Vaslav Nijinsky*, p 15.
14 Geoffrey Whitworth, *The Art of Nijinsky*, p 49.
15 Illustrated in color in Tamara Karsavina *Theatre Street*, frontispiece.
16 Alexandre Benois, *Reminiscences of the Russian Ballet*, pp 339–40 .
17 Prince Peter Lieven, *The Birth of Ballets-Russes*, pp 159–60.
18 The wardrobe mistress of the company.
19 Romola Nijinsky, *Nijinsky*, p 136 .
20 Romola Nijinsky, *ibid*, pp 136–7.
21 Letter dated 29 March 1911, quoted by Richard Buckle from his collection, in *Nijinsky*, p 202.
22 Romola Nijinsky, *Nijinsky*, p 136.
23 This was the spelling of his name that he finally settled on.

8*   Costume for the Rose

Peach silk knit leotard, painted pink with rose petal outlines, with appliquéd silk petals dyed and painted in shades of red and purple. Heavily darned matching tights, with painted vine, leaf, and petal motifs have elastic shoulder straps. Wig base with ear flaps, maker's label "L. Gustave, 10 Long Acre, London." Elastic armbands decorated with matching petals.
1996.7.3.a-e

Provenance: Diaghilev and de Basil's Ballets Foundation Ltd. Sotheby's London, lot 16, 17 July 1968. Castle Howard Estate Ltd. Sotheby's London, lot 11, 14 December 1995.

This costume is based on the original worn by Nijinsky although, with fewer and smaller leaves, it exposes more of the dancer's body. The colors correspond

Le Dieu Bleu (The Blue God)

Hindu ballet in 1 act by Jean Cocteau and Federigo
    de Madrazo
Composer: Reynaldo Hahn
Conductor: Désiré-Emile Inghelbrecht
Choreographer: Michel Fokine
Designer (set and costumes): Léon Bakst
Principal dancers:
    Young Man: Max Frohman
    Young Girl: Tamara Karsavina
    The Goddess: Lydia Nelidova
    The Blue God: Vaslav Nijinsky
    The High Priest: Michel Fedorov
    The Drunken Bayadère: Bronislava Nijinska
Company: Diaghilev's Ballets Russes
First performance: 13 May 1912, Théâtre du
    Châtelet, Paris

Synopsis

From the program, unacknowledged but by Jean
Cocteau:

"A warm evening in mythical India. The outer
court of a temple hewn out of rock and open to
the sky. A basin in the centre in which floats the
Lotus. On the left a great door, or rather a semi-
circular golden trap-door. In the background,
behind a grating which shuts off the sanctuary, the
plain of the Ganges. Wild flowers and creepers
covering columns and cornices in heavy masses.
Sacred serpents hanging along the walls. Giant
tortoises with painted shells sleeping round the
water.

A young man is about to be made a priest.
There are crowds, offerings, cermonial ritual. Three
women carry peacocks on their shoulders, others
flowers and fruits on metal plates. The young
man's ordinary garments are removed and he is
clad in the saffron robe of the priesthood in the
midst of wild evolutions [sic] of dancers and yogis.
There is a sudden tumult. A young girl brushes past
the guards and throws herself at the young priest's
feet, entreating him not to leave her for the
priestly life. He gently pushes her away and
remains in a state of ecstasy. The priests insult her
and try to drive her off. She takes no heed of their
threats, and dances to win back the lost joy of her
love. The priests are indignant at this disturbance
of their mysteries, and they surround the girl; but
she escapes them, and improvises a sorrowful
dance of memories. She reminds him of their
journey together on the banks of the Ganges.
Gradually the young man begins to look at her,
and is troubled. She sees this, and her acting
increases in intensity. All at once he rushes to her
side. The priests are scandalised and furious. The
young man is taken away, and the high priest
threatens the young girl with a terrible vengeance;
he makes her understand that she is to suffer
martyrdom.

While the crowd disperses they tie the girl's
wrists together. The gates between the pillars are
closed. There is complete solitude and silence. The
serpents begin to uncoil themselves, the tortoises
go to the water and drink, the Milky Way floods
the sky. The girl creeps about trying to find a way
out. The gates are fast; but she sees a ray of hope.
Under the trap door there is a faint light. She lifts
it, but suddenly recoils, stupefied with horror. It is
the den of the monsters belonging to the temple.
They come out, and go round the temple in a slow
procession. Some crawl, some spring, some bound,

and some fly. They try to push her into their den.
Then she remembers the Lotus, and sinks down
and prays to it.

The monsters pause, uneasy. Slowly the basin
fills with light; the Lotus opens. The Goddess
appears. Motionless, with a grave smile, she
appears, crouched in the unfolding petals. One
finger of her right hand points to the water; almost
touching her hand, but coming up from the water,
is another finger and hand, then an arm. The arm
and hand are blue, and gradually the God emerges.
He is entirely blue, with lips and nails of silver.

The Goddess shows him the martyr. He walks
on the water, leaps to the ground, and turns to the
monsters, scatters them, and prepares to charm
them.

The movements of the Blue God are gentle and
frenzied by turns. He disperses the groups of
monsters and plays among them, regardless of
their angry growls. He evades them; he crawls
when they jump, and he jumps when they crawl.
By his order the branches of the creeper come
down and wind themselves round the monsters,
rendering them powerless to move. Some of them
inhale the perfume of the flowers and sink sense-
less to the ground.

He shows the Goddess the tamed monsters. He
runs from one to the other, and charms one last
rebel, asserting his decisive power. Then, radiant,
he dances round with gradually decreasing frenzy,
and sinks down.

Priests rush in with torches to see the result of
their vengeance. At the sight of the miracle they
fall with their faces to the ground.

The Goddess orders them to untie the girl. They
tremble and obey. An atmosphere of exquisite
happiness fills the temple. The lovers embrace.

At a sign from the Goddess a gigantic golden
staircase appears, whose steps are lost in the
clouds. And as she sinks into the heart of the Lotus
the Blue God flies up to heaven."

Diaghilev intended to follow up the
exotic ballets, *Cléopâtre* of 1909 and
Schéhérazade (see pp 62–66) of 1910 which
had so impressed Parisian audiences, with
another startling production inspired by the
orient for the 1911 season, in which this
time he would ensure that Nijinsky would
predominate. He settled on *Le Dieu Bleu*,
commissioning the libretto from Jean
Cocteau and Federigo de Madrazo, and the
music for the first time from a non-Russian,
the French composer Reynaldo Hahn.

Le Dieu Bleu was one of six new ballets
planned for the 1911 season: the others were
Narcisse,[1] *La Péri*,[2] *Le Spectre de la Rose* (see
pp 67–70), *Sadko*[3] and *Petrushka* (see pp
117–27). Fokine was to be responsible for
the choreography of all the ballets. The first
four were to be designed by Bakst. It
proved to be an over-ambitious plan, especially as at the same time Fokine and Bakst
were also working on *Le Martyre de Saint

Sébastien[4] for Ida Rubinstein, who had
formed her own separate company for
producing a few grandly lavish gala performances in which she gave herself the starring role. Diaghilev was particularly
irritated by what he saw as Fokine's and
Bakst's treachery in agreeing to work for
someone else. However, while accepting
that they could not possibly cope with so
many new productions simultaneously, he
only realized that *Le Dieu Bleu* could not be
included in his plans by the end of May
1911, a few weeks before the Paris season
opened. It was postponed to the 1912 season.

The postponement was not entirely
Bakst's fault. He had been as diligent as he
could be, but he never received the information he needed. Stage designers have to
work to an agreed plan—they need precise
instructions, they do not invent in the
abstract. Bakst tried hard to receive his
instructions. As late as 15 (28) April 1911 he
wrote from Paris complaining and explain-
ing to Diaghilev in Monte Carlo: "I have
sent you the sketch for *Péri* for which two
costumes are needed, but, working on them,
I am changing them, as with everything by
the way. But remember, after you receive
the design send it back within 3 hours, so
that I don't have to ask everyone, you,
Shura [Benois], Fokine, a hundred times as I
do now to send me the staging plan for *Le
Dieu Bleu*, without which I am not prepared
to do any more work. Apart from the few
arbitrary and vague instructions which you
gave me when the priority was to work on
Thamar[5] and *Après-midi d'un faune* I have
received nothing—no libretto, no number of
characters, nor number of scenes, no definite budget, no cast list. I always repeat (but
I may as well be singing to the wind) that
the whole essence of my designing for the
theater is based on the most calculated
arrangement of patches of color against the
background of a set with costumes which
correspond directly to the physique of the
dancers. Even so, I am doing a lot of work
on *Le Dieu Bleu*, but blind, without knowing
what band of color will come out of it. It's
awful. Once again, I earnestly and urgently
ask you to send me details of the staging for
Le Dieu Bleu, the number of characters, how
many in each costume, and the names of the
artists according to the libretto, the libretto
itself, the number—precisely worked out, in
full, the fixed number of monsters etc.
Fokine with Shura and you can work it out,
but as I have already told you more than

once I cannot design sets in one country, travel to another to help with the staging, and then to a third to do all the lighting and make adjustments to the scenery. It's too much. Every second here is dear to me, and you should know from my parcels of *Rose* and *Narcisse* how conscientious and honest I am working on productions, and how I can be trusted more than a little, especially as every artist can only work in his own characteristic manner and style. Once again I remind you that Muelle[6] needs the exact measurements of the dancers, those who have not been cast as well as those who have, and, most important, the shoe sizes for Crait. Once again I ask you to send me without delay the details for the staging of *Le Dieu Bleu* because I cannot work on something I know nothing about. The consequences will be fatal. Ask Serov, he'll tell you how much I am working for you—and so I ask you to help me a little, and not sit back indifferent to what I am doing here. After all, it is for you. Once again, I repeat, the costumes of the main characters appear dominant, like flowers in the bouquet of the other costumes. If my backgrounds remain uncertain then I cannot finish the work. It is pointless for me to go on repeating 'send me, send me *Le Dieu Bleu*,' when I am obstinately refused the rudiments of my work."[7]

There is no record of Diaghilev's reply, but he probably ignored Bakst's letter, dismissing it as mere unnecessary fussing. Diaghilev hardly ever wrote letters, preferring to communicate with everyone by telegram. Having accepted the postponement of the production, he probably also lost some of his enthusiasm for it, although he still lavished a huge budget on it and continued to hope that it would provide Nijinsky with another sensational role. Fokine began rehearsing his choreography during the winter of 1911–12 in St Petersburg. In his ideas for *Le Dieu Bleu* he was much influenced by the dancing he had seen by the ballet troupe of the Royal Siamese Court which had visited Russia in 1900. According to Prince Lieven, Fokine also made "a very thorough study of India and its plastic art," but "in spite of visits to museums and the examination of many documents and much material"[8] the result was unconvincing and uninspired. Cyril Beaumont thought the choreography appeared to be uninspired because of Reynaldo Hahn's dull score. It may well have been the reason. Prince Lieven was slightly more complimetary but also thought that "the music seemed very fine, though actu-

ally it was a little flat, charming enough but lacking in interest and importance—India seen through the eyes of Massenet, sweet and insipid."[9]

All the critics agreed that the best things about *Le Dieu Bleu* were the set and the costumes designed by Bakst. Because of the postponement, Bakst had to make copies of a number of his costume designs as he had sold the originals during an exhibition at the Musée des Arts Décoratifs in Paris.[10] This did not, however, prevent him from finding his "band" of color with which, as Beaumont wrote, he could "evoke all the cruelty and voluptuousness of the East" and "conjure up the mystery and sense of awe produced in the East in a mood of religious exaltation."[11] The main colors were purples, mauves, pinks, greens, pale blues, yellows, set in white, the brilliant, basic white of the costumes backed by the bright orange and deep blue of the set. It was magnificent, but it was not enough. The greatest disappointment was obviously the wasted opportunity with Nijinsky. Beaumont again: "His role seemed to consist of posing, there was very little dancing. It was difficult to dispel the impression that for the first time Nijinsky's artistry and rare abilities had been wasted."[12]

Le Dieu Bleu was a failure. It aroused no enthusiasm in the audiences. It was performed three times in Paris in 1912, three times in London in 1913 during the spring season at the Royal Opera House, Covent Garden,[13] and never revived.

9* Costume for a Temple Servant

Plum facecloth robe adorned with vertical bands of gold embroidery, gold button-front opening, ivory wool panels applied and raised gold arabesques, the elbow length sleeves edged in white wool and applied with blue triangles, the hem with broad white band stencilled with blue and green triangles and arches, the front and back inset with painted satin panels with gilded studs
Stamped "2002"
1996.7.4

Provenance: Diaghilev and de Basil's Ballets Foundation Ltd. Sotheby's London, lot 1, 17 July 1968. Castle Howard Estate Ltd. Sotheby's London, lot 20, 14 December 1995.
Exhibitions: Strasbourg 1969, No 150; San Francisco 1988–9, No 115.

There were six Servants of the Temple, Mmes Iezerska, Dombrowska, Kowalewska, Rozumowicz, Hubert, and Zulicka, but in the absence of any label it is impossible to determine who wore this costume.

Notes

1 *Narcisse*, with music by Nicholas Tcherepnine, was first produced at the Théâtre de Monte-Carlo on 26 April 1911.
2 *La Péri* was planned with music by Paul Dukas who intended it as a vehicle for his mistress Natasha Trouhanova. The production did not take place because after both Diaghilev and Fokine agreed that Trouhanova was incapable of dancing the part Dukas, highly offended, withdrew his score. Two costume designs by Bakst were, however, reproduced in the season's souvenir program.
3 *Sadko*, scene 6 from the opera, "The kingdom under the sea," by Nikolai Rimsky-Korsakov, with sets and costumes by Boris Anisfeld, was first produced at the Théâtre du Châtelet, Paris on 6 June 1911.
4 *Le Martyre de Saint Sébastien* by Gabriele d'Annunzio, directed by Armand Bour, with music by Claude Debussy, and Ida Rubinstein as the Saint was first performed at the Théâtre du Châtelet, Paris on 22 May 1911, just before Diaghilev's sixth season began there on 6 June.
5 *Thamar*, with music by Mily Balakirev, choreography by Michel Fokine, and Tamara Karsavina in the title role was also produced only in 1912, on 20 May at the Théâtre du Châtelet.
6 Marie Muelle was the costumier in Paris who worked most closely with Bakst.
7 Bakst to Diaghilev, quoted in I. S. Zilberstein and V. A. Samkov, *Sergei Diaghilev*, Vol 2, pp 116–7.
8 Prince Peter Lieven, *The Birth of Ballets-Russes*, p 170.
9 Prince Peter Lieven, *ibid*, p 170.
10 The exhibition at the Palais du Louvre, Pavillon de Marsan, 6 July–15 October 1911, was Bakst's first one-man show in the West.
11 Cyril W. Beaumont, *The Diaghilev Ballet in London*, p 58.
12 Cyril W. Beaumont, *ibid*, p 60.
13 The season was from 4 February to 7 March. *Le Dieu Bleu* was first performed on 27 February.

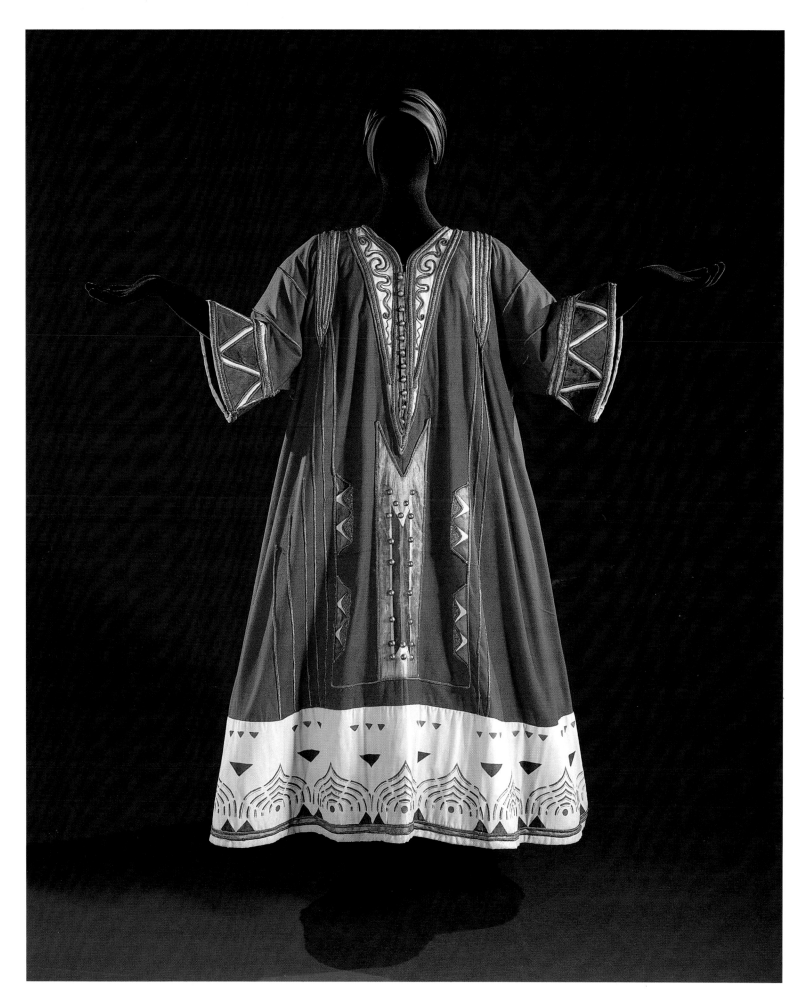

L'Après-midi d'un faune (The Afternoon of a Faun)

Ballet in 1 scene by Vaslav Nijinsky after the poem
by Stéphane Mallarmé[1]
Composer: Claude Debussy (*Prélude à l'Après-midi
d'un faune*)
Conductor: Pierre Monteux
Choreographer: Vaslav Nijinsky
Designer (set and costumes): Léon Bakst
Dancers:
    The Faun: Vaslav Nijinsky
    The Nymphs: Lydia Nelidova, Bronislava
        Nijinska, Olga Khokhlova, Tcherepanova,
        Maikerska, Klementovitch, Kopytsinska
Company: Diaghilev's Ballets Russes
First Performance: 29 May 1912, Théâtre du
    Châtelet, Paris

Synopsis

The program stated: "This is not Stéphane Mallarmé's *The Afternoon of a Faun*; it is a short scene
based on the musical prelude to this pan-like
episode which precedes it

> A Faun sleeps:
> Nymphs trick him;
> A forgotten scarf satisfies his desire
> the curtain falls so that the poem can begin in
> everyone's memory."[2]

"A Faun reclines on a rock playing his pipes and
sucking the juice from a bunch a grapes. Seven
nymphs wander through the wood below him. The
Faun watches their arrival, climbs down from his
rock, approaches them and begins to woo them.
Frightened, the nymphs escape two by two; the
leader of the nymphs and the last one to escape
leaves a scarf behind. The Faun returns to his rock
bearing the scarf in front of him on outstretched
arms. He lays the scarf out on the ground and
lowers himself face downwards onto it with a
gesture whose symbolism was plain."

No one is definite about how long
Nijinsky took to prepare his first
choreographic work. Bronislava Nijinska
said there were 90 rehearsals for this short
ballet,[3] Romola Nijinsky said there were
120, "of which at least ninety were taken up
training the dancers in the method."[4] And
that was the difficulty: Nijinsky invented a
new technique of movement based not at all
on the classical dancing technique of the
five positions, but on one inspired by two-
dimensional Greek vase and Egyptian frieze
painting with the bodies of the dancers
facing the audience while their heads and
limbs were in profile. Peter Ostwald also
makes the interesting suggestion that a
further source of inspiration for Nijinsky
may have been the pathological movements
associated with "neurological deformities"
which he had witnessed in his elder
brother's asylum.[5] In fact, the source of
inspiration is almost irrelevant when assess-
ing the ballet, which was revolutionary and

marked a crucial turning point in the
development of the Ballets Russes. "This
production," wrote Prince Lieven, "was
Diaghileff's first departure from the principles for which he strove, together with his
friends, during his youth and early man-
hood. He abandoned the artistic principles
which *Mir Iskusstva* (*The World of Art*) had
fought to uphold. In addition, and this is
extremely important, the production of this
ballet brought with it the inevitable rupture
with Fokine. What is important here is not
so much the advancement of Nijinsky as a
choreographer and the resulting resignation
of Fokine, as the jettisoning of Fokine's
main choreographic principles, the break
with tradition which Fokine had developed
but had never sought to overthrow."[6]
Diaghilev was never an impresario to rely
exclusively on safe and tested productions
but was, on the contrary, always restless to
experiment and promote new artists. He
took risks. *L'Après-midi d'un faune* was,
however, a dead-end revolution which led
nowhere beyond Nijinsky's own new choreography. He was, without question, an
innovative choreographer of genius, but he
made only three other ballets—*Jeux, Le Sacre
du Printemps* (see pp 291–95), and *Til Eulenspiegel*, which was the only ballet Diaghilev
never saw.[7]

No one is definite either about who first
thought of the ballet—Nijinsky, Diaghilev,
or Bakst. As with so many of the ballets
produced by the Ballets Russes (and as with
so much in the theater), the genesis of this
one was probably in conversations between
the three of them discussing various ideas.
In this case, all three were on holiday
together on the Lido in Venice during the
summer of 1910. What is certain is that
Diaghilev, becoming disenchanted with
Fokine as the company's choreographer in
spite of the huge success of *Schéhérazade* and
other ballets, was already hoping to replace
him with Nijinsky, his lover and the star of
his company. To that end, during the company's tour in Dresden at the the beginning
of 1912, he took Nijinsky to visit Emile
Jaques-Dalcroze at his school at Hellerau,
where he was developing and teaching his
theories of musical training through
rhythm, "Eurythmics," in which Diaghilev
had become very interested. As Grigoriev
said: "Diaghilev was determined that Nijinsky should imbibe the teaching and apply it
to the composition of a ballet."[8] Igor
Stravinsky, who was very much one of the

"closed circle" of friends at the time,
described the ballet's creation: "Diaghileff
made up his mind that year that he would
spare no effort to make a choreographer of
Nijinsky. I do not know whether he really
believed in his choreographic gifts, or
whether he thought that his talented dancing, about which he raved, indicated that he
would show equal talent as a ballet master.
However that may be, his idea was to make
Nijinsky compose, under his own strict
supervision, a sort of antique tableau conjuring up the erotic gambols of a faun
importuning nymphs. At the suggestion of
Bakst, who was obsessed by ancient Greece,
this tableau was to be presented as an
animated bas-relief, with the figures in
profile. Bakst dominated the production.
Besides creating the decorative setting and
the beautiful costumes, he inspired the
choreography even to the slightest movements. Nothing better could be found for
this ballet than the impressionist music of
Debussy, who, however evinced little enthusiasm for the project."[9] While dismissing the
theme, Stravinsky credits Bakst with the
main creative impulse.[10] Bakst shared his
enthusiasm for Greek art with Nijinsky by
showing him the painted Greek vases in the
Louvre upon which many of the movements of the ballet were subsequently
modeled.[11] Certainly, Mallarmé's poem (or
eclogue) as a basis for the work was not
chosen by Nijinsky, who at the time could
neither read nor speak French; and the
music, an existing well-known piece by a
celebrated composer, was chosen by
Diaghilev. When Debussy was asked if his
prelude could be used for a ballet he merely
said: "Why?" but then agreed.

Nijinsky first began to work on his ballet
in the autumn of 1910. From Bronislava
Nijinska's contemporary notes, it appears
that Nijinsky had plenty of ideas of his
own: "At the very beginning of the ballet
the Faune [sic] has a series of poses, reclining on a rock, sitting up, or kneeling . . .
Vaslav is creating his Faune by using me as
his model. I am like a piece of clay he is
molding, shaping into each pose and
change of movement . . . I can't grasp at
once and render correctly his own choreographic scheme . . . It is amazing how
Vaslav himself, from the very beginning,
without any preparation, is in complete
mastery of the new technique of his ballet.
In his own execution, each movement, each
position of the body, and the expression of

each choreographic moment is perfect."[12] These notes were written when she was nineteen and an adoring sister. She would probably not have known or been told of any ideas that may have been passed to Nijinsky by Bakst or Diaghilev. However, it seems to me that only Nijinsky, as a dancer, having absorbed any theories that may have been suggested to him, could work out what his body and the bodies of the other dancers could do in practice. It was he, after all, who eventually wrote down the choreographic score.[13] In spite of all the early concentrated work with his sister, Nijinsky was not ready to present the ballet during the 1911 season, and it was replaced in the program by *Le Spectre de la Rose* (see pp 67–70). Work on the ballet was therefore stopped; it resumed only in Berlin in January 1912 with so-called "unofficial" rehearsals, to keep them a secret from Fokine. Rehearsals continued in Monte Carlo by which time Fokine, who was rehearsing *Daphnis and Chloë*, knew all about Nijinsky's ballet and bitterly resented Diaghilev's favoritism: "What extreme efforts were made to assure the success of *L'Après-midi d'un Faune*, this first experiment of his favorite, and what measures were taken to diminish the success of *Daphnis*!"[14]

Before the first performance, Diaghilev said to Bronislava Nijinska: "I have never seen Bakst so enthusiastic. Levushka [Bakst's pet name] said that *L'Après-midi d'un faune* is a 'super-genius' creation and we are all fools not to have understood it."[15] No one is definite about how long the ballet was; timings vary between eight minutes and twelve.[16] Grigoriev described the first night: "the audience were electrified from the start. The ballet was watched with intense interest, and at the end one half of the spectators broke into frantic applause, and the other into equally frantic protests. Diaghilev was visibly put out; for, although forewarned by his friends, he had scarcely expected so violent a reaction . . . He appeared on the stage flushed and agitated—when suddenly we heard shouts of 'Bis, bis!' from the auditorium, which quite drowned the hissing of the objectors. Diaghilev seized on this demonstration to order a repetition of the performance."[17] Much has been made of the final moment of the ballet, when Nijinsky jerked himself on the scarf in a simulated orgasm, apparently scandalising the audience. It seems to me, however, from reading the reports, that the "scandal" at the time was much more to do with the audience's (and the critics') reac-

tion to Nijinsky's choreography as a whole than to his apparently obscene single final gesture. Cyril Beaumont, writing later, summed up the general impression: "I well remember the gasp that went up from the audience at Nijinsky's audacity. Yet the movements and poses were performed so quietly, so impersonally, that their true character, with their power to offend, was almost smoothed away. It was an intriguing study in erotic symbolism."[18] Indeed, *Le Figaro* was the only newspaper seriously to

object to the ballet, with the editor, Gaston Calmette, suppressing his critic's notice and writing a piece himself instead under the heading of "A Faux Pas": "We are shown a lecherous faun, whose movements are filthy and bestial in their eroticism, and whose gestures are crude as they are indecent. That is all."[19] M. Calmette, throughout his article, was also referring to all the movements and gestures, not just the final one. Diaghilev was quick to reply, by including a supportive letter from Odilon Redon[20] and an

Below: Vaslav Nijinsky as the Faun and his sister Bronislava as a Nymph.

admiring article by Auguste Rodin from *Le Matin* which *Le Figaro* was honorable enough to print the next day. The controversy was a welcome bonus to Diaghilev's normally effective publicity machine.

In her restoration of Nijinsky's choreography from a close study of his notated score, Ann Hutchinson Guest accurately summarizes the originality of the work: "What was truly daring about the work went unobserved in the tumult of unbridled emotional reaction . . . Nijinksy's novel way of interrelating movement and music produced short movement phrases culminating in frieze-like tableaux that contrasted with Debussy's fluid music; above all Nijinsky's choreographic concept departed from traditional theatrical precepts of scenic representation and audience response."[21]

In general the ballet was received with calm praise by the critics. By the time it was shown in America during the company's tour in 1916, the hysteria had died down, and its genuine innovation was appreciated; the critic Oliver M. Sayler wrote: "Of course, there are infinite possibilities of interpretation in this ballet. You may read into it what you like. I prefer to think of it as a whimsical joke, a satire on sex. In our western puritanism we permit no satires on sex outside 'the Follies' and the Winter Garden entertainments. Possibly that is why this extremely reserved and deliciously suave and polished fable has caused so much uneasiness. Genuine art has herein found a new field of expression."[22]

Léon Bakst had designed a beautiful but inappropriate set which Bakst and Diaghilev both liked very much, but which Nijinsky did not. The original program quoted Stéphane Mallarmé: "*L'Après-midi d'un faune* should be danced in the middle of a landscape with zinc trees." Zinc was not the color used by Bakst. Instead he used soft autumnal reds, greens, and ochres, described by Louis Schneider in *Comoedia* as "something like a primitive tapestry, rather than a realistic evocation." But he continued: "One difficulty became apparent: the tapestry in question is so close to the proscenium arch that the dancers have only just enough room for their movements, no more than two meters, including the mound on which the Faun is resting when the curtain goes up and upon which, at the end of this disturbing scene, enamoured, he goes to sleep inhaling, intoxicated, the hot scent emanating from the veil of one of the nymphs he pursued. With rare good fortune M. Léon Bakst has realised that atmosphere

which brings out the 'thickly wooded sleep' of the Faun . . . he has imagined the 'beautiful country' perfectly. In this deep forest where we know that the burning light of mid-day has made its mark, there is something better than color, there is reverie, rhythmic clarity, an exact transcription of the spoken word into the language of sounds."[23] The scenery may have pleased M. Schneider, but when Nijinsky came to write down the notation he gave explicit instructions about the set and the costumes: "the set consists of a back-cloth, truck, drapes and floor cloth. Depicted on the back-cloth is a torrid summer landscape in Greece. On the right, from the audience's point of view, there should be a stream, and to the left a hillock, which can be made with the aid of a truck."[24] For the revival in 1922, after Nijinsky had gone mad and with Bronislava Nijinska as the Faun, the set was redesigned by Picasso but so unsuccessfully that it remained anonymous.

Bakst's costumes, on the other hand, were perfect creations for this ballet and its production—that is, both for the choreography and for its setting. The costumes for the nymphs, modeled on the Greek peplum, were armless diaphanous dresses of finely pleated gauze bordered at the hem with tiny squares or wavy lines of blue or dull red, the white overskirt being decorated also with wavy lines, bands of ivy leaves, or dots of the same color as the squares. The nymphs also wore tightly fitting wigs made of cord painted gold with Grecian locks falling to their waists. They wore no tights and were naked under their costumes. These costumes became standard for Bakst's "Greek style" productions. For Nijinsky Bakst designed a closely fitting body-stocking which he painted in a café-au-lait color with big brown spots which continued over his bare arms and hands giving the impression of the skin of a faun. There were garlands of leaves and flowers round his loins and his neck, and on his head he had a wig of the same gold-painted cord as the nymphs but twisted at the side into two little horns. Romola Nijinsky thought that the whole effect was "the very image of an adolescent Faun, a young being half animal, half human. In the costume, as in Nijinsky's expression, one could not define where the human ended and the animal began."[25]

Nijinsky was one of those performers who needed to spend a long time getting ready in the dressing room before curtain up, always arriving at the theatre several hours before the obligatory "half," and one

who slowly eased himself into any given part by gradually transforming his appearance through the use of make-up.[26] Romola also described in detail the make-up which changed his face completely: "He underlined the obliquity of his eyes, and this brought out and gave a slumberous expression. His mouth, chiselled by nature, he made heavier. Here also was an infinite languor and bestial line. His face, with its high cheek bones, lent itself admirably to the transformation. His ears he elongated with flesh-coloured wax and made them pointed like a horse's. He did not imitate; he merely brought out the impression of a clever animal who might almost be human."[27] That was Nijinsky's great trick.

10* Costume design for Vaslav Nijinsky as the Faun

Graphite, tempera and/or watercolor, gold paint on illustration board
15¹¹⁄₁₆ x 10¹¹⁄₁₆ in: 39.8 x 27 cm
Signed in pencil lower right: "Bakst"
Inscribed upper right in pencil: "'L'Après Midi d'un Faune' / (Nijinsky)"
1935.37

Provenance: The Marchioness of Ripon; Leonide Massine; Marie Harriman Gallery.
Exhibitions: London 1912, No 65; Chicago 1934, No 2; Middletown 1935; New York 1937–8, No 698; Boston 1938; Paris 1939, No 22bis (illustrated p 12); Los Angeles 1939–40; Williamsburg 1940; Cambridge 1942; Boston 1945; Hartford 1949, No 38; Edinburgh 1954, No 84; London 1954–5, No 99; Sarasota 1958, No 4; New York 1958; Hartford 1959; San Francisco 1959; Indianapolis 1959-60, No 15a; Lisbon 1962, No 270; New London 1963; Eindhoven 1964; Hartford 1965, No 6; Houston 1965; New York 1965–6, No 6 (illustrated in color frontispiece); Spoleto 1966; New York 1966–7; Princeton 1968; Frankfurt-am-Main 1969, No 45; Strasbourg 1969, No 156 (illustrated in color on cover); Philadelphia 1970; Blommenholm 1971, No 5; Amherst 1974; Hartford 1974; Chicago 1975, No 31; New York 1979, No 6; Coral Gables 1982; Frankfurt-am-Main 1986, No 137 (illustrated in color p 217); Hartford 1988; Worcester 1989
Illustrations: Alexandre, pl 13 (color); Beaumont 1946, p 121; *The Bellman*, 27 January 1917, p 103; Buckle 1971, cover (color); *Comoedia Illustré*, 15 May 1912, cover (color)[28]; Detaille, cover and facing p 40 (both color); Gadan & Maillard, p 9 (color); Hartford Symphony 97/98 Season prospectus, p 5 (color); Haskell 1968, cover (color); Kirstein, p 200 No 381; Krasovskaya; Lister 1954; Lynham, pl XXVII p 131; Pozharskaya, pl 145; Pozharskaya and Volodina, p 96 (color); Schouvaloff 1991, p 151 (color); *Serge de Diaghileff's Ballet Russe*, a tour of America October 1916 to February 1917, inside back cover (color); Souvenir Program, American tour 1916.

With this design Bakst reached a peak of perfection, both in terms of what a costume design should be and what a ballet costume should be. The design, cleverly composed to cover the whole sheet, is full of sensuous and languorous movement, an effect achieved by the weaving scarf (although it was not part of the Faun's costume), the crossed legs and the relationship between the arms, the back, and the tilt of the head. The feet are human, the oddity of the foot on the ground in a sandal and the other bare accentuating the sybaritic feeling, but the hands, malformed and disproportionately large (or just badly drawn), grabbing at the vine and the fruit, are bestial. The face, indefinite but smiling with satisfaction, is neither quite human nor quite beast. The description above of Nijinsky's make-up shows that he achieved Bakst's requirement. The descriptions of the costume and the wig also show this to be a faultless working drawing, but it is at the same time an interpretation of the mood of the ballet.

A ballet costume should not only give the right outward appearance of the character for whom it is designed, but should also be easy to dance in by not inhibiting the dancer's movements. Here Bakst, perfectly aware of Nijinsky's choreographic intentions, designed a minimal and therefore ideal costume. Moreover, the photographs of Nijinsky and the nymphs in their angular poses confirm the suitability of the costumes in relation to each other. Whether they were suitable or not in relation to the set is not clear, since the exisiting "action" photographs were all studio shots taken in front of a different background.

Bakst made at least one copy of this design; there is a photograph of him painting one in his studio in about 1922. A hand-painted lithograph was also made at some time, but since the edition was unnumbered the size is not known.

Notes

1 Although this is the official credit line, Nijinsky admitted to never having read the poem, or any poems by Mallarmé.
2 This note was almost certainly written by Jean Cocteau.
3 Bronislava Nijinska, *Early Memoirs*, p 427.
4 Romola Nijinksy, *Nijinsky*, p 165.
5 Peter Ostwald, *Vaslav Nijinsky*, p 58. When Vaslav was still a small child his elder brother, Stanislav, suffered severe brain damage after a fall out of a window and had to be permanently hospitalized.
6 Prince Peter Lieven, *The Birth of Ballets-Russes*, p 174.
7 *Jeux* with music by Claude Debussy was first performed on 15 May 1913 at the Théâtre des Champs-Elysées, Paris; *Til Eulenspiegel* with music by Richard Strauss was first performed on 23 October 1916 at the Manhattan Opera House, New York.
8 Serge Grigoriev, *The Diaghilev Ballet*, p 72.
9 Igor Stravinsky, *Chronicle of My Life*, p 64.
10 Corroborated by Arnold Haskell in *Diaghileff*, p 269: "as far as the central idea was concerned, they [Diaghilev and Bakst] resolved to make the ballet a moving bas-relief, all in profile, a ballet with no dancing but only movement and plastic attitude—the insprration for all this being solely Bakst's."
11 Jean-Michel Nectoux in *L'Après-midi d'un faune* has identified several vases in the Louvre by comparing photographs of Nijinsky dancing with the figures in the paintings.
12 Bronislava Nijinska, *op cit*, p 316.
13 In August–September 1915 in Budapest.
14 Michel Fokine, *Memoirs of a Ballet Master*, p 203. See pp 79–81 on *Daphnis and Chloë*.
15 Bronislava Nijinska, *Early Memoirs*, p 431.
16 Serge Grigoriev in *The Diaghilev Ballet* says 8 minutes, p 77; Arnold Haskell in *Diaghileff* says 10 minutes, p 269; Romola Nijinsky in *Nijinsky* says 12 minutes, p 173.
17 Serge Grigoriev, *op cit*, p 79.
18 Cyril Beaumont, *The Diaghilev Ballet in London*, p 54.
19 The title is a play on words, literally "a false step," as *pas* is a choreographic term meaning a single complete movement of a leg, or a dance for one or more dancers in similar costume. The article, published on 30 May 1912, is quoted in Richard Buckle *Nijinsky*, p 285.
20 He had originally been thought of as designer of the ballet.
21 Ann Hutchinson Guest, *Nijinsky's Faune Restored*, p 5.
22 Oliver M. Sayler, "'The Faun' and 'Scheherazade' Escape the Censorial Eye— Diaghileff Ballet Reaches New Heights" in *The Indianapolis News*, 11 March 1916.
23 Louis Schneider in *Comoedia*, 30 May 1912, p 2.
24 Vaslav Nijinsky, *L'Après-midi d'un Faune*, notation, MS in the British Library (Additional MSS 47215).
25 Romola Nijinsky, *op cit*, p 172.
26 The length of time Nijinsky needed to spend in his dressing room before an evening of performances was in order to prepare himself psychologically for whatever roles he was to dance, while the intervals between the ballets were long enough for him to change his make-up without haste.
27 Romola Nijinsky, *op cit*.
28 This cover has also been reproduced many times.

Daphnis and Chloë

Choreographic symphony in 1 act, 3 scenes by
    Michel Fokine based on a pastoral by Longus
Composer: Maurice Ravel
Conductor: Pierre Monteux
Choreographer: Michel Fokine
Designer (sets and costumes): Léon Bakst
Principal dancers:
    Chloë: Tamara Karsavina
    Daphnis: Vaslav Nijinsky
    Darkon: Adolf Bolm[1]
    Lykanion: Ludmilla Schollar
Company: Diaghilev's Ballets Russes
First Performance: 8 June 1912, Théâtre du
    Châtelet, Paris

Synopsis

Scene 1: a sacred cypress grove with an altar to Pan guarded by three nymphs. Greek maidens enter bearing gifts of flowers and grapes. They are followed by shepherds who join them in their ritual dancing. Daphnis leads the dancing surrounded by the maidens. Chloë, to draw his jealous eye, dances with the shepherds whose leader is Darkon. Darkon tries to kiss Chloë against her will. Daphnis leaps to her aid and a fight threatens. Instead, the crowd suggests a dancing competition between the two, with the prize for the winner being a kiss from Chloë. Darkon begins but his clumsiness is mocked by the crowd. Daphnis wins and for his grace Chloë rewards him with a kiss. She leaves with the maidens and the shepherds. Daphnis, left alone, lies down to rest. Lykanion, the temptress, tries to seduce Daphnis with an alluring dance, but he remains faithful to Chloë and angrily drives her away. Suddenly the clash of arms and warlike shouts are heard as Chloë, panting for breath and looking for shelter, runs across the grove pursued by brigands. One of them seizes her and carries her away. Daphnis searches for Chloë but can only find "a piece of her torn garment."[2] In despair, he curses the gods and falls to the ground. Suddenly the nymphs come to life and descend from their pedestals to dance. They catch sight of Daphnis and, waking him up, call upon Pan to come to the aid of the lovers.

Scene 2: the brigands' camp. During a war-like dance Chloë is brought on and ordered to dance. She tries to escape but the chief brigand carries her triumphantly back. Suddenly the atmosphere changes and the menacing shadow of Pan appears in silhouette. All the brigands flee in terror, leaving Chloë alone to offer her thanks to the gods.

Scene 3: the sacred grove towards morning. Daphnis is still stretched out on the grass. A group of herdsmen enter in search of Daphnis and Chloë. They awaken Daphnis. Chloë appears surrounded by shepherds. Daphnis realizes that what has happened has been a dream. The two lovers fall into each other's arms and, in front of the altar guarded by the nymphs, swear eternal love. Everyone joins in celebrating their betrothal.

Fokine, while still a student, became convinced that ballet needed modernizing, but he realized that it could progress no further as long as it continued to be governed by strict rules of tradition. In 1904 he came across *Daphnis and Chloë* by the fourth-century Greek writer, Longus, and, as soon as he had read "this most beautiful love story of the shepherd and the shepherdess on the island of Lesbos,"[3] he wrote his first ballet. He submitted the script to the Director of the Imperial Theaters, Vladimir Teliakovsky, with an introduction in which he outlined his ideas for the reform of ballet and of which the following is an extract:

"In the ballet the whole meaning of the story can be expressed by the dance. Above all, dancing should be interpretative. It should not degenerate into mere gymnastics . . . it should express the whole epoch to which the subject of the ballet belongs.

"For such interpretative dancing the music must be equally inspired. In place of the old-time waltzes, polkas, pizzicati, and galops, it is necessary to create a form of music which expresses the same emotion as that which inspires the movements of the dancer. The harmony which these dances must have with the theme, the period, and the style, demands a new view-point in the matter of decoration and costume. One no longer demands the eternal short skirts, pink tights, and satin ballet-shoes . . .

"The ballet must no longer be made up of 'numbers,' 'entries,' and so forth. It must show artistic unity of conception. The action of the ballet must never be interrupted to allow the *danseuse* to respond to the applause of the public.

"In place of the traditional dualism, the ballet must have complete unity of expression, a unity which is made up of a harmonious blending of the three elements—music, painting, and plastic art.

"The great, the outstanding, feature of the new ballet is that in place of acrobatic tricks designed to attract applause, and formal entrances and pauses made solely for effect, there shall be but one thing—the aspiration of beauty.

"Through the rhythms of the body the ballet can find expression for ideas, sentiments, emotions. The dance bears the same relation to gesture that poetry bears to prose. Dancing is the poetry of motion."[4]

The only reaction from the Imperial Theaters was a notice, a few days later, that artists should no longer acknowledge applause during opera performances. As for the rest, and the scenario of the ballet, they were forgotten. Forgotten, that is, until 1909 when Diaghilev asked Fokine for ideas for new ballets and was enthused by his suggestion of *Daphnis and Chloë*. Diaghilev, primarily interested in the musical aspect, decided with his customary flair to commission a score from the French composer Maurice Ravel.[5] This was a particularly surprising choice after only the first season, but no doubt he thought that it would please the French critics and audiences. Fokine was thrilled with the suggestion because "to begin with, Ravel was not involved with the old tradition of ballet. And, in the second place . . . he was already very well aware that polkas, pizzicatos, waltzes, and galops—so indispensable in the old ballet—were completely out of place in the new."[6] Ravel himself stated that his intention was to compose: "a vast musical fresco, less concerned with archaism than fidelity to the Greece of my dreams which corresponds closely to the one imagined and painted by French artists of the end of the eighteenth century," and that the work was constructed symphonically: "according to a very rigorous plan, using a small number of motifs whose development ensured the symphonic homogeneity of the work."[7] The ballet was originally planned for the 1910 season. However, in spite of the fact that the choreographer and composer worked closely together, Ravel found the composition difficult. On 10 May 1910 he wrote to Mme Godebska (Misia Sert): "*Daphnis* does not progress very quickly. It's not through lack of working on it. I have been clamped to it since morning."[8] Ravel did not finish the score in time for the 1910 season, nor even for the 1911 season.

When it became obvious that Ravel would not deliver, Bakst persuaded Diaghilev to produce a different "Greek" ballet based on the theme of Narcissus and Echo, simply called *Narcisse*, and a score was commissioned from Tcherepnine. The substitution annoyed Fokine, because he had been developing his choreographic ideas for *Daphnis and Chloë* and now found that he had to adapt them hurriedly for *Narcisse*, a ballet for which he had no particular enthusiasm. "What angered me greatly," he wrote, "and seemed to me most inartistic was Diaghilev's use in *Narcisse* of the Bakst scenery designed for *Daphnis*. All the paraphernalia I needed for *Daphnis*—the green meadow, the grove with the statues of three nymphs; wreaths; sacrificial offerings of the shepherds—were all in *Narcisse*. The nymphs played an important part in *Daphnis* but had no relation whatsoever to the story of *Narcisse*."[9] It annoyed Fokine even more when Bakst's set design for scenes 1 and 3 of *Daphnis and Chloë*—with the nymphs, Daphnis, Chloë, and a herd of sleepy sheep—was reproduced in *Comoedia Illustré* on 15 June 1911 under the caption *Décor de "Narcisse"*. *Narcisse*, first performed on 26 April 1911 in Monte Carlo, was neither a triumph nor a disaster, but was not repeated.

By 5 April 1912, when the score of *Daphnis and Chloë* was finally ready, Diaghilev was totally preoccupied with making Nijinsky into a choreographer and therefore did everything to obstruct Fokine. Furthermore, he realized that Nijinsky would not be required to dance in one of the three scenes. Grigoriev, the company manager, wrote: "it was my impression that he [Diaghilev] would have abandoned it altogether, but that he did not wish to offend Ravel and that the scenery and costumes were now ready and singers for the accompanying chorus engaged. As it was, he deferred its production to the very end of the Paris season, on the pretext that Fokine was unlikely to complete it sooner; and this in itself militated against its success."[10] In fact, in the spring of 1912, Diaghilev was so determined not to produce the ballet that he did not mind offending Ravel after all, by calling on the composer's publisher, Jacques Durand, to say that the score was inadequate. Durand, using all his powers of argument, persuaded him to change his mind and "Mr de Diaghilev after consideration said simply 'I'll put on *Daphnis*.'"[11] His agreement, however, did not prevent him from using other means of trying to thwart the production. He deliberately allowed Fokine very little rehearsal time, with priority always given to Nijinsky for *L'Après-midi d'un faune*, so that the first night of *Daphnis and Chloë* had to be postponed from 5 to 8 June. As a final insult, according to Fokine, Diaghilev put *Daphnis and Chloë* first in the running order, and directed that the performance begin half an hour earlier than usual, which would ensure that neither critics nor audience saw it.[12] Whether this is true or not, and it does seem unlikely to me, Fokine finished the ballet, the curtain went up at the usual time, *Daphnis and Chloë* was performed first, and the house was full.

Critics, unaware of the behind-the-scenes row between Diaghilev and Fokine, probably made matters worse by praising the production. Louis Schneider in *Comoedia* thought that Bakst's sets did not "summarise the action, but determined the

meaning, the atmosphere and the character; and, what is more, the one was in contrast with the other. Thus the painter with his palette has realised the triptych dreamt of by the choreographer and the composer. The set for the first and third scenes is idyllic . . . the set for the second scene is in a completely different color scheme . . . wild, violent, savage. It is not conventional, School of Fine Art Greece with a blue sky and soft sunlight. The costumes are also by M. Léon Bakst: to go on about magical polychromy is to repeat oneself. The tunics of the shepherds and the brilliant costumes of the pirates stand out against the scenery, just as the scenery makes a wonderful background for the variously colored materials of the costumes."[13] A lone, dissenting voice was André Boll's; he wrote later about Bakst's setting that "its brutal and vigorous harmonies in a somewhat outmoded mythological spirit only corresponded superficially with the musical spirit of the score. In future *Daphnis and Chloë* should find a setting more in harmony with 'ravelian' art."[14] This was a reaction against the excessive "painterliness" of the Ballets Russes settings which was not shared by other critics. Robert Brussel in *Le Figaro* summed up the general opinion of the whole production: "*Daphnis and Chloë* then is a genuine work of art which, in a setting enriched by the most noble tradition, concedes nothing or almost nothing to present fashion, does not court easy access, and, being, neither reactionary nor falsely prophetic of the future, is in the best taste of the present day as works should be which aspire to influence profoundly their epoch. Michel Fokine, at once author and producer, has afforded in *Daphnis and Chloë*, a new proof of his extraordinary talent."[15] But it was not proof enough for Diaghilev to want to retain him, nor for Fokine to stay. He resigned from the company immediately after the curtain came down.[16]

The Ballets Russes repeated *Daphnis and Chloë* in Paris in 1913, and took it to London in 1914 when Fokine danced the part of Daphnis after his reconciliation with Diaghilev—the only appearance of Fokine as a dancer in London. The anonymous critic of *The Times* wrote: "The dancing of M. Fokine as Daphnis matched that of Mme. Karsavina in its grace and suppleness, and their scene of reunion had a joyousness of movement which seemed the exact counterpart to the rich melody and orchestral colour of the music to which it belongs."[17]

The London performances were also marked by a quarrel between Diaghilev and Ravel, conducted through the newspapers. Ravel, in a letter that appeared on the morning of the first night (9 June) in *The Times*, *Morning Post*, *Daily Mail*, and *Daily Telegraph* (in English not his own), stated that although he had agreed to make an arrangement of the score without chorus for performance only in "certain minor centres," he was "deeply surprised and grieved" when he discovered that "what will be produced before the London public is not my work in its original form" but "the new version without chorus." Diaghilev's reply, published the following day (10 June), justified his action: "The experiment of giving *Daphnis and Chloë* with chorus was tried two years ago . . . and it was clearly proved that the participation of the chorus was not only useless but actually detrimental."[18] This justification was, of course, made on artistic grounds, but in fact Diaghilev had dropped the chorus for financial reasons. He ended his letter with characteristic cunning: "I had the pleasure of asking M. Ravel to write *Daphnis et Chloe* for my ballet; more, the composer did me the honour to dedicate this remarkable work to me, and it would be very extraordinary in view of this if I had not made every effort to present it in the most perfect manner possible to the London public, to whom I owe a very great debt of admiration and gratitude." This effectively put a stop to any further objections by the composer or the public.

In 1921 Fokine revived the ballet with his own company at the Opéra in Paris. When the ballet was revived by Diaghilev on 1 January 1924 at the Théâtre de Monte-Carlo, Daphnis, danced by Anton Dolin, had a new costume designed by Juan Gris.

A final economy made by Diaghilev was his use of Bakst's set for scenes one and three for *The Gods Go A-Begging*, the ballet to Handel's music, which was first performed at His Majesty's Theatre in London on 16 July 1928.

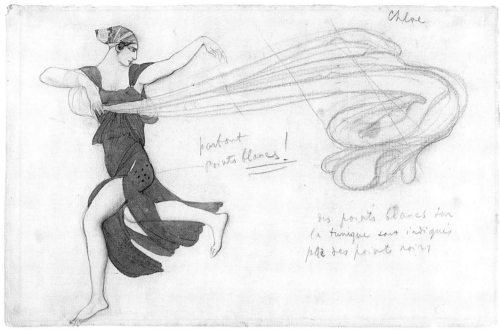

11   Costume design for Tamara Karsavina as Chloë

Graphite, tempera and/or watercolor on paper
11⅛ x 17¹¹⁄₁₆ in: 28.2 x 44.7 cm
Unsigned and undated
Inscribed in pencil top right: "Chloe," centre:
   "partout / points *blancs*!" ("*white* spots everywhere"), bottom right: "des points blancs sur /
   la tunique sont indiqués / par des points noirs"
   ("the white spots on the tunic are shown by
   black dots")
1933.392

Exhibitions: New York 1933 (ex catalogue); Chicago
   1933, No 4; Northampton 1934, No 4; Hartford
   1934b; New Haven 1935; San Francisco
   1935–6; Paris 1939, No 27 (illustrated p 12);
   Poughkeepsie, New York 1940; Williamsburg
   1940; Cambridge 1942; Edinburgh 1954, No
   91; London 1954–5, No 106; Michigan 1957;
   Elmira 1958, No 3; Indianapolis 1959, No 16;
   Rowayton 1960; Storrs 1963; Hartford 1965,
   No 3 (described as "Chloë's costume for
   Koravine"); Houston 1965; New York 1965–6,
   No 4 (illustrated p 15); New York 1966–7;
   Princeton 1968; Strasbourg 1969, No 167
   (illustrated No 39); Frankfurt-am-Main 1969,
   No 50; Blommenholm 1971 (?); Hartford 1973;
   Hartford 1974; Hempstead 1974, No 10;
   Chicago 1975, No 33; Hartford 1979; Coral
   Gables 1982; Columbus 1989; Worcester 1989.
Illustrations: Percival, p 90; Schouvaloff 1991,
   p 153.

Bakst has drawn this design showing the moment, in scene one, when Chloë runs across the grove pursued by brigands, with her scarf billowing behind her. As noted in the synopsis above, historians are uncertain about what Daphnis finds when he searches for Chloë. This drawing might be considered to be evidence that he finds the scarf, since it is given such prominence in the composition, but for the fact that it remains unpainted, and is indeed crossed out, as if Bakst was having second thoughts. However, it is the exisiting composition, with the figure running off to the left of the paper while looking back to the right, as well as that scarf, which together create the illusion of fearful movement. Although Bakst has taken great care with the face and head-dress, and corrected the line of the arms and the legs, he has left the hands and feet with fingers and toes like carrots. This was a characteristic trait of his drawing, but occasionally he would take enough trouble to prove that he too was able to draw hands and feet with exquisite correctness. But he obviously considered this drawing to be incomplete, hence it was annotated and left unsigned, although it is sufficiently detailed to serve as a costume design.

1 Later often spelt "Adolph".
2 This is according to Fokine's own version in
   Memoirs of a Ballet Master, p 198. In other
   descriptions this is sometimes her torn scarf
   (Beaumont, *Michel Fokine*, p 98), sometimes a
   sandal (Buckle, *Nijinsky*, p 296).
3 Michel Fokine, *Memoirs of a Ballet Master*, p 71.
   Fokine has transposed the place as the original
   story was set in Sicily.
4 Quoted in Cyril W. Beaumont, *Michel Fokine*,
   p 23. See also Introduction, pp. 36–7.
5 Diaghilev, in a letter to Benois dated 12 (25) June
   1909 (quoted in I. S. Zilberstein and V. A.
   Samkov, *Sergei Diaghilev*, vol 2, p 103), states that
   he has already commissioned *Daphnis and Chloë*.
   Roland-Manuel in *Maurice Ravel et son oeuvre
   dramatique* puts the birth of the project at 1906,
   which is unlikely. But Fokine gives 1910 as the
   date in his *Memoirs* (p 195), which is confirmed
   by Bronislava Nijinska in *Early Memoirs*
   (p 328–9). Ravel, in his *Esquisse autobiographique*
   (p 214), supported by Serge Lifar in *Diaghilev*
   (p 267), gives the surprisingly wrong date of
   1907. Haskell, quoting Nouvel, in *Diaghileff*
   (p 217), gives 1909 but adds that "it was not
   ready till 1911" which was not the case.
6 Michel Fokine, *op cit*, p 196.
7 Maurice Ravel, "Esquisse autobiographique" in
   La Revue Musicale, Paris December 1938, pp
   213–4.
8 Quoted in René Chalupt, *Ravel au miroir de ses
   lettres*. See also Introduction, p 53, note 17.
9 Michel Fokine, *op cit*, p 201.
10 Serge Grigoriev, *The Diaghilev Ballet*, p 77.
11 Jacques Durand, *Quelques Souvenirs d'un Editeur
   de Musique*.
12 Michel Fokine, *op cit*, p 203, but Richard Buckle
   states in *Diaghilev* (p 229) that he cannot believe
   this to be so. Both say that first performances of
   ballets were never first in the program, but this
   statement is not borne out by the contemporary
   newspaper notices that show that *Daphnis and
   Chloë* was not the only new production to be
   performed first.
13 Louis Schneider, *Comoedia*, Paris 10 June 1912,
   p 2.
14 André Boll in *La Revue Musicale*, Paris December
   1938, p 253.
15 Robert Brussel, 9 June 1912, quoted by Cyril
   Beaumont in *Michel Fokine*, pp 100–1.
16 It is not clear whether this was after the first or
   the second, and last, performance.
17 Anon, "Ravel's 'Daphnis et Chloe'" in *The Times*,
   London 10 June 1914.
18 Maurice Ravel's letter from Paris dated 7 June
   appeared in *The Times*, London 9 June 1914;
   Diaghilev's reply appeared after the notice
   above.

Les Femmes de Bonne Humeur (The Good-Humored Ladies)

Ballet in 1 act after the play *Le Donne di Buon Umore* by Carlo Goldoni adapted by Vincenzo Tommasini

Composer: Domenico Scarlatti, orchestrated by Vincenzo Tommasini

Conductor: Ernest Ansermet

Choreographer: Leonide Massine

Designer (sets and costumes): Léon Bakst

Principal dancers:

Luca: Enrico Cecchetti

Silvestra: Josephine Cecchetti

Constanza: Lubov Tchernicheva

Mariuccia: Tamara Karsavina

Leonardo: Leonide Massine

Company: Diaghilev's Ballets Russes

First Performance: 12 April 1917, Teatro Costanzi, Rome

Synopsis

The scene is a square in a small town near Venice. Old Marquise Silvestra sits on her balcony, primping for the Carnival, while her maid, Mariuccia, mimics her behind her back. Count Rinaldo, a languid young man betrothed to Silvestra's niece Constanza, comes into the square and sinks into a café chair. Niccolo, the waiter, brings him a drink. Mariuccia comes from the house and presses a *billet-doux* into the Count's hand. He reads that a lady, infatuated with him, wants to meet him and will come wearing a pink bow in her hair. This is Constanza's test of his fidelity. Now, four masked ladies appear—Constanza, Felicita, Dorotea, and Pasquina—all wearing pink bows. Constanza quickly disappears as one by one the others flirt with the Count, but as he approaches each of them he is repulsed. Last comes the old Marquise who is also wearing a pink bow. The Count invites her to join him in a glass of wine and coquettishly she agrees. However, when she raises her mask he is dismayed to see she is old, and tries to escape. She clings on to him and drags him to the Carnival.

In her mistress's absence Mariuccia invites her admirer, Leonardo, to supper. His friend Battista joins them. The old Marquis of Luca totters in and eyes Mariuccia. The other three invite him to join them and they all have a hilarious time. The climax is a *pas de trois* by Mariuccia and the two young men while the Marquis nods happily and falls asleep. Felicita and Dorotea interrupt the dance. Leonardo quickly escapes at the sight of his wife Felicita. The ladies seize Battista telling him that his fiancée has been flirting all evening with Captain Faloppa. Incredulous, he is only convinced when Pasquina passes by on the Captain's arm. Battista, racing after them, knocks over the table and wakes up the Marquis. The ladies tie a mask over the old man's eyes and escape into the house.

The clock in the tower strikes four. Constanza emerges to dance a lament for her lover and then sees the Marquise, glowing in her triumphs, with the Count on one arm and the Captain on the other. Leonardo and Battista return dressed as women with veils hiding their faces. They flutter round the old Marquis and lead him round the square back to the café. He is delighted by their attentions and, seating them down, goes to order wine. They throw back their veils and burst into roars of laughter. The old man collapses.

Meanwhile the young ladies have dressed up the waiter Niccolo as a rich prince and posed him

in the doorway to await the Marquise. She arrives with her dashing escorts. The young ladies draw her attention to the Prince in the doorway who, coming forward, bows magnificently and asks for her hand. Overcome with joy the Marquise announces her forthcoming marriage to the Prince, but Mariuccia springs forward and takes off Niccolo's mask. The Marquise is furious, pounces on Niccolo and starts hitting him while the rest of the company bursts out laughing. Their laughter wakes the Marquis who appears in his nightcap and gown and in turn starts hitting everyone with his stick. The stick falls on the Marquise's head and knocks off her magnificent wig to reveal her bald head. She sinks to the ground while everyone laughs at the ridiculous spectacle.

After their tour in America in 1916, the Ballets Russes found refuge first in Spain and then in Italy. In 1917 Diaghilev, with his "headquarters" in Rome, prepared a new and revolutionary season for Paris. He was determined that his company should change course again and, according to Grigoriev, thought that Massine, as his new choreographer, was "capable of becoming the very incarnation of all that was modern in art and of putting Diaghilev's own ideas into practice."[1] Among the new ballets proposed were a revised production of *The Fairy Doll*, to be called *La Boutique Fantasque* (but plans to produce it were postponed; see pp 182–84); *Parade* by Erik Satie and Jean Cocteau as a Cubist ballet to be designed by Picasso, his first work for the theatre, and *Les Femmes de Bonne Humeur* designed by Bakst. *Parade* was rehearsed in Rome but first produced in Paris at the Châtelet theater on 18 May 1917. Thus *Les Femmes de Bonne Humeur* was Massine's first major ballet.

Diaghilev had the idea of basing a ballet on a play by Goldoni and using music by Scarlatti. Diaghilev and Massine listened to "about five hundred of his sonatas, finally choosing about twenty which would . . . enhance the comic situations in the play."[2] Tommasini was commissioned to orchestrate the selected pieces. Massine was given several months in which to arrange the choreography, and it was during these rehearsals that he learnt and mastered his craft. As he describes in his autobiography: "I learned the value of concentrating on detail, and giving full significance to even the most minute gesture. I also discovered that the body includes various more or less independent structural systems, each answerable only to itself, which must be co-ordinated according to choreographic harmony. This led me to invent broken, angular

movements for the upper part of the body while the lower limbs continued to move in the usual harmonic academic style . . . I created entirely new body movements in my imagination, profiting largely by the effect of rhythmic forces, and varying, according to the nature of the movement, its rhythmic value as well as its tempo in order to attain, in the composition of choreographic phrases, the strongest possible effect."[3] Where Fokine had begun the choreographic revolution by turning his back on the traditional technique of ballet, Massine took the revolution a stage further. He still believed in the technique, but once it was mastered, he would use and pose the body in any shape or form which he considered suited and best expressed the music. The "Sitter Out" in *The Dancing Times* described Massine as a choreographer as "a futurist," and continued: "Dancing as understood by him is something different to the dancing of the Traditional School. He poetically described it to me as a marriage of choregraphy [*sic*] and plastique, a statement which M. Diaghileff amplified by adding that the ballets of Fokine show choreography, the later ones of Nijinsky, plastique, but those of Massine a happy blend of the two."[4] The dancers certainly responded brilliantly to Massine's ideas, and, under the watchful eye of Diaghilev who "was present at all rehearsals, and took an active part in them, making suggestions and criticising passages he disapproved of,"[5] were pleased to be given so much time to perfect the ballet. It was, by all accounts, a great pleasure to dance in it. Lydia Sokolova, who danced the part of Felicita in London, wrote that she thought it "was the most perfect and complete ballet of its type ever invented . . . Nothing could have been gayer or more fun to dance."[6] *Les Femmes de Bonne Humeur* became known as the ballet "of perpetual motion," and although audiences loved it they had great difficulty in following the rather trite but infinitely intricate plot. The "Sitter Out," in his next article, was not so impressed, describing the dancing as "unusual," and saying that: "The whole thing is a trick—a most amusing and clever one it is true, but I decline to recognise it as great Art."[7]

By 1917 Bakst was almost the only one left of the original company. He sensed the move to modernity, but had no intention of ceding his place as innovator in design for the Ballets Russes to Picasso, Larionov, or anyone else. As if to emphasize his own ability and desire to keep up with the times, he contributed an important introductory article to the 1917 Souvenir Program with the title "Choreography and Settings of the New Ballets Russes." In it he discussed the choreography of Massine and the design by Larionov for *Midnight Sun* (see pp 230–32) and *Contes Russes* (see p 233) before introducing Picasso's *Parade*. He then rather portentously introduced his own work for *Les Femmes de Bonne Humeur*: "The reconstruction of a certain period on the stage is a fiction. I do not think that one should be able to undertake such a task without incurring the risk of being accused of parody. That is the reason why I preferred, instead of imitating Italian eighteenth century stage decoration, to offer a personal interpretation of the age of Goldoni. I had to emphasise the farcical character of the burlesque, and Italian gaiety, which is so evident in the work of the Italian writer's work (and often in Scarlatti's music). Besides which, in order to emphasise the characters and make them stand out, I tried to design a setting (in rather dark tones) as if it were seen through a hemispherical glass so popular in the eighteenth century. The optical effect I managed to achieve pleased me greatly (is that the only respectable point of departure for an artist?) in that it distorted the lines of perspective so that concentric curves emphasised the vertical axes of the characters. Massine, in turn, in his singularly attractive choreography, sought to emphasise the burlesque nature of the piece. The great variety of movement, the frenetic fury of the dances, a sort of dionysiac ecstasy made *Les Femmes de Bonne Humeur* an admirable capriccio. Its merriment often approaches the limits of Hogarthian laughter." The scene represents a square in a small town near Venice enclosed by the false proscenium of a green and white curtain. Buildings are on three sides of the square with a white *campanile* (clock tower) in the center background against a deep blue sky. The first sketch which Bakst made was much too extreme: the convex distortion of the perspective did not work at all and the trick appeared to be merely pointless and ridiculous. Diaghilev asked Bakst to make another drawing and, for the performances in Rome and Paris, the distortion of the buildings was only slight. Benois remembered the ballet: "Bakst had made charming costumes (it was before his break with Diaghilev) and they reminded one of the dresses of old-fashioned marionettes. The décor, in brownish tones, was in full harmony with the costumes and only

betrayed the influence of the modern fashion—very naively—by the slight forward tilt of the houses. The marionette character of the choreography openly smacked of the grotesque, for the interpreters of Goldoni's ballet moved about and gesticulated as if pulled by strings. Nevertheless *Les Femmes de Bonne Humeur* made an enchanting impression; it had charm very similar to the charm of our first ballets—*our* ballets."[8]

Whatever Benois said, no one much liked or was ready for what was thought to be quirky scenery; otherwise, the ballet was always considered to be great fun. Diaghilev relied on the continued success and popularity of *Les Femmes de Bonne Humeur* and, therefore, when the company went to London in 1918, their first visit since 1914, he asked Bakst to redesign his set so that all the buildings appeared to stand up straight. Bakst wrote to Diaghilev on 18 July 1918: "Here is my new sketch, the second, and also as yet unpaid (the price is 2000 francs), for *Donne di bon umore*. Although it disgusts me to produce tidy little houses, I accept your need to curry favour with your audience. But one thing I implore you not to do: do not make the color of the sky any lighter, for that would *ruin* everything, because it would be impossible to concentrate on the artists *below it*, and instead of Goldoni and Italy, as seen through Hogarth, we should have nothing but Werther and Massenet . . . The scenery is unbelievably simple, the houses pure Italian, though unfortunately I did them on the table where the sketch looks miles better than on the easel. Enfin!"[9] While Bakst may have thought that his scenery was simple, it presented problems for the scene painter, Vladimir Polunin. He described his work: "To transfer a design by Bakst into suitable proportions for the stage proved to be a difficult task, for he often painted his effective designs with more regard for their pictorial effect than for the use of the scene painter, and so it was in this case. If his design were to be transferred to the prepared canvas in the same proportions, the nearest houses of the back-cloth would have appeared so small that the heads of the dancers would have been on a level with the roofs, which would have destroyed the veracity of the effect. On the other hand, if the buildings were to be of normal size, the top of the tower would have been cut off by a sky-border."[10] There are two kinds of set design: one which is perfectly to scale and which only needs "squaring up" by the scene painter in order to transpose it exactly onto the canvas, and one which, without

necessarily being accurately drawn, nevertheless accurately transmits the atmosphere required by the set thereby allowing the scene-painter scope for his own imagination. Bakst always tended, as Polunin says, toward making the second kind of design; at the same time he was astute enough to realize that such designs would have greater commercial possibilities in exhibitions. Polunin continued: "Diaghileff, who came several times a day to the studio where the work was in progress, immediately decided that the tower should be 27 feet high, and he was right; the sky-border did not spoil the effect and the nobility of the tower gave the proper dimensions to the surrounding buildings. He looked over the details of the drawings, criticised the height of the buildings . . . chose another type of fountain instead of that depicted by Bakst, which was not to his taste, took an interest in all the details, and did his best to appreciate the point of view of the executors," and, finally, "Diaghileff said to me: 'Thank goodness, at last I have a scene in accordance with what I wanted.'"[11] Diaghilev was a stickler for detail and determined to have his own way, a trait which often irritated his colleagues. They put up with it and, sometimes not without a struggle, changed what he wanted changed because they were persuaded that his perfectionism led to good notices and appreciative audiences. An anonymous critic in 1919 gave a typical assessment of *Les Femmes de Bonne Humeur*: "This Hogarthian piece is the true ballet-pantomime, and last night delighted those familiar with it and astonished those to whom it was new. The wonderful pantomime at the supper table, the extraordinary delicacy of the solos, and the effect of novelty and freshness of the whole—much improved in its effect by condensation—won an instant success—a success well justified. The farcical element was never excessive; the whole was delicious comedy with a gentle reminder that it was make-believe supplied by the busy figure seated at the spinet at the corner of the stage. The delicious Scarlatti music was neatly played, and the whole number an immediate triumph."[12] It would be hard to find a more enthusiastic notice. It certainly justified the ballet's frequent revival. Florence Grenfell, a devoted friend of the Ballets Russes, noted in her diary for 20 November 1925: "We all went to the Coliseum to see Lydia [Lopokova] in the 'Good Humoured Ladies.' She was absolutely adorable, danced it perfectly, & the Ballet became with her as enchanting as of old."

drawings for *Les Femmes de Bonne Humeur* he tried something new and unfamiliar by appearing to be influenced by a "Cubist" manner. He was not to be left out of the latest trend, even though he probably had little sympathy for it. The figures are flat, stiff, and angular, with exaggerated hands and awkward feet; actually, however, they much less Cubist than a successful conveying of Massine's choreography through imitation of the dancers' marionette-like, grotesque positions. The drawings were so appreciated for their color and amusing liveliness that Bakst made copies of several of them.

*

Enrico Cecchetti was born in a dressing room in Rome in 1850, the son of two dancers. He was a great teacher of ballet, and taught in St Petersburg from 1890. Among his pupils were Karsavina, Pavlova, Fokine, and Nijinksy. In 1910 he became the resident teacher for Diaghilev's Ballets Russes and every dancer in the company benefited from his teaching. He also danced in a number of important roles. In 1923 he returned to La Scala, Milan, and it was to Cecchetti in Italy that Diaghilev sent the young Serge Lifar to perfect his dancing technique. He died in Milan in 1928.

12* Costume design for Enrico Cecchetti as the Marquis of Luca

Graphite, tempera and/or watercolor, silver and gold paint on paper
26⅝ x 19 in: 67.6 x 48.2 cm
Signed and dated in pencil bottom right: "Bakst / 1917"
Inscribed top right in pencil: "'Les Dames de bonne Humeur' / 'Luca' (Marquis)"
1939.431

Provenance: Your Secretary Inc.
Exhibitions: London 1917, No 24; Poughkeepsie 1940; New York 1944; Edinburgh 1954, No 109; London 1954–5, No 118; Hartford 1957; New York 1965–6, No 5 (illustrated p 14); New York 1967; Hartford 1974; Hartford 1979; Coral Gables 1982; Hartford 1988.
Illustrations: Lister 1954; Percival, p 89 (a copy dated "17"); Pozharskaya and Volodina, p 163b (color; a copy dated "17").
There are at least three more or less identical versions of this design, including a smaller (45 x 29 cm) preliminary version, dated 1916. This latter remained in the collection of Serge Lifar, was exhibited at Strasbourg in 1969 as No 254, and sold at Sotheby's in 1984 as lot No 15.

Bakst frequently changed his style of drawing costume designs, suiting the drawing to the production. In the series of

Notes

1 Serge Grigoriev, *The Diaghilev Ballet*, p 127.
2 Leonide Massine, *My Life in Ballet*, p 96.
3 Leonide Massine, *Ibid*, pp 95–6.
4 The Sitter Out in *The Dancing Times*, October 1918, p 5.
5 Serge Grigoriev, *The Diaghilev Ballet*, p 125.
6 Lydia Sokolova, *Dancing for Diaghilev*, p 98.
7 The Sitter Out in *The Dancing Times*, November 1918, p 31.
8 Alexandre Benois, *Reminiscences of the Russian Ballet*, pp 379–80.
9 Quoted in Serge Lifar *Diaghilev*, p 210.
10 Vladimir Polunin, *The Continental Method of Scene Painting*, pp 39–40.
11 Vladimir Polunin, *ibid*, p 40.
12 Anonymous cutting in unidentified newspaper, "The Russian Ballet: Alhambra Season Opened." Therefore probably dated 11 April 1919.

Aladin ou la Lampe Merveilleuse (Aladin or the Magic Lamp)

Fairy story in 3 acts and 11 scenes by Rip
(Georges Thenon)
Composer: Willy Redstone
Conductor: Léo Pouget
Director: M. Signoret
Designer (sets and costumes): Léon Bakst
Principal Characters:
    Barbizon: Albert Brasseur
    Aladin: M. Clermont
    Fouilloche: M. Signoret
    Suzy: Yvonne Reynolds
    The Tiller Girls
First Performance: 22 May 1919, Théâtre Marigny,
Paris

Synopsis

A "modern" fairy story performed as a revue.

Aladin, a pasha, is a Parisian banker who became rich because of the lamp he inherited from an ancestor. He commands the Bolshevik Fouilloche to ruin Barbizon, a rich factory owner, by organizing a strike of his workers. By doing this he will have Miss Suzy Barbizon, who has refused to marry him, at his mercy. Barbizon is indeed ruined, but because he accepts his collapse cheerfully, he is rewarded by finding Aladin's lamp and becomes, as he says, richer than Aroun-al-Rothschild. He transforms Aladin and Fouilloche into policemen, and when they want to arrest him he invites them to a party he is proposing to give in his magnificent palace. During the party Fouilloche makes off with the lamp, organizes a soviet, and transforms society. Barbizon achieves eternal happiness by becoming a plumber, that is to say all-powerful. But his old secretary, who is in love with Miss Suzy, acquires the lamp and makes her disappear for ever.

The eleven scenes were titled as follows: "Aladin's lamp," "The strike," "Decadence and grandeur of Barbizon," "The thousand-and-second night," "Paris-Bagdad," "The harem," "Retrieving the lamp," "Barbizon entertains," "The new society," "The Devil vanquished," "The lamp is extinguished."

Georges Thenon, under the pseudonym Rip, was the author and producer of a successful series of revues at the Marigny Theater in Paris. In *Aladin* he was taking advantage of the continuing vogue for "orientalism" and the new vogue for the Russian Bolshevik revolution. During an interview before the first night Rip was reported as saying: "*Aladin ou la Lampe Merveilleuse*, contrary to what some people believe, is a modern fairy story. The action takes place during the present day. The transformations brought about by Aladin's lamp make very varied transitions possible. Here and there I have introduced some current jokes. Revue is an extendible art form which fits in well with fairy stories. In *Aladin* there is a scene on music, another on fashion, and another on Bolshevism. We will see the Bolshevik Signoret claiming the

right for all workers to be millionaires, and the beggar Albert Brasseur suddenly in charge of a fortune which he doesn't know what to do with."[1]

It was M. Trébor, the Director of the Marigny Theater, who had the inspired idea of engaging Léon Bakst as designer. Renowned as Bakst was for his sets and costumes for the Ballets Russes, no one had had the audacity of commissioning him to design something so supposedly lightweight and trivial as a revue. The timing was right. Bakst had little else to do at the time. The effects of the upheaval of the First World War and the Russian Revolution were still being felt, and Diaghilev was producing fewer new ballets. He was also turning toward other designers. Indeed, he had jumped at Bakst's infuriated but unintentioned suggestion of getting someone else to design *La Boutique Fantasque* by immediately commissioning André Derain (see pp 182–84). This "treachery," as Bakst saw it, severed their relationship for some time. However, it left him free to concentrate on *Aladin* which required, in addition to eleven set designs, over three hundred costume designs.

In this revue, Bakst continued to develop his ideas of scenic innovation but in a completely different vein from the one he pursued unsuccessfully in *Les Femmes de Bonne Humeur* (see pp 82–84). In *Aladin* he reduced the scenery to backcloths only, with all the architectural details, furnishings, props, and any other decoration painted on them. The cloths were like eleven primitive paintings in a "pointilliste" style. In some of the set drawings he did not particularly tax his imagination but reworked earlier ideas, which has led to their often being confused with designs for earlier ballets, especially *Thamar*. The stage was left bare except for token stylized tables, chairs, and props necessary for the action made out of unpainted wood. One of the essential ingredients of revue or pantomime is the apparently magical transformation from one scene to the next. Bakst's method of staging, the exchange of one backcloth for another during a lighting change, was not in itself innovative, but certainly made the transformations easy and effective. However, the total absence of realism was disconcerting, and stretched the audience's (and the critics') imaginations beyond their capacity.

The three hundred costumes required for the different scenes, which switched

from one extreme to another in both setting and period, were in an extensive variety of different styles. There was, however, a limit even to Bakst's imagination about the number of variations he could give to an "oriental" costume, and so he reused and redrew many of the designs he had made for earlier ballets for Diaghilev. He particularly copied previous designs for *Schéhérazade* and *Le Dieu Bleu*, although his "orientalism" for *Aladin* extended to China and Japan. One of the scenes was a fancy dress party of the period of Louis XIV, and for this Bakst both used a number of the designs he had made for Anna Pavlova's *The Sleeping Beauty* in New York in 1916, and made new designs which he later used for Diaghilev's *The Sleeping Princess* (see pp 87–101) in London in 1921. This partly explains the confusion surrounding the drawings for *Aladin*; the other reason is quite simply that *Aladin* is probably one of Bakst's least-known works, and considered by many to be merely an embarrassing episode in the artist's distinguished career. Bakst, on the other hand, clearly enjoyed the challenge of designing a complete revue, as he found that it was the perfect medium in which to continue his scenic experiments.

The first night was postponed from 11 May to 20 May 1919 because of a strike by the tailors and embroiderers, but whether this was caused by Bakst being over-fussy as usual is not known. The first night was then again delayed until 22 May (with a public dress rehearsal on 21 May).

The comments about the revue followed a general pattern: surprise at first about Bakst, then, on the whole, praise. "It is a surprise," wrote Régis Gignoux, "to see the set of a street in Belleville by the painter of *Schéhérazade*."[2] "But never mind the play!" wrote André Rivoire, "It is only the pretext for a sumptuous spectacle. The sets and costumes are by Bakst. I prefer the costumes which are charming, in pleasing colors, and of original design, to the sets which I find a little depressing."[3] But Louis Schneider gives the clearest and most generous point of view: "But it is the painter of the Ballets Russes, M. Léon Bakst, who is the genie of this magic lamp. It is he who takes us from a picturesque corner of the suburbs of Paris to the enchanted gardens of the Thousand and One Nights; it is he who dresses the various minor and major characters in gowns, breeches, turbans grouped together according to principles of good taste which are simultaneously both daringly novel and harmoniously controlled. His is the melodious spirit of this beautiful show in which Rip, with his occasionally bitter and aggressive zest, and his satirical observation on current events, used his imagination as a writer of revues."[4]

13*   Costume design for a minor character

Graphite, tempera and/or watercolor on paper
12 x 6 in: 30.4 x 15.2 cm
Signed and dated, lower right in pencil: "Bakst / 1918"
Gift of Mr and Mrs Alexis Zalstem Zalessky
1959.262

Exhibitions: Indianapolis 1959, No 12; New York 1965–6, No 3 (illustrated p 14); New York 1966–7; Princeton 1968; Strasbourg 1969, No 61 (described as "Shah Schariar" in *Schéhérazade*); Blommenholm 1971; Hartford 1974; Chicago 1975, No 10; Houston 1976; Hartford 1979; Coral Gables 1982; Columbus 1989; Worcester 1989.

Hitherto, this costume design has been exhibited as being for *Schéhérazade*, but this has been wishful thinking. While everyone expects (or hopes) that a design by Bakst, however remotely "oriental," is for his most famous and trend-setting ballet, a more than merely casual glance at this drawing confirms that it is not only not for *Schéhérazade* but not even for a ballet. Could anyone dance in such a costume? First, it is nothing like any of the other designs for *Schéhérazade* which resemble delicate Persian miniatures (see p 64). Secondly, the colors here are also quite different from the colors Bakst used for *Schéhérazade*. Thirdly, the date is wrong. Bakst did redesign some of the costumes for *Schéhérazade* in 1915, including the costume for Flora Revalles as Zobeida for the American tour by the Ballets Russes in 1916, but he did no more work on the ballet in 1918, the date of this drawing.

Although this design is for a minor character in a relatively unknown production it is nevetheless full of vigour. The drawing and the painting, though sketchy and quick, has been controlled in a masterly way: the clothes sit firmly on the portly figure. It is essentially a working drawing, but Bakst, the artist, extended the original short beard to the present long, thick, black one in order to balance better the head with the headdress. The pencil shading on the right is characteristic of the period.

Notes

1 Rip quoted in unidentified newspaper, Paris, 17 May 1919 (all cuttings in the Bibliothèque de l'Arsenal, Département des Arts du Spectacle, Paris).
2 Régis Gignoux in unidentified newspaper, Paris, 22 May 1919.
3 André Rivoire in unidentified newspaper, Paris, 22 May 1919.
4 Louis Schneider in unidentified newspaper, Paris, 22 May 1919, but probably from *Comoedia* as Schneider was the critic on that newspaper at the time.

The Sleeping Princess

Ballet in 5 acts after the fairy story by Charles Perrault[1]
Composer: Piotr Ilyitch Tchaikovsky, with the prelude to act 3, the symphonic interlude *The Dream* between acts 3 and 4, and *Aurora's Variation* in act 3 orchestrated by Igor Stravinsky
Conductor: Gregor Fitelberg
Choreographers: Marius Petipa, reproduced by Nicholas Sergueieff [sic], with choreography for the action scenes, *Hunting Dances*, *Aurora's Variation* in act 3, and *Tales of Bluebeard*, *Schéhérazade*, and *Innocent Ivan* in act 5 by Bronislava Nijinska
Designer (sets and costumes): Léon Bakst
Principal dancers:
    King Florestan XXIV: Leonard Treer
    The Queen: Vera Sudeikina
    Cantalbutte, Master of Ceremonies: Jean Jazvinsky
    Princess Aurora: Olga Spessiva (Spessivtseva)[2]
    The Lilac Fairy: Lydia Lopokova[3]
    The Blue Bird: Stanislas Idzikowski
    Carabosse, the Wicked Fairy: Carlotta Brianza
    Prince Charming: Pierre Vladimiroff
Company: Diaghilev's Ballets Russes
First Performance: 2 November 1921, Alhambra Theatre, London

Synopsis

Act 1: the Christening. The scene is the royal palace of King Florestan XXIV during the christening of his infant daughter Princess Aurora. All the fairies have been invited to attend as godmothers. Each has a special present for the baby. Just as everyone is rejoicing a page rushes on to announce the arrival of the Wicked Fairy, Carabosse, whom the Master of Ceremonies had forgotten to invite. The Wicked Fairy arrives in her chariot drawn by six rats, and, refusing to accept any apology, insists on seeing the baby. She prophesies that one day the child will prick her finger on a spindle and on that day she will die. But the Lilac Fairy, who still has to give her present to the baby, promises that she will not die but fall into a sleep from which she will wake only when a certain Prince comes to give her a kiss.

Act 2: the Spell. Sixteen years later Aurora has grown into a beautiful young girl. The King and Queen prepare festivities in honour of the Princes who have come to woo her. The villagers are also invited, but, to his horror, the Master of Ceremonies sees that some of them have come with spindles, in spite of a law which prohibits them. An old woman approaches Aurora and shows her a spindle. While she is examining it she pricks her finger. The old woman reveals herself as the Wicked Fairy and vanishes. But the Lilac Fairy appears and with a wave of her wand everyone falls into a deep slumber. An impenetrable forest grows round the palace.

Act 3: the Vision. Twenty years later Florimond, known as Prince Charming, is hunting in the forest. He becomes separated from his companions and rests beneath a tree. The Lilac Fairy appears and shows him Aurora in a vision. Prince Charming implores the Fairy to lead him to her and, out of compassion, she invites him to step into her fairy boat made of mother-of-pearl.

Act 4: the Awakening. The Lilac Fairy leads Prince Charming to the palace where the King is sleeping at the foot of Aurora's bed. Prince Charming tiptoes to her side and breaks the spell by waking her with a kiss. There is great rejoicing, and the King and Queen bestow the hand of their beautiful daughter upon the Prince.

Act 5: the Wedding. Characters from fairy tales arrive, dance and pay their respects to the bride and groom. The whole assembly joins in a great dance in their honour.

(Acts 3 and 4 were combined after the first few performances; see below and note 1.)

On 10 March 1911 *The Times* in London published a letter from Diaghilev in answer to a criticism that he should produce a classic Russian ballet: "as for *The Sleeping Beauty*, this interminable ballet on a subject taken from a French fable, composed on French themes, staged in the style of Louis XIV, does not possess a single national element which might justify the idea of presenting this Franco-Italian fairy story in London." It was tongue-in-cheek, of course, because Tchaikovsky was a favorite composer for all Russians.

But by 1921 everything had changed. It was after the war and after the Russian Revolution. Diaghilev and his colleagues were stranded in the West like displaced persons, unable or unwilling to return to Russia. He had to regroup his team, find and train new dancers, and, as he had long ago quarrelled with Fokine, had seen Nijinsky go mad, and had now parted company with Massine, he was without a choreographer. His attitude to the Revolution was ambivalent: on the one hand he welcomed the new artistic freedom and even had a red star brandished for a while at the end of *The Firebird* instead of the double-headed eagle, but on the other hand he felt very strongly that as his company had come to symbolize the art of ballet he had a duty to maintain the classical tradition of Russian ballet and that it should no longer be despised but glorified. He also needed money even more than usual. Aware of the long-running success of the musical comedy *Chu-Chin-Chow*, he thought that one huge, spectacular, star-studded production of a popular "classical" ballet would make him enough money to guarantee the continuity of the Ballets Russes. For this fail-safe production Diaghilev, with Stravinsky's eager support, chose Tchaikovsky's *The Sleeping Beauty*, the most classical and perfect of ballets, the pinnacle of Petipa's art. And he chose Lon-

don, the city where his ballets had been so well appreciated, in which to produce it. He arranged the necessary financial backing by Sir Oswald Stoll, who advanced £10,000 and agreed to present the ballet at the Alhambra Theatre for a run of at least six months. Diaghilev retitled the ballet *The Sleeping Princess*, allegedly because he thought that none of his dancers was a beauty, but actually because he did not want it to be confused in the audience's mind with the traditional English Christmas pantomime which was regularly staged during the winter season.

The production had to be prepared quite quickly. Diaghilev, surprisingly, first thought of André Derain as designer who, fortunately, refused. He then thought of Benois, who had a special affinity with the period of Louis XIV, but he was still living in Russia employed as curator at the Hermitage Museum. Finally, in spite of having quarrelled with him over *La Boutique Fantasque*, he turned to Léon Bakst because he knew that of all his designers he was the one capable of producing exactly the right kind of sumptuous spectacle. Diaghilev probably also knew that Bakst had designed *The Sleeping Beauty* for Anna Pavlova in New York in 1916,[4] and may have seen his exhibition of 22 designs for that production at the Fine Art Society in London in 1917. Bakst agreed to the commission on condition that he would also design Stravinsky's opera *Mavra* (see pp 318–22), because he saw that as an opportunity for being recognized as a "modern" designer.

In his luxuriously produced book, *The Designs of Léon Bakst for "The Sleeping Princess,"* André Levinson did not mention either the Pavlova production or the exhibition, and exaggerated when he wrote: "In less than six weeks—his time was necessarily restricted—Léon Bakst composed, or, rather, improvised the six scenes and the three hundred costumes (a whole world of pictorial fiction) which the ballet contains. A less bold, more timorous worker, seeking the exact historical document, nosing about in portfolios, compiling dossiers, would have succumbed to the difficulties. Bakst, above all else an imaginative artist, triumphed." Bakst actually had longer than six weeks and anyway had done all his "nosing about in portfolios" when designing Pavlova's *The Sleeping Beauty* five years earlier. He had also designed a series of costumes of the same period for one of the scenes in *Aladin* (see pp 85–86), the Paris revue of 1919. He had studied the costume designs of Jean Bérain the elder (1640–1711), Jean-Baptiste Martin (1659–1735), and Louis Boquet (1717–1814), designers at the French court, for his designs of the seventeenth-and eighteenth-century costumes. A number of his drawings appear at first sight to be either exact copies or mirror images (as if tracings) of the earlier artists' work. A second look, however, reveals that Bakst has not exactly imitated the original sources, but has interpreted them in his own grandiose fashion, introducing his own special palette of colors while remaining faithful to the period. Deborah Howard commented: "The evocation of the atmosphere of the periods of Louis XIV and XV was achieved without pedantic adherence to historical sequence required by the scenario. In each act the costumes cover a range of historical periods."[5] For his set designs Bakst drew inspiration from the Bibiena family. His design for the first act, for example, faithfully reproduces in part a project drawn by Ferdinando Galli da Bibiena (1657–1743), of which there is an engraving in his volume *Varie Opere di Perspectiva*.[6]

It is therefore apparent that in designing *The Sleeping Princess* Bakst took a number of short cuts and used many of the designs he had previously made for both the earlier productions but, to be fair, he also had to do a great deal of new work, and very fast. On 4 October, a month before the first performance, Bakst complained in a letter to Diaghilev: "You must remind your directors [of the Alhambra] in London that they took a year and a half to stage this ballet at the Imperial Theaters[7] and yet I, in two months, between 10 August and 10 October, have to do with my own hand more than two hundred designs for costumes and sets, not counting the props, wigs, shoes, armor, jewelry, etc., that makes about four watercolors a day, work beyond human and creative strength . . . the fact that we are mounting *The Sleeping Princess* in two months is certainly a record for energy and speed which has never been seen in the theater before."[8] He was not telling Diaghilev the whole truth: in addition to using many previous designs, he employed at least two copyists as assistants who made his work a lot easier. The same standard figure, mostly for male and female courtiers, was used several times, differently colored for separate costumes (see No 27, p 98). More copies were made for *The Sleeping Princess* than for any other production. Also,

Bakst was not starting from scratch: *The Sleeping Beauty* and *The Sleeping Princess* were scenically essentially the same. The main difference, affecting the whole scale of the production, was the size of the stage, the Alhambra's in London being half the size of the Hippodrome's in New York. Bakst's sets were more suited to the smaller stage, because the scenery and props were less cluttered and the special effects were easier to achieve. The design principle used by Bakst for this production was described in *The Dancing Times*: "This principle was a simple one and an obvious one, but it was so dextrously used that the effect was magnificent. It solely consisted in arranging the sets in dull colours, and grouping the dancers on opposite sides of the stage costumed in opposing or contrasting colours . . . *The Sleeping Princess* is an example to all producers of theatric decor. It possesses originality to the extent of genius, it preserves unity between costume and set, and it creates that most difficult of all decorative results, a sense of rhythmic perfection."[9]

This perfection was achieved with difficulty, according to Vladimir Polunin who painted three of the five acts: "The numerous acts of this ballet had been prepared in Paris; some of the scenes were painted there and others in London. Bakst, like a field-marshal, sent out from his headquarters in Paris his instructions to the various studios. Those intended for us arrived by air mail, but his explanations were frequently contradictory. Three acts fell to our share but, as Bakst was not present, it was often difficult to fathom his meaning so that the work had to be held up pending explanations. To add to these difficulties it was found that the canvas, which had been purchased in great quantity, was worthless; the priming fell off, while the colours peeled away and changed in tone before our eyes . . . Although each piece was repainted five or six times, which improved the tone for a short while, it was impossible to obtain a satisfactory result."[10] So a technical fault thought by the scene painter to be disastrous was, to the critic, an inspired intention.

However brilliant the sets and costumes, a vital consideration for the success of the production was, of course, the question of choreographer and dancers. Diaghilev was fortunate in being able to engage Nicholas Sergueeff, formerly the company manager of the Mariinsky Theater and familiar with the ballet, to recreate Petipa's choreography, because he happened conveniently then to

be living in Paris. He also engaged Bronislava Nijinska, who had recently arrived from Kiev, to devise certain numbers, especially in the final act. Diaghilev was also able to engage several famous dancers from the Mariinsky Theater who had emigrated to Paris, including Vera Trefilova, Liubov Egorova, Pierre Vladimirov, and Anatole Vilzak. Finally, Diaghilev also discovered that Olga Spessivtseva had arrived in Latvia from Russia; although he had never seen her dance, he knew of her reputation and immediately engaged her for Aurora.[11] Boris Kochno[12] described watching a rehearsal: "When I came into the studio with Diaghilev, Spessivtseva was working at the barre . . . She began to rehearse Aurora's variation. The others, who were working all over the room, stopped one by one and stood motionless, watching her dance. Smiling, she moved with extraordinary serenity and ease, and the virtuoso steps she was executing seemed simple and natural. She never had to reach for balance; she seemed sustained by an invisible thread. At the end of the variation, there was a long, admiring silence, and then the room exploded into applause—company rules forbade it, but that day it was Diaghilev himself who first gave the signal."[13] Diaghilev, thinking her name would be too difficult for English audiences to pronounce or remember, shortened it to Spessiva. Two other dancers were engaged to fulfil Diaghilev's superstitious link with the past: Carlotta Brianza, Aurora in the original production, danced the part of the Wicked Fairy Carabosse, and Enrico Cecchetti, the original Carabosse, danced one performance on 5 January to celebrate his fifty years on the stage.

Diaghilev lavished every care on the production. As the company manager, Grigoriev, noted: "During the period of preparation, Diaghilev displayed amazing energy. He entered into every detail of the production, endeavouring to make it as perfect as possible."[14] He also lavished Sir Oswald Stoll's money on it. Not only did he spend the original advance of £10,000, but a further two payments of £5,000 as well, the final one given most reluctantly. Only full houses throughout the scheduled six-month run would recoup the investment, let alone show a profit. In spite of Diaghilev's care and the attention of the entire technical staff, the first night had to be postponed from 31 October to 2 November. According to Diaghilev: "The dress rehearsal was a disaster. The stage machinery did not work;

the trees in the enchanted woods did not sprout; the backdrop shifts did not come off; the tulle skirts got tangled in the flats."[15] The first night was even worse: "a catastrophe. There was a sound of cracking, creaking wood, and the enchanted forest refused to grow, ruining the curtain of the second act. This spoilt the reception of the work to a certain extent, but its effect was still more far-reaching. After the performance Diaghileff broke down completely and sobbed. He was exhausted by the struggle, and saw in the mishap an omen of ill fortune. From that moment, perhaps for the first time in his life, he was a beaten man, with no confidence in the success of his great creation."[16]

In fact, the technical failures were less obvious from the auditorium. *The Sleeping Princess* was a huge *succès d'estime*, with balletomanes going mad over it. But in spite of their going to see it night after night it was a financial flop. What went wrong? Most of the critics at first gave the production a cool reception. Typical was J. T. Grein in *The Illustrated London News* who summed up the evening: "It was all very beautiful, very vivid, but the touch of the fairy-wand was missing. I would call it the perfection of technique overwhelming inspiration . . . At any rate, I came away in admiration of the feast of the eye and the ear, for the colossality—if I may coin the word—of the canvas, but not enchanted. I had dwelt in marble halls instead of fairyland."[17] More cruel was Ernest Newman: "In common with some hundreds of other people, I was present on Wednesday at the Alhambra at the suicide of the Russian Ballet. It was buried with fitting pomp . . . The Russian Ballet, as an art force, has ceased to be."[18] Although *The Dancing Times*, appealing to the balletomanes, said: "you must make a point of visiting the Alhambra as soon as you can, the haunting melodies of Tchaikovsky, the sumptuous colouring by Bakst, the wonderful marches of the *corps de ballet*, and the brilliant dancing of the principals all combine to make a never-to-be-forgotten spectacle,"[19] the truth was that the English audience of 1921, apart from those balletomanes, was not ready. *The Sleeping Princess* may well have been Petipa's greatest achievement in the demonstration of technical virtuosity, but choreography which shows off pure technique requires a trained audience capable of appreciating it. English audiences on the whole knew nothing of classical ballet, and cared very little.

For once, Diaghilev's judgement had been wrong. Sir Oswald Stoll, to cut his losses, took the ballet off on 4 February 1922 after only 114 performances, and sequestered the sets and costumes.[20] The result was that the production could not move to the Opéra in Paris as originally planned but, in order to fulfil his contract there, Diaghilev cunningly and hastily arranged a one-act selection of excerpts, using some of the scenery and costumes from the 1909 production of *Le Pavillon d'Armide* (see pp 108–16) designed by Alexandre Benois, with some new costumes designed by Nathalie Gontcharova, and called this new ballet *Le Mariage de la Belle au Bois Dormant* or *Aurora's Wedding*. This proved to be a most popular ballet and remained in the repertory for many years.

The experience of *The Sleeping Princess* was not a happy one for Diaghilev. Boris Kochno quotes him in his book: "This misadventure taught me a lesson. I see in it an occult hint—for our whole life is full of these warnings—which is that it is not my business and it is not up to me to concern myself with revising the triumphs of days gone by."[21] It was a perceptive thought. From then on Diaghilev concentrated on producing new and original works.

Florence E. Grenfell (later Lady St Just) was an enthusiastic devotee and patron of the Ballets Russes, who went regularly and frequently to their performances. Being also a friend of Diaghilev and many of the dancers, she was not only allowed to attend rehearsals but was also treated as a confidante. She kept a diary in which she noted her impressions. They have an immediacy unmatched in other reports or reminiscences. Here are some extracts from previously unpublished entries referring to *The Sleeping Princess*:

1921
Thursday 29th September
I went on afterwards to watch a repetition of the new Ballet "The Enchanted Princess." I got such a wonderful welcome from the members of the corps de ballet I was quite embarrassed. Some of the numbers in the Ballet are v. attractive, & the music pretty, but I don't believe it will run for 6 months as Diaghileff hopes.

Thursday 13th October
I spent the morning at a Ballet repetition. They are really making no progress now, & can't get on until Diaghileff arrives.

Saturday 15th October
Lopokova & Leon [Woizikovsky] arrived down very late. Diaghileff has at last arrived & strenuous rehearsing has started.

Friday 21st October
I looked in at Volodio's [Vladimir Polunin, the scene painter] studio on my way back. The Bakst scenery for the Sleeping Princess is now finished & really very beautiful.

Tuesday 25th October
I went by myself to the Alhambra & watched a rehearsal of the Ballet, I sat with Mrs Bewicke. It was frightfully exciting & I really think is going to be lovely. The Bakst scenery is beautiful & I went up with Hilda [Sokolova] afterwards to the dressing room and saw many of the dresses, they are really dreams.

Thursday 27th October
I had an interview with the Polunins after that. Diaghileff is behaving v. badly to them, & they say they are going to a lawyer about it wh: I think for their sake is a mistake [Presumably Diaghilev was refusing to pay them].

Friday 28th October
I took Teddy [her husband] to a repetition at the Alhambra after dinner & he manfully sat through 3½ hours of it! Many of them were wearing their costumes. I can't say how lovely I think it is going to be & the new ballerina Spezzizzova [sic] is a dream, I can't say the rehearsal went v. well, & it doesn't look hopeful for the 1st night to be on Monday.

Sunday 30th October
I went to see a parade of all the costumes for the new Ballet in the morning, they are perfectly marvellous I must say.

Tuesday Nov: 1st
I went off after dinner to see the dress rehearsal of the Ballet, but no one at all was being admitted, so I came back to C. P. [Cavendish Place].

Wednesday 2nd November
We went on to the 1st performance of the new Ballet the "Sleeping Princess," one must not judge of it yet. It did not go well, the scenery stuck, & the artists were over tired & nervous, as a spectical [sic] it is astounding, but *much* too long & monotonous. Sepzifsova [sic] was a disappointment, & was frightfully nervous. Lopokova skored [sic] the big hit of the evening. There were grt: applause at the end, but more for the artists than the Ballet I think. Teddy came in for the last act after a business dinner. I went round to see all my friends afterwards. Diaghileff

I thought gloomy, & the artists v. anxious to know what the feeling of the public was.

Thursday 3rd November
Sokolova lunched with me v. depressed about the Ballet. Both she & Leon have really nothing to do in it & feel they are waisting [sic] their time.

Friday 4th November
Edward & I went to the Ballet in the evening. It is already much better & Sepzifsova [sic] danced beautifully & looked divine without the monstrous tow coloured wig she wore the 1st night.

Monday 9th November
Rosalind and Con dined with me & we went to the Ballet. It is going better every time & the house was fuller. Egorova took the part of the Princess, she danced well but has no charm & is too old for the part.

Saturday 12th November
We went on to the Ballet, Leda [Lopokova] was taking the part of the Princess, she did it v. deliciously, but it doesn't really suit her. Nijinska was the "Lilac Fairy," her acting of the part was wonderful, but she couldn't dance it.

Saturday 19th November
I took Mrs Roots to the Ballet in the afternoon, they have altered it a lot, but I don't think it has improved it.

Tuesday 6th December
Nevile who is back on leave from Constantinople dined with me & we went to the Ballet. He enjoyed it v. much, he had often seen it before in Petrograd.

Wednesday 7th December
I went to the Ballet with Mrs Bewicke, I do like her most awfully. To my joy Sepzifsova [sic] was dancing the Princess, goodness she is a darling.

Friday 16th December
I dined with John A. S. & went to the Ballet. Spezzifsova [sic] dancing & altogether the best performance I have yet seen. John gave a supper party afterwards in his flat, for Lopokova, Hilda, Leon & me. John was very highbrow & long winded & I thought we never should get away.

1922
Wednesday 4th January
In the late afternoon I went with Lopokova, & one of the men of the Ballet to choose a presentation gift for old Maestro Giachetti's [sic] jubilee, 50 years on the stage. After endless discussion a plated tea tray & tea service were chosen.

Thursday 5th January
Clare Wortley dined with us & came to the Ballet, it was a grt: night as old Giachetti [sic], to celebrate his jubilee, took the part of the Bad Fairy, wh: part he had created in Petrograd. Although v. nervous he was wonderfully good, & got a tremendous ovation. He was presented at the end by countless wreaths, & a long address from the Russian Ballet, & my choice of the silver tea set, wh: was presented to him from all the artists. He was cheered both by the artists, & the public, until he quite broke down, poor old man.

Monday 30th January
I went to tea with Hilda Bewicke in the afternoon. The Ballet ends on Saturday, but Diaghileff will not say what is going to happen then.

Saturday 4th February
Teddy and I went to the last night of "The Sleeping Princess." There was the greatest enthusiasm all through, & wild applause at the end, & the ballerinas literally covered in flowers. The audience refused to leave until Leda & Idzikovsky had made speeches & all the other leading dancers had to appear. No one knows what now will happen to the Ballet. The artists have been given a holiday, & put on half pay for a month, but then what is to happen. Diaghileff has again disappeared.

14 Costume design for the *corps de ballet* in the Mazurka, scene 5

Graphite, tempera, gold and silver paint on paper
11⁷/₁₆ x 8¾ in: 22.2 x 29 cm
Signed and dated, lower right in pencil: "Bakst / 1921"
1933.393

Exhibitions: Paris 1925, (possibly No 165); London 1927, (possibly No 11 or 13); New York 1933, No 2; Chicago 1933, No 5; Northampton 1934, No 5; Hartford 1934b; New Haven 1935; San Francisco 1935–6; Poughkeepsie 1940; Williamsburg 1940; Paris 1939, No 63; New York MoMA 1944a; Edinburgh 1954, No 245; London 1954–5, No 282; Michigan 1957; Elmira 1958, No 46; Richmond 1959; Storrs 1963; Hartford 1964; Hartford 1965, No 4; Houston 1965; New York 1965–6, No 11 (illustrated p 17); New York 1966–7; Hartford 1974; Houston 1976; Hartford 1979; Coral Gables 1982; Hartford 1988; Worcester 1989.
Illustrations: Buckle 1955, p 77 No 94; *Hartford Times* 28 September 1934; Levinson 1922, pl. 34 (color).

This is Bakst being provocatively sexy. The bare nipples are accentuated by the brazen gaze; and the parted lips promise pleasure. The figure is drawn with all the

bravura characterizing the mazurka in the final scene for which it was intended. Lydia Sokolova described the end of the ballet: "Then followed the beautiful *pas de deux* of Aurora and Prince Charming, danced on the first night by Spessivtseva and Vladimirov, which seemed the quintessence of classical dancing. After this the centre of the stage remained empty for a moment, but with the King and Queen on their thrones, the pages, and the huge Negro guards with their pikes and feathered turbans, there must still have been a dozen or more people grouped on either side. Suddenly all the rest of the company, the dancers in the fairy tales, the male and female courtiers, and eventually the Prince and Princess, came shooting from the wings to wheel and wheel around the stage in a splendid Mazurka."[22]

This design is almost certainly adapted from one by Jean Baptiste Martin, as many of his designs were for this production. An important difference is that unlike Martin, who always indicated the floor or a shadow from the foot, Bakst never did. Bakst's figures are always as if suspended in space.

This design was still in the artist's possession when Levinson produced his book. There is no record of when Serge Lifar acquired it. As it was not exhibited for the first time until 1933, it is supposition alone

that it was shown in Bakst's posthumous exhibitions in Paris in 1925 or in London in 1927, included in the exhibitions list above, because the catalogues of both include works with the same title: "Mazurka."

15* Costume for a Lady of the Court in the Mazurka, scene 5

Based on Polish national costume, the off-white velvet coat with hanging sleeves is meant to be worn on the right shoulder. It is trimmed with brown swansdown, gold frogs and gold lamé buttons.
Lining inscribed "Mazzurka Evina"
Gown has a tighly fitted silver lamé bodice with short sleeves and peplum over a panniered white satin skirt with silver appliqués, embroidery and swags around hemline
Lining of bodice inscribed "Rostova, Natova"
Square-crowned hat, based on Uhlan officer's, is silver lamé trimmed with silver braid and tassels from two corners.
Labeled "Polouchina"
1996.7.12a-c

Provenance: Diaghilev and de Basil Ballets Foundation Ltd; Sotheby's London, lot 149 (iv), 17 July 1968; Castle Howard Estate Ltd; Sotheby's London, lot 61, 14 December 1995.

The ballet was first produced in five acts or scenes. However, when Diaghilev realized that the technical difficulties in some of the scene changes were proving excessive and making the evening longer than even balletomanes could endure, he simplified the staging and made scenes 3 and 4 (the Vision and the Awakening) continuous. Therefore, after the first few performances, scene 5 (the Wedding) became scene 4 (see Synopsis and note 1).

The female dancers in the mazurka were identified in the program as Ladies of the Court. There were twelve mazurka girls: Mmes Klementowicz, Maicherska, Nemtchinova, Antonova, Komarova, Allanova, Rosenstein, L. Sumarokova, Coxon, Evina, Gostemilova, Astafieva II. All their costumes matched, but, from the inscriptions, the separate pieces here are not necessarily from the same single costume. Many of the dancers had several parts in the production. Evina was also one of the Ladies-in-Waiting in scene 1, a Village Maiden in scene 2, and a Marchioness in scene 3.

Lubov Rostova was with de Basil's Ballets Russes from 1932–37, Nina Natova and Helen Polouchina were in de Basil's second company in Australia in 1936–37.

De Basil's company did not perform Tchaikovsky's whole five-act ballet, but followed Diaghilev's invention by performing only the one-act version which was called either *Le Mariage d'Aurore* or *Aurora's Wedding*. De Basil revived the ballet in this form for the first time at the Academy of Music, Philadelphia on 12 November 1924, and the second company in Australia first performed it at the Theatre Royal, Adelaide on 27 October 1936.

When Diaghilev first staged the one-act version at the Opéra in Paris on 18 May 1922, he had been obliged to use costumes from *Le Pavillon d'Armide* designed by Alexandre Benois, and have some new ones designed by Nathalie Gontcharova because, after the financial disaster of *The Sleeping Princess* in London, all the costumes and scenery had been sequestered by the management of the Alhambra Theatre. Bakst's costumes and scenery were stored under the stage of the London Coliseum, and it was rumored that they had all perished after being soaked from a leaking water tank which had been installed on stage for an aquatic show. It has been assumed, therefore, that the de Basil Company also used only Benois's and Gontcharova's costumes for their revival. In fact, however, Diaghilev recovered all the costumes by repaying the debt by 1925, and the labels inside these costumes show that de Basil acquired the original costumes for this production along with all the others.

16* Costume for a Dignitary of the Court in the Mazurka, scene 5

Based on Polish national costume, the double-breasted tunic of cream-colored cotton faille has painted gold scrolls, gold frogs and braid which also trims revers and cuffs of long sleeves.
Inscribed in Russian "Tova," "Khoziarski"
Short sleeve bolero of Prussian-blue plush, has a black velvet coat attached at the shoulders which is trimmed with gold frogs and black marabou around collar and cuffs. Its slashed hanging sleeves are lined with "ermine"-painted white velvet.
Inscribed in Russian "Tovaroff"
Breeches of Prussian-blue plush
Inscribed "Tovaroff"
1996.7.16a-c
Provenance: Diaghilev and de Basil Ballets Foundation Ltd; Sotheby's London, lot 149 (iii), 163 (x),17 July 1968; Castle Howard Estate Ltd; Sotheby's London, lot 73, 14 December 1995.
The male dancers in the mazurka were identified in the program as Dignitaries of the Court. There were twelve mazurka boys, who also wore matching costumes: MM. Serguieff, Addison, Pavlov, Savitsky, Ochimovksi, Winter, Yalmoujinski, Lukine, Patrikeeff, Koziarski, Stepanov, Komissarov. Koziarski was also the King's

Herald in scene 1, a Village Youth in scene 2
(see No 19), and a Duke in scene 3.
Tovarov was in de Basil's second company on the
Australian tour of 1936–7.

17* Dorothy Coxon's costume as a Lady-in-Waiting, scene 1

Early eighteenth-century court dress, panniered
open robe. Bodice of burnt orange satin, has a
white stomacher, gold fringe at neckline,
orange sleeves caught at upper arm and elbow
by "pearls" and off-white chiffon engageants.
Orange satin overskirt is pulled back to reveal
lime-green satin "petticoat" trimmed with
white satin bands, metallic medallions and
tassels. An olive-green velvet train trimmed
with marabou is attached at one shoulder.
Lining of skirt is inscribed "Coxon 1 act"
1996.7.13

Provenance: Diaghilev and de Basil Ballets Foundation Ltd; Sotheby's London, lot 170, 3 March
1973; Castle Howard Estate Ltd; Sotheby's
London, lot 62, 14 December 1995.

The principle which Bakst used throughout his design for *The Sleeping Princess*
was to have settings in muted, monochrome
colors against which the dancers, costumed
in strong, bright colors, would be positioned in various contrasting groups. The
effect was described in *The Dancing Times*:
"scene I was performed in a wide hall, the
ceilings of which were supported by pillars
of marble of smoky black and dull white in
irregular patterns . . . Against this dull
coloured background the dancers paraded
and arranged themselves. When the movements of the crowd, including the king and
queen, had been completed and all was
prepared for the entrance of the fairies, it
was found that on the left of the stage
facing the royalties were the bright red and
scarlet costumes, while on the king's side all
was blue and white. Naturally this brilliant
background formed a delightful environment for the dances of the fairies, and an
element of humour was introduced by the
rat-drawn chariot of the wicked fairy,
although her intentions were far from being
humorous."[23]

18* Plotnikova's costume as a Lady-in-Waiting, scene 1

Late seventeenth-century chrome-yellow velvet gown. Bodice has gold lamé stomacher with lace tucker and engageants. Matching skirt has apron front and long lamé train. Gold lamé hemline panels are trimmed with large metal studs.
On petersham: "Maison Muelle Rossignol, Costumier de l'Opéra, 42 rue de la Victoire, Paris"
Inscribed in pencil and purple ink "Plotnikova"
1996.7.14a-b

Provenance: Diaghilev and de Basil Ballets Foundation Ltd; Sotheby's London, lot 135 (ii), 17 July 1968; Castle Howard Estate Ltd; Sotheby's London, lot 62, 14 December 1995.
Exhibitions: San Francisco 1988–9, No 126.
The Ladies-in-Waiting in scene 1 (the Christening) were Mmes D'Albaicin, Coxon, Damaskina, Plotnikova, Savitska, Rosenstein, Antonova, Evina, Gostemilova, A. Sumarokova, L. Nemtchinova, Grekulova, Poplavska and Astafieva II.

The costumier Muelle, always preferred by Bakst, executed most of the costumes for the production, although some were made by Pierre Pitoeff. They were made in Paris under Bakst's supervision before being sent to London. The meticulous attention to detail is astonishing, but more remarkable, considering that these costumes are only for ladies-in-waiting, is the lavishness. But Bakst made no distinction between minor and major characters: they were all members of the same court and all, in his view, had to be equally expensively dressed. After seeing the costumes, one has no surprise that the production went way over budget.

Cyril Beaumont, who had been allowed the privilege of attending some rehearsals, described a costume parade: "A few days later we arrive at the third stage of rehearsal. The dances are repeated, but now the piano is replaced by an orchestra. Then the costumes must be considered. This time Diaghilev is seated in a large cane armchair placed in the centre of the stage. Each dancer finds in his dressing room his costume and the original drawing mounted on card and protected by a sheet of transparent talc.[24] When dressed he walks upon the stage and hands the design to the director, who compares it with the realisation. Nothing is left to chance. The dancer is required to perform such and such a 'variation.' Does the costume prevent free movement of the arms? Does its weight prevent the execution of such a step? Notes are made and orders given for the necessary alterations."[25] Grace Lovat Fraser and Miss Norman made the alterations, as well as making some new costumes required at the last minute. They were also helped by Vera Sudeikina (later the second wife of Stravinsky).

19*   Anton Dolin's costume as a Village Youth, scene 2

Livery suit of orange wool felt. Jacket has white wool attached waistcoat, painted green striped white silk collar and cuffs. Epaulettes, slashed sleeves and jacket front are decorated with domed silver buttons
Lining inscribed in purple "Luca"
A belt of apricot velvet edged with gold braid
Knee-length orange breeches sewn at the side with steel buttons
Inscribed in purple "Patrikeev"
A black felt hat trimmed with green feathers
1996.7.18a-d

Provenance: Diaghilev and de Basil Ballets Foundation Ltd; Sotheby's London, lot 152 (ii), 17 July 1968; Castle Howard Estate Ltd; Sotheby's London, lot 78, 14 December 1995.
Exhibitions: San Francisco 1988–9, No 135.
The Village Youths were MM. Kremneff, Fedorov, Bourman, Semenov, Mikalaichik, Patrikeeff, Koziarski, Ochimovsky, Winter, Karnecki, Yalmoujinsky, Savitzki, Pavlov, Lukine, Singaievski, and Stepanov. They all had identical costumes.
"Patrikeev" (Patrikeeff in the program) was the name given by Diaghilev to the young Irish dancer Patrick Healey-Kay who in 1923 gave himself the name Anton Dolin by which he became famous. Patrikeeff was also one of the

Royal Pages in scene 1, and one of the Dignitaries of the Court in scene 5 who danced the mazurka.
"Luka" refers to Lukine who was also one of the Four Rats in scene 1, and one of the Dignitaries of the Court in scene 5.

20*   Costume for a Village Youth, scene 2

Not illustrated. For description see previous item without hat and belt.
The jacket indistinctly inscribed "V . . . tann"
The breeches inscribed "Mika . . ."
1996.7.24a-c

Provenance: Diaghilev and de Basil Ballets Foundation Ltd; Sotheby's London, lot 163 (ix), 17 July 1968; Castle Howard Estate Ltd; Sotheby's London, lot 84, 14 December 1995.
This costume was worn in part by Bourman and in part by Mikalaichik. Bourman was also a Royal Page in scene 1, and a Marquis in scene 3. Mikolaichik was also a Royal Page in scene 1, a Marquis in scene 3, and the Wolf in scene 5.

21*   Costume for a Village Maiden, scene 2

Based on French peasant costume, the gown has a blue velvet bodice with bright yellow stomacher laced with gold ribbon. White organdy collar and undersleeves are painted with red and green motifs. White taffeta underskirt with painted motifs has red silk gauze overdrape.
Bodice inscribed in purple "KK," and Komarova
1996.7.19a-b

Also a bodice inscribed in purple "KK," and "Soumarokova"
1996.7.22a-b

Provenance: Diaghilev and de Basil Ballets Foundation Ltd; Sotheby's London, lots 163 (viii), 149 (ii), two from 153 (ii), 17 July 1968; Castle Howard Estate Ltd; Sotheby's London, lot 79, 14 December 1995.

The Village Maidens were Mmes Allanova, Rosenstein, A. Sumarokova, L. Sumarokova, Evina, L. Nemtchinova, Antonova, Krasovska, Coxon, Moreton, Gostemilova, Komarova, Plotnikova, Poplavska, Damaskina, Astafieva II.
As there is no initial with the inscription, it is not possible to determine which Sumarokov girl wore the second bodice.

22*   Costume for a Duchess, scene 3

Riding habit. Redingote of bright yellow satin with
gold stencilled scrolling patterns. Bright green
velvet lapel and facings with navy velvet and
gold braid decoration on deep cuffs. Faux off-
white silk waistcoat has gold lace trim. Yellow
faille sash is trimmed with gold fringe.
Bodice inscribed three times in Russian and English
"Klementovich"
Trained skirt brown silk with gold stencilled
scrolling patterns. Gold fringe and velvet trim
at hemline.
Indistinctly inscribed in Russian "Tanya"?
Broad-brimmed felt hat adorned with pale yellow
ostrich plumes
Inscribed in purple "Allanova Duchesse III act"
1996.7.17a-d

Provenance: Diaghilev and de Basil Ballets Foundation Ltd; Sotheby's London, lot 163 (ii), 17 July
1968; Castle Howard Estate Ltd; Sotheby's
London, lot 77, 14 December 1995.
There were five Duchesses in identical costumes:
Mmes Klementowicz, Dubrovska, Allanova,
Komarova, Majcherska. Klementowicz was also
the Fairy of the Song-Birds in scene 1, one of
Princess Aurora's Friends in scenes 2 and 4, and
one of the Ladies of the Court in scene 5.
Allanova was also one of the Royal Nurses in
scene 1, a Village Maiden in scene 2, and one
of the Ladies of the Court in scene 5.

Three parts of this costume were worn by three
different dancers: Klementowicz, Majcherska,
and Allanova.
Bakst's palette for scene 3, known as the "Hunting
Scene," was a wide range of both subtle and
garish autumnal colors: browns, greens,
yellows, golds, with occasional blues.

23*   Costume for a Duke, scene 3

Tunic and petticoat breeches. Knee-length tunic of
bright yellow velvet with gold stencilled
scrolling patterns is trimmed with gold braid
and green velvet accents on pockets. Short
oversleeves trimmed with marabou over gold
silk sleeve with pleated cuffs at wrist.
Labelled "Vinter Duc"
Breeches of yellow satin edged with tabbed fringe
of green silk
Inscribed in purple ink "Koziarsky"
1996.7.23a-b

Provenance: Diaghilev and de Basil Ballets Foundation Ltd; Sotheby's London, lot 163 (iii), 17 July
1968; Castle Howard Estate Ltd; Sotheby's
London, lot 81, 14 December 1995.
There were five Dukes in identical costumes:
Koziarsky, Winter, Pavlov, Fedorov, Semenov.
According to the label and inscription this is
made up of two separate costumes: the jacket
was worn by Winter, the breeches by Koziarsky.

Winter was also one the Wicked Fairy's two
Pages in scene 1, a Village Youth in scene 2,
and a Dignitary of the Court in scene 5.
Koziarsky was the King's Herald in scene 1, a
Village Youth in scene 2, and a Dignitary of the
Court in scene 5.

24* Vera Nemtchinova's costume as a Baroness, scene 3

Riding habit. Redingote of grey blue cotton flannel with gold stencilled scrolling patterns has faux waistcoat of turquoise satin with gold braid and buttons. Deep cuffs of white moire are trimmed with brown velvet ribbon and gold braid.

Lining inscribed in purple ink "AB Vera Baronesse"

Skirt of dark brown flannel stencilled overall with gold to match the pattern of the jacket

Inscribed "Baronesse Nemchinova"

Lemon yellow chemise with dark brown pleated jabot neck

Dark brown tricorn hat

Lining inscribed "Vera Baronesse"

1996.7.25a-d

Provenance: Diaghilev and de Basil Ballets Foundation Ltd; Sotheby's London, lot 152, 17 July 1968; Castle Howard Estate Ltd; Sotheby's London, lot 87, 14 December 1995.

Exhibitions: San Francisco 1988–9, No 132.

There were four Baronesses in identical costumes: V. Nemtchinova, Schollar, Sokolova, and Bewicke. This is Nemtchinova's complete costume. She was also the Carnation Fairy in scene 1, one of Princess Aurora's Friends in scenes 2 and 4, and Columbine in scene 5.

25* Costume for a Beater, scene 3

Yellow velvet tabard has slashed sleeves and painted scarlet buttons with loops at center front.

Inscribed in pencil "Mr Savitski, Taille au dessus du Modèle" ("Mr Savitski, Height above [greater than] the Pattern")

Waistcoat, white cotton faille with bright pink painted stripes covered at center front by white silk ribbons.

Inscribed in pencil in Russian "N. Семенов" ("N. Semyonov")

Pair of brown facecloth breeches adorned with silver buttons

Yellow felt hat with broad brim, scarlet band and feathers

Inscribed in pencil in Russian "Павлов" ("Pavlov") and in a mixture of English and Russian "Рачлов".

1996.7.15a-d

Provenance: Diaghilev and de Basil Ballets Foundation Ltd; Sotheby's London, lot 152 (iv), 17 July 1968; Castle Howard Estate Ltd; Sotheby's London, lot 72, 14 December 1995.

The program does not specify who the beaters were in scene 3, nor how many there were, but they all wore identical costumes.

According to the program, Savitski was a Marquis in scene 3 not a Beater, and the inscription above would seem to indicate that he had to be recast after the costume arrived in London. Savitski was also one the Wicked Fairy's Four Rats in scene 1, a Village Youth in scene 2, and a Dignitary of the Court in scene 5.

According to the program, Semenov was a Duke in scene 3, not a Beater. He was also a Minister of State in scene 1, a Village Youth in scene 2, and the Shah in scene 5.

26*   Copy costume design for the Pages of the Princess

Graphite transfer, tempera and/or watercolor, gold
   paint on illustration board (background painted
   out in cream paint)
36⅜ x 19⅛ in: 92.5 x 48.5 cm
Stamped signature, undated
Label on reverse inscribed in the artist's hand "N
   102 Série A bis," "La Belle"
Gift of Nikita D. Lobanov
1967.23

This is an unfinished copy of the design
which is reproduced in André Levinson's *L'Oeuvre de Léon Bakst pour La Belle au Bois Dormant* (*The Designs of Léon Bakst for "The Sleeping Princess"*) as plate XXXVII. Bakst has copied his own design exceedingly accurately by using a transfer method, but it is larger than the original. Intended for exhibition, he was obviously dissatisfied with it, and left it. It is one of the many drawings that was found in his apartment after his death by G. Rasamatt, the husband of one of Bakst's nieces. He had a stamp made of Bakst's signature and stamped every drawing he found whether it was by Bakst or not. In this case he stamped a correct one, even though the artist had discarded it.

Studio of Léon Bakst

27* Costume design for the Maids of Honor, scene 1

Graphite, tempera, and silver paint with black ink notations on paper

11⅜ x 8½ in: 28.9 x 21.5 cm (cut round the bottom and right hand edge cut)

Unsigned and undated

Inscribed by Bakst in ink in French top right and erased with pencil: "Prologue / Les Dames d'Honneur] / au moins 4 costumes" ("Prologue, Maids of Honor, at least 4 costumes"), and clockwise from top "cornet [sic] en / etoffe [sic] d'argent / avec perles" ("headdress in silver material with pearls"), "cache col en / soie très fine / avec perles / et argent" ("very fine silk scarf with pearls and silver"), "gants blancs" ("white gloves"), "corsage en velours bleu vif / avec devant en soie et g[cut]" ("vivid blue velvet bodice with silk and [cut] front"), "manches avec larges dente[lles]" ("sleeves with wide lace-work"), "tablier en etoffe [sic] d'argent" ("apron in silver material"), "jupe en soie vert [crossed out] / avec passement" ("skirt in green silk with gold silk lace"), "Traine en [cut] / avec mouche / de soie ou [cut]" ("Train in [cut] with patches of silk or [cut]"), "bijou" ("jewel"), "ruban / soie" ("silk ribbon"), "collier des / grosses perles" ("necklace of large pearls"), "boucles d'oreilles" ("earrings").

1939.433

Provenance: Your Secretary Inc.

Exhibitions: Edinburgh 1954, No 244; London 1954–5, No 281; Houston 1965; New York 1965–6, No 9 (illustrated p 10); New York 1966–7; Princeton 1968; Los Angeles 1969; Hartford 1974; Houston 1976; Hartford 1979; Coral Gables 1982; Oberlin 1985; Worcester 1989.

Illustration: Bremser, vol I p 77 (described as by Bakst).

Although the inscription in the top right hand corner has been crossed out, indicating that the costume may have been used for some other character, there were four Maids of Honor, played by Leokadia Klementowicz, Hilda Bewicke, Ursula Moreton, and Luba Sumarokova.

This design and the next are copies by assistants, although they have hitherto been exhibited as being by Bakst himself. Copies (not obvious fakes) of Bakst's work have caused endless confusion. It is a minefield. When Bakst realized quite early in his theatrical career that there was a lucrative market for his designs he began to make them with greater care, and to leave them "clean"—that is, without additional notes. Sometimes he copied his designs, enlarging them for exhibition (as with No 26) or varying the color for a different character in the same or another production. More often he would have his designs copied by assistants specifically for the costumiers' workshops, but himself write extensive notes and instructions, as in these two designs. The fact that the notes are in Bakst's hand has led people wrongly to assume that the whole design is also by him. The presence of notes, however, does not mean that Bakst definitely did not do the drawing. Sometimes Bakst later painted out his written instructions, and either left his original signature or signed the work again. Sometimes the drawings and notes were signed by Bakst as "Copie d'après Bakst" ("Copy after Bakst") and unscrupulous dealers have been known to paint or cut out the words "Copy after." It is usually obvious when this has happened. Bakst was not deceitful and generally signed his own copies with the right date: he signed and dated nearly all his work. Nervous about his contract with Diaghilev for *The Sleeping Princess*, he signed the slightest scrap of paper containing any hint of a design he made for this production. Therefore, in the absence of any signature, both these drawings are the work of assistants, although Bakst may have added a strengthening line or two here and there, as in the head, right shoulder, and left arm of the Maid of Honor, and in the mustache and beard of the courtier. The drawing, generally, is weak, especially the body of the Maid of Honor at the waist, as well as all the decorative detail. The painting in both is clearly not up to Bakst's own standard. The trimming of both sheets is very suspect. What is there to hide? No wonder Bakst signed neither of these designs.

Studio of Léon Bakst

28*   Costume design for a courtier, scene 3

Graphite, tempera and/or watercolor, gold paint and black ink notations on paper
12⅛ x 6¾ in: 31 x 17.1 cm
Unsigned and undated
Inscribed by Bakst in ink in French, clockwise from top right (the right-hand edge of the design has been trimmed, cutting through several words): "plumes dans / cet esprit" ("feathers in this style"), "Acte [cut]," (in pencil) "1 Cost[ume]," "D [cut]," "feutre / plume d'autru / che" ("felt, ostrich feather"), "collerette à l'espag[ne]" ("muslin collar in Spanish style"), "veste en satin / brodé d'or" ("short satin jacket embroidered with gold"), "chaine massive [en] / medaillon" ("solid chain with locket"), "cape en soie" ("silk cloak"), "panatalons b[ouffants] / brodé d'or avec de la / [cut] / les baies" ("baggy trousers embroidered with gold and [cut] the openings"), "pantalon vel[ours]" ("velvet trousers"), "bas soie tete [sic]" ("silk stocking top"), "soulier en [cut] agraffes [sic] or [cut]" ("shoe in [cut] with gold buckle"), "gants blancs" ("white gloves"), "boutons ronds / en or" ("round gold buttons").
1939.432

Provenance: Your Secretary Inc.
Exhibitions: Cambridge 1942; Edinburgh 1954, No 243; London 1954–5, No 280; New York 1965–6, No 10 (illustrated p 17); New York 1966–7; Princeton 1968; Los Angeles 1969; Amherst 1974; Hartford 1979; Worcester 1989.

29* Unfinished design for an angel

Graphite pencil transfer, tempera and/or watercolor, silver paint on illustration board
19¹/₁₆ x 12¹⁵/₁₆ in: 48.5 x 32.8 cm
Stamped signature, undated
Gift of Nikita D. Lobanov
1967.22

This unfinished drawing is not for a theatrical
production. Bakst probably intended it for
exhibition in New York. The date is circa 1922.
Bakst has again used a transfer method for the
drawing from some other original, but was
again dissatisfied with his work. See also No
26, p 97, concerning the stamped signature.

Notes

1 After the first few performances the ballet was
shortened to 4 acts by combining acts 3 and 4.
The acts were then called "scenes" in the program as follows: scene I, the Christening; scene
II, the Spell; scene III, the Vision; scene IV, the
Wedding. The designs and costumes in this
collection are designated according to the
original numbering of the scenes.

2 The cast list is for the first night. Princess Aurora
was also danced alternately by Lydia Lopokova,
Vera Trefilova, and Liubov Egorova.

3 When Lopokova danced the part of Princess
Aurora, Bronislava Nijinska danced the part of
the Lilac Fairy.

4 This production was very different from the one
planned by Diaghilev: it was a 40-minute
version included as act 2 of a large-scale revue
called *The Big Show* at the Hippodrome.

5 Deborah Howard, "A Sumptuous Revival" in
Apollo, April 1970, p 305. In her discussion of the
influences of the French designers on Bakst she
seems unaware of his production of *The Sleeping
Beauty* in New York.

6 Illustrated in Deborah Howard, *ibid*, p 302.

7 *The Sleeping Beauty* was first performed at the
Mariinsky Theater, St Petersburg on 15 January
1890.

8 Quoted from an unknown source.

9 "Notes on Decor" in *The Dancing Times*, December 1921, p 283.

10 Vladimir Polunin, *The Continental Method of
Scene Painting*, p 67.

11 Diaghilev tried to engage Tamara Karsavina, but
she preferred to remain in Bulgaria with her
husband, Mr Bruce, who was attached to the
Reparations Committee, *The Dancing Times*,
October 1921, p 2.

12 Boris Kochno, as a young man of seventeen, was
engaged by Diaghilev to be his secretary in
February 1921. He quickly became indispensable, and later wrote the librettos of many of the
Ballets Russes ballets.

13 Boris Kochno, *Diaghilev and the Ballets Russes*,
p 171.

14 Serge Grigoriev, *The Diaghilev Ballet*, p 179.

15 Quoted by Boris Kochno in *Diaghilev and the
Ballets Russes*, p 172.

16 Arnold Haskell, *Diaghileff*, p 320.

17 J. T. Grein, "The World of the Theatre" in *The
Illustrated London News*, 19 November 1921, p 690.

18 Ernest Newman, *The Sunday Times*, 6 November
1921, quoted in Nesta Macdonald *Diaghilev
observed*, p 276.

19 The Sitter Out in *The Dancing Times*, December
1921, p 184.

20 115 performances according to Boris Kochno, *op
cit*, p 173. Even so, until then no ballet had been
performed in England so many consecutive
times. Diaghilev resisted the request to vary the
program by including evenings of some of his
short ballets because, foreseeing the sequestra-
tion, he did not want to lose the scenery and
costumes for his other ballets as well. The
finances are described in detail in Nesta Macdonald's *Diaghilev Observed.*

21 Boris Kochno, *op cit*, p 172.

22 Lydia Sokolova, *Dancing for Diaghilev*, p 193.

23 "Notes on Decor" in *The Dancing Times*, December 1921, p 283.

24 This is extremely unlikely. Bakst was most
possessive of his original designs and, as he was
perfectly aware of their commercial value, he
would not have risked putting them into the
hands of others. It is much more likely that
Beaumont saw copies made by assistants.

25 Cyril W. Beaumont, "Rehearsing the Alhambra
Ballet" in *The Dancing Times,* December 1921, p 208.

André Bauchant

French
born 1873 Château Renault (Indre et Loire)
died 1958 Montoire-sur-le-Loir (Loir et Cher)

**30   Persée délivrant Andromède
(Perseus releasing Andromeda)**

Oil on canvas (extended to fit frame)
24⅝ x 34⅛ in: 64.5 x 87 cm (extended to 89.3 cm)
Signed and dated lower right in oil: "A. Bauchant /
    1926"
Label on reverse of canvas inscribed in ink "A.
    Bauchant / Persée délivrant / Andromède"
    ("Perseus releasing Andromeda")
Stamp on canvas and stretcher (twice) "Douanes
    Exposition Paris" ("Customs Exhibition Paris")
Label on reverse on stretcher: "Lucien Lefebvre-
    Foinet / 19 rue Vavin / 2 rue Bréa / Paris VI /
    couleurs et toiles fines," stamped No "5264"
    and inscribed in pencil "Bauchand [sic] / Décors
    / Persée" ("Bauchand Set design Perseus")
1933.397

Exhibitions: Paris 1929, No 4; London 1930, No 4;
    New York 1933, No 7; Chicago 1933, No 9
    (Described as "Decor pour Persée"); Northamp-
    ton 1934, No 9; Hartford 1934b; New Haven
    1935; San Francisco 1935–6; Richmond 1959;
    New York 1965–6, No 12 (illustrated p 18);
    New York 1966–7; Princeton 1968; Hartford
    1974

Andromeda is chained to a rock while Perseus,
    holding the Gorgon's head, is approaching on
    his winged horse to slay the sea monster.

André Bauchant and his elder brother Hippolyte were both nurserymen. André, however, always believed that he would one day be called upon "to do something other than help plants grow out of the ground."[1] During the First World War, after returning from Greece, discovering that he could draw, he had been engaged in making accurate drawings of the landscape for range-finding. He was entirely a self-taught painter, but this experience gave him a lot of practice. In 1919, at the age of forty-seven, he decided to devote himself exclusively to painting; although he knew and cared little or nothing about the history of art, he was fascinated by classical history. *Les Ruines* by Constantin Volney, *L'Histoire de la Grèce Ancienne* by Victor Duruy and *Histoire des Empereurs Romains* by Jacques Royou, the standard authoritative works, were inspirational reading for him. His subject matter, therefore, was flowers, mythology, classical history, and, being a good catholic, holy scripture, but he never looked at any reference material while painting, and painted only in his studio. His biographer, Maximilien Gauthier, described his method of working: "He sketches

extremely quickly with a pencil, at a single stretch, with fine comma-like lines, without lingering over varying the tones of shadows; it is very mysterious; not much is discernable and yet everything is there; as he reaches the completion of a work one gradually becomes aware that his painting was conceived in total, down to the last detail, before the first stroke of the brush."[2] However, Gauthier also adds quoting the artist: "But note that it doesn't all come by itself; I remember that I have taken a lot of care before reaching that point."[3] At the same time he had an essentially "amateur" or untrained way of working. He always began a painting from the bottom and worked up. Bauchant, the gardener, explained this: "A plant only lives by its roots, a house is not built without foundations, it is all in the base, if it is solid then the picture will succeed, if not it will not live."[4]

By 1921 nine out of sixteen works he submitted to the Salon d'Automne were accepted, and when Bauchant visited the Grand Palais to see his paintings he overheard someone saying about his work: "It's like Rousseau, improved by Marie Laurençin."[5] While it is true that his work does have a certain resemblance to Rousseau's, even in the way he writes his signature with the line underneath, Bauchant is supposed

not to have seen anything by Rousseau until 1927. He does not, to my mind, have the wide-eyed exuberance of Rousseau, nor does he share the fey quality of Laurencin's work. He is a pure naif painter, possessing a strange and mesmerizing quality of classicism, a sort of "primitivized" Poussin. He is also a melancholy painter.

The inscription on the reverse suggests that this painting is a decor, and Serge Lifar, in his biography of Diaghilev,[6] quoting from the notebooks which were in his possession, states that the one for 1923–4 contains lists of possible future productions including Méhul's opera *Persée et Andromède*. However, this was only an idea of Diaghilev which never came to anything, and this painting has nothing to do with the theater. It is one of a series of paintings that Bauchant was doing at the time based on classical themes.

Notes

1   Maximilien Gauthier, *André Bauchant*, p 14.
2   Maximilien Gauthier, *ibid*, pp 39–40.
3   André Bauchant quoted in Maximilien Gauthier, *ibid*, p 40.
4   André Bauchant quoted by Anne Devroye-Stilz in *André Bauchant*.
5   André Bauchant quoted in Maximilien Gauthier, *op cit*, p 28.
6   Serge Lifar, *Diaghilev*, p 322.

Apollon Musagète (Apollo)

Ballet in 2 scenes by Igor Stravinsky
Composer: Igor Stravinsky
Conductor: Igor Stravinsky
Violin solo: Marcel Darrieux
Choreographer: George Balanchine
Designer (sets and costumes): André Bauchant
   (New costumes in 1929 by Gabrielle Chanel)
Principal dancers:
   Apollo: Serge Lifar
   Terpsichore: Alice Nikitina
   Calliope: Lubov Tchernicheva
   Polyhymnia: Felia Dubrovska
   Leto : Sophie Orlova
   Company: Diaghilev's Ballets Russes
First Performance: 12 June 1928, Théâtre Sarah-
   Bernhardt, Paris

Commissioned by Elizabeth Sprague Coolidge, the
original performance of the work—with choreography by Adolf Bolm who also danced the
part of Apollo, and with designs by Nicholas
Remisov—was at the Library of Congress in
Washington D.C. on 27 April 1928. The other
dancers were Ruth Page (Terpsichore), Elise
Reiman (Calliope), and Bernice Holmes (Polyhymnia). Stravinsky did not see this production.

Synopsis[1]

The following note, in French, appeared in the
original program above Igor Stravinsky's
signature:

"*Apollo* is a piece without plot. It is a ballet whose
choreography follows the theme of Apollo, in
other words the leader of the muses inspiring
each of the others with their art.

"The ballet begins with a short prologue representing the birth of Apollo. Leto is seized with
childbirth. She throws her arms round a tree,
she kneels on soft grass and the child leaps
into the light. Two goddesses run forward to
greet Apollo, giving him as swaddling clothes a
white veil and a gold belt. They give him nectar
and ambrosia and lead him towards Olympus.
End of the prologue; a new setting. Apollo, left
alone, dances (*Variation*). At the end of his
dance Calliope, Polyhymnia and Terpsichore
appear: Apollo bestows a gift upon each one
(*Pas d'action*). Thus Calliope becomes the muse
of Poetry, Polyhymnia of Mime, and Terpsichore
of Dance. Each in turn exhibits her art to him
(*Variations*). Apollo receives them with a dance
in honor of these new-born arts (*Variation*).
Terpsichore, uniting Poetry and Mime, finds
herself in the place of honor beside Apollo (*Pas
de deux*). The other muses join Apollo and
Terpsichore thereby grouping all three round
their leader (*Coda*). These allegorical scenes end
with an apotheosis in which Apollo leads the
muses, with Terpsichore first, towards Parnassus which in future will be their abode."

Scene 1. Leto gives birth to the god Apollo. Atten-
dant handmaidens dance to him and bring him
a lute.

Scene 2. The three Muses, Calliope (poetry), Polyhymnia (mime), and Terpsichore (dancing) pay
homage to Apollo. He gives them gifts, symbols of their art: a tablet to Calliope, a mask to
Polyhymnia, and a lyre to Terpsichore. Apollo
leads the Muses in a procession up towards
Parnassus.

It has often been given as evidence that
during the last years of the 1920s
Diaghilev's treasure hunt in search of rare
Russian books was a new passion that
replaced the one for producing original
ballets. This was not so. Indeed, during
those last years he was just as innovative
and involved as ever. He was particularly
thrilled when he learned that Stravinsky
had composed a new score. He wrote excit-
edly to Lifar on 30 September 1927 about a
day he had spent with Stravinsky: "After
lunch he played me the first half of the new
ballet. It is, of course, an amazing work,
extraordinarily calm, and with a greater
clarity than anything he has so far done; a
filigree counterpoint round transparent,
clear-cut themes, all in the major key; somehow music not of this world, but from
somewhere above." According to Diaghilev
the ballet at this stage had no particular
theme, for he concluded that: "When the
train was already moving out, he shouted to
me: 'Find a good title!'"[2] As Lifar states, this
is at variance with Stravinsky's own
account in his later memoirs where he
writes that the welcome commission from
Elizabeth Sprague Coolidge "enabled me to
carry out an idea, which had long tempted
me, to compose a ballet founded on
moments or episodes in Greek mythology
plastically interpreted by dancing of the so-
called classical school. I chose as theme
Apollo Musagetes, that is to say as master
of the Muses, inspiring each of them with
her own art. I reduced their number to
three, selecting from among them Calliope,
Polyhymnia, and Terpsichore as being the
most characteristic of choreographic art."[3]

With the title agreed, Diaghilev
entrusted the choreography to Balanchine.
Lifar was always to dance the title role, but
there was an argument over who should
dance Terpsichore. Balanchine wanted
Danilova, with whom he was now in love,
but Diaghilev insisted on Nikitina as she
was Lord Rothermere's "favorite," and
Diaghilev needed his patronage. The
necessary cheque would only be forthcoming if Nikitina would dance. Balanchine had
to agree, with the result that Nikitina alternated the part with Danilova. Nikitina
described Balanchine's method of setting a
ballet: "Balanchine, who is intensely musical and sensitive, is chiefly inspired by the
personality of the artists. He indicates a step
and then says: 'Try something else!' And he
goes on doing this until he finds his chore-

ography through the dancers. Balanchine
senses instinctively the artists whom he is
working upon; he unconsciously works for
that artist . . . there is little technique in his
choreography and the steps are simple.
Everything is concentrated upon expression,
beauty, grace."[4]

Balanchine, who had for the last few
years performed the role of "master-of-all-
trades" for Diaghilev as dancer and choreographer, admitted to finding his artistic
salvation in *Apollo*. After a variety of slight,
entertaining but not very memorable or
lasting works, Balanchine returned to a
strict and pure classicism. He evolved a
new classical style which "serenely embodied the classical virtues of clarity and
grandeur and yet in spirit and in style of
movement was more up to date and adventurous than the run of ultramodern
ballets."[5] *Apollo* was the first of many ballets
created by Balanchine and Stravinsky, the
collaboration which Richard Buckle has
called "the most blessed partnership in the
history of ballet."[6] Stravinsky was certainly
well pleased with Balanchine's work, writing that "his beautiful choreography clearly
expressed my meaning."[7] *Apollo* is also the
first of Balanchine's ballets still to be regularly performed, and so it is no wonder that
he later considered it to have been a turning
point in his career.

In order to avoid a traditional classical
look which he feared might be just pastiche,
Diaghilev, with characteristic daring, commissioned the primitive painter André
Bauchant to design the sets and costumes.
Diaghilev first noticed this painter's work at
the Salon d'Automne in Paris in 1927 at
which Bauchant exhibited three paintings
on classical themes, *Bataille de Marathon*,
Periclès, and *Incendie au Temple d'Ephèse*. By
arrangement with Jeanne Bucher, the gallery
director who was sponsoring Bauchant,
Diaghilev went with Serge Lifar to visit the
artist at his house at La Blutière, near his
birthplace Château-Renault, in January
1928, and subsequently commissioned him
to design the sets for *Apollo*. In a letter dated
30 March 1928 Bauchant agreed to design
the sets, costumes and props, and that the
designs would remain Diaghilev's
property.[8] On 12 April 1928 Bauchant went
to Monte Carlo at Diaghilev's invitation,
and stayed until 9 May.[9] In view of these
dates, Boris Kochno's statement that "We
never did meet Bauchant; he lived in the
country and never came to town,"[10] is very

surprising. Besides, it is firmly contradicted by Nicolas Nabokov who had also gone to Monte Carlo in April 1928 to work on his ballet *Ode* (see pp 323–31), which was to be presented in the same year. Nabokov describes meeting Bauchant: "a funny-looking man with thick glasses, in disorderly dress and endowed with a crooked goatee," and relates a story of an argument between Diaghilev and Bauchant: "It appeared that on the morning of my arrival Diaghilev walked into the studio where Bauchant was supposed to be painting the sets for *Apollon*. He found Bauchant putting the last touches on a still life of his own. Looking about, Diaghilev saw a few other "contraband" still lifes. There wasn't a trace of *Apollon* around. Bauchant proudly acknowledged having painted the pictures since his arrival two weeks previously in Monte Carlo. Diaghilev got furious; he informed M. Bauchant-*jeune*[11] that he had not been invited to Monte Carlo to paint pictures but to prepare sets; that he, Diaghilev, was not a provider of free studios for M. Bauchant-*jeune* and that M. Bauchant-*jeune* had better stop painting his silly pictures immediately. Bauchant listened carefully to this diatribe and riposted with indignation. He said that his pictures weren't silly at all and that if M. de Diaghilev did not undertsand them it was the fault of that '*saltimbanque*' Picasso and all the Russian barbarians round M. de Diaghilev in his ballet troupe."[12] All this detail could not have been invented by Nabokov, which makes Kochno's denial even more curious, particularly since, according to Nabokov, he was in Monte Carlo at the same time. Kochno goes on to say: "And although he [Bauchant] had accepted Diaghilev's commission, he never delivered any sketches. Diaghilev then decided to use for the sets the landscapes from two of Bauchant's canvases, which Prince Schervashidze adapted for the stage."[13] This version of events was also denied by Diaghilev himself, when he was quoted at length in a newspaper article which appeared the day before the first performance: "In painting, among the newcomers, I only see old young, old men who are young, that is to say who have kept a fresh spirit which emanates from their painting. Bombois . . . and Beauchant [sic]. I was very pleased to meet the latter. I had been told about a peasant, and I saw a man with a superb Napoleon III head. In Monte Carlo, where I made him come to design the sets for *Apollon* (they are marvellous, a

primitive sky, you will see for yourselves next week), he walked to the Casino dressed in pale olive trousers, a black cloth jacket with flowing tails and brown leather gloves, large travelling gloves which he always had with him. There was something else he always had with him: a bulky envelope with photographs of his pictures. He was sometimes introduced to a Princess. Then his first move would be to take the famous envelope out of the pocket of his jacket, show his photographs and say: 'Here is my life's work.' What a delicious painter! His large compositions, in such a classical manner, the delicay of his flowers, the rustic feeling in his landscapes. And always, in everything, a literary point of departure. Then he paints with simplicity. He finds most of his themes in the Larousse dictionary."[14]

Bauchant painted at least two versions of Apollo's chariot flying through the sky; the one in this collection was used for the main set. The painting called *Champs-Elysées* had indeed been painted earlier (see below), which perhaps explains in part Kochno's statement. Bauchant had problems with designing the costumes, and admitted it.[15] Alice Nikitina got quite confused, however, in writing about her costume later: "Diaghilev, who did not like the Grecian robes which Rouault had designed for me, asked Chanel to make me a sort of tutu of uneven length, much shorter behind than in front."[16] Rouault had nothing to do with *Apollo*; he designed *The Prodigal Son* only in 1929 (see pp 300–5). Bauchant did design the original costumes for *Apollo*, and they were replaced, but not until 1929, by new ones designed by Gabrielle Chanel.

In an interview published two days before the first night, Diaghilev said that "Stravinsky has aimed for majestic tranquility," and that Balanchine's choreography "is in total accord with the spirit of Stravinsky's music. It is classicism in a contemporary mould." Of Bauchant he said that he belonged to the "Douanier" Henri Rousseau group of painters, which, though not strictly true, suited Diaghilev's sense of publicity, and he added that "his approach was naïf, sincere, completely individual, and in sharp contrast to the stereotyped Greek productions."[17]

The main talking point of the ballet was naturally the score by Stravinsky. But Balanchine's choreography and the dancing also received a lot of praise—none higher than Diaghilev's for Lifar, as Lifar himself recalled in his book: "Sergei Pavlovich,

profoundly moved, impulsively kissed my leg after the performance. 'Remember it, Seriozha, for the rest of your days. I am kissing a dancer's leg for the second time in my life, the last was Nijinsky's after *Le Spectre de la Rose*.'"[18] Other critics describing Lifar's performance would confirm that such a gesture was not exaggerated.

Edward Gordon Craig, who had often been highly critical of Diaghilev's ballet, was this time moved to report favorably when he saw the ballet in the following year: "I can imagine no more delicate piece of work than the arrangement of the different sections of this second ballet, this 'Apollo.'[19] Everything conspires in it to cheat us—but all is done openly and beautifully. The arrangement of this Ballet was by *Georges Balanchine*, a man of a fine creative talent. The dancers were Serge Lifar and the three ladies, Danilova, Tchernicheva and Doubrovska, and all four enchanted me."[20] Of Bauchant's work there was no mention.

31   Design for the front cloth: Champs-Elysées

Oil on canvas (extended to fit frame)
39⅛ x 45½ in (sight): 100 cm extended to 101.8 x 132.4 cm
Signed and dated bottom right in oil: "A. Bauchant / 1927"
Stamped on reverse on canvas "Douane Exposition Paris" ("Customs Exhibition Paris") and "Douane Centrale Exposition Paris"
Label on reverse on stretcher: "Lucien Lefebvre-Foinet / 19 rue Vavin / 2 rue Bréa / Paris VI / couleurs et toiles fines," stamped No "5267" and another label with typed inscription "Bauchant / Apollon / Décor / (Les Champs Elysées) / Coll. S. Lifar" stamped "Douane Centrale Exposition Paris"
1933.395

Exhibitions: Paris 1928; London 1928; Paris 1929, No 8; Paris 1930 No 13; London 1930, No 1; New York 1933, No 5; Chicago 1933, No 7; Northampton 1934, No 7; Hartford 1934b; New Haven 1935; San Francisco 1935–6; Paris 1939, No 87 (illustrated p 37); Williamsburg 1940; New York 1941–2; Minneapolis 1953; Indianapolis 1959, No 22; New York 1962; New York 1965–6, No 13 (illustrated p 18); Spoleto 1966; New York 1966–7; Hempstead 1974, No 23 (illustrated); Hartford 1974, No 23.
Illustrations: Amberg, pl 78; Clarke and Crisp *Design for Ballet*, pl 106a; Hammond, Richard "Ballets Russes, 1928" in (?) *Theatre Arts*, facing p 25; Hansen, fig 65; Spencer, p 127; Taper, facing p 112.

This painting, with its date of 1927, was bought by Diaghilev before he had decided to commission Bauchant to design the sets for the ballet, and may well have been included in the exhibition at the Jeanne Bucher gallery "Fleurs et Paysages d'André Bauchant" (21 December 1927–6 January 1928). Diaghilev was keen to avoid the traditional "classical" look in the production, and this primitive vase of flowers was about as far away from that look as it was possible to get.

Vases of flowers on a table or stand are a recurrent theme in Bauchant's work, sometimes with a plain background, sometimes, as here, with a river meandering through a landscape with trees and figures.[21] Bauchant, being a nurseryman and a gardener, painted real flowers with considerable accuracy, although these would not all have been in flower at the same time. It is a floral fantasy.

The actual curtain, painted by Prince Schervashidze, was without the figures because Diaghilev did not like them. In the production this was used as a front cloth hung only before the beginning of the action, and not for scene 1 as has been thought hitherto. The initial idea had been for the huge vase to fall apart and become a grotto for the birth of Apollo, but for practical reasons this was abandoned, and the first scene of the ballet was changed and simplified. The critic of *The Times* described the birth: "A young woman sits astride an archway from which hangs a muslin curtain; a young man swathed in silk hops behind the muslin. He is Apollo. Two young women remove the swathings; he now has very little on and hops more freely; the lights go out; when they go up again he has put on a red garment."[22] The same basic set was used for both scenes of the ballet (see No 32).

Right: the final moment, as Apollo, played by Serge Lifar, leads the Muses toward Parnassus.

32   Set design

Oil on fabric, wax-lined
23⅝ x 27¾ in: 60 x 73 cm
Signed and dated lower left in oil: "A. Bauchant / 1928"
Label on reverse on stretcher: "Lucien Lefebvre-Foinet / 19 rue Vavin / 2 rue Bréa / Paris VI / couleurs et toiles fines," stamped No "2624" and another label with typed inscription "Bauchant / Apollon / Décor (ciel) [sky] / Coll. S. Lifar" inscribed in pencil "1928"
1933.396

Exhibitions: Paris 1928; London 1928; Paris 1929, No 9; Paris 1930, No 14; London 1930, No 2; New York 1933, No 6; Chicago 1933, No 8; Northampton 1934, No 8; Hartford 1934b; New Haven 1935; Middletown 1935; Boston 1938; Paris 1939, No 87 (illustrated); Poughkeepsie 1940; Williamsburg 1940; New York 1941–2; Minneapolis 1954, No 8; Indianapolis 1959, No 23; New York 1962 (illustrated p 55, pl. 28); New York 1965–6, No 14 (illustrated p 18); Spoleto 1966; New York 1966–7; Princeton 1968; Strasbourg 1969, No 442 (illustrated No 110); Frankfurt-am-Main 1969, No 129; Hartford 1974; Hempstead 1974, No 24; New York 1980.
Illustrations: Cohen, pl. 28 no 2 p 55; Komisarjevsky, p 50; Oswald, No 2 p 28.

Apollo was a favorite subject for Bauchant. In 1925 he had painted *Apollon apparaissant aux Bergers* (*Apollo appearing to the Shepherds*) which already has a similar chariot (top right) drawn by four horses, with angels (top left) and a similar rock formation below. The inspiration for the shape and color of the rocks comes from a ridge near the artist's home at La Blutière rather than from anything he saw in Greece.

This is one of two known versions of the painting,[23] and is the one most closely resembling the finished set. Again, as for the previous painting, Diaghilev required all the figures to be left out of the set. The rocks were built as a ground row in the background, with the massive central rock built as a hollow rostrum large enough for Serge Lifar to emerge from in scene 1, and with steps behind for the final ascent in scene 2. They were positioned in front of a sky cloth. The chariot and four horses on a cloud were flown in at the end from the audience's right in front of the sky cloth.

Notes

1 For a detailed choreographic synopsis see George Balanchine and Francis Mason *Balanchine's Festival of Ballet*.

2 Quoted in Serge Lifar, *Diaghilev*, p 453.

3 Igor Stravinsky, *Chronicle of my Life*, pp 218–9.

4 Alice Nikitina, *Nikitina*, pp 89–90.

5 Bernard Taper, *Balanchine*, p 96.

6 Richard Buckle, *Diaghilev*, p 495.

7 Igor Stravinsky, *op cit*, p 234.

8 Sotheby's catalogue, *Serge Lifar Collection* 9 May 1984, lot 145.

9 The precise dates are given in Maximilien Gauthier, *André Bauchant*, p 32.

10 Boris Kochno *Diaghilev and the Ballets Russes*, p 266.

11 He always insisted on introducing himself as "Bauchant-*jeune*" to distinguish himself from his elder brother, since they both carried on a business as nurserymen.

12 Nicolas Nabokov, *op cit*, pp 83, 86–7.

13 Boris Kochno, *op cit*, p 266.

14 Serge Diaghilev quoted by E. T. in *L'Intransigeant*, Paris 11 June 1928.

15 Bauchant's great-niece, Mme Renault-Bauchant, told me that is what he had told her.

16 Alice Nikitina, *op cit*, p 91.

17 Serge Diaghilev quoted in *Vozrozhdenie (Renaissance)*, Paris 10 June 1928, quoted in I. C. Zilberstein and V. A. Samkov *Diaghilev* Vol 1, p 250.

18 Serge Lifar, *Diaghilev*, p 468.

19 He states that had also seen *The Firebird*, but this was not performed in 1929.

20 Edward Gordon Craig from "A Letter on Recent Travels through Europe" in *The Mask* Vol XV No 2, April–May–June, quoted in Arnold Rood, *Gordon Craig on Movement and Dance*, p 162. He saw a performance when Nikitina was replaced by Danilova.

21 This painting is similar to *L'Eté*, dated 1928.

22 *The Times*, London 26 June 1928.

23 Another version was reproduced (along with *Champs Elysées*) in Richard Hammond's article "Ballets Russes, 1928" in ? *Theatre Arts*. There were, however, three other paintings of Apollo included in the exhibition in Paris at the Magellan Gallery in 1928, in addition to those made for *Apollo*. The critic in *Cahiers d'Art* No 5–6 1928 (p 262) summed up the artist's work by saying: "Beauchant [sic] can, in no way, be compared to Rousseau. He lacks that divine inspiration which is present throughout the work of the 'Douanier.' Furthermore, he lacks that unconsciousness about the finished work which is wonderful in Rousseau. Beauchant, as Mme Bucher presents him to us, is a somewhat rustic painter who enjoys looking at paintings of old, and who enjoys recasting them in his own style."

Alexandre Benois

Russian
born 1870 St Petersburg
died 1960 Paris

Le Pavillon d'Armide (Armida's Pavilion)

Ballet-Pantomime in 1 act, 3 scenes by Alexandre Benois, after the story *Omphale* by Théophile Gautier
Composer: Nicholas Tcherepnine
Conductor: Nicholas Tcherepnine
Choreographer: Michel Fokine
Designer (sets and costumes): Alexandre Benois
Principal dancers:
    Viscount René de Beaugency: Michel Mordkine
    The Marquis of S—: Alexis Bulgakov
    Baptiste: Serge Grigoriev
    Armide: Vera Karalli
    Confidantes of Armide: Tamara Karsavina, Alexandra Baldina, Alexandra Fedorov, Elena Smirnova
    The Favorite Slave: Vaslav Nijinsky
Company: Diaghilev's Ballets Russes
First Performance: 19 May 1909, Théâtre du Châtelet, Paris

Synopsis

Scene 1. Armida's pavilion. The Viscount de Beaugency, on his way to visit his fiancée, has been caught in a storm and invited by the Marquis to spend the night. He is shown into a room with a magnificent tapestry upon which the beautiful Marquise is represented as Armida surrounded by her court. The room also has a huge clock upheld by the figures of Love and Time. The Viscount falls asleep while staring at the tapestry. Midnight strikes. The figure of Time moves, turning his hourglass upside down. The two figures come down from the clock and Love drives Time away. Then twelve small figures, the twelve hours, step out of the clock, perform a dance, and return to the clock. The Viscount is woken by the sounds and gazes at the tapestry as it begins to change.

Scene 2. The scene is that of the tapestry, a garden in front of a palace where Armida is surrounded by her court. The Viscount appears as her lover René. She chides him for his absence and orders festivities to celebrate his return. King Hidraot, having an uncanny resemblance to the Marquis, enters. René is completely captivated by Armida who gives him her scarf as a token of her love. The King blesses their union. Daybreak interrupts the festivities, and the dream vanishes.

Scene 3. Armida's pavilion. The Viscount awakes to be greeted by his host the Marquis. The Viscount prepares to leave and continue his interrupted journey when he suddenly catches sight of Armida's scarf draped over the clock. In the tapestry Armida is now without her scarf. Tormented between dream and reality, the Viscount swoons while the Marquis gloats over the success of his sorcery.

When Diaghilev and his "committee" decided to take ballet as well as opera to Paris for their Russian season in 1909, they immediately agreed to include *Le Pavillon d'Armide* which had already had a try-out in Russia.[1] The development of this production has a somewhat protracted history. Alexandre Benois had long intended to create a three-act ballet. In about 1900, his friend the painter Constantin Somov suggested one of Théophile Gautier's stories, *Omphale*, as a suitable subject. The romantic Hoffmanesque story, a mixture of reality and fantasy, greatly appealed to Benois as "the dramatic quality of *Omphale* would give my ballet sufficient seriousness to save it from being merely commonplace and gay as the fashion of the times prescribed."[2] Curiously, however, in describing the story in his *Reminiscences* much later, Benois gets it wrong when he states that "the hero finds a lock of hair in an old chest of drawers and falls in love with the beautiful woman, portrayed on an ancient Gobelins."[3] Benois took the idea to the composer Nicholas Tcherepnine, his nephew by marriage, who, enthused, immediately began to compose a score. In 1902, thinking the time was propitious after Benois's successful production of *Götterdämmerung* at the Imperial Theaters, he and Tcherepnine offered *Le Pavillon d'Armide* to the director, Vladimir Teliakovsky. According to Benois, he merely enquired "Are there any waltzes?"[4] When he was assured that there were, Teliakovsky accepted the ballet and paid Benois for the libretto. However, soon afterwards Benois and Teliakovsky fell out. The reason, as described by Benois, seems trivial in the extreme, but then everything I read about him tells me that although he was extraordinarily knowledgeable and charming, he was also very touchy. Apparently he took offence when some observations he sent from Rome were replied to by a subordinate instead of by Teliakovsky himself, and so he withdrew his ballet.

Nothing more happened until 1907, when Michel Fokine heard the suite from *Le Pavillon d'Armide* at a concert. He was always looking for suitable music for ballets and, attracted by what he had heard, approached the composer Tcherepnine who was then also one of the conductors at the Mariinsky Theater. Fokine, by this time already highly regarded as a choreographer by the younger members of the Imperial Theaters company, needed to produce something for the annual Students' Recital. Tcherepnine was understandably not too flattered by the idea of having his music used for a students' performance, and explained besides that his suite was only for the middle scene of an intended three-act ballet, and that Benois's approval for such a shortened version would also have to be sought. Fokine, however, was persuasive, saying that he only wanted one scene, and that the students would not let him down. Tcherepnine and Benois agreed, and the ballet, called *The Animated Tapestry*,[5] was produced without scenery and with costumes from the wardrobe stock on 15 April 1907. A few days after the performance, which was a success, Alexander Krupensky, Director of the St Petersburg Office of the Imperial Theaters, approached Fokine with the request: "Would it not be possible to produce this on the stage of the Imperial [Mariinsky] Theatre with real artists?"[6] Krupensky also suggested that the first and third scenes should be included as well as the second scene, but that the whole ballet should be shortened to one act. Benois at first expressed his displeasure at the suggestion of shortening his ballet as he "had intended to create something imposing, something that would resurrect the tradition of former ballets"[7] which he loved so much. But Tcherepnine and Fokine persisted. Fokine explained his attitude towards the one-act ballet: "I adopted the one-act ballet not through any newly created theories, but because of my natural disposition . . . It seems to me that the concentration of the means of expression strengthens them, and that the stretching of these means weakens them."[8] Eventually Benois gave way, probably feeling that the chance to have the ballet produced at the Imperial Theater was not to be easily foregone. The production therefore went ahead as a one-act ballet with three scenes, although Fokine still regretted that the libretto called for too much old-fashioned mime and not enough pure dancing. Benois designed the sets and costumes, majestically evoking the sumptuous epoch of Louis XIV. Mathilde Kshessinska was to dance the part of Armida, and even though the venerable Pavel Gerdt, asked to dance the part of

René de Beaugency, thought it ludicrous that at sixty he should appear as a young man of twenty, he was finally persuaded to do so.

The rehearsal period was not all plain sailing, as the Imperial Theaters at the time were riddled with intrigue. At Benois's invitation Diaghilev attended one of the rehearsals, but after half an hour was asked by the police to leave the theater because, since his dismissal in 1901, he was *persona non grata* there. A week before the first night Kshessinska, for no apparent reason except to please the Directorate, refused to take any further part in the production. Fortunately, Anna Pavlova immediately offered to take her place. Then Krupensky refused to allow the *corps de ballet* to rehearse in costume before the dress rehearsal so that "when the artists now appeared in costumes they had not seen before, with their pompous wigs and complicated head-dresses, there was a great bustle and confusion."[9] Fokine and Benois demanded an extra dress rehearsal. The management refused, saying everything had been announced and the programs printed. Benois then arranged to be interviewed by Isaiah Rosenberg, Léon Bakst's brother, who wrote a daily column in the *St Petersburg Gazette*. According to Benois, "the gist of the interview consisted of a characterisation of the ways of a directorate utterly bound by red tape, showing that such a directorate alone was sufficient to make the complete failure of my work almost inevitable."[10] Surprisingly, the opposition collapsed and Teliakovsky immediately ordered the first night to be postponed for a week, giving the company two extra dress rehearsals.

The first performance of *Le Pavillon d'Armide* finally took place without a hitch at 11.15 p.m. on 25 November 1907, after a mediocre performance of *Swan Lake*, and was most enthusiastically received. Audiences had greater stamina then than now. Diaghilev greeted Benois by saying: "This must be shown to Europe."[11]

Benois's close collaboration with Fokine on this production had a decisive effect on the establishment of the Ballets Russes, because when it was agreed that ballets as well as operas should be included in the repertory to be taken to Paris Fokine was engaged as ballet-master. The final program consisted of his ballets only: *Le Pavillon d'Armide*, *Les Sylphides* (see pp 153–54), *Cléopâtre*, *Polovtsian Dances* from *Prince Igor* (see pp 225–29), and, with some choreography by others, *Le Festin*, a suite of *divertissements*.

Valerian Svetlov, the distinguished critic, was an eye witness of the company's "get-in" and the usual organized chaos during rehearsals at the Châtelet Theater. He described vividly what he saw: "In the vast basement great trunks of props, costumes, tights, and scenery were being unpacked. Forty thousand kilos. On stage behind the backcloth the sheep which appear in the third scene of *Armide* were roaming around.[12] Tcherepnine, the composer, conducted the orchestral rehearsals of *Armide*. Cooper, the conductor from Moscow, conducted *Igor* and *Festin*. Fokine was tireless and the dancers were tireless. Everyone worked with only brief interruptions from morning till midnight. Everyone was exhausted and became excitable as before a decisive battle but the work progressed in an atmosphere of amicable harmony. Sometimes there were little upsets, the conductor would not give way to the choreographer and vice-versa. But everything was usually settled in a friendly way. Everyone recognized how important it was to work together and without argument for the sake of their art."[13]

Several improvements were made to *Le Pavillon d'Armide* for Paris. Some of the music was re-arranged and about a quarter of an hour was cut. Benois changed some of the costumes and the decor. "In the St

Below: Tamara Karsavina as Armida, when she danced the part in 1909, and Michel Mordkine as the Viscount.

Petersburg version I had been worried by the neighbourhood of lilac, pink and yellow, and by the somewhat motley details of the décor for the second scene. These defects I now corrected."[14] Benois also writes of the introduction of "two gigantic water pyramids" at the end of the second scene.[15] There were also important cast changes: Mordkine replaced Gerdt, and Bulgakov replaced Solianikov. Kshessinska refused to go to Paris when she learned that Armida was to be her only part and that she would have to share it with Karalli. So Pavlova was engaged instead to repeat her performance but, as she did not arrive in Paris until later, Karalli danced the role of Armida at both the public dress rehearsal[16] and the first night on 18 and 19 May 1909. Finally, a new number was introduced, a *pas de trois*. Richard Buckle has described the importance of this moment in the ballet: "The conquest of Europe by Russian dancing and the reign of Diaghilev as Director of the Ballets Russes can be said to begin at the moment Nijinsky takes the stage with his two partners."[17]

The French impresario Gabriel Astruc had invented a series of publicity stunts, including filling the front row of the dress circle with ravishingly pretty girls alternately blond and brunette, in order to make sure that the first evening was a brilliantly glittering occasion. He succeeded, as Ernest La Jeunesse reported: "I was forgetting that this performance was so crowded that four celebrities fought over every seat. All eyes were on the dress circle, on all the necks, coiffures and bosoms covered in all the jewels of Paris, on all the boxes with all the Highnesses and Excellencies and the Russian Ambassador, on all the audience, in fact, sparkling and brimming over with such distinction, splendour and opulence that the Field of the Cloth of Gold was like some provincial fair or market in Nizhni-Novgorod by comparison."[18]

The press, on the whole, gave the Russians an enthusiastic reception. Robert Brussel in *Le Figaro* typified the general appreciation: "The groups, figures and steps of the choreographer M. Fokine reveal a rich and versatile imagination and, what is still more rare, a very informed artistic taste. There is a most attractive combination of tradition and modernism in his composition. As for success, it was enormous and recalled the most wonderful evenings of *Boris*."[19] On the other hand, while *Le Pavillon d'Armide* "fulfilled its mission in Paris"[20] according to Benois, it was,

according to Arnold Haskell, "a comparative failure." "The French," he continued, "may well have thought it daring of these strangers to show them the France of Louis XIV when they were looking to the Russians for something altogether exotic."[21] And so it was the second item of the evening, the barbaric and frenetically thrilling dances from *Prince Igor*,[22] followed by the exotic "orientalism" of *Cléopâtre* on 2 June, which really took Paris by storm.

33   Set design for scene 2: Armida's garden

Graphite, crayon, pen and ink, and tempera and/or
    watercolor on paper
15¼ x 20¾ in: 38.8 x 52.7 cm
Signed on base of fountain left in ink: "Alexandre
    Benois"
Undated
Inscribed bottom left in ink: "Le Pavillon d'Armide
    II Tableau"; bottom right: "Pas de trois dansé
    par Mlles Karsavina et A[lexandra] Fedorova et
    par M. Nijinksy 1909"
1933.398

Exhibitions: Paris 1929, No 9; Paris 1930, No 14;
    London 1930, No 2; New York 1933 (ex cata-
    logue); Chicago 1933, No 10; Northampton
    1934, No 10; Hartford 1934b; New Haven
    1935; Middletown 1935; New York 1937–8, No
    699; Paris 1939, No 88 (illustrated p 4); ? Los
    Angeles 1939–40; Williamsburg 1940; Cam-
    bridge 1942; New York 1944; Lawrence 1949;
    Edinburgh 1954, No 12; London 1954–5, No
    15; Michigan 1957; Elmira 1958, No 15;
    Indianapolis 1959, No 68; New York 1965–6,
    No 17; Spoleto 1966; New York 1966–7;
    Princeton 1968; Strasbourg 1969, No 3 (illus-
    trated No 2); Hartford 1973; Hartford 1974;
    Hempstead 1974, No 27; Chicago 1975;
    Houston 1976; Hartford 1979; Coral Gables
    1982; Hartford 1988; Worcester 1989.
Illustrations: Bablet, p 37 No 42; Beaumont, p 104;
    Buckle 1955, p 46 No 49; Clarke and Crisp
    1978, pl 82 pp 112–3; *Dance and Dancers*
    October 1955, p 23; *Dance and Dancers* March
    1984, p 10; de Mille, p 140 (color); Kirstein,
    p 184 No 343; Palmer, p 18; Percival, p 77;
    Pozharskaya and Volodina, p 49a; Williams
    1981, No 35 (color).

The problem with all the famous set and costume designs by Alexandre Benois is that he made later copies and tended to inscribe and date them with the date of the first performance rather than with the date of execution. This often makes it difficult to ascribe them accurately. Benois, the punctilious academic and historian, was not averse to misleading future writers about his own work.

This is one of the designs which became famous. Benois changed his mind several times about whether the second scene of his ballet, the garden, should be set on the diagonal or symmetrically on the center line, both being standard classical conventions of eighteenth-century baroque theater design. The first design for the 1907 production was symmetrical of a rustic and simple character, with a modest central pavilion, no fountains, and no topiary. This was changed for the original production at the Mariinsky Theater to a garden set on the diagonal,[23] with a more imposing two-storeyed

pavilion on top of a hill above a cascade on the right, a pyramid with palm trees in the center background, and two small fountains in front of topiary bays on the left. One of the "improvements" Benois made to his design for Paris was to set it again symmetrically on the center line. This perspective creates a greater sense of grandeur: the pavilion has the addition of a spire,[24] the topiary is larger and more formalized, and on either side of the stage there are two huge fountains gushing almost to the flies. The French technicians at the Châtelet theater, as well as being lazy, were notoriously unhelpful and had simply stated that water for fountains was impossible. After his trying experiences of the year before with French technicians, Diaghilev had decided to take his own chief technician, Karl Valtz, from the Bolshoi Theater, Moscow, to ensure efficient fit-ups. Prince Lieven described the situation during rehearsals when Benois spoke to Valtz:

"'What a pity that we can't create the effect of spraying water.' 'What do you mean? Can't? Your word is law. Give the order, and it shall be done.' 'But how can you manage it?' 'Don't worry. It will all be ready in time.' And so it was. In the Paris production two beautiful fountains played on stage, each superior to the St Petersburg one. The murmur of water could be heard through the whole theatre."[25]

There are at least five versions of this design for Armida's garden for the Paris production, with minor differences between them. As noted in the details above, this design is undated. This is deliberate on Benois's part as the drawing was almost certainly made after, rather than before, the first performance. Therefore, technically, it is not a "set design" but an impression of the setting. The reason for this conclusion is the presence of the three figures. They also occur, in different positions, in most of the other versions. In one version, however,

reproduced in *Apollon* in September 1910,[26] the same scene is shown with King Hidraot standing center at the bottom of the steps, with an urn on each side but no fountains. This is undoubtedly the original set design, as it shows one of the main characters with no fountains (which were only included in Paris at the last minute), and, as far as I can tell, was the first to be reproduced. As Benois could not have foreseen that the *pas de trois* with Nijinsky would be the sensation of the ballet, he would not have highlighted this moment in his drawings until the production had taken place. But who took part in the *pas de trois*?

The inscription is clear: "Karsavina and Fedorova dancing with Nijinsky." Furthermore, Benois, in his *Reminiscences* (which he wrote much later), stated: "We had seen at rehearsals how effective Nijinsky's appearance was going to be. He was to be Armida's slave, who accompanied her two confidantes, T. Karsavina and A. Fedorova.

But when Vaslav appeared in the white, silver and yellow costume I had designed for him, that harmonised so well with the gold and yellow dresses of his ladies, the effect surpassed everything we had expected."[27] No one disputes that Nijinsky was one of the three. However, Karsavina states that she danced with Nijinsky and his sister.[28] Bronislava Nijinska states that the others were Alexandra Fedorova and Alexandra Baldina.[29] Richard Buckle and other historians state that the two confidantes with Nijinsky were Karsavina and Baldina.[30] Buckle is repeating Robert Brussel of *Le Figaro* whom he quotes: "They rehearse the *pas de trois* with la Karsavina, la Baldina and Nijinsky."[31] Brussel, as a journalist, was the only one writing at the time and presumably recorded accurately what he saw. In all, there were four confidantes: Karsavina, Baldina, A. Fedorova and Smirnova. Alden Murray, supporting Buckle, suggests that the answer as to who danced the *pas de trois* is provided by the Astruc Papers in the Dance Collection of the New York Public Library, which contain an inventory of the costumes with the names of the dancers who wore them.[32] The inventory shows that Karsavina's and Baldina's costumes consisted of "orange silk bodice with gold lace decoration, orange silk and yellow tulle skirt trimmed and embroidered with gold appliqué, spangles and precious stones, yellow tarlatan underskirt, green silk head-dress with white ostrich feathers," and that Smirnova's and Fedorova's costumes consisted of "blue satin bodice with white chiffon sleeves trimmed with gold, black and blue silk skirt with gold appliqué and fringe, white tarlatan and tulle underskirt trimmed with gold braid, grey-blue silk head-dress with garlands of roses."[33] The inventory would seem therefore to confirm that Karsavina and Baldina danced the *pas de trois* with Nijinsky. But it is not so simple. During the run, the company was disrupted by love affairs—one was Karalli eloping with the tenor Sobinov. As Anna Pavlova had not yet arrived, Karsavina took over the part of Armida on 25 May, and Fedorova replaced Karsavina in the *pas de trois*, except that, according to Buckle, Karsavina "was allowed to retain her old solo from the *pas de trois*, because it suited her and she considered it the most effective choreography in the ballet; and Feodorova danced something else."[34] So, although both Karsavina and Fedorova danced in the *pas de trois* they did not dance in it together, at least not then. Why did Benois include them

both in his inscription? Alden Murray's opinion that "Benois may have been thinking of Fedorova because she staged a version of *Le Pavillon d'Armide* in Riga in1931"[35] is obviously incorrect; this drawing had already been exhibited in Paris and London by then as the property of Serge Lifar. The explanation may be simple after all. Pavlova, who was due to dance the part of Armida, arrived late and did not dance with the company until 2 June in *Les Sylphides* and *Cléopâtre*. She took over the part of Armida from Karsavina on 7 June, when presumably Karsavina returned to her original part of one of the confidantes along with Fedorova. Benois could not have mistaken who danced with Nijinsky, but this explains why the drawing must have been done some time after 7 June 1909, although the labels in the costumes, and therefore the inventory, showed the original cast.

34 Costume design for Alexis Bulgakov as the Marquis of S— in scenes 1 and 3

Graphite, black ink, and tempera and/or watercolor with white highlights on paper
11 x 8⅝ in: 27.9 x 22 cm
Signed and dated lower left in pen in Russian: "Alexandre Benois / 1909"
Inscribed in pencil at top: "Le vieux Marquis de S. *Le Pavillon / d'Armide*"
Inscribed in pencil in French top right of figure: "bandeau en taffeta" ("headband in taffeta"), "brocard [sic] que j'ai obtenu / moi même" ("brocade which I have got myself").
Inscribed in pencil in French bottom right with sketch detail of hat: "feutre noir" ("black felt"), "point d'argent" ("silver stitching"), "chapeau" ("hat").
Inscribed in pencil in French left of figure top to bottom: "fichu en / foulard à / dentelles" ("neckerchief in silk lace"), "batiste" ("cambric"), "gilet en / satin rose / à broderie / de moquette" ("waistcoat in pink satin with moquette embroidery"), "pantalons / en бумага" ("bumaga cotton trousers"), "velours / gris / foncé" ("dark grey velvet").
1933.401

Exhibitions: Chicago 1933, No 11; Northampton 1934, No 11; San Francisco 1935; Paris 1939, No 93; ? Los Angeles 1939–40; Poughkeepsie 1940; Cambridge 1942; Washington D.C. 1950–51; Edinburgh 1954, No 15; London 1954–5, No 18; New York 1965–6, No 18 (illustrated p 20; not shown in New York); Spoleto 1966; New York 1966–7; Amherst 1974; Hempstead 1974, No 29; Houston 1976; Hartford 1979; Columbus 1989; Worcester 1989.
Illustrations: Beaumont, p 105; Palmer, p 18.

35 Costume design for Alexis Bulgakov as the Marquis of S— as King Hidraot in scene 2

Graphite, black ink, tempera and/or watercolor, silver paint with white highlights and brown ink notations on paper
11¼ x 8⅞ in: 28.6 x 22 cm
Signed and dated lower right in ink: "Alexandre Benois 1909"; and in pencil: "A. Benois"; and inscribed below signature in Russian: "Павил" ("Pavil" [for "Pavillon"]).
Inscribed in pencil in French right of figure from top to bottom: "Le Marquis de S... / en Roi / Hidraot" "satin," "broderies" ("embroidery"), "rangée de perles" ("row of pearls"), "broderie d'or / sur velours / noir" ("gold embroidery on black velvet"), "pluche" ("plush"), "foulard" ("foulard silk"), "brocard [sic] (que j'ai obtenu moi-même)" ("brocade [which I have got myself]"), "gand [sic] en / peau à revers / en бумага [bumaga]" ("leather glove with cotton back"), "satin rose / à passementerie / d'argent et broderies / d'argent" ("pink satin with silver trimmings and silver embroidery"), "velours / noirs / parrure [sic] / de / paillettes / bleues" ("black velvet adorned with blue spangles"), "gape argent / drap d'argent" ("silver [?] silver cloth"); and left of figure: "Le Pavillon d'Armide," "gland en / laine noire / interculée de fils d'argent" ("tassel in black wool intertwined with silver thread"), "manteau en / brocard [sic] avec / un / immense / soleil / brodées [sic] en / fleur au / milieu" ("brocade coat with a huge sun embroidered like flower in the center").
1933.406

Exhibitions: Chicago 1933, No 13; Northampton 1934, No 13; San Francisco 1935; Paris 1939, No 90; Los Angeles 1939–40; Poughkeepsie 1940; Washington D.C. 1950–51; Edinburgh 1954, No 16; London 1954–5, No 19; Michigan 1957; Indianapolis 1959, No 70; New York 1965–6, No 19 (illustrated p 20; not shown in New York); Spoleto 1966; Strasbourg 1969, No 4; Hartford 1974; Hartford 1979; Columbus 1989; Worcester 1989.

Benois designed the two costumes for the Marquis, one in real life, the other in dreamland, to be as contrasting as possible, accentuated by the drawing of the two figures: the "real life" Marquis is an aged, gaunt, stooping man relying heavily on his stick, whereas the "dreamland" Marquis is upright, bold and regal.

In all his costume designs for *Le Pavillon d'Armide,* Benois made extensive annotations for the costumiers and, where words were inadequate, he made detailed marginal drawings. Although they are essentially working drawings, they are full of character and unmistakably purvey the intended atmosphere of the piece. There is also no doubt about when they were drawn; the Russian signature especially is a sign (or even a guarantee) that the drawings were made when stated.

Another, more finished, version of the design for the "real life" Marquis, without annotations, is in the Theater Museum in St Petersburg.

The inventory in the Astruc Papers (see note 33) describes the two costumes as follows:

Pavillon d'Armide
Boulgakow (Marquis)

1er costume
1 habit régence étoffe brochée bleue
1 gilet Louis XV satin crevette garni argent
1 collante étoffe noire
1 paire bottes velours noir
1 chapeau feutre noir Louis XVI
1 paire manchettes batiste avec guipure
1 cravate
2 foulards soie orange (de tête et de poche)

2e costume (en roi)
1 habit Louis XV satin crevette garni point d'Espagne et brandebourge d'argent avec pierreries
1 large pantalon velours coton noir pailleté
1 paire bottines drap d'or avec pierreries
1 coiffure fantaisie drap d'or et satin crevette
1 grand manteau à piérine en hermine avec traîne velours coton noir avec application peintes

1st costume
1 regency coat in blue brocade
1 Louis XV satin shrimp-colored waistcoat with silver trim
1 skin-tight vest in black cloth
1 pair black velvet boots
1 black felt hat Louis XVI
1 pair cambric cuffs with point-lace
1 cravat
2 orange silk scarves (head and pocket)

2nd costume (as king)
1 Louis XV satin shrimp-colored coat trimmed with Spanish stitch and silver frogs and loops with precious stones
1 pair wide black cotton velvet spangled trousers
1 pair gold brocade ankle boots with precious stones
1 fantastic gold brocade and shrimp-colored satin headdress
1 large cloak bordered with ermine with black cotton velvet train with painted decorations

When the drawings are compared with these inventory descriptions, we can see how accurately the costumiers interpreted them.

36 Costume design for members of King Hidraot's suite, scene 2

Graphite, black ink, tempera and/or watercolor, silver paint with white highlights on paper
17⁹⁄₁₆ x 12¹¹⁄₁₆ in: 44.5 x 32.2 cm
Signed twice bottom left and right in pencil: "Alexandre Benois"
Inscribed in pencil in French top right to bottom: "4 costumes pareilles / pour / la suite du Roi Hidraot" ("4 identical costumes for the suite of King Hidraot"), "plumes" ("feathers"), "plumes," "pattis / blanc / brodé d'or" ("white . . . embroidered with gold"), "perruque noir" ("black wig"), "noeud en / battiste [sic] agrementé / de dentelles / argent" ("knot in cambric embellished with silver lace"), "chemise battiste [sic]" ("cambric shirt"), "écharpe / en soie / blanche brodé d'argent" ("scarf in white silk embrodered with silver"), "doublure bleu [sic]" ("blue lining"), "robe en / taffeta / peinte de rouge / mauve et argent" ("taffeta dress painted red mauve and silver"), "fringe d'argent" ("silver fringe"), "pantalon à la / turque / en satin bleu / peint de bleu foncé / et paillettes d'argent" ("Turkish trousers in blue satin dyed dark blue with silver spangles"), "souliers argent" ("silver shoes")." Inscribed in pencil in French left from top to bottom: "couronne / de / perles" ("crown of pearls"), above pencil sketch detail: "motif des / agraffes [sic] / en argent / (passementerie)" ("design for silver clasps [trimmings]"), "pierre diamant" ("diamond stone"), "costume en / drap d'or / en argent or en / drap jaune brodé / d'argent" ("costume in gold cloth, silver, gold, yellow cloth embroidered with silver").
1933.399

Exhibitions: ? Chicago 1933, No 13; ? Northampton 1934, No 13; San Francisco 1935; Paris 1939, No 91; ? Los Angeles 1939–40; Edinburgh 1954, No 18; London 1954–5, No 21; Indianapolis 1959, No 69; Storrs 1963; New York 1965–6, No 20 (illustrated p 21; not shown in New York); Spoleto 1966; Princeton 1968; Strasbourg 1969, No 5; Amherst 1974; Hartford 1979; Hartford 1988; Worcester 1989.

The four members of the King's suite are hardly less regal than the King himself. The costumes are not listed in the inventory, but the drawing is nevertheless clearly of the same date.

These costumes, and others from *Le Pavillon d'Armide*, were used in 1922 for *Aurora's Wedding* in Paris after all the costumes for *The Sleeping Princess* had been sequestered in London (see Léon Bakst, pp 87–101).

37 Costume design for Tamara Karsavina as Armide, 1911

Graphite, tempera and/or watercolor, black ink, silver paint with white highlights, and brown ink notations on paper, mounted on board
16⅛ x 12¹⁵⁄₁₆ in: 41 x 32.9 cm
Unsigned and undated
Inscribed in pen, upper left: "Costume d'Armide / Pavillon d'Armide / pour Mlle [changed to 'Mme'] Karsavina"
Inscribed in pencil in French top left pointing to headdress: "saphires / entourés de / perles" ("sapphires surrounded by pearls"), "pierre / saphir" ("sapphire stone"), "satin." Inscribed in pencil in French right top to bottom: "diadème en métal ou en drap d'or sur / carcasse" ("diadem in metal or gold cloth on a frame"),"[?] esparte d'argent" ("[?] in silver"),"galon d'or" ("gold braid"), "dentelles

argent" ("silver lace"), "saphire," "revers satin crême" ("cream satin facings"), "[?] barrelet de perles" ("pearl [?]"), "battiste [sic]" ("cambric"), "dentelles" ("lace"), "echarpe en / gaze rose [word crossed out] / brodé de / bleu, argent, argent / et or (frange / or)" ("scarf in pink gauze embroidered with silver, silver and gold and gold [gold fringe]"), "frange or" ("gold fringe"), "tunique / de ballet / [illegible] / la robe" ("ballet costume [?] dress"). Inscribed in pencil in French right of detail drawing of clasp upper left: "motif des / agraffes [sic] drap / d'argent [word crossed out] / découpé et cousu / d'or" ("design of the clasps in silver cloth cut out and sown with gold"), "perle" ("pearl)." Inscribed in pencil in French left from top to bottom: "dentelle" ("lace"), "robe taffeta" ("taffeta dress"), "guirlande de fleurs / bleus (foncé), blanches / à feuilles d'or / se terminant à / la taille" ("garland of [dark] blue and white flowers with gold leaves finishing at the waist").
1933.400

Exhibitions: Chicago 1933, No 12; Northampton 1934, No 12; Hartford 1934b; New Haven 1935; Middletown 1935; New York 1937–8, No 700; Paris 1939, No 92 (illustrated p 4); ? Los Angeles 1939–40; Cambridge 1942; Edinburgh 1954, No 17; London 1954–5, No 20; Indianapolis 1959, No 71; New York 1965–6, No 21 (illustrated p 21; not shown in New York); Spoleto 1966; New York 1966–7; Princeton 1968; Strasbourg 1969, No 6; Amherst 1974; Hempstead 1974, No 28; Hartford 1974; Chicago 1975, No 2; Hartford 1979; Columbus 1989; Worcester 1989.

Illustration: Kirstein, p 185 No 345.

Benois redesigned Armide's costume for Tamara Karsavina when she danced the part at the first performance of Diaghilev's Ballets Russes in London, at the Royal Opera House, Covent Garden, on 21 June 1911. The other principal dancers on that occasion were as follows:

Viscount René de Beaugency: Adolf Bolm
Marquis of S—: Enrico Cecchetti
Baptiste: Serge Grigoriev
Confidantes of Armide: Elsa Will, Ludmilla Schollar, Bronislava Nijinska, Alexandra Vassilevska
The Favorite Slave: Vaslav Nijinsky.

This design is not to be confused with the costume Karsavina wore as one of Armide's confidantes in 1909; there is a photograph of her wearing that in her book *Theatre Street* (facing p 198). Another photograph of her wearing the same 1909 costume is reproduced in Arnold Haskell's *Diaghileff* (facing p 228) with the wrong caption "London, 1911"; Boris Kochno in *Diaghilev and the Ballets Russes* (p 27) makes the same mistake.

Benois's original costume for Pavlova as Armide in 1909 was also blue, in silk with applied silver lace, pearl spangles, and precious stones. Karsavina's actual costume for Armide in London, however, appears from illustrations to have been rather more heavily decorated with precious stones than is apparent in this design.

Fokine made this general interesting comment about the costumes. He writes, of course, as a choreographer, not a designer: "The problem of adapting style to the requirements of the dance Benois solved in the usual way. He designed highly authentic and beautiful costumes in the style of Louis XIV, and shortened them to knee length. I would have preferred to have dancers' costumes in style from head to foot, not in the upper part of the body only.

Part of the cast could have been in costumes of lighter weight, but still authentic—as, for example, those of the dancers of the waltzes and variations, which required 'ballet style' dancing and therefore a compromise costume."[36]

Notes

1 In an interview, published on 30 July 1908 in *Peterburgskaya Gazeta* (*The Petersburg Gazette*), Diaghilev also included Tchaikovsky's *Nutcracker* with Kshessinska in his plans, and in another interview, published on 1 October 1908 in *Teatr* (*Theatre*), he included Glazunov's *Raymonda* and Tchaikovsky's *The Sleeping Beauty*, as well as *Le Pavillon d'Armide* in both interviews.

2 Alexandre Benois, *Reminiscences of the Russian Ballet*, p 225.

3 Alexandre Benois, *ibid*, p 225. There is no lock of hair in a chest of drawers in the original story. The word "Gobelins" has also caused problems. Gautier described the tapestry as being "Beauvais," but Benois was not being specific: *gobelins* is the generic word in Russian meaning simply "tapestry."

4 Alexandre Benois, *op cit*, p 227. Vladimir Arkadievitch Teliakovsky was the last director of the Imperial Theaters from 1901–1917.

5 Sometimes also called *The Animated Gobelins*, but see note 3 above.

6 Quoted in Cyril Beaumont, *Michel Fokine and his ballets*, p 30.

7 Alexandre Benois, *op cit*, p 242.

8 Michel Fokine, *Memoirs of a Ballet Master*, p 109.

9 Alexandre Benois, *op cit*, p 262.

10 Alexandre Benois, *op cit*, p 243.

11 Quoted in Alexandre Benois, *op cit*, p 266.

12 Live sheep were brought in to replace the cardboard ones in St Petersburg. According to Prince Lieven in *The Birth of Ballets Russes*, p 89, the sheep were "stored underneath the stage and . . . forgotten. The poor animals died of hunger, and the pastoral scene had to be played without them."

13 Valerian Svetlov, *Le Ballet Contemporain*.

14 Alexandre Benois, *op cit*, p 291–2.

15 See No 33.

16 In France, the public dress rehearsal, treated like a gala performance, is considered to be as important as the official first night.

17 Richard Buckle, *Diaghilev*, p 141.

18 Ernest La Jeunesse, *Des soirs, des gens, des choses . . .*, p 46.

19 Quoted by Cyril Beaumont in *op cit*, p 45. *Boris* refers to *Boris Godunov* performed in the previous year, 1908, with Fedor Chaliapine in the title role.

20 Alexandre Benois, *op cit*, p 292.

21 Arnold Haskell, *Diaghileff*, p 212.

22 The dances from *Prince Igor* were performed almost every season, and were also the last item of the last performance in Paris by the Ballets Russes on 12 June 1929.

23 This design is illustrated in Alexandre Benois, *Reminiscences of the Russian Ballet*, facing p 292.

24 Alden Murray in "A Problematical Pavilion: Benois' First Ballet" in *Russian History*, p 33,

states that it was possibly inspired by "Rinaldi's 1764 toboggan pavilion at Oranienbaum".

25 Prince Peter Lieven, *The Birth of Ballets-Russes*, p 88.

26 *Apollon*, St Petersburg September 1910, facing p 28.

27 Alexandre Benois, *Reminiscences of the Russian Ballet*, p 288.

28 Tamara Karsavina, *Theatre Street*, p 197.

29 Bronislava Nijinska, *Early Memoirs*, p 270.

30 Richard Buckle, *Nijinsky*, pp 91, 95, and *Diaghilev*, pp 139, 141,

31 *Le Figaro*, 11 May 1909 quoted by Richard Buckle in *Nijinsky*, p 87.

32 Alden Murray, *op cit*, p 33. The inventory of sets and costumes was drawn up when Diaghilev offered them as collateral to the Société des Bains de Mer de Monte-Carlo in return for an urgently needed loan of 20,000 francs. (The inventory is not, however, in Diaghilev's handwriting as Murray states, but in Grigoriev's, the company manager, and a copy in typescript).

33 Astruc Papers (Folder 29), Dance Collection, New York Public Library. "Mmes Karsavina et Baldina / 2 corsages soie orange, broderies appliqués or / 2 jupes soie orange et tulle jaune, garnies the brodées application or, paillettes et pierreries / 2 jupons tarlatane jaune / 2 coiffures soie verte à plume d'autruche blanches / Mmes Smirnova et Fedorova / 2 corsages satin bleu, manches mousseline blanche garnis or / 2 jupes soie noirs et bleue, application or frange or / 1 jupon tarlatane et tulle blanc galonné or (manque 1) / 1 coiffure soie gris bleu avec guirlande de roses."

34 Richard Buckle, *Nijinsky*, p 106.

35 Alden Murray, *op cit*, p 34.

36 Michel Fokine, *Memoirs of a Ballet Master*, p 112.

Petrushka

Burlesque ballet in 1 act, 4 scenes by Igor
    Stravinsky and Alexandre Benois
Composer: Igor Stravinsky
Conductor: Pierre Monteux
Choreographer: Michel Fokine
Designer (sets and costumes): Alexandre Benois
Principal dancers:
    The Ballerina: Tamara Karsavina
    Petrushka: Vaslav Nijinsky
    The Moor: Alexandre Orlov
    The Showman:[1] Enrico Cecchetti
Company: Diaghilev's Ballets Russes
First Performance: 13 June 1911, Théâtre du
    Châtelet, Paris

Synopsis

Scene 1. Admiralty Square in St Petersburg, the
Butter Week (or Shrovetide) Fair in 1830. A crowd
is enjoying the fair. A drumroll heralds the appearance of the Showman from behind a curtained
booth. The curtains open to reveal three puppets:
a Moor, a Ballerina, and Petrushka. At a command
from the Showman, the puppets begin to dance.
The Moor and Petrushka are both in love with the
Ballerina. She prefers the Moor. Petrushka, jealous,
attacks the Moor. The Showman ends the performance. The puppets collapse motionless.

Scene 2. Petrushka's room. Petrushka is kicked
into the room by the Showman. He tries in vain to
escape. The Ballerina appears. Petrushka expresses
his love awkwardly. The Ballerina does not respond,
and leaves him alone in despair.

Scene 3. The Moor's room. The Moor, alone, is
happy playing with a coconut. The Ballerina enters
and dances to excite him. He embraces her.
Petrushka enters and threatens the Moor. He
chases Petrushka away.

Scene 4. Admiralty Square (the same as scene
1, but later). The crowd is still dancing. Suddenly
Petrushka rushes out of his booth chased by the
Moor brandishing a scimitar. The Moor stabs and
kills Petrushka. A policeman arrives, but the Showman picks up the body and to everyone's relief
shows that Petrushka was only a puppet. The
Showman is left alone, holding the puppet. As he
goes back toward the booth the spirit of Petrushka
appears above it, and threatens the Showman for
refusing to believe that he is not just a puppet.

While Stravinsky was finishing *The
Firebird* (see pp 212–16) he wrote that
he suddenly had the idea of a ballet based
on a pagan rite of elders watching a girl
dance herself to death. He described it to
his friend Nicolas Roerich and it was subsequently developed into *Le Sacre du Printemps* (*The Rite of Spring*; see pp 291–95). He
also described this theme of a ballet to
Diaghilev who immediately saw its potential. However, as Stravinsky himself
describes: "Before tackling the *Sacre du
Printemps*, which would be a long and
difficult task, I wanted to refresh myself by
composing an orchestral piece in which the
piano would play the most important
part—a sort of *Konzertstück*. In composing
the music, I had in my mind a distinct
picture of a puppet, suddenly endowed
with life."[2] Stravinsky called his puppet
Petrushka, the name of the "immortal and
unhappy hero of every fair in all
countries."[3]

When Diaghilev visited Stravinsky at
Clarens in Switzerland in the autumn of
1910 he heard this new work or, rather,
what became the second scene of *Petrushka*,
instead of parts of *Le Sacre du Printemps*
which he was expecting. He was delighted
and urged Stravinsky to develop it into a
whole ballet. Together, they worked out the
bones of the plot and agreed that the scene
of the action should be in St Petersburg
during one of the famous Butter Week fairs.
They also agreed to ask Benois to write the
scenario and design the sets and costumes.
They foresaw some difficulty in persuading
him to take on the work on account of his
extreme pique over the crediting of the
scenario of *Schéhérazade* to Bakst instead of
to him a few months earlier (see p 62), but
they thought, correctly, that his sympathy
for the idea of the new ballet would overcome his reluctance to work for Diaghilev
again. Benois describes his eager reaction to
Diaghilev's offer and how he began to see
the staging of the ballet: "Petrouchka,[4] the
Russian Guignol or Punch, no less than
Harlequin, had been my friend since my
earliest childhood . . . I immediately had the
feeling that 'it was a duty I owed to my old
friend' to immortalise him on the real stage.
I was still more tempted by the idea of
depicting the Butter Week Fair on the stage
. . . I suddenly *saw* how this ballet ought to
presented. It at once became plain that
Guignol-Petrouchka screens were not
appropriate to a stage performance . . . Once
the screens were abolished from the stage,
they had naturally to be replaced by a small
theatre. The dolls of this theatre would have
to come to life without ceasing to be dolls—
retaining, so to speak, their doll's nature.
The dolls should come to life at the command of a magician, and their coming to life
should be somehow accompanied by suffer-
ening. The greater the contrast between the
real, live people and the automatons who
had just been given life, the sharper the
interest of the action would be."[5] Diaghilev
was right in his supposition: Benois could
not resist the commission. He had designed
for Diaghilev in the previous two seasons
Les Sylphides and *Giselle*, two dreamily

romantic ballets, so now, as James Laver
wrote: "In *Petrushka* [sic] he had an opportunity of breaking away from his moonlit
groves and melancholy ghosts, and was
able to show how racily Russian it was
possible for him to be."[6]

Petrushka became Benois's most famous
work for the theater, and his highly successful original designs make any production of
the ballet almost unimaginable without
them. Between 1911 and 1958 Benois himself designed many productions all based
on his original designs; and it is still one of
the few Diaghilev ballets to be regularly
performed by companies throughout the
world. Yet, while saying in his *Reminiscences*
that he "continued to collaborate, actively
and harmoniously, in the creation of the
new ballet,"[7] he seems to have conveniently
forgotten that he almost did not design the
ballet at all because he wrote to Diaghilev
on 31 January 1911 that for financial reasons
he should stop working. He ended his letter
by writing: "You know you are dear to me,
and your project is dear to me, but it's
necessary, before it's too late, to part, to go.
I think, while it's not too late you can still
find a replacement for me who will finish
the production of *Petrushka*. Either Sapunov
or Sudeikine."[8] There is no record of
Diaghilev's reply, but he obviously persuaded Benois to continue working. The
scenario and the final score were finished in
Rome in the spring of 1911. Rehearsals,
under Fokine, also began in Rome while the
company was appearing at the Teatro
Costanzi.

Fokine described Stravinsky's difficult
music as "sounds tormenting the ear and
yet stimulating the imagination and stirring
the soul."[9] As usual he worked quickly, but
most of the dancers found the music incomprehensible and unsuitable for dancing.
Fokine admitted "that with Stravinsky's
music, composition cannot progress so
rapidly as with Chopin or Schumann. It was
necessary to explain the musical counts to
the dancers. At times it was especially
difficult to remember the rapid changes of
the counts," and "the mistakes made by the
dancers in counting retarded the progress of
the work."[10] But Fokine mastered the
unusual rhythms of Stravinsky's music and
eventually instilled them into his dancers.
Petrushka was an entirely original creation,
with Stravinsky and Benois providing the
means for Fokine to redefine the meaning of
ballet. Indeed, André Levinson said that

Petrushka was not a ballet at all, but a mime drama: "the dance is at no time treated as an end in itself, but is used as a means of psychological expression."[11] This applies particularly to the choreography for the doll puppets, the Ballerina, the Moor, and especially for Petrushka himself. The Ballerina and the Moor remain doll-like throughout, but Petrushka becomes almost human, because he falls in love. He tries to express himself, but to no purpose. *Petrushka* also gave Fokine the opportunity to put into effect one of the major principles for the production of ballet included in the statement he had submitted in 1904 to the Imperial Theaters for the reform of ballet. This was that "the group is not merely an ornament. The new ballet advances from the expressiveness of the face or the hands to that of the whole body, and from that of the individual body to groups of bodies and the expressiveness of the combined dancing of a crowd."[12] Stravinsky completely misunderstood Fokine's intentions when he criticized the crowd by saying: "it was a pity that the movements of the crowd had been neglected. I mean that they were left to the arbitrary improvisation of the performers instead of being choreographically regulated in accordance with the clearly defined exigencies of the music."[13] Although Fokine had some trouble with the French extras who were engaged to "fill out" the crowd and who found it difficult to convert themselves into convincing Russians, he did not neglect the movements of the crowd but deliberately choreographed them against the music which he used as a background accompaniment, almost as "muzak." This was an aspect of the production which did not go unnoticed by the critic of *The Dancing Times,* reviewing a later production, but one that was rehearsed by those who knew it well from the original: "To me one of the joys of the Russian Ballet is the remarkable way in which the choreographers treat the crowds. It is difficult to realise that the crowd of merry-makers who surround the booths in Admiralty Square, Petrograd, are going through a series of evolutions which they have rehearsed many times in the class-room and performed frequently in public. Everything comes so naturally, and there is an entire absence of those formal groupings with which the choreographer usually burdens his ballet."[14] From time to time, fitting in with the music, various groups from the regular company formed for popular dances which, according to Cyril Beaumont, were "full of variety and national character. Who can forget the hand-claps and lusty rhythmic stamps of the fat coachmen, the semi-stupid movements of the nurses, the frenzied dances of the gypsies . . . and the terrifying gestures of the masked revellers who pretend to frighten the women."[15] Fokine's manipulation of the crowd, individuals and groups, was one of the most original aspects of the choreography, and yet he wrote that he only had one two-hour rehearsal for the crowd scenes.[16]

Nijinsky, in the title role, must have felt some special empathy for Petrushka. His starting point, as with all his characterizations, was simply solving the technical problem of finding the right make-up. Once he had found it, he could begin to inhabit the mask he had created and transform himself into the individual character. Ottoline Morrell, who discussed the part of Petrushka with Nijinsky, wrote: "He said he made up in this part as an old traditional Russian figure—the mythical outcast in whom is concentrated the pathos and suffering of life, one who beats his hands against the walls, but always is cheated and left alone outside."[17] All commentators, including Stravinsky, have said that his interpretation has never been surpassed. "The perfection," wrote Stravinsky, "with which he became the very incarnation of this character was all the more remarkable because the purely saltatory work in which he usually excelled was in this case definitely dominated by dramatic action, music, and gesture."[18] The "incarnation" was accidental in the sense that it was not thought out by Nijinsky but instinctively acquired from Fokine's instructions. Fokine described working with him: "Nijinsky was not too strong musically and counting was a problem for him. On the other hand, he grasped the movements and their inner meaning, and therefore work with him always progressed pleasantly."[19] Although Fokine gave him the movements and their meaning, it required some other indefinable quality contributed by Nijinsky to transform them into that "insurpassability" with which so many observers credit him. Perhaps this is defined as Nijinsky's genius. As Prince Lieven wrote: "His unerring creative sense enabled him, in spite of his lack of rational intelligence, to create profound and completely satisfying dramatic images. And perhaps the most powerful and satisfying of all his parts was Petrushka."[20] One observer, Cyril Beaumont, who not only saw Nijinsky many times as Petrushka, but also saw many Petrushkas, stated that he never saw anyone approach Nijinsky's performance because "he suggested a puppet that sometimes aped a human being, whereas all the other interpreters conveyed a dancer imitating a puppet."[21]

As always before a first night, everyone concerned in the production was affected by an almost hysterical nervous tension, and Benois was affected more than the others, but with reason. The scenery for Petrushka's room, which had been painted in St Petersburg, was badly damaged while in transit to Paris, with most of the damage being suffered by the portrait of the Showman which was to have glared from the middle of one of the walls, constantly reminding Petrushka that he was in the Showman's power. Unfortunately, Benois could not repaint it himself as he was suffering from an abscess on his elbow. According to him. he accepted Bakst's offer to repaint the portrait "having no doubt that he would do it perfectly."[22] According to other versions, Diaghilev did not like the portrait and asked Bakst to repaint it. This may explain why Bakst repainted the Showman in profile instead of full face as in the original. At any rate, when Benois came to the theater and saw the new portrait he flew into a rage: "My fury expressed itself in a loud shout across the theatre . . . 'I shall not allow it! Take it down immediately! I can't bear it!' After which I flung my portfolio full of drawings on the floor and rushed out into the street and home."[23] Bakst's "retouching" added unbearable insult to injury, after the previous year when Benois had been ignored in favour of Bakst as the librettist of *Schéhérazade.* It also caused the final rift between Bakst and Benois. Bakst wrote to his wife on 28 May (10 June) 1911: "Benois and I have broken up for ever. You were right when you said that he was jealous of me. His behaviour towards me during these last two years and especially now in Paris has resulted in having to call (at his request) something like a court of arbitration, and unanimously Serov, Nouvel and Diaghilev said, 'Benois's behavior towards Bakst for the past year and a half has been scandalous . . .' I have put a cross to Shura [Benois], and, as always in such cases, will never return to him."[24] Valentin Serov[25] tried to patch things up by offering to repaint the portrait once again according to the original design, and even though he "executed it with touching diligence,"[26] he was unable to mollify Benois, who sent his resignation to Diaghilev, giving up his post of Artistic Director of the Ballets Russes.

NOTE
The usual chronological order of the drawings has been abandoned for this production in favor of a purely logical order.
Benois designed many productions of
Petrushka in many different countries, which
were all based on and had similarities to the
original 1911 production. He also made
many other drawings, especially of the first
scene and the costume designs for
Petrushka and the Ballerina, based on productions but unrelated to any of them, all of
which he almost invariably dated 1911, the
date of the first production, rather than the
date of execution.

**38   Set design for the Butter Week
        Fair, scenes 1 and 4**

Graphite, tempera and/or watercolor and crayon
    on paper
17¹¹⁄₁₆ x 24³⁄₁₆ in: 44.8 x 61.5 cm
Signed, and dated lower left in pen: Alexandre
    Benois 1911
1933.402

Exhibitions: Paris 1930, No 16; Chicago 1933, No
    14; Northampton 1934, No 14; New Haven
    1935; Middletown 1935; New York 1937–8;
    Boston 1938; Paris 1939, No 111 (illustrated p
    11); Williamsburg 1940; New York 1944;
    Edinburgh 1954, No 28; London 1954–5, No
    32; Michigan 1957; Sarasota 1958, No 5
    (illustrated p 68); Elmira 1958, No 13; Indi-
    anapolis 1959, No 71; New York 1962 (illus-
    trated p 16); Eindhoven 1964, No 26; Houston
    1965; New York 1965–6, No 22 (illustrated p
    22; not shown in New York); Spoleto 1966;
    New York 1966–7; Princeton 1968; Strasbourg
    1969, No 130; Frankfurt-am-Main 1969, No 39;
    Blommenholm 1971; Hartford 1973; Hartford
    1974; Hempstead 1974, No 30; Chicago 1975;
    New York 1976; Hartford 1978–9; New York
    1979; Basel 1984, No 58; Hartford 1988;
    Worcester 1989.

Illustrations: A. E. A., Jr., p 31; Bablet, p 36 No 41;
    Buckle 1955, p 50 No 57; Cogniat 1930, pl 2
    (color); Gontcharova, p 43; Haskell 1968, p 41;
    Kirstein, p 196 No 374; Lynham pl XXIV p 117.

This is not the original design for the set,
but a later, embellished variation. It was
almost certainly made after the production
had taken place and, since the signature is
not in Russian, made outside Russia. Most
of the elements in this painting were also
featured in the original version. Blue was
also generally the predominant color.

A common element in all the designs is
the false proscenium. A pen and ink drawing dated 1910, reproduced in Mark
Etkind's book,[27] is clearly the first sketch. It
already shows the false proscenium with
shuttered windows, with the *balagani*, temporary wooden structures housing various
fairground entertainments, arranged on the
stage with the little curtained theater in the
centre. The general arrangement is the same
in all drawings; the details differ.

A design captioned "Principal décor for *Petrouchka*" is reproduced in Benois's *Reminiscences*,[28] and is therefore presumably the correct version for the set. And yet it shows that the false proscenium is of clapboard whereas the original set is seen, from the photograph of the scene in the theater, to have a false proscenium with false windows and shutters as in this Lifar version. The scale, too, was different in the actual set, so that every element in the drawing appears to have more space than it really did on stage, caused largely by the marionette theater having to be wider than drawn in order to accommodate the three living "puppets."

The merry-go-round, shown in both the design and in the actual set, was a genuine one of horses of the time of Napoleon III acquired by the company at a fair. During the Company's tour of South America in 1917 it slipped off the unloading crane in Buenos Aires and fell irretrievably into the sea. It was also during this tour, on 26 September, that Nijinsky danced for the last time at the Colón Theater in *Le Spectre de la Rose* and *Petrushka*.

NOTE
The following three set designs are for the revival at Det Kongelige Theater (Royal Theater), Copenhagen, Denmark, on 14 October 1925 by the Royal Danish Ballet when the main credits were as follows:

Choreographer: Michel Fokine
Designer (sets and costumes): Alexandre Benois
Conductor: Georg Hoeberg
Principal dancers:
The Ballerina: Elna Hansen
Petrushka: Svend Aage Larsen
The Moor: John Andersen
The Showman: Karl Merrild

Above: the Butter Week Fair in scene 1, when the puppets are revealed in the booth. The scene on stage at the 1911 production, Théâtre du Châtelet, Paris.

39 Design for the front cloth (1925 Copenhagen production)

Black ink and tempera and/or watercolor on paper
11⁹/₁₆ x 15¹³/₁₆ in: 29.2 x 40.2 cm
Signed and dated bottom right in ink: "Alexandre Benois, 1925"
1933.405

Exhibitions: Chicago 1933, No 17; Northampton 1934, No 17; San Francisco 1935; Paris 1939, No 110 (described as being for 1911); Williamsburg 1940; Edinburgh 1954, No 27 (described as being for 1911); London 1954–5, No 31 (described as being for 1911); Elmira 1958, No 24; Indianapolis 1959, No 74; New York 1962, No 6; Eindhoven 1964; Hartford 1965, No 8; New York 1965–6, No 25 (illustrated p 23); Spoleto 1966; New York 1966–7; Princeton 1968; Strasbourg 1969, No 129; Frankfurt-am-Main 1969, No 38; Hartford 1973; Hartford 1974; Hempstead 1974, No 31; Hartford 1978–9; New York 1980; Coral Gables 1982; Basel 1984; Hartford 1988; Worcester 1989.
Illustrations: Bremser, vol I p 132; Oswald, No 6 p 17 (detail).

The design for this front cloth is different from the original one. The idea for this one, with its grotesque and menacing\figures flying through the sky above St Petersburg, goes back to Benois's first thoughts which he describes in his *Reminiscences*: "Petrouchka, the Russian Guignol or Punch, no less than Harlequin, had been my friend since my earliest childhood. Whenever I heard the loud, nasal cries of the travelling Punch and Judy showman: 'Here's Petrouchka! Come, good people, and see the Show!' I would get into a kind of frenzy to see the enchanting performance, which consisted, as did the *balagani* pantomimes, in the endless tricks of an idle loafer, who ends up by being captured by a hairy devil and dragged off to Hell."[29] The childhood recollection was very strong, and this is captured in the design of the grotesque creatures which is very childlike.

The original design for the front cloth of the snow-covered Fair in St Petersburg by moonlight was rejected by Diaghilev, because he wanted to emphasize the character of the Showman. In the cloth finally used for the first production, the Showman dominated the design.

40 Set design for Petrushka's room, scene 2 (1925 Copenhagen production)

Graphite, tempera and/or watercolor with white
  highlights, black ink, and brown ink notations
  on illustration board
12⁹⁄₁₆ x 19¼ in: 32.1 x 49 cm
Signed and dated bottom left in ink: "Alexandre
  Benois 1925"
Inscribed in ink bottom right: "La Chambre de
  Petrouchka"
1933.404

Left: Enrico Cecchetti as the Showman kicking
Vaslav Nijinsky as Petrushka into his room at the
beginning of scene 2. Scene from the original
1911 production at the Théâtre du Châtelet, Paris.

Exhibitions: New York 1933, No 8 (described as
  being for 1911); Chicago 1933, No 16;
  Northampton, No 16; San Francisco 1935; Paris
  1939, No 112 (described as being for 1911);
  Poughkeepsie 1940; Edinburgh 1954, No 29
  (described as being for 1911); London 1954–5,
  No 33 (described as being for 1911); Michigan
  1957; Indianapolis 1959, No 76; New York
  1962 (illustrated p 16); Eindhoven 1964, No 27;
  Hartford 1965, No 7; New York 1965–6, No 24
  (illustrated p 23); Spoleto 1966; New York
  1966–7; Strasbourg 1969, No 131; Frankfurt-
  am-Main 1969, No 40; Hartford 1974; Hartford
  1978-9; Basel 1984, No 59; Columbus 1989;
  Worcester 1989.
Illustrations: Bablet, p 37 No 42; Benois, facing
  p 334.

41 Set design for the Moor's room, scene 3 (1925 Copenhagen production)

Graphite, tempera and/or watercolor with white highlights, black ink, and brown ink notations on illustration board
12½ x 19³⁄₁₆ in: 31.9 x 48.9 cm
Signed and dated bottom left in ink: "Alexandre Benois 1925"
Inscribed in ink bottom lower right: "La Chambre du Negre"
1933.403

Exhibitions: New York 1933, No 9 (described as being for 1911); Chicago 1933, No 15; Northampton 1934, No 15; San Francisco 1935; Paris 1939, No 113 (described as being for 1911); Williamsburg 1940; Edinburgh 1954, No 30 (described as being for 1911); London 1954–5, No 34 (described as being for 1911); Michigan 1957; Indianapolis 1959, No 76; New York 1962 ; New York 1965–6, No 23 (illustrated p 23) (not shown in New York); Spoleto 1966; New York 1966–7; Princeton 1968; Strasbourg 1969, No 132 (illustrated No 30); Frankfurt-am-Main 1969, No 41; Hartford 1974; Hartford 1978-9; New York 1980; Allentown 1986; Columbus 1989; Worcester 1989.
Illustration: Benois, facing p 335.

The designs for Petrushka's room (or cell) and the Moor's room were intended as enlargements of their cells in the marionette theatre, to be seen like close-ups in a movie and in sharp contrast to each other. Petrushka's room is all claustrophobic cold black, with the portrait of the Showman glaring from the center of the wall symbolizing the powerful hold he has over the miserable and lonesome puppet, and the two painted devils protecting the door preventing escape. This design emphasizes the coldness by a skirting of ice-capped mountains and a frieze of billowing clouds. Petrushka is drawn as a gawky, lonely, frightened puppet. The original design was more stark: the walls were painted like a midnight sky with a new moon, no mountains, no clouds, and the controversial portrait (see photograph, opposite).

The Moor's room is like a red hot jungle with tigers and snakes peeping through blue and green palm trees, a captivating childlike image of Africa—friendly, not frightening. The Moor is drawn sitting on his tiger-skin divan with the Ballerina on his knees. The decoration of the walls of this scene was the most varied in all the produc-

tions Benois designed. In the original design, the trees were much more fantastical with huge hanging bunches of imaginary fruits and large camellia-like flowers above a wide skirting painted like a field with rabbits skippeting about hither and thither. The decoration on the door was not a snake but a six-point star. The original design was more charming.

The Copenhagen production was the third designed by Benois, the second being in 1920 for the Kirov Ballet in Petrograd. W. A. Propert thought that Benois's 1911 designs for *Petrushka* showed him "freed from all academic fetters leaping forward with the youngest of the moderns. Specially was this noticeable in the cells of the Moor and Petrushka where the fruit, flowers and animals in the one, and the sinister portrait of the magician in the other are as vivid and convincing as anything ever done by his successors of the newer school."[30] First ideas were best: the simplicity and directness of the original designs so appropriate to the straightforward but touching narrative were spoiled by over-elaboration in the designs for subsequent productions.

42 Costume design for Petrushka

Graphite, tempera and/or watercolor and silver
 paint on paper
17¾ x 12⁷⁄₁₆ in: 45 x 31.6 cm
Signed, lower right in pencil: Alexandre Benois
Inscribed upper right: "Petrouchka" / Paris, 1911
1933.407

Exhibitions: New York 1933, No 10; Chicago 1933,
    Nos 18–26 (not identified); Northampton 1934,
    Nos 18–25 (not identified); Hartford 1934b;
    New Haven 1935; Middletown 1935; San
    Francisco 1935-6; New York 1937–8; Paris
    1939, No 115 (illustrated p 11); Poughkeepsie
    1940; London 1954–5, No 36; Indianapolis
    1959, No 76; New York 1962 ; New York 1965-
    6, No 32 (illustrated p 24); Spoleto 1966; New
    York 1966–7; Princeton 1968; Strasbourg 1969,
    No 134 (illustrated No 28); Chicago 1975, No
    23; New York 1976; Hartford 1978–9; Coral
    Gables 1982; Basel 1984, No 60; Columbus
    1989; Worcester 1989.
Illustrations: Bremser, vol II p 1120; Haskell 1968,
    p 41; Kirstein, p 197 No 377; Percival, p 78;
    New York Times, 24 December 1965.

Benois derived his design for Petrushka's
costume from his childhood memories
of seeing itinerant performances in the
balagani (temporary wooden theaters) of the
Butter Week fairs. He remembered seeing
true pantomimes with the traditional characters of Pierrot, Harlequin, and Columbine.
Petrushka's costume is a combination of
Pierrot's customary white top with pom-

Below: Vaslav Nijinsky as Petrushka.

pom buttons and Harlequin's patchwork
trousers, with another memory of someone's pointed hat and tassel.

As this was probably the most famous
costume in the history of the Ballets Russes,
and as Nijinsky was for ever identified with
creating the part of Petrushka in the original
production, Benois repeated his costume
design in many different variations, often
inscribing a later version, whether it was for
a production or not, with "Nijinsky" and
"1911." This idiosyncrasy on his part makes

it difficult, if not impossible, to date all his
designs accurately. One of the clues is that
most of the early designs for *Petrushka* were
made in Russia and are therefore signed
and inscribed in Russian; most of these have
also remained in Russia.[31] This design,
rather brisk and mechanical, and somewhat
unusual in that the inscription does not
include the word "Nijinsky," was probably
made in the 1920s as a present for Serge
Lifar and is not a costume design for any
specific dancer. This is why I have not

included the name Nijinsky or any other dancer's name in the title of the drawing. Designs showing the puppet on a stand are also rare. Another version of this design (without the stand), belonging to Serge Lifar, was sold at Sotheby's, London on 9 May 1984, Lot No 9.

43   Costume design for Tamara Karsavina as the Ballerina

Graphite, tempera and/or watercolor, gold paint, and ink on paper
17⁷⁄₁₆ x 12½ in: 44.3 x 31.8 cm
Signed, lower right in pencil: "Alexandre Benois"
Inscribed upper right in pencil: "*Petrouchka* / Paris 1911 / La Balerine [sic] / pour / Mme Karsavina"
Inscribed in pencil round costume from top left clockwise: "peluche" ("plush"), "velours" ("velvet"), "tulle," "velours," "satin," "taffetas," "velour," "grosse dentelles (coarse lace)," "[illegible] les / [?] points teintés de noir / et agrémentés / d'un petit noeud" ("[?] points colored black and embellished with a small knot")
1933.408

Exhibitions: New York 1933, No 10; Chicago 1933, Nos 18–26 (not identified); Northampton 1934, Nos 18–25 (not identified); Hartford 1934b; New Haven 1935; Middletown 1935; Paris 1939, No 116; Edinburgh 1954, No 32; London 1954–5, No 38; Michigan 1957; Indianapolis 1959, No 79; New York 1962 ; Störrs 1963; Houston 1965; New York 1965–6, No 32 (illustrated p 25); Spoleto 1966; New York 1966–7; Princeton 1968; Strasbourg 1969, No 135; Chicago 1975, No 24; New York 1976; Hartford 1978–9; Basel 1984, No 61; Columbus 1989; Worcester 1989.
Illustrations: Bremser, illustrated vol II p 1120; Kirstein, illustrated p 197 No 378.

As I have noted elsewhere, Benois tended to date his designs for *Petrushka* with the date of the first performance not with the date of execution. So, in spite of the date written on this drawing, Benois made it for the revival of the ballet in 1926 when Karsavina again danced the part of the Ballerina; since there are instructions to costumiers, it is a genuine design for a remake of her costume. The fact that this design, unusually, also shows the Ballerina puppet on a stand as in the previous drawing for Petrushka, and that it is of similar size, suggests that they were both made at the same time.

There are as many versions of the design for the Ballerina as there are for Petrushka, but they are all very similar. The same hat, the same long-sleeved shirt and jacket, the same wide skirt and striped trousers with lace frill underneath appear in all the designs. The color, shades of red and mauve with blue, and the decorative details of the dress are also always the same. The only differences are in the features of the face, the tilt of the head, and the position of the arms.

Petrushka was revived again for two performances in Paris in December 1928 with Karsavina as the Ballerina. Grigoriev wrote: "Diaghilev was haunted by the memory of her *début* in this ballet with Nijinsky; and from that he was led to wonder whether, if Nijinsky were to be shown *Petrushka* again, it might not produce so strong an impression on his mind as perhaps to set him on the way to recovery. So, on 27 December, the unfortunate Nijinsky was brought to the Opéra, where, very gently, as if he were some precious object that might easily be broken, he was escorted by Diaghilev across the stage to a box."[32] Karsavina herself takes up the story: "'He is in good spirits to-night,' Diaghileff said, 'and seems to like watching the ballet. Wait for him on the stage.' It was the interval before *Petroushka* [sic], the scene set, the company ready to go on. For one moment I hoped that the familiar situation and myself in the costume in which he so often saw me dancing at his side might reclaim the lost thread of remembrance in the mind of Nijinsky."[33] But there was no spark of recognition; Nijinsky remained in his private world. It must have been the most poignant performance ever given by a ballet company.

44   Costume design for a policeman, scenes 1 and 4

Graphite and tempera and/or watercolor on paper
13¹¹⁄₁₆ x 8¾ in: 34.8 x 22.1 cm
Signed and dated lower right in pencil in Russian:
    "Александр Бенуа / 1911" ("Alexandre Benois / 1911")
Inscribed upper right in pencil in Russian:
    "квартальный" ("kvartalnii / non-commissioned police officer"), centre right: "25"
Inscribed on reverse in blue pencil in Russian:
    "В.А.Д." ("V.A.D.")
1933.413

Exhibitions: Chicago 1933, Nos 18–26 (not identified); Northampton 1934, Nos 18–25 (not identified); San Francisco 1935; Paris 1939, No 121; Washington DC 1950–1; Edinburgh 1954, No 36; London 1954–5, No 42; Indianapolis 1959; Hartford 1965, No 11; Houston 1965; New York 1965–6, No 30 (illustrated p 22) (not shown in New York); Spoleto 1966; New York 1966–7; Amherst 1974; New York 1976; Hartford 1978–9; Basel 1984, No 63; Hartford 1988; Worcester 1989.
Illustration: de Mille, p 140 (color).

Apart from the main characters, Benois, as writer of the scenario, invented all the other characters in the ballet as well. In the original programme the following characters were played by named dancers in the Ballets Russes company: Wet-nurses (9),[34] coachmen (5), stable boys (2), a roistering merchant (1), gypsies (without respect for the law or religion) (2), street dancers (2), organ-grinders (2), fairground barker

(1), telescope demonstrator (1). The rest of the crowd—made up of merchants, officers, soldiers, lords, ladies, children, maids, cossacks, policemen, and a bear trainer—was played by other Russian dancers and French extras. The first group had special dances choreographed for them, while the second group were given individual and characteristic movements.

These costume designs show the characters either in movement or in typical poses as if they are illustrations to a story. They were all made for the first production. Their very sketchiness gives them a kind of delightful dash.

Boris Kochno described the importance Diaghilev attached to some of these "extra" characters: "Because, in 1914, Massine made his debut with the Diaghilev company in the supporting role of the Policeman in *Petrouchka*, to Diaghilev's superstitious mind it became a matter of prime importance that new recruits to the company appear in this ballet. He was convinced that this secondary role brought luck to a dancer who was making his debut, that it guaranteed a brilliant future. When Anton Dolin and, later, Serge Lifar joined the Diaghilev company, he immediately cast them as extras in *Petrouchka*."[35]

45 Costume design for the water-seller, scenes 1 and 4

Graphite, tempera and/or watercolor, and ink notations on paper
12³⁄₈ x 9¼ in: 31.4 x 23.7 cm
Signed and dated lower right in pencil in Russian: "Александр Бенуа / 1911" ("Alexandre Benois / 1911")
Inscribed upper right in pencil illegibly in Russian
Inscribed on reverse in Russian: "В.А.Д." (V. A. D.)
1933.409

Exhibitions: Chicago 1933, Nos 18–26 (not identified); Northampton 1934, Nos 18–25 (not identified); San Francisco 1935; Paris 1939, No 119; Edinburgh 1954, No 38; London 1954–5, No 44; New York 1965–6, No 26 (illustrated p 22) (not shown in New York); Spoleto 1966; Amherst 1974; New York 1976; Columbus 1989; Worcester 1989.

46 Costume design for peasant women, scenes 1 and 4

Graphite and tempera and/or watercolor on paper
9¹⁵⁄₁₆ x 7³⁄₁₆ in: 25.2 x 18.3 cm
Signed in pencil in Russian bottom left: "А Б. со [illegible]" ("A. B. so [illegible]" "A[lexandre] B[enois] with [?]")
Inscribed upper right in pencil in Russian over previous erased and now illegible inscription: "Баба" ("Baba" "Peasant woman"), and lower right in Russian: "кратное" ("kratnoe" "multiple")
On reverse pencil sketch of man and house
1933.410

Exhibitions: Chicago 1933, Nos 18–25 (not identified); Northampton 1934, Nos 18–25 (not identified); San Francisco 1935; Paris 1939, No 118; Williamsburg 1940; Edinburgh 1954, No 40; London 1954–5, No 46; Elmira 1958, No 48; Rowayton 1960; New York 1965–6, No 26 (illustrated p 22) (not shown in New York); Spoleto 1966; Amherst 1974; New York 1976; Basel 1984, No 63; Hartford 1988; Worcester 1989.
Illustration: Kirstein, p 197 No 376.

47 Costume design for peasant men, scenes 1 and 4

Graphite and tempera and/or watercolour on paper
11⁷⁄₁₆ x 7¹³⁄₁₆ in: 29 x 19.8 cm
Unsigned and undated
Inscribed upper left and upper right in pencil in Russian erased: "No 34," "4 [illegible]"
Inscribed in pencil illegibly in Russian upper centre
On reverse inscribed in pencil: "No 45"
1933.411

Exhibitions: Chicago 1933, Nos 18–26 (not identified); Northampton 1934, Nos 18–25 (not identified); San Francisco 1935; New York 1937–8, No 702; Paris 1939, No 117; Williamsburg 1940; Washington DC 1950; Edinburgh 1954, No 39; London 1954–5, No 45; Michigan 1957; Elmira 1958, No 49; Hartford 1965; New York 1965–6, No 26 (illustrated p 22) (not shown in New York); Spoleto 1966; New York 1976; Hartford 1978–9; Columbus 1989; Worcester 1989.

48 Costume design for a woman, scenes 1 and 4

Graphite, tempera and/or watercolour, and silver and gold paint on paper
12³⁄₈ x 9¹⁄₈ in: 31.5 x 23.1 cm
Signed bottom left in watercolour in Russian: "Александр Бенуа с Т [illegible]" ("Alexandre Benois with T[illegible]")
Dated lower right in pencil: 1911
Inscribed right in pencil in Russian: "сукно" ("sukno" "cloth" [crossed out]) "парча" ("parcha" "brocade"), "бумага" ("bumaga" "cotton"), "30." Inscribed on reverse in blue pencil: "No 43," "В.А.Д.." ("V.A.D.")
1933.412

Exhibitions: Chicago 1933, Nos 18–26 (not identified); Northampton 1934, Nos 18–25 (not identified); San Francisco 1935; Paris 1939, No 120; Edinburgh 1954, No 37; London 1954–5, No 43; Michigan 1957; Elmira 1958, No 47; Hartford 1965, No 10; New York 1965–6, No 26 (illustrated p 22) (not shown in New York); Spoleto 1966; New York 1966–7; Hartford 1974; New York 1976; Hartford 1978–9; Columbus 1989; Worcester 1989.

Notes

1 This character is also sometimes referred to as the Charlatan or the Magician.
2 Igor Stravinsky, *Chronicle of My Life*, p 56.
3 Igor Stravinsky, *ibid*, p 57.
4 The French spelling.
5 Alexandre Benois, *Reminiscences of the Russian Ballet*, pp 324–6.
6 James Laver, "The Russian Ballet: A retrospect" in *The Studio* May 1927, p 307.
7 Alexandre Benois, *op cit*, p 328.
8 Alexandre Benois quoted in I. S. Zilberstein and V. A. Samkov, *Diaghilev*, Vol 2, p 114. Nikolai Sapunov (1880–1912) was a *World of Art* painter and theatre designer, as was Sergei Sudeikine, married to Vera Sudeikine who later became Stravinsky's second wife.
9 Michel Fokine, *Memoirs of a Ballet Master*, p 184.
10 Michel Fokine, *ibid*, pp 185, 186.
11 André Levinson, "Stravinsky and the Dance" in *Theatre Arts* Vol 8, New York, Nov 1924, p 744.
12 Quoted in Arnold Haskell, *Balletomania*, p 137.
13 Igor Stravinsky, *op cit*, pp 61–2.
14 The Sitter Out in *The Dancing Times*, London June 1919, p 363.
15 Cyril Beaumont, *Michel Fokine and his ballets*, p 81.
16 Michel Fokine, *op cit*, p 190.
17 Ottoline Morrell, *The Early Memoirs*, pp 227–8.
18 Igor Stravinsky, *op cit*, p 61.
19 Michel Fokine, *op cit*, p 186.
20 Prince Peter Lieven, *The Birth of Ballets-Russes*, p 146.
21 Cyril W. Beaumont, *Bookseller at the Ballet*, p 114.
22 Alexandre Benois, *op cit*, p 334 .
23 Alexandre Benois, *ibid*.
24 Quoted in I. S. Zilberstein and V. A. Samkov *Diaghilev*, p 189.
25 Serov painted his front cloth for *Schéhérazade* with Efimov at the end of May/beginning of June 1911 in Matisse's old studio-workshop which Bakst had arranged to rent for them. The cloth was first shown in Paris on 13 June 1911, on the same night as the first night of *Petrushka*. It continued to be shown until 1914, when Diaghilev said it had become too valuable to be used as a piece of scenery. Serov died on 22 November 1911 aged 46. (See also Léon Bakst p 64.)
26 Alexandre Benois, *op cit*, p 334.
27 Mark Etkind, *A. N. Benois i Russkaya Khudozhestvennaya Kultura (A. N. Benois and Russian Artistic Culture)*, p 263.
28 Alexandre Benois, *Reminiscences of the Russian Ballet*, facing p 330.
29 Alexandre Benois, *op cit*, p 324.
30 W. A. Propert, *The Russian Ballet in Western Europe*.
31 The original design (or one of the early designs) with the signature in Russian is illustrated in N. Lapshina's *Mir Iskusstva*, p 240,
32 Serge Grigoriev, *The Diaghilev Ballet*, pp 254–5.
33 Tamara Karsavina, *Theatre Street*, p 243.
34 "Nourrices," usually mistranslated as "Nursemaids."
35 Boris Kochno, *Diaghilev and the Ballets Russes*, p 69. Serge Lifar's first part in *Petrushka* was as the telescope demonstrator on 13 June 1923 at the Gaité-Lyrique, Paris.

Le Rossignol (The Nightingale)

Opera in 3 scenes by Igor Stravinsky and Stepan
 Mitusov, after the story by Hans Christian
 Andersen
Composer: Igor Stravinsky
Conductor: Pierre Monteux
Choreographer: Boris Romanov
Directors: Alexandre Benois, Alexander Sanine
Designer (sets and costumes): Alexandre Benois
Principal singers:
 The Emperor of China: Paul Andreev
 The Nightingale: Aurelia Dobrovolska
 Death: Elisabeth Petrenko
Company: Diaghilev's Ballets Russes
First Performance: 26 May 1914, Théâtre national
 de l'Opéra, Paris

Synopsis

Act 1. A forest by the sea. A fisherman sings in his
boat about the beauty of the Nightingale's song.
Then the Nightingale herself is heard. Her song is
interrupted by the arrival of the High Chamberlain,
the Cook, the Bonze (High Priest), and other
courtiers from the Emperor's palace. They invite the
Nightingale to sing to the Emperor in his palace.

 Act 2. The palace. The royal procession enters,
the Nightingale sings, and the Emperor, moved to
tears, offers it any honor it may desire. The bird
replies that it is honor enough to please the
Emperor. Three envoys from the Emperor of Japan
arrive, bringing a mechanical nightingale. When it
begins to sing, the real Nightingale flies away. The
Emperor of China is so angry that he banishes the
real Nightingale from his empire. The fisherman is
heard singing of the coming of death.

 Act 3. The Emperor is dying. He is watched
over by Death wearing the Emperor's crown and
accompanied by ghosts. The Emperor feebly calls
for his musicians. None comes, but the Nightingale
returns and sings so beautifully that Death and the
ghosts are chased away. When the courtiers arrive
to pay their last respects, they are astonished to
see the Emperor quite well again in all his splendid
robes. The fisherman proclaims that the song of
the Nightingale has conquered death.

Stravinsky began composing *The Nightingale* in 1908. At that time he was still
regularly seeing and discussing his work
with Rimsky-Korsakov, and later wrote: "I
remember with pleasure his approval of the
preliminary sketches."[1] But Rimsky-
Korsakov was never to hear the completed
work, because he died in June 1908. *The
Nightingale* was put to one side until the
summer of 1909 when Stravinsky finished
the first act. He then did no more work on
it until 1913 when he was asked by the Free
Theater of Moscow to finish it. By then he
had composed not only *The Firebird*, but
Petrushka and *Le Sacre du Printemps*[2] as well,
and his musical language had completely
changed. He therefore suggested that they
perform only the first act "as an indepen-

dent little lyrical scene,"[3] but they insisted
and eventually persuaded him to compose
the other two acts. Stravinsky worked on
the score through the winter of 1913–14, but
by the time he had finished the opera the
Free Theater had folded. Stravinsky then
offered it to Diaghilev instead who "jumped
at the chance" of producing it because he
had already engaged singers for other
operas.[4]

 In 1913 Gabriel Astruc, Diaghilev's
impresario in Paris, overstretched himself
when he built the beautiful new Théâtre des
Champs-Elysées, and went bankrupt. Sir
Joseph Beecham came to Diaghilev's aid by
offering to sponsor a season at the Theatre
Royal, Drury Lane, in London. But as
Beecham was more interested in opera than
ballet Diaghilev promised four new produc-
tions, *The Golden Cockerel* and *A Night in
May* by Rimsky Korsakov, *Prince Igor*[5] by
Borodin, and the first performance of
Stravinsky's *The Nightingale*. In an interview
as late as November 1913, Diaghilev is
quoted as saying that the program with *The
Nightingale* would also include Rimsky-
Korsakov's *Mozart and Salieri* with
Chaliapine singing Salieri in English, and
Schéhérazade with Chaliapine miming the
part of Shahriar.[6]

 Diaghilev was entirely unscrupulous in
so far as his productions were concerned—
that it is to say, he always strove fiercely
and unremittingly for the best, and second-
best was never good enough. Inevitably this
perfectionism led to explosive rows and
flaming quarrels, but as Haskell wrote:
"Diaghileff never allowed personal questions to interfere with the work he had
planned, never bore a grudge for any length
of time. One day he might quarrel, bitterly,
violently; insult and be insulted by his
opponent; but a week or two later the
whole matter would be forgotten, and he
would greet him with the remark, "What
about our collaboration?"[7] This is exactly
what he did with Benois when he asked
him to design *The Nightingale*. They had had
more than mere friendly tiffs in the past:
Benois had been deeply hurt by Diaghilev
on more than one occasion, most notably
about having been left out of the credits for
Schéhérazade (see pp 62–66), and about the
repainting of the portrait in *Petrushka* (see
pp 117–27). But when Diaghilev asked
Benois to undertake the design of *The
Nightingale* and *The Golden Cockerel* the latter
was beguiled and accepted, or, as he wrote

"after wavering slightly, I accepted
Diaghilev's proposal."[8] One of the reasons
he took the commission was because he saw
the possibility, with *The Golden Cockerel*, of
realizing an experimental idea he had had
for some time about the production of
opera, "to present an opera in which the
dramatic action should be entrusted completely to ballet artists, but the vocal element preserved."[9] Opera singers, he
thought, were usually hideous and (apart
from Chaliapine) incapable of acting, and
therefore made it impossible to believe in
the action of the opera. He wanted to hide
the singers, and use dancers, who were
usually good-looking and could move well,
to mime the action. Diaghilev, never one to
dismiss an experiment, approved of the
idea. "Our first plan," wrote Benois, "was to
place all the solo-singers and the chorus in
the orchestra, but on second thoughts it was
decided to follow my alternative suggestion—to place them on the stage itself and
turn their presence to decorative effect."[10]
Unfortunately, during the winter of 1913–14,
he was also very busy designing and directing Goldoni's *La Locandiera* (*The Innkeeper*)
for the Moscow Art Theater, and he decided
that he could not undertake both productions. According to him he was then
"deeply infatuated with the work of N. S.
Gontcharova,"[11] and suggested to Diaghilev
that she should be asked to undertake the
design of *The Golden Cockerel* while maintaining the method of production that they
had agreed upon. This does not ring quite
true, for nothing could be further from
Benois in spirit or in technique than
Gontcharova's work, and his sensibility was
totally opposed to hers. Benois probably
decided on his attitude to Gontcharova's
work only when he came to write his memoirs, as she was then a famous artist. It
seems more likely that Diaghilev saw
Gontcharova's gigantic exhibition of 768
works in Moscow in August 1913 and
approached her himself. Mary Chamot
supports such a view: "In choosing Goncharova as designer for the Paris production
of Rimsky-Korsakov's opera *Le Coq d'Or*
Diaghilev showed his usual artistic flair and
foresight. He was always one step ahead of
fashion by encouraging the latest movement
in art, even anticipating the next craze."[12]

 Benois concentrated instead on *The
Nightingale*. He described his ideas for the
design of the opera: "The sea and landscape
of the first act, the throne-room and the

golden bedroom in the Emperor's palace, gave me an opportunity to express all my infatuation with Chinese art. At first I hoped to keep to the style of the somewhat ridiculous Choinoiseries fashionable in the eighteenth century, but as the work advanced I became irritated by their insipidity. My love for genuine Chinese Art began more and more to permeate my production. My collection of popular Chinese colour-prints, which had been brought for me from Manchuria, served as valuable material for the costumes. The final result was a Chinoiserie *de ma façon*, far from accurate by pedantic standards and even, in a sense, hybrid, but undoubtedly appropriate to Stravinsky's music."[13]

In the end Benois thought that *The Nightingale* was one of his most successful productions, but he conveniently does not mention in his *Reminiscences* that he was so annoyed with Diaghilev that he might well not have finished his work. He wrote on 13 March 1914 complaining to his friend Valerian Svetlov that it was impossible to reach Diaghilev, and, after accusing him of being a grasping robber and charlatan, continued: "I could simply plead that Diaghilev has not fulfilled our contract (the terms were that I should have received ¾ of the agreed amount on delivery of the set designs, but so far I have not received a penny), and take away the designs, but I am just not in a position to decide to do that, for the simple reason that Diaghilev is after all 'Seriozha' and I can't sue him. But this is what I can do: if the execution of the sets and costumes for *The Nightingale* turns out to be disgraceful, then I'll just demand that my name is taken off the posters. From now on I consider that all the conditions of work are absolutely impossible, and so that is why I decline to take any further active part in the present business. Diaghilev does not want to listen to my (our) advice, and so let him devise a way of saving the situation. I will not concern myself with the scenic production (opera and ballet) until I receive the money that is already owed to me."[14] Recollections written much later are often unreliable, tempered to suit revised opinion, but the problem was presumably resolved (Diaghilev must have paid, at least something, at the last minute) and Benois finished the job.

The sets and costumes were all built and made in St Petersburg and, although paid for by Sir Joseph Beecham and the Drury Lane management on the understanding that the opera would be produced first in London, the scenery was all made to fit the Opéra in Paris. Diaghilev imperiously ignored the niceties of his contract and had the first night in Paris. How Diaghilev "succeeded in persuading 'his' Englishmen to consent to this remains a mystery."[15]

The opera was performed only twice in Paris, and four times in London. Coming as it did after the furore of *Sacre* in the previous year, *The Nightingale* did not cause much of a stir. Maurice Ravel, in an article, tried hard to defend and recommend *The Nightingale* by declaring it to be a "masterpiece," and "I can cite few theatrical works which have more moving passages than the last scene of *The Nightingale* . . . I believe I have never seen more perfectly harmonious sets and costumes. As a measure perhaps of his French origins, M. Alexandre Benois blends a delicate taste with the asiatic splendor of his compatriots."[16] In London, the *Daily News* thought that "the scene in the Emperor's palace, with the gold-clad ruler on a very lofty throne, surrounded by courtiers in every conceivable kind of gorgeous robe, is a masterpiece of stage effect. The scene and costumes place M. Benois on a level with the other artists who have done so much to make the Russian Ballet memorable in the annals of art, and to make Drury Lane the rendezvous of all the distinguished painters in London."[17] This critic seems to have forgotten Benois's earlier productions *Le Pavillon d'Armide*, *Giselle*, and *Petrushka*. Drury Lane may indeed have been a "rendezvous" for painters, but unfortunatley it did not always look after their work: because Beecham had paid for them, the sets and costumes for *The Nightingale* were put in store in the cellars of the theater, where most of them perished during the war. (See also Henri Matisse *Le Chant du Rossignol*, pp 257–61.)

49 Costume design for a Chinese guard

Graphite, tempera and/or watercolor, and ink, with brown ink notations on paper
19¹⁵/₁₆ x 14⅛ in: 50.7 x 35.8 cm
Signed and inscribed, lower right in pencil: "A mon cher ami Sert (To my dear friend Sert) / Alexandre Benois"
Illegible erased inscription upper left includes number "4"
1933.414

Provenance: José-Maria Sert
Exhibitions: Chicago 1933, Nos 27–8 (not identified); Northampton 1934, Nos 27–8 (not identified); San Francisco 1935; Paris 1939, No 127; Poughkeepsie 1940; Williamsburg 1940; Edinburgh 1954, No 58; London 1954–5, No 68; Michigan 1957; Richmond 1959; Rowayton 1960; New York 1962; New York 1965–6, No 15 (illustrated p 19); New York 1966–7; Princeton 1968; Strasbourg 1969, No 288 (illustrated No 55; exhibited as being for the later ballet *Le Chant du Rossignol*); Frankfurt-am-Main 1969, No 69; Hartford 1974; Basel 1976; Hartford 1988; Worcester 1989.
Illustrations: Zilberstein and Samkov, No 100; Buckle 1955, p 80 No 101 (shown hanging on a wall with the following design).

T his design was for four costumes. As with all the costume designs for this production it was adapted by Benois from a collection of drawings in his possession. He changed the color to suit the general palette of the production, which was based on ultramarine and cobalt blues combined with yellow and gold. Benois's *chinoiserie* was based on the Russian perception of it at the end of the eighteenth century which is particularly evident in Oranienbaum and Tsarskoe Selo.

Twelve other costume designs are reproduced in the 1914 Souvenir Program.

This design was given by Benois to José-Maria Sert, the Spanish artist, who was responsible for designing the sets for Richard Strauss's *The Legend of Joseph*[18] in the same season (Léon Bakst designed the costumes). Sert was the first non-Russian artist to be commissioned by Diaghilev to design a production, and was chosen, according to Diaghilev, because he was "a specialist in architecturally decorative work, in other words in the sphere necessary for Richard Strauss's sets." For the Ballets Russes, Sert also designed the costumes for *Las Meninas*[19] and sets and costumes for *Le Astuzie Femminili* (see pp 311–14).

50 Costume design for a Chinese woman

Graphite, tempera and/or watercolor with white highlights, gold paint, and ink with brown ink notations on paper
18 x 11⁷/₁₆ in: 45.8 x 29 cm
Inscribed and signed lower left: "A Madame / Misia Edwards / Patronne des Ballets russes / souvenir d'amitié / et de gratitude (To Madame Misia Edwards, patron of the Ballets Russes, as a token of friendship and gratitude) / Alexandre Benois"
Inscribed upper left in pencil: "Autres dames / [illegible] (Other women [?])"
1933.415

Provenance: Mme Alfred Edwards
Exhibitions: Chicago 1933, Nos 27–8 (not identified); Northampton 1934, Nos 27–8 (not identified); San Francisco 1935; Paris 1939, No 128; Williamsburg 1940; Edinburgh 1954, No 59; London 1954–5, No 69; Richmond 1959; New York 1962; Houston 1965; New York 1965–6, No 16 (illustrated p 19) (not shown in New York); New York 1966–7; Princeton 1968; Strasbourg 1969, No 289; Frankfurt-am-Main 1969, No 70; Hartford 1988; Columbus 1989; Worcester 1989.
Illustrations: Buckle 1955, p 80 No 101 (shown hanging on a wall with previous design); Hartford Symphony 97/98 Season Prospectus, p 13 (color).

B enois gave this design to Misia when she was married to her second husband, the owner of the newspaper *Le Matin*; it was a marriage of convenience, as he was conveniently rich enough for her to be a significant patron of the Ballets Russes and to be able "yearly to perform conjuring tricks to help Serge [Diaghilev] accomplish the miracle of making both ends meet."[20] Polish, née Godebska, her first husband was Thadée Natanson, owner and publisher of *La Revue Blanche*, and her third was the painter José-Maria Sert (see pp 311–14).

Jacques-Emile Blanche exaggerated only slightly her importance in Diaghilev's life: "José-Maria Sert and his wife, Misia Godebska, were closely associated with Diaghileff's ventures. Indeed, she was called 'the godmother of the Russian ballets' just as Diaghileff called me the 'godfather.' It was her taste that decided whatever Diaghileff undertook, and he never embarked upon a production without her sanction. She was an amateur musician and painter, and one of the Parisians whose portrait everyone had painted—among them Toulouse-Lautrec, Renoir, Bonnard, and Vuillard."[21]

Misia Sert was present at Diaghilev's death in Venice in 1929, and arranged his funeral.

Notes

1 Igor Stravinsky, *Chronicle of my life*, p 43.
2 Stravinsky always favored the French title which had been given to the work by Léon Bakst (see pp 291–95).
3 Igor Stravinsky, *op cit*, p 87.
4 Andreev and Petrenko were engaged to sing in *Prince Igor*, and Dobrovolska and Petrenko in *The Golden Cockerel*.
5 Although the dances in Act 2 were well known and very popular, Diaghilev had not previously given the whole opera.
6 Interview in *Teatr* (*Theater*), dated 27 November 1913, quoted in I. S. Zilberstein and V. A. Samkov, *Diaghilev* Vol 1, p 234.
7 Arnold Haskell, *Diaghileff*, p 272.
8 Alexandre Benois, *Reminiscences of the Russian Ballet*, p 353.
9 Alexandre Benois, *ibid*, p 354.
10 Alexandre Benois, *ibid*, p 356.
11 Alexandre Benois, *ibid*, p 356.
12 Mary Chamot, *Goncharova*, p 14.
13 Alexandre Benois, *op cit*, p 359.
14 Quoted in I. S. Zilberstein and V. A. Samkov, *op cit* Vol 2, pp 199–200.
15 Prince Peter Lieven, *The Birth of Ballets-Russes*, p 203.
16 Maurice Ravel, "Les Nouveaux Spectacles de la Saison 1914" in *Collection des plus beaux numéros de Comoedia Illustré*, 1914 Season.
17 *Daily News* 19 June 1914, quoted in Nesta Macdonald, *Diaghilev Observed*, p 118.
18 First performed on 14 May 1914 at the Opéra, Paris.
19 Composed by Gabriel Fauré, first performed on 25 August 1916 at the Teatro Eugenia-Victoria, San Sebastian, Spain.
20 Misia Sert, *Two or Three Muses*, p 133.
21 Jacques-Emile Blanche, *Portraits of a Lifetime*, p 262.

Giselle ou Les Wilis (Giselle or the Wilis)

Fantastic ballet in 2 acts by Théophile Gautier,
    Vernoy de Saint-Georges, and Jean Coralli
Composer: Adolphe Adam
Conductor: Henri Büsser
Choreographers: Jean Coralli and Jules Perrot,
    revived by Nicolas Serguéev
Designer (sets and costumes): Alexandre Benois
Principal dancers:
    Giselle: Olga Spessivtseva
    Albrecht: Albert Aveline
    Berthe, Giselle's mother: Blanche Kerval
    Hilarion: P. Raymond
    The Prince of Courland: Ryaux
    Wilfrid, Albrecht's equerry: Serge Peretti
    Countess Bathilde: Olga Soutzo
    Myrtha, Queen of the Wilis: De Craponne
First Performance of revival: 26 November 1924,
    Théâtre national de l'Opéra, Paris

Created on 28 June 1841 at the Opéra (Théâtre de
    l'Académie Royale de Musique), Paris
Conductor: François Habeneck
Choreographers: Jean Coralli and Jules Perrot[1]
Designer (sets): Pierre Ciceri
Designer (costumes): Paul Lormier
Principal dancers:
    Giselle: Carlotta Grisi
    Albrecht: Lucien Petipa
    Berthe, Giselle's mother: Mlle Roland
    Hilarion: M Simon
    The Prince of Courland: M Quériau
    Wilfrid, Albrecht's equerry: Jean Coralli
    Bathilde: Mlle Forster
    Myrtha, Queen of the Wilis: Adèle Dumilâtre

Synopsis

Act 1. A village on the Rhine at vintage time. Giselle lives in a cottage with her mother. Opposite is Albrecht, Duke of Silesia, posing as Loys, a villager. Hilarion, a gamekeeper in love with Giselle, appears just as Albrecht, in peasant dress, emerges from his cottage with Wilfrid, his squire. Giselle dances with Albrecht while Hilarion watches jealously. Village girls join them. Giselle's mother, Berthe, warns her that she will dance herself into her grave. Hearing the horn of an approaching hunting party, Albrecht leads the girls to their work in the vineyard. Giselle and her mother return to their cottage. Hilarion, alone, steals into Albrecht's cottage and comes out carrying a cloak and sword which he carries away. The villagers return, and Giselle joins them in their festivities. At the height of their celebrations the Prince of Courland arrives with his daughter, Bathilde, and other huntsmen. Giselle confides that she is betrothed and the Princess also admits that she is betrothed. The Princess, charmed by Giselle, puts her necklace round her neck. Hilarion then shows Giselle the cloak and sword. Albrecht appears and is recognized by the Princess as her fiancé. Giselle recoils from the knowledge that he is not the villager Loys. The unhappy Giselle seizes the sword and tries to stab herself, but Albrecht prevents her. But grief has unhinged her mind, and pitifully she begins to dance the steps they danced so happily together until, more and more frenzied, she falls dead at Albrecht's feet.

Act 2. The tomb of Giselle. A party of huntsmen arrive seeking refuge. Hilarion joins them. A clock strikes midnight and the darting lights of the will-o'-the-wisps drive Hilarion and the huntsmen away. Myrtha, the Queen of the Wilis, a ghost-like figure, glides out of the shadows. Wilis are the ghosts of betrothed girls who have died before their marriages and, unable to rest, seek their revenge. Myrtha calls her band together to welcome a new member. They summon Giselle, who rises from her grave, and they dance away. They return with Hilarion whom they have trapped and drive him into the lake. Now Albrecht, bearing lilies, comes grief-stricken to Giselle's grave. He follows her ghostly form which appears before him. The Wilis return and the Queen commands Giselle to lure Albrecht into the dance which will mean his death. Giselle pleads for him in vain but they continue to dance. At four o'clock the Wilis must vanish, for they are powerless as day breaks. Giselle rejoices that Albrecht has been saved, and sinks into her tomb. Albrecht follows her but before he reaches the tomb she has vanished and he, in despair, falls to the ground. Wilfrid, his faithful servant, finds him fallen by the grave.

Giselle has been performed more or less continuously in one country or another with most of the same music and much of the original choreography for over a hundred and fifty years. No other ballet has such long-lived distinction. The story is rather silly, the music is undistinguished, the choreography is often dull, and yet it touches some deep sentiment in everyone. Giselle is the essence of Romanticism, and somehow we can all still be enraptured by "sighing swains and midnight graveyards."[2] Not yet all devoured by cynicism, we can still be made to believe in simplicity and innocence. Alicia Markova, a renowned and exquisite Giselle, explained that she "takes care of Albrecht because she really loves him. That's very simple, and that's a constant that everybody understands."[3] Furthermore, the part of Giselle, as Nicholas Dromgoole pointed out, "has become the touchstone against which ballerinas are judged. A ballerina who cannot convince in Giselle is somehow seen as not having quite made the grade."[4]

Théophile Gautier (1811–72) had the idea for the ballet when he was reviewing Heinrich Heine's book De l'Allemagne and came across a passage describing the Wilis. This was reprinted in the scenario of the ballet: "There exists a tradition of nocturnal dancing known in Slav countries under the name of Wili. Wilis are fiancées who have died before their wedding day; these poor young creatures cannot remain at peace in their graves. In their extinguished hearts and lifeless feet remains that love of danc-ing which they could not satisfy in their lifetime. At midnight they rise up and gather together in groups on the high road, and pity the young man who meets them, for he must dance with them until he falls down dead. Dressed in their wedding gowns, with garlands of flowers on their heads, and brilliant rings on their fingers, the Wilis dance in the moonlight like elves; their faces, though white as snow, are beautiful in their youthfulness. They laugh with such treacherous joy, they lure you so seductively, they look so sweetly inviting, that these lifeless Bacchantes are irresistible."[5] This gave Gautier the material for the second act of his ballet but, not being an experienced librettist, he approached Jules Henri Vernoy, Marquis de Saint-Georges, to help him set it in an appropriate context. The first act is therefore almost certainly all by Saint-Georges. Their synopsis was accepted by Léon Pillet, the director of the Opéra, within three days. Gautier probably showed the synopsis to Jules Perrot (1810–92) in the hope of attracting, through him, Carlotta Grisi (1819–99), his mistress, to create the part of Giselle. According to Cyril Beaumont, "it is easy to imagine how such a subject would have appealed to his lively imagination and sensitive feeling for dramatic situations."[6] Perrot, in turn, approached Adam who persuaded Pillet to postpone another ballet of his, La Jolie Fille du Canal, in order to produce Giselle instead, for which he would write the music within a week.[7] Perrot was not credited with any of the choreography in the original program because Coralli was already employed by the Opéra as resident choreographer. However, Pillet accepted Perrot's services as well in view of his relationship with Grisi. This is confirmed by Adam, who wrote in a letter the day after the first performance to Vernoy de Saint Georges: "Perrot has arranged all his wife's [sic] pas and has performed his task with real talent."[8] There is no doubt that the ballet was the work of both choreographers. It was immediately a huge success and remained in the repertory at the Opéra in Paris where it was regularly performed until 1868.

Giselle was first performed in Russia on 18 December 1842 at the Bolshoi Theater in St Petersburg in a version copied from Paris. Jules Perrot himself worked in St Petersburg from 1848 to 1859, and Giselle was among the ballets he produced. It was a completely new production as Perrot, hitherto an anonymous choreographer, was now in sole charge. According to the historian Natalia Roslavleva: "He considerably strengthened the dramatic action of the ballet, deepened Giselle's mad scene, and made all the secondary characters more convincing."[9] Perrot's first Giselle in St Petersburg was Fanny Elssler in 1848, but she proved wrong for the part. In 1850 Perrot again produced the ballet successfully with Carlotta Grisi, the original creator, during her tour in St Petersburg. This was the version which was regularly performed in Russia, and passed down the generations through Marius Petipa.

Alexandre Benois, who saw this version in 1885, remembered: "The sets on that occasion were old and shabby and so were the costumes; the part of Giselle was taken by the unattractive, long-limbed and bony Gorshenkova,[10] who was not favoured by the management because she did not draw a public. Her movements were angular and clumsy and she lacked the charming *naïveté* the part demands. But in spite of all this, the performance moved me so deeply that the memory of it has remained fresh to this day. This, my first impression of *Giselle*, was not wiped out even after I had seen it perfectly performed by Pavlova, Karsavina and Spessiva. When, in 1910, I insisted that *Giselle* should be included in the programme of the second season of our ballets, it was chiefly my youthful memories of the matinée in 1885 that prompted me to do so."[11] Indeed, it was audacious of Diaghilev to take this French ballet to Parisian audiences. Even though they had ignored it themselves for a long time, they did not take too kindly to being shown up by some Russians, and received it with indifference. They would have much preferred more performances of *Schéhérazade*. Of all Diaghilev's collaborators at the time, it was natural that Benois should undertake the design as he was both most in sympathy with the central-European Romantic spirit, and the most respectful of tradition. The production was intended as a recreation rather than a new version. The Perrot–Petipa version had survived through a combination of memory and regular performance. Benois, however, felt that "although the version used undoubtedly bore the stamp of a certain tradition, it was far from being in keeping with the style of 1840. Yet it would, I felt, have been highly interesting to see this ballet—faded yet eternally fresh—in the form in which it had been presented to its contemporaries, Théophile Gautier and Adolphe Adam."[12]

In 1924 Jacques Rouché (1862–1957), director of the Paris Opéra, decided to revive *Giselle* for the first time since 1868 as part of the celebrations commemorating the fiftieth anniversary of the present building designed by Charles Garnier. His decision was possible only because a dance score of the Mariinsky Theater version[13] was in the possession of Nicolas Sergeyev, former stage director of the Russian company, who had emigrated to Paris.

After the Revolution, Alexandre Benois stayed in Russia, where he was director of the graphic arts department at the Hermitage Museum, until the autumn of 1923 when Diaghilev, anxious to renew his old friendship, commissioned him to design two operas by Gounod—*Le Médecin malgré lui* and *Philémon et Baucis*.[14] Rouché then also decided to invite Benois to design *Giselle*, believing correctly that his temperament suited the ballet. Indeed, Benois clearly still retained the same feelings about *Giselle* because his designs for this later production resemble those he made for 1910. They are discussed below.

There are two conflicting accounts as to how Olga Spessivtseva came to dance the name part in Paris. She had first danced Giselle, with Pierre Vladimirov as Albrecht, on 30 March 1919 at the Mariinsky Theater when "the tremendous ovation that greeted the end of the ballet left no doubt in the minds of those who witnessed it that they had seen a unique and perfect interpretation . . . Olga was rivalled by no-one, not even Pavlova or Karsavina. Indeed, she had surpassed them both in the extraordinary pathos of her mime in the first act and her unbelievably ethereal dancing in the second."[15] So wrote Anton Dolin, and he added that "*Giselle* was going to be revived specially for her after her triumph in Russia."[16] In other words, she was simply invited by Rouché.

The other account is by Serge Lifar which, in view of the existing documents, is undoubtedly more accurate or, rather, more complete. Lifar states that Diaghilev had invited Spessivtseva to rejoin his company in 1924. She had had a great personal success dancing Aurora for him in *The Sleeping Princess* in London during the winter of 1921–2 (see pp 87–101), after which she had returned to Russia. Diaghilev now felt that his company needed strengthening and set about trying to engage a number of new dancers, among whom was Spessivtseva.

He wrote to Lifar some time in July 1924 from Monte Carlo: "Spessivtseva has arrived in Paris, and Boris [Kochno] is having talks with her, but she is behaving badly, putting on airs, like a true 'star' . . . moreover she got her visa through me, but for three years they didn't let her into France."[17] She was no doubt "behaving badly" at the time because Léon Bakst, out of spite for Diaghilev with whom he had finally separated over *Mavra* (see pp 318–22), was trying hard to persuade her to work for Rouché instead. Besides, Bakst was infatuated with Spessivtseva, albeit in a platonic way. Lifar quotes two letters Bakst wrote to Spessivsteva.[18] In the first, dated 2 June 1924, Bakst wrote, after reviling Diaghilev personally: "The dancing in his company is beneath criticism, and the productions monstrously lack taste. That's why he needs you. As always he has money behind him and, above all, he will do all he can to tie you up for a long period. It would—my dear, wonderful and noble, but not very practical, Olia[19]—be a great mistake on your part to sign a contract for more than one or two months . . . A. Levinson has told me that Rouché, of the Grand Opéra, is ready to sign a contract with you now, and this would not be a mistake, because once you have conquered the Opéra (and such a conquest is respected differently from that of the Théâtre des Champs-Elysées), you will be able to have a more solid hold over them both, Rouché as much as D[iaghilev]. He is prepared to do anything to take you away from Rouché, because D's ballet is in a real mess just now, in terms of true ballet. The dancing that goes on there would never have been tolerated even in the Theater in Warsaw. On the other hand, the classical dancing and the *corps de ballet* at the Opéra at the moment are excellent. So, dear Olia, wait a few days. There will probably be a telegram from Rouché, or at least I will write to you again." In the second letter, dated 28 June 1924, Bakst wrote: "I am hurrying to say that I have had a fairly long and decisive interview with Rouché. The outcome is that he wants very much to sign a long term contract with you. He asks if you would write to him setting out your conditions because he does not know whether to engage you for one year, or by the production. I advise the contract for a year; but you have to specify what he can present from your repertoire, apart from new ballets . . . I could not tell Rouché exactly what your roles were. I only know *The Sleeping Beauty* and *Giselle*, but I was not

sure if you dance *La Fille mal Gardée*." The upshot was that Spessivtseva, persuaded by Bakst, danced for Rouché and not for Diaghilev in 1924.

Anton Dolin quotes from a letter by Mme Salamon in which there is a moving description of the devastating effect of Spessivtseva's dancing, not in performance, but in rehearsal, without costume, without make-up, watched by the writer from just a few feet away: "We had arrived towards the end of the first act and for the first time Olga Spessivtseva mimed and danced before the entire corps the famous *scène de folie*, in a silence that was so profound that the rehearsal room seemed more like a church in its solemn and holy atmosphere of religion. At the end of this wonderful scene of ballet no one moved, a deathly quiet prevailed. The agony and sorrow of the lost love that she had so almost terrifyingly recalled in her mime and action kept us all transfixed, motionless, except for the tears in our eyes . . ."[20]

51   Set design for Act 1: a village on the Rhine

Graphite, tempera and/or watercolor, and brown ink on illustration board
19⅞ x 25 in: 48.7 x 63.6 cm
Signed and inscribed, lower right in ink: "Alexandre [overpainted] Benois 7 X 1924 [and two illegible overpainted words]"
Inscribed on back in Benois's hand in ink: "N8 / Décor de l" Acte I / de / "Giselle" (première idée). / pour l" Opéra de Paris"
1933.417

Exhibitions: Chicago 1933, No 29; Northampton 1934, No 29; San Francisco 1935; Poughkeepsie 1940; Williamsburg 1940; New York MoMA, 1944a; Minneapolis 1953; Elmira 1958, No 12; Richmond 1959; Hartford 1964; New York 1965–6, No 33 (illustrated p 26); New York 1966–7; Spoleto 1966; Princeton 1968; Strasbourg 1969, No 76 (illustrated No 6); Frankfurt-am-Main 1969, No 21; Hartford 1974; Hartford 1979; Hartford 1988; Worcester 1989.
Illustrations: Amberg, pl 2; Goode 1939, between pp 118–9 (color).

In the twentieth century, the problem facing any designer of *Giselle*, or any other "museum" piece, is to devise a plausible evocation of the period in which the original was created while avoiding the temptation of pastiche because taste and fashion now are so different from then. Benois's impeccable taste, as well as his knowledge and understanding of an earlier period, were probably thought to be enough to

ensure a successful resolution to this problem with *Giselle* at the Opéra in 1924. In my opinion, Benois failed because he tried too hard to avoid pastiche.

The original libretto is vague about the setting for act one. All it says is: "The scene represents a pleasant valley in Germany. At the back of the stage are hills covered with vines, and a mountain road leading to the valley."[21] There is one further clue at the beginning of the description of the action: "Hilarion appears, looks about him as if searching for someone; then he lovingly points out Giselle's cottage, and angrily that of Loys."[22] It is also made clear that both cottages have to have practical doors. There is no specific indication of period or time, but as it is vintage time it must be early autumn, perhaps September.[23]

The original setting by Ciceri, as interpreted by an engraving, was published in *Les Beautés de l'Opéra* in 1844. It shows two thatched cottages, each shaded by the branches of a tree growing next to them. The branches meet above the center, creating a leafy canopy. Between the cottages a road winds back past smaller trees toward the vine-covered hills. In the far distance, on top of a rocky hill, stands a castle. The romantic, rustic atmosphere is bright and cheerful. Two figures, Giselle and Albrecht, are shown dancing in the foreground.

By contrast, Benois's set for this act is doom-laden. The castle, perched on a craggy, inaccessible rock, dominates the scene against a stormy sky. The two cottages are like paupers' huts, not pretty, and that of Loys is almost a ruin. The trees are starkly scraggy with leafless branches. No vines are tended here, no vines would even grow. This setting is wrong: the beginning should not so obviously anticipate the tragedy at the end.

Benois himself must have thought he was overdoing the doom, because he painted another version for the same production which is reproduced in Prince Lieven's *The Birth of Ballets-Russes*.[24] In this design the trees have more leaves, there are no scraggy fir trees, the sky is not so stormy, there is another castle behind the tree center right, the cliffs are gentler, and the cottages, especially the one on the right, are not so dilapidated. There are also two figures in the foreground, Giselle and Albrecht, recognizable by their costumes. This modified, and more successful, design, made after the Lifar version which is acknowledged to have been only the "first idea," was the one used in the production.

52 Set design for Act 2: within a forest glade

Graphite, tempera and/or watercolor, and ink on illustration board
18⁷/₁₆ x 24⁵/₁₆ in: 46.7 x 61.7 cm
Signed and inscribed center in ink: "Alexandre Benois 1924 Giselle Acte II"
1933.416

Exhibitions: Chicago 1933, No 30; Northampton 1934, No 29a; San Francisco 1935; Paris 1939, No 98 (exhibited as being for *Giselle* 1910); Williamsburg 1940; Cambridge 1942; New York 1944; Michigan 1957; Richmond 1959; New York 1965–6, No 34 (illustrated p 26) (not shown in New York); New York 1966-7; Spoleto 1966; Princeton 1968; Strasbourg 1969, No 77; Amherst 1974; Hartford 1974; Hartford 1979; Hartford 1988; Worcester 1989.
Illustrations: Beaumont, p 112 (as being for the 1910 production); Palmer, p 11.

The original libretto has much fuller instructions about act two than act one:

"The scene represents a forest by the banks of a pool. A damp and cool spot where rushes, reeds, clumps of wild flowers and water plants grow; birch trees, aspens, and weeping willows bow their pale foliage. To the left, under a cypress tree, stands a white marble cross on which is carved the name 'Giselle.' The grave is almost buried under a thick growth of grasses and wild flowers. The blue glimmer of a very bright moon lights this set with a cold and misty appearance."[25]

The engraving for this act, after the setting by Ciceri, also published in *Les Beautés de l'Opéra* in 1844, shows that he followed the instructions to the letter. Indeed, according to Beaumont, he had been over-zealous for "this setting was carried out in the realistic style then in vogue, and the stage must have been rather crowded for, in connection with his scheme, the designer used some 200 bullrushes and 120 branches of flowers with their leaves."[26]

Benois, quite the contrary to his avowed intention to reproduce the original design as closely as possible, has ignored the instructions in every detail except the cross and the "blue glimmer" of moonlight. His flora are quite incorrect; there is no feeling of dense vegetation—indeed, it appears to be deep midwinter. The pool is hardly noticeable. But the most serious fault is the introduction of the small, ruined church in the center of the backcloth. Not only is this completely irrelevant, but its illuminated presence disastrously detracts attention away from the cross. The romanticism inherent in this scene is quite lacking in this design. On the other hand, the critic André Tessier was flattering in the usual French way: "Above all we relished his set for the second act: under huge dark trees, the vista on a blue night, the tragic poetry of a moon-beam bathing the stones of the cemetery and the inevitable ruins of a monastery church."[27]

53   Costume design for Olga Spessivtseva as Giselle, Act 1

Graphite, tempera and/or watercolor, ink, and silver paint on paper
9⁹⁄₁₆ x 6³⁄₁₆ in: 24.3 x 15.8 cm
Signed and dated bottom left in ink: "Alex. Benois 1924"
Inscribed top left in ink: "*Giselle* / Giselle"
Inscribed in pencil upper left: "A[ct]. 1"
Inscribed in pencil round body clockwise from top right: "satin," "faille" ("coarse grained silk"), "satin avec / dentelles d'argent" ("satin with silver lace"), "taffetas," "velours" ("velvet"), "velours."
1933.420

Exhibitions: ? New York 1933[28]; Chicago 1933, Nos 31–37 (not identified); Northampton 1934, Nos 30–37a (not identified); San Francisco 1935; Paris 1939, No 103 (exhibited as being for *Giselle*, 1910); Williamsburg 1940; Cambridge 1942; New York 1944; Washington D.C. 1950–1; Michigan 1957; Richmond 1959; Storrs 1963; Hartford 1964; New York 1965–6, No 37 (illustrated p 27) (not shown in New York); Hartford 1966; Spoleto 1966; New York 1966–7; Princeton 1968; Amherst 1974; Hartford 1979; Columbus 1989; Worcester 1989.
Illustrations: Beaumont 1944, facing p 68; Beaumont, p 113; Goode 1939, between pp 118–9 (color).

There are no precise indications of either period or dress in the original libretto of *Giselle*, but in his costume designs Benois wanted to be faithful to the tradition initiated by Lormier for the first production in 1841 while interpreting that tradition in his own style. Benois therefore almost certainly looked at Lormier's designs and read his notes which are preserved in the Bibliothèque de l'Opéra. He also looked at other contemporary illustrations.

Benois first considered the problem of designing *Giselle* in 1910 when he made the production for Karsavina and Nijinsky and the Ballets Russes. He subsequently wrote in his *Reminiscences*: "When it came to the costumes I became suddenly afraid that my idea of resuscitating old scenic images would be thought retrogressive and ridiculous, or a proof of the poverty of my imagination. I therefore decided, as a compromise, not to make use of the piquant possibilities of deliberate 'lack of taste.' Nijinsky's was the only costume I designed in exactly the correct style—the so-called troubadour style."[29]

By 1924 Benois was no longer afraid of "resuscitating old scenic images." All his costumes are much closer to the original in spirit while having none of their "stagey" elaborations. He managed to maintain a convincing naturalistic simplicity, with a muted palette of browns and various shades of blue, which was totally appropriate to the rustic realism of the first act. Thus his costume for Giselle is a "tasteful" and more naturalistic version of the costume originally worn by Carlotta Grisi.[30] The naturalism did not, however, extend to the choice of materials: the original bodice of brown velvet was perhaps more natural than Benois's blue silk.

In act two the ethereal quality of all the Wilis was enhanced by their having longer skirts than was shown in the design, as can be seen in the photograph of Spessivtseva. In fact, this follows the original instruction more closely which specifies a "low-necked white dress reaching to the top of the calf."[31] Benois's "Hamlet style" costume for Albrecht in act two in black velvet seems more appropriate than the original "jerkin of primrose velvet embroidered in gold."[32]

Giselle

Les Wilis

J.

Graphite, tempera and/or watercolor, silver paint, and ink with brown ink notations on paper
9⅝ x 6¼ in: 24.3 x 15.9 cm
Signed and dated bottom left in ink: "Alex. Benois / 1924"
Inscribed top left in ink: "*Giselle* / Les Wilis / [in pencil] J"
Inscribed in pencil round costume clockwise from top right: "courronne [sic] de myrthes [sic]" ("wreath of myrtle", "la jupe / légèrement / paillettée [sic] de / grosses paillettes" ("the skirt lightly spangled with large spangles"), "satin / recouvert de tule [sic]" ("satin covered with net"), "Le reste Mlle Craponne / 2 Willis [sic]. / 24 (?) Willis [sic]. / Giselle en Willis [sic]," "Des voiles / [word crossed out] pour / tout le monde" ("veils for everyone")
1933.426

Exhibitions: ? New York 1933; Chicago 1933, Nos 31–37 (not identified); Northampton 1934, Nos 30–37a (not identified); San Francisco 1935; Paris 1939, No 109 (exhibited as being for *Giselle*, 1910); Michigan 1957; New York 1965–6, No 43 (illustrated p 27); Spoleto 1966; New York 1966–7; Princeton 1968; Strasbourg 1969, No 80; Hartford 1974; Hartford 1979; Hartford 1988; Worcester 1989.
Illustrations: Beaumont 1944, facing p 68; Beaumont, p 113; Palmer, p 13.

All the designs are drawn in Benois's characteristically classical, traditional manner showing the figures in various poses. Although his drawing is quite sketchy, the figures are full of verve; all, that is, except the design for the Wilis which, perhaps significantly, gave Benois some trouble. The line is unsure and has been redrawn several times. Nineteen other costume designs for this production from Lifar's collection were sold at Sotheby's, London on 9 May 1984.

Right: Olga Spessivtseva as Giselle in act 2.

56 Costume design for Albert Aveline as Albrecht, Act 2

Graphite, tempera and/or watercolor, ink, and
   brown ink notations on paper
9⅝ x 6¼ in: 24.4 x 15.6 cm
Signed and dated lower right in ink: "Alex. Benois /
   1924"
Inscribed top left in ink: "*Giselle* / Albrecht sur la /
   Tombe / de / Giselle / [in pencil] C"
Inscribed top right in pencil: "Mr. Aveline," and
   round costume clockwise from top right:
   "faille" ("coarse grained silk"), "velours"
   ("velvet"), "Nanson / soie"
1933.425

Exhibitions: ? New York 1933; Chicago 1933, Nos
   31–37 (not identified); Northampton 1934, Nos
   30–37a (not identified); San Francisco 1935;
   Paris 1939, No 108 (exhibited as being for
   Giselle, 1910); Cambridge 1942; Richmond
   1959; Hartford 1964; New York 1965–6, No 42
   (illustrated p 27; not shown in New York);
   Spoleto 1966; New York 1966–7; Hartford
   1974; Hartford 1979; Hartford 1988; Columbus
   1989; Worcester 1989.
Illustrations: Beaumont, p 113; Goode 1939,
   between pp 118–9 (color).

55 Costume design for Albert Aveline as Albrecht, Act 1

Graphite, tempera and/or watercolor with white
   highlights, and ink on paper
9½ x 6⅜ in: 24.2 x 16.2 cm
Signed and dated bottom left in ink: "Alex. Benois /
   1924"
Inscribed upper left in ink: "*Giselle* / Albrecht / [in
   pencil] B. bis"
1933.421

Exhibitions: ? New York 1933; Chicago 1933, Nos
   31–37 (not identified); Northampton 1934, Nos
   30–37a (not identified); San Francisco 1935;
   Paris 1939, No 104 (exhibited as being for
   Giselle, 1910); Poughkeepsie 1940; New York
   1944; Washington D.C. 1950–1; Michigan
   1957; Richmond 1959; Storrs 1963; Hartford
   1964; New York 1965–6, No 38 (illustrated p
   27; not shown in New York); Spoleto 1966;
   New York 1966–7; Princeton 1968; Hartford
   1979; Columbus 1989; Worcester 1989.

57 Costume design for Blanche Kerval as Berthe, Giselle's mother, Act 1

Graphite, tempera and/or watercolor with white highlights, ink, and brown ink notations on paper

9⅝ x 6¼ in: 24.5 x 15.7 cm

Signed and dated bottom right in ink: "Alex. Benois / 1924"

Inscribed top left in ink: "*Giselle* / Berthe / (La mère de / Giselle) / [in pencil] E." ; upper right in pencil: "Mme. Kerval"

Inscribed round costume clockwise from top right: "toile" ("linen"), "chemise" ("shirt"), "lainage / velours" ("wool / velvet"), "rubicane" ("horse, black flecked with white"), "toile," "borderie [?sic] / de / laine" ("wool border")

1933.424

Condition: average. Support is brittle and discolored with mat burn and surface soil. Ink and pigments are abraded and flaking, exhibiting some losses.

Exhibitions: ? New York 1933; Chicago 1933, Nos 31–37 (not identified); Northampton 1934, Nos 30–37a (not identified); San Francisco 1935; Paris 1939, No 107 (exhibited as being for *Giselle*, 1910); Washington D.C. 1950–1; Hartford 1964; New York 1965–6, No 41 (illustrated p 27; not shown in New York); Spoleto 1966; New York 1966–7; Hartford 1979; Columbus 1989; Worcester 1989.

58 Costume design for P. Raymond as Hilarion, Act 1

Graphite, tempera and/or watercolor, silver paint, ink, and brown ink notations on paper

9½ x 6¼ in: 24 x 15.9 cm

Signed and dated bottom left in ink: "Alex. Benois / 1924"

Inscribed top left in ink: "*Giselle* / Hilarion. / [in pencil] H."

Inscribed in pencil round costume clockwise from upper right: "drap" ("cloth"), "drap," "drap," "cuir" ("leather"), "toile" ("canvas"), "fourrure" ("fur")

1933.422

Condition: average. Support is brittle and discolored with mat burn, light damage and surface soil; abrasions; fraying, tears and losses at corners. Flaking, abrasions and losses to ink and tempera.

Exhibitions: ? New York 1933; Chicago 1933, Nos 31–37 (not identified); Northampton 1934, Nos 30–37a (not identified); San Francisco 1935;

Paris 1939, No 105 (exhibited as being for *Giselle*, 1910); Michigan 1957; Richmond 1959; Hartford 1964; New York 1965–6, No 39 (illustrated p 27; not shown in New York); Spoleto 1966; New York 1966–7; Hartford 1979; Columbus 1989; Worcester 1989.
Illustration: Beaumont 1944, facing p 68.

59   Costume design for Giselle's friends, Act 1

Graphite, tempera and/or watercolor, silver paint, ink, and brown ink notations on paper
9⁷/₁₆ x 6¼ in: 23.9 x 15.9 cm
Signed and dated bottom left in ink: "Alex. Benois / 1924"
Inscribed top left in ink: "*Giselle* / Les amies / de Giselle / [in pencil] N / *V. dos* / 6 ?"
Inscribed in pencil round costume clockwise from upper right: "flannelles blancs et / argent" ("white and silver flannel"), "(en revenant des / vendanges / elles portent des / couronnes de / feuilles de vigne et / des raisins" ("returning from grape picking they wear wreaths of vine leaves and grapes"), "crêpe de chine," "velours," "taffetas," "satin," "taffetas," "velours," "marron / bis" ("greyish brown")
1933.423

Exhibitions: ? New York 1933; Chicago 1933, Nos 3137 (not identified); Northampton 1934, Nos 3037a (not identified); San Francisco 1935; Paris 1939, No 106 (exhibited as being for *Giselle*, 1910); Washington D.C. 19501; Michigan 1957; Richmond 1959; Hartford 1964; New York 19656, No 40 (illustrated p 27; not shown in New York); Spoleto 1966; New York 19667; Princeton 1968; Hartford 1979; Columbus 1989; Worcester 1989.

60   Costume design for a lady, Act 1

Graphite, tempera and/or watercolor, silver and gold paint, and ink on paper
9⁷/₁₆ x 6¼ in: 24 x 16 cm
Signed and dated lower left in ink: "Alexandre / Benois / 1924"
Inscribed top left in ink: "*Giselle* / Une Dame / [in pencil P"
Inscribed in pencil round costume clockwise from top center: "Battiste [sic]" ("cambric)", "satin / et / perles," "lainage / fin" ("fine wool"), "velours," "satin [crossed out] / taffetas," "lainage"
1933.418

Exhibitions: ? New York 1933; Chicago 1933, Nos 31–37 (not identified); Northampton 1934, Nos 30–37a (not identified); San Francisco 1935; Paris 1939, No 101 (exhibited as being for *Giselle*, 1910); Williamsburg 1940; Michigan 1957; Hartford 1964; Houston 1965; New York 1965–6, No 35 (illustrated p 27; not shown in New York); Spoleto 1966; New York 1966–7; Strasbourg 1969, No 78; Hartford 1979; Columbus 1989; Worcester 1989.
Illustration: Palmer, p 12.

61 Costume design for peasants, Act 1

Graphite, tempera and/or watercolor, ink, and
  brown ink notations on paper
9⅛ x 6⅛ in: 23.1 x 15.5 cm
Signed and dated bottom left in ink: "Alex. / Benois
  / 1924"
Inscribed top left in ink: "*Giselle* / Paysans / [in
  pencil] L bis"
Inscribed in pencil left of costume from top to
  bottom: "fourrure," "drap," "drap [crossed out]
  / toile," "drap," "et l'autre / moitié / comme ça"
  ("and the other half like this") and on right of
  costume: "drap"
1933.419

Exhibitions: ? New York 1933; Chicago 1933, Nos
  3137 (not identified); Northampton 1934, Nos
  3037a (not identified); San Francisco 1935;
  Paris 1939, No 102 (exhibited as being for
  Giselle, 1910); Poughkeepsie 1940; Washington
  D.C. 1950¹; Michigan 1957; Richmond 1959;
  Storrs 1963; Hartford 1964; New York 1965⁶,
  No 36 (illustrated p 27; not shown in New
  York); Spoleto 1966; New York 1966⁷; Prince-
  ton 1968; Strasbourg 1969, No 81; Frankfurt-
  am-Main 1969, No 23; Amherst 1974; Hartford
  1979; Columbus 1989; Worcester 1989.

1 Perrot was not credited in the original program.
2 Arnold Haskell, *Balletomania*, p 69.
3 Alicia Markova quoted in Ismene Brown,
  "Giselle? Join the queue" in *The Daily Telegraph*,
  London 26 October 1994.
4 Nicholas Dromgoole, "Love means never being
  able to say you're happy" in *The Sunday Telegraph*, London 4 February 1995.
5 Henri Heine, "Tradition Allemande" in de Saint-
  Georges *Giselle ou Les Wilis*, p 4.
6 Cyril Beaumont, *The Ballet Called "Giselle"*, p 22.
7 According to Cyril Beaumont, *ibid*, p 55, Gautier
  wrote "less than a week," and Adam, in unpublished memoirs, wrote "eight days" in one place
  and "three weeks" in another.
8 Quoted from a letter published in Serge Lifar,
  Ballet Traditional to Modern, pp 233–4.
9 Natalia Roslavleva, *Era of the Russian Ballet*, p 65.
10 Maria Gorshenkova, 1857–1938.
11 Alexandre Benois, *Reminiscences of the Russian
  Ballet*, p 69.
12 Alexandre Benois, *ibid*, p 317.
13 Notated after the Stepanov system, published in
  Paris in 1891, adopted in St Petersburg 1893, and
  in Moscow in 1895. With this system Sergeyev
  brought twenty-one classics out of Russia. Now
  no longer used.
14 *Le Médecin malgré lui* first performed 5 January
  1924, and *Philémon et Baucis* first performed 10
  January 1924, both at Monte Carlo.
15 Anton Dolin, *The Sleeping Ballerina*, p 18.
16 Anton Dolin, *ibid*, p 36.
17 Letter undated, quoted in I. S. Zilberstein and
  V. A. Samkov, *Diaghilev* Vol 2, p 138.
18 Léon Bakst letters, quoted in French in Serge
  Lifar, *Les Trois Grâces*, pp 240–4.
19 Diminutive of Olga.
20 Letter from Mme Colette Salamon, quoted in
  Anton Dolin, *op cit*, p 38.
21 Saint-Georges, *Giselle ou Les Wilis*, p 9.
22 Saint-Georges, *ibid*, p 9.
23 Vintages in Germany can go on late into the
  year, especially for *eiswein* when the grapes are
  picked after the first frosts. Most wine festivals
  are in August or September.
24 Prince Peter Lieven, *The Birth of Ballets-Russes*,
  reproduced facing p 83. In this book the illustration is included in the chapter on 1909 back to
  back with a reproduction of Benois's design for
  Pavillon d'Armide. The misleading assumption is
  that the design for *Giselle* is for the 1910 Ballets
  Russes production, whereas the date "1924" is
  clearly visible beside the signature.
25 Saint-Georges, *Giselle ou Les Wilis*, p 14.
26 Cyril W. Beaumont, *The Ballet called "Giselle"*,
  p 60.
27 André Tessier, *L'Oeuvre*, Paris, Winter 1924–5.
28 This note applies to Nos 53–61. Some costume
  designs were exhibited as No 11 but it is not
  possible to identify which or how many.
29 Alexandre Benois, *Reminiscences of the Russian
  Ballet*, p 317.
30 Engraving by H. Robinson after the painting by
  A. E. Chalon reproduced in Cyril Beaumont, *The
  Ballet called "Giselle"*, facing p 65.
31 Quoted in Cyril W. Beaumont, *The Ballet called
  "Giselle"*, p 66.
32 Cyril W. Beaumont. *ibid*.

Christian Bérard

*French
born 1902 Paris
died 1949 Paris*

Night

Ballet in 1 act by Boris Kochno
Staged as scene 26 of 30 in *Charles B. Cochran's
    1930 Revue*
Composer: Henri Sauguet
Conductor: Charles Prentice
Choreographer: Serge Lifar
Designer (set and costumes): Christian Bérard
Principal dancers:
    The Lady: Alice Nikitina
    The Man with the Bag: Constantin
        Tcherkas
    The Cripple: Nicolas Efimoff
    The Man with the Sack: Richard
        Domonsky
    Woman in window: Sipha Treble
    Woman in cart: Peggy Cartwright
    Her coachman: Edward Coventry
    A Harlequin: K.L. Prince
    A Baker: Serge Lifar
    A Child: Freddie Springett
First Performance: 4 March 1930, Palace Theatre,
Manchester

First performance at the London Pavilion,
    27 March 1930
With Nicolas Efimoff as a Harlequin and André
    Verdi as the Cripple

Synopsis

From the London program:
    "The Scene is Paris at dawn, and the figures
who first appear are symbolic of the early workers,
relieved by a tragic silhouette of Harlequin returned
to his garret. There enters a young baker, bearing
on his shoulders a child. The Scene is next occupied
by a rich woman coming home from a ball. She
and the young baker are mutually attracted. But
between them is a perpetual barrier, represented
by a semi-transparent wall, on either side of which
men vainly beckon. We may call the curtain Fate,
Chance, Reality, as we will—its significance is the
same—the symbol of thwarted desire. Finally the
wall descends completely, shutting out both man
and woman from all hope of romance."

When Diaghilev died on 19 August 1929
the Ballets Russes died with him. The
distraught company, left leaderless, floun-
dered in tears and tried to persuade Serge
Lifar and Boris Kochno to assume command. Lifar, Diaghilev's latest star, and
Kochno, his trusted confidant and manipu-
lator, who had both been with Diaghilev in
Venice when he died, considered their
position but finally concluded not to continue the company. They issued an "act of
abdication" (see Appendix C) which they
both signed but which, incomprehensibly,

was wrongly dated 5 August instead of 5
September. "We do not want to take on the
responsibility of carrying on Diaghilev's
work," they wrote, and left all their colleagues to fend for themselves.[1]

Lifar and Balanchine were both
approached by Jacques Rouché, Director of
the Paris Opéra, with an offer to participate
in a production of Beethoven's *Les Créatures
de Prométhée* (see pp 306–10) as part of the
centenary commemoration, two years late,
of the composer's death. At the same time
they were both engaged by Charles
B. Cochran, the flamboyant English impresario, to take part in his forthcoming *1930
Revue*. Lifar's version of the events, flattering himself, is at variance with the facts, as
is so often the case with his published
statements. Reading Lifar it would seem
that he took all the initiatives: "A few days
after my interview with Jacques Rouché, I
met Cochran. We had a very commonplace
business conversation about my appearing
in his London review [sic]. I was to be paid
£200 a week (in those days that was a large
sum) in addition to my rights in the choreography of a short ballet I agreed to direct.
It was called *La Nuit* and I advised him to
ask Sauguet for the music, Bérard (one of
Diaghilev's last discoveries) for the décors
and Kochno for the book. My contract with
Cochran bound me for ten months in
1930."[2] Sauguet and Kochno had been
responsible for the music and book of *The
Cat* produced by Diaghilev in 1928; Bérard,
now living with Kochno, had been ignored
by Diaghilev.

The three stars of the revue were Maisie
Gay, Ada-May, and Alice Nikitina who was
engaged after Lord Rothermere, her
admirer, had suggested her to Cochran.
Nikitina, although bedevilled by injury, had
become an important star during
Diaghilev's final seasons and a particular
favorite owing to her influence over Lord
Rothermere who, infatuated with her, not
only heaped luxurious presents upon her
but also provided the Ballets Russes with
generous financial patronage. Cochran
planned two other ballets in his revue
besides *Night*: *Luna Park* or *The Freaks*, with
music by Lord Berners, choreography by
George Balanchine, and set and costumes

by Christopher Wood; and *Piccadilly 1830,*
with music by Ivor Novello, choreography
by Balanchine, and set and costumes by
Oliver Messel. Nikitina was responsible for
Cochran's engaging the other members of
the team, as she states in her undoubtedly
more accurate recollection of the sequence
of events: "I suggested that Cochran should
engage my usual partner, Lifar, with whom
I was accustomed to dance and who suited
me better than anybody else, because of his
height which conformed with mine. I asked
him, too, to approach Balanchine and
Kochno so that the Diaghilev team would
be fully reconstructed."[3] Kochno introduced
her to Bérard and showed her some of his
work. She in turn suggested Bérard to
Cochran. Her version rings true because she
had the necessary influential connections,
and she would have known better than
Cochran about who might be a suitable
partner for her. Lifar proved to be a tough
negotiator. He asked for the same salary as
Nikitina and to do the choreography of one
of the ballets. Cochran was annoyed and
said that England was full of good dancers
capable of being her partner. Nikitina loyally defended Lifar: "I supported Lifar's
case as best I could and we finally achieved
what we wanted. Lifar was to do the choreography of *La Nuit*, a new ballet to the
music of Sauguet, Kochno wrote the text
and Bérard made costumes and a décor of
miraculous beauty, as he alone could do. I
was proud to have been the Egeria of this
great theatrical event."[4]

But *Night* did not prove to be the anticipated "great theatrical event." Kochno has
written that he was inspired by his "nocturnal rambles through Paris,"[5] but they must
have been rather befogged—the meaning of
the ballet baffled almost everyone. The
program for the Manchester try-out did not
include a synopsis, but the critic of the
Manchester Evening News tried to respond
enthusiastically to the ballets as distinct
from the rest of the revue: "Dancing of
another kind is the art of Serge Lifar, and
with him, Nikitina. Mr Cochran has done a
great service in perpetuating this essence of
the Russian ballet. Lifar is magnificent; agile
strength allied to leaping grace. The ballets
in which he and Nikitina appear are all

interesting; they range from a queer fantasy *Luna Park* . . . to the strangely effective *Night* . . . *Night* will have to be seen again before we understand what it is all about. At the moment the main impression that remains is of eerie strength and superb lighting and staging."[6] C. B. C. (Charles B. Cochran himself) went further: "Christian Bérard is a young genius. A first class discovery for the theatre . . ."[7] This was only Bérard's second work for the theater, his first having been a production of *La Voix Humaine,* a monologue by Jean Cocteau performed by Berthe Bory at the Comédie Française, but his unique aptitiude for stage design was widely noticed. The art critic of the *Daily Mail*, less concerned with the performances of the dancers or the content of the ballets than with the design of the whole revue, complimented Cochran on apparently inheriting Diaghilev's flair for discovering and employing artistic talent: "The combination of Lifar's choreography, Sauguet's music and C. Bérard's setting and costumes maintains the best tradition of the Russian Ballet; and not the least attraction is due to the ingenious stage designs of the young Frenchman, whose talent, jealously secreted by some Paris art dealers, has not escaped Mr Cochran's watchful eye."[8]

Cochran, always fanning the press for publicity, seized on the obscurity of *Night* as a talking point. The *Daily Mail* carried a story in which the explanations given by him and Nikitina did not, however, reveal any particular philosophical depths in the piece: "Nikitina, poised like a butterfly on the settee in her sitting room, was amused. There was no deeply hidden meaning. 'There is not even very much story in it,' she said; 'just a dream. Just a *chic* lady in Paris in the early morning, dreaming about a young man whom she never sees except behind a wall. When she thinks it is not a dream and wants to touch and kiss him the wall becomes dark again between them, and she goes away terribly disappointed. The dirty little people behind the wall are only dream figures, the small people who pass along the street in the early morning; and Harlequin goes by in grief at his own story. The droll child has no meaning. He is only the small brother of the baker who just represents a handsome youth. It is all like a modern picture."[9] For the most part audiences remained baffled and critics unenthusiastic. The synopsis (printed above) which was added to the program when the revue opened in London did little to illuminate this short, episodic ballet. The critic of *The*

Star: "*Night* seemed to me peculiarly dull and meaningless,"[10] was echoed by John Martin in the *New York Times*: "*Night* . . . is almost as beclouded as its title would seem to indicate . . . Its meaning is quite obscure and its composition diffuse and scrappy."[11] Another anonymous critic went even further in his condemnation of *Night* after rapturously praising the rest of the revue by calling it a "semi-symbolic, semi-pretentious affair . . . concerning a baker and a woman of fashion [which] would in any entertainment not notoriously sophisticated be merely dismissed as silly. The vulgar would, I think, have given this 'the bird.'"[12] This critic's assumption proved to be accurate, except that apparently 'the bird' was not given only by the vulgar. Serge Lifar, who for once was only half-indulging in exalted self-flattery, admitted that "it was thoroughly well booed except for the episode where I appeared carrying on my shoulders a six-year-old child."[13] Of course.

Theater critics are hardly ever unanimous in their praise or condemnation: that is why we value them but, paradoxically, why we often also ignore their criticism. The one critic who liked *Night* also gave the best impression of it: "Outstanding on the more serious side of the evening were what I may call the Diaghileff legacy, three ballets danced by a group of the finest of the Russian dancers. Alice Nikitina's classic grace and poise, and the lithe athleticism of Serge Lifar, are displayed in settings of the most delicate and expressive simplicity. My favourite of the three was *Night* an impression of the mood of the black hour before dawn, when sinister figures creep home with sacks and carts; and when the lady homeward bound from the ball and the flour-smeared baker are parted by symbolic barriers of fate and circumstance. Nikitina's white, agonised arms swaying in piteous surrender before the impenetrable wall, are an unforgettable example of the mute eloquence of the dance."[14]

This sympathetic "rave" review was not enough to change the general opinion of the ballet. *Night* was withdrawn after a month in London, and replaced by a *pas de deux*, arranged by George Balanchine to music by Tchaikovsky, danced by Nikitina and Lifar in costumes designed by Oliver Messel.

Night, as *La Nuit*, was restaged at the Théâtre des Champs-Elysées on 19 April 1949 by the Ballets des Champs-Elysées, with new choreography by Janine Charrat with Irene Skorik and Youly Algaroff.

convincing, an artist has to be in total control of his line, and his line has to be guided by an innate and indefinable good taste. That Bérard was such an artist is demonstrated clearly by the costume drawings which follow. The figures are merely sketched, but they are all alive and have their own characters. (The drawing in ink of the head and arm of a figure lying prone, to the left of the inscription and signature, is unrelated to the set design.)

63 Costume sketch design of Serge Lifar as the Baker carrying Freddie Springett as the Child

Graphite and ink on paper
10³/₁₆ x 6⁷/₈ in: 25.9 x 17.5 cm
Signed bottom right in ink: "C. Bérard'
1933.428a

Exhibitions: New York 1933, No 13 (described as "costumes" for *Cochran's Revue*); Chicago 1933, No 39 (described as "'La Nuit' 3 costumes"); Northampton 1934, No 39; New Haven 1935; Middletown 1935; Williamsburg 1940; Michigan 1957; New York 1965–6, No 45 (illustarted p 29); New York 1966–7; Princeton 1968; Hartford 1988; Columbus 1989; Worcester 1989.
Illustration: Kochno 1988, p 149 No 2.

62 Design for the set: a dark street

Graphite and ink on paper
7¼ x 6¹¹/₁₆ in: 18.4 x 17 cm
Inscribed and signed bottom right in ink: "à mon cher / Lifar— / C. Bérard"
1933.427

Exhibitions: London 1930, No 8; New York 1933, No 12; Chicago 1933, No 38; Northampton 1934, No 38; Poughkeepsie 1940; Williamsburg 1940; New York 1965–6, No 44 (illustrated p 28); New York 1966–7; Hartford 1979; Columbus 1989; Worcester 1989.

This is a preliminary design showing the solid windowless walls of the street. The drawing of the proscenium arch cleverly determines their scale on the stage. The final design was a single wall made of gauze, which became transparent when lit from behind.[15] It is a set of the utmost simplicity; there is nothing romantic or even attractive about it. Although it functioned perfectly as the set for the story of the piece, it was inappropriate within the context of an

entertaining revue. Even Boris Kochno remarked that "the melancholy atmosphere of his setting and the miserable and mysterious characters were disconcerting."[16]

The composer of *Night*, Henri Sauguet, recalling the production of that work, paid a tribute to Bérard after his death which encapsulated his essential quality as a theater designer: "To this brief tableau Bérard brought his magical touch combining a refined taste and an extreme economy of means with a stupefyingly audacious sense of fantasy never seen before, which characterized his singular art, both so human and imaginative. Few artists understood the requirements of the stage better than he (and for the ballet, they are perhaps even more exacting than for plays, operas or musicals), or contributed to them with such grace without compromising personal vision. His clarity was stunning."[17]

"Economy of means" by itself is, of course, not enough. For the reduction of an idea to its minimum essential to be

64 Costume design for Alice Nikitina as the Lady

Graphite and ink on paper
10³/₁₆ x 6⁷/₈ in: 25.9 x 17.3 cm
Signed bottom center right in ink: "C. Bérard'
1933.428b

Exhibitions: New York 1933, No 13 (described as
    "costumes" for *Cochran's Revue*); Chicago
    1933, No 39 (described as "'La Nuit' 3 cos-
    tumes"); Northampton 1934, No 39; New
    Haven 1935; Middletown 1935; Williamsburg
    1940; Michigan 1957; New York 1965–6, No 46
    (illustrated p 29); New York 1966–7; Princeton
    1968; Amherst 1974; Hartford 1979; Hartford
    1988; Worcester 1989.
Illustrations: Clarke and Crisp, p 134 No 170;
    Kochno 1988, p 149 No 3.
The actual dress, a traditional ballet dress, was
    made of a mauve-red silk.

65 Design sketch of scene with Peggy Cartwright, as the Woman in the Cart, being pulled by Edward Coventry, her Coachman

Graphite and ink on paper
7 x 9¹⁵⁄₁₆ in: 17.9 x 25.2 cm
Signed lower left in ink: "C. Bérard"
1933.428c

Exhibitions: New York 1933, No 13 (described as "costumes" for *Cochran's Revue*); Chicago 1933, No 39 (described as "'La Nuit' 3 costumes"); Northampton 1934, No 39; New Haven 1935; Middletown 1935; Williamsburg 1940; New York 1965–6, No 47 (illustrated p 28); New York 1966–7; Princeton 1968; Hartford 1979; Hartford 1988; Worcester 1989.
Illustration: Kochno 1988 p 149 No 1.
This cannot be considered to be a proper costume design, unless it did not matter what Peggy Cartwright wore as she was covered up in the cart.

66 Costume design for K. L. Prince (and Nicolas Efimoff) as Harlequin

Graphite, tempera and/or watercolor, and ink on paper
14⅞ x 12⅛ in: 37.8 x 30.8 cm
Signed, inscribed and dated lower right in pencil: "à Lifar / C. Bérard 1930"
1933.429

Exhibitions: New York 1933, No 14 (described as being for *Comédie Française* 1931); Chicago 1933, No 40 (described as "Arlequin"); Northampton 1934, No 40; Elmira 1958, No 39; Richmond 1959; New York 1965–6, No 48 (illustrated p 29); New York 1966–7; Hartford 1974; Hartford 1979; Hartford 1988; Worcester 1989.
Illustrations: Amberg, pl 65; Bremser, vol I p 134.

*N*ight includes a Harlequin among its characters (Prince created the part in Manchester, Efimoff followed in London). However, this drawing, with its inscription and border, being larger and the most finished of Bérard's designs, was obviously made specially as a present for Lifar—perhaps for the first night.

This has been described as being for the Comédie Française, but Bérard's production for that theatre was Cocteau's *La Voix Humaine* which, being a monologue by a woman, does not include the character of a Harlequin.

Notes

1 The full text, in translation, of the "abdication" is printed in Appendix C. See also Schervashidze p 306 for a fuller description of the immediate aftermath of Diaghilev's death.
2 Serge Lifar, *Ma Vie*, p 88.
3 Alice Nikitina, *Nikitina by herself*, p 99.
4 Alice Nikitina, *ibid*, p 99.
5 Boris Kochno, *Christian Bérard*.
6 *Manchester Evening News*, 5 March 1930.
7 C. B. C., *Manchester Evening Chronicle*, 5 March 1930.
8 Our Art Critic, "Mr Cochran's Finds" in *Daily Mail* (1st Yorkshire Edition), 5 April 1930".
9 'Ballet Puzzle Solved" in *Daily Mail* (Manchester edition), 12 March 1930.
10 *The Star*, 28 March 1930.
11 John Martin, "The Dance: Diaghileff's Group" in the *New York Times*, 8 June 1930.
12 Anonymous cutting, "Cochran's 1930 Revue', 28 March 1930.
13 Serge Lifar, *op cit*, p 97.
14 *The Evening News*, 28 March 1930.
15 The design remained in Lifar's collection. It was exhibited in Lausanne in 1986 as No 74 in *Serge Lifar: une vie pour la danse*, and illustrated in the catalogue of that exhibition, p 62.
16 Boris Kochno, *Le Ballet*, p 211–2.
17 Henri Sauguet in *Labyrinthe*, Paris, February 1950, quoted in Boris Kochno, *Christian Bérard*, p 144.

Georges Braque
French
born 1882 Argenteuil
died 1963 Paris

Les Fâcheux (The Society Bores)

Ballet in 1 act by Boris Kochno, after the comedy-
    ballet in 3 acts by Molière
Composer: Georges Auric
Conductor: Edouard Flament
Choreographer: Bronislava Nijinska
Designer (set and costumes): Georges Braque
Principal dancers:
    Orphise: Lubov Tchernicheva
    Naïade: L. Krassovska[1]
    Eraste: Anatole Wilzak
    L'Elégant (The Dandy): Anton Dolin
    La Montagne: Nicolas Zverev
    Lysandre, the Dancing Master: Bronislava
        Nijinska[1]
    The Card Player: Leon Woizikovsky
    The Tutor: Jean Jazvinsky
Company: Diaghilev's Ballets Russes
First Performance: 19 January 1924, Théâtre de
    Monte-Carlo

Synopsis

Eraste, in love with Orphise, is constantly frustrated in his efforts to be alone with her by the intrusions of a series of different bores. First, he sees her with the Dandy. Jealous, he orders his servant La Montagne to follow her and bring her back. Then a maniac dancer arrives and executes a new dance in front of Eraste which he then proceeds to teach him. La Montagne returns to announce the imminent arrival of Orphise. The dancer leaves but then Eraste is accosted by some shuttlecock players who force him to join them in their game. They lose the shuttlecock and ask Eraste to go and look for it. Orphise returns and dances by herself. Eraste enters and is about to join her when his way is barred by two gossips. Orphise escapes into her guardian's house and reappears at the window. Then boule players followed by a card player come to annoy Eraste. Finally he is alone and Orphise joins him. But he is now frustrated by Orphise's guardian who, with his valet, begins to attack him. Orphise again escapes to her window. La Montagne comes to the rescue with some friends and finally the police arrive to stop the brawl. Eraste rescues Orphise's guardian. Now all the boring intruders return while Orphise, who sees that all is quiet, comes out of the house and falls into her lover's arms. Her guardian, in gratitude, gives the couple his blessing.

The comedy-ballet by Molière, upon which this ballet is based, was first performed privately before the King, Louis XIV, at Vaux-le-Vicomte near Paris on 17 August 1661. The first public performance was at the Théâtre du Palais-Royal in Paris on 4 November 1661 by the Company of Monsieur, the King's brother.

In 1924 Diaghilev, more by accident than calculated design, celebrated Louis XIV in three of the new works presented during that year: *Les Tentations de la Bergère* (see pp 217–22), Gounod's opera *Le Médecin malgré lui*, also after Molière, and Kochno's ballet-only version of *Les Fâcheux*.[2]

Diaghilev had signed his first contract with the Société des Bains de Mer in Monaco in the autumn of 1922. For the first time the Company had a base from which to operate and at last, after the difficulties of war and the traumas of the Revolution, felt reasonably secure. Diaghilev began to plan a French Festival which was not realized until 1924.[3] Influenced by Jean Cocteau, Diaghilev approached Georges Auric, one of the group of young French composers known as "Les Six,"[4] for a ballet score. Auric agreed to expand his score for the incidental music he had written for a production of *Les Fâcheux* at the Théâtre de l'Odéon in Paris. He tried to avoid pastiche by keeping to the style of the seventeenth century in a contemporary fashion, but he did not entirely succeed. Although the score, according to Robert Brussel, was like "scattered dry twiglets," the conductor managed to hold it together, and "the performance, as is usual with M. Diaghilev, is delightful."[5]

Bronislava Nijinska was responsible for the choreography. She, too, turned to the seventeenth century. She studied engravings of dancers of the period whose poses and movements she incorporated in a modernized form. Grigoriev, the company manager, recounts that rehearsals were, however, beset by disagreements. First, she disregarded any of the suggestions made by Kochno, who, as librettist, was supposed to be working with her. "Then, on watching a rehearsal, Diaghilev would not approve what he saw; and this would result in long and heated arguments between him and Nijinska, which would go on till rehearsals would have to be cancelled and the dancers sent home. Nijinska would then do her best to carry out Diaghilev's instructions; but this not only wasted a lot of time, it also caused her to lose interest."[6] One of Diaghilev's and Kochno's suggestions was that Anton Dolin, as the Dandy, should dance his variation on point. Grigoriev, understandably, disapproved of this suggestion as being nothing but a stunt. But Dolin, judging from contemporary notices, was obviously able to convince enraptured audiences without being effeminate.

Nijinska also disregarded Braque's design ideas. There appears to have been no consultation between them, as if each of them was working on a different production—a fault only too often prevalent today, but unexpected then, especially given Diaghilev's normally autocratic attitude. Braque also studied seventeenth-century design and closely followed Molière's instructions, but chose a palette of greens and browns for his sets and costumes. Although the design of the costumes was accurately based on seventeenth-century dress, Braque had the eccentric and novel idea of making the backs of all the women's costumes a uniform brown with the intention that the dancers would disappear when they turned round. This idea came to him from his experience as a Camouflage Service artist during the First World War. While guns and tanks painted brown and green may have disappeared in the field, costumes on the stage remained only too visible. It did not help that Nijinska completely ignored this feature of the costumes. Braque also, in being too faithful to the seventeenth century, did not appreciate the needs of dancers. Lydia Sokolova later plaintively recollected: "The costumes were Louis XIV and very difficult to dance in. Some of them were one colour in front and another behind, mostly in greens, greys, yellows and browns; they were unbecoming and with heavy flat hats tilted over the eyes, and heavy wigs, they gave an impression of weight."[7] While paying scant attention to the needs of dancers, Braque insisted on meticulous execution of his designs and had the costumes dyed and "washed several times in an effort to achieve the exact tint of his drawing."[8] Stanislas Idzikowski, cast in the minor role of Lysandre, complained after a dress rehearsal that the dye in his costume had been still wet and had left marks on his skin, and that as he had been up half the night trying to wash it off he refused to go on with the part. Diaghilev, seeing this as an ultimatum which he did not accept, dismissed Idzikowski and asked Nijinska herself to dance the part.

Braque's set designs began with a drawing for a front cloth for a prologue showing a naked naiad in a green grotto, although Kochno's libretto did not include such a scene. However, Diaghilev liked the drawing so much that he decided to insert a prologue, but, as Kochno stated, "the dancers Diaghilev selected for the nymph refused, one after another, to appear on stage in a costume they considered indecent."[9] Finally, Henrietta Maikerska, whose name is printed in the program, was replaced as the Naiad by L. Krassovska, but only for the first night, because after that Braque replaced the dancer with a painted figure (see the design below).

The set, like the costumes, was in the same color scheme of greens and browns which, according to Robert Brussel "appears at first to be grey and lifeless; but it loses its dreariness as soon as the costumes of the characters give it its true value."[10] Braque's concept of stage design was to have a dominant color tone, usually brown, acting as a background for costumes in a variety of colors which, without being uniform, would have the same tonal value as the background and therefore blend in with it. This concept seems to have worked, if not for the dancers, then at least for this critic. Jean Cocteau went further, and emphasized the importance of Braque's contribution from his point of view: "I have written that Georges Braque got the better of the choreography. I should have said that he was the real choreographer and that Madame Nijinksa could only follow where he led. The true dance of Les Fâcheux takes place between the beiges, the yellows, the chestnut browns, the greys."[11] He may have been correct in flattering Braque, but the result was obviously an unbalanced production.

Les Fâcheux was tinkered with too much for its own good, and so the dancers suffered. As Anton Dolin observed: "This ballet was never the success it could or should have been, and was one of the rare instances where not only a good deal of the dancing was changed more than once but new scenery was created and other ideas interpolated in to it by Georges Braquex [sic]."[12]

In 1927 the ballet was revived with no greater success, with new choreography by Leonide Massine, with the same set and costumes which he described as "a sombre abstraction of an eighteenth-century street scene, with elaborately authentic costumes."[13]

67 Design detail for the front cloth

Graphite and tempera and/or watercolor on paper (on the back of a color reproduction of paintings by Francis Picabia, *Jeune Fille Américaine* and a fragment of another)
12 x 12 in: 30.5 x 30.5 cm
Signed and dated lower right in pencil: "G Braque / 24"
1933.431

Exhibitions: Paris 1930 No 26; London 1930, No 12; New York 1933, No 15; Chicago 1933, No 42; Northampton 1934, No 41; San Francisco 1935; Paris 1939, No 142 (illustrated p 26); Chicago 1939–40; Poughkeepsie 1940; New York 1941–2; Detroit 1948; Edinburgh 1954, No 278 (illustrated p 51); London 1954–5, No 318 (illustrated p 61); Michigan 1957; Elmira 1958, No 19; Sarasota 1958, No 13; Indianapolis 1959, No 108; Storrs 1963; Hartford 1965, No 12; New York 1965–6, No 49 (illustrated p 30); Princeton 1968; Strasbourg 1969, No 401 (illustrated No 90); Frankfurt-am-Main 1969, No 115; Hartford 1973; Hartford 1974; Hempstead 1974, No 33; Hartford 1979; Hartford 1988; Worcester 1989.
Illustrations: Amberg, pl. II (color); Buckle 1955, p 107 No 143; *Daily News and Chronicle*, 17 September 1930; Hansen, fig 47; Haskell, p 95; Pozharskaya and Volodina, p 242; Rischbieter, p 86a.

Although Krassovska had valiantly agreed, when others had refused, to appear as the naiad on the first night she was not prepared to continue thereafter, and so the idea of having a semi-naked dancer standing provocatively on a scallop shell was abandoned. The dancer was then replaced by a figure painted on canvas. This drawing, the design for that replacement, was therefore made after the first night.

It is not a good drawing, but there is a deftness about it which is most appealing: all, that is, but the legs and feet which Braque painted thickly over in white before trying crudely to correct them without success. Those legs belong to another body altogether. This uncertainty in the drawing is surprising since Braque at this time painted a whole series of masterly paintings of the female figure, no longer in the cubist vein, from the *Canéphores* in 1922 to the *Grand Nu* in 1926.

This is a version of the same subject reproduced in the two-volume work on this ballet, *Les Fâcheux*, with an introduction by Jean Cocteau (see Select Bibliography). The set design, a project and several costume designs are reproduced in the same work. The projected set design and fifteen costume designs are in the collections of the Victoria and Albert Museum, London.

Notes

1 In the printed program Naïade is given as Henrietta Maikerska and Lysandre as Stanislas Idzikowski. The reason for the change is explained in the text.
2 This ballet always kept its French title: any version of the English was considered to be too unappealing.
3 This festival also included *Les Biches* by Francis Poulenc (see pp 242–46).
4 The group of young composers, influenced by Erik Satie, so called by the critic Henri Collet in 1920. The other members were Louis Durey, Arthur Honegger, Darius Milhaud, Francis Poulenc, and Germaine Tailleferre.
5 Robert Brussel in *Le Figaro*, Paris 7 June 1924.
6 Serge Grigoriev, *The Diaghilev Ballet*, p 199.
7 Lydia Sokolova, *Dancing for Diaghilev*, p 218.
8 Boris Kochno, *Diaghilev and the Ballets Russes*, p 211.
9 Boris Kochno, *ibid*, p 210.
10 Robert Brussel, *op cit*.
11 Jean Cocteau, *Les Fâcheux*.
12 Anton Dolin, *Divertissement*, p 107.
13 Leonide Massine, *My Life in Ballet*, pp 170–1.

Zéphire et Flore

Ballet in 1 act by Boris Kochno
Composer: Vladimir Dukelsky
Conductor: Marc-César Scotto
Choreographer: Leonide Massine
Designer (set and costumes): Georges Braque
Principal dancers:
    Flore: Alice Nikitina
    Zéphire,[1] her husband: Anton Dolin
    Borée, his brother: Serge Lifar
Company: Diaghilev's Ballets Russes
First Performance: 28 April 1925, Théâtre de
    Monte-Carlo
Revised version: 27 May 1926, Théâtre Sarah-
    Bernhardt, Paris

Synopsis

The original version was in nine scenes. The action takes place on Olympus.

Scene 1. Dance of the Muses and appearance of Borée, who avoids the Muses and looks for Flore.

Scene 2. *Entrée* by Zéphire and Flore. Borée, in love with Flore, intervenes and tries to separate the couple.

Scene 3. Blind man's buff, a game invented by Borée to remove Flore.

Scene 4. Flore joins in the game and falls into the arms of Zéphire. But Borée, jealous, intervenes and draws Zéphire away who, blindfolded, mistakes him for Flore. Unseen by Flore, Borée shoots an arrow at Zéphire.

Divertissement by the Muses. They dance with Flore and then leave her alone.

Scene 5. Borée pursues Flore, who thrusts him aside. Flore disappears and Borée escapes.

Scene 6. Bearers carry Zéphire, wounded by his brother, to the top of Olympus.

Scene 7. Tears of the Muses and Flore, who rush up to the lifeless body of Zéphire.

Scene 8. Zéphire's recovery and dance. The Muses bind the arms of the couple together so that they will not leave one another.

Scene 9. Zéphire and Flore leave, abandoning Borée to be punished for his love by the Muses.

Diaghilev, always on the lookout for new composers, was persuaded by Walter Nouvel,[2] to listen to a concerto composed by a young Russian, Vladimir Dukelsky,[3] just twenty years old, who had recently arrived from America. Dukelsky, excessively nervous, gave a private audition, with Diaghilev himself turning the pages. At the end, Diaghilev clapped his hands "thunderously," according to Dukelsky, and said *"Bravo, jeune homme,* and congratulations. Best new music I've heard in years. Now— what shall we call your ballet?"[4] And with that he commissioned him to compose a ballet "combining classicism with Russian overtones—tutus with *kokoshniks."*[5] Boris Kochno, Diaghilev's secretary and Dukelsky's friend, also twenty, was asked to provide the libretto for an updated version of *Flore et Zéphire,* the ballet by Didelot[6] first performed in London in 1796. Kochno states that Diaghilev called the ballet his "kindergarten"[7] because, apart from him and Dukelsky, the principal dancers were to be the youngest in the company, with Serge Lifar, only nineteen, being given his first major part.

Kochno's original idea was to stage the ballet as if it were a performance given by Russian serfs disguised as gods in the private theater of some nobleman. But when Diaghilev could find no suitable Russian painter to design the sets, he turned to Georges Braque who initially designed a single set.

According to Serge Lifar, Nijinska was first asked to do the choreography, but when she discovered that he was to dance Borée she left the company because she considered that he was not up to it. Diaghilev then gave the choreography to Lifar who wrote: "I set eagerly to work. I would lie awake at night thinking up new steps, new attitudes. I did so much of it indeed that a doubt began to creep into my mind. I did not want to devote myself entirely to a job I was far from knowing thoroughly. Choreography might make me lose signs [*sic,* surely 'sight'] of my real objective—the Dance. I did not want to sacrifice time I needed to become a dancer, to an occupation in which I might never be anything but a very poor creator."[8] This surfeit of false modesty infuriated Diaghilev, who then turned to Massine. The facts are expressed differently by Boris Kochno, who stated that Diaghilev, "after attending one rehearsal during which Lifar struggled in vain to devise a *pas de deux,"*[9] realized that he was not competent to do the choreography and so turned to Massine. It may well be that Massine did not know that Lifar had already made an attempt at choreographing the work, since the sessions had been conducted in a private studio with two trustworthy friends, but according to him Diaghilev had already approached him in the summer of 1924 to choreograph two new ballets, *Zéphire et Flore* and *Les Matelots* (see pp 279–85). Massine's version of the facts appears to be confirmed by Arnold Haskell, who stated: "For some time Massine had been seeking to rejoin the Ballet, and Diaghileff found that it would now be wise to make the peace. Nouvel and Wollheim [Diaghilev's London agent] were entrusted with the negotiations, and they proved almost interminable, for Massine had learnt the value of independence. Finally a contract was signed by which he was engaged as choreographer only, and entrusted with the novelties for the next Paris season."[10] As Haskell got his information from Nouvel this is the truest version— which is not to say, however, that Diaghilev was not capable of, and often did exercise, great duplicity. In any event, Massine rejoined the company. He wrote: "I accepted his [Diaghilev's] offer and agreed to join him later in the year at Monte Carlo. When I arrived there . . . I began to work at once on a new ballet, *Zéphire et Flore,* in which Kochno planned to re-create a *ballet d'action* of the eighteenth century . . . The music contained interesting echoes of Bach fugues . . . We encountered few problems in the preparation of the ballet. I found the dancers quick to assimilate the courtly movements which I devised, and Serge Lifar, dancing his first solo as Boréas, showed wit and instinctive control. Nikitina was enchanting as Flore; her slim, elegant figure was ideally suited to the part, and her dancing was delicate and expressive. As Zéphire Dolin had excellent elevation and striking stage presence. I was pleased with the final result of my work, but perhaps the mythological subject was too remote, for the ballet never became popular with our audiences."[11]

The production was plagued by injury. Diaghilev, determined to transform Lifar into a star with this ballet, so overworked and exhausted his dancers at the dress rehearsal that Lifar fell heavily, dislocating both his ankles. Diaghilev was horrified. Lifar wrote that he "spent a sleepless night at my bedside, while my ankles were being set,"[12] but that the following day Diaghilev said he would have to transfer the part to Slavinsky in order to honor his contract which required him to produce a new ballet. Lifar would not hear of it, and, in typically melodramatic style, said, "No, Sergei Pavlovitch, I cannot give up my part to anybody. Make *Flore et Zéphire* [sic] our last performance: I shall either dance in *Zéphire* or throw myself from the rock of Monaco, but I will never allow another to do my Boreas."[13] Diaghilev agreed to postpone the production for a week. Lifar was well aware of the chance being offered him, and, quite determined to go on, showed enormous guts in doing so. According to him, "nobody in the audience had the least idea of the state of my feet, nothing at all was noticed,"[14] and with justification he added, "this ballet was the first of my triumphs."[15] This was confirmed by Diaghilev, who inscribed his program: "To dear Boreas, the young and irresistible wind, on the day when he first swept through Monte Carlo."[16]

Zéphire et Flore was performed only once in Monte Carlo. The company then went to Barcelona before appearing at the Gaîté-Lyrique Theater in Paris. Alice Nikitina records in her memoirs that, on the first night in Paris, "at the beginning of the performance there was a *pas de trois* between Dolin, Lifar and myself at the end of which I had to make a great *jeté* in a high, gliding *arabesque*, then stop in this *arabesque* in a position *en plié*. It so happened that my foot rested on a hole and turned inside out. I heard a bone crack and felt an abominable pain pierce my ankle. I resolved to go on as though nothing had happened . . . Nobody in the auditorium, nor even on the stage, had noticed anything and our success was enormous."[17] The toughness of dancers is extraordinary, but Nikitina could no longer dance in Paris. She taught her part to Danilova, but danced it again herself in London. Diaghilev, although encouraged by some of the flattering notices of Dukelsky's score, was not entirely satisfied with the ballet and changed it before presenting it in London, by having Braque design two more backdrops to make the ballet three acts instead of one. Florence Grenfell went to the first night: "Thursday 12th November: We all went to see the new Ballet 'Zephyr & Flore.' I had heard it so criticised I must say I was most pleasantly surprised. Some of it I like v. much indeed, the Braque scenery & costumes are a joy to look on, the 1st impression of Dukelsky's music was pleasing & the Miassine[18] choreography interesting. Lifar was wonderful as Boreas but I was disappointed with Tcherkas & Nikitina. It had a v. good reception."

Zéphire et Flore was repeated in 1926, but as it was never entirely successful it was thereafter dropped from the repertoire. However, it did achieve Diaghilev's aim in establishing Lifar as a star.

68   Costume design for Alice Nikitina as Flore

Graphite and tempera and/or watercolor on paper
11⅛ x 9¾ in: 28.4 x 24.7 cm (maximum)
Unsigned and undated
1933.433

Exhibitions: Paris 1930 No 29; London 1930, No 14; New York 1933, No 16; Chicago 1933, Nos 43–44 (not identified); Northampton 1934, No 44; Edinburgh 1954, No 285; London 1954–5, No 327; Indianapolis 1959, No 114; Houston 1965; New York 1965–6, No 51 (illustrated p 31); New York 1966–7; Princeton 1968; Hartford 1974; Hempstead 1974, No 34; Hartford 1979; Hartford 1988; Columbus 1989; Worcester 1989
Illustrations: Buckle 1955, p 106 No 141 (titled "Boréas"); Hansen, fig 49; Rischbieter, p 86b; *Souvenir Program*, Théâtre de Monte-Carlo 1926.

The costumes for *Zéphire et Flore*, according to the composer Dukelsky, were "attended to" by Coco Chanel who "was then in 'residence' aboard the Duke of Westminster's yacht lying in the Monaco harbor, and often came to lunch with Diaghilev and his satellites."[19] The phrase he uses is ambiguous because these designs show that Braque made the original drawings. In fact, Chanel was responsible only for making up the costumes, although she did have some influence on the design because, as can be seen from the existing photographs, the tutu was quite rightly all but eliminated from the final costume. In other respects the costume is an accurate interpretation of the drawing. Chanel was not responsible for everything; Nikitina remembered how, after the performance in which she cracked her ankle, she "slumped on a chair in the beautiful grey-blue tights on which Braque himself had painted flowers."[20]

This design is merely a quick sketch and yet the information it contains for the costumier is entirely adequate. The main figure began as a front view, but Braque changed it to a back view by painting out the unfinished face with a dash of color. Braque then included a sketch for the headdress in the bottom right corner. The way the sketch is cut on the right and bottom shows that it must originally have been on a larger piece of paper. The cut-away corners may also have had other drawings on them. The little figure study on the left is irrelevant to the design.

Left: Anton Dolin as Zéphire and Alice Nikitina as Flore.

69 Costume design for Lydia Sokolova, Lubov Soumarokova, and Nina Devalois [sic] as three of the Muses

Graphite and tempera and/or watercolor on white card stock
12¹³⁄₁₆ x 9¾ in: 32.6 x 24.9 cm
Unsigned and undated
Inscribed in pencil top left: "2 tuniques colorées (2 colored dresses)," centre right: "crêpe de chine blanc (white crêpe de chine)," lower right: "crêpe de chine," lower left: "voile / brillant (sparkling voile)'
1933.432

Exhibitions: Paris 1930 No 30; London 1930, No 13; New York 1933, No 16; Chicago 1933, Nos 43–44 (not identified); Northampton 1934, No 43; San Francisco 1935; Chicago 1939; Paris 1939, No 144; Edinburgh 1954, No 284; London 1954–5, No 326; Michigan 1957; Indianapolis 1959, No 113; Storrs 1963; New York 1965–6, No 50 (illustrated p 31); New York 1966–7; Princeton 1968; Hartford 1974; Hartford 1979; Hartford 1988; Columbus 1989; Worcester 1989.
Illustrations: Buckle 1955, p 106 No 138; Komisarjevsky, p 51 (described as being for *Les Fâcheux*); Rischbieter, p 87; *Souvenir Program*, Théâtre de Monte-Carlo 1926.

Although the inscription states that this design was for two costumes, existing photographs show that the three dancers mentioned wore the same costume.

The Muses in the first production were danced by Lubov Tchernicheva, Lydia Sokolova, Alexandra Danilova, Felia Doubrovska, Nina Devalois,[21] Tamara Gevergeeva, Henriette Maikerska, Lubov Soumarokova, and Tatiana Chamié. Their costumes were all similar in cut and design but made in different colors.[22] Alexandra Danilova described her role and costume: "As muses, we were part of the landscape on Olympus; our job was to provide the background. Our costumes were awful—wool dresses with drop waists that made us look as if we were wearing burlap sacks."[23] Lydia Sokolova, who wore a costume made from this design, was no more flattering: "We wore 'sack' dresses, with tiaras resembling Russian head-dresses and long dangling earrings. Massine gave us each an angular, and uncomfortable little solo and these were danced in rapid succession."[24] The reference to the "sack" dresses is right, but the tiaras are not like Russian head-dresses and there are no earrings in this deft design.

Notes

1 This is the spelling in the original program, but the name is often spelt Zéphyr.
2 Walter Nouvel (1871–1949) was one of the original group of *The World of Art*. Neither as talented nor as flamboyant as Diaghilev but his equal in erudition and taste, Nouvel had the role of "second in command" throughout the period of Diaghilev's activities.
3 The Russian composer, Vladimir Dukelsky, was referred to by Diaghilev as his "third son," the other two being Stravinsky and Prokofiev. He later emigrated to America where he assumed the name Vernon Duke and wrote many successful songs including *April in Paris*. He referred to the production of the ballet in a poem, *Epistle to V. F. Markov*, in which he recalled how Diaghilev had written in his notebook that "he was handing over Glinka's lyre to him as a gift to Flora and Zephyr."
4 Vernon Duke, *Passport to Paris* p 117.
5 Vernon Duke, *ibid* p 121. *Kokoshnik* is a traditional, highly decorated and often bejeweled Russian woman's headdress.
6 Charles Louis Didelot (1767–1836), French dancer and choreographer, was born in Stockholm, and moved to St Petersburg in 1801 where he stayed until his death except for a break between 1811–16 when he worked in Paris and London.
7 Boris Kochno, *Diaghilev and the Ballets Russes* p 223.
8 Serge Lifar, *Ma Vie* p 46.
9 Boris Kochno, *op cit* p 227.
10 Arnold Haskell, *Diaghileff*, p 332.
11 Leonide Massine, *My Life in Ballet* p 163–4.
12 Serge Lifar, *Diaghilev*, p 408.
13 Serge Lifar, *ibid*, p 409.
14 Serge Lifar, *ibid*, p 409.
15 Serge Lifar, *ibid*, p 409.
16 Serge Lifar, *ibid*, p 410.
17 Alice Nikitina, *Nikitina by herself*, p 52. Nikitina incorrectly states that the theater was the Sarah-Bernhardt, which was where the revival took place.
18 The original transliterated spelling of his name.
19 Vernon Duke, *Passport to Paris*, p 136.
20 Alice Nikitina, *Nikitina by herself*, p 52.
21 This is the spelling in the program. She later became famous as Ninette de Valois, founder of Sadler's Wells Ballet in London, now The Royal Ballet.
22 Other similar designs in different colors are in the Kochno collection at the Musée de l'Opéra in Paris.
23 Alexandra Danilova, *Shoura*, p 78.
24 Lydia Sokolova, *Dancing for Diaghilev*, p 231.

Les Sylphides

Romantic reverie in 1 act by Michel Fokine
Composer: Frédéric Chopin, seven piano pieces
    orchestrated by Alexander Glazunov, Igor
    Stravinsky, Sergei Taneyev, Anatole Liadov,
    Nicholas Tcherepnine
Conductor: Marc-César Scotto
Choreographer: Michel Fokine
Designer (set): Georges Braque
Designer (costumes): Alexandre Benois
Principal dancers:
    Vera Nemtchinova, Lubov Tchernicheva,
    Alice Nikitina, Stanislas Idzikowski
Company: Diaghilev's Ballets Russes
First performance of revival using Braque's setting:
    21 January 1926, Théâtre de Monte-Carlo

Synopsis

A plotless ballet, a series of abstract dances, using Chopin's *Nocturne*, opus 32, No 2 danced by the *corps de ballet*; *Waltz*, opus 70, No 1 danced by Vera Nemtchinova; *Mazurka*, opus 33, No 3 danced by Alice Nikitina *Mazurka*, opus 67, No 3 danced by Stanislas Idzikowski; *Prelude*, opus 28, No 7 played as the overture and repeated here danced by Lubov Tchernicheva; *Waltz*, opus 64, No 2 danced by Vera Nemtchinova and Stanislas Idzikowski; and *Waltz*, opus 18, No 1 danced by Vera Nemtchinova, Lubov Tchernicheva, Alice Nikitina and Stanislas Idzikovsky.

Fokine, the choreographer, confirmed the abstractness of this ballet: "On numerous occasions I have had the opportunity to write the synopsis of *Les Sylphides*. I have known many critics who had a greater mastery of words, and who described it better than I did. I have read many descriptions of this ballet in programs compiled by experts—and yet I have never been able to find a satisfactory verbal elucidation of this ballet."[1]

*L*es Sylphides was one of the most popular ballets produced by the Ballets Russes.[2] As it was also reputedly Diaghilev's favorite, it was performed almost every season from the first in 1909 until the last in 1929. He was always very particular about how it should be danced and insisted on perfection from his dancers. No one was allowed to be in it until they had been in the company for at least six months and had watched the ballet many times. Lydia Sokolova (who had joined the company as Hilda Munnings in 1913) recalled: "Endless pains were always taken with this lovely work, and every performance of it had to be an absolutely perfect unity. Every girl who danced in that ballet was chosen not only for her grace, but also for her ability to move in unison with her fellow artists . . . When we were allowed to appear in it we felt as if we had been given a special promotion, even though we had no solos."[3]

The first version of the ballet, using four pieces by Chopin orchestrated by Alexander Glazunov, was called *Chopiniana*. The pieces were a polonaise, nocturne, mazurka, and tarantella. To these Fokine, the choreographer, persuaded Glazunov to add an extra waltz because he "wanted to create at least one dance on toes and in the long skirts of the Taglioni period,"[4] whereas the other pieces suggested character dancing. Fokine was aware of being criticized for apparently being interested only in developing character dancing and renouncing classical dancing on point. He was determined to scotch that criticism for, while he was indeed primarily concerned with freeing ballet from its rigid "classical" rules of mime, he nevertheless respected classical dancing on point, or "toe" as he called it. He stated: "From the outset I myself pictured the ballet as most varied in content and form, expressive of life. I recognized the dramatic, the abstract, the character, and the classic dance . . . I wished to demonstrate, therefore, that I loved not only the dramatic, but the dance in its pure form; that I recognized the toe dance, and the ballet skirts—but only in their proper place, and not in the place they then occupied in the ballet."[5] *Chopiniana* had a vague story, with characters suggested by an incident in Chopin's life. The extra waltz was danced by Anna Pavlova as Taglioni and Mikhail Obukhov as Perrot,[6] but the characters in this case were irrelevant because the choreography of the *pas de deux* was conceived as pure movement expressing the music and nothing else. As Fokine wrote: "When composing, I placed no restrictions on myself; I simply could not conceive of any spectacular stunts to the accompaniment of the poetic, lyrical Waltz of Chopin. I was totally unconcerned whether this romantic duet would bring applause or satisfy the audience or the ballerina, for I did not think of methods for guaranteeing success. As a matter of fact, I did not think of success at all. That is probably why I was rewarded with one of the greatest successes which had fallen to any of my compositions."[7] *Chopiniana* was performed on 10 (23) February 1907 at the Mariinsky Theatre, St Petersburg as a charity performance in aid of the Society for the Prevention of Cruelty to Children. The costumes, except for Pavlova's in the waltz, which was designed by Léon Bakst, were from the theater's stock of tutus "à la Taglioni"—that is, a white muslin skirt coming midway between knee and ankle.

The waltz in *Chopiniana* inspired Fokine to revise his whole ballet into one without any plot or character—the first abstract ballet. This second version, called *Ballet to the Music of Chopin*, consisted of a nocturne, a waltz, a mazurka, another mazurka, a prelude, another waltz, and a final waltz now orchestrated by Maurice Keller as well as Glazunov. It was presented at a charity performance in aid of the Imperial Patriotic Society on 8 (21) March 1908 at the Mariinsky Theater. The costumes, which cost 25 roubles, were all modeled on Bakst's design for Pavlova of the previous year. "The result was," according to Fokine, "that the *corps de ballet* looked like no other that had ever been seen before. I was surrounded by twenty-three Taglionis."[8] The set used was a section of the panorama backcloth designed by Botcharov for the original production of Tchaikovsky's *The Sleeping Beauty*. The same version, called *Grand Pas to Music by Chopin*, was presented at the graduation exercises of the Imperial Ballet School on 19 February 1909 also at the Mariinsky Theater. It was this version which was taken to Paris by Diaghilev during the first season of ballet in 1909.[9]

Chopiniana was renamed *Les Sylphides*, deliberately recalling the ballet *La Sylphide* created by Taglioni in 1832.[10] Benois says that the title was changed at his "instigation,"[11] but Grigoriev writes that it was Diaghilev who insisted on changing the title and that "no one objected except Fokine, who was reluctant to forgo the title he had chosen, but in the end he too consented."[12] *Les Sylphides* was an inspired choice of title, whoever was responsible for the change. Diaghilev also wanted the orchestration changed, but Fokine's wish to keep it as it was prevailed. The set, a romantic ruin of a church in a cemetery surrounded by trees under a starlit sky, and the costumes, still "à la Taglioni," were designed by Alexandre Benois. The impression Benois intended to give on the stage was a "languid vision of spirits of dead maidens, dancing their dreamy dances among the moonlit ruins and mausoleums."[13] The set was perhaps too reminiscent of the second act of *Giselle*, but Cyril Beaumont wrote: "All the dances breathe an intense sadness, save only the last which is full of rapture, a joy of quick movement; and just as the spectator feels he must join in to free himself from the intense strain on his emotions, the curtain falls. Then, so torn is he between the conflicting emotions of sadness and rapture, that a few moments elapse before he can applaud."[14]

The first performance was on 2 June 1909 at the Théâtre du Châtelet, Paris. The principal dancers were Anna Pavlova, Tamara Karsavina, Alexandra Baldina, and Vaslav Nijinsky. In 1917 a new set by Carlo Sokrate, an avenue of green trees relieved by a stone fountain set in the central pathway,[15] replaced the set by Benois.

In 1926 Diaghilev used a new setting designed by Braque, while still using costumes designed by Benois. Boris Kochno wrote that Diaghilev converted the Salle Ganne in the theater in Monte Carlo into "an experimental theatre for his company, where he presented dance recitals, entrusting the roles currently performed by his premiers danseurs to the young hopefuls of his troupe," and that "for one of these performances, Braque designed a new set for *Les Sylphides*, but he forbade Diaghilev to use it elsewhere."[16] Braque may have tried to forbid him from using his setting, but Diaghilev used it anyway. After the first performances in Monte Carlo, the ballet was revived in Paris on 25 May at the Théâtre Sarah-Bernhardt with the new setting. Braque was right in trying to forbid its use because it was dismissed by André Levinson: "The set, harsh and scant, with rust-colored wings framing a starry background, is by George Braque."[17] It is an inappropriate setting. The brown sky and the crude grey stars jar with the required romantic atmosphere of this most ethereal of ballets.

70   Design for the set

Graphite and tempera and/or watercolor on paper
8⅞ x 24 in: 22.5 x 61 cm
Unsigned and undated
Inscribed on reverse in pencil: "Braque / Les Sylphides"
1933.434

Exhibitions: London 1930, No 11; Munich 1931; New York 1933, No 17; Chicago 1933, No 45; Northampton 1934, No 45; Hartford 1934; Middletown 1938 (?); Paris 1939, No 145; Chicago 1939–40; New York MoMA 1944; Edinburgh 1954, No 281; London 1954–5, No 323; Elmira 1958, No 43; Indianapolis 1959, No 115; New York 1965–6, No 52 (illustrated p 30); Princeton 1968; Strasbourg 1969, No 24; Frankfurt-am-Main 1969, No 3; Hartford 1973; Hartford 1974; Hartford 1979; Coral Gables 1982; Hartford 1988; Worcester 1989.
Illustrations: de Mille p 140 (color); Komisarjevsky, p 50.

Notes

1 Michel Fokine, *Memoirs of a Ballet Master*, p 131.
2 There were two perennially popular ballets, *Les Sylphides* and *Polovtsian Dances*, each quite different in style.
3 Lydia Sokolova, *Dancing for Diaghilev*, pp 35–6.
4 Michel Fokine, *Memoirs of a Ballet Master*, p 99. Marie Taglioni (1804–84) was the greatest dancer of the Romantic period.
5 Michel Fokine. *ibid*, p 105.
6 Jules Perrot (1810–92) was one of the greatest male dancers, who danced with Taglioni until she became too jealous of the applause he received.
7 Michel Fokine, *op cit*, p 101.
8 Michel Fokine, *op cit*, p 129.
9 There is some confusion between the versions and when they were staged. Boris Kochno in *Diaghilev and the Ballets Russes* (p 32) states that *Dances to Music by Chopin* [sic] on 8 March 1908 was the same as *Chopiniana*, and that *Grand Pas to Music by Chopin* on 19 February 1909 was the new version orchestrated by Keller and Glazunov. Cyril Beaumont in *Michel Fokine and his Ballets* (pp 35, 39) states that the first version of *Chopiniana* was staged on 8 March 1908 and the second version, performed by students, on 6 April, but Beaumont also notes, quoting a letter he received from Fokine (p 37), that the first version was staged on the same evening as *Eunice* (10 February 1907) and the second on the same evening as *Egyptian Nights* (8 March 1908). Fokine is correct, as his dates are confirmed by announcements in contemporary newspapers.
10 In Paris. She first danced the part at the Mariinsky Theater in St Petersburg in 1837.
11 Alexandre Benois, *Reminiscences of the Russian Ballet*, p 275.
12 Serge Grigoriev, *The Diaghilev Ballet*, p 17.
13 Alexandre Benois, *op cit*, p 293.
14 Cyril Beaumont, *Michel Fokine and his Ballets*, p 51.
15 Cyril Beaumont, *The Diaghilev Ballet in London*, p 126.
16 Boris Kochno, *op cit*, p 226. But *Les Sylphides* was performed in the main theater.
17 André Levinson, "Barabau—Les Sylphides" in *Comoedia*, Paris 27 May 1926, p 2.

Giorgio de Chirico

Greek–Italian
born 1888 Volo (Greece)
died 1978 Rome

Le Bal (The Ball)

Ballet in 2 scenes by Boris Kochno, after a story by
    Count Vladimir Sollogub
Composer: Vittorio Rieti
Conductor: Marc-César Scotto
Choreographer: George Balanchine
Designer (sets and costumes): Giorgio de Chirico
Principal Dancers:
    The Young Man: Anton Dolin
    The Lady: Alexandra Danilova
    The Astrologer: André Bobrow
    The Spanish Entrée: Felia Dubrovska,
        Leon Woizikovsky, George Balanchine
    The Italian Entrée: Eugenia Lipkovska,
        Serge Lifar
Company: Diaghilev's Ballets Russes
First Performance: 7 May 1929,[1] Théâtre de
    Monte-Carlo

Synopsis

Scene 1, Prologue. Among the crowd of guests at a ball, a Young Man, struck by the beauty of a Lady escorted by an Astrologer, follows the couple.

Scene 2, the Ball. A general dance, a Spanish *entrée*, the Lady's variation, an Italian *entrée*, repeat of the general dance. In the middle of the repeat, the Young Man enters in search of the Lady whom he has lost in the crowd. The Lady appears wearing a mask which the Young Man begs her to remove. She agrees and terrifies the Young Man by uncovering the face of an old woman. In her turn the Lady pursues the Young Man until he hides. The guests begin to leave. The Young Man is left alone in the empty ballroom. As he is about to go the Lady, having replaced her mask, returns accompanied by the Astrologer. She surprises the Young Man by removing her mask to reveal an old woman and then with a quick gesture shows that this was only another mask. The Astrologer in turn removes his disguise and his beard and appears as a beautiful young man. He takes the Lady by the arm and they leave together while the Young Man falls in a faint.

"Every year it gets more difficult to work." So said Diaghilev in an interview,[2] and continued: "Earlier, there was a rich source of musical material, comparatively unknown in the West, which was available for productions. But now we have to find new compositions, and something truly first class is not created every year." Diaghilev cared more about a good score as the starting point of a ballet than any other aspect. For one of the two new productions in 1929 he again commissioned Vittorio Rieti, the young Italian composer who had written *Barabau* for him in 1925,[3] but he was so fussy and insisted on so many changes to the score that Rieti eventually lost his

patience and wrote to Diaghilev: "Here is *Le Bal*. It is dedicated to you; it is yours; you can do what you like with it, but above all don't expect me to work any more on it!"[4] Presumably Diaghilev was satisfied with the score because he called it a "brilliant composition, thematically Italian with all its attributes."[5] Diaghilev's insistence on getting the score completed to his satisfaction belies the often-held opinion that he had lost interest in his ballet productions by the late 1920s.

As the scenario by Boris Kochno was based on a short story by the Russian Romantic writer, Count Vladimir Sollogub, Diaghilev's first idea was to set the ballet in the Romantic period.[6] However, according to Kochno, no suitable designer could be found "capable of carrying out this idea, and so he approached de Chirico."[7] Kochno does not explain why Diaghilev chose de Chirico. Once again it was an inspired choice, but ultimately overpowering. After getting a score right, Diaghilev was next most interested in finding the right designer. For the last six years of the Ballets Russes's existence Diaghilev commissioned painters mostly from the School of Paris[8] to design the sets and costumes for his ballets, often giving them their first opportunity of working in the theater and thereby introducing them to a wider public. This search for new designers also shows that Diaghilev, essentially a man of the theater, was an impresario whose enthusiasm was always fired by the prospect of finding someone new and being able to establish a new reputation. De Chirico already had a reputation as a painter, had been an original member of the Bureau Central de Recherches Surréalistes in 1925, and in February–March 1928 had an exhibition, against his wishes, of his early work at the Galerie Surréaliste in Paris. Perhaps Diaghilev saw this exhibition, perhaps not, but he was at least familiar enough with de Chirico's work to recognize that his persistent theme of a classical Greek dreamland with its architectural fragments of broken columns, pilasters, capitals, scorched rocks, and a mysterious white horse would provide an appropriately romantic (and surreal) setting for his ball. The ballet became

imbued with, even dominated by, the spirit of de Chirico. The architectural elements extended into many of the costumes, giving a monumental unity to the whole production which was alleviated by the subtle use of pale, sunny colors—fawn, pale blue, pink, and white, most of all white, the most difficult color to use on stage. "The sets and the costuming are all in his characteristic manner," wrote Florence Gilliam, "an atmosphere of ruined temples and the sculpture of antiquity made to animate a modernism that is far from being a mere parody of the past."[9] Along with most critics, the writer for *The Times* noticed that "the *ballet* is remarkable for the beauty of its *décor* . . . Under the various pastel shades lies white as a foundation; white often comes to the surface, though the prevailing tone is biscuit brown; elaborate tracery in black adds linear interest," and "the total effect has that touch of the bizarre which is characteristic of modern design, yet is beautiful in the old-fashioned sense of grateful to the eye."[10] His very emphasis on the design shows that it was probably too obtrusive, and when the ballet was revived in 1935 (see p 167) with new choreography by Massine using the same set and costumes, the critic of the *Dancing Times* wrote perceptively: "Everybody should see *Le Bal* for the sake of Chirico's *décor*, for it is so delightful a picture, wherein lies its danger, and in which we can read the story of the strange and unsatisfactory paths along which the artists of Paris were leading Serge Diaghileff."[11] But Diaghilev was not being led, he always did the leading—although, in this case, de Chirico may have overbalanced the production.

Choreography (except when he wanted his favorites to shine as choreographers) and dancing were, curiously, always of less importance to Diaghilev than the other elements of a production. Indeed, Anton Dolin, returning to the company after an absence of three years to dance the part of the Young Man, wrote later: "It always seemed to me that the last thing he ever thought about was the dancers."[12] Lydia Lopokova, the famous dancer who had retired from Diaghilev's company in 1926 knowing more about choreography and

dancing than most critics, reviewed the ballet, which she called "a sort of *patisserie* in a lighter vein," in *The Nation and Athenæum*: "I find the ingenuity of M. Balanchine's poses and movements over-startling—there are so many different elements in his composition, steps and positions coming once and never repeated or developed, that they seem, sometimes, to lose significance. The choreography was lively, muscular and pretty, but not inspiring; though the *pas de deux* of Dolin and Danilova, who danced very well indeed, and the tarantella of Lipkowska and Lifar were excellent set pieces."[13] Lifar, on the other hand, dismissed *Le Bal* as being "an utterly insignificant ballet which anyone might have created,"[14] but this was written later, out of pique and his subsequent jealousy of Balanchine. Dolin, however, earned his accolade because, as he himself revealingly admitted: "I loved my role having danced it in Monte Carlo several times and was less nervous about it than I would have

been otherwise; and so, which is unusual for me at a first performance anywhere, I danced well."[15]

Some ballets are not meant to be taken too seriously; above all they are meant to be enjoyed, and the anonymous critic of *The Literary Digest* certainly enjoyed himself: "The fun begins in the first scene, where we see the guests on their way to the ball. The costumes and scenery, designed by M. Giorgio de Chirico, convey a plastic, three-dimensional solidity, even to the pilasters painted round the top hats of the men and the architectural designs on the ladies' dresses. We laugh at the odd movements of the guests."[16]

Toward the end of the London season,[17] Dolin gave a large party for the company and his friends. Diaghilev, too, had been invited. Lydia Sokolova described his appearance: "There was a hush as he appeared standing in the doorway. His face was ashen, the flesh was loose round his cheeks, his eyes were sunken and his grey

Above: scene 1, the Prologue, on stage in Monte Carlo.

hair showed through the dye. He sat down on a chair near the door and folded his hands on the top of his cane, just as I remembered him doing when I went for my audition at Covent Garden sixteen years before. He looked as if he was suffering and spoke very little."[18] It was the last time that most of those at the party saw Diaghilev. The company dispersed for the summer vacation. Diaghilev died in Venice on 19 August 1929.

71   Set design for scene 1: The Prologue

Graphite and tempera and/or watercolor with lead
    white highlights on paper
11 x 15⅝ in: 28 x 39.6 cm
Signed, lower right in watercolor: "G. de Chirico"
1933.435

Exhibitions: Paris 1929, No 14 (illustrated pl II);
    Paris 1930 No 31; London Claridge 1930, No
    71; London Tooth 1930, No 15; Paris 1933;
    New York 1933, No 18; Chicago 1933, No 46;
    Northampton 1934, No 46; Hartford 1934;
    New Haven 1935; Middletown 1935; New York
    1936; Paris 1939, No 149; Cambridge 1942;
    Washington D.C. 1950–1; Edinburgh 1954, No
    366; London 1954–5, No 401; Michigan 1957;
    Elmira 1958, No 1; Indianapolis 1959, No 150;
    Storrs 1963; Eindhoven 1964, No 47 ; New York
    1965–6, No 54 (illustrated p 33); Spoleto 1966;
    New York 1966–7; Strasbourg 1969, No 443;
    Frankfurt-am-Main 1969, No 146; Hartford
    1973; Hartford 1974; Hempstead 1974, No 36;
    Hartford 1979; Indianapolis 1985; Worcester
    1989.
Illustrations: Bablet, p 169 No 311; Buckle 1955,
    facing p 112 (color); Hansen 1985, fig 66;
    Komisarjevsky, p 47; Pozharskaya and Volodina,
    p 257b (color); Spencer, p 131.

The Lifar Collection is particularly remarkable for containing several almost complete sets of designs for a number of Ballets Russes productions. This group for *Le Bal* is one of them.[19] These designs, however, are not exactly what Diaghilev was expecting, because at the end of November 1928 he wrote to Lifar: "Yesterday I signed the Chirico contract for Rieti's ballet (*Le Bal*). The sketches are to be done in oils, so that a certain collection will be richer by a number of good things."[20] Lifar then adds: "That 'certain' collection, i.e. my own, was even then a very rich one."[21] Although Lifar was clearly delighted by this important addition to his collection, he does not explain how the designs finally came to be made in tempera or watercolor rather than oil. De Chirico obviously worked in oil, but it is not a medium much used by theater designers as it is a much slower process. Besides, tempera and watercolor are more suitable mediums, especially for set designs, as the pigment can be more

accurately interpreted for color when it is mixed with glue or size, as it should be for scene painting, instead of oil as for easel painting.

In this design for the prologue, the two large classical figures have been cut out of other sheets of paper and pasted onto the large sheet. A likely reason for this is that de Chirico revised his ideas about the scale of the figures in relation to the doors and the dancers using them. He made the painted figures truly massive, almost crushing the dancers into insignificance. The color range of pale brown and pale blue over a predominant white was continued in the design for the main set and in the costumes. The pediments above the standard-sized doors in the actual set were much more ornate than in the design.

72   Set design for scene 2: The Ball

Graphite and tempera and/or watercolor with lead
    white highlights on paper
11 x 15⅝ in: 28.2 x 40.4 cm
Signed, lower right in watercolor: "G. de Chirico"
1933.436

Exhibitions: Paris 1929, No 15; Paris 1930 No 32;
    London Claridge 1930, No 72; London Tooth
    1930, No 16; Paris 1933; New York 1933, No
    19; Chicago 1933, No 47; Northampton 1934,
    No 47; Hartford 1934; New Haven 1935;
    Middletown 1935; Poughkeepsie 1935; New
    York 1936; New York 1937–8, No 704; Boston
    1938; Paris 1939, No 150; Los Angeles
    1939–40; Williamsburg 1940 ; New York
    1941–2; Edinburgh 1954, No 367; London
    1954–5, No 402; Michigan 1957; Indianapolis
    1959, No 151; Hartford 1965, No 13; New York
    1965–6, No 55 (illustrated p 33); Spoleto 1966;
    New York 1966–7; Princeton 1968; Strasbourg
    1969, No 444; Frankfurt-am-Main 1969, No
    147; Blommenholm 1971; Wellesley 1972, No
    49; Hempstead 1974, No 37; Harford 1974;
    Chicago 1975, No 66; Hartford 1979; Coral
    Gables 1982; Frankfurt-am-Main 1986, No 207
    (illustrated in color p 259); Hartford 1988;
    Worcester 1989.

Illustrations: Amberg, pl 79; Bablet, p 169 No 312;
    Buckle 1955, facing p 113 (color); Cogniat
    1930, pl 46; *Das Kunstwerk* February 1959,
    p 19; Gontcharova, p 93; Hansen 1985, fig 67;
    Haskell, p 111 (top); Percival, p 111 (top);
    Pozharskaya and Volodina, p 258a (color;
    Rischbieter, p 181; Williams, No 14 p 19.

De Chirico remembered seeing pieces of
    furniture discarded in the street or
during removals, and was so struck by the
incongruity of the scene that he was
inspired to make a series of paintings in
which he put exterior objects into an interior setting and *vice versa*. He became fascinated by the surreal ambiguity this created
between the outside and the inside.[22] In this
room, the elements of classical architecture
and Greek landscape are grouped into the
two corners to leave the center of the stage
free for dancing, a necessary requirement of
any design for a ballet. The sills of the two
windows on either side provided benches
for the "Guests" at the ball to sit on, while
watching the Entrées. The horse galloping
over the bridge back stage center, and the
oval-headed, faceless mannequin on the
right are two other recurring themes in de
Chirico's work.

The window and the figure on the right,
the small temple and the archway on the
left, have been pasted on.

Above: scene 2, the Ball, with Serge Lifar and
Eugénie Lipkovska in the Italian entrée, on stage
in Monte Carlo.

73 Design for detail of the backcloth, scene 2

Graphite and tempera and/or watercolor on paper
5³⁄₈ x 6¹¹⁄₁₆ in: 13.7 x 17 cm
1933.437

Exhibitions: Paris 1929, No 16; Chicago 1933, No
    48; Northampton 1934, No 48; Hartford 1934;
    Paris 1939, No 151; Poughkeepsie 1940;
    Minneapolis 1953; Edinburgh 1954, No 368;
    London 1954–5, No 403; Michigan 1957;
    Indianapolis 1959, No 152; Storrs 1963; Eind-
    hoven 1964 ; New York 1965–6, No 56 (illus-
    trated p 33); Spoleto 1966; New York 1966–7;
    Strasbourg 1969, No 445; Frankfurt-am-Main
    1969, No 148; Hartford 1974; Hartford 1979;
    Indianapolis 1985; Hartford 1979; Worcester
    1989.
The drawing is in three separate pieces: the back-
    cloth, the horse, and the bridge. The horse was
    originally pinned with a thumb tack under its
    belly.

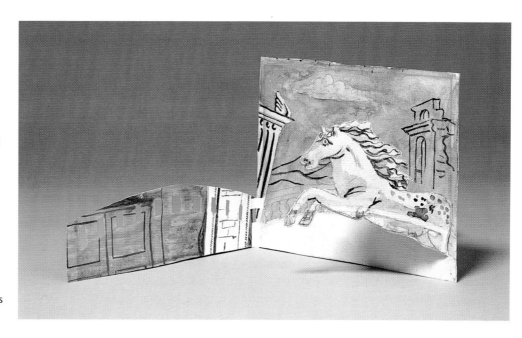

74 Costume design for Anton Dolin as the Young Man

Graphite and tempera and/or watercolour with
    white highlights on paper
10¹⁵⁄₁₆ x 7⅞ in: 27.9 x 20 cm
Signed lower left in watercolour: "G. de Chirico"
Detail of design for back inscribed lower right:
    ". . . dos" ("back")
1933.439

Exhibitions: Paris 1929, No 17;[23] London Tooth
    1930, Nos 17–24;[24] Paris 1930, Nos 33–36;[25]
    New York 1933, No 21;[26] Chicago 1933, Nos
    50–65;[27] Northampton 1934, No 51–65;[28]
    Hartford 1934; San Francisco 1935; Paris 1939,
    No 157; ? Los Angeles 1939–40; New York
    MoMA 1944;[29] Washington D.C. 1950–1;
    Edinburgh 1954, No 370; London 1954–5, No
    405; Indianapolis 1959, No 154; New York
    1965–6, No 58 (illustrated p 35; not shown in
    New York); Spoleto 1966; New York 1966–7;
    Princeton 1968; Strasbourg 1969, No 450;
    Frankfurt-am-Main 1969, No 153; Hartford
    1979; London 1981; Indianapolis 1985; Colum-
    bus 1989; Worcester 1989.
Illustration: Buckle 1955, p 118 No 160.

De Chirico continued his classical "architectural" theme through to many of the
costumes, which gave them a coherence and
unity within the overall design scheme.
Using architectural elements to decorate
dance costumes was not a novel idea. It had
been used to striking effect by Jean Berain
(1638–1711) in a symbolic costume for an
architect for a ballet for Louis XIV.[30] Whether
de Chirico was aware of this or not is irrelevant, because his use of architecture was for
a different purpose: unifying the surrealism
rather than accentuating the symbolism. In
this design the back of the jacket introduces
a decorative architectural detail, while the
front, with the medals, is straightforward
but symbolically military. It is not a true
uniform, although vaguely inspired by the
Greek army.

There is an incomplete pencil sketch of a
similar figure on the reverse.

75 Costume design for Alexandra Danilova as the Woman

Graphite and tempera and/or watercolour on paper
    overlay for design change
10⅞ x 7⅞ in: 27.6 x 20 cm
Signed lower right in watercolour: "G. de Chirico"
Detail of design for back inscribed in watercolour
    upper right: ". . . dos" ("back")
1933.444

Exhibitions: Paris 1929, No 17;[23] London Tooth
    1930, Nos 17–24;[24] Paris 1930, Nos 33–36;[25]
    New York 1933, No 21;[26] Chicago 1933, Nos
    50–65;[27] Northampton 1934, No 51–65;[28]
    Hartford 1934; San Francisco 1935; Boston
    1938; Paris 1939, No 161;[31] ? Los Angeles
    1939–40; Washington D.C. 1950–1; Edinburgh
    1954, No 375 (illustrated p 27); London
    1954–5, No 410 (illustrated p 24); Michigan
    1959; Indianapolis 1959, No 154; Hartford
    1965; New York 1965–6, No 63 (illustrated p
    35); Spoleto 1966; New York 1966–7; Hartford
    1973; Hempstead 1974, No 44; Hartford 1979;
    Boston 1982–3; Indianapolis 1985; New York
    1987–8; Columbus 1989; Worcester 1989.
Illustrations: Amberg, pl 81; Buckle 1955, p 118 No
    159; Pozharskaya and Volodina, p 259a.

Alexandra Danilova found this a difficult
ballet to learn: "The positions were
angular, with the elbows and knees bent.
The steps were very syncopated. On each
note, I had somehow to do a double movement." She was not helped by her costume:
"Our costumes were very modern—
painterly and rather awkward. I wore a
dress, not a tutu, and a white wig."[32] The
red design on the skirt is pasted on.

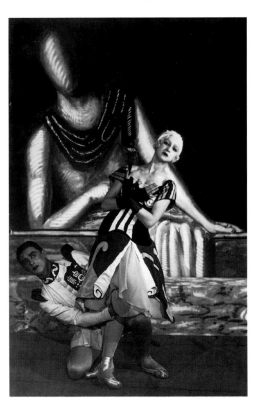

Right: Anton Dolin as the Young Man and
Alexandra Danilova as the Woman in scene 2.

...dos

J. de Chirico

76 Costume design for André Bobrow as the Astrologer

Graphite and tempera and/or watercolor on paper
11 x 7¹⁵/₁₆ in: 27.7 x 20 cm
Signed lower right in watercolor: "G. de Chirico"
Detail of design for back inscribed at bottom in
    watercolor with arrow: "dos" ("back")
1933.443

Exhibitions: Paris 1929, No 17;[23] London Tooth
    1930, Nos 17–24;[24] Paris 1930, Nos 33–36;[25]
    New York 1933, No 21;[26] Chicago 1933, Nos
    50–65;[27] Northampton 1934, No 51–65;[28]
    Hartford 1934; San Francisco 1935; Paris 1939,
    No 161;[31] ? Los Angeles 1939–40; Cambridge
    1942; Edinburgh 1954, No 374; London
    1954–5, No 409; Michigan 1957; Indianapolis
    1959, No 158; New York 1965–6, No 62 (illus-
    trated p 35); Spoleto 1966; New York 1966–7;
    Blommenholm 1971; Wellesley 1972; Amherst
    1974; Hempstead 1974, No 42; Hartford 1979;
    Coral Gables 1982; Hartford 1988; Worcester
    1989.
De Chirico has corrected the legs and feet, but the
    right foot is still weak.
The detailed design for the mask remained in
    Lifar's collection and was sold at Sotheby's
    London in 1984, Lot 58.

77* Costume worn by André Bobrow as the Astrologer

Two-piece wool suit. Flannel tail coat has black
    front with appliquéd stars and signs of the
    Zodiac in white, orange, and yellow silks. The
    white back has appliquéd outlined astronomi-
    cal motifs. White flannel trousers with tapered
    legs.
Gift of James Junius Goodwin and a Special Gift
    Account
1968.111 (a-b)

Provenance: Sotheby's London, lot 98 (i), 17 July
    1968.
In the revival by de Basil's Ballets Russes in 1935
    this costume was worn by Roland Guerard as
    the Astrologer. For note on this revival see No
    90 p 167.

78 Costume design for Serge Lifar as the man in the Italian entrée

Graphite and tempera and/or watercolor on paper
10⅞ x 7¹⁵⁄₁₆ in: 27.5 x 20.2 cm
Signed lower right in watercolor: "G. de Chirico"
Inscribed in pencil on turban: "rose," and right: "repeter [sic] dans le dos / les mêmes motifs" ("repeat the same designs on the back")
Preliminary incomplete pencil sketch of the same figure on reverse
1933.441

Exhibitions: Paris 1929, No 17;[23] London Tooth 1930, Nos 17–24;[24] Paris 1930, Nos 33–36;[25] New York 1933, No 21;[26] Chicago 1933, Nos 50–65;[27] Northampton 1934, No 51–65;[28] Hartford 1934; San Francisco 1935; Paris 1939, No 155; ? Los Angeles 1939–40; Poughkeepsie 1940; Edinburgh 1954, No 372; London 1954–5, No 407; Michigan 1957; Indianapolis 1959, No 156; New York 1965–6, No 60 (illustrated p 35); Spoleto 1966; New York 1966–7; Princeton 1968; London 1981; Indianapolis 1985; Columbus 1989; Worcester 1989.
Illustration: Buckle 1955, p 118 No 157.
This is the finished design. An earlier, fussier version remained in Lifar's collection and was sold at Sotheby's London in 1984, Lot 57. See note 19 on p 169.

79 Costume design for Eugénie Lipkovska as the woman in the Italian entrée

Graphite and tempera and/or watercolor with white highlights on paper
11 x 8 in: 27.6 x 20 cm
Signed lower right in watercolor: "G. de Chirico"
1933.442

Exhibitions: Paris 1929, No 17;[23] London Tooth 1930, Nos 17–24;[24] ? London Claridge 1930; Paris 1930, Nos 33–36;[25] New York 1933, No 21;[26] Chicago 1933, Nos 50–65;[27] Northampton 1934, No 51–65;[28] Hartford 1934; New York 1937–8, No 705; Paris 1939, No 156; ? Los Angeles 1939–40; Poughkeepsie 1940; Cambridge 1942; ? New York MoMA 1944;[28] Washington D.C. 1950; Edinburgh 1954, No 373; London 1954–5, No 408; Michigan 1957; Indianapolis 1957, No 157; New York 1965–6, No 61 (illustrated p 35); Spoleto 1966; New York 1966–7; Princeton 1968; Hartford 1974; Hempstead 1974, No 45; Hartford 1979; Coral Gables 1982; Indianapolis 1985; New York 1987–8; Hartford 1988; Worcester 1989.
Illustrations: Buckle 1955, p 118 No 158; Pozharskaya and Volodina, p 259b.

L ydia Sokolova, who danced the Italian entrée with Lifar, but some time after the first night, said that: "Half the point of this dance was destroyed by the heavy costumes. Chirico's dresses were undoubtedly the most striking part of the ballet, being covered with architectural motifs and simulated parchment scrolls to give the impression of being made out of plaster or paper: but their weight and stiffness made them hard to dance in."[33]

80 Costume design for Felia Doubrovska as the woman in the Spanish entrée

Graphite and tempera and/or watercolor on paper
11 x 7⅞ in: 28 x 20 cm
Signed lower right in watercolor: "G. de Chirico"
1933.448

Exhibitions: Paris 1929, No 17;[23] London Tooth 1930, Nos 17–24;[24] Paris 1930, Nos 33–36;[25] New York 1933, No 21;[26] Chicago 1933, Nos 50–65;[27] Northampton 1934, No 51–65;[28] Hartford 1934; San Francisco 1935; Paris 1939, No 161;[29] ? Los Angeles 1939–40; Williamsburg 1940; Edinburgh 1954, No 379; London 1954–5, No 414; Michigan 1957; Indianapolis 1959, No 163; New York 1965–6, No 67 (illustrated p 36; not shown in New York); Spoleto 1966; New York 1966–7; Indianapolis 1985; Columbus 1989; Worcester 1989.
On the reverse there is a pencil and watercolor drawing of a mask with a wrinkled face similar to No 88, p 166.

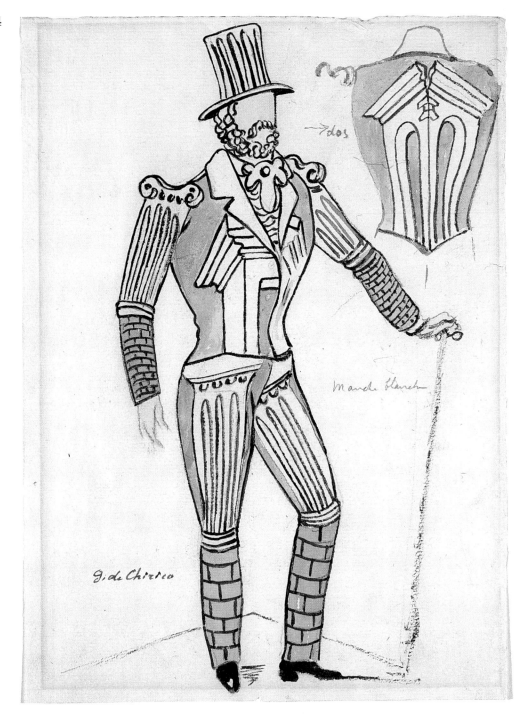

81 Costume design for a male guest

Graphite and tempera and/or watercolor on paper
10¹³⁄₁₆ x 7⁷⁄₈ in: 27.5 x 20 cm
Signed lower left in watercolor: "G. de Chirico"
Detail of design for back inscribed in watercolor left with an arrow: "dos" ("back"), and inscribed right in pencil: "manche blanche" ("white sleeve")
1933.440

Exhibitions: Paris 1929, No 17;[23] London Tooth 1930, Nos 17–24;[24] Paris 1930, Nos 33–36;[25] New York 1933, No 21;[26] Chicago 1933, Nos 50–65;[27] Northampton 1934, No 51–65;[28] Hartford 1934; San Francisco 1935; Paris 1939, No 157; ? Los Angeles 1939–40; Washington D.C. 1950–1; Edinburgh 1954, No 37;[23]

London 1954–5, No 406; Michigan 1957; Indianapolis 1959, No 155; New York 1965–6, No 59 (illustrated p 35); Spoleto 1966; New York 1966–7; Hempstead 1974, No 46; Hartford 1979; Indianapolis 1985; New York 1987–8; Columbus 1989; Worcester 1989.
Illustrations: Amberg, pl 80; Cogniat 1930, pl 45 (color).
On the reverse there is a portion of an incomplete pencil sketch of the same figure.
This design relates to the seated figure on the cover of the Souvenir Program, No 94, p 170.

82 Costume design for Hoyer II and Ignatov as the two classical statues

Graphite, tempera and/or watercolor, and ink on paper
11 x 8 in: 27.9 x 20.2 cm
Signed lower centre right in watercolor: "G. de Chirico"
1933.445

Exhibitions: Paris 1929, No 17;[23] London Tooth 1930, Nos 17–24;[24] Paris 1930, Nos 33–36;[25] New York 1933, No 21;[26] Chicago 1933, Nos 50–65;[27] Northampton 1934, No 51–65;[28] Hartford 1934; San Francisco 1935; Paris 1939, No 161;[31] ? Los Angeles 1939–40; Edinburgh 1954, No 376; London 1954–5, No 411; Indianapolis 1959, No 160; New York 1965–6, No 64 (illustrated p 36); Spoleto 1966; New York 1966–7; Princeton 1968; Hempstead 1974, No 43; Indianapolis 1985; New York 1987–8; Columbus 1989; Worcester 1989.
Chirico here cleverly varies his theme by using a linear decoration which gives the effect of being partly sculptural, partly architectural, and partly skeletal.
This design relates to the standing figure on the cover of the Souvenir Program, No 94, p 170.

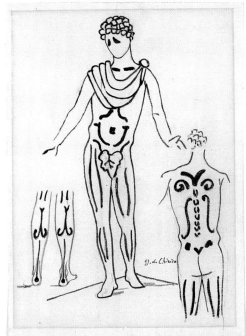

83 Costume design for Alicia Markova, Dora Vadimova, Branitska, and Soumarokova as the Sylphs

Graphite and tempera and/or watercolor on paper
9³/₁₆ x 7¹³/₁₆ in: 24.7 x 19.7 cm
Signed lower left in watercolor: G. de Chirico
1933.447

Exhibitions: Paris 1929, No 17;[23] London Tooth
1930, Nos 17–24;[24] Paris 1930, Nos 33–36;[25]
New York 1933, No 21;[26] Chicago 1933, Nos
50–65;[27] Northampton 1934, No 51–65;[28]
Hartford 1934; San Francisco 1935; Paris 1939,
No 161;[31] ? Los Angeles 1939–40; Edinburgh
1954, No 378; London 1954–5, No 413; Indianapolis 1959; New York 1965–6, No 66
(illustrated p 36; not shown in New York);
Spoleto 1966; New York 1966–7; Indianapolis
1985; Columbus 1989; Worcester 1989.

84 Costume design for a female guest

Graphite and tempera and/or watercolor on paper
10⁷/₈ x 7⁷/₈ in: 27.5 x 20 cm
Signed, lower right in watercolor: G. de Chirico
1933.446

Exhibitions: Paris 1929, No 17;[23] London Tooth
1930, Nos 17–24;[24] Paris 1930, Nos 33–36;[25]
New York 1933, No 21;[26] Chicago 1933, Nos

50–65;[27] Northampton 1934, No 51–65;[28]
Hartford 1934; San Francisco 1935; Paris 1939,
No 156; ? Los Angeles 1939–40; Edinburgh
1954, No 377; London 1954–5, No 412; New
York 1965–6, No 65 (illustrated p 36); Spoleto
1966; New York 1966–7; Strasbourg 1969, No
448; Frankfurt-am-Main 1969, No 151; Indianapolis 1985; Columbus 1989; Worcester
1989.
The Female Guests at the first performance were
Mmes Marra, Maikerska, Slavinska, Chamié,
Karlevska, Klemetska, Gouluk, Miklachevska,
Obidennaia, Pavlova, Barash, and Tarakanova,
but it is not possible to determine who wore
any particular costume, or even how many
costumes were made from a single design.

85 Costume design for a female guest

Graphite and tempera and/or watercolor on paper
11¹/₈ x 7¹³/₁₆ in: 28.2 x 19.9 cm
Signed lower right in watercolor: "G. de Chirico"
1933.451

Exhibitions: Paris 1929, No 17;[23] London Tooth
1930, Nos 17–24;[24] Paris 1930, Nos 33–36;[25]
New York 1933, No 21;[26] Chicago 1933, Nos
50–65;[27] Northampton 1934, No 51–65;[28]
Hartford 1934; San Francisco 1935; Paris 1939,
No 161;[29] ? Los Angeles 1939–40; Edinburgh
1954, No 377; London 1954–5, No 412; Michigan 1957; Elmira 1958, No 36; Indianapolis
1959; Hartford 1965; New York 1965–6, No 70
(illustrated p 37; not shown in New York);
Spoleto 1966; New York 1966–7; Columbus
1989; Worcester 1989.
This design was drawn on a sheet of paper torn
down to the present size from a larger sheet.
On the reverse is part of a preliminary colored
drawing with the same design for the figures
as No 72, p 158, except that here the seated
figure is standing and the classical figure has
his right arm raised above his head.

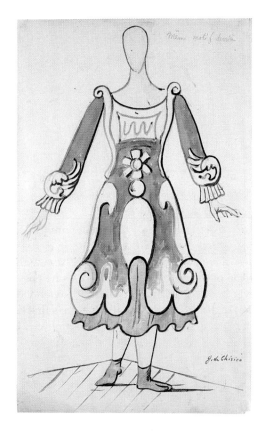

86   Costume design for a female guest

Graphite and tempera and/or watercolor on illustration board
13³⁄₈ x 8³⁄₁₆ in: 34.0 x 20.8 cm
Signed lower right in watercolor: "G. de Chirico"
Inscribed upper right in pencil: "même motif derrière" ("the same design behind")
1933.453

Exhibitions: Paris 1929, No 17;[23] London Tooth 1930, Nos 17–24;[24] Paris 1930, Nos 33–36;[25] New York 1933, No 21;[26] Chicago 1933, Nos 50–65;[27] Northampton 1934, No 51–65;[28] Hartford 1934; San Francisco 1935; Paris 1939, No 161;[29] ? Los Angeles 1939–40; Washington D.C. 1950; Indianapolis 1959, No 168; Storrs 1963; Eindhoven 1964; New York 1965–6, No 72 (illustrated p 37); Spoleto 1966; New York 1966–7; Strasbourg 1969, No 451; Frankfurt-am-Main 1969, No 154; Hartford 1974; Hartford 1979; Indianapolis 1985; Columbus 1989; Worcester 1989.

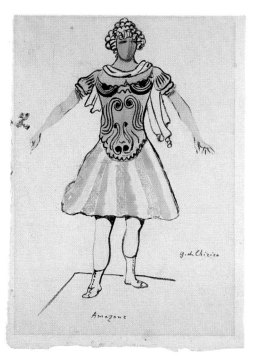

87   Costume design for a female guest, an Amazon

Graphite and tempera and/or watercolor on paper with paper overlay for design change
11 x 8 in: 28.0 x 20.3 cm
Signed lower right in watercolor: "G. de Chirico"
Inscribed bottom center in watercolor: "Amazone"
1933.454

Exhibitions: Paris 1929, No 17;[23] London Tooth 1930, Nos 17–24;[24] Paris 1930, Nos 33–36;[25] New York 1933, No 21;[26] Chicago 1933, Nos 50–65;[27] Northampton 1934, No 51–65;[28] Hartford 1934; San Francisco 1935; Paris 1939, No 160; ? Los Angeles 1939–40; Edinburgh 1954, No 374; London 1954–5, No 409; Michigan 1957; Indianapolis 1959, No 169; Storrs 1963; Eindhoven 1964; New York 1965–6, No 73 (illustrated p 37; not shown in New York); Spoleto 1966; New York 1966–7; Strasbourg 1969, No 449; Frankfurt-am-Main 1969, No 152; Amherst 1974; Indianapolis 1985; Columbus 1989; Worcester 1989.

88   Design for the inner mask for a female guest

Graphite and tempera and/or watercolor on paper
6⁵⁄₁₆ x 4¹³⁄₁₆ in: 16.0 x 12.2 cm
Signed lower left in watercolor: "G. de Chirico"
1933.452

Exhibitions: Paris 1929, No 17;[23] London Tooth 1930, Nos 17–24;[24] Paris 1930, Nos 33–36;[25] New York 1933, No 21;[26] Chicago 1933, Nos 50–65;[27] Northampton 1934, No 51–65;[28] Paris 1939, No 159; ? Los Angeles 1939–40; Indianapolis 1959; New York 1965–6, No 71 (illustrated p 37; not shown in New York); Spoleto 1966; New York 1966–7; Hartford 1974; Hartford 1979; Indianapolis 1985; Columbus 1989; Worcester 1989.
The mask is drawn on an erased pencil drawing of a figure the other way up. On the reverse is a pencil and watercolor drawing of the lower part of a woman's costume (see below).

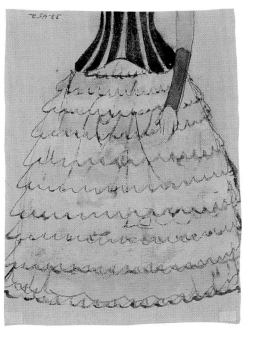

Right: reverse of No 88, a preliminary idea for No 80, p 163.

89 Costume design for a male guest, a General

Graphite and tempera and/or watercolor on paper
10⅞ x 7¾ in: 27.7 x 20 cm
Signed lower left in watercolor: "G. de Chirico"
1933.449

Exhibitions: Paris 1929, No 17;[23] London Tooth
1930, Nos 17–24;[24] Paris 1930, Nos 33–36;[25]
New York 1933, No 21;[26] Chicago 1933, Nos
50–65;[27] Northampton 1934, No 51–65;[28]
Hartford 1934; San Francisco 1935; Paris 1939,
No 154; ? Los Angeles 1939–40; Edinburgh
1954, No 380; London 1954–5, No 415; Michigan 1957; Indianapolis 1959, No 164; New
York 1965–6, No 68 (illustrated p 37; not
shown in New York); Spoleto 1966; New York
1966–7; Princeton 1968; Blommenholm 1971;
Amherst 1974; Hartford 1979; Indianapolis
1985; Hartford 1988; Worcester 1989.

90* Costume for a male guest, a General

Two-piece wool suit. Gabardine tail coat has gray
front with white stand collar, cuffs and painted
fish-scale pattern from chest to waist. Two
medals appliquéd on the left breast, terracotta
epaulettes stand on the shoulder and a silk
sash of the same color is draped across the
chest. The white flannel back has a yellow silk
grenade with painted terracotta lightning bolts
outlined in black.
Pre-printed label "A. Ingrato, Monte-Carlo,"
inscribed on collar "BLAT" and, in purple ink
"24QA"
White flannel trousers with a stripe divided into
alternate salmon-pink and garter-blue elongated triangles
Pre-printed label "A. Ingrato, Monte-Carlo,"
inscribed in black "Efimoff" with superscription
in purple in Russian "Лиса" ("Lisa")
Gift of James Junius Goodwin and a Special Gift
Account
1968.113 (a-b)
Provenance: Sotheby's London, lot 98 (iii), 17 July
1968

The Male Guests at the the first performance were
Mssrs Tcherkas, Efimow [sic], Kremnew,
Borovsky, Jazvinsky, Kochanovsky, Fedorow,
Lissanevitch, Hoyer, Petrakevitch, Ladré,
Matouchevsky, and Yovanovitch.
From the inscription, this costume was worn by
Lissanevitch (but see also No 93, p 169).
The Male Guests for the revival were Mssrs Alexan-
droff, Bousloff, Belsky, Guerard, Hoyer,
Ismailoff, Katcharoff, Kosloff, Matouchevsky,
Lazovsky, Tovaroff, and Alonsono (Hoyer and
Matouchevsky were in the original production.)
There is no inscription to identify who wore this
costume in the revival.

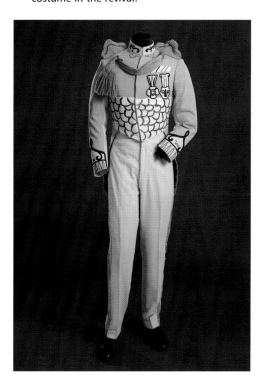

The ballet was revived by de Basil's
Ballets Russes on 8 March 1935 at the
Auditorium, Chicago, with new choreogra-
phy by Leonide Massine using the original
sets and costumes by de Chirico. Tatiana
Riabouchinska was the Young Lady and
Roman Jasinsky was the Young Man.

The London[34] critics tried hard to like
Massine's new version and blamed the
composer rather than the choreographer for
the production's failings. The *Sunday Times*
was the most outspoken: "The music, by
Rieti, is one of the worst specimens that
have come down to us of a bad genre in a
bad epoch. Its emptiness and boring ugli-
ness have evidently posed Mr Massine with
some of the most difficult problems he has
ever had to face; and it cannot be pretended
that he has solved them all. But one's first
feelings of indifference or repulsion gradually give way to a detached interest in some
of the lines and combinations of lines projected in this curiously acrobatic choreography."[35]

Once again, the most effective, in the
sense of most obtrusive, aspect of the production was de Chirico's design: much
admired, but clearly overpowering and to
the ultimate detriment of the ballet. The
critic of *The Times* noted the failing: "Signor
Chirico's cool colours are delightful to the
eye, but his treatment of the human figure is
always in the manner of a *nature morte*, and
to bring the figures to life is a contradiction
in terms."[36]

Massine himself found de Chirico's
design very restricting, and working within
it confirmed his feeling that he should not
have attempted "to re-do work that had
already been done."[37]

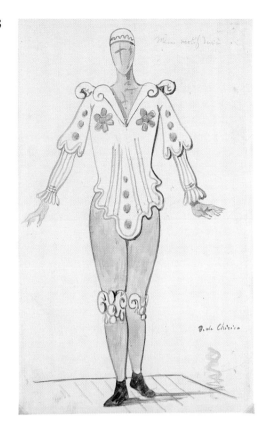

91   Costume design for a male guest

Graphite and tempera and/or watercolor on paper
13³/₈ x 8¹/₈ in: 34 x 20.7 cm
Signed lower right in watercolor: "G. de Chirico"
1933.450

Exhibitions: Paris 1929, No 17;[23] London Tooth
1930, Nos 17–24;[24] Paris 1930, Nos 33–36;[25]
New York 1933, No 21;[26] Chicago 1933, Nos
50–65;[27] Northampton 1934, No 51–65;[28]
Hartford 1934; San Francisco 1935; Paris 1939,
No 161;[29] ? Los Angeles 1939–40; Williamsburg
1940; Washington D.C. 1950; Elmira 1958, No
35; Indianapolis 1959; Storrs 1963; Eindhoven
1964; New York 1965–6, No 69 (illustrated p
37); Spoleto 1966; New York 1966–7; Princeton
1968; Amherst 1974; Hempstead 1974, No 47;
Hartford 1979; Boston 1982–3; Indianapolis
1985; Hartford 1988; Worcester 1989.

92*   Costume for a male guest

Doublet, tights, and knee pads. Cream taffeta
waist-length doublet with extended center
front, appliquéd with blue silk flowers and
spots outlined in brown embroidery. Short
sleeves are over a blue ribbon-striped long
sleeve. Stiff wings on shoulders.
Inscribed twice in ink "Belsky."
Inscribed in purple in Russian "Качар" ("Katchar")
and "Bousl."
Two cream silk knee-pads in brown with a pattern
suggesting armor.
One inscribed "Bousl," the other "Лепс ("Leps")
and "Izm."

Gift of James Junius Goodwin and a Special Gift
Account
1968.114 (a-d)
Provenance: Sotheby's London, lot 98 (iv), 17 July
1968

The inscriptions do not identify who wore this
costume in the original production: they
indicate, however, that it was worn by both
Belsky and Bousloff, and possibly by Katcharoff
and Ismailoff as well in the revival.

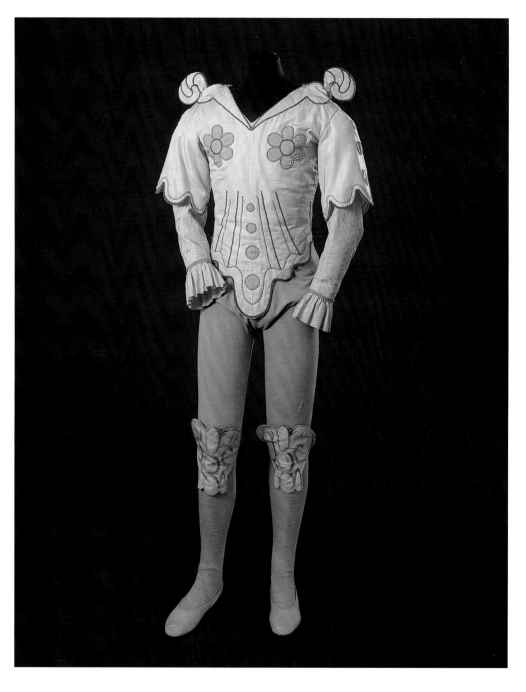

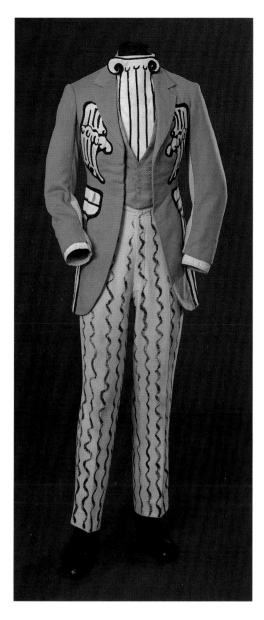

93* Costume for Nicolas Efimov as a male guest

Three-piece wool suit. Flannel tail coat has a terracotta front with green wool attached waistcoat showing at the front opening. Pale blue back has appliquéd white architectural motifs outlined in black braid and a pattern of terracotta briocks on the skirt.

Pre-printed label "A. Ingrato, Monte-Carlo" and inscription "M. Effimoff."

White twill dicky appliqué with an Ionic column outlined in black braid in lieu of a tie.

White flannel trousers, hand-painted with wavy stripes in black.

Pre-printed label "A. Ingrato, Monte-Carlo" and indistinct inscription, probably "M. Effimoff."

1968.112 (a–c)

Provenance: Sotheby's London, lot 98 (ii), 17 July 1968

There is no inscription to indicate who wore this costume in the revival.

Notes

1 This date is according to the program. A number of books give the date incorrectly as 9 May.

2 Serge Diaghilev, quoted in interview by Lev Dmitrievich Liubimov in *Vozrozhdenie* (*Renaissance*), Paris, 16 May 1929, quoted in I. S. Zilberstein and V. A. Samkov, *Sergei Diaghilev*, vol 1, pp 252–3.

3 Vittorio Rieti (1898–1994) was the librettist as well as the composer of *Barabau*. The ballet, with choreography by George Balanchine, was first performed at the Coliseum Theatre, London, on 11 December 1925. Rieti was also helping at the time to orchestrate the piano concerto by Igor Markevitch, Diaghilev's latest "favorite," which was given its first performance at the Royal Opera House, Covent Garden, on 15 July 1929.

4 Letter (in French) dated 27 February 1929, quoted in Serge Grigoriev, *The Diaghilev Ballet*, p 257.

5 Interview *op cit*, p 254.

6 According to Boris Kochno, *Diaghilev and the Ballets Russes*, p 270. But in the Kochno collection, sold at Sotheby's, Monaco on 11–12 October 1991, lot 393 was described as an "autograph working manuscript of the the scenario for *Le Bal*" by Rieti which showed that "the composer actively participated in the planning of the ballet."

7 Boris Kochno, *ibid*, p 270.

8 A loose, but useful, term describing all those artists, not necessarily French, who were working in Paris in the 1920s.

9 Florence Gilliam in "*The Boulevardier'*, ? New York July 1929, p 41.

10 Anon, *The Times*, London 9 July 1929.

11 G. E. G., *The Dancing Times*, London August 1935, p 529.

12 Anton Dolin, *Divertissement*, p 198.

13 Lydia Lopokova in *The Nation and Athenæum*, London 13 July 1929, quoted in Nesta Macdonald, *Diaghilev Observed*, pp 374–5.

14 Serge Lifar, *Diaghilev*, p 340.

15 Anton Dolin *op cit*, p 201

16 Anon, "Modernism in the Russian Ballet" in *The Literary Digest,* 24 August 1929.

17 At the Royal Opera House, Covent Garden, from 29 June–26 July 1929.

18 Lydia Sokolova, *Dancing for Diaghilev* , pp 278–9.

19 The costume design for George Balanchine in the *pas de trois Espagnol* is in the collections of the Theatre Museum, London. Serge Lifar kept a version of the design for his own costume and sold it at Sotheby's, London, in 1984, Lot 57. Other almost complete productions represented in the collection are *Mavra* (see pp 318–22), *Les Matelots* (see pp 279–85), and *Jack-in-the-Box* (see pp 185–90).

20 Quoted in Serge Lifar, *Diaghilev*, p 480.

21 See Appendix B, works listed in the catalogues of exhibitions, for an indication of the richness of the collection at that time.

22 For example, in "My Mediterranean Bedroom," painted during the winter of 1927–8, there is a copse of five pine trees in the middle of the room, the carpet is like the sea, the outside of the house is on the back wall, and an unmade bed is in the bottom right-hand corner.

23 Notes 23–29 and 31 apply to this and the following costume designs: Nos 74–76, 78–89, 91. In none of the catalogues is any costume identified

The catalogue states that No 17 was "19 costumes." There are 16 costume designs in the Wadsworth Atheneum's collection.

24 The catalogue describes Nos 17–24 as "Eight costumes."

25 The catalogue describes Nos 33–36 as "costumes."

26 The catalogue states that No 21 was "Costumes."

27 The catalogue describes No 50–65 as "'Le Bal' costumes."

28 The catalogue describes Nos 51–65 as "costumes."

29 The catalogue lists "2 designs for costumes."

30 Illustrated in Cyril W. Beaumont, *Five Centuries of Ballet Design*, p 45 and *Ballet Design Past and Present*, p 13. Another symbolic costume by Berain was, for example, for a Silversmith festooned with forks and spoons.

31 The catalogue describes No 161 as "Sept costumes divers."

32 Alexandra Danilova, *Choura*, p 102.

33 Lydia Sokolova, *Dancing for Diaghilev*, pp 273–4.

34 *Le Bal* was first performed at the Royal Opera House, Covent Garden, London on 20 June 1935.

35 "The Ballets Russes" in *The Sunday Times*, London 23 June 1935.

36 "'Le Bal'" in *The Times*, London 21 June 1935.

37 Leonide Massine, *My Life in Ballet*, p 200.

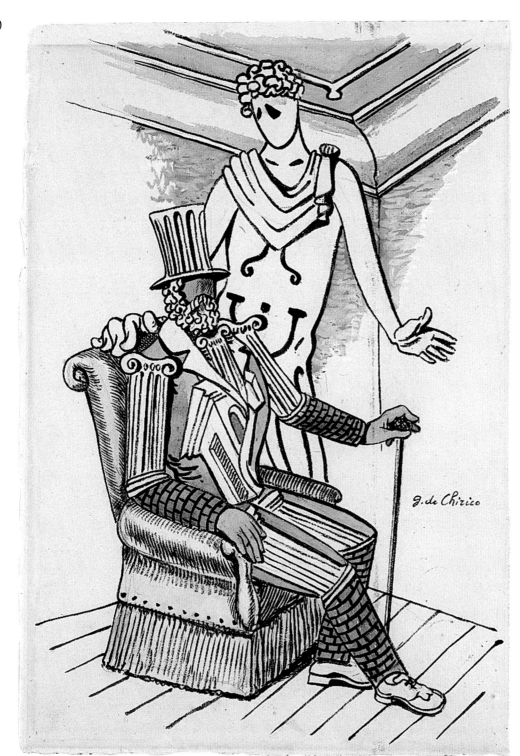

94   Design for the cover of the souvenir program of Diaghilev's Ballets Russes for the 1929 season in Monte Carlo and Paris

Graphite and tempera and/or watercolor on paper
15⅞ x 10¹⁵⁄₁₆ in: 40.4 x 27.7 cm
Signed center right in watercolor: "G. de Chirico"
1933.438

Exhibitions: London 1930, No 25; New York 1933, No 20; Chicago 1933, Nos 49; Northampton 1934, No 49; Hartford 1934; Paris 1939, No 152; Washington D.C. 1950–1; Edinburgh 1954, No 369; London 1954–5, No 404; Michigan 1957; Elmira 1958, No 5; Indianapolis 1959, No 153; Hartford 1961, No 17; Hartford 1965; New York 1965–6, No 57 (illustrated p 34); Spoleto 1966; New York 1966–7; Princeton 1968; Strasbourg 1969, No 446; Frankfurt-am-Main 1969, No 149; Hartford 1973; Hartford 1974; Hartford 1979; Coral Gables 1982; New York 1987–8; Hartford 1988; Worcester 1989.
Illustrations: Buckle 1955, p 119 No 161; Gadan & Maillard, p 22 (color); Garafola, No 46; Pozharskaya and Volodina, 257a.

The surreal cover of the Souvenir Program sets the scene for the ballet by incorporating the main design motifs, but in a topsy-turvy way. The seated figure on the armchair in an interior introduces the exterior architectural elements. It is almost a copy of the costume design for one of the guests (No 81, p 164), the only difference being the cravat, which here is also a column. The standing figure, emphasizing the white and creating mystery, is a copy of the design for the classical statues (No 82, p 164). This design also accurately sets the mood for the obviously lighthearted and amusing ballet.

A similar pair of figures, one standing, one seated, called *Il ritorno del figlino prodigo* (*The return of the prodigal son*), is plate 1 of a suite of 6 lithographs in *Metamorphosis* which de Chirico also made in 1929.

The Paris season was at the Théâtre Sarah-Bernhardt from 21 May to 12 June.

95*   Trophy, c. 1929

Graphite and tempera and/or watercolor with
    white highlights on paper
8¹¹⁄₁₆ x 13¾ in: 22 x 34.8 cm
Signed bottom right in watercolor: "G. de Chirico"
1937.88
Provenance: Julien Levy Gallery, New York

Exhibitions: Stamford 1957; Storrs 1963;
    New York 1965–6, No 53 (illustrated p 32; not
    shown in New York); Princeton 1968; Stras-
    bourg 1969, No 447 (as "Projet pour un décor
    du *Bal*?"); Frankfurt-am-Main 1969, No 150;
    Hartford 1973; Hartford 1974; Coral Gables
    1982; Columbus 1989.

This has previously been thought to be
"possibly for a stage setting." Indeed, as
can be seen from the exhibitions list above,
it was shown at Strasbourg and catalogued
as being a project for *Le Bal*. In fact, this
painting has nothing to do with either *Le
Bal* or any stage setting but, perhaps
because of the curtains, has deceptively
appeared to be theatrical.

This work is similar to the series of
paintings called "Trophies" which became a
recurring theme for de Chirico toward the
end of the 1920s. In these "trophies" he
assembled centrally a group of his favorite
objects, often behind curtains or scraps of
curtain, usually apparently in a desert with
miniature temples on the horizon on either
side, putting the objects into a grandiose
scale. This painting, unusually, has a faceless mannequin and figures with faces as
well as the usual bric-à-brac of a broken
column, wings, plumed helmets, and a
leaping horse.

Bacchus et Ariane (Bacchus and Ariadne)

Ballet in 2 scenes by Abel Hermant
Composer: Albert Roussel
Conductor: Philippe Gaubert
Choreographer: Serge Lifar
Designer (sets and costumes): Giorgio de Chirico
Principal Dancers:
    Bacchus: Serge Lifar
    Ariane: Olga Spessivtseva
    Thésée: Serge Peretti
First Performance: 22 May 1931, Théâtre national
    de l'Opéra, Paris

Synopsis

From the English version in the program.

"Scene 1. The scene is Naxos. Theseus, delighted with his victory over the Minotaur, frolics with Ariadne in the company of seven young men and seven virgins. Bacchus arrives whom Ariadne takes for an acrobat sent from Olympus to join in the victory celebrations. When she approaches him he envelops her with his cloak which has hypnotic powers and she falls asleep. Theseus, remembering that he has conquered the Minotaur, and the young men approach Bacchus aggressively. But Bacchus is unafraid and lays Ariadne under a rock. He then points the way of escape to Theseus and his young men by the sea where his ship with black sails is waiting. Zeus comes to his son's aid by filling the mountain with his thunder and the sky with his lightning. Bacchus celebrates his easy victory by dancing round Ariadne who rises, still asleep, and dances in her turn until he lays her down on a bed and disappears.

Scene 2. Ariadne awakens as if from a dream and realizes that Theseus has gone. She looks towards the sea and gazes at the ship with the black sails disappearing. In despair she is about to throw herself into the sea when Bacchus takes her in his arms. Their dance ends in the spell of love as priests and priestesses crowned with vines and flowers appear and dance with them. A faun and a bacchante present Ariadne with a gold cup into which they squeeze the juice from a bunch of grapes. Ariadne lifts the cup to her lips and is seized with a sacred delirium. She begins to dance, alone at first, but then with Bacchus, and then accompanied by the priests and priestesses until Bacchus rises into the sky carried aloft in a chariot."

After the unexpected death of Diaghilev in August 1929, and after Lifar and Kochno had declared that they would not continue with the Ballets Russes company, Lifar was approached by Jacques Rouché, the Director of the Paris Opéra, to participate in the planned revival of Beethoven's *Les Créatures de Prométhée* (*The Creatures of Prometheus*) in December 1929.[1] The production was a "triumph" for Lifar (according to Lifar), and after the first performance Rouché, embracing him, said: "Lifar, I am going to put into your hands the future of the National Ballet and of the Dance at the Opera . . . Henceforth this is your home . . . stay here!"[2] Lifar stayed at the Opéra,

except for a brief interlude after the Second World War, until 1958. He not only choreographed many of the ballets during that time, with himself usually in the leading role, but he completely revitalized ballet in France. After *Prometheus* Lifar had to fulfil an engagement with C. B. Cochran in Manchester and London,[3] before continuing his contract with the Opéra by choreographing and dancing in *Prelude Dominical*[4] and *L'Orchestre en Liberté* (see pp 178–81), two lightweight and even rather frivolous ballets.

Bacchus et Ariane was the first major work planned entirely by Lifar for the Opéra. Although audiences in Paris had admired Diaghilev's Ballets Russes and had enthusiastically supported their seasons, they had not accepted their "modernist" style which they considered to be quite alien to the French tradition and the current practises then prevailing at the Opéra. With *Bacchus et Ariane* Lifar intended to show those audiences the new direction he proposed that French ballet should take. "I was filled with the idea of organising a veritable homage to Diaghilev's memory. Not some work in the manner of Massine, Nijinska or Balanchine, but an entirely original ballet so as to perpetuate, in my own way, the aesthetic tradition of the *Ballets Russes*, and this was *Bacchus et Ariane*. I had conceived it on a very large scale. In order to remain faithful to Diaghilev's instructions I had to have everything new, the décor, the costumes, even the curtain. Giorgio de Chirico undertook the task. The book was written by Abel Hermant and the music by Albert Roussel. If one adds that I was responsible for the choreography, it would be difficult to imagine a whole that was more original, more 'new' for the Paris Opera."[5]

Classical mytholgy has been the most persistent and enduring influence on French writing, especially dramatic writing. In his scenario for *Bacchus et Ariane* Abel Hermant has gone further than Racine in his *Phèdre*. He has not taken the myth at its face value, but has tried to explain why Theseus abandons Ariadne. Although he extended the myth, the classical knowledge of the audience made the scenario comprehensible, and accepted by the critics. The classical legend of Ariadne in Naxos had also already inspired several composers, from Monteverdi to Massenet and Strauss. There was praise too for this version by Albert Roussel, and the musical interpretation by

the conductor. The score, according to Raymond Balliman, was "lively, sinewy, flawlessly constructed, and asserted itself through its diversity, strains, curious rhythms, great inspiration, and noble material. The writing confirms the composer's mastery of his pen."[6]

De Chirico was mostly ignored by the critics, but when noticed was criticized for "designing grotesque figures, cabalistic signs on superfluous cloths or curtains, and disconcertingly whimsical costumes. Oh! That Bacchus, like Puss in Boots, and with gloves on, and those virgins in jerseys decorated with their breasts drawn in charcoal!"[7]

Serge Lifar, as dancer, was praised, but more as if he were an acrobat or gymnast rather than dancer: the jump he made from the top of a rostrum into the wings was six meters.

Serge Lifar, as choreographer, or *choreauthor*, a term he invented and preferred, received a battering from all the critics. None was more vitriolic than André Levinson who, although an admirer of Lifar the dancer, had battled ceaselessly against the very principles of Diaghilev's Ballets Russes: "The present and the future of French ballet have found themselves to be tied to the career of a young Russian dancer, a beautiful and talented boy, busy perfecting an already remarkable craft. But nothing qualifies him to be employed as a choreographer except the capricious kindness that the late Diaghilev once bestowed upon him.[8] And it is by virtue of this that M. Serge Lifar, whom I have praised from his very first performances for his gifts as an interpreter, but who had the greatest need to be directed, is the director in charge of the ballet company at the Opéra leading a courageous and charming troupe, which does not know whether to laugh or cry as it proceeds from one failure to the next. Even those who are unrepentant in their vulgar infatuation with anything that is 'all the rage' are puzzled by the inanity of his invention and the forbidding monotony of the distortions in which he takes pleasure."[9]

But Serge Lifar survived the battering. He thought, as a *choreauthor*, that *Bacchus et Ariane*, a classical myth staged in contemporary way, was his "first leap into space before the birth of *Icare*,"[10] a revolutionary neo-classical ballet which Lifar choreographed in 1935 to "rhythms" by George Szyfer.

96   Set design for scene 1: The storm, with Jupiter

Graphite and tempera and/or watercolor with
    white highlights on paper
9⅝ x 12½ in: 24.4 x 31.8 cm
Unsigned
1933.455

Exhibitions: New York 1933, No 22; Chicago 1933,
    No 66; Northampton 1934, No 66; Williams-
    burg 1940; Elmira 1958, No 18; Indianapolis
    1959, No 170; Hartford 1965, No 17; New York
    1965–6, No 74 (illustrated p 38); New York
    1966–7; Princeton 1968; Hartford 1973; Hart-
    ford 1978–9; Worcester 1989.
Illustration: Rischbieter, p 182f.

The set was criticized for not being obviously Naxos, and yet Chirico has introduced elements of rock, sea, sand, and a fragment of a Greek column which, with his appropriate color scheme of pink and brown, red and yellow, give the desired atmosphere for the setting. These three designs are preliminary sketches for the two sets and drop curtain between the scenes, as is evident from their unfinished quality and imprecision with areas left unpainted. In the two set drawings the rostra and the ship are not properly defined, and the drawing for the cloth, though more precise, is still only a sketch. Scene painters and carpenters require drawings of greater definition. Indeed, a more refined and finished drawing for the backcloth to scene 1 remained in the Lifar collection until it was sold at Sotheby's, London in 1984, Lot 59.

97 Design for the drop curtain, prelude to scene 2: Sleeping Ariadne

Graphite and tempera and/or watercolor with
   white highlights on paper
9⁷⁄₁₆ x 12¼ in: 24.0 x 31 cm
Unsigned
1933.457

Exhibitions: New York 1933, No 23; Chicago 1933,
   No 67; Northampton 1934, No 67; Poughkeep-
   sie 1940; Williamsburg 1940; Baltimore 1941,
   No 20; Indianapolis 1959, No 172; Hartford
   1961; Hartford 1965, No 19; New York 1965–6,
   No 76 (illustrated p 39); New York 1966–7;
   Princeton 1968; Hartford 1973; Amherst 1974;
   Frankfurt-am-Main 1986, No 209 (illustrated
   p 260); Columbus 1989; Worcester 1989.
Illustration: Rischbieter, p 182e.
Both the groups of figures and the rocks have been
   pasted on.

Above: scene 2, after the storm, on stage at the Opéra, Paris.

98 Set design for scene 2: After the storm

Graphite and tempera and/or watercolor with white highlights on paper
9⅝ x 12½ in: 24.5 x 31.8 cm
Unsigned
1933.456

Exhibitions: Chicago 1933, No 68; Northampton 1934, No 68; Williamsburg 1940; Indianapolis 1959, No 171; Rowayton 1960; Hartford 1965, No 18; New York 1965–6, No 75 (illustrated p 38); New York 1966–7; Princeton 1968; Hartford 1973; Hartford 1978–9; Columbus 1989; Worcester 1989.

Notes

1 For details about the background to this production see Schervashidze, *Prométhée*, pp 306–10.
2 Serge Lifar, *Ma Vie*, p 95.
3 See Christian Bérard, *La Nuit*, pp 140–44.
4 The full title is *Prélude Dominical et les six pièces à danser pour chaque jour de la semaine* by Guy Ropartz with set and costumes by Paul Colin, first performed at the Opéra on 16 February 1931.
5 Serge Lifar, *op cit*, p 111.
6 Raymond Balliman, "A l'Opéra" in *L'Ami du Peuple*, 24 May 1931.
7 Anon, *L'Est Républicain*, 12 June 1931.
8 He is referring to Stravinsky's *Renard* which was revived by Diaghilev in 1929 with new choreography by Lifar (see Larionov, pp 235–38).
9 André Levinson, "La Danse" in unidentified newspaper (but probably *Comoedia*), 28 May 1931.
10 Serge Lifar in Paul Valéry, *Serge Lifar à l'Opéra*.

Jean Cocteau

French
born 1889 Maisons Lafitte (Seine-et-Oise)
died 1963 Milly-la-Forêt (Essonne)

99 Serge Lifar

Graphite on gray board
19⅝ x 17⅝ in: 50 x 44.7 cm
Signed, inscribed, and dated in pencil lower left:
    "Jean / * / à mon / cher ami / Serge / * / 1931"
1933.460

Exhibitions: New York 1933, No 24; Chicago 1933,
    No 71; Northampton 1934, No 71; Paris 1939,
    No 183; Williamsburg 1940; Baltimore 1941,
    No 17; New York 1944; Edinburgh 1954, No
    470; London 1954–5, No 479; Elmira 1958, No
    57; New York 1965–6, No 79 (illustrated p 8) ;
    New York 1966–7; Princeton 1968; Hartford
    1974; Hartford 1988; Worcester 1989.
Illustration: Buckle 1955, p 120 No 164.

Cocteau, who at the age of eighteen recognized a good bandwagon when he saw it, jumped on it, and so became one of the earliest and most ardent sycophants of the Ballets Russes after they took Paris by storm in 1909. With his heavily rouged cheeks and lipstick, he gave the immediate impression of being merely a frivolous but fashionable young man. His immense charm and clever conversation, however, confounded that impression, and he was adopted by the company as a kind of fairy jester. It also quickly became evident that he had an astonishing and lively talent for drawing.

Cocteau began by drawing, writing came later. He is best remembered now for his films, but he always thought of himself as a poet and described all his work as poetry, "poésie," as well as "poésie de théâtre, poésie cinématographique, poésie graphique" and so forth. "Drawing," he wrote in a letter in 1922, "greatly amuses me. It's a relief when I am writing, or *not* writing."[1] Through his early study of the caricatures by Sem, a famous cartoonist, Cocteau developed his skill for capturing a character by means of a single line. He knew he had the ability to catch a likeness but he wrote: "A line must live at each point along its course in such a way that the artist's presence makes itself felt above that of the model."[2]

Cocteau began his long association with the Ballets Russes by drawing sympathetic caricatures of Diaghilev, Misia Sert his great friend and confidante, Nijinsky, Stravinsky, Bakst, and later, Picasso, Erik Satie, Francis Poulenc, and others either separately or together. In 1910, in adoration of Nijinsky, he published a thin book of poems, *Vaslav Nijinsky, six vers de Jean Cocteau, six dessins de Paul Iribe*. In 1911 Bakst persuaded Diaghilev to commission Cocteau to design two posters, one featuring Nijinsky and the other Karsavina in *Le Spectre de la Rose* (see pp 67–70) which had its first performance that year during the season in Monte Carlo. Cocteau mischievously made Karsavina uncannily resemble himself. He wrote the libretto, with Federigo de Madrazo, for the unsuccessful ballet *Le Dieu Bleu* (see pp 71–73) which had its first performance postponed from 1911 to 13 May 1912. In 1913 he contributed synopses of some of the major ballets to a luxuriously produced book on Léon Bakst's art.[3] He wrote two more ballets for Diaghilev, both highly original, revolutionary, and much discussed: *Parade* in 1917 with cubist designs by Picasso, his first work for the theatre, and *Le Train Bleu* in 1924. Nothing came of *David*, a project in which Cocteau tried to interest Stravinsky in 1914, but they finally did collaborate on *Oedipus Rex*, intended as a birthday present for Diaghilev and produced by him in 1927, for which Cocteau's text was translated into Latin.

Cocteau obviously fell in love with Lifar, as did everyone else, when he arrived as a beautiful boy and aspiring dancer from Kiev in 1923. But although all biographies are strangely reticent about the relationship between them, it was surely one of more than mere friendship and mutual admiration. Lifar himself gives the most revealing clue in his biography of Diaghilev: "I had been invited by friends to one of our own performances, although it was against the rules for any of us ever to be seen in front of the curtain. My seat was next that of Cocteau, Auric, Trubnikov and others. Diaghilev came in, and, adjusting his monocle, saw us all: whereupon the right side of his face began nervously twitching, his eyebrows rose, and moving towards us, in a perturbed and irritated voice, he began to address me as follows: 'If I am not mistaken, you, young man, are in your second year in the company, and should be aware that the management has forbidden members of the *corps-de-ballet* to occupy seats intended for the paying public.' During the entr'acte he met me in the foyer, and literally threw me out: 'I forbid you, once and for all, to be seen in a theatre. If you don't choose to obey me, you're at liberty to leave the company, and spend all your nights in the front row with Jeanchik.'"[4] But perhaps this story is more revealing about Diaghilev's jealousy and fiery temper. Lifar sat no more in the auditorium, but the relationship with "Jeanchik" continued. After Diaghilev's death they collaborated on several projects: Cocteau designed the poster and catalogue cover for Lifar's Pushkin exhibition in 1937, wrote a "souvenir" for his Diaghilev exhibition in 1939, and designed the sets and costumes for his ballet *Phèdre* in 1950.

This drawing is a masterly exercise of draftsmanship. The double line (apart from being extremely difficult to do) accentuates the three-dimensional effect of the drawing without blurring the definition. Behind the intimate and affectionate nature of the pose, with Lifar at first glance apparently asleep, we can detect an uneasy nervousness. His eye is only partly closed, he is warily watch-

Above: reverse of No 99, showing more studies of Serge Lifar.

ing the draftsman, and we are made to feel that he would be ready to pounce like a panther if needs be.

On the reverse of this drawing there is an unfinished pencil sketch, also of Lifar asleep with his head in the same position but with his arm over his head, and another sketch of Lifar's head, signed in pencil "Jean."

A head and torso portrait, in the same "double-line" style, of the dancer wearing a similar vest was used by Lifar as the frontispiece to *A l'aube de mon destin: chez Diaghilev, sept ans aux Ballets Russes* (*At the dawn of my destiny: with Diaghilev, seven years with the Ballets Russes*), published in Paris 1949.

Notes

1 Quoted by Pierre Chanel, "A Thousand Flashes of Genius" in Arthur Peters, *Jean Cocteau and the French Scene*, pp 107–8.
2 From "De la ligne" in *La Difficulté d'être* (*The Difficulty of being*).
3 See Arsène Alexandre, *The Decorative Art of Léon Bakst*.
4 Serge Lifar, *Diaghilev*, p 371.

Paul Colin

*French
born 1892 Nancy
died 1985 Paris*

L'Orchestre en Liberté

Choreographic farce in 1 act by Frantz Gautier and
    Paul Gsell
Composer: Henry Sauveplane
Conductor: J.-E. Szyfer
Choreographer: Serge Lifar
Designer (set and costumes): Paul Colin
Principal Dancers:
    Solo violin: Serge Lifar
    Flute: Suzanne Lorcia
    Cymbals: Serge Peretti, Mlle Lamballe
First Performance: 11 February 1931, Théâtre
    national de l'Opéra, Paris

Synopsis

From the program in which it was printed in
English as well as French.

"A performance at the Opéra is just drawing to
an end and the closing bars of an emphatic finale
are heard.

The spectator is supposed to be placed at the
back of the stage and therefore is facing the
reverse side of the scenery. An electrician crosses
the stage and the lights are extinguished.

After a short while, however, a bluish light
gradually dissipates the gloom and extraordinary
happenings take place.

Freed from their bondage to man, the instruments left in the orchestra pit and reposing against
the scenery are suddenly animated by a new and
strange life.

The solo violin calls to the flute and the other
instruments, tuba, bassoon, double-bass, oboe,
cymbals, and horns, dance without constraint,
when suddenly the conductor's baton interrupts
them and essays to force them to perform well-
worn melodies. They revolt and turn him out in a
fury. At this moment various instruments of the
negro music make their way onto the stage, drive
off the traditional orchestra, form themselves into
a barbaric jazz and give themselves up to savage
contortions. But musical taste soon has its revenge.
The solo violin re-appears with his comrades, and
together they wage a fierce battle against the
Negroes, who retire discomfited.

Peace reigns once again, celebrated by a joyous
bourrée. Fraternity and felicity succeed in establishing a harmony which the stereotyped and conserv-
ative authority of the conductor's baton had been
unable to obtain. From the heavens the harp
descends, quivering, bringing with it the grace
which alone should inspire all art and all love. As
the violin and flute embrace tenderly the final
perfect chord is heard."

Serge Lifar described this ballet as
"Music-hall at the Opéra."[1] It was meant
as an amusing ballet, with no very profound intentions, on the theme of the battle
between jazz and classical music. Furthermore, the jazz instruments were personified
by black dancers while the symphony

Above: Serge Lifar as the Violin.

orchestra instruments were personified by
white dancers. Such a theme would be
unthinkable and outlawed for being racist
today, especially as the blacks apparently
lose, but in 1931 Paris was still enthralled by
jazz and all black culture.

In 1920 Rolf de Maré, a rich Swedish
aristocrat passionately interested in ballet
and folk art, founded the Ballets Suédois for
his friend, the dancer and choreographer,
Jean Börlin, and took on a lease of the
Théâtre des Champs-Elysées. In 1923 he
produced the "Negro ballet" *La Création du
Monde* (see pp 247–50). At the end of 1924
de Maré wound up the Ballets Suédois and
turned the Théâtre des Champs-Elysées into
a music hall. The true spirit of the "jazz
age" in Paris was given substance by Rolf
de Maré on 2 October 1925 when he presented a troupe of black musicians and
performers straight from Broadway under
the title of *Revue Nègre*. Paul Colin's poster
featuring two black musicians and "a very
pretty girl" in the company brilliantly
interpreted the exuberance of the revue, and
launched Josephine Baker's inimitable
career. A year later, in July 1926, Colin
designed the poster for the *Revue des Black
Birds* by another troupe of black performers.

In 1927 Colin produced and published *Le
Tumulte Noir*, an album of 44 lithographs in
a series of caricatures giving an affectionate
and gently satirical view of black entertain-
ers, including Johnny Hudgings and
Josephine Baker, as well as other personalities such as Mistinguett, and Ida Rubinstein
doing the Charleston under a palm tree.

In view of his sympathetic affinity with
the black craze, Colin was a natural choice
as designer for *L'Orchestre en Liberté*. The
idea of symbolizing musical instruments as
theatrical costumes was not a new idea; it
was a device that had been successfully
used for a number of court ballets during
the reigns of Louis XIII and Louis XIV in the
seventeenth and eighteenth centuries. The
novelty in Colin's case was the symbolic use
of jazz instruments on black players. Jean
Laurent and Julie Sazonova, in their naturally biased account, thought that "this
ballet, reminiscent of the games of the
eighteenth century with the instruments
painted on the costumes, was a charming
entertainment, an amusing prank, a caprice
against jazz wanting to take hold of the
domain established by classical music, with
Lifar-violin relaxing in a refined and stately
dance."[2] But André Levinson, a sterner
critic, was dismissive of the ballet saying
that "the choreographic material of the
piece appears to be so thin and its humour
so forced that the spectators remain puzzled
by it, afraid that they might not have understood it, but suspecting a little that there
was nothing to understand."[3]

Although the ballet was performed only
seven times, it was an undoubted success
for Paul Colin, if not much for anyone else.

100 Project for a poster based on the 179
costume design for Serge Lifar
as the Violin

Charcoal, tempera and/or watercolor on card stock
23³/₁₆ x 15⅛ in: 59.2 x 38.4 cm
Signed lower right in gouache: "Paul / Colin"
1933.458

Exhibitions: Chicago 1933, No 69; Northampton
    1934, No 69; Williamsburg 1940; Cambridge
    1942; Michigan 1957; Richmond 1959; New
    York 1965–6, No 77 (illustrated p 40); New York
    1966–7; Princeton 1968; Hartford 1974;
    Hartford 1978–9; Worcester 1989.
Illustration: Hartford Symphony 97/98 Season
    prospectus, cover (color).

This is almost certainly a preliminary
sketch for a poster based on the original
costume design for Serge Lifar as the solo
violin which is in the Bibliothèque-Musée
de l'Opéra, Paris.[4] Observing his principle
that a poster's "message should be understood at 100 kilometers an hour," Colin has
made a bolder (both in drawing and in
color) and more simplified version of the
costume design. The original design, on a
white, unpainted background, and
unsigned, is very delicate and includes the
inscription "Serge Lifar," whereas this
drawing is boldly signed as Colin signed all
his poster work, and the background is
painted in appropriate colors for the necessary letters to be added. It is doubtful,
however, if this sketch was further developed for a poster, or indeed if a poster was
ever made specially for the production.

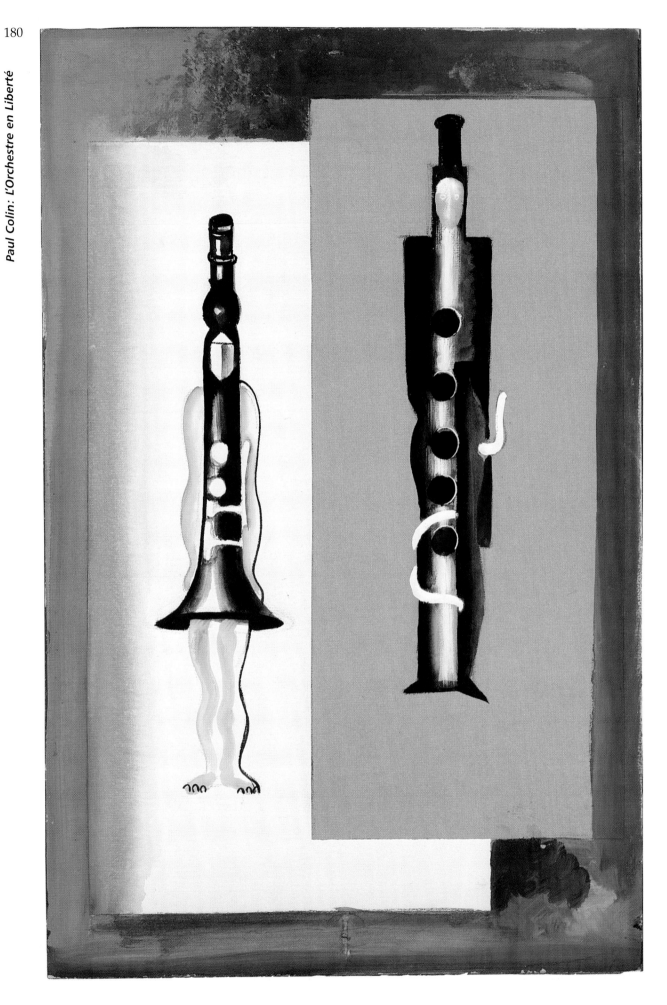

101 Collage based on the costume designs for the Oboe and the Flute

Graphite, tempera and/or watercolor, and chalk on collage of paper mounted to heavy cardboard
23½ x 15¼ in: 59.7 x 38.9 cm
The reverse of the board inscribed in blue crayon "P Colin / costumes / L'Orchestre en Liberté / à l'Opéra"
1933.459

Exhibitions: Chicago 1933, No 70; Northampton 1934, No 70; Richmond 1959; New York 1965–6, No 78 (illustrated p 40); New York 1966–7; Princeton 1968; Hartford 1974; Hartford 1978–9; Coral Gables 1982; New York 1987–8; Columbus 1989; Worcester 1989.
Illustration: Hartford Symphony 97/98 Season prospectus, p 7 (color).

These are stylized versions of the original costume designs for the Oboe and the Flute which are in the Bibliothèque-Musée de l'Opéra, Paris.[5] These drawings, in spite of the arms and legs on the oboe, are less obviously for theatrical costumes than the originals, and their execution is duller.

The costumes were made up of a head-dress for the mouthpieces and the main part painted on a leotard. They were successful and practical as dance costumes, although it required some imagination to interpret the symbolism.

Notes

1 Paul Valéry, Jean Cocteau, Serge Lifar, *Serge Lifar à l'Opéra.*
2 Jean Laurent and Julie Sazonova, *Serge Lifar, Rénovateur du ballet français*, p 59.
3 André Levinson, *Les Visages de la Danse*, pp 133–4.
4 Inventory number: D.216 (85. Folio 66).
5 Inventory numbers: Oboe D.216 (85. Folio 51), Flute D.216 (85. Folio 58).

André Derain

French
born 1880 Chatou (Yvelines)
died 1954 Chambourcy (Yvelines)

La Boutique Fantasque (The Fantastic Toy Shop)

Comic ballet in 1 act, 3 scenes by Serge Diaghilev, Léon Bakst and Leonide Massine based on *The Fairy Doll*[1]
Composer: Gioacchino Rossini orchestrated by Ottorino Respighi
Conductor: Henry Defosse
Choreographer: Leonide Massine
Designer (set and costumes): André Derain
Principal Dancers:
    The Shopkeeper: Enrico Cecchetti
    Russian Merchant: Serge Grigoriev
    His wife: Josephine Cecchetti
    Can-can dancers: Lydia Lopokova,
        Leonide Massine
    Tarantella dancers: Lydia Sokolova,
        Leon Woizikovsky
    Cossack chief: Nicholas Zverev
    Dancing poodles: Vera Clark, Nicholas Kremnev
Company: Diaghilev's Ballets Russes
First Performance: 5 June 1919, Alhambra Theatre, London

Synopsis

The action takes place in about 1865. Scene 1. Customers enter a toy-shop and the shopkeeper shows them his latest novelties in dolls. Among them are Tarantella dancers, a snob, a street hawker, kings and queens from a pack of cards, two poodles, cossacks, and two can-can dancers. The customers are two English ladies, an American family, and a large Russian family of the rich merchant class. They are all particularly fascinated by the can-can dancers. The parents of each family buy one of the dolls which are put into boxes. The families leave, arranging to call for their purchases in the morning. Pleased with their sale, the shopkeeper and his assistant lock up the shop and depart.

Scene 2. At nightfall the dolls are left lamenting the fate of the two dancers who are lovers and are about to be separated, having found different buyers. The lovers make up their minds to escape. They take an affectionate farewell of their companions and leave at dawn.

Scene 3. In the morning the shopkeeper and his assistant come to open the shop. The buyers return to collect their purchases. They are annoyed at not having received them the previous evening as promised, but the shopkeeper reassures them, and tells them they are packed and ready to be taken away. When he goes to fetch them he finds nothing but paper, and is completely disconcerted. The customers, who believe that he has fooled them, revenge themselves by attacking him and throwing the shop into disorder, but the shopkeeper cannot explain what has happened. The dolls, returning to life, frighten the customers out of the shop.

Nothing delighted Diaghilev more than finding unknown music by famous composers. In 1917, while staying in Rome, he discovered[2] a large collection of unpublished lighthearted piano pieces by Rossini, called *Les Riens* (*Nothings*), which he had composed for the entertainment of his guests at dinner parties. These "merry compositions, full of irony" are described, anonymously, but actually by Diaghilev himself, in the Souvenir Program: "From the Albums we may take an 'Anti-dancing Valse,' a 'Funeral as Carnival,' and 'Asthmatic Study,' and 'Abortive Polka,' a piece called 'Ugh! Peas!' a 'Convulsive Prelude,' and even a Petite Valse: 'Castor Oil.' In the Russian vein, Rossini composed a Siberian Dance, a Slav March (which serves as prelude to 'La Boutique Fantasque'), and even a Tartar Bolero . . . Of these delightful pages which sparkle with satire, and are so little expected from the composer of the 'Barber,' having more in common with Chopin, Delibes, or Glinka, the music of 'La Boutique Fantasque' is composed."[3] The central piece was a can-can dedicated to his favorite composer, Offenbach.

These pieces immediately struck Diaghilev as being eminently suitable for a revival of a ballet on the theme of *The Fairy Doll* (dolls coming to life) which had been suggested to him by Grigoriev.[4] Ottorino Respighi was commissioned to orchestrate the pieces, and Massine was given the choreography. Massine, compressing events, described his enthusiasm for the project: "The gaiety and variety of the music inspired me with the idea of choreographing a series of dances by animated toys, and it was agreed to create a ballet within the framework of a toyshop which offered its customers a wide range of dancing dolls. Diaghilev sensibly urged me to keep to a comparatively simple libretto which would follow Rossini's music closely."[5] The ballet was given the new title of *La Boutique Fantasque*, with the libretto of *The Fairy Doll* (see pp 59–61) being revised by Diaghilev himself and Léon Bakst, who, in view of his previous production in Russia, was asked at first to design the sets and costumes. It proved to be an unfortunate decision, for it resulted in an acrimonious quarrel and a rift between them which lasted for two years.

La Boutique Fantasque was a long time in preparation. For Bakst it led to nothing except a valuable set of drawings. He worked on the production during the early part of 1918. A design for the set and thirty-one costume designs were exhibited in The Hague from 19 May until July 1918 in an exhibition sponsored by Mrs Alice Warder Garrett whose husband, John Work Garrett, was then the American ambassador to The Netherlands. It is therefore strange that Bakst wrote to Diaghilev on 18 July 1918 in a postscript to a letter mostly about *Les Femmes de Bonne Humeur*: "I am drawing the costumes for *Boutique Fantasque* in little easy stages: reviving the Naples of 1858."[6] Bakst deliberately concealed his exhibition from Diaghilev, who would not have allowed the designs for a ballet to be shown anywhere before its first performance. But Bakst could not resist the commercial opportunity of an important exhibition. While he was exploiting his designs as fine art, there was silence from Diaghilev about the production until the spring of 1919 when he suddenly asked for the remainder. Diaghilev may have thought that Bakst had done no work on the ballet so that the rush which he now imposed upon him would force him to resign, or he may have discovered that Bakst had already exhibited his designs which infuriated him. In either case Diaghilev's deviousness had its desired effect in allowing him to commission someone else, because, in a letter dated 24 March 1919, Bakst, somewhat tongue-in-cheek, wrote: "Since you are in such a hurry, ask another painter to design this production for you. Perhaps he will cook up something for you quickly."[7] Bakst, in making this suggestion, never supposed that Diaghilev would take him up on it. But he did; he commissioned André Derain. Bakst did not speak to Diaghilev again until he worked on *The Sleeping Princess* in 1921 (see pp 87–101).

Massine gives a different, and incorrect, explanation: "When the preliminary sketches arrived he [Diaghilev] was disappointed. He felt that they lacked charm and gaiety."[8] But he was correct in stating: "Diaghilev was ruthless in anything that affected the work of the company. The artistic perfection of his productions was the most important thing in his life and he would allow nothing, not even a long-standing friendship, to stand in the way of it."[9] Diaghilev, sensing that the artistic climate had changed after the First World War and, perhaps particularly, after the Russian Revolution, realized that he could not merely return to the old days and repeat past successes, but that he had to advance with the times and embrace the modern school more firmly. In a rather quaint translation, he explained his choice of Derain in the *Souvenir Program*: "André Derain, the great *fauve*, the leader, with Matisse, of the new French school, is essentially a painter of easel pictures. He is a renovator of the purest French classical painting without being a mere reconstructor. This Italian primitive, in the guise of the modern French movement, is at the same time a great revolutionist in the region of colour. Deriving, like Matisse, from the Impressionists and Divisionists, Derain's point of departure is that at which Matisse ended his quest. Derain has progressed in the direction of conscious colour. He has begun to measure out colour in careful doses. To the bacchanalian splendour of the Russian decorators he has opposed the classic harmony of colour, aided by the well-balanced taste of a Latin deriving from Giotto and Leonardo. That is why, in the harmony of the scenery and costumes of "La Boutique Fantasque," we are agreeably surprised at the application of this broad view and at the admirable result of his quest of harmonies that are tender and calming."[10]

Derain produced an appropriately whimsical, delightful and child-like setting which charmed everyone except the scene painter, Vladimir Polunin, who began by showing his disapproval that a mere easel painter had been engaged instead of a theater designer. "His design," he wrote, "painted in oils, at first glance seemed to me so untheatrical that I could hardly conceive how it might be used for the stage. Diaghileff, too, seemed to have some doubts, so that a certain perceptible mutual uneasiness existed between the designer and the executor at the very outset, which did not seem to promise satisfactory results."[11] Although the uneasiness continued, with Polunin never quite appreciating the painter's intentions and Derain never quite fathoming the requirements of the scene painter, they managed to work together well enough to convince Gilbert Cannan, the critic of *Theatre Arts*, into writing of Derain: "His designs are flawless and he has an exquisite sense of the theatre,

every touch, every combination of form and color is intriguing."[12] What can have Polunin have thought if he read this notice? But the scene painter is used to being ignored.

La Boutique Fantasque was Massine's first essay in devising a new form of naturalistic realism in ballet inspired by his study of Spanish folk-dancing, especially flamenco. Diaghilev, in the same *Souvenir Program*, explained Massine's theory: "Adopting as principle the absolute perfection of the style of dancing in Spain, which is what is termed in pictorial art a 'miniature,' Massine presents himself as a choreographist [sic] of easel pictures. Massine is a realist in three dimensions. He is a choreographist in space . . . Massine transforms reality in his imagination, but in all that he does he starts directly from nature, which he interprets with a vision that is full of vitality, opposed to all formula, and perhaps even to all principle."[13]

Designer and choreographer worked closely together. For Derain's setting Massine devised an uninterrupted sequence of hilariously witty dances for the toys: Sokolova and Woizikovsky as the Tarantella Dancers, Idzikowski as the Snob, Zverev as the Cossack Chief and Istomina as his Sweetheart, Clark and Kremnev as the Poodles, culminating in a can-can danced by Lydia Lopokova and Leonide Massine himself which anyone who saw them never forgot. Certainly not Cyril Beaumont, who wrote that it had been "presented with the utmost brilliance and fire."[14] But the secret of the success of the choreography was, as Sokolova remarked, that "Massine had seized the opportunity to type-cast every dancer with absolute precision. The interpreters of even the smallest part could flatter themselves that Massine had taken as much trouble to show them off to advantage as if they had been the stars of the ballet."[15] Such was the huge popular success of the ballet that Cyril Beaumont reported that when the curtain fell on the first performance "the applause was literally deafening. But when the collaborators came forward to take a call in their turn, Derain was frightened at the warmth of his welcome and had to be dragged upon the stage; Massine made repeated graceful bows; while Lopokova, half-crying, half-laughing, seemed divided between sadness and delight."[16] The ballet was a huge popular success. Everyone agreed with Gilbert Cannan who "felt with a sense of intense relief that a sense of humor had been

restored to a tortured world. Men and women could be allowed once more to smile to themselves."[17] And Cyril Beaumont boasted, as did everyone else who could: "I was there, I saw the first night of *La Boutique Fantasque*."[18]

Postscript: in 1920, Raoul Gunsbourg, Director of the Société des Bains de Mer at Monte Carlo, tried to claim authorship of *La Boutique Fantasque* through a lawyer, Maurice Coolus, saying that his idea had been plagiarized. Diaghilev, in a reply dated 20 February 1920 wrote: "On the subject of M. Raoul Gunsbourg's claim on the libretto of the *Boutique Fantasque*, I have to inform you that I commissioned this ballet from M. Respighi in Rome in December 1916. I took as an idea the theme of toys which come to life in a toy shop, a theme which I had known since childhood and which has been used in an innumerable number of ballets, notably in *Puppenfee*."[19]

102* Design for a detail of the cut cloth

Graphite and tempera and/or watercolor on paper
7 x 9¹¹⁄₁₆ in: 17.6 x 24.6 cm
Inscribed top left and top right in pencil: "N 7"
Inscribed center right in pencil: "Table plus
    cafetière"
Purchased of Marie Harriman Gallery from J. J.
    Goodwin Fund
1935.35
Provenance: Leonide Massine

Exhibitions: New York 1937–8, No ? 708 ; Paris
    1939, No 192; Los Angeles 1939–40; Williams-
    burg 1940; New York 1941–2; Edinburgh 1954,
    No 268; London 1954–5, No 308; Stamford
    1957; Indianapolis 1959; New York 1965–6,
    No 80 (illustrated p 41) (not shown in New
    York); Hartford 1974; Columbus 1989; Worces-
    ter 1989.
Illustrations: Souvenir Programme for Alhambra
    Theatre 30 April–30 July 1919; Buckle 1955,
    p 33, No 35; Haskell, p 85.

This table was painted straight onto one of the arches of the cut cloth (on the audience's right), representing the arches of the shop front seen from the inside beyond which could be seen the backcloth. W. A. Propert, who thought that Derain's set was the most interesting aspect of the production, described the scene: "It was at first sight frankly uncouth and almost defiantly ugly—the pervading colours a hot brown against a cold grey, with chairs and tables that defied all the laws of perspective roughly painted on the background and the wings—and far behind, seen through the

arches of the shop-front, a child's dream of houses, hills and trees, and a little river with a gigantic paddle-steamer that filled it from end to end. It was like the work of a ten-year-old schoolgirl, and yet the simplicity of its design was so transparently sincere, there was such a feeling of air and space everywhere—the colour of the background was so clear and cool as seen through the brown screen—and above all there were

such enchanting arrangements of fruits and flowers painted on the wings, that one forgave all those yards of ugly colour and impossible furniture."[20]

Who painted the table on the cloth? Massine wrote: "With its bright colours and *trompe l'oeil* chairs and tables, which Derain painted on the drop-cloth himself, the *boutique* had the right atmosphere of a toyshop seen through the eyes of a child."[21] But Vladimir Polunin, the scene painter, wrote that he had painted "the pieces of furniture straight on to the walls of the *boutique*," although he disapproved of the fact that "their perspective did not correspond with the normal perspective employed in the general scene."[22]

Polunin also wrote that Derain did paint some of the set himself but that in "introducing new details, he paid no heed to warnings of a technical character, but used such thick colours that he ran the risk of their cracking and peeling off."[23] According to him, Derain painted only some minor details. The very existence of this design, which is clear, precise, and detailed, suggests that Derain made it for Polunin to transfer to the canvas.

Left: the scene on stage showing the painted table.

Notes

1 See Léon Bakst, pp 59–61.
2 According to Serge Grigoriev in *The Diaghilev Ballet*, p 142: "In various libraries in Paris and Rome he [Diaghilev] had discovered a number of little known compositions by Rossini." This was confirmed by Cyril W. Beaumont in *The Diaghilev Ballet in London*, p 134, and partly confirmed by Arnold Haskell in *Diaghileff*, p 298: "Diaghileff, who had been making further finds, decided to make a ballet out of certain pieces that Rossini had composed." Leonide Massine, however, in *My Life in Ballet*, p 119, states: "Ottorino Respighi had brought to his [Diaghilev's] notice a series of little-known works by Rossini." This is endorsed by Richard Buckle in *Diaghilev*, p 337, and by Vicente García-Márquez in *Massine*, p 114.
3 [Serge Diaghilev], *Souvenir Programme* for the Alhambra Theatre, London 30 April–30 July 1919. Cyril W. Beaumont in *The Diaghilev Ballet in London*, p 132, referring to this program, wrote: "One evening, however, Diaghilev showed me an advance proof of a little illustrated monograph he had prepared, which dealt in a witty manner with the new ballet."
4 Serge Grigoriev, *op cit*, p 142, although Arnold Haskell, *op cit*, p 298 states that the first idea for the ballet had been on the theme of a pack of playing cards.
5 Leonide Massine, *op cit*, p 119.
6 Quoted in I. S. Zilberstein and V. A. Samkov, *Sergei Diaghilev* Vol 2, p 128.
7 From a French translation of the original letter in Russian in the Kochno Collection at the Bibliothèque nationale.
8 Leonide Massine, *op cit*, p 132.
9 Leonide Massine, *op cit*, p 133.
10 [Serge Diaghilev], *Souvenir Programme, op cit*.
11 Vladimir Polunin, *The Continental Method of Scene Painting*, p 56.
12 Gilbert Cannan, *Theatre Arts* Vol IV, January ?1920, p 77.
13 [Serge Diaghilev], *Souvenir Programme, op cit*.
14 Cyril W. Beaumont *The Diaghilev Ballet in London*, p 137
15 Lydia Sokolova, *Dancing for Diaghilev*, p 136.
16 Cyril W. Beaumont, *op cit*, p 136.
17 Gilbert Cannan, *op cit*.
18 Cyril W. Beaumont, *op cit*, p 139.
19 Quoted from a letter written from the Hôtel Continental, Paris, in a private collection.
20 W. A. Propert, *The Russian Ballet in Western Europe*, pp 52–3.
21 Leonide Massine, *My Life in Ballet*, p 133.
22 Vladimir Polunin, *The Continental Method of Scene Painting*, p 58.
23 Vladimir Polunin, *ibid*, p 57.

Jack-in-the-Box

Ballet in 1 act
Composer: Erik Satie orchestrated by Darius
    Milhaud[1]
Conductor: Roger Desormière
Choreographer: George Balanchine
Designer (set and costumes): André Derain .
Principal Dancers:
    Jack in the Box: Stanislas Idzikowski
    The Black Ballerina: Alexandra Danilova
    The White Ballerinas: Lubov Tchernicheva,
        Felia Dubrovska
Company: Diaghilev's Ballets Russes
First Performance: 3 June 1926, Théâtre Sarah-
    Bernhardt, Paris

Synopsis

Suite of three dances. Three Ballerinas, two white,
one black, play with a Jack-in-the-Box as if with a
ball while, at the back of the set, clouds cut out of
cardboard are moved about by Cloud Carriers.

The following note by E. E. [Edwin Evans] was
printed in the program for the first performance in
London at His Majesty's Theatre on 5 July 1926:
"The music of 'Jack in the Box' consists chiefly of
three dances, which were composed for piano
about a quarter of a century ago as incidental
music to a scenario by Jules Déparquit. The composer always believed that he had left the MS. in a
cab, but he was in the habit of accumulating his
discarded suits, of which a large number were
found at his death, and in the pocket of an old
jacket were discovered the long lost dances, which
have since been orchestrated by Darius Milhaud.
The preceding Fanfare and the two connecting
entr'actes are Satie's own orchestration, the latter
being part of a strange experiment which he called
musique d'ameublement. Music was to become as
much part of interior decoration as the paper on
the walls, which adds to the amenities without
anybody being conscious of its presence. Satie
thought the idea had wonderful commercial
possibilities, because he believed that everybody
who could afford it would have his own musique
d'ameublement. But at a supper party which he
organised on these lines the guests annoyed him
exceedingly by insisting upon listening attentively
to the music instead of being subconsciously
soothed by it, and the experiment was a fiasco. The
first entr'acte is derived from a song heard in these
islands. The second is based upon the well-known
air 'Connais-tu le pays?' from 'Mignon,' and a
theme from Saint-Saëns 'Dans[e] Macabre.'"

Erik Satie, composer of the ballets Parade[2]
and Mercure,[3] died on 1 July 1925. Conrad Satie, Erik's brother, asked Darius Milhaud and three friends to help him go
through the effects left in his brother's
apartment before selling them at auction.
Milhaud described the experience: "A
narrow corridor, with a washbasin in it, led
to the bedroom into which Satie had never
allowed anyone, not even his concierge, to
penetrate. The idea of entering it upset us.
What a shock we had on opening the door!

It seemed impossible that Satie had lived in
such poverty. This man, whose faultlessly
clean and correct dress made him look
rather like a model official, owned almost
literally nothing: a wretched bed, a table
covered with the most incongruous objects,
one chair, and a half-empty wardrobe in
which were a dozen old-fashioned corduroy
suits, brand new, and absolutely identical.
In each corner of the room were piles of old
newspapers, old hats and walking sticks.
On the ancient, broken-down piano, with its
pedals tied up with string, there was a
parcel whose postmark proved that it had
been delivered several years before; Satie
had merely torn a corner of the paper to see
what it contained—a little picture, some
New Year's present, no doubt . . . Behind
the piano we found an exercise book containing Jack-in-the-Box and Geneviève de
Brabant, which Satie thought he had lost in
a bus."[4]

Satie had composed Jack-in-the-Box in
1899 for a pantomime, now lost, by Jules
Dépaquit. When the score was rediscovered,
Satie's brother Conrad gave the rights to it
for five years to Comte Etienne de Beaumont who planned to include it in a "Festival Erik Satie" in memory of the composer.

At the same time, Diaghilev also
planned an evening "in memory of Erik
Satie," by wanting to revive Parade and
create Jack-in-the-Box. He signed a contract[5]
with Etienne de Beaumont on 14 January
1926 to the effect that "Monsieur de
Diaguileff" [sic] would "revive Mercure,
give Parade, and create a special new number Jack-in-the-Box by Erik Satie orchestrated
by Darius Milhaud." The contract also
specified that de Beaumont would commission and pay Picasso to design the set and
costumes, but that Diaghilev would pay for
all the production costs. De Beaumont
would pay for the choreographer, who,
although not named, was assumed then to
be Massine, and Diaghilev would pay for
the rehearsal costs. When Massine left the
company for another engagement in London with C. B. Cochran, Picasso, who
wanted only to work with Massine, also
withdrew, and the choreography was given
instead to Balanchine. André Derain, who
had had a misunderstanding with Etienne
de Beaumont over the production of
Geneviève de Brabant (the other score found
by Milhaud), was given Jack-in-the-Box in
compensation. After all the ins and outs of
trying to get the ballet staged, Diaghilev

decided he did not want to coproduce with
de Beaumont. So the score was first performed alone at the Théâtre des Champs-
Elysées, Paris, on 17 May 1926. On 20 May
1926 Diaghilev signed a further contract
with de Beaumont for the exclusive theatrical use of Jack-in-the-Box for five years.

During 1921–2 Satie and Derain had
discussed a number of different projects,
including one called Archidanses which
Derain described as: "Project related to the
composition of a ballet. Until further notice
this ballet is called Suite d'archidanses,
entirely created by Monsieur Erik Satie,
distinguished musician, and Monsieur
Derain, suitable painter."[6] Derain was the
main originator, and no music was written
except possibly a few bars entitled Pour
Derain in 1923. Derain's notes on Archidanses
include that it was to be in two parts separated by an interlude, and that six dancers
in the first part wear "a tutu of which half is
white, and the other half black; the white
has black spots and the black white spots,"
and as for the men "they are black behind
and white in front."[7] Archidanses remained
merely a project, but when Derain was
offered Jack-in-the-Box by Etienne de Beaumont he wrote to him in April 1926: "I am
thinking of staging a fragment of Archidanses with three characters. I can prepare
everything quite quickly and it will be very
simple. But the choreography cannot be
made until after I have been consulted
about the successive positions of the
dancers. Let Diaghilev write to me with his
requirements. I will reply, and a week later I
will send him the designs."[8] Derain therefore not only considerably influenced the
choreography of Jack-in-the-Box, but also
largely used the design scheme he had
previously devised for Archidanses. He did
not finish the designs within a week as he
said he would, for as Boris Kochno relates
(with slight exaggeration, perhaps): "When
Diaghilev and I came to his house to pick
up the designs, Derain shut himself up in
his studio on the pretext of looking for them
among his other sketches. After we had
waited for an hour in the entrance hall, he
opened the studio door, and inside we
found, spread over the floor, the water
colors he had just finished. We carried them
off still damp."[9]

Although very short and slight, the
ballet was prepared with the care that
Diaghilev gave to every production.
Balanchine's choreography exploited

Idzikowski's acrobatic technique and gave him the opportunity to dazzle with his virtuosity. Grigoriev, the company manager, hit the nail on the head when he wrote: "In spite of their brilliant execution and the impressive list of collaborators responsible for it, *Jack-in-the-Box* was not a ballet for the general public, whom it rather bored. Its appeal was rather to a small circle, for whom it had 'snob' value."[10]

Jack-in-the-Box had three performances in Paris, a few in London, and was never repeated. Florence Grenfell, who saw it in London, called it a "v. small ballet . . . light but rather charming."[11]

103   Design for the set (Introduction)

Graphite, ink, and tempera and/or watercolor on paper
9⅞ x 12⅞ in: 25.1 x 32.9 cm
Unsigned
Inscribed on reverse in pencil: "Scenery of 'Jack in the Box' by Derain / Serge Lifar Collection"
1933.461

Exhibitions: London 1926, No 1; Paris 1929, No 18 (illustrated No III); London Tooth 1930, No 28; Munich 1931–2; New York 1933, No 25; Chicago 1933, No 72; Northampton 1934, No 72; New York 1937–8, No 706; Paris 1939, No 195; Los Angeles 1939–40; Williamsburg 1940; New York 1941–2; Washington D.C. 1950–1; ? Minneapolis 1953; Edinburgh 1954, No 269; London 1954–5, No 309; Michigan 1957; Elmira 1958, No 22; Indianapolis 1959, No 210; Hartford 1965, No 20; New York 1965–6, No 81 (illustrated p 42) (not shown in New York); New York 1966–7; Princeton 1968; Strasbourg 1969, No 425; Frankfurt-am-Main 1969, No 131; Hartford 1973; Amherst 1974; Hartford 1974; Hempstead 1974, No 60; Frankfurt-am-Main 1986, No 206 (illustrated in color p 257); Columbus 1989; Worcester 1989.
Illustrations: Bremser, vol I p 369; Buckle 1955, p 101 No 126 (all the designs for this production are illustrated on one page described "A wall at Forbes House with designs by André Derain for *Jack-in-the-Box*"; Chabert, p 359; Pozharskaya and Volodina, p 252a; Rischbieter, No 101a.

Derain's design concept for this ballet of three short dances was simple and effective: black and white as for a game of checkers. The dancers make their appearance through either the white or the black arches, according to their color. Derain originally also wanted a checkerboard floor cloth, but this design omits that.

104 Design for the set with the two blue Ballerinas and the two white Cloud Carriers

Graphite, ink, and tempera and/or watercolor on paper
9½ x 12⅝ in: 24.3 x 32.1 cm
Unsigned
1933.463

Exhibitions: London 1926, No 3; Paris 1929, No 20; London Tooth 1930, No 30; New York 1933, No 27; Chicago 1933, No 73; Northampton 1934, No 73; San Francisco 1935; Paris 1939, No 196; Cambridge 1942; Washington D.C. 1950–1; Edinburgh 1954, No 271; London 1954–5, No 311; Michigan 1957; Richmond 1959; Hartford 1965, No 22; New York 1965–6, No 83 (illustrated p 42); New York 1966–7; Strasbourg 1969, No 428 (illustrated No 100); Frankfurt-am-Main 1969, No 134; Hartford 1974; Hempstead 1974, No 62; Hartford 1978–9; Coral Gables 1982; Columbus 1989; Worcester 1989.
Illustrations: Chabert, p 358; Pasi, p 203; Pozharskaya and Volodina, p 252b; Rischbieter, No 101c.

The dance with the white cloud background preceded the one with the black cloud (see No 105). Derain understood that black in the theater is a dead color, and so his "black" ballerinas are in fact in dark blue, a color which has depth and vibrancy under theatrical light. These two drawings are also more in the nature of sketches for the choreographer than set designs: Derain considerably influenced the nature and sequence of this ballet.

Two working drawings for the set by Prince Alexandre Schervashidze, the scene painter, which remained in the Lifar collection,[12] show that the set was made up of flats of legs and borders, with pieces added to make three irregular arches diminishing in size upstage.

105 Design for the set with the two white Ballerinas and the two black Cloud Carriers

Graphite, ink, and tempera and/or watercolor on paper
9½ x 12¹¹⁄₁₆ in: 24.1 x 33 cm
Unsigned
Inscribed on reverse in pencil: "Groupe / from / 'Jack in the Box' / by Derain / Serge Lifar Collection"
1933.462

Exhibitions: London 1926, No 2; Paris 1929, No 19; London Tooth 1930, No 29; New York 1933, No 26; Chicago 1933, No 74; Northampton 1934, No 74; San Francisco 1935; Paris 1939, No 196; Poughkeepsie 1940; Washington D.C. 1950–1; Edinburgh 1954, No 270; London 1954–5, No 310; Michigan 1957; ? Indianapolis 1959, No 211; Rowayton 1960; Storrs 1963; Hartford 1964; Hartford 1965; New York 1965–6, No 82 (illustrated p 42); New York 1966–7; Princeton 1968; Strasbourg 1969, No 427; Frankfurt-am-Main 1969, No 133; Hartford 1974; Hempstead 1974, No 61; Hartford 1978-9; Coral Gables 1982; Frankfurt-am-Main 1986, No 205 (illustrated p 256); Hartford 1988; Worcester 1989.
Illustrations: Chabert, p 358; Clarke and Crisp 1978, pl 101 p 145; Rischbieter, No 101b.

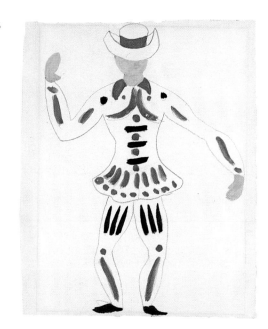

106 Costume design for Stanislas Idzikowski as Le Pantin (Jack in the Box)

Graphite, ink, and tempera and/or watercolor with
    white highlights on paper
12½ x 9⅝ in: 31.5 x 20.3 cm
Unsigned
1933.466

Exhibitions: London 1926, No 9; Paris 1929, No 21
    (described as 6 costumes); London Tooth 1930,
    Nos 31–3;[13] New York 1933, No 28;[13] Chicago
    1933, No 75–80 (not identified); Northampton
    1934, Nos 75–80 (not identified); San Francisco
    1935; Paris 1939, No 197;[13] Poughkeepsie
    1940; Williamsburg 1940; New York MoMA
    1944 (lists "Two designs for costumes");
    Edinburgh 1954, No 277; London 1954–5, No
    317; Michigan 1957; Indianapolis 1959; Storrs
    1963; Hartford 1965 No 23; New York 1965–6,
    No 89 (illustrated in color facing p 1); New York
    1966–7; Princeton 1968; Hartford 1973; Hart-
    ford 1974; Hempstead 1974, No 59; London
    1981; Columbus 1989; Worcester 1989.

For this costume, and the following one
(No 107) for the Black Ballerina, Derain
introduced other colors apart from black
and white. In this one, he adapts the traditional harlequin costume of colored patches.

The costume was modified for the stage
by the addition of a white fur trim to make
it stand out more clearly against the background.

107 Costume design for Alexandra Danilova as the Black Ballerina

Graphite, ink, and tempera and/or watercolor on
    paper
12⅜ x 9¾ in: 31 x 24.3 cm
Unsigned
1933.464

Exhibitions: London 1926, No 4; Paris 1929, No 21
    (described as "6 costumes"); London Tooth
    1930, Nos 31–3;[13] New York 1933, No 28;[13]
    Chicago 1933, No 75–80 (not identified);
    Northampton 1934, Nos 75–80 (not identified);
    San Francisco 1935; New York 1937–8, No 707;
    Paris 1939, No 197;[13] Poughkeepsie 1940;
    Williamsburg 1940; Washington D.C. 1950–1;
    Edinburgh 1954, No 273; London 1954–5, No
    313; Michigan 1957; Elmira 1958, No 32;
    Indianapolis 1959, No 212; Hartford 1964; New
    York 1965–6, No 84 (illustrated p 42); New York
    1966–7; Princeton 1968; Hartford 1973; Hart-
    ford 1974; Hempstead 1974, No 57; Hartford
    1978–9; London 1981; Coral Gables 1982;
    Hartford 1988; Worcester 1989.

This costume was inspired by Joséphine
Baker's famous (or, rather, notorious)
"banana" costume in the Revue Nègre,
which delighted Paris in 1925. Danilova did
not "black up" her face for the performance,
as this would have made the quick change
afterwards too difficult.

Left: studio photograph of Alexandra Danilova as the Black Ballerina and Stanislas Idzikowski as Jack-in-the-Box.

109 Costume design for one of the two White Ballerinas

Graphite, ink, and tempera and/or watercolor on paper
12¹/₁₆ x 9¾ in: 30.7 x 24.7 cm
1933.465

Exhibitions: London 1926, No 6; Paris 1929, No 21; London Tooth 1930, Nos 31–3;[13] New York 1933, No 28;[13] Chicago 1933, No 75–80 (not identified); Northampton 1934, Nos 75–80 (not identified); San Francisco 1935; Paris 1939, No 197;[3] Washington D.C. 1950–1; Edinburgh 1954, No 274 or 275; London 1954–5, No 314 or 315; Michigan 1957; Indianapolis 1959, No 213; Storrs 1963; New York 1965–6, No 86 (illustrated in color facing p 1); New York 1966–7; Princeton 1968; Hartford 1974; Coral Gables 1982; Columbus 1989; Worcester 1989.
Illustrations: Chabert, p 369; Gontcharova, p 89; Volta, p 150; Rischbieter, No 102c.

108 Costume design for one of the two White Ballerinas

Graphite, ink, and tempera and/or watercolor on paper
12⅛ x 9⅝ in: 30.6 x 24.5 cm
Unsigned
1933.468

Exhibitions: London 1926, No 7; Paris 1929, No 21; London Tooth 1930, Nos 31–3;[13] New York 1933, No 28;[13] Chicago 1933, No 75–80 (not identified); Northampton 1934, Nos 75–80 (not identified); Paris 1939, No 197;[13] Cambridge 1942; Washington D.C. 1950–1; Edinburgh 1954, No 274 or 275; London 1954–5, No 314 or 315; Indianapolis 1959, No 216; Hartford 1965, No 25; New York 1965–6, No 87 (illustrated in color facing p 1); New York 1966–7; Hartford 1974; Hartford 1978–9; Coral Gables 1982; Columbus 1989; Worcester 1989.
Illustrations: Chabert, p 369; Volta, p 150 (color); Rischbieter, No 102a.

Notes

1 The credit line for the composer includes the note that the music was "put at the disposition of Serge Diaghilev by Comte Etienne de Beaumont, the owner of the work."
2 Ballet in 1 act by Jean Cocteau, choreography by Leonide Massine, front cloth, set and costumes by Pablo Picasso, produced by Diaghilev's Ballets Russes at the Théâtre du Châtelet, Paris on 18 May 1917.
3 "Plastic poses" in 1 act, choreography by Leonide Massine, set and costumes by Pablo Picasso, produced by Comte Etienne de Beaumont at his *Soirées de Paris* at the Théâtre Cigale, Paris on 15 June 1924.
4 Darius Milhaud, *Notes without Music*, pp 177–8.
5 In the Bibliothèque-Musée de l'Opéra, Paris, Fonds Kochno, pièce 10.
6 Quoted in Ornella Volta, *Satie et la danse*, p 101.
7 Quoted in Ornella Volta, *ibid*, p 104.
8 Quoted in Ornella Volta, *ibid*, p 154.
9 Boris Kochno, *Diaghilev and the Ballets Russes*, p 243.
10 Serge Grigoriev, *The Diaghilev Ballet*, p 228.
11 Florence E. Grenfell, unpublished diaries, 5 July 1926.
12 The drawings were sold at Sotheby's, London on 9 May 1984, lot 38 i and ii, and bought by the Dance Collection, New York Public Library at the Lincoln Center.
13 This note applies to Nos 106–111. The exhibition catalogues do not specify which costumes were exhibited.

110 Costume design for a white Cloud Carrier

Graphite, tempera and/or watercolor with clear surface coating on paper
12½ x 10³⁄₁₆ in: 31.5 x 25.7 cm
Unsigned
1933.469

Exhibitions: London 1926, No 5; Paris 1929, No 21; London Tooth 1930, Nos 31–3;[13] New York 1933, No 28;[13] Chicago 1933, No 75–80 (not identified); Northampton 1934, Nos 75–80 (not identified); San Francisco 1935; Paris 1939, No 197;[13] Cambridge 1942; Washington D.C. 1950–1; Edinburgh 1954, No 276 or 277; London 1954–5, No 316 or 317; Michigan 1957; Indianapolis 1959, No 217; Hartford 1965, No 26; New York 1965–6, No 85 (illustrated in color facing p 1); New York 1966–7; Princeton 1968; Hartford 1974; Hempstead 1974, No 58; Hartford 1978–9; Columbus 1989; Worcester 1989.
Illustrations: Volta, p 150 (color); Rischbieter, No 102d.

111 Costume design for a black Cloud Carrier

Graphite, ink, and tempera and/or watercolor on paper
13 x 9⅞ in: 32.9 x 25 cm
Unsigned
1933.467

Exhibitions: London 1926, No 8; Paris 1929, No 21; London Tooth 1930, Nos 31–3;[13] New York 1933, No 28;[13] Chicago 1933, No 75–80 (not identified); Northampton 1934, Nos 75–80 (not identified); San Francisco 1935; Paris 1939, No 197;[13] Washington D.C. 1950–1; Edinburgh 1954, No 276 or 277; London 1954–5, No 316 or 317; Michigan 1957; Elmira 1958, No 53; Indianapolis 1959, No 215; Hartford 1964; Hartford 1965, No 24; New York 1965–6, No 88 (illustrated in color facing p 1); New York 1966–7; Hartford 1974; Hartford 1978–9; Hartford 1988; Worcester 1989.
This and the previous costume (No 110) were originally designed for Derain's and Satie's ballet project *Archidanses*.

Mstislav Dobujinsky

Russian
born 1875 Novgorod
died 1957 New York

Papillons (Butterflies)

Pantomime Ballet in 1 act by Michel Fokine
Composer: Robert Schumann, orchestrated by
    Nicholas Tcherepnine
Conductor: Pierre Monteux
Choreographer: Michel Fokine
Designer (set): Mstislav Dobujinsky
Designer (costumes): Léon Bakst
Principal Dancers:
    The Young Girl: Tamara Karsavina
    Pierrot: Michel Fokine
    Ludmilla Schollar, Lubov Tchernicheva
Company: Diaghilev's Ballets Russes
First Performance: 14 April 1914, Théâtre de
    Monte-Carlo

Synopsis

The scene is Carnival night in 1830. A melancholy Pierrot wanders in the park when a group of girls, with little wings attached to their shoulders, enter and dance round him. Pierrot, believing them to be butterflies, tries to attract them with a candle flame. He succeeds in capturing one, but is so rough with her that her wings break and she falls down dead. Her companions return and the distraught Pierrot appeals to them for help. They succeed in re-attaching her wings and she comes back to life. Pierrot is happy again and they all dance joyously.

Suddenly a clock strikes to denote the end of the Carnival. All the girls, including Pierrot's captive, disappear, to return accompanied by their chaperones. The last to leave is a young masked girl escorted by a gentleman. Pierrot looks at her, and as she passes him she half-raises her mask and smiles. Pierrot, realizing that he has been tricked, stares after her, overcome with bitterness. Finally he turns and falls to the ground stricken with grief.

When Diaghilev dismissed Nijinsky toward the end of 1913, ostensibly for breaking his contract by not performing in Rio de Janeiro,[1] but actually for having improbably and impudently married Romola Pulszky in Buenos Aires, he was left without his chief dancer and choreographer. Diaghilev then reluctantly came to the conclusion that, in order to salvage the 1914 season which was to include the important new ballet *La Légende de Joseph* by Richard Strauss,[2] he had no alternative but to make it up with Fokine and persuade him to return to the Company. Grigoriev writes how Diaghilev spent five hours on the telephone persuading Fokine and that "as he replaced the receiver Diaghilev heaved a sigh of relief. 'Well, that's settled, I think,' he said. 'He was a tough nut to crack, though, all the same!'"[3] Fokine, on the other hand, does not mention the telephone, but says Diaghilev paid him a visit. Given Diaghilev's character, Grigoriev's version, even if exaggerated, sounds the truer.

The Paris season at the Opéra was short, only ten days but, in addition to *La Légende de Joseph*, Diaghilev, ambitiously determined to impress Parisians with further novelties, planned three other premieres: *Le Coq d'Or*,[4] *Le Rossignol* (see pp 128–31), and *Midas*,[5] as well as a new, complete version of *Schéhérazade*. He would have liked a fourth premiere, but Fokine demurred. As he was to be the main choreographer and was also going to be the main dancer in several ballets, he wisely did not want to overstretch himself. He therefore first persuaded Diaghilev to engage Boris Romanov as choreographer for *Le Rossignol*, and then suggested reviving *Papillons*. This short ballet to Schumann's music of the same name had been given first at a charity performance in aid of the Literary Fund at the Mariinsky Theater, St Petersburg on 10 (23) March 1912. The set and costumes had been designed by Léon Bakst. In *Papillons*, Fokine concentrated the style he had developed in *Les Sylphides* and *Carnaval*. It had that same pervading atmosphere of deep romanticism as *Carnaval* and, though slight, was more sublime.

In 1914 Bakst had a nervous collapse. In his memoirs, Dobujinsky stated that he thought also "that there had been another of his recurrent tiffs with Diaghilev."[6] Although Bakst managed to design a series of extraordinary costumes for *La Légende de Joseph* in the style of Veronese, the task of designing his own ballet *Midas* was handed over to Dobujinsky; while Bakst's existing costumes were used for the revival of *Papillons*, Dobujinsky was commissioned to design a new set.[7] He described his task: "As Fokine had already prepared the choreography I did not have much contact with him. My problem was to provide a suitable 'romantic' background and harmonize the colors of the set with the colors of Bakst's costumes. What I invented—a moonlit park with a little temple to Cupid by a lake and two pink-colored side pavilions with lighted windows and stairs for access— successfully coincided with Fokine's staging. This charming ballet of his (which was in some ways a continuation of *Carnaval*) had a great success and remained in the repertory of Diaghilev's ballets for a long time."[8]

Objective critics tended to agree with Dobujinsky's subjective assessment of the ballet. Charles Ricketts, writing about the whole 1914 season, believed that: "The New Ballets have been admirable and have made up for the loss of Nijinsky, who is replaced by Fokine, his master and the begetter, practically, of the whole series. (Fokine is an older man, admirable also, but lacking the spontaneity and flame of Nijinsky.) *Papillons* has proved a pendant to *Carnaval*, a thing of moonlight, gossamer, and tender irony, swift and delicate like a sudden breeze."[9] Cyril Beaumont, a more professional critic, in the sense of being more knowledgeable about ballet, was a great admirer of Fokine's particular style of classicism but he had reservations about *Papillons* and considered that it lacked originality: "*Papillons* is a charming, ingenious composition, delicate and fragile as a butterfly's wing. The groups, the miming, the *pas de deux*, and the scene of the death and reanimation of the butterfly are full of that poetry and tender lyricism characteristic of Fokine's work in this vein, but the impression afforded is slight and the piece naturally suffers from being a repetition of style."[10] Fokine was criticized for the very quality for which he was most admired. Critics are often impatient with genius and are only satisfied with something entirely new each time. But *Papillons* was never meant to be anything other than a charming curtain-raiser: it was always performed first in a program before more substantial ballets like *La Légende de Joseph*, *Schéhérazade*, or *La Boutique Fantasque*.

Dobujinsky was right, it was a popular ballet, but it did not remain in the repertoire after 1920.

112* Design for the set

Graphite, tempera and/or watercolor and ink on
card stock
4⁵/₁₆ x 7⁵/₁₆ in: 11.0 x 18.5 cm (7³/₈ x 9⁷/₈ in: 18.9 x
25.1 cm overall)
Signed in pencil on design bottom right:
"M. Douboujinsky"
Signed in pencil on larger sheet below mat
decoration: "M. Douboujinsky"
Inscribed in pencil: "'Papillons'" 1914
1963.498
Provenance: Rostislav Dobujinsky

Exhibitions: Paris 1939, ? No 206 (described as
"Deux décors"); London 1959, No 8; New York
1965-6, No 90 (illustrated p 43); Spoleto 1966;
Strasbourg 1969, No 180; Frankfurt-am-Main,
No 52; Hartford 1974; Hartford 1978-9; Coral
Gables 1982; Columbus 1989; Worcester 1989.
Illustration: Hansen, fig 21.

This is a classically symmetrical set
design of great simplicity: a painted
back cloth and two side "trucks" for the
pavilions. The blue/green/rose effect in
moonlight depends as much on lighting as
on painted canvas. But the black cut-cloth
curtain making a false proscenium is Dobujinsky's touch of brilliant invention: it concentrates the attention at the same time as it
increases the mystery. It also underlines the

mood of the piece, which is the prime
function of set design.

There are at least two other versions of
this design. One of them is illustrated in
color in Cyril W. Beaumont, *Five Centuries
of Ballet Design*, p 109. This and the
Wadsworth drawing both have figures
in them.

The most authentic design, in the sense
of being closest to the actual set, is the one
that was illustrated in the *Souvenir Program*
of the *Ballets Russes*, ninth season, May–June
1914. This has no figures, but in every other
respect is almost identical to the Wadsworth
drawing.

Notes

1 Serge Grigoriev in *The Diaghilev Ballet*, p 100,
refers to a contract quoting the telegram reply
sent to Nijinsky by Diaghilev but which Grigoriev was asked to sign on his behalf: "In reply
to your telegram to Monsieur Diaghilev I wish
to inform you of the following. Monsieur
Diaghilev considers that by missing a performance at Rio and refusing to dance in the ballet
Carnaval you broke your contract. He will not
therefore require your further services. Serge

Grigoriev, *Régisseur* of the Diaghilev Company."
Richard Buckle, however, in *Nijinsky*, p 396,
states: "But Nijinsky had not had a contract
since 1909," and Bronislava Nijinska in her *Early
Memoirs*, p 482, gives a different and probably
more accurate wording of the telegram (originally in French): "The Ballet Russe has no
further need of your services. Do not rejoin us.
Serge Grigorieff."
2 Ballet in 1 act by Count Harry Kessler and Hugo
von Hofmannsthal, set by José-Maria Sert and
costumes by Léon Bakst, first performed at the
Opéra, Paris on 14 May 1914.
3 Serge Grigoriev, *op cit*, p 103.
4 Opera in 3 scenes by Rimsky Korsakov with
libretto by V. Bielsky revised by Alexandre
Benois, scenery and costumes by Nathalie
Gontcharova, first performed at the Opéra,
Paris, on 24 May 1914.
5 Ballet in 1 act by Maximilien Steinberg with
libretto by Léon Bakst after Ovid's *Metamorphoses*, scenery and costumes by Mstislav
Dobujinsky, first performed at the Opéra, Paris,
on 2 June 1914.
6 Mstislav Dobujinsky, *Vospominaniya (Memoirs)*,
p 394.
7 A set design by Bakst for *Papillons* dated 1914
was exhibited in Strasbourg in 1969.
8 Mstislav Dobujinsky, *op cit*, p 395.
9 Charles Ricketts, *Self Portrait*, p 204 (in a letter
dated 21 July 1914 to Gordon Bottomley).
10 Cyril W. Beaumont, *Michel Fokine and his ballets*,
p 86.

Max Ernst

German
born 1891 Brühl (near Cologne)
died 1976 Paris

113   Still Death, 1925

Oil on fabric
25⅝ x 21½ in: 65.3 x 54.3 cm
Signed lower left in oil: "max ernst"
Label on reverse on stretcher inscribed in pencil:
   "Projet de mise en scène." Stamped on frame,
   canvas, and stretcher on reverse: "Douanes
   Exposition Paris"
1933.474

Exhibitions: ? Paris 1929, No 29; Chicago 1933, No
   85 (described as "Projet de mise en scène");
   Northampton 1934, No 85; San Francisco 1935;
   New York 1941–2; Indianapolis 1959, No 231;
   New York 1961; Eindhoven 1964, No 61; New
   York 1965–6, No 91 (illustrated p 44); New York
   1966–7; Amherst 1974; Worcester 1989.
Illustrations: Ernst, p 50 (described as "Still Death,"
   but credited wrongly to "Private Collection,
   Paris"); Schneede, No 138 p 79 (described as
   "Still life"); Spies 1976, No 941 p 77 (described
   as "Nature morte").

The label on the reverse incorrectly describes this painting as a "Project for a set design." It was not intended for the theater and has no connexion with it, but is one of a series of still lifes which Ernst painted after he discovered the technique of *frottage* (see No 114, p 195). In this series of oil paintings, using the same technique as in his pencil rubbings, he opposed a positive painted image of fruit with either its negative image or the negative image of another fruit. The painted cherries here appear to be solid and real, but the rubbed grapes appear to be only an insubstantial impression: the positive confronting the negative. *Frottage* for Ernst was "nothing other than a technical means of intensifying the hallucinatory faculties of the spirit in such a way that 'visions' automatically appear."[1] Here we have the illusion of a vision of a real bunch of grapes beyond the wall because we are made aware of the 'beyond' by the partially painted, partially rubbed circular hole. There is, therefore, a further unseen dimension to the painting. However, Uwe Schneede's explanation that by using such a technique Ernst "highlights the dialectic of presence and absence"[2] stretches the point beyond reasonableness: the painting is not as interesting as all that.

Historians have ignored Ernst's witticism of playing on the French term for a still life, *nature morte*, in calling this painting "Still death," even though it is a meaningless title.

Notes

1 Max Ernst in catalogue *Max Ernst*, Wallraf-
   Richartz Museum, Cologne 1962–3 quoted in
   Uwe M. Schneede, *The Essential Max Ernst*, p 73.
2 Uwe M. Schneede, *ibid*, p 79.

Romeo and Juliet

A rehearsal without scenery in 2 acts by Boris
    Kochno based on the play by William
    Shakespeare[1]
Composer: Constant Lambert
Conductor: Marc-César Scotto
Choreographers: Bronislava Nijinska; for the
    entr'acte: George Balanchine
Painting: Max Ernst, Joan Miró[2]
Costumes: Made by Mme Vialet from sketches by
    Joan Miró
Principal Dancers:
    Romeo: Serge Lifar
    Juliet: Tamara Karsavina
    The Nurse: Lydia Sokolova
    The Dancing Master: Thadée Slavinsky
Company: Diaghilev's Ballets Russes
First Performance: 4 May 1926, Théâtre de Monte-
    Carlo

Synopsis

From the program.

"Act 1: The action takes place during a class of
the Russian Ballet. Enter Karsavina and Lifar, who
noticing that they are late, quickly change into
their rehearsal clothes and start work. The dancing
master teaches them a *pas de deux* during which,
forgetting their steps, they do not conceal their
love for one another. Their scandalised friends
separate the lovers and drag them off to the
theatre where a rehearsal is about to begin.

Act 2. Preparations for a rehearsal of scenes
from *Romeo and Juliet*

    1. Romeo and Juliet's first meeting at the
Capulets' ball

    2. The Nurse and Peter, Capulet's servant[3]

    3. Duel between Romeo and Tybalt

    4. The balcony scene

    5. Paris, with musicians, looks for Juliet, his
fiancée

    6. The death of Juliet

The curtain falls in front of the enthusiastic
actors[4] who imitate and applaud the hero and
heroine. The curtain rises, the actors go on stage
and search for Romeo and Juliet. The lovers elope
by aeroplane."

The music was always the starting point
for Diaghilev when planning a new
production, and he was also always keen to
discover new talent in young artists. There
are several conflicting explanations as to
why he chose a score by Constant Lambert,
then a twenty-year-old student at the Royal
College of Music in London. Diaghilev
undoubtedly thought he would have
greater success in persuading the English
newspaper tycoon, Lord Rothermere, to
sponsor his London seasons if his programs
were to include specifically "English" ballets. He therefore relied on advice from
Sacheverell Sitwell who, with his brother
Osbert and sister Edith, was at the center of
London artistic life and whose circle
included the composers Lord Berners[5] and
the young William Walton as well as Con-

stant Lambert. It was, however, through the
painter Charles Ricketts, a friend of the
family, and his friend the illustrator
Edmund Dulac, that Lambert was introduced to Diaghilev in 1925.[6] He played him
his dance suite *Adam and Eve*. Diaghilev was
impressed and commissioned Lambert, but
changed the title to *Romeo and Juliet* because
it sounded "more English" than the book of
Genesis. Boris Kochno, who wrote the
libretto, an adaptation of Shakespeare based
on a rehearsal of the play, wrote that
Diaghilev commissioned the composer
"after he had attended a concert at which
early works by Lambert were played (this
concert presenting new musicians was
called, I believe, 'Promenades')."[7] This
statement is refuted by Richard Shead in his
biography of Lambert, who wrote: "If
Kochno means Henry Wood's Promenade
Concerts (and he can hardly mean anything
else) . . . no work of Lambert's was played
at these until 1929."[8] A less likely, but nevertheless plausible and amusing account of
how Diaghilev commissioned Lambert, one
containing more than a grain of truth, was
given by Vladimir Dukelsky. The young
Russian composer had been responsible for
the successful *Zéphire et Flore*[9] produced by
Diaghilev in 1925, and had remained in his
entourage as an "unofficial musical secretary." He became friends with William
Walton and, through him, became
acquainted with Lambert. Dukelsky
described how Lambert, flamboyantly
dressed in an orange shirt with a black tie
which irritated Diaghilev, "used to haunt
the corridor outside Diaghilev's door at the
Savoy Hotel and sit on the floor with the
determination to waylay the great man and
obtain a hearing. Diaghilev, who had an
efficient bodyguard in Boris [Kochno], was
used to ducking composers and creditors
alike, and outsmarted poor Lambert daily
by sneaking into his suite before the boy
had a chance to open his mouth."[10] Eventually, when Dukelsky managed to persuade
Diaghilev to listen to Walton's *Portsmouth
Point*, Walton generously suggested that
Lambert join him in his audition. "Willie
played first—he was no pianist, and got an
icy reception from Sergei Pavlovitch, who
told me what he thought of *Portsmouth Point*
in Russian, and it wasn't much.[11] Lambert, a
self-assured and efficient performer, went
on next, gave an excellent account of his
skimpy piece and—miracle of miracles—
was rewarded by a beatific smile by the

listener. 'Are you English?' he queried. 'Yes,
I am, why?' countered Lambert. 'That's
most surprising. I don't like English music,
yet I like your little ballet. I'm going to
produce it, but not with that silly title,'
Diaghilev went on. He took a big red pencil,
crossed out *Adam and Eve* and wrote *Romeo
and Juliet* over it. Constant burst into uncontrollable tears."[12]

Bronislava Nijinska was engaged by
Diaghilev to choreograph the ballet.
Although she had resigned from the company at the beginning of 1925 after having
been the resident choreographer for three
years, Diaghilev forgot his quarrel with her
and re-engaged her for *Romeo and Juliet*
because, as he explained to Grigoriev:
"Neither Massine nor Balanchine seem to
me suited to this ballet."[13] Diaghilev was
always prepared to forget quarrels for the
sake of his art, just as he was always prepared to have them.

Diaghilev rejected Lambert's first suggestion of Augustus John as designer
because he considered him to be too dull.
Instead, after some indecision, he decided in
favour of an alternative (and young) English painter, Lambert's friend Christopher
Wood, recommended by Jean Cocteau and
whose work was also familiar to Picasso.
We know from a letter Wood wrote to his
mother that it was not until 27 March 1926,
less than six weeks before the first night,
that he received the official commission. He
had, however, already been given the brief
that the ballet should be set at a rehearsal,
and he had done a number of drawings. He
wrote: "My long anxiety has come to an end
today. Diaghilev asked me definitely to do
the ballet after lunch . . . they saw my
designs which they discussed and asked me
many questions, trying to change several
things which I quite firmly refused, and
which I think they appreciated as they saw I
understood and meant what I had drawn.
Apparently he was more or less decided I
should do it over a month ago . . . the whole
of Paris is talking about it."[14] Wood was
thrilled by receiving the commission—
believing, correctly, that working for
Diaghilev and his renowned company
would be a great fillip for his career. Sadly,
at least for him, it all went wrong. By
9 April, only two weeks after his official
appointment, he wrote that Diaghilev "is
impossible to work for knowing nothing
about painting, he wishes to poke his nose
into everything, and makes the most ridicu-

lous and useless changes. He has driven me so mad I feel I would almost like to chuck the whole thing."[15] On 11 April Diaghilev wrote to Wood: "Finally, I have taken a decision which will probably surprise you, but it is the best of all. I will not make any scenery at all for *Romeo*. This ballet is a sketch, a rehearsal as it says in the program. We therefore have to find some dodge, and this dodge is to play it outside any theatrical convention, however artistic it may be. Apart from anything else it is the only way of getting near the choreography outlined by Madame Nijinska."[16] This continuing interference by Diaghilev confirmed Wood in his resolve to resign, in which he was supported by both Picasso and Cocteau. The decisive straw for Wood was on 14 April when Max Ernst arrived in Monte Carlo at Diaghilev's invitation because, as Wood wrote, "he decided to have the curtain of my ballet painted by a young modern painter who had nothing to do with it, but who Diaghilev wished to employ to add another novelty to his season."[17]

Before they left Paris for Monte Carlo, Diaghilev had sent Boris Kochno and Serge Lifar to look at an exhibition of surrealist painters, including Ernst and Miró. Lifar recalled: "When he was seeing us off at the station: 'How did you like the surrealists?' asked Diaghilev . . . 'I didn't like Ernst and Miró, and I didn't understand surrealism at all, but you'd perhaps better go and see for yourself.' A few days later Diaghilev arrived in Monte Carlo . . . with Ernst and Miró, whom he had commissioned to paint the sets for *Roméo et Juliette* [sic]. He was wholly wrapped up in his new friends . . . In gratitude for my advice to go and see the surrealists for himself, Diaghilev had brought from Paris some paintings by both Miró and

Ernst which had particularly taken his fancy, and these he presented to me, thus laying the foundation of my collection."[18] Lifar does not mention Christopher Wood, so he was obviously unaware of his engagement and his resignation; he is also telescoping events because, according to Wood's letters, Diaghilev was already in Monte Carlo when Ernst arived alone. Furthermore, Ernst's and Miró's greater participation in the production than just a single curtain could only have been hastily arranged after Wood's departure. In Ernst's case this was the enlargement, by the scene painter Prince Schervashidze, of more than one of the paintings bought by Diaghilev and brought by him to Monte Carlo: in Miró's case this included some minimal costume designs in addition to some props and two of his abstract paintings used for the front cloth and back cloth (see below and pp 262–65).

While Christopher Wood's projected designs were appropriate, showing a rehearsal stage viewed at an angle from the back toward the auditorium, Ernst's and Miró's contributions were wholly inappropriate and unconnected to the ballet. Lambert was angered by the change of designer and wrote to his mother two weeks after the first night: "When I arrived in Monte Carlo I found that the first performance was in 2 or 3 days' time and that far from doing the ballet without a décor Diaghilev had chosen two 10th-rate painters from an imbecile group called the 'surréalistes.' I cannot tell you how monstrous the décor is, both in itself and as an accompaniment to my music and the choreography of Nijinska. As you know, I am not academic in my point of view about painting but never in my life have I seen anything so imbecile."[19] What-

ever Lambert's feelings, the sets and costumes went unnoticed in Monte Carlo.

Lambert was also angered by changes that Diaghilev had apparently made to the choreography. His letter to his mother continued: "Diaghilev has introduced disgraceful changes in the choreography, altering bits that Nijinska declared she would never be induced to change . . . I was so upset by all this that I asked for and with great difficulty obtained an interview with Diaghilev. Instead of giving it to me alone he had Kochno and Grigoriev (the stage manager) with him. To frighten me, I suppose . . . I then tried to speak about the choreography but he said 'I have known Madame Nijinska for 20 years and I forbid you to mention her name in my presence.' I naturally lost my temper and said I would withdraw the music entirely. I'm afraid it was rather a dreadful scene but then it is impossible to remain calm with a man like that."[20] Lambert in fact consulted a lawyer in Nice, but was advised that he could not withdraw from his contract. In the event this was fortunate because the production certainly helped to establish Lambert as a significant composer at a remarkably young age.

When Nijinska was told by Diaghilev that Romeo was to be danced by Serge Lifar she insisted on an examination first, because she had very little confidence in his ability. Lifar's indignation was calmed by Diaghilev: "'Don't fuss, and don't get angry. Nijinska wants an examination; well, she shall have it . . .' Examination day came. Our teacher, Legat, was at the piano, and, noticing how nervous and agitated I was—I had gone as white as a sheet—he did his best to reassure and encourage me . . . My 'examination' took half an hour, and I danced as I had never danced before. Legat began by setting me small variations, then, noticing how enthusiastically I soared and the ease with which I accomplished my twelve *pirouettes*, my three *tours en l'air*, led me through more and more complicated steps. The 'examination' ended with Legat abruptly leaving the piano and kissing me in his delight, to be followed by Sergei Pavlovitch, who also embraced and congratulated me, saying: 'Tomorrow we begin the production.' Nijinska herself was obviously troubled."[21]

Wanting to re-establish a connection with the past, Diaghilev first tried unsuccessfully to get Mathilde Kshessinska for the role of Juliet, but then approached Tamara Karsavina who agreed. Like

Below: Serge Lifar as Romeo and Tamara Karsavina as Juliet, center stage in rehearsal in front of the back cloth for scene 1 by Joan Miró (see pp 262–65).

Nijinska, she did not share Diaghilev's confidence in Lifar. Lydia Sokolova, playing the Nurse, noticed: "It was not so funny for Mme Karsavina, who was out of practice, to find herself landed with Lifar as a partner. The great dancer, used to the support of such artists as Fokine and Nijinsky, discovered that the inexperienced young man hardly knew how to lift her. She never complained. Her manners were as beautiful as her face. She would just raise her eyebrows and say, 'But Serge, if you will do it this way it will work.'"[22] Most of the rehearsals setting the ballet, however, were performed by Alice Nikitina as Juliet, who subsequently alternated the part with Karsavina. Nikitina, who with an unsurprising lapse of memory forgot to mention Karsavina, described working on the ballet: "We had no time to waste as Nijinska was to leave us soon again for another assignment. Some of the scenes were really beautiful and full of invention."[23] Karsavina, on the other hand, remembered that her part was "choreographically insignificant."[24] Jean Cocteau was also critical of Nijinska's work: "Her return was not a success. She took off from the premise that she was choreographing a dramatic work, and, by undertaking simply to substitute gestures for words she repeated for the greater part of the ballet the error she had made with *Les Fâcheux* and foundered in a conventional, realistic pantomime."

After the first night in Monte Carlo, and some time after Nijinska had left for South America, Diaghilev thought that the division between the two scenes would be better marked by the introduction of an *entr'acte*. Lambert reported this to his mother in the same previously quoted letter: "Kochno came to see me and asked if I had any music for an entr'acte as they thought it would be more 'vivante' if there was a passage of dancers from the classroom to the theatre. I was very annoyed at their trying to spoil Nijinska's work any more, so I said I would give him music for an entr'acte but only on the understanding that not a note of it was to be danced. So they have now added a sort of comic march-past of the characters (without music) in very dubious taste and in a style which is the complete opposite of Nijinska's."[25] Lambert's condition was not met, but the *entr'acte* was introduced anyway, choreographed by George Balanchine. The "sort of comic march-past" consisted of just the dancers' legs being seen below the knee behind an almost-lowered house curtain.

"This idea," commented Lydia Sokolova, "was thought to be very ingenious by the powers that be, but the public sometimes tittered, thinking that the machinery had gone wrong."[26]

While the first night in Monte Carlo had been uneventful, the first night in Paris at the Théâtre Sarah-Bernhardt on 18 May 1926 was a riot. The scene was described by a representative of *The Dancing Times*: "The lights were lowered to commence, M. Roger Desormières [sic], the young conductor, had just picked up his baton, when some thirty or forty young men surged up the central gangway blowing whistles as loudly as possible, whilst confederates posted all over the house howled and shrieked at the top of their voices. From the top boxes showers of printed leaflets rained down on the heads of the people below. For fully ten minutes pandemonium reigned. Not one note could be heard from the orchestra, which, however did not stop playing, and the *corps de ballet* carried on bravely in the face of the tumult. By this time, however, the majority of the audience who had no interest in the sectarian squabbles of the artistic coteries of Montparnasse, and who wished to hear the music, decided to take a hand in the matter themselves and eject the disturbers, whereupon the *mêlée* developed into a free fight which only ceased when the police arrived and pounced upon the manifestors, who were dragged off to the nearest *commissariat* looking rather the worse for wear."[27] When the police had removed the troublemakers, Diaghilev gave the sign to re-start the performance, which then took place with little reaction. The protest had only been against Ernst and Miró, for participating in Diaghilev's Ballets Russes. The ringleaders, and the writers of the leaflet, were Louis Aragon and André Breton, the founders of the surrealist movement. This was the leaflet's pedantic and rather stilted text:

Protest

It is inadmissable that ideas should be at the behest of money. Not a year goes by but that someone whom one thought to be unshakeable submits to forces to which he was opposed until then. Those individuals who capitulate to the point of disregarding social distinctions are of no importance, for the ideal to which they paid allegiance before their abdication survives without them. That is why the participation of the painters Max Ernst and Joan Miró in the forthcoming production of the Russian Ballet can never imply that although they have abandoned their class the *surrealist* ideal has done likewise. It

is essentially a subversive ideal which cannot come to terms with such enterprises, whose goal has always been to tame the dreams and rebellions of physical and intellectual hunger for the profit of the international aristocracy.
It may have seemed to Ernst and Miró that their collaboration with M. de Diaghilev, legitimised by the example of Picasso, would not have serious consequences. However, it puts us under the obligation—we who have all the worry of maintaining slave-ships of every kind of advanced thought out of reach—of denouncing, without consideration of the people involved, an attitude which arms the worst partisans with questionable ethics.

We know that we are only making out a very relative case for our artistic relationship with such and such. Give us the honor of believing that in May 1926 we are more than ever incapable of sacrificing our sense of real revolution.[28]

Such a protest, especially since it was not directed against either the dancers or the composer but was widely reported in the newspapers, was only welcome publicity for Diaghilev. Although the furore made the audience biased in the ballet's favor, critics on the whole did not give it flattering notices. Victor Glover was glum: "In *Romeo and Juliet* the modernist 'decors,' which caused the excitement on the opening night, are not calculated to rejoice the eyes. All is very severe. Dancers are rehearsing behind the scenes, dressed in their costumes de travail, a pirouette here, a few evolutions there of the two stars, and in another corner of the stage a couple rehearse the Shakespearian drama. The ball at the Capulet mansion, the love duo between Romeo and Juliet, the tomb, and the rehearsal is over. Romeo puts on his street clothes and carries the resuscitated Juliet off the stage. It is supposed to be highly diverting, but it ceases to be amusing after the first few minutes. It is all so colorless. Once the rule of the Ballet Russe [sic] used to be wealth of color, richesse, harmony and volupte. Today it appears to be strictly black and white and sharp angles with grace entirely banished. The splendor that was has departed. Once it was a social crime not to have seen the Russian Ballet at least once in a season, to-day we are excused if we miss it occasionally."[29]

Romeo and Juliet was not much better appreciated in England, although *The Times* critic must have known about the *contretemps* with Christopher Wood: "The decoration of the ballet had been entrusted to two Frenchmen of the latest 'advanced' school, which seems to be quite as silly as its predecessors. We wish that M. Diaghilev had seen fit to commission an English artist to provide the scenery for his first English ballet."[30] On the other hand, Diaghilev must have felt that his desire to produce an "English" ballet was vindicated when he read another of the London critics: "*Romeo and Juliet* belongs to the soufflé order of divertissements. It is a midsummer joke, as daintily ephemeral as foam left by the ebbing tide on sunlit sands—the sands of Deauville, let us say."[31] It is often difficult to believe that different critics have seen the same production.

114 The Sea (Act 1 act-drop)

Oil paint, graphite incised in paint, black crayon or chalk on thin card stock
12¾ x 15¾ in: 32.5 x 40 cm
Signed and dated bottom right in pencil: "max ernst / 1926"
Inscribed on reverse in pencil: "Max Ernst Romeo & Juliet 44-865"
1933.471

Exhibitions: London 1926, No 14;[32] Paris 1929;[33] Munich 1931–2, No 226; Chicago 1933, No 82; Northampton 1934, No 82; San Francisco 1935; Paris 1939, No 226; New York MoMA 1944a; Washington D.C. 1950–1; Edinburgh 1954, No 321; London 1954–5, No 364; Indianapolis 1959, No 228; Storrs 1963; New York 1965–6, No 93 (illustrated p 44); New York 1966–7; Princeton 1968; Strasbourg 1969, No 417; Frankfurt-am-Main 1969, No 124; Blommenholm 1971; Hartford 1973; Hartford 1974; Hempstead 1974, No 67; Hartford 1978–9; Coral Gables 1982; Frankfurt-am-Main 1986, No 203 (illustrated in color p 255 top); Hartford 1988; Worcester 1989.
Illustrations: Bablet, p 163 No 302; Hansen, fig 56; Percival, p 108; Rischbieter, p 117 (color); Spies 1976, No 998 p 107 (described as "La Mer").

Max Ernst described exactly when (on 10 August 1925) and how he discovered his technique of *frottage* or rubbing: "One rainy day at an inn by the seaside, I discover myself recalling how in childhood the panel of imitation mahogany opposite my bed had served as the optical stimulant to visions in somnolence. Now I am impressed by the obsession imposed upon my excited gaze by the wooden floor, the grain of which had been deepened and exposed by countless scrubbings. I decide to investigate the symbolism of this obsession and, to aid my meditative and hallucinatory powers, I take from the boards a series of drawings. At random I drop pieces of paper on the floor and then rub them with black lead. By examining closely the drawings thus obtained, I am surprised at the sudden intensification of my visionary capacities. My curiosity awakened, I marvel and am led to examine in the same way, all sorts of materials that fall into my field of vision—leaves and their veins, the ragged edges of sack cloth, the palette knife's markings on a 'modern' painting, thread unrolled from its spool and so forth."[34] To the technique of *frottage* Ernst added *grattage* (scraping): his paintings at this time often combined both techniques. By introducing irrational and unconscious (or automatic) subject matter into art, and by liberating himself from the formal rigidity of cubism Ernst became one of the original surrealists. His ideas coincided with those of André Breton who published his Surrealist Manifesto in October 1924, and he participated in the first Surrealist exhibition at the Galerie Pierre in Paris in November 1925.

The paintings by Max Ernst and Joan Miró which Diaghilev chose as decorations for *Romeo and Juliet* were either those he acquired at the exhibition at the Galerie van Leer in Paris which opened on 10 March 1926,[35] or were made specially later in Monte Carlo after he had decided to do without Christopher Wood. Diaghilev was fascinated by this new "surrealism," and, as Lifar observed, was "interested in discussing art with Ernst, talks which began at evening and often went on till five next morning."[36]

In the absence of revealing photographs or precise descriptions of the scenes it is almost impossible to determine which paintings were used for which scenes. It is known, however, that Miró was largely responsible for the decorations for act one,[37] and Ernst for act two. The works by Ernst, enlarged in each case onto scenic canvas by

Prince Schervashidze, the scene painter, were all simple compositions related in both subject matter and title to his series of drawings called *Histoire Naturelle,* in which a frequently recurring image is a sun floating between the horizontals of earth and sky.

This painting called "The Sea" was used for the act-drop for act one. It was described accurately by Serge Grigoriev, who was totally unsympathetic to Diaghilev's artistic experiment: "To make up for the absence of scenery there were no less than two act-drops, by the *Surréaliste* painters Max Ernst and Joan Miró; but their design had no relation to the subject, the music, or the choreography. Diaghilev took enormous pains over lighting these act-drops; and at one of these lighting rehearsals, when I was as usual sitting next to him, he asked me if I did not think the first act-drop particularly lovely. What I saw hung in front of me was a huge plain pale-blue expanse of canvas, in the centre of which was painted a large disc resembling a gramophone record, of which three-quarters were distinct and the remainder lost in a haze. I certainly could not go into ecstasies over it and said so; at which Diaghilev all but lost his temper. 'I can't understand you,' he said, 'After all these years you've worked with me, and all you've seen, you don't seem to be able to grasp the idea of modern painting!'"[38]

Only one critic, Henry Malherbe, bothered to describe in some detail what was to be seen on stage because, as he put it: "The spectators appeared to be less interested in the music than in the surrealist painting by Mssrs Max Ernst and Joan Miró."[39] He identified four cloths. He appeared, however, to be confused about the first which he described as "made of parallel lines, circles, and a few clumsy, colored commas." This could be either the painting by Ernst or one of the paintings by Miró. He then described other elements designed by Miró[40] before stating: "The cloth for the second scene is divided into three equal parts, one grey, another beige, and the third acid yellow. The third scene is black and violet and embellished with several concentric circles. The final curtain is funereal black."[41]

The painting described for the second scene is not in the Wadsworth Atheneum but, in different colors, remained in Serge Lifar's private collection. Under the title "Horizon" it was included in the sale of Lifar's collection at Sotheby's in 1984, but remained unsold.[42]

The painting described for the third scene (the Duel) was also perhaps the same as this one but lit differently: we have Grigoriev's evidence of Diaghilev's painstaking lighting, and the minimal painting may well have been changed out of immediate recognition by a change in the lighting.

O ne of the few production photographs shows this painting (enlarged) to have been used as the background to the Balcony scene. The photograph shows Karsavina sitting on the balcony which Ernst also designed in *grattage,* but the balcony is merely a barrier, as she is on the same stage level as Lifar. This incongruity was apparently no more remarkable than the scenery itself. Even Lydia Sokolova, who danced the part of the Nurse, retained only the vaguest memory of the sets: "There were two drop curtains by Max Ernst painted with abstractions which I think were meant to represent Day and Night."[43]

The whole canvas has been lightly painted over in pale gray-yellow to give a shimmering, translucent effect.

115　The Night (act 2 scene 4: Balcony scene)

Oil on fabric
24 x 18⅛ in: 61 x 46 cm
Signed (scratched in paint) bottom center: "max ernst"
Inscribed on reverse on stretcher in pencil: "Max Ernst" with framing instructions; stamped on reverse on stretcher and on canvas (twice) "Douane Centrale Exportation Paris." Typed label on stretcher "Max Ernst / Roméo et Juliette / Rideau / Coll. S. Lifar" inscribed in pencil "La Nuit 1926"
1933.470

Exhibitions: London 1926, No 12; Paris 1929, No 23; Paris 1930, No 43; Munich 1931–2, No 225; New York 1933, No 29; Chicago 1933, No 81; Northampton 1934, No 81; San Francisco 1935; Paris 1939, No 225; Poughkeepsie 1940; Williamsburg 1940; New York 1941–2; Indianapolis 1959, No 227; Eindhoven 1964, No 61; New York 1965–6, No 92 (illustrated p 44); New York 1966–7; Princeton 1968; Strasbourg 1969, No 416; Frankfurt-am-Main 1969, No 123; Hartford 1974; Hartford 1978–9; Frankfurt-am-Main 1986, No 202 (illustrated p 254); New York 1986, No 91 (illustrated p 45); Worcester 1989.
Illustrations: Hansen, fig 57; Haskell, p 96 (top); *Souvenir Program* of 1926 Season; Spies 1976, No 997 p 106 (described as "La Nuit").

116　The Sun

Oil paint, crayon or charcoal, and tempera and/or watercolor on thin card stock
12¾ x 19¾ in: 32.5 x 50.1 cm
Signed and inscribed bottom center right in pencil: "à Serge Lifar, pour qu'il danse sur / les lignes de sa main / affectueusement / max ernst" ("To Serge Lifar, let him dance on the lines of his hand, affectionately, Max Ernst")
1933.472

Exhibitions: London 1926, No 16; Paris 1929, No 27 or 28;[44] London Claridge 1930, No 74; Paris 1930, No 43; Munich 1931–2, No 227; New York 1933, No 30; Chicago 1933, No 83; Northampton 1934, No 83; San Francisco 1935; Paris 1939, No 227; Williamsburg 1940; New York 1941–2; New York MoMA 1944a; Washington D.C. 1950–1; Edinburgh 1954, No 322; London 1954–5, No 365; Michigan 1957; Sarasota 1958, No 26; Indianapolis 1959, No 229; Eindhoven 1964, No 64; New York 1965–6, No 94 (illustrated p 45); New York 1966–7; Princeton 1968; Strasbourg 1969, No 418; Frankfurt-am-Main 1969, No 125; Blommenholm 1971; Hartford 1973; Hartford 1974; Hempstead 1974, No 68; Hartford 1978–9; Coral Gables 1982; Frankfurt-am-Main 1986, No 204 (illustrated in color p 255 bottom); Hartford 1988; Worcester 1989.
Illustration: Spies 1976, No 999 p 107 (described as "Le Soleil")

T his painting was not used in the ballet, and, from the inscription, was a present from the artist to Serge Lifar at the time of the production. The color has faded over the years from blue to brown.

117 Design for a hanging in scene 6: The death of Juliet

Oil paint over gesso incised with graphite pencil or point on heavy brown cardboard
13¾ x 10¹¹⁄₁₆ in: 35.2 x 27 cm
Signed (incised in the paint) lower right: "max ernst"
Inscribed on reverse in pencil: "Drawing for Romeo and Juliet 1927 by Max Ernst / Hanging for the death scene of Juliet / Serge Lifar Collection"
1933.473

Exhibitions: Paris 1929, No 24; Chicago 1933, No 84; Northampton 1934, No 84; Munich 1931–2, No 228; Paris 1939, No 228; New York 1941–2; New York MoMA 1944a; Washington DC 1950–1; Edinburgh 1954, No 333; London 1954–5, No 366; Michigan 1957; Elmira 1958, No 31; Indianapolis 1959, No 230; Rowayton 1960; Eindhoven 1964, No 64; New York 1965–6, No 95 (illustrated upside down p 44); New York 1966–7; Strasbourg 1969, No 419; Frankfurt–am–Main 1969, No 126; Hartford 1974; Hempstead 1974, No 66; Munich 1979, No 120; San Francisco 1986; Hartford 1988; Worcester 1989.
Illustrations: Haskell, p 96 (bottom; Spies 1976, No 1000 p 108 (described as "La Mort de Juliette").

In his catalogue of Ernst's work, Werner Spies dates this painting 1926. However, the date on the reverse, as well as the fact that this was not exhibited in London in 1926, indicates that it was made for the revival of *Romeo and Juliet* in 1927, when it was performed three times at the Théâtre Sarah-Bernhardt in Paris on 28 May, 9 and 10 June, and at the Prince's Theatre in London. Furthermore, the fact that Ernst has not used his *frottage* technique but only *grattage* in this painting helps to confirm the later date.

On the other hand, it also fits Henry Malherbe's description, albeit very vague, quoted earlier, of the final curtain being "funereal black"—the dark blues would have appeared black on stage.

Notes

1 The ballet was always officially known by its English title *Romeo and Juliet*, and not translated.
2 The artists were credited specifically as painters, not as designers.
3 This scene was cut before the first performance in London on 21 June 1926 at His Majesty's Theatre.
4 In later programs this word was inexplicably changed to "audience." Since the ballet was meant to be a rehearsal there should not have been an audience!
5 Gerald Hugh Tyrwhitt-Wilson, Lord Berners (1883–1950) composed *The Triumph of Neptune* to a libretto by Sacheverell Sitwell, first performed by Diaghilev's Ballets Russes on 3 December 1926 at the Lyceum Theatre, London.
6 According to David Chadd in *The Diaghilev Ballet in England*, p 52, corroborated by Andrew Motion in *The Lamberts*, pp 143–4.
7 Boris Kochno, *Diaghilev and the Ballets Russes*, p 234.
8 Richard Shead, *Constant Lambert*, p 37.
9 See pp 147–52.
10 Vernon Duke, *Passport to Paris*, p 172.
11 But Diaghilev had it played as interval music.
12 Vernon Duke, *op cit*, p 173.
13 Serge Grigoriev, *The Diaghilev Ballet*, p 222.
14 Quoted in David Chadd and John Gage, *op cit*, p 52. One surviving design is in the Graves Art Gallery, Sheffield, and there are four designs in Kettle's Yard Gallery, Cambridge, England.
15 Quoted in David Chadd and John Gage, *op cit*, p 53.
16 Quoted in *Diaghilev: Les Ballets Russes*, exhibition catalogue, p 136. Bibliothèque nationale, Fonds Kochno, pièce 108.
17 Quoted in David Chadd and John Gage, *op cit*, p 53.
18 Serge Lifar, *Diaghilev*, pp 433–4.
19 Quoted in Richard Shead, *op cit*, p 38.
20 Quoted in Richard Shead, *op cit*, pp 38–9.
21 Serge Lifar, *op cit*, pp 434–4
22 Lydia Sokolova, *Dancing for Diaghilev*, p 244.
23 Alice Nikitina, *Nikitina by herself*, p 58.
24 Tamara Karsavina, "Serge Lifar and the last Diaghilev seasons" in *The Dancing Times* London, March 1967, p 302.
25 Quoted in Richard Shead, *op cit*, p 41.
26 Lydia Sokolova, *op cit*, p 245.
27 Anon,"A stormy night at the Russian Ballet" in *The Dancing Times* London, May 1926, p 267.
28 The text was reprinted in *La Révolution Surréaliste*, Paris, No 7, 15 June 1926. The French text is as follows: "*Protestation*: Il n'est pas admissible que la pensée soit aux ordres de l'argent. Il n'est pourtant pas d'année qui n'apporte la soumission d'un homme qu'on croyait irréductible aux puissances auxquelles il s'opposait jusqu'alors. Peu importent les individus qui se résignent à ce point à en passer par les conditions sociales, l'idée de laquelle ils se réclamaient avant, une telle abdication subsiste en dehors d'eux. C'est en ce sens que la participation des peintres Max Ernst et Joan Miró au prochain spectacle des ballets russes ne saurait impliquer avec le leur le déclassement de l'idée *surréaliste*. Idée essentiellement subversive qui ne peut composer avec de semblables entreprises, dont le but a toujours été de domestiquer au profit de l'aristocratie internationale les rêves et les révoltes de la famine physique et intellectuelle.

"Il a pu sembler à Ernst et à Miró que leur collaboration avec Monsieur de Diaghilew, légitimée par l'exemple de Picasso, ne tirait pas à si grave conséquence. Elle nous met pourtant dans l'obligation, nous qui avons tout souci de maintenir hors de portée des négriers de toutes sortes de positions avancées de l'esprit, elle nous met dans l'obligation de dénoncer, sans considération de personnes, une attitude qui donne des armes aux pires partisans de l'équivoque morale.

"On sait que nous ne faisons qu'un cas très relatif de nos affinités artistiques avec un tel ou tel. Qu'on nous fasse l'honneur de croire qu'en mai 1926 nous sommes plus que jamais incapables d'y sacrifier le sens que nous avons de la réalité révolutionnaire."
29 Victor Glover, "Pandemonium at Paris Premiere" in unidentified American newspaper, byline dated Paris 27 May [1926].
30 Anon, *The Times*, London, 22 June 1926, p 14.
31 H. H. in *The Observer*, London, 27 June 1926.
32 Nos 14–15 in the catalogue described as "The Sea" dated 1925.
33 Nos 25–26 in the catalogue described as "La Mer" dated 1925.
34 Max Ernst quoted in the catalogue of the Tate Gallery, London, exhibition, p 11. Of the several versions of this account, this is the least unintelligible.
35 Which Diaghilev was urged to see by Kochno and Lifar, see pp 19–20.
36 Serge Lifar, *Diaghilev*, p 434.
37 See *Joan Miró*, pp 262–65, for a fuller description of his participation.
38 Serge Grigoriev, *The Diaghilev Ballet*, p 225.
39 Henry Malherbe in *Le Temps*, Paris, 2 June 1926, p 3.
40 See *Joan Miró*, pp 262–65.
41 Henry Malherbe, *op cit*.
42 *Ballet Material and Manuscripts from the Serge Lifar Collection*, Sotheby's, London, 9 May 1984, lot 50.
43 Lydia Sokolova, *Dancing for Diaghilev*, p 245.
44 Both called "Le Soleil" in the catalogue.

Fedor Fedorovsky

Russian
born 1883 Černigov (Ukraine)
died 1955 Moscow

Khovanshchina (The Khovansky Affair)

Unfinished opera in 3 acts and 4 tableaux by
   Modest Mussorgsky and Vladimir Stassov
Composer: Modest Mussorgsky completed and
   orchestrated by Nikolai Rimsky-Korsakov, with
   alterations and additions by Igor Stravinsky and
   new orchestrations by Maurice Ravel[1]
Conductor: Emile Cooper
Director: Alexander Sanine
Choreographer: Adolf Bolm[2]
Designer (sets and costumes): Fedor Fedorovsky
Principal Singers:
   Dositheus (Chief of the Old Believers):
      Fedor Chaliapine
   Prince Ivan Khovansky (Chief of the Streltsy):
      M. Zaporojetz
   Prince Andrew Khovansky (his son):
      Vasili Damaev
   Chaklovity (a Nobleman): Paul Andreyev
   Marfa (a young mystic, one of the Old
      Believers): Elisabeth Petrenko
   The Scribe: Nicolas Andreev
   Emma: Marie Brian
   Varsonofiev (a follower of Khovansky):
      Alexander Belianin
   Kouska (a Streltsy): Nicolas Bolshakov
   Three Streltsy: MM. Belianin, Alexandrovitch,
      Strobinder
   Suzanne (an Old Believer): Hélène Nikolaeva
Principal Dancers:
   Mlles Astafieva, Tchernicheva, Maicherska,
      Konietska, Bonietska, Dombrovska,
      Khokhlova, Wassilewska, Maningsova[3]
Company: Diaghilev's Ballets Russes
First Performance: 5 June 1913, Théâtre des
   Champs-Elysées, Paris

Synopsis

From the program.

"Act 1, First Tableau 'The Old Believers':[4] Dawn is breaking on Moscow, and the growing light reveals the great square and the church built in the days of Ivan the Terrible. A Streltsy sentry, humming a song, is preparing to go off duty, and is joined by two friends who come to bring him the latest news. A scribe instals himself in his booth, where Chaklovity seeks his assistance in concocting a malicious indictment of the Khovansky family who are accused of a desire to usurp the throne. In the meantime the town is beginning to wake up; people come into the square and make the scribe read the notices posted on the walls. The scribe demands payment for doing this, and thereby comes in for some rough handling, but at last he reads the ukase which contains severe repressive measures against a large number of noblemen. The crowd voices its anger and then its sadness in face of these cruelties.

But now Ivan Khovansky, head of the Streltsy, and his brilliant train make their appearance. On him are centred the hopes of Old Russia, and he comforts the people and encourages them to hope on before he passes on to the Kremlin. His son, Prince Andrew, arrives on the scene in pursuit of a young Lutheran girl, Emma. He is confronted by Marfa, one of the Old Believers, who takes Emma under her protection. Marfa loves Andrew, who also loves her: she reproaches him with his faithlessness, disarms him when he threatens her with a dagger, and predicts that a different kind of death awaits him, which will reunite him to her. Ivan Khovansky returns from the Kremlin at this moment, and witnesses the scene. He is struck by Emma's beauty, and gives orders to his soldiers to carry her off to his palace. Andrew, in despair, tries to stab her rather than let her belong to his father, when Dositheus, the austere chief of the Old Believers, appears. He is filled with indignation at the scene and bitterly reproaches the princes, reminding them of the unhappy state of Russia, and urging on them the necessity of union and devout adherence to the faith. He confides Emma to Marfa's care, sends away the Streltsy, and prays with his fellow believers in a state of mystic exaltation while the bells of the Kremlin call the people to worship.

Act 1, Second Tableau 'The Streltsy Quarter': Before the palace of Ivan Khovansky, which Dositheus has just entered, there passes a procession of the Old Believers, singing a hymn of faith and hope. Marfa is seated in front of the palace, musing over the past and recalling the happy hours spent with her lover, Andrew Khovansky. This frank avowal scandalises old Suzanne, who is shocked at what she considers sin on Marfa's part. Marfa vindicates her conduct with great nobility, and receives the approval of Dositheus, who unexpectedly appearing between them defends the rights of true love and indignantly drives Suzanne away. He knows what Marfa is suffering and comforts her, then, left alone, he prays for his unhappy country which is threatened with dangers fromn every quarter.

The Streltsy now come out of their houses. Most of them are drunk, and are quarrelling noisily with their wives. Their disputes are interrupted for a time by a song which one of them starts and which the others try to sing in chorus. They are beginning to dance, when the old scribe appears, half mad with terror. He warns them that the troops of the Tsar Peter are entering the Streltsy quarter and laying waste everything on their way. It is the end of the military faction of Old Russia. The crowd, at first incredulous, then terror-stricken, implores the counsel and protection of Prince Ivan Khovansky and begs to march against the invaders. But the Old Prince has lost all hope; he believes resistance is useless, and predicts the downfall of Old Russia. All the people unite in a fervent appeal to divine mercy.

Act 2, Third Tableau 'The End of the Streltsy (The Old Militia)': Prince Ivan Khovansky has retired to one of his estates. His serfs are singing a lament which saddens them; he tells them to choose more cheerful music. A stranger enters, who tries to warn the old Chief of the Streltsy of the dangers which threaten his life. Ivan is annoyed at the message, and does not believe that anyone would dare to attack him on his own estate. After having punished the messenger, whose insolence has disgusted him, he sends for his Persian slaves and orders them to dance for him. The dance is interrupted by the arrival of the nobleman, Chaklovity. This false friend gives him to understand that the Princess Regent wishes to summon a council where a place has been reserved for Ivan Khovansky. The old Prince is angry at first, but at last consents to go, and sends for his state apparel. Just as he is crossing the threshold, however, a man who has been stationed there by the treacherous Chaklovity starts forward and stabs him while Chaklovity rejoices in his triumph.

Act 3, Fourth Tableau 'The End of the Old Believers': The Tsar's troops surround a convent where Dositheus and his followers are preparing for death. The funeral pyre is prepared. The Old Believers envelop themselves in their shrouds before marching voluntarily to martyrdom. Marfa sees Andrew Khovansky arriving. The approach of death re-unites them; she lights a torch and performs the funeral rites which Mussorgsky called the Requiem of Love. The hour of martyrdom has sounded. The march to death begins. The Old Believers mount the funeral pyre which is lighted by Dositheus, and their sublime suicide is accomplished while their hymns of exaltation rise to heaven."

Diaghilev was particularly ambitious in his plans for his eighth season in Paris. With Fokine's resignation as choreographer after *Daphnis and Chloë* at the end of the 1912 season, which he had accepted with alacrity, Diaghilev could concentrate on his desire to see Nijinsky accepted and confirmed as a masterly and original choreographer. His plans for the ballet included two new works. Nijinsky would stage *Jeux*[5] and *Le Sacre du Printemps* (see pp 291–95). But Diaghilev also planned to return, for the first time since 1909, to his love of opera by presenting a revival of *Boris Godunov*,[6] which had so impressed Parisian audiences in 1908, and a new production of *Khovanshchina*,[7] both with Fedor Chaliapine. A spur to Diaghilev's ambition may have been that the season was to celebrate the opening of the smartest theater in Paris, the Théâtre des Champs-Elysées, under the management of Gabriel Astruc. Diaghilev, cunning as ever in matters of business, realized that Astruc needed his company for the prestige it would bring to his new theater. He drove a hard bargain. It was reported by Arnold Haskell: "'I had said to Diaghileff,' says Astruc, 'This year no more Opéra, no more

Châtelet! You are coming to me.' 'But my dear friend, the directors of the Opéra want me.' 'So. And how much are they offering you? Doubtless twelve hundred francs, your usual price.' 'Yes, but you must understand that for six years now people say that Astruc invented the Russian Ballet. That, my dear friend, must be paid for.' 'How much?' 'At least 25,000 francs a performance.' 'Even for twenty performances?' 'Even for twenty performances.' The signing of this contract, Astruc goes on to say, meant his death warrant, for to those 25,000 francs it was necessary to add as much again for incidental expenses, and no success could cover such a strain. Gallantly he says, 'That mad act, that I had not the right not to commit, allowed the creation of *Sacre*, and cost me the life of my management.'"[8] The season was, of course, a huge success in many ways, although, at the time, the audience's hostile reaction to *Le Sacre du Printemps* on 29 May caused the company much anguish. Astruc had indeed overreached himself, and was declared bankrupt in August.

Khovanshchina, originally scheduled for 30 May, was postponed for technical reasons until 5 June. As Grigoriev commented: "The product of so much combined talent, could scarcely fail to achieve an outstanding success; nor did it; and the encouragement this afforded us overlaid the distress of our experience with *Sacre*."[9] In order to achieve that success, Diaghilev did not hesitate to tinker drastically with Mussorgsky's score, and justified his tinkering by the fact that the opera was unfinished. He cut Mussorgsky's second act completely and therefore cut the character of Prince Galitsin, councillor and former lover of the Tsarevna, an enlightened and cultured man who is opposed to Prince Khovansky. Lost from this act also was Marfa's fine song in which she foretells Galitsin's downfall. Diaghilev's aim in omitting this act and this character was to concentrate the attention on Khovansky and Dositheus. This change gave greater prominence to Chaliapine as Dositheus, a change which would have had his full support. However, the balance of the original opera in which the aim was to show the opposing forces of Khovansky and Galitsin, and the influence of Dositheus on both of them, was therefore lost. Chaklovity's song praying for Russia in the third act was also left out. But Diaghilev (and Chaliapine) knew that audiences came primarily to listen to Chaliapine, and not to operatic interpretations of Russian history

sung in Russian.[10] He ignored the Russian critics who reported that the opera was performed to French audiences in a scandalously cut version. More to the point, wrote Lunacharsky, would be to "curtail the hideously long intervals."[11]

It was Valentin Serov, the painter, who recommended Fedorovsky as designer for *Khovanshchina*. It was typical of Diaghilev to engage a young man at the beginning of his career to design such an important and complicated production, with so many scenes and costumes. Fedorovsky did not let him down. He avoided designing a series of historically accurate Russian scenes and costumes of the late seventeenth century, and he avoided a stylization which he thought "untruthful" and "lifeless." Instead, he designed almost symbolic sets and costumes which were imbued with the atmosphere of the period through their color range. They gave the impression of being historically accurate without necessarily being so. As Fedorovsky stated: "I want color to express sound, I want truthfulness in colors expressing the word."[12] He therefore looked for colors which he thought would be equivalent to the musical notes. He expressed visually what Mussorgsky had expressed in his score, but their starting point was an historical fact. The symbolism was probably lost on the audience, but theater design is to do with creating a truthful atmosphere by whatever means, rather than historical accuracy. Fedorovsky succeeded. He also devised an original technique in his designs. Many of them, both sets and costumes, are drawn in a perspective with the vanishing point almost at the bottom of the page so that we appear to look up at the scenes and the figures which consequently appear more awesome. He also always drew several characters in the same design, which has the advantage of letting the costumier (and us) see the color range of groups of figures together.

While Astruc was going bankrupt in Paris because of his extravagances in the Théâtre des Champs-Elysées, Sir Thomas Beecham took a lease on the Theatre Royal, Drury Lane, in London to present a season of Diaghilev's opera and ballet productions because he was "becoming more convinced every day that nothing but the discovery of some new and vitalizing force could lift opera out of the deplorable stagnation in which it was languishing. It was impossible to overlook the undiminished popularity of the Ballet, and it was at least imaginable that another one hundred per cent Russian

institution might be the key to the enigma."[13] He does not add that he was also convinced it would do his career no harm to conduct *Boris Godunov* and *Khovanshchina* himself, and that he had convinced his father, Sir Joseph Beecham, to pay for it all. It was worth it. Grigoriev commented that "rumours of our triumphs in Paris had provoked most eager expectations . . . Both *Boris* and *Khovanshchina*, with Chaliapine, conducted in turn by Cooper and Thomas Beecham, were resounding successes."[14] More objectively, the critic of *The Times* enthusiastically confirmed that opinion about *Khovanshchina*: "M. Chaliapin was magnificent from first to last, and his singing put the crown upon the restrained dignity of his acting. M. Zaporojetz as the leader of the Streltsy, too, was very fine. His voice had the power of command in it, and he gave the essence of the character in his proud, unbending bearing. Mme. Petrenko's beautiful voice had plenty of scope in the part of the visionary Martha, and M. Damaev, though he has not a beautiful voice, played the part of the licentious young Khovansky admirably. But, after all, it is the wonderful chorus which makes the most overwhelming impression and draws the strongest line of distinction between this and any other operatic company which London has seen in recent years."[15]

118* Costume designs for M. Zaporojetz as Ivan Khovansky, Alexander Belianin as Varsonofiev, and Paul Andreev as Chaklovity

Graphite, charcoal, tempera, and gold paint on paper mounted on canvas and stretched (cream background painted in later by another hand)
31¾ x 39¾ in: 81 x 101 cm
Signed in Russian and dated: "Федоровски (Fedorovsky) 1912/1913"
Inscribed bottom right: "Inv Nr 983"
Gift of Nikita D. Lobanov
1970.123

Fedorovsky's costume designs are often on an unusually large scale, which probably made them cumbersome to work from by the costumier. However, as noted above, the inclusion of several figures in one design made the interpretation, particularly of color, more accurately balanced.

119* Costume design for twelve figures (six women and six children) of the chorus

Graphite and tempera on paper mounted to canvas and stretched (cream background painted in later by another hand)
30 x 52 in: 76.2 x 131.8 cm
Signed in Russian and dated: "Федоровски (Fedorovsky) 1913"
Inscribed bottom right: "Inv 976"
Gift of Nikita D. Lobanov
1970.124

Notes

1 Stravinsky provided a new final chorus which was not, however, performed on the first night as Diaghilev, sensing the hostility toward the changes in the score, did not want the critics to hear it. Ravel orchestrated the reading of the *ukases*, the hymn to Prince Khovansky, the duet between Khovansky and Emma in act 1, and Marfa's song and the song of Kouska and the Chorus in act 2.

2 Bolm choreographed the Persian Dance in act 2.

3 Real name Hilda Munnings, later Lydia Sokolova.

4 The reforms of the Russian Orthodox church carried out by Patriarch Nikon (1605–81) in the seventeenth century—concerned with liturgy and ritual, involving the correction of the texts of the Bible and service books in accordance with the best Greek manuscripts and Greek practise—were denounced as innovations and opposed by those who saw them as a challenge to the fundamental position of the Russian church. These opponents called themselves "Old Believers."

5 *Jeux* with music by Claude Debussy conducted by Pierre Monteux, set and costumes by Léon Bakst, Vaslav Nijinsky as the Young Man and Tamara Karsvaina and Ludmilla Schollar as the Young Girls was first performed at the Théâtre des Champs-Elysées, Paris on 15 May 1913.

6 The revival of *Boris Godunov* was first performed on 22 May 1913. There were six performances alternating with evenings of ballet.

7 This now usual spelling is used although Diaghilev simplified the transliteration of the title to *Khovantchina*.

8 Arnold Haskell, *Diaghileff*, pp 242–3.

9 Serge Grigoriev, *The Diaghilev Ballet*, p 94.

10 Diaghilev had cut a number of scenes for the performances of *Boris Godunov* in 1908 but, after protestations from a more knowledgeable audience, was forced to reinstate them for the performances in 1913.

11 V. A. Lunacharsky quoted in N. Gilyarovskaya, *F. F. Fedorovsky*, p 48. For a full evaluation of the extent of Diaghilev's tinkering with the score, see Richard Taruskin, *Stravinsky and the Russian Traditions,* Vol 2 pp 1039–68.

12 Quoted in N. Gilyarovskaya, *ibid*, p 50.

13 Sir Thomas Beecham, *A Mingled Chime*, p 161.

14 Serge Grigoriev, *op cit*, p 94.

15 Anon, "Khovanstchina" in *The Times*, London 2 July 1913, p 10.

Naum Gabo

Russian
born 1890 Briansk
died 1977 Waterbury (Connecticut)

La Chatte (The Cat)

Ballet in 1 act by Sobeka (Boris Kochno),[1] after the fable by Aesop
Composer: Henri Sauguet
Conductor: Marc-César Scotto
Choreographer: George Balanchine
Designers (architectural and sculptural constructions): Naum Gabo[2] and Antoine Pevsner
Designer (costumes): Naum Gabo
Principal Dancers:
    The Cat: Olga Spessivtseva[3]
    The Young Man: Serge Lifar
Company: Diaghilev's Ballets Russes
First Performance: 30 April 1927, Théâtre de Monte-Carlo

Synopsis

A young man, in love with a cat, abandons his friends and prays to Aphrodite to change the animal into a girl so that he can express his love for her. The goddess agrees, the cat becomes a girl, and the young man succeeds in winning her affection. But during their lovemaking the goddess tests the girl's constancy by tempting her with a mouse which scampers across the bridal chamber. The girl sees the mouse and immediately abandons her lover. Aphrodite then turns her back into a cat to the great grief of her lover, who dies.

Always on the lookout for new composers Diaghilev saw *Les Roses*—a dance divertissement by the twenty-three year old Henri Sauguet with choreography by Leonide Massine and designed by Marie Laurencin—produced during Comte Etienne de Beaumont's Soirées de Paris at the Théâtre de la Cigale in 1924. (Diaghilev may have also seen the same composer's one-act comic opera, *Le Plumet du Colonel*, produced in the same year at the Théâtre des Champs-Elysées.) He was impressed, but commissioned Sauguet only two years later to write a ballet. Sauguet first thought of asking Paul Eluard for a libretto, but then wrote to Diaghilev: "Abandoning the too dangerous idea of working with Paul Eluard, which he would have certainly refused, I have spoken to René Crevel about our ballet project."[4] But Diaghilev decided to ask Boris Kochno to devise a suitable libretto from Aesop's fable about a cat transformed into a woman. Sauguet rightly saw Diaghilev's commission as a ratification of his talent and a guarantee of his future, but he did not let it go to his head because, as Schneider wrote: "He did not forget the fickleness of human nature or the whims of luck."[5] *La Chatte* suffered from both,

although it was ultimately a huge success and remained in the repertory of the Ballets Russes until Diaghilev's death.

The ballet is supposedly based on Aesop's fable, but Kochno turned the whole story upside down. In the original fable it is the cat who falls in love with a handsome young man and prays to Aphrodite to change her into a woman. The temptation of the mouse introduced by Aphrodite makes sense in the original fable, but becomes meaningless in this upside-down version. Apparently no one noticed the incongruity.

The choreography was entrusted to George Balanchine. It was the only new ballet he made in 1927, but it was one of his most imaginative creations and, according to Bernard Taper, "a thoroughly modern statement."[6] That the modernism was really Balanchine's is questionable because the set and costumes, being truly revolutionary, affected the appreciation and evaluation of the ballet as a whole.

Sauguet initially wanted Christian Bérard to be the designer and took Diaghilev and Kochno "to the eminently bourgeois town house of the painter's father, which in no way resembled the setting in which Diaghilev's imagination placed every young, unknown artist."[7] Diaghilev thought that any worthwhile artist should be impoverished and live in a miserable garret. However, when the prosperous Bérard finally showed him some canvases, they were "apparently unfinished [and] represented some melancholy characters—street acrobats in dirty tights, youths on crutches lounging in front of brick walls, and so on";[8] Diaghilev, however, was unimpressed. He told Sauguet that he did not want his ballet set in "some concierge's hovel,"[9] and again ignored the composer's request.

Instead of commissioning Bérard, Diaghilev pursued his own avant-garde interests by deciding to approach Naum Gabo whose "constructivist" work, together with that of his brother Antoine Pevsner, he had seen at the Galerie Percier in Paris in 1924.[10] Another of Gabo's brothers, Alexei Pevsner, recalled that "Gabo protested strongly against any 'isms'" and that Antoine agreed with him. Gabo called the

ideas he was standing for in art "constructive ideas" or "ideas of spatial construction."[11] And yet Gabo and Pevsner called themselves "constructivists," although they defined their artistic ideas in 1920 in a broadsheet (written by Gabo but signed by both) called *Realist Manifesto,* in which they stated that "art should stop being imitative and try instead to discover new forms."[12] During the autumn of 1924 Diaghilev visited Gabo in Berlin and suggested to him the idea of designing a ballet. After a further visit a year later Gabo signed a contract at the beginning of 1926 with the condition that his brother, Antoine, who was very depressed at the time, be included in the contract and given equal credit for the set. Gabo in fact designed the whole set except for the quasi-figurative, symbolic sculpture of the goddess Aphrodite which was the work of Pevsner. Steven Nash has described the design concept as being a "severe environment of geometry and light to act as a foil for the ancient theme, rather sweet music, and athletic grace of the dancers."[13] Gabo made a model of the set during the summer of 1926 while staying in Paris at his brother's flat. Richard Buckle, who talked to Gabo about his design, quoted him saying how "Diaghilev climbed the stairs to examine the gleaming construction of transparent planes and curves against a curtain of shining black 'American cloth.' It took him no time at all to pass judgement. Looking up at the sculptor, he exclaimed, 'That's a real temple.'"[14] The main material used for both the model and the finished set was Celon, "a cellulose acetate preferable to celluloid because it was less flammable (available at the time in Germany from its manufacturer, Celonwerke.)"[15] The finished set, which was an exact enlargement of the model, was a complex construction of different transparent, rectangular shapes, platforms, and boxes erected round the symbolic rhomboid figure of Aphrodite, which all gleamed and sparkled under the spotlights. Cyril Beaumont, though incorrectly calling the plastic material "talc," wrote that "the multiform units suggested a constructional game for the child of an architect of the modernist school, or, better still, 'parts of a —— greenhouse,' as one of the stage-hands commented."[16] The minimal costumes were constructed of the same material, as well as other plastics and silver cloth. The mouse, which was clockwork, proved quickly to be so unreliable that it had to be left to the imagination.

Diaghilev originally intended the ballet as a modern showpiece for Olga Spessivt-seva whom he successfully enticed away from the Paris Opéra where she had been dancing regularly for the previous two years, and most sublimely in *Giselle*.[17] Spessivtseva's training had been entirely classical and so her style was not suited to Massine's or Nijinska's modern ballets; however, Diaghilev thought that Balanchine might be able to coax her into his style, but warned him, according to Richard Buckle, "that if she disliked the ballet it must be good, but if she liked it it would be awful."[18] After a while Diaghilev congratulated Balanchine because although he saw that Spessivtseva hated the ballet he could see that she was going to be marvelous in it. And she was. The first night in Monte Carlo was a sensational success. Anton Dolin wrote that: "She had, in some uncanny way, with no exaggeration of body or face, transformed herself into a cat, feline and seductive. One forgot the lovely face to admire in its place the suppleness and expression of her body."[19]

Before the ballet was produced in Paris, Diaghilev took the unusual step of a issuing a statement which was published in *Le Figaro* on the eve of the first night. Part of this statement was: "At the first night of the Russian Ballet tomorrow a new dancer, Olga Spessiva, will make her début. It is true that for two seasons a ballerina, whose name was almost the same, has been dancing at the Opéra, but fate dictated that for one reason or another Spessivtseva from the Opéra was not "appreciated" by the keenest audience in the world, the Parisian audience . . . Our great ballet master Cecchetti, who created Nijinsky, Karsavina and many others, said only this winter during one of his classes at La Scala in Milan: 'One apple came into the world, it was cut in two, one half became Pavlova, the other Spessiva.' And I would add that for me Spessiva is the half of the apple that was turned to the sun . . . Having begun twenty years ago with Pavlova and Nijinsky my joy is all the greater now that I have come to Spessiva and Lifar. The former have become legendary. The latter, very different from their predecessors, are now before us waiting for their turn to pass into legend. The legend of

the glory of the Russian Ballet is a beautiful legend."[20] Pavlova never forgave Diaghilev for this stated preference, even though she had never been eclipsed by Spessivtseva. In an ironic retribution, Spessivtseva twisted her ankle so badly at the dress rehearsal that she was prevented from dancing on the first night in Paris. Some historians have written that she feigned injury after quarreling with Diaghilev because she hated the ballet so much, but this has been denied by Serge Lifar who recalled that he saw her at her flat, clearly in great pain, being attended by a Doctor Dalimier.[21] Walter Nuvel, Diaghilev's friend and collaborator, also confirmed in a subsequent letter to him that Doctor Dalimier continued to treat Spessivtseva.[22]

Balanchine wanted Danilova, his mistress, to replace Spessivtseva. In spite of his threat to withdraw the ballet if his wish was refused, Diaghilev imperiously insisted on Alice Nikitina. It was late afternoon before Nikitina began to learn her part, without a piano, in a corridor of the Mogador theater: "It was 5.30 p.m. and not a minute to lose. We managed to sweep a little bit of free space and Lifar started to show me the *pas de deux*, humming an incredibly false tune. I tried in spite of everything to memorise what he was showing me, resolved at any price to get this crazy situation in control. For the next variation they sent me Balanchine who, very reluctantly, showed me hurriedly the actual dance of the *Chatte*. It was thus, on this slippery and dusty linoleum, amidst all the disorder, without music, that the greatest success of Diaghilev's last years was born and became my greatest personal triumph—that is the reason that up to now I am nicknamed *La Chatte!*"[23] Thus, although Diaghilev had carefully planned the ballet for Spessivtseva's reincarnation, it actually confirmed Nikitina's stardom and, furthermore, "became a milestone in the process of deifying Lifar."[24]

There was another misadventure when the company reached London: the first night had to be postponed by one day because the scenery failed to be delivered in time by the railroad company. When it was finally shown, the ballet was no less successful in London than in Monte Carlo and Paris. Nikitina naturally over-flattered herself, but with some justification because the ballet was indeed an immense success and was repeated everywhere in the following seasons.[25] Cyril Beaumont was particularly ecstatic in his appreciation of the

effectiveness of the dancing: "The chief merit of *The Cat*, paradoxical as it may seem in so advanced a production, was its power to convey much more forcefully than ballets directly inspired by classical mythology, something of that ideal of physical beauty which was the dominant motive in the dance festivals of the ancient Greeks. There was something intensely refreshing and exhilarating in the sight of those trained, well formed, lissom brown bodies, worthy of a Grecian frieze, leaping, bending, twirling, finally to mass into an impressive group. Those figures were further enhanced and almost deified whenever the talc in their costumes caught the light and reflected it back in a myriad flashes."[26] While the reputations of Nikitina and Lifar were greatly enhanced by this ballet, it was undoubtedly Gabo's contribution (with his brother's help) which not only made that enhancement possible but also became the chief talking point of the production. The critic, W. H. Haddon Squire, summed it up exactly: "The most novel feature of the new ballet is its stage setting. Here, instead of the scene painter and his flat, painted surfaces, we have the architect-sculptor and three-dimensional forms. Painted canvas, and the old picture stage, give only the illusion of three dimensions, but these three-dimensional volumes, derived from simple geometric forms, not only heighten the spectator's sense of space but enrich the rhythmical variety of the dancers' movements. In *The Cat* Gabo and Pevsner use sheets of mica, held together by metal strips, for their volumes, and these, being transparent, provide opportunities for some extraordinarily beautiful lighting."[27] The comment about the lighting, which was undoubtedly arranged by Diaghilev himself, confirms his restless inquisitiveness and persistent experimentation in the art and technique of theater.

120 Costume sketch design for Serge Lifar as the Young Man

Graphite with ink notations on transparent graph paper
11¹⁄₁₆ x 8⅝ in: 28 x 21.8 cm
Signed lower right in Russian in pencil: "Габо (Gabo)", and dated in ink: "1.VI.27"
Inscribed top left in Russian in ink: "Прекрасному / Лифарю / от Габо в память о 'La Chatte' (To the excellent Lifar from Gabo in memory of 'La Chatte')"
1933.475

Exhibitions: Chicago 1933, No 86; Northampton 1934, No 86; San Francisco 1935; Paris 1939, No 232 (described as "Deux costumes"); Williamsburg 1940; Edinburgh 1954, No 348; London 1954–5, No 381; Michigan 1957; Elmira 1958, No 58; Indianapolis 1959, No 259; Storrs 1963; Eindhoven 1964, No 75; New York 1965–6, No 96 (illustrated p 46); New York 1966–7; Princeton 1968; Strasbourg 1969, No 430; Frankfurt-am-Main 1969, No 135; Hartford 1974; Hempstead 1974, No 69; London 1981; Frankfurt-am-Main 1986, No 192 (illustrated p 249 bottom right, not as indicated in catalogue); Hartford 1988; Worcester 1989.
Illustrations: Kochno 1970 (a similar drawing on p 248); Rischbieter, p 136a.

Gabo made several drawings of the costumes, and most are on the same tracing graph paper. Some drawings remained the property of the artist; two, including one of the Cat, belonged to Lifar until his collection was sold in 1984;[28] four others, originally belonging to Boris Kochno, are now in the Musée de l'Opéra in Paris.

These drawings, being apparently unfinished, give the illusion of being preparatory drawings for figurative sculptures as they could easily be enlarged in construction in scale to any size. At the same time, as drawings they are all in a style which harmonizes closely with the setting; the faceless and feetless figures are reduced to a minimal outline but, although insubstantial and transparent, they are full of vigour and character. As costume designs, however, all the drawings are most uninformative and inadequate, because there is no indication about the material that should be used or how the individual costumes should be made. Presumably, therefore, Gabo himself carefully supervised the making of each of the costumes, and almost certainly made the headdresses. The finished costumes, conceived as closely corresponding to the set while showing off the bodies of the dancers, were successful for, as Lydia Sokolova remarked: "The form of these costumes was simple, and although Spessivtseva's talc *tutu* and Lifar's breastplate were sometimes distracting, there have been few ballets in which the beauty of young people's bodies in motion were shown to better effect."[29] Henning Rischbieter described this effect of the transparent costumes within the set as: "creating a clinical, Utopian atmosphere that seemed at the time ambiguous."[30]

The original costume (with some modern additions) and the headdress worn by Lifar were sold in 1984. The catalogue gave

Right: Serge Lifar as the Young Man, being carried away by his six comrades.

the following description: "Short one sleeved (left) yellow silk jersey top with bold padded silver cloth shoulder piece from which front and back hang triangular cellulose acetate panels to form a breast-plate bordered with silver ribbon, fastened with button at right side . . . The original helmet of celluloid is composed of a head band, a band over the head supporting two sculptured shapes slotted together, the supporting one having a circle removed, the slotted two lozenges removed, chinstrap."[31] The costume also included white knitted shorts and a wide silver ribbon belt.

Gabo made this drawing in 1926 together with the others. The date, in ink, on this one was written at the same time as the inscription and is therefore the date that Gabo gave the drawing to Lifar in Paris, after three performances of the ballet, and not when he made the drawing.

On the reverse of this drawing there is a partial tracing of the same figure.

121 Costume design for the Young Man's (Lifar's) six comrades

Graphite with ink notations on transparent graph paper
11¹¹⁄₁₆ x 8⅝ in: 27.5 x 21.8 cm
Signed lower right in Russian in pencil: "Габо (Gabo)"
Inscribed top right in Russian in ink: "Сергею Павловичу / Дягилеву / в знак уважения / Н. Габо / Paris 1 июнь 1927 (To Serge Pavlovitch Diaghilev as a mark of respect, N. Gabo, Paris, 1 June 1927)"
1933.476

Exhibitions: Chicago 1933, No 87; Northampton 1934, No 87; San Francisco 1935; Paris 1939, No 232 (described as "Deux costumes"); Williamsburg 1940; Edinburgh 1954, No 349; London 1954–5, No 382 (described as "Costume: woman'"); Michigan 1957; Elmira 1958, No 58; Indianapolis 1959, No 260; Storrs 1963; Eindhoven 1964, No 76; New York 1965–6, No 97 (illustrated p 47); New York 1966–7; Princeton 1968; Strasbourg 1969, No 431; Frankfurt-am-Main 1969, No 136; Hartford 1973; Hartford 1974; Hempstead 1974, No 70 Frankfurt-am-Main 1986, No 193 (illustrated p 249 bottom left, not as indicated in catalogue); Worcester 1989.
Illustration: Rischbieter, p 136b.

The six comrades were Nicolas Efimov, Constantin Tcherkas, Richard Domansky, Mezeslaw Borovsky, Boris Lissanevitch, and Marjan Ladré. Their costumes were not as in the drawing. The tops and shorts were not made to simulate chainmail, but were similar to Lifar's costume in the previous drawing, except that the tops were sleeveless and had no breastplates.

Gabo gave this drawing to Diaghilev on the same day as he gave the previous one to Lifar. Lifar acquired it after Diaghilev's death. On the reverse is a tracing of the same figure, in outline only.

Notes

1 Kochno invented this pseudonym by using the initial letters of the three collaborators Sauguet, Balanchine, and Kochno himself, and by playing on the Russian word "собака (sobaka)" meaning dog, because Diaghilev often called him his faithful watchdog.
2 Pseudonym for Neemia Pevsner.
3 Diaghilev simplified her name to "Spessiva," which is the version printed in the program.
4 Letter dated 12 November 1926 quoted in Nicole Wild and Jean-Michel Nectoux, *Diaghilev: Les Ballets Russes*, p 143.
5 Marcel Schneider, *Henri Sauguet*, p 18.
6 Bernard Taper, *Balanchine*, p 90.
7 Boris Kochno, *Diaghilev and the Ballets Russes*, p 252.
8 Boris Kochno, *ibid*, p 252.
9 Boris Kochno, *ibid*, p 253. For once, Diaghilev did not recognize the potential greatness of a theater designer: he never commissioned Bérard. But Sauguet, Kochno, and Bérard, with Serge Lifar as choreographer, were together responsible for *La Nuit*, see pp 142–46.
10 *Constructivistes Russes: Gabo et Pevsner*, Galerie Percier, Paris 19 June–5 July 1924.
11 Alexei Pevsner, *A biographical sketch of my brothers*, p 42.
12 Herbert Read in Ruth Olson and Abraham Chanin *Gabo/Pevsner*, p 10.
13 Steven A. Nash, *Naum Gabo: Sixty Years of Constructivism*, p 30.
14 Richard Buckle, *Diaghilev*, pp 483–4.
15 Steven A. Nash, *op cit*, p 30.
16 Cyril W. Beaumont, *The Diaghilev Ballet in London*, p 273.
17 See Alexandre Benois, *Giselle* pp 130–39.
18 Richard Buckle, *op cit*, p 485.
19 Anton Dolin, *The Sleeping Ballerina*, p 47.
20 Serge Diaghilev in *Le Figaro*, Paris, 26 May 1927, translated from the original Russian, quoted in I. S. Zilberstein and V. A. Samkov, *Sergei Diaghilev*, p 246. The full text, in different translations, is quoted in Serge Lifar, *Serge Diaghilev*, p 448, and in Richard Buckle, *op cit*, pp 487–8.
21 Serge Lifar, *Les Trois Grâces*, p 251.
22 Dated 28 June 1927, quoted in I. S. Zilberstein and V. A. Samkov, *op cit*, p 475.
23 Alice Nikitina, *Nikitina*, p 76.
24 Richard Buckle, *op cit*, p 484.
25 In the subsequent seasons Nikitina alternated the part of the Cat with Alicia Markova.
26 Cyril W. Beaumont, *The Diaghilev Ballet in London*, p 276.
27 W. H. Haddon Squire, "A Cat in a Musical Easy Chair," in *The Christian Science Monitor*, 9 July 1927.
28 Sotheby's London, *Ballet Material and Manuscripts from the Serge Lifar Collection*, 9 May 1984, Lots 53–4.
29 Lydia Sokolova, *Dancing for Diaghilev*, p 259.
30 Henning Rischbieter, *Art and the Stage*, p 128.
31 Sotheby's London, *op cit*, lot 51.

Nathalie Gontcharova

Russian
born 1881 Ladizhno (Tula)
died 1962 Paris

Les Noces (Svadebka or The Wedding)

Russian choreographic scenes by Igor Stravinsky
Composer: Igor Stravinsky
Conductor: Ernest Ansermet
Choreographer: Bronislava Nijinska
Designer (set and costumes):
    Nathalie Gontcharova[1]
Principal Dancers:
    The Bride: Felia Dubrovska
    The Bridegroom: Leon Woizikovsky
Solo Singers:
    Helen Smirnova, Maria Davidova,
        Michel d'Arial, Georges Lanskoy
Pianists:
    Hélène Léon, Marcelle Meyer, Georges Auric,
        Edouard Flament[2]
Company: Diaghilev's Ballets Russes
First Performance: 13 June 1923, Théâtre de la
    Gaîté-Lyrique, Paris

Synopsis

A cantata with dances, in two parts and four scenes, showing an old Russian peasant wedding, performed without pause.
    Part One, Scene 1. Blessing the Bride (The Tresses).
        Scene 2. Blessing the Bridegroom.
        Scene 3. The Bride's Departure.
        Part Two, Scene 4. The Wedding Feast.

From its inception to its first performance *Les Noces*[3] took longer than any other ballet to complete. Stravinsky stated that he first had the "idea for a choral work on the subject of a Russian peasant wedding early in 1912,"[4] and that the title occurred to him at the same time. He made a few sketches in 1913, but was at that time fully engrossed in *Le Sacre du Printemps* (see pp 291–95). He began seriously to work on the libretto and composition in June 1914 after the premiere of *Le Rossignol* (see pp 128–31), first visiting Russia in search of suitable material. He found it in Peter Kireevsky's ten-volume collection of Russian popular songs, from which he adapted the words of the cantata. Stravinsky drafted the first part by the end of 1914 and, according to him, when he played it to Diaghilev in the spring of 1915 "he wept and said it was the most beautiful and the most purely Russian creation of our Ballet."[5] Stravinsky did not finish the short score, however, until 1917, and only completed the final instrumentation, after several changes, on 6 April 1923 when the looming first performance of the ballet in June made it imperative that he should do so.

Diaghilev's original intention was for Nijinsky to make the choreography, as he made clear to Stravinsky in a letter dated 25 November 1914: "The invention of movement for *Noces* is definitely for Nijinsky, but I will not discuss the thing with him for several months yet. As for Massine, he is still too young."[6] But by the time the production of the ballet was finally to take place, Nijinsky had gone mad and Massine had left the company. The choreography was given to Nijinsky's sister, Bronislava.

Meanwhile, Nathalie Gontcharova who, with Michel Larionov, had been invited to join Diaghilev and Stravinsky in Switzerland in 1915, began very soon to work on the designs for *Les Noces*. The development of the design went through almost as many phases and took almost as much time as the composition of the score. Gontcharova herself described in some detail the various concepts she tried out. At first, as she wrote: "It was the festive, folk aspect of weddings that stood out for me, the colourful costumes and dances that connect weddings with holidays, enjoyment, abundance and happy vitality. Therefore the costumes I designed were derived from peasant forms and vivid colours, harmonized sometimes in unison, sometimes by opposites, almost without intermediates, and this applied to decorations and curtains as well."[7] But the bright and garish colors and the bold peasant patterns worried her; soon they no longer seemed right. Instead, she decided to transpose the action from the peasant class to the provincial and suburban petty bourgeoisie. She "made new sketches for the costumes, curtain and scenery. Stripes, circles, squares and splashes replaced floral ornamentation. The heavy immobile corset replaced the thick pliant chemise, hair and hats took the place of head-scarves. The skirts became longer in accordance with the somewhat outmoded town fashions."[8] But, in spite of the complete change of atmosphere and feeling, Gontcharova's uneasiness remained. She then remembered country weddings in early spring in northern Russia when "almost all the spring flowers are cold in tone, except for a few yellow ones, which appear very early and recall the Sun, the others are the colour of

the sky and of clouds."[9] Her third set of costume designs used pastels in clear, cool colors with silver and lace, but these, too, she thought unsatisfactory.

When Diaghilev finally announced a firm date for the production, Gontcharova was at last able to concentrate her mind and resolve the problem of the sets and costumes which had caused her so much anxiety. A theater deadline is a powerful determinant. She discarded all her previous ideas. The great colorist decided to confine herself to the muted colors of the sky and the earth for the sets, with blue signifying hope, gray the past, and yellow ochre anxiety, and brown and white for the costumes, all the colors symbolizing different states in a marriage. In an interview on the day of the first night Gontcharova said: "Reviving my way of doing things, which I had already shown in the costumes of *La Belle au Bois Dormant*[10] produced at the Opéra, I wanted, for *Noces*, to reach the extreme limit of simplicity. While maintaining the atmosphere of Russia and its local color, I synthesized my country's costumes and tried to refine the outline. I made the settings of *Noces* in neutral colors. No garish colors this time. It is a great fault of many modern designers that they confine themselves to a formula once they have found one without ever escaping from it. Just as the costumes and sets which I designed for the *Coq d'Or* shimmered in vivid colors, so this time the tones are restrained. As for the costumes for *Noces* I restricted myself to designing only two: one for all the men, the other for all the women. Mme Nijinska, that great artist of choreography, was thus able to arrange the dances not for distinct characters with a definite role but for identical and, so to speak, interchangeable components. She used them as mobile constructions, in the most rigorous and boldest manner ever seen on stage."[11]

Although Gontcharova claims the final simplification of the sets and costumes as her idea, Bronislava Nijinska has stated that it was she who conceived the ballet in this way. Their different accounts vary considerably. Nijinska states how she saw Gontcharova's "Northern Russian" version in 1921; when she rejected it Diaghilev decided to postpone the production. (This is unlikely, since the score had not been completed by then.) Diaghilev finally decided to produce the ballet in 1923, and when he discussed it with Nijinska again she reassured him by saying: "*Noces* is a ballet that must be danced on point. That will elongate the dancers' silhouettes and make them resemble the saints in Byzantine icons."[12] She did not see a Russian peasant wedding as a happy or even optimistic occasion: her choreography was designed as an abstract interpretation of the feelings of the bride and bridegroom without individual characterization. As Nijinska explained: "The choreography of *Les Noces* allowed me to resume my new path—the raising of the so-called corps de ballet to the highest artistic level, expressing the whole ballet-action. In *Les Noces* there would not be any leading parts; each member would blend through the movement into the whole . . . The action of the separate characters would be expressed, not by each one individually but, rather, by the action of the whole ensemble."[13] Nijinska also had very definite ideas about which design would be most appropriate for her choreography. Therefore, according to her, Gontcharova and Larionov were to be invited "to see the choreography, talk about it and then design new simple sets and costumes. I explained to Gontcharova my ideas for this choreography and the necessity for simple Russian costumes, all being of the same color, in order to maintain the integrity of my choreographic composition."[14] Nijinska added that she and Diaghilev had already agreed on the design concept. Nijinska wanted the costumes to be in dark blue with beige blouses, reminiscent of proletarian workers, but deferred to Gontcharova's preference for brown as it was "her realm as the artist-painter."[15] The final costumes, based on Russian peasant clothes, were brown trousers and white shirts for the men, and white blouses and brown scarves and dresses for the girls made of parachute silk. In spite of the obviously visible color, many critics and commentators saw the costumes as being black.

In view of Nijinska's certainty and Gontcharova's vagueness in each of their statements, and the fact that the designs for *Les Noces* are unique in Gontcharova's work on account of their sobriety and monochrome quality, it seems to me that Nijinska's version has the greater verisimilitude. What is also true, however, is that in the end both artists were in complete agreement with each other about the final form and visual presentation of the production. Gontcharova certainly saw the rehearsals on the roof of the theater in Monte Carlo, because she made drawings of the groups of dancers which correspond to some of the existing photographs.

Lydia Sokolova complained that: "*Les Noces* was difficult to dance. The women moved about mostly in *pas de bourrée*—that is to say on point, but rising and falling on and off the toes at high speed—forming into straight lines facing the audience, then packing themselves into strange congested groups."[16] Stravinsky, without showing much enthusiasm, thought that the first staging of his ballet "was generally compatible with my conception of the ritualistic and non-personal."[17] Part of the impersonal conception was to have the pianos and orchestra on stage, so that there would be an alienating contrast between the dancers in their costumes and the musicians in their evening dress. Stravinsky had used this stage arrangement for his *Soldier's Tale* to great effect; but Diaghilev hated *The Soldier's Tale*. In the end, Diaghilev had to agree to placing the four pianos on stage (two on either side of the dancing area, as shown in No 122), because there was no room for them in the orchestra pit.

As was so often the case with a new and unfamiliar work, especially one in which tradition was eschewed in favour of experiment, critics were divided in their opinions. Louis Schneider (in spite of seeing the wrong color) was very moved by the production and sincere in his praise: "Those black and white costumes against sets in the same tones manage not to be funereal, but give, rather, the impression of some lunar ceremony. It all makes for very refined artistry."[18] But Henry Malherbe saw something different: "M. Stravinsky, Mmes Nijinska and Gontcharova wanted us, I suppose, to undertsand everything that is tragic, savage, tyrannical and bitterly comic about the marriage ceremony in Russia . . . But I must confess that this *Noces* only has the lugubrious air of a funeral."[19]

The technical difficulty in staging the ballet and the expense of engaging a chorus delayed the production of *Les Noces* in London until 1926, when it caused even more controversy than in Paris. Critics and audiences were ranged fiercely against one another. The staunchest defender of the ballet was H. G. Wells, who—in a long letter apparently intended for the press, but not published, and distributed instead at performances at His Majesty's Theatre—wrote in part: "I do not know of any other ballet so interesting, so amusing, so fresh or nearly so exciting as 'Les Noces.' I want to see it again and again, and because I want to do so I protest against this conspiracy of wilful stupidity that may succeed in driving it out of the programme."[20]

122 Design for the set: Part One, scenes 1 and 3

Graphite and tempera and/or watercolor on paper
26½ x 38¾ in: 67.6 x 98.2 cm
Signed bottom left in ink over pencil:
   "N. Gontcharova"
Inscribed on reverse in black watercolor:
   "N. Gontcharova," "N. G," (in black over blue),
   "N 29," in blue watercolor in Gontcharova's
   hand, "N. Gontcharova / 'Noce' [sic] / 43 rue de
   Seine / Paris 6ᵉ," and stamped "Douane Cen-
   trale Paris"
1933.479

Exhibitions: Paris 1930, No 56; Paris 1933; New
   York 1933, No 32; Chicago 1933, No 90;
   Northampton 1934, No 90; San Francisco 1935;
   Paris 1939, No 254; Williamsburg 1940; Indi-
   anapolis 1959, No 281; New York 1962–3; New
   York 1965–6, No 98 (illustrated p 48; not
   shown in New York); New York 1966–7; Stras-
   bourg 1969, No 370 (illustrated No 97); Frank-
   furt-am-Main 1969, No 104; Hartford 1973;
   Hartford 1974; Hemsptead 1974, No 79;
   Hartford 1978–9; Boston 1982–3; New York
   1986, No 57 (illustrated p 34).
Illustrations: Chamot, p 83 No 69; Gontcharova,
   fig 8 p 139; Kirstein, p 224 No 425;
   Pozharskaya and Volodina, p 220.

Gontcharova made many versions of the set, some with pianos, incorrectly drawn, some without; some with one window, some with two. Some historians have assumed, presumably without reading the synopsis or seeing the ballet, that all the versions are for the same set, and that the set did not change for each scene. Not so.

This set design, for the first optimistic scene when the bride is blessed and the third scene when she leaves, is blue because "in blue there is something of the serenity, the hope of always being together."[21]

The backcloth for these scenes in the bride's house had one little window, whereas the backcloth for the second scene in the bridegroom's house had two little windows. These cloths were dropped in just behind center stage. For the final scene the backcloth was at the back of the stage revealing a little wooden house and a matrimonial bed covered with six eiderdowns.

While the background cloth changed for each of the scenes the wings did not, for, as

Gontcharova said: "that is the framework for all the settings of life, something that remains the same all the time . . . The three scenes enframed by these wings—the first sky blue, second gray and the third ochre— are also almost without ornament. There are only one or two little windows, placed very high up in order not to look out too much and also not to be seen from outside, because conjugal life is sacred and closed, it is a kind of sanctuary."[22] She had stipulated that the wings should be brown, the color of earth, but expediency (and financial considerations) dictated that they were in fact black as in this design.

As discussed above, neither this design, nor any of the others, is in the artist's customary scheme of bright and even garish colors. It is also deliberately out of scale in order to emphasize the desired feeling of space. But the pencil "squaring-up" markings show that the placing of the window in relation to the door has been meticulously planned.

123   Choreographic costume design for two of the women

Ink with white highlights on paper
9¹³/₁₆ x 10¾ in: 25 x 32.5 cm
Signed bottom left in ink: "N. Gontcharova"
1933.480

Exhibitions: Chicago 1933, No 91; Northampton
   1934, No 91; San Francisco 1935; Paris 1939,
   No 255; Edinburgh 1954, No 171; London
   1954–5, No 187; Michigan 1957; Indianapolis
   1959, No 282; New York 1962–3; Hartford
   1964; New York 1965–6, No 99 (illustrated p
   49); New York 1966–7; Strasbourg 1969, No
   376; Frankfurt-am-Main 1969, No 107;
   Amherst 1974; Chicago 1975, No 52; Boston
   1982–3; New York 1986, No 57; Worcester
   1989.
Illustrations: Chamot, p 84 No 70; Hansen, fig 43.

Gontcharova made four distinct groups of so-called "choreographic designs" for *Les Noces* after she had seen the rehearsals of the ballet in Monte Carlo. The first group are sketches of the dancers, both men and women, in various positions within the set indicated by a single window. The second group are full-length figures of the women in costume in different positions, with some drawings more finished than others. The third group are outline drawings of the men and women in certain choreographic positions matching existing photographs taken during rehearsal.

This drawing is from the fourth group, which are head and torso drawings only of the women in costume in different positions, and as such are not costume designs at all. A more accurate description, therefore, is "choreographic drawing." They were the last to be made and were probably done after the first performance. The corrections in white in this drawing indicate that it was made specifically for reproduction. Three other examples from this group showing different positions are in the collections of the Victoria and Albert Museum, London: one shows two women looking left each with one arm above her head and the other arm as in this drawing, another one similar but looking right, and the third similar to this drawing with the two women looking in opposite directions.

It has been assumed that because the drawings are in black and white the actual costumes for the women were also black and white, whereas they were in fact brown and white. This is confirmed not only by Serge Grigoriev,[23] the stage manager for the original production, but also by an early remake in the collections of the Whitworth Art Gallery, Manchester.

Notes

1   This is the French form of the artist's name which she used for her signature. In English the name is spelled "Goncharova."

2   At short notice Flament replaced Francis Poulenc who had an "unlucky attack of jaundice" (*My Friends and Myself*, p 137).

3   Originally the ballet was called *Noces,* without the definite article which was added some time later. Stravinsky said in *Expositions and Developments* (p 114) that although usually known by the French title, "Little Wedding" would be the best equivalent of the Russian title, if "little" could be made to mean not "small" but "peasant."

4   Igor Stravinsky and Robert Craft, *Expositions and Developments*, p 114.

5   Igor Stravinsky and Robert Craft, *ibid*, p 118.

6   Quoted in Richard Buckle, *Diaghilev*, p 287, from the Stravinsky Archives.

7   Natalia Goncharova [sic], "The Metamorphoses of the Ballet 'Les Noces'" in *Leonardo* Vol 12 No 2 (Spring 1979), p 137.

8   Natalia Goncharova, *ibid*, p 139.

9   Natalia Goncharova, *ibid*, p 140.

10 Gontcharova is referring to *Aurora's Wedding*, the retitled one-act version of *The Sleeping Princess* (see pp 87–101), produced in Paris with new costumes she had designed after the original ones by Bakst had been sequestered following the financial collapse of the production in London

11 A.-G. d'E., "Mme Gontcharova nous parle du décor et des costumes de 'Noces,' Les Ballets Russes" in *Le Parisien*, Paris 14 June 1923.

12 Boris Kochno, *Diaghilev and the Ballets Russes*, p 189.

13 Bronislava Nijinska, "Creation of 'Les Noces'" in *Dance Magazine* December 1974, p 59.

14 Bronislava Nijinska, *ibid*, p 61.

15 Bronislava Nijinska, *ibid*, p 61.

16 Lydia Sokolova, *Dancing for Diaghilev*, p 204.

17 Igor Stravinsky and Robert Craft, *op cit*, p 117.

18 Louis Schneider in *Le Gaulois*, Paris 17 June 1923.

19 Henry Malherbe in *Le Temps*, Paris 20 June 1923.

20 H. G. Wells in letter signed and dated 18 June 1926; copies were inserted in the Ballets Russes program.

21 Natalia Goncharova, *op cit*, p 141.

22 *Ibid*.

23 Serge Grigoriev in Tatiana Loguine, *Gontcharova et Larionov*, p 113.

L'Oiseau de Feu (The Firebird)

Russian fairy story in 2 scenes adapted by Michel
    Fokine
Composer: Igor Stravinsky
Conductor: Henry Defosse
Choreographer: Michel Fokine[1]
Designer (scenery and costumes):
    Nathalie Gontcharova
Principal Dancers:
    The Firebird: Lydia Lopokova
    The Beautiful Tsarevna: Lubov Tchernicheva
    Ivan Tsarevitch: Serge Lifar
    Koshchei: Georges Balanchin [sic]
Company: Diaghilev's Ballets Russes
First performance of this revival: 25 November
    1926, Lyceum Theatre, London

The first production by the Ballets Russes was on
25 June 1910 at the Théâtre national de
l'Opéra, Paris, when the differences in the main
credits were as follows:
Conductor: Gabriel Pierné
Designers: Alexander Golovine (sets and costumes),
    Léon Bakst (costumes for the Firebird, Ivan
    Tsarevitch, and the Beautiful Tsarevna)
Principal Dancers:
    The Firebird: Tamara Karsavina
    The Beautiful Tsarevna: Vera Fokina
    Ivan Tsarevitch: Michel Fokine
    Koshchei: Alexei Bulgakov

Synopsis

Ivan Tsarevitch strays into Koshchei's garden at
night and sees the Firebird, enticed there by a tree
with golden apples. He catches the bird. She begs
him to let her go, but he releases her only after she
has given him a magic feather. He then meets
thirteen beautiful princesses who are captive under
the magic spell of Koshchei, and falls in love with
one of them. At dawn they have to return to the
palace. Ivan Tsarevitch breaks open the gates to
follow them but is taken prisoner by Koshchei's
monster guards. He remembers the feather and
waves it three times. The Firebird appears and
forces Koshchei and his monsters to dance until
they fall exhausted. The Firebird then shows Ivan
the egg which contains the life and death of
Koshchei. Ivan Tsarevitch breaks the egg on the
ground. Koshchei dies, and the princesses are
freed. The two lovers are reunited and celebrate
their betrothal.

In 1910 *The Firebird* made Igor Stravinsky
famous overnight. But it was as early as
1908 that Diaghilev wanted to include a
ballet on a Russian theme by a Russian
composer in his first program, because he
considered that Parisian audiences should
be shown something specifically Russian.[2]
Nothing, however, came of this initial plan
except that the hurriedly arranged suite of
dances under the general title of *Le Festin*, to
fill out the 1909 program, included a number called *L'Oiseau de Feu (The Firebird)*.[3]
This was not the Firebird he intended; and
so it was only after the first season that the
new production was planned. Alexandre

Benois claimed credit for thinking of the
idea, but conceded that others participated
in its development: "The fundamental
elements of the subject were inspired by the
young poet Potiomkin. The working out of
these elements were undertaken by a sort of
conference in which Tcherepnine, Fokine,
the painters Steletzky [sic], Golovin and I
took part. Our excellent writer Remizov,
who was not only a great crank but also a
great lover of all things Russian, was carried
away with our idea."[4] Theater is often a
cooperative and collaborative effort.
According to Benois, it had already been
decided that Tcherepnine (married to
Benois's niece) should be the composer.
This, however, is contradicted by Prince
Lieven, who stated that Diaghilev first
commissioned Liadov. It was only when
Liadov apparently told Diaghilev three
months later that all he had done was buy
the music paper that Diaghilev approached
Tcherepnine. However, "the sketches composed by him were not satisfactory. Quite
by accident, at a symphonic concert, the
friends heard a short symphonic poem by a
young composer. This composition was
called *Fireworks*, and the name of the composer was Igor Stravinsky. Diaghileff went
into raptures."[5]

Diaghilev at once commissioned a score
from Stravinsky, by which time the libretto
had been worked out in detail. Stravinsky
later confessed: "Although alarmed by the
fact that this was a commission for a fixed
date, and afraid lest I should fail to complete the work in time—I was still unaware
of my own capabilities—I accepted the
order. It was highly flattering to be chosen
from among the musicians of my generation, and to be allowed to collaborate in so
important an enterprise side by side with
personages who were generally recognised
as masters in their own spheres."[6] Fokine,
who from the beginning had been designated as the choreographer, was alone
credited with the libretto in spite of the fact
that it was undoubtedly, as Benois wrote, a
joint achievement. Remizov's contribution
was the invention of the "Bellyboshkies,"
who were "evil sort of creatures, some with
tails and some without,"[7] Koshchei's servants and followers. Fokine studied the
scenario in detail with Stravinsky; he gave
him precise instructions and "the exact
measurements required of the music."[8]

The design of the first production was
finally given to Golovine. His sets and

costumes generally pleased everyone except
Benois, who wrote: "Unfortunately Golovin,
a wonderful colorist and a lover of ancient
Russian art, remained true to himself and
his work did not harmonise either with
Stravinsky's music or with what Fokine,
under its inspiration, was 'modelling' with
his dancers. It must be admitted that
Golovin's first sketch for the décor was, in
itself, enchanting . . . But although this
sketch of Golovin's was indeed a masterpiece, it was absolutely unsuitable as a
décor."[9] Benois was alone in his opinion. On
the other hand, Prince Lieven thought the
scenery was "very fine, vivid, and effective,"[10] and Grigoriev, the company manager, thought it was "entrancing:
diaphanous and magical."[11] However,
Diaghilev was not satisfied with the costumes for the Firebird herself, the Tsarevitch, and the Tsarevna when he first saw
them at a dress rehearsal in Paris; he asked
Léon Bakst to design new ones. The replace-
ments were entirely successful.

Stravinsky got a wonderful production
from his collaborators and appreciated their
individual contributions, although he was
rather grudging in his appreciation of
Fokine: "Karsavina's rendering of the bird's
part was perfect, and that beautiful and
gracious artiste had a brilliant success in it.
The performance was warmly applauded
by the Paris public. I am, of course, far from
attributing this success solely to the score; it
was equally due to the spectacle on the
stage in the painter Golovin's magnificent
setting, the brilliant interpretation by
Diaghileff's artistes, and the talent of the
choreographer. I must admit, however, that
the choreography of this ballet always
seemed to me to be complicated and over-
burdened with plastic detail, so that the
artistes felt, and still feel even now, great
difficulty in co-ordinating their steps and
gestures with the music."[12] The composer's
reservations were not shared by the Parisian
critics, whose views may be summed up by
Henri Ghéon: "*L'Oiseau de Feu*, being the
result of an intimate collaboration between
choreography, music and painting, presents
us with the most exquisite miracle of harmony imaginable, of sound and form and
movement . . . Stravinsky, Fokine, Golovin,
in my eyes, are but one name."[13]

This first production of *The Firebird* was
regularly performed until its final performances in Paris and London during the
1921 season. By this time the scenery, in

spite of having been repainted twice by Vladimir Polunin, and the costumes were in such a poor state of repair that Diaghilev realized he would have to have a new production if the ballet were to be retained in the repertoire as he wished. He decided to commission new designs from Nathalie Gontcharova. Diaghilev was precise in his brief, which he outlined in a letter to Boris Kochno: "First scene: A dark night, with phosphorescent apples. The stage is full of apples, and not a single tree; the garden (orchard) is dark brown. The décor must be worked out in minute detail—like Mantegna's 'hunt' in Mantua, or like the Avignon frescoes. Then, for the second scene the back cloth is changed: the garden is transformed into the Holy City, the apples become the gilded onion domes of churches, a countless swarm of churches crowded together."[14]

The new scenery pleased no one except the stage hands and, presumably, Diaghilev. Lydia Sokolova described how Gontcharova had eliminated a cumbersome rostrum which "was a very high, steep wooden structure which had to be securely built and bolted before every performance, as every member of the company came running down its steps in the course of the ballet . . . We now made our entrance through cutouts in the forest set; and the big tree which used to shine with a magic light and from which the chief Princess used to take down the golden apples, was now a flat with the fruit heaped at its foot."[15] The rostrum had been necessary for some of the choreography, and its removal unfortunately destroyed some striking effects, especially the entrances of the Princesses and Koshchei's monsters. Sokolova, one of the Princesses, reminisced sadly: "The beautiful groupings when the Princesses appeared on that high platform and ran down the steps with the moonlight on their hair were never to be seen again. From 1926 onwards they continued to make some of the movements Fokine had planned specially for the old production, but as Gontcharova gave them head-dresses and tucked up their hair, the backbending and stroking movements became pointless."[16] Fokine, who had not been asked to revise his choreography or indeed have anything to do with the revival, was even more severe about the new design: "Nathalie Gontcharova, at Diaghilev's request, painted scenery having no connection with my plot. Gontcharova . . . dealt a deathblow to *Firebird*. The interference of Diaghilev in the building of the

scenery was responsible for making the plot meaningless. Amidst trees in the garden stands a gate which can be easily bypassed. It is bypassed by all the participants except Ivan Tsarevitch. There is no fence connected with the gate. For what good reason is the Tsarevitch trying to break in? Why does he have to hack at the gate with his sword?"[17] The questions have no answer. Fokine was right.

The audience, too, seems not to have been as spellbound by the new production as the old. While the anonymous critic of *The Times* praised Gontcharova for having "seized her opportunities and provided a wonderful spectacle, in which the grotesque and the beautiful are imaginatively compounded,"[18] he was unaware of the incongruous set. The absurdity pinpointed by Fokine, however, did not escape the keen-eyed Cyril W. Beaumont, who wrote an illuminating comparison between the two productions, coming down firmly in favor of the original. After describing the opening, he wrote: "The original entrance to Kostchei's castle was guarded by a palisade formed of intruding knights petrified to stone by Kostchei's magic—a palisade broken by a pair of gates facing the audience. The gates opened to allow the Princesses to emerge, and when they retired closed upon them. When Ivan Tsarevitch attempted to follow them and shook the gates, they flew open to disgorge a horde of monsters. In the present setting there is no palisade, but a kind of hedge with gaps, through which one can see the Princesses advance and retire, and through which the Prince could easily have entered."[19] A balanced view from a member of the audience, albeit a biased one, was expressed by Florence Grenfell: "Maynard [Keynes] & I went on to the Ballet; grt: excitement to see Lydia in the "Fire Bird." She in spite of grt: nerves danced it beautifully & my idea of long trousers in her new costume were v. successful. The Ballet as a whole struck me afresh by its beauty, the new costumes are magnificent but not as good as the old ones."[20]

124 Costume design for Koshchei's four guards

Graphite, tempera and/or watercolor with ink signature, and two adhered textile samples on paper
19 x 15 in: 48.3 x 38 cm
Signed bottom left in watercolor over pencil: "N. Gontcharova," and top left: "N.G."
Inscribed upper left in pencil: "'Oiseau de Feu' / Garde de Kachei [sic]," and left center: "4 figurants (4 supernumeries or dancers)"
Two material swatches (brown velvet and cream silk) pasted on sheet
1933.477

Exhibitions: Paris 1929, No 31; London Clardige 1930, No 47; Paris 1930, No 57; London Tooth 1930, No 35; New York 1933, No 31 (described as "Costumes for *L'Oiseaux* [sic] *de Feu*"); Chicago 1933, Nos 88–89; Northampton 1934, Nos 88–89; Paris 1939, No 259; ? Los Angeles 1939–40; Poughkeepsie 1940; Cambridge 1942; Edinburgh 1954, No 183; London 1954–5, No 201; Elmira 1958, No 41; Storrs 1963; New York 1965–6, No 100 (illustrated p 49); New York 1966–7; Princeton 1968; Strasbourg 1969, No 88 (illustrated No 19 incorrectly attributed to Larionov); Frankfurt-am-Main 1969, No 25; Hartford 1973; Amherst 1974; Coral Gables 1982; Allentown 1986; Columbus 1989; Worcester 1989.

There is not a great distinction between Koshchei's guards and monsters in Gontcharova's designs for their costumes: the autumnal colors of brown and rust blended rather than contrasted with the coloring of the set, and the masks based on recognizable animal heads made the figures benign, and almost comical, rather than terrifying.

Gontcharova's drawing of the designs emphasizes her light-hearted approach, but perhaps she thought that in 1926 such characters could no longer be taken seriously. This was not an opinion shared, apparently, by Diaghilev. According to Boris Kochno, Balanchine's capers as Koshchei "often won him sharp reprimands from Diaghilev, because some evenings, in interpreting this evil genie whom Fokine's scenario describes as a 'foul, green-fingered giant who terrorised travellers and held them prisoners within his unyielding walls,' Balanchine would make him a hilarious character and send the audience into gales of laughter with his pranks."[21] In the original production designed by Golovin, the monsters were demons suggesting "evil distortions and malformations of the human form,"[22] and therefore, while being strangely repulsive yet retaining recognizable human features, conformed more closely to Fokine's scenario than Gontcharova's non-human designs.

125   Costume design for a monster in Koshchei's suite

Graphite, tempera and/or watercolor with black ink signature, and two adhered textile samples on paper
17¾ x 13⅝ in: 45 x 34.6 cm
Signed bottom right in watercolor over pencil: "N. Gontcharova," and top left: "N. G."
Inscribed upper left in pencil: "4 / figurants / F," top right: "'Oiseau de Feu' / Personnage de / la suite / de Kachei [sic] (character in the suite of Koshchei)," and center right "P"
Two material swatches (yellow silk and rust velvet) pasted on sheet
1933.478

Exhibitions: Paris 1929, No 31; London Claridge 1930, No 48; Paris 1930, No 58; London Tooth 1930, No 36; New York 1933, No 31 (described as "Costumes for *L'Oiseaux* [sic] *de Feu*"); Chicago 1933, Nos 88–89; Northampton 1934, Nos 88–89; New York 1937–8, No 709; Boston 1938; Paris 1939, No 260; ? Los Angeles 1939–40; Williamsburg 1940; Cambridge 1942; Edinburgh 1954, No 182; London 1954–5, No 200; Michigan 1957; Elmira 1958, No 44; Rowayton 1960; New York 1965–6, No 101 (illustrated p 49); New York 1966–7; Princeton 1968; Strasbourg 1969, No 89; Frankfurt-am-Main 1969, No 26; Amherst 1974; Hempstead 1974, No 81; Coral Gables 1982; Allentown 1986; Hartford 1988; Worcester 1989.
Illustration: Chamot, p 90 No 77.

126* Costume for an Enchanted Princess

A-line shift, pale gray-green nun's veiling. Bateau neckline edged with metallic trim, painted gold leaf forms outlined with gold braid. Long sleeves have elongated cuffs.
Label inscribed "Morris, Obidenna, Sidorenko"
1996.7.26
Provenance: Diaghilev and de Basil Ballets Foundation Ltd; Sotheby's London, lot 89, 3 March 1973; Castle Howard Estate Ltd; Sotheby's London, lot 95, 14 December 1995

In the 1926 revival of *The Fire Bird* by Diaghilev's Ballets Russes, the Enchanted Princesses were Mmes Sokolova, Danilova, Petrova, Maikerska, Soumarokova, Slavinska, Chamie, Vadimova, Branitska, Klemetska, Orlova, and Obidennaia [sic].
De Basil's Ballets Russes revived the ballet, with choreography after Fokine using Gontcharova's sets and costumes, at the Théâtre de Monte-Carlo on 28 April 1934; at the Royal Opera House, Covent Garden, London, on 25 June

1934, and at the Auditorium, Chicago, on 27 December 1934. It was then known by its French title, followed by the English title in brackets. The conductor was Antal Dorati. Alexandra Danilova was the Fire-Bird, Tamara Grigorieva the Beautiful Tsarevna, Léonide Massine Ivan Tsarevitch, and David Lichine the Immortal Koshchei. The Enchanted Princesses were Mlles Branitska, Chamié, Morosova, Nelidova, Obidenna [sic], Osato, Razoumova, Serova, Strakhova, Strogova, Tchinarova, and Volkova.
From the spelling of the inscription, this costume was worn by Obidenna in de Basil's revival, but she also wore it earlier in Diaghilev's revival.
Morris was in de Basil's company in 1946–7. Sidorenko, whose real name was Galina Razoumova, was in de Basil's company from 1933–41.

127* Costume for an Enchanted Princess

Not illustrated. For description see No 126*
Label inscribed "Osato," "Lloyd" and, underneath,
    an illegible name but possibly "Gueneva"
1996.7.30
Provenance: Diaghilev and de Basil Ballets Founda-
    tion Ltd; Sotheby's London, lot 89, 3 March
    1973; Castle Howard Estate Ltd; Sotheby's
    London, lot 95, 14 December 1995

There is no label to identify who wore this costume
    in Diaghilev's revival.
The label identifies that this costume was worn by
    Osato in de Basil's revival. Lloyd was in the
    company 1947–9. As Gueneva was in the
    company in 1933, before the revival, she may
    have been intended for the part, but did not
    perform it.

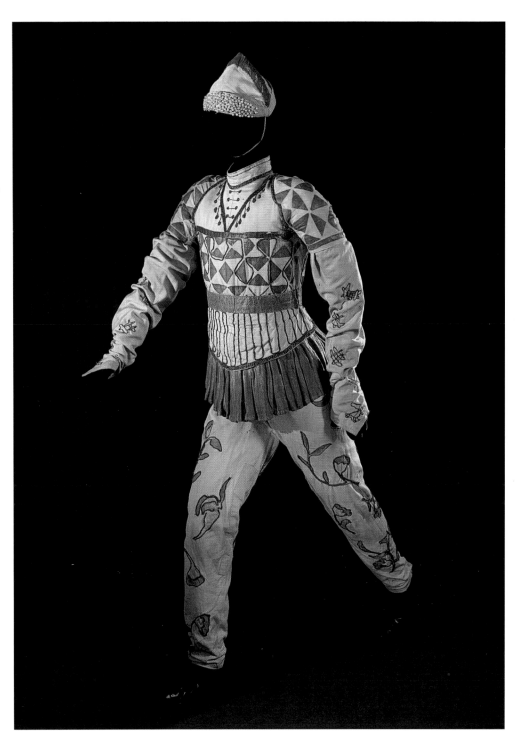

128* Costume for one of Koshchei's attendant guards

Tunic, trousers, and hat of off-white faille. Tunic
    has gold lamé pleated skirt and is decorated
    with painted gold triangles and twisted gold
    braid
Label inscribed "Joukovsky"
Tapered trousers have painted gold floral forms
    outlined with gold braid
The hat is embellished on one side with pearls
Indistinct label, possibly "Loubert"
1996.7.27a–c
Provenance: Diaghilev and de Basil Ballets Founda-
    tion Ltd; Sotheby's London, lot 91, 3 March
    1973; Castle Howard Estate Ltd; Sotheby's
    London, lot 96, 14 December 1995

There is no label to identify who wore this costume
    in Diaghilev's revival.
Joukovsky was in de Basil's company in 1948–9,
    Loubert in 1947.

129* Costume for one of Koshchei's servants

Cloth of gold robe with orange velvet collar and wide sash. Beige faille, elongated sleeves match dickie with Russian stand collar
Dickie labeled "W. Clarkson, Perruquier & Costumier, London W.1."
1996.7.28a–c
Provenance: Diaghilev and de Basil Ballets Foundation Ltd; Sotheby's London, lot 91, 3 March 1973; Castle Howard Estate Ltd; Sotheby's London, lot 97, 14 December 1995

There is no label to identify who wore this costume in either Diaghilev's or de Basil's revival.

130* Robe for one of Koshchei's Attendants

Red wool robe appliquéd with symmetrically placed blue roundels, interspaced with white felt squares, and embellished at hemline with white felt appliqués outlined with jet beads. Rose cotton sleeves taper over hand
1996.7.29
Provenance: Diaghilev and de Basil Ballets Foundation Ltd; Sotheby's London, lot 89, 3 March 1973; Castle Howard Estate Ltd; Sotheby's London, lot 99, 14 December 1995

There is no label to identify who wore this costume in Diaghilev's revival.
Koshchei's Attendants in the 1926 revival were Fedorov and Vinter, and in the 1934 revival Platoff and Smirnoff.

Notes

1 Although Fokine was credited with the choreography it was, strictly speaking, *after* Fokine in this revival.
2 The evidence for this is in a letter Léon Bakst wrote to his wife dated 24 July 1908.
3 Danced by Karsavina and Nijinsky to Tchaikovsky's music for the Blue Bird *pas de deux* from *The Sleeping Beauty*.
4 Alexandre Benois, *Reminiscences of the Russian Ballet*, p 304.
5 Prince Peter Lieven, *The Birth of Ballets-Russes*, p 107. Prince Lieven was wrong in stating that the composition was *Fireworks,* which was not performed until 1910. The composition, in fact, was *Scherzo Fantastique*; hearing it persuaded Diaghilev to commission Stravinsky to orchestrate some of *Les Sylphides*. It was this successful commission which led to *The Firebird*. Earlier, sensing that Liadov might not produce anything, Diaghilev had thought of approaching Glazunov.
6 Igor Stravinsky, *Chronicle of my Life*, p 47.
7 Prince Peter Lieven, *op cit*, p 107.
8 Igor Stravinsky and Robert Craft, *Expositions and Developments*, p 129.
9 Alexandre Benois, *op cit*, p 306.
10 Prince Peter Lieven, *op cit*, p 109.
11 Serge Grigoriev, *The Diaghilev Ballet*, p 44.
12 Igor Stravinsky, *op cit*, pp 53–4.
13 Henri Ghéon in an unidentified newspaper quoted in Serge Lifar, *Diaghilev*, p 244.
14 Serge Diaghilev to Boris Kochno in a letter dated 7 August 1926, quoted in Boris Kochno, *Diaghilev and the Ballets Russes*, p 54.
15 Lydia Sokolova, *Dancing for Diaghilev*, p 255–6.
16 Lydia Sokolova, *ibid*, p 255–6.
17 Michel Fokine. *Memoirs of a ballet master*, p 174.
18 Anon, *The Times* London, 26 November 1926.
19 Cyril W. Beaumont, "Arena-Fokine: Cyril W. Beaumont Answers" in *Dance and Dancers* London, March 1962, p 20.
20 Florence Grenfell diaries, 25 November 1926. Lydia Lopokova was married to Maynard Keynes.
21 Boris Kochno, *Diaghilev and the Ballets Russes*, p 55.
22 Cyril W. Beaumont, *op cit*, p 20.

Juan Gris *(José Victoriana Gonzalez)*

Spanish
born 1887 Madrid
died 1927 Paris

Les Tentations de la Bergère, ou l'Amour Vainqueur
(The Temptations of the Shepherdess, or Vanquishing Love)

Ballet in 1 act by Boris Kochno[1]
Composer: Michel Pignolet de Montéclair
   (1666–1737), restored and orchestrated by
   Henri Casadesus
Conductor: Edouard Flament
Choreographer: Bronislava Nijinska
Designer (set and costumes): Juan Gris
Principal Dancers:
   The Shepherdess: Vera Nemtchinova
   The Shepherd: Leon Woizikovsky
   The King: Anatole Wilzak
   The Marquis: Théodore Slavinsky
   Counts: Nicolas Zverev, Anton Dolin,
      Jean Jazvinsky
Company: Diaghilev's Ballets Russes
First Performance: 3 January 1924, Théâtre de
   Monte-Carlo

Synopsis

Courtiers bow to each other as chandeliers are lit. A procession of peasants celebrates the betrothal of the Shepherdess and the Shepherd. Enter a Marquis and three Counts. The Marquis fancies the Shepherdess and dances with her. He offers her sumptuous gifts which are brought on by black attendants. The Shepherdess abandons the Shepherd. But she soon takes pity on her despairing loved one. She leaves the Marquis and throws herself into the arms of the Shepherd. The Marquis wants revenge. Then the King appears. He reunites and protects the rustic lovers. The Counts and other courtiers celebrate their joy.

Diaghilev first thought of engaging Juan Gris to design a set when he was planning to present a suite of Spanish dances in 1921 with the title of *Cuadro Flamenco* but, because Gris delayed replying, Diaghilev changed his mind and asked Picasso instead.[2] Gris, who realized that designing a ballet for Diaghilev would do wonders for his reputation, was very disappointed. Not prone to being affected by other people's feelings, Diaghilev nevertheless asked Gris to draw the portraits for that year's souvenir program of Maria d'Albaïcin and Thadée Slavinsky, the leading dancers, and, later, also portraits of Boris Kochno and Michel Larionov.

In the autumn of 1922 Diaghilev negotiated successfully with the Société des Bains de Mer, the organization responsible for the theater in Monte Carlo, for his company to be based there for several months every winter. At the same time, he began to plan a completely French season of opera and ballet to take place at the beginning of 1924. He had already commissioned the young French composers Georges Auric and Francis Poulenc to write ballets,[3] and he now added three neglected operas by Gounod—*La Colombe, Le Médecin malgré lui,* and *Philémon et Baucis*—and an opera by Chabrier, *Une Education Manquée.*[4] In order to represent an earlier age, Diaghilev then added a new ballet devised from music by the early eighteenth-century composer, Montéclair, to a libretto based on the divertissement in Tchaikovsky's *The Queen of Spades,* which he called *Les Tentations de la Bergère.* Diaghilev commissioned Gris to design this ballet in the style of Louis XIV. Gris did not let a second chance escape him, and accepted the commission although he was at the time preparing for an exhibition in Paris arranged for the spring of 1923. He still thought that working for Diaghilev would be a profitable way for him to become better known as an artist, although, as Kahnweiler, his friend and agent, wrote: "He was not attracted by the material profit, for he received only a small sum—four or five thousand francs, if I remember rightly—such as might suffice for a hack, but which meant nothing in terms of the amount of time that Gris was forced to take off from his real work."[5] Subsequently he was forced to take even more time off, because Diaghilev asked him to design *La Colombe* and, at the last minute, the set and two costumes for *Une Education manquée.*

On the face of it, Diaghilev's choice of Gris, a Cubist painter, as designer for a ballet in the style of Louis XIV was eccentric, but he knew what he was doing. Gris was essentially an "architectural" painter and Diaghilev required, and got, a solidly stylized architectural set as a credible background for an essentially artificial and frivolous ballet. The costumes, based on the research Gris did of the period, were also stylized and in pale, but glittering, colors. According to Kahnweiler, Diaghilev was a pernickety taskmaster: "Diaghilev used to come and discuss with him . . . I must admit that I can imagine nothing more demoralising. Diaghilev, with an air of friendly charm, would scrap, or at least modify, all Gris' original ideas."[6] Gris made a scale model of the set and designed all the costumes by the early summer of 1923.

When Diaghilev was asked by the impresario Gabriel Astruc and by Henry Lapauze, a rich fundraiser for Versailles, to provide the entertainment at a grand charity gala (in aid of the upkeep of the palace and the restoration of the park), which was planned to take place in the Hall of Mirrors on 30 June 1923, his first thought was to include *Les Tentations de la Bergère* in the program. This idea was confirmed in an article in *Le Gaulois* on 3 June which stated: "Another 'enticement' planned for the program is a ballet interlude to the music of Montéclair played by Henri Casadesus' Society of Ancient Instruments."[7] Unfortunately, Diaghilev had to abandon this idea because the music could not be prepared in time. One or two other items in the proposed program mentioned in *Le Gaulois* were also later changed. In his general assessment, however, the reporter was accurate when he concluded his article by saying that the evening, which became known as *La Fête Merveilleuse,* promised to be a "festivity of such variety, brilliance and splendor as to be truly worthy of the most beautiful palace and the most famous park in the universe . . . The great Parisian dressmakers are making up true marvels, and the rue de la Paix is in a state of excitement. The festivity of 30 June could well be called 'Diadem evening.'"[8]

Diaghilev asked Gris to provide a suitable setting for the evening's entertainment, and suggested that several of the costumes which he had already designed for *Les Tentations de la Bergère* should be made up for the pageant: the Master of Ceremonies, two Heralds, six black pages, and the Sun King himself. Gris first thought of constructing a Cubist setting but then, according to a report, "Suddenly a revelation of the purity and beauty of Versailles changed his mind. Wonder came after irony, enthusiasm came after contempt."[9] The Hall of

UN DIVERTISSEMENT DE LA « FÊTE MERVEILLEUSE »

DONNÉE AU CHATEAU DE VERSAILLES, LE 30 JUIN

Above: the scene for the *Fête Merveilleuse* in the Hall of Mirrors at Versailles, with one of the Heralds shown at the extreme right; by René Lelong, reproduced in *L'Illustration*.

Mirrors is a vaulted gallery of unusual and difficult proportions—238 feet long and 35 feet wide—with seventeen arched mirror panels reflecting the arched windows overlooking the park. Gris divided the space into one third for the stage area and two thirds for the thousand spectators. Gris's setting was described in *Le Figaro*: "With the collaboration of the Keeper and the Architect of the Château, Juan Gris has created a décor worthy of Mansart.[10] Imagine a great staircase, covered in mirror from Saint Gobain, and completely embellished with glittering adornments; spun-glass fountains, baskets, hedges, flowerbeds, dazzling swags and garlands—all leading gradually to a stage some ten meters square, on which the ballets were to be performed. In front of all this was a low fountain with mirror representing the water in the basin, and more spun-glass jets, catching the light from the great chandeliers originally installed in the *Galerie*."[11]

The *Fête Merveilleuse* started at 10 p.m., when an invisible orchestra (hidden behind the staircase) began to play, and the Master of Ceremonies, surrounded by pages, was heralded on to the stage. The entertainment began with a short version of *Le Mariage d'Aurore,* adapted by Bronislava Nijinska from Tchaikovsky's *The Sleeping Beauty*. The ballet, which was received with tumultuous applause and cries of admiration, was followed by two arias from *La Serva Padrona*

by Paisiello, *L'Hymne au Soleil* by Rameau, and *La Chanson de la Galanterie* from *Carnaval de Versailles* by Lully, sung by Maria Kousnezoff and Daniel Vigneau. Idzikowski then danced *L'Oiseau Bleu*, and the final numbers were a pavane from Fauré's *Masques et Bergamasques* danced in Spanish costumes designed by José-Maria Sert, and a tarantella by Cimarosa danced in Neapolitan dress. The end of the entertainment was marked by Wiltzak, as the Sun King, in a magnificent blue and gold costume climbing the stairs to his throne at the top with his enormous blue velvet cloak embroidered with *fleur de lys* covering the stairway.[12] Then there were fireworks in the park and a candle-lit supper in the Galerie des Batailles. Unromantically, however, the candelabras had to be lit by electricity because candles were not allowed by the fire officers. Pierre Plessis, reporting the event for *Le Gaulois*, was ecstatic: "Everything blended together in spontaneously creating an extraodinary atmosphere: the liveliness, the harmoniousness, the mellowness of the coloring, the splendor of the representation and the costumes, the general stylishness, even the smiles on the faces of the Russian company. We were all astonished. We could not immediately understand how these dancers from the steppes with their slav melancholia rich in violence could pierce the secret of a kingdom so different from their own and understand

the legend of the Sun King better than many French."[13] His opinion seems to have been echoed by all those who attended the evening—"the great and the good" of *tout Paris* who had scrambled for the highly priced tickets in order to make sure of being seen at Versailles for the great occasion. There was, however, one dissenting voice, Henry Malherbe in *Le Temps*, who wrote with some irony an attack directed at Diaghilev: "M. de Diaghilef [sic] has made himself the master of fashion and taste to such an extent that only he is considered to be worthy of arranging, in this majestic place, an entertainment to equal the stately displays of old. Did the great Russian artist not have time to arrange an entertainment more suited to such a rare occasion? It seems to me that *Le Mariage d'Aurore*, of which we were promised the first performance, was not made up of unexpected things. I remember that the company of slav dancers performed last season on the stage of the Opéra a ballet by the very trite Tchaikovsky called *La Belle au Bois Dormant*. M. de Diaghilef could therefore put to the test that the need for always appearing to be original is just as importunate as never appearing to be so . . . Not being able to perfect a ballet by Montéclair, he only showed us a quaint muscovite music-hall number, a true pot-pourri of song and dance."[14] Malherbe loved the fireworks, though, and the "anachronistic but crackling" jazz band after supper in the Galerie des Battailles.

Les Tentations de la Bergère had to wait another six months before being produced. Gris did not much enjoy his first experience of working in the theater. He wrote to Kahnweiler on 6 January 1924, three days after the first night in Monte Carlo: "The Montéclair ballet has been a great success. The costumes for it are all so badly made but they go well with the setting. I had to take a curtain call, and Nijinska says that she has never seen such complete harmony. But Oh! how frantic I was during the last days. Apart from Nijinska, who takes her work seriously, and Diaghilev who knows his job, nobody uses his brains or foresees anything. No one has any common sense. I cannot wait to get away from this infuriating milieu. If one doesn't keep one's eye on every little detail, something is certain to go wrong; and if one keeps one's eye on everything, one is interfering. What an unbearable atmosphere!"[15]

By the time *Les Tentations de la Bergère* was performed in Paris[16] Henry Malherbe was much more complimentary about Diaghilev: "M. Serge de Diaghilew [sic] is a collector and a patron who questions without ceasing. He could have continued to live in glory and innocence if, in choreographic art, he had stuck to the first formulas which he showed us. But his natural daring drives him to battle and rebellion. He is at the head of the battallion of modernists. He does not want to relinquish this command. He has become our greatest experimenter."[17] Malherbe's remarks about Diaghilev were, however, not so much in connection with *Les Tentations de la Bergère* as with *Les Biches* (see pp 242–46), which he went on to discuss later in his article.

Les Tentations de la Bergère was not, indeed, one of Diaghilev's great experiments. Gris's setting, while being stylistically appropriate, was very cumbersome, complicated, and overpowering in its effect on the stage. More damning was Lydia Sokolova who stated perceptively: "Nijinska's talent was for inventing vigorous and forceful movements: she was not really at home in the stilted artificialities of that period, and the Montéclair music needed a lighter touch."[18] Even the composer did not come out of the production unscathed: Grigoriev thought that "The weak point of the ballet . . . was Montéclair's music, which turned out rather dull and monotonous."[19] Florence Grenfell, dazzled perhaps by Monte Carlo in winter, wrote that the ballet was "delicious & lovely costumes by Gris," but by the time she saw it again in London she had changed her mind: "it had been a good deal altered, but is still dull."[20] *Les Tentations de la Bergère* did not stay long in the repertory, mainly because the set took too long to fit up and strike.

131 Costume design for two Heralds

Graphite, tempera and/or watercolor, gold and copper paint with white highlights on paper
13½ x 12 in: 34.2 x 25.3 cm
Signed lower left in pencil: "Juan Gris"
Unfinished sketch in pencil on reverse of same figure and detail of costumed figure with train-bearers. Inscribed on reverse in blue pencil: "2 casques" ("2 helmets"), "1 trousse" ("1 trunkhose"), "1 costume," "1 chemise" ("1 shirt")
1933.483

Exhibitions: Paris 1930, No 61; New York 1933, No 35; Chicago 1933, No 94; Northampton 1934, No 94; Edinburgh 1954, No 318; London 1954–5, No 361; Michigan 1957; Elmira 1958, No 45; Indianapolis 1959, No 302; Storrs 1963; New York 1965–6, No 103 (illustrated in color facing p 12); New York 1966–7; Princeton 1968; Hartford 1974; Hempstead 1974, No 83;

Hartford 1978–9; London 1981; Madrid 1985, No 182 (illustrated in color); New York 1986, No 61; Hartford 1988; Worcester 1989.
Illustrations: Cooper 1977, p 457; Green, p 275; Hansen, fig 46.

Although Gris originally made this design specifically for *Les Tentations de la Bergère,* the costume was first made up for the two Heralds in *La Fête Merveilleuse,* the gala benefit pageant which took place on 30 June 1923 in the Hall of Mirrors at Versailles (see above).

Boris Kochno, Diaghilev's secretary, recounts how Gris designed the costume "for two heralds, the dancer Singayevsky[21] and me. Attired as a Roman warrior (after seventeenth-century paintings) and accompanied by the blazing of trumpets, I strode onto the platform to announce the beginning of the entertainment. It was to be my one appearance in a theatrical performance."[22]

The architectural quality of the design of the set is carried through by Gris to the design of this costume, especially in the drawing of the skirt and banner with their sun-burst motifs symbolizing Louis XIV, the Sun King. At the same time, the design is in a similar, though rougher, style to authentic seventeenth- and eighteenth-century costume designs made for the King's pageants.

132* Costume for Nicholas Singaevsky as a Herald

Roman type armor based on ballet costume by Jean Berain (1637–1711). Fitted cuirass of gold lamé scallops. Mauve and grey silk appliqué on epaulette-like sleeves and kilt-like skirt decorated with rose metal laurel wreaths and golden suns. Interior muslin tag inscribed in purple possibly "Krouvkoff."
Gift of James Junius Goodwin and a Special Gift Account
1968.115
Provenance: Diaghilev and de Basil Ballets Foundation Ltd; Sotheby's London, lot 93a, 17 July 1968

This costume was first worn by Singaevsky as one of the two Heralds announcing the entrance of the King in the *Fête Merveilleuse* at Versailles. The name on the tag is not identified.

133 Design for the front cloth: Offrandes à la Bergère

Graphite, tempera and/or watercolor, gold and
   silver paint clear medium on paper
9⅝ x 12¹⁄₁₆ in: 24.5 x 30.5 cm
Signed lower left in pencil: "Juan Gris"
Inscribed lower right in pencil: "statue de 2,60 x
   6,45"
1933.481

Illustrations: Bablet, (color); Buckle 1955, p 103 No
   130; Cooper 1977, p 458; Souvenir Program of
   the Ballets Russes de Diaghilev, Monte Carlo,
   January 1924, and Paris, May–June 1924.

This has previously been described as "a
detail, probably for the setting." However, the photograph of the scene on stage
shows no such detail, nor, given the actual
setting as it was, any reason for such a
detail. Furthermore, the fact that the drawing has been bisected by a vertical center
line indicates that it was intended for a
painted cloth and not for a construction.
This is therefore the design for the front
cloth, setting the atmosphere of the piece
about to be performed. The still legible
inscription of the measurements in meters
also indicates that the vignette was meant to
be enlarged. Diaghilev used the painted

front cloth as a device by which he encouraged his designers to show off—the same
reason that the design was reproduced in
the Souvenir Pogram.

Gris wrote from Monte Carlo to Daniel-
Henry Kahnweiler on 9 December 1923: "I
have given permission here for the photographs of *Colombe* and the Montéclair,
which I have slightly touched up, to be
reproduced in the programme. Diaghilev
has also asked me for a drawing for the
cover and two others for the inside. I have
done them, but I don't think they are very
good. I am wondering if it wouldn't be
better to reproduce some of the drawings
you have at home. I still don't know when
we are coming back. It is not for lack of
wanting to. I loathe this part of the country
more and more, but I feel that to leave
would mean a split with Diaghilev, who

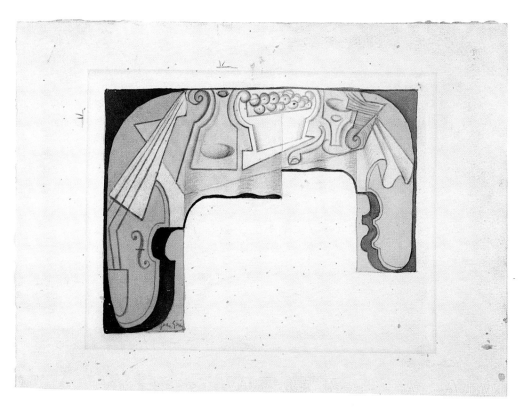

134   Design for cut cloths

Graphite and tempera and/or watercolor on paper
9¹⁄₁₆ x 12¹⁄₁₆ in: 23.1 x 31.5 cm
Signed bottom right of the left leg in pencil: "Juan
    Gris"
1933.482

Exhibitions: New York 1933, No 34; Chicago 1933,
    No 93; Northampton 1934, No 93; Paris 1939,
    No 261 (Described as "Décor: Deux détails");
    Minneapolis 1953; Edinburgh 1954, No 311;
    London 1954–5, No 354; Michigan 1957;
    Indianapolis 1959, No 300; Westport 1963;
    New York 1965–6, No 105 (illustrated p 50);
    New York 1966–7; Princeton 1968; Strasbourg
    1969, No 390; Frankfurt-am-Main 1969, No
    109; Hartford 1973; Hartford 1974; Hartford
    1978–9; Coral Gables 1982; Frankfurt-am-Main
    1986, No 213 (illustrated p 264); Hartford
    1988; Worcester 1989.
Illustrations: Buckle 1955, p 103 No 131; Green,
    p 277; Madrid 1985 catalogue, fig 4 p 67;
    Rischbieter, p 85 (color).

would read into my departure a gesture of scorn for his ballets."[23]

This is one of the drawings to which Gris referred. It is evident, however, that instead of making a new drawing he used an existing one, and merely washed over with white previously written inscriptions and measurements prior to its reproduction in the Souvenir Program. The writing is still visible, but now illegible. Gris then signed the drawing in pencil over the wash.

As with all his work for this production, this vignette is based on authentic baroque illustration but in a different style from his usual Cubism.

There are several unfinished pencil sketches on the reverse.

The previous catalogue stated that according to Serge Lifar this design was for *Les Tentations de la Bergère*. Karin von Maur suggests that this design is an "alternative" to the previous one, and correctly states that "the contrast between the two could not be more extreme, either in content or in style . . . The difference shows just how much Gris must have had to hold his own style and his own originality in check in order to accommodate himself to the period flavour of the scenario and the score."[24] But this design bears no relation to the finished set, and there is no evidence to suggest that Gris ever thought of designing a Cubist setting for the ballet, particularly as his brief from Diaghilev was for one in the style and period of Louis XIV. It is therefore not an "alternative" to the previous design, and, furthermore, has no connexion with it. The only connexion that this design may have to *Les Tentations de la Bergère* is if it were done as a preliminary project either before the brief for the ballet was finalized, or for *La Fête Merveilleuse* when Gris was thinking of a Cubist setting for the pageant.

Vladimir Polunin, who was responsible for painting the set after it was built, wrote: "The setting for *La Tentation de la Bergère* [sic], which consists of seven planes and numerous flats, can be classed with mixed types of scenery, that is one part is hung while the other consists of a complicated built construction."[25]

This drawing is for a "hanging" part of a set: a horizontal cloth is called a "border" and a vertical a "leg." In this case, Gris has not separated them; furthermore, he has cleverly drawn his design in perspective to indicate his intention of having two hangings, one behind the other, with the decoration overlapping. For which production, however, remains uncertain.

135 Design for the cover of the Souvenir Program for Diaghilev's Ballets Russes season at Monte Carlo, 1924

Graphite and tempera and/or watercolor on paper
11⅝ x 8½ in: 29.7 x 21.9 cm
Signed bottom left in pencil: "Juan Gris"
1933.484

Exhibitions: New York 1933, No 36 (described as "Costume for a Pierrot"); Chicago 1933, No 95 (described as "Projet de costume de Pierrot"); Northampton 1934, No 95; San Francisco 1935–6; Paris 1939, No 262 (described as "Esquisse de costume pour Pierrot" in *Les Tentations de la Bergère*²⁶); New York, 1944–5; Sarasota 1949, No 20; Edinburgh 1954, No 312; London 1954–5, No 355; Sarasota 1958, No 38; Elmira 1958, No 59; Indianapolis 1959, No 303; Storrs 1963; New York 1965–6, No 102 (illustrated p 50); New York 1966–7; Princeton 1968; Hartford 1973; Hartford 1974; Hartford 1978–9; Coral Gables 1982; Madrid 1985, No 180 (illustrated in color); Hartford 1988; Worcester 1989.
Illustrations: Amberg pl 48 (described as being for *La Colombe*²⁷); Cooper 1977, p 461; Rischbieter, No 91.

This is the original drawing for the cover, to which Gris refers in his letter to Kahnweiler quoted above. The figure of a Pierrot had become a recurring image in Gris's work round about the time of Diaghilev's commission. It was therefore natural for him to exploit this theatrical figure for the cover of the program, although it seems not to have occurred to him that a *commedia dell'arte* character is not exactly the appropriate figure to use for illustrating a ballet company. Especially not a pipe-smoking, beer-drinking one. However, this seems not to have occurred to Diaghilev either, because he used the drawing.

In another respect, Gris was at this time developing his Cubist theories by humanizing the purely architectural side of his painting. Although he stated in a lecture that "the only true pictorial technique is a sort of flat, coloured architecture," he developed this idea by stating later in the same lecture that "there is no form more expansive than the circle and none more concentrated than the triangle . . . some forms also have a very accentuated centre of gravity, whereas in others it is much weaker. Symmetrical forms are heavier in relation to their centre of gravity than complicated, asymmetrical ones. Geometrical figures and forms with a vertical axis have more gravity than forms with an unpronounced or non-vertical axis."²⁸ He did not mention the human form, but he used it in this drawing (and in others) not so much to represent a figure as merely a form—just as, in the previous drawing, he used the violin and guitar, other recurring images in his work.

Notes

1 Kochno is not credited in the program of the first performance.
2 According to Daniel-Henry Kahnweiler in *Juan Gris: His life and work* (p 38), Diaghilev sent Gris the offer telegram on 14 April 1921. Gris wrote to Kahnweiler on 26 April: "The ballet project has not come off. Diaghilev told me that my reply to his telegram arrived too late and so he made other arrangements." *Cuadro Flamenco* was first performed at Théâtre de la Gaîté-Lyrique, Paris on 17 May 1921.
3 *Les Fâcheux* by Auric (see pp 147–49), and *Les Biches* by Poulenc (see pp 242–46).
4 The operas were all first produced by Diaghilev at the Théâtre de Monte-Carlo: *La Colombe* on 1 January 1924, *Le Médecin malgré lui* on 5 January, *Philémon et Baucis* on 10 January, and *Une Education Manquée* on 17 January.
5 Daniel-Henry Kahnweiler, *op cit*, p 49.
6 Daniel-Henry Kahnweiler, *op cit*, p 50.
7 Laurent Saint-Raymond, "La Saison de Versailles" in *Le Gaulois*, Paris 3 June 1923, p 1.
8 Laurent Saint-Raymond, *ibid*.
9 Pierre Plessis, "Une Nuit Triomphale chez le Roi Soleil" in *Le Gaulois*, Paris 2 July 1923, p 1.
10 François Mansart (1598–1666) was one of the architects of Versailles. Jules Hardouin-Mansart (1646–1708), his great-nephew and Louis XIV's chief architect, was responsible for the Hall of Mirrors.
11 From *Le Figaro*, Paris 30 June 1923 quoted in Nesta Macdonald, *Diaghilev Observed*, pp 290–1.
12 Gabriel Astruc, who was there, states in *Le Pavillon des Fantômes* (p 277) that the cloak was given by the Galeries Lafayette and that Wiltzak ascended the stairs, and not descended as some historians write.
13 Pierre Plessis, *op cit*, p 1.
14 Henry Malherbe, "Chronique Musicale: Au château de Versailles: les ballets russes dans la galerie des Glaces" in *Le Temps*, Paris 4 July 1923.
15 Juan Gris to Daniel-Henry Kahnweiler, quoted in *Juan Gris: His life and work*, p 52.
16 The first performance in Paris was on 26 June 1924 at the Théâtre des Champs-Elysées.
17 Henry Malherbe, "Chronique Musicale: Au Théâtre des Champs-Elysées: Ballets russes" in *Le Temps*, Paris 11 June 1924.
18 Lydia Sokolova, *Dancing for Diaghilev*, p 214.
19 Serge Grigoriev, *The Diaghilev Ballet*, p 198.
20 Florence E. Grenfell, unpublished diaries 2 January and 1 December 1924.
21 Bronislava Nijinska's second husband.
22 Boris Kochno, *Diaghilev and the Ballets Russes*, p 197.
23 Quoted in Daniel-Henry Kahnweiler, *Juan Gris: his life and work*, p 51.
24 Karin von Maur, "Music and Theatre in the Work of Juan Gris" in Christopher Green, *Juan Gris*, pp 276–7.
25 Vladimir Polunin, *The Continental Method of Scene Painting*, p 68.
26 There is no Pierrot character in *Les Tentations de la Bergère*.
27 There is no Pierrot character in *La Colombe*.
28 Juan Gris, "On the possibilities of painting," a lecture first published in 1924, quoted in Daniel-Henry Kahnweiler, *Juan Gris: his life and work*, p 195–201.

Constantin Korovine

Russian
born 1861 Moscow
died 1939 Paris

Skazanie o Nevidemom Grade Kitezhe i Deve Fevronii
(The Legend of the Invisible City of Kitezh and of the Maiden Fevronia)

Opera in four acts and six scenes by Vladimir Belsky
Composer: Nikolai Rimsky-Korsakov
Conductor: Felix Blumenfeld
Director: V. P. Shkaffer
Designers (sets): Constantin Korovine (act 1 and act 4, scene 1), Apollinari Vasnetsov (acts 2 and 3, act 4 scene 2)
Designer (costumes): Constantin Korovine
Principal singers:
  King Yuri: M. Philippov
  Prince Vsevolod: Andrei Labinsky
  Fevronia: Maria Kuznetsov
  Grisha: Ivan Ershov
  Feodor Poyarok: Vasili Sharonov
First performance: 7 (20) February 1907, Mariinsky Theater, St Petersburg

Synopsis

Act 1. Prince Vsevolod, joint ruler with his father King Yuri of the sacred city of Kitezh, is riding through the forest when he meets Fevronia, a simple peasant girl. He is so struck by her beautiful simplicity that he asks her to become his wife. He does not reveal his identity, though Fevronia later discovers it for herself.

Act 2. As the bridal procession wends its way through the village it is halted by the curses of Grisha, the village drunkard. Fevronia addresses him gently and he falls back. As the procession moves on, a horde of Tartars swoops on the village, pillages and sets fire to everything in its way. Vsevolod is killed and Fevronia and Grisha are taken prisoner. Grisha is made to act as a guide to the sacred city of Kitezh.

Act 3, scene 1. The news is brought to King Yuri in Kitezh, but his informant believes it is Fevronia who leads the Tartar horde. King Yuri calls a meeting in the square in front of the cathedral and exhorts his people to save the city with their prayers. A miracle occurs: a glowing cloud of golden mist descends upon the city and Kitezh rises to heaven. There is no trace of where it stood, except a burning cross.

Act 3, scene 2. The Tartars have set up camp by the side of a lake. The two commanders are quarrelling over Fevronia. Grisha hears the bells of the sacred city and, conscience-stricken, confesses to Fevronia that her anguish is due to his evil deeds. She forgives him. Taking her hand he rushes away with her, determined to reach the sacred city.

Act 4. Grisha and Fevronia are lost in the depths of the forest. She is exhausted. A strange group of goblins and devils appears and Grisha is terrified. Suddenly the bells of Kitezh are heard again. Grisha falls dying in mystic ecstasy. Flowers spring up and hide Fevronia. The shadow of Prince Vsevolod leans down from heaven and leads Fevronia into the sacred city. The people of the city and the King rejoice as the prince and his bride appear.

Kitezh, written mainly during 1903–4 and published in 1906, was Rimsky-Korsakov's last opera to be produced in his lifetime. Full of musical invention and unusual orchestration, and imbued with mystical feeling, it gave expression to his deeply held faith in the Russian people. The opera became his *Parsifal*, as it were, an opera in which the psychological drama was more important than the dramatic action. The whole legend of the invisible city of Kitezh is an artistic symbol for the great future that awaits the Russian people as a reward for their suffering. (Rimsky-Korsakov did not live to see the irony of such a sentiment.)

As *Kitezh* was the only new production to be mounted by the Imperial Theaters during the season, the Directorate made every effort to give it a lavish and glorious staging. Vladimir Teliakovsky, the director, allocated the design between two painters, Vasnetsov and Korovine. This was not an unusual practice at the time because it was recognized that some painters were better at some kinds of scene than others. Korovine's talent for painting trees was known, and he was therefore asked to design the naturalistic forest sets, as well as the costumes. Vasnetsov, an academic painter, was asked to design the other scenes, as well as the fantastical set for the final scene of the invisible city. The choice of designers was felicitous, and both were praised. The critic of *Rech* (identified only by his initials) was particularly impressed by the 'transformation of the city of Kitezh. The cathedral, whose walls are shot with multicolored mother-of-pearl, is most fabulous. In general, the stamp of art nouveau is on the production, but not to extreme."[1] The lavishness of the production not only did not go unnoticed by the press, but was even exaggerated. As Telyakovsky noted in his diary: "*Novoe Vremya* [*New Times*], not knowing what to say, informs us that the brilliant production cost 75,000 roubles, when in fact it cost 12,000 roubles as most of the costumes were made in our wardrobe workshops."[2]

The critics were not quite so rapturous about the performers. In *Rech* again, Maria Kuznetsov as Fevronia was reproached for "not yet being sufficiently inspired in her role. She played it more like a simple pious girl instead of a saintly maiden imbued with mystical ecstasy. She did not always follow the vocal part accurately; as usual, she was out of tune on the top notes and sounded rather harsh and strained. But all the same, she can hold her own in this part. Mr Ershov was excellent . . . He gave a vivid characterization, and the vocal execution, apart from a few unfortunate shrieks on the top notes, was distinguished by its expressiveness and naturalness."[3]

The opera pleased the audience. They applauded loudly, even shouted their approbation, and presented Rimsky-Korsakov with several garlands.

Constantin Korovine: The Legend of Kitezh

136 Costume design for the Tartar bowmen

Graphite, ink, tempera and/or watercolor, crayon, blue stamp with ink notations on thin card stock
13¼ x 8¹¹⁄₁₆ in: 33.6 x 22 cm
Signed in Russian in ink lower left: "К. Коровин (K. Korovin)"
Inscribed in Russian in ink top right: "Китеж / Татары (Kitezh Tartars)", in blue pencil top center: "Китеж (Kitezh)," "83"
Inscribed in Russian in ink clockwise round costume from top right: "кончик / красноватый" ("reddish tip)","кордонъ" ("cord"), "холст" ("linen", "кожа" ("leather"), "шелк" ("silk"), "сукно" ("broadcloth"), "No 83," "кордонъ"
Stamped in Russian upper left: "С. Петербургская контора Императорских Театров (The St Petersburg Office of the Imperial Theaters)," dated "4 November 1906," and stamped bottom right: "Опись Музея / Госуд. С. Петербурга / Отд II Ном 39/83 (Inventory of the Museum of the State of St Petersburg, Dept. II No 39/83)" [Roman and Arabic numerals inscribed in ink]
Reverse stamped with Imperial Theaters stamp "Монт. Б. С.П.Б. ИМП. ТЕАТРОВ (Ballet production of the Imperial Theaters in St Petersburg)," inventory stamp with number inscribed in ink: "Инв (Inv) No 1191," and year in red ink "1906г (g[od])," and Control Commission stamp "Коммисия / по контролю / для вывоза за границу / предметов / искусства и старины (Control Commission for the Export Abroad of Works of Art and Antiques)"
1933.486

Exhibitions: New York 1933, No 37 (described as "Russian Costumes [Marinsky Theatre, St Petersburg] 1908)"; Chicago 1933, Nos 96–101 (described as "Costumes Russes pour le Theatre de St Petersbourg"); Northampton 1934, No 97; Washington D.C., 1950–1; Elmira 1958, No 50; Richmond 1959; Hartford 1964; New York 1965–6, No 106 (illustrated p 51); New York 1966–7; Hartford 1974; Worcester 1989.

Of all the designers represented in the Lifar collection, Korovine is, in many ways, the most professional and the least flamboyant. Although he was initially an easel painter (and, indeed, remained one to the end of his life), his most significant work was for the theater—especially opera and ballet. But that significance was really apparent on the stage and not on paper. He learnt his art with Savva Mamontov's Private Opera Company[4] where he also met and befriended Chaliapine. The three of them shared and developed ideas about opera production which insisted on musical and vocal interpretation, acting and design having equal status. Their ideas had a strong influence on Diaghilev.

Korovine moved to the Imperial Theaters and his allegiance remained with them, which is why he did not do much work for Diaghilev.[5] Another reason is probably that Diaghilev was not attracted by his very lack of flamboyance. There is a similarity or, rather, a definite sameness in the execution of all his costume designs. They are nothing but working drawings—efficient, clear, with detailed instructions usually written round the figure. They are without painterly frills or embellishments; they never imitate another style of painting. Any costumier would have no difficulty in making up a costume from any of the designs. This is Korovine's professionalism.

He also understood very clearly the difference between dress or street clothes and theatrical costume. All his costume designs are based on careful research, either by studying illustrated books on national or regional costume or, often, by traveling to the particular region and observing for himself. He then adapted what he saw to suit not only the production but also the performer. Korovine wanted to get away from the traditional ballet costume. He worked particularly closely on several productions with Alexander Gorsky, the choreographer, at the Bolshoi Theater in Moscow who encouraged him to develop his ideas about designing suitable costume for ballet which, while remaining true to a style and period, would both harmonize with the overall color scheme of the production and be comfortable to dance in. Korovine then applied these principles to all his work for the theater.

This design, and especially the ones following for *Prince Igor*, are typical examples of Korovine's design, based on authentic costume but allowing the performer great freedom of movement. They are bold, vigorous, detailed, quickly executed, but never slapdash.

There are many other similar examples of Korovine's designs in the Bakhrushin Theater Museum, the Museum of the Bolshoi Theater in Moscow, and the Theater Museum in St Petersburg. Quite a number of designs such as these finished up in private collections, although they all began by being the property of the wardrobe of the Imperial Theaters. Official stamps, however, show that they were all exported legally.

Notes

1 G. T. in *Rech* (*Speech*), St Petersburg 10 (23) February 1907, p 5.
2 Vladimir Telyakovsky diary entry for 8 February 1907, quoted in D. Kogan, *Konstantin Korovin*, p 309.
3 G. T., *op cit*, p 5.
4 He worked for Mamontov during the seasons 1885–91 and again from 1896–8.
5 For Diaghilev he designed the set and some costumes for *Le Festin* in 1909, and *Les Orientales* in 1910, and the sets for *Swan Lake* which had first been designed in 1901 for the Mariinsky Theater and which Diaghilev acquired, together with the costumes, for his production in 1911.

Knyaz Igor (Prince Igor)

Opera in 3 acts with a prologue by Alexander
 Borodin, after a scenario by Vladimir Stasov
Composer: Alexander Borodin, completed and
 partly orchestrated by Nikolai Rimsky-Korsakov
 and Alexander Glazunov
Conductor: M. Krushevski
Director: M. Melnikov
Choreographer: Michel Fokine
Designers (sets): Constantin Korovine (prologue),
 G. Solov (act 1, scenes 1 and 2, and act 3),
 P. Y. Ovchinnikov (act 2, The Polovtsian Camp)
Designer (costumes): Constantin Korovine
Principal Singers:
 Prince Igor: M. Andreev
 Princess Yarolsavna: Elena Nikolaeva
 Vladimir Igorevitch: Andrei Labinsky
 Vladimir Yaroslavitch: M. Smirnov
 Kontchak: M. Philippov
 Kontchakovna: Elisaveta Petrenko
Principal Dancer:
 Chief Polovtsian Warrior: Adolph Bolm
First performance of revival: 24 September (7
 October) 1909, Mariinsky Theater, St Petersburg
First produced on 23 October (4 November) 1890
 at the Mariinsky Theater

Synopsis

Prologue. The town square of Pultivl. A large crowd
is assembled to acclaim Prince Igor and his son
Vladimir as they set forth at the head of a great
army. Igor gives the command to march when an
eclipse of the sun takes place. The crowd and the
warriors take it as an evil omen and beg Igor not
to go ahead. He is adamant even after Yaroslavna
has added her entreaties to those of the crowd.
The eclipse passes, the army moves off to loud
cheers. Yaroslavna's brother, Prince Galitzky, is left
in charge.

Act 1, scene 1. Galitzky takes advantage of
Igor's absence to indulge in wild orgies which
terrify the townspeople. He tries to win them over
with the help of Eroshka and Skoula, two deserters
from Igor's army, who propose to place him on the
throne instead of Igor.

Act 1, scene 2. Yaroslavna, in her room, hears
of Galitzky's reprehensible behaviour and summons
him to her. He laughs in her face, insults her, and
makes her very angry. Hardly has he gone when
Boyards enter to announce that Igor and his army
have been defeated, that he and Vladimir have
been taken prisoner and that the pagan hordes are
now marching on Pultivl. The loyal Boyards swear
to protect the city and their princess.

Acts 2. The camp of the Polovtsy. The return of
the Polovtsian army under their leader Khan Konchak is greeted with excitement. Vladimir falls in
love with Khan Kontchak's beautiful daughter
Konchakovna. Prince Igor is overcome by the
disaster which has befallen him. Ovlour, a soldier of
the enemy camp, offers to help him escape, but
Prince Igor refuses to repay Khan Konchak's hospitality so unchivalrously. The Khan, distressed to see
Prince Igor so unhappy, orders a grand entertainment in his honor.

(Act 3. The same scene. The victorious Polovtsian army returns with the spoils of war and
prisoners from Pultivl. Prince Igor now agrees to
escape. Konchakovna gets to know of the plans,
reproaches Vladimir and holds him until his father
has disappeared. Soldiers rush to kill Vladimir in

revenge for his father's escape but Khan Konchak
orders them to leave him alone so that he can be
united with Konchakovna and also not to follow
Prince Igor.)

Act 4. Square in Pultivl. Yaroslavna, in despair,
suddenly catches sight of her husband. She rushes
forward to embrace him. Amid great rejoicing they
go into the Kremlin of Pultivl together.

The printed program stated that the
opera was in three acts and a prologue,
instead of four acts and a prologue. Even
while Rimsky-Korsakov was still alive, the
Directorate of the Imperial Theaters, for
some reason, began by cutting parts of act 3,
and then omitted the act altogether, thereby
apparently denying its very existence.
Rimsky-Korsakov was very upset by what
he called "the unscrupulousness of the
Mariinsky Theater" and rightly thought that
the cuts did the opera "considerable harm."[1]
However, it was immediately popular with
audiences and remained so in spite of the
ruthless cut.

This revival was especially remarkable
and memorable for the performance of the
Polovtsian Dances at the end of act 2. It is
often stated with some surprise that
Diaghilev's Russian Ballet never performed
in Russia.[2] While this is technically true—in
the sense that his company, before and after
it was officially called the Ballets Russes,
performed only outside Russia— many of
the early ballets choreographed by Fokine
had their original performances at the
Mariinsky Theater. And one of the greatest
sensations of the first Russian Season of
ballet in Paris, *The Polovtsian Dances*, first
performed in May 1909, was repeated in its
correct place during this opera. The conductor, Krushevski, in spite of obviously knowing every detail of the complicated score,
was criticized for giving a rather soulless
performance, except in the *Dances* when the
orchestra, fired by the beauty of the music,
fulfilled the composer's wishes. Fokine was
singled out for praise: "Fokine showed a lot
of taste and talent. There was so much
freedom and variety in the grouping of the
dancers, so much beauty and originality in
the movements interpreting their oriental
character, so much brilliance in the motley
combinations of the bright costumes, and so
much fire and genuine passion in the performance that these dances truly appeared
to be in great contrast to the general musical
interpretation which was colorless by comparison. The audience was greatly enthused
and gave M. Fokine an ovation."[3] The same

critic thought that Korovine had excellently
sustained the ancient style of Russian architecture in his settings, and that the costumes
were very successful in their diversity. But
this was not an opinion shared by everyone.

The performance in Paris had also
included scenes from the opera with
Sharonov as Prince Igor and Elisaveta
Petrenko as Kontchakovna who repeated
her role in this revival a few months later,
together with some of the other singers. In
the *Dances* the only differences between
Paris and St Petersburg were that there
were fewer dancers in Paris, although many
were the same, and that the set and costumes had been designed by Nikolai
Roerich, not Korovine.[4] When the opera was
given in Russia this difference was noted
and compared by a critic who saw both
performances: "Instead of Roerich's remote,
smoky, sunset steppe with a reddish glow
from the dying embers of camp fires,
Korovine produced a setting of a kind of
mountainous landscape with huge branchy
trees. And after the dense, carpet-like colors
of the Paris costumes there was something
disagreeable about the banal, rather too
bright, and sometimes sickly colors of
Korovine's costumes. But above all, the
setting for the *Dances* with its monotonously
insistent redness was very irritating, after
the incomparable, and henceforth famous,
Paris 'gamut' which so enraptured J.
Blanche!"[5] In spite of such noticeable differences, the important factor in the two productions was that the choreographer,
Fokine, and the Chief Warrior, Adolph
Bolm, were the same. The effect, however,
of the *Dances* on the Russian audience was
not as stunning as on the Parisian. Russians,
while admiring the high artistic quality and
brio of the dancing, did not by then consider it to be particularly novel, unlike the
French who had never seen anything like it
before. Fokine explained his intention in
choreographing the *Dances* and why it was
new: "About the staging of the *Polovetzian
Dances* [sic]—which I consider one of the
most important of all my works— . . . I
wished to illustrate the feasibility of the
expressiveness of a group dance. Prior to
this, the task of the *corps de ballet* in a performance had narrowed down to acting as a
background accompaniment for the performing soloist. There existed *corps de ballet*
numbers without soloists, but still its role
did not go beyond being a moving ornament of dancers tied together by the same

tempo. These were groups and movements pleasing to the eye; but the expression of feelings, ecstasies, spiritual loftiness, and temperament were terms never used in connection with the *corps de ballet*. My goal was to create an excitement-arousing dance for the *corps*."[6]

Fokine obviously achieved his goal, for the reception given to *The Polovtsian Dances* was invariably ecstatic. The *Dances* were the most performed of all Diaghilev's ballets. They were included in every season in Paris (except 1914, 1925, 1926), and in London (except 1914), as well as in both American tours. Cyril W. Beaumont, praising Fokine's genius, described their effect: "The spectators were carried away by the wild throbbing frenzy of Borodin's music, that maddening passion contrasted with periods of deep lassitude so characteristic of the Slav temperament. Fokine has exactly interpreted in his choreographic medium that marvellous evocation of 12th century Russia, even to the least modification of its themes and rhythms. The music and dances seem inseparable, it is impossible to believe that they ever existed apart . . . No one who has seen this dance will deny its right to be acclaimed a masterpiece. Nothing could be more removed from the traditions of the old ballet and nothing could be more indicative of Fokine's genius as a choreographer."[7]

There was a lone voice which disagreed with the universal acclaim, and in view of the *Dances'* subsequent popularity, it is now amusing to read the report: "The first presentation of *Prince Igor* . . . was followed by half the audience walking out of the theatre, while the manager of Covent Garden could be heard shouting 'Monsieur Diaghileff you have compromised your debut. This is not dancing, but the capering of savages.'"[8]

On 14 (27) December 1909, Fedor Chaliapine took over the role of Prince Vladimir.[9] Chaliapine's astonishing vocal range meant that he could sing with equal effectiveness three different roles in this opera—Prince Igor himself, Kontchak, and Vladimir Yaroslavitch, as in this revival. As was so often the case, Chaliapine's performance was truly impressive. The critic of *Rech* wrote: "Only Chaliapine, great artist that he is, was able to give the part its due. His Prince Vladimir never lost his princely manner. Youthful, handsome, with a princely gait, he maintains his bearing, his princely appearance even when he is intoxicated. And what a master of make-up Chaliapine is. His face, framed in curly reddish hair and a smallish beard, has noble features . . . Chaliapine does not make a single

unnecessary accentuating gesture, does not sing a single phrase with a mannered expression."[10] Very few singers ever get such rapturous acclaim for their acting.

137 Costume design for Adolph Bolm as the Polovtsian Chief Warrior

Graphite, tempera and/or watercolor, silver paint with brown ink and crayon notations on thin card stock
13⅛ x 8⁵⁄₁₆ in: 33.5 x 21.1 cm
Signed in Russian in ink lower left: "К. Коровин (K. Korovin)"
Inscribed in Russian in pencil top left: "Игорь / Г. Больм (Igor / Mr Bolm)"
Inscribed in Russian in ink round costume clockwise from top right: "павлинныя / перья" ("peacock feathers"), "парик" ("wig"), "сукно полосанами" ("striped broadcloth"), "рукава / можно / убрать" ("the sleeves can be deleted"), "шелк" ("silk"), "кожа" ("leather"), "парча" ("brocade"), "золотая / парча" ("gold brocade"), "и кисти бляхи" ("and plated tassels"), "ремни" ("thongs")
Stamped in Russian upper right: "С. Иетербургская контора Императорских Театров (The St Petersburg Office of the Imperial Theaters)," dated "13 September 1909," and stamped bottom center in Russian, now illegible except for the inscriptions in ink: "Опись Музея / Госуд. С. Петербурга / Отд II Ном 39/83 (Inventory of the Museum of the State of St Petersburg, Dept. II No 100/35)" [Roman and Arabic numerals inscribed in ink]
Reverse stamped with Imperial Theaters stamp "Монт. Б. С.П.Б ИМП. ТЕАТРОВ (Ballet production of the Imperial Theaters in St Petersburg)," inscribed in pencil: "No," "No 61"
Inscribed in pencil in another hand: "на куртку

сукна ар 12" ("for the jerkin 12 arshins [1 arshin = 28 in: 70 cm] of broadcloth"), "на штаны канаусе 9 арш" ("for the trousers allow 9 arsh[ins]"), "на кушак канаусе 5 арш" ("for the belt allow 5 arsh[ins]")
1933.485

Exhibitions: New York 1933, No 37 (described as "Russian Costumes (Marinsky Theatre, St Petersburg) 1908"); Chicago 1933, No 96 (described as "Costumes Russes pour le Theatre de St Petersbourg"); Northampton 1934, No 96; Washington DC 1950–1; Richmond 1959; New York 1965–6, No 107 (illustrated p 51); New York 1966–7; Princeton 1968; Strasbourg 1968, No 18; Frankfurt-am-Main 1969, No 2; Amherst 1974; Hartford 1978–9; Coral Gables 1982; Allentown 1985; Columbus 1989; Worcester 1989.

It is not generally realized that Adolph Bolm created the Polovtsian Chief Warrior in Russia as well as in Paris in Fokine's choreography. The only difference was in his costume. However, there were even some similarities between the costumes designed by Roerich for Paris and Korovine for St Petersburg, as both designers developed their designs after careful research into Polovtsian dress of the twelfth century. The main difference was in the coloration: Roerich was bolder than Korovine, who favored more muted tones. One critic, however, was scathing about Korovine's costume designs: "Unfortunately the production at the Mariinsky Theater impaired their [Fokine's and Bolm's] inspired work. The costumes are completely unsuited to the character of the scene and the ideas of the choreographer, not only because of their tonal range but in their style. They are somehow heavy and have none of the primitive quality of the Paris production: the dancers feel awkward and appear to be dolled up. Particularly incongruous are the wide, puffed up sharovary (wide trousers) of the Polovtsian girls which completely hide their legs. Owing to this banal and conventional 'orientalism' some pearls and details of Fokine's staging were lost."[11] Fokine, who himself frequently danced the part, was full of praise for Bolm: "The leading part was danced by Adolph Bolm. He was marvelous. It was his best role, and he remained its best performer. I have seen a great many Leading Warriors in this ballet, but to me Bolm has always remained incomparable . . . The main power of the *Polovetzian Dances* lies, not in the central part, but in the dancing of the ensemble, which does not represent the background, is not an accompaniment, but is a collective, participating personnel. Bolm, however, outshone the dancers surrounding him."[12]

138 Costume design for a Polovtsian woman

Graphite, crayon, ink, and tempera and/or water-color on off-white card stock
13³/₁₆ x 8⁵/₁₆ in: 33.5 x 21 cm
Signed in Russian in ink lower center left:
"К Коровин (K. Korovin)"
Inscribed in Russian in ink top left: "Кн Игорь (Pr Igor)," top right: "Балет / Половцы (Ballet of the Polovtsians)," in pencil top: "Балет (Ballet)," "28," in blue pencil upper left: "Князь игорь (Prince Igor)," in pencil bottom center right: "? Соворкина (Sovorkina)"
Inscribed in Russian in ink round costume clockwise from top right: "браслеты" ("bracelets"), "шелк" ("silk"), "? бохрома (?)," "шелк", "браслеты", "шелк", "крашено / ярко золотой" ("painted bright gold"), "бляхи" ("plates"), "полосные / кисти" ("striped tassels"), "металлные / бляхи" ("metal plates"), "бусы" ("beads"), "бляхи" ("plates"), "бляхи"
Stamped bottom center, now illegible except for Roman and Arabic numerals inscribed in ink: "Опись Музея / Госуд. С. Петербурга / Отд II Ном 100/37 (Inventory of the Museum of the State of St Petersburg, Dept. II No 100/37)"
Reverse stamped with Imperial Theaters stamp "Монт. Б. С.П.Б ИМП. ТЕАТРОВ (Ballet production of the Imperial Theaters in St Petersburg)," inventory stamp with number inscribed in ink: "Инв (Inv) No 1243," and year in pencil "1908г (g[od])," and Control Commission stamp "Коммисия / по контролю / для вывозда за границу / предметов / искусства и старины (Control Commission for the Export Abroad of Works of Art and Antiques)"
1933.489

Exhibitions: New York 1933, No 37 (described as "Russian Costumes (Marinsky Theatre, St Petersburg) 1908"); Chicago 1933, No 96 (described as "Costumes Russes pour le Theatre de St Petersbourg"); Northampton 1934, No 100; Williamsburgh 1940; Washington D.C. 1950–1; Michigan 1957; Storrs 1963; New York 1965–6, No 111 (illustrated p 52); New York 1966–7; Princeton 1968; Strasbourg 1969, No 17; Frankfurt-am-Main 1969, No 1; Hartford 1974; Hartford 1978–9; Coral Gables 1982; Worcester 1989.

Constantin Korovine: Knyaz Igor

139 Costume design for a Polovtsian soldier

Graphite, ink, and tempera and/or watercolor with crayon and brown ink notations on card stock
13⅛ x 8⁵⁄₁₆ in : 33.3 x 21 cm
Signed in Russian in ink lower right: "Константин Коровин (Konstantin Korovin)"
Inscribed in Russian in blue pencil top center: "Князь Игорь (Prince Igor)," "39," top left: "Кн. Игорь (Pr Igor)," and top right: "Народ / Половцы (Polovtsian[s] / people)"
Inscribed in Russian in ink round costume clockwise from top right: "войлочная" ("felt hat"), "мех" ("fur"), "парик", "холст" ("linen"), "холст," "холст," "холст," [illegible] туфли" ("slippers")
Stamped bottom right, now illegible except for Roman and Arabic numerals inscribed in ink: "Опись Музея / Госуд. С. Петербурга / Отд II Ном 100/40 (Inventory of the Museum of the State of St Petersburg, Dept. II No 100/40)"
Reverse stamped with Imperial Theaters stamp Монт. Б. С.П.Б. ИМП. ТЕАТРОВ (Ballet production of the Imperial Theaters in St Petersburg), inventory stamp with number inscribed in ink: (Inv) No 1243," and year in pencil "1908г (g[od])," "N 45," and Control Commission stamp "Коммисия / по контролю / для вывозда за границу / предметов / искусства и старины (Control Commission for the Export Abroad of Works of Art and Antiques)"
1933.487

Exhibitions: New York 1933, No 37 (described as "Russian Costumes (Marinsky Theatre, St Petersburg) 1908"); Chicago 1933, No 96 (described as "Costumes Russes pour le Theatre de St Petersbourg"); Northampton 1934, No 98; Williamsburgh 1940; Washington D.C. 1950–1; Michigan 1957; Hartford 1964; New York 1965–6, No 108 (illustrated p 51); New York 1966–7; Hartford 1978–9; Columbus 1989; Worcester 1989.

140 Costume design for an armed Polovtsian

Graphite, ink, and tempera and/or watercolor with crayon and brown ink notations on card stock
13⅛ x 8⅜ in: 33.4 x 21.2 cm
Signed in Russian in ink lower right: "Константин Коровин (Konstantin Korovin)"
Inscribed in Russian in blue chalk top center: "Князь игорь (Prince Igor)," in pencil top right: "Половец (a Polovtsian)," in ink top left: "Кн. Игорь (Pr Igor)," and in ink top right: "Половец (a Polovtsian)"
Inscribed in Russian in ink round costume clockwise from top right: "кольчуга" ("chain mail"), "металл" ("metal"), "металл," "колчуга," "толстое / сукно [illegible]" ("thick broadcloth [illegible]"), "холст" ("linen"), "металл," "бутафору" ("prop"), "холст," "холст," "кожа" ("leather")
Stamped lower center, now illegible except for Roman and Arabic numerals inscribed in ink: "Опись Музея / Госуд. С. Vетербурга / Отд II Ном 100/39 (Inventory of the Museum of the State of St Petersburg, Dept. II No 100/39)"
Reverse stamped with Imperial Theaters stamp "Монт. Б. С.И.Б ИМП. ТЕАТРОВ Инв (Ballet production of the Imperial Theaters in St Petersburg)," inventory stamp with number inscribed in ink: "Инв (Inv) No 1243," and year in pencil "1908г (g[od]) / N 42," in pencil "В И (V I)"
1933.488

Exhibitions: New York 1933, No 37 (described as "Russian Costumes (Marinsky Theatre, St Petersburg) 1908"); Chicago 1933, No 96 (described as "Costumes Russes pour le Theatre de St Petersbourg"); Northampton 1934, No 99; Williamsburgh 1940; Washington D.C. 1950–1; Michigan 1957; Hartford 1964; New York 1965–6, No 109 (illustrated p 52); New York 1966–7; Amherst 1974; Hartford 1978–9; Columbus 1989; Worcester 1989.

141 Costume design for a Polovtsian soldier

Graphite, ink, tempera and/or watercolor with pastel, with crayon and brown ink notations on thin stock
13³⁄₁₆ x 8¼ in : 33.5 x 21 cm
Signed in Russian in ink lower right: "Константин Коровин (Konstantin Korovin)"
Inscribed in Russian in pencil top: "Народ Половцы (Polovtsian[s] [people])," in blue crayon center: "Князь Игорь (Prince Igor)," in ink top right: "Народ Половцы," in ink top left: "Кн. Игорь (Pr Igor)"
Inscribed in Russian in ink round costume clockwise from top right: "точно / парик" ("exact wig"), "овчина" ("sheepskin"), "холст" ("broadcloth"), "кожа" ("leather"), indicating staff "бутафору" ("prop"), indicating shield "кожа над коже" ("leather over leather")
Stamped bottom center, now illegible except for Roman and Arabic numerals inscribed in ink: "Опись Музея / Госуд. С. Петербурга / Отд II Ном 100/42 (Inventory of the Museum of the State of St Petersburg, Dept. II No 100/42)"
Reverse stamped with Imperial Theaters stamp "Монт. Б. С.П.Б ИМП. ТЕАТРОВ (Ballet production of the Imperial Theaters in St Petersburg)," inventory stamp with number inscribed in ink: "Инв (Inv) No 1243," and year in pencil "1908г (g[od]) / No 45," and Control Commission stamp "Коммисия / по контролю / для вывозда за границу / предметов / искусства и старины (Control Commission for the Export Abroad of Works of Art and Antiques)"
1933.490

Condition: average to poor. Support is brittle, discolored with mat burn and surface soil. Corners are damaged with creases, folds, and tears; losses to lower right corner. Pigment exhibits flaking, cracking and losses. Yellow sash is flaking.

Exhibitions: New York 1933, No 37 (described as "Russian Costumes (Marinsky Theatre, St Petersburg) 1908"); Chicago 1933, No 96 (described as "Costumes Russes pour le Theatre de St Petersbourg"); Northampton 1934, No 101; Williamsburgh 1940; Washington D.C. 1950–1; Hartford 1964; New York 1965–6, No 110 (illustrated p 52); New York 1966–7; Strasbourg 1969, No 14; Amherst 1974; Columbus 1989; Worcester 1989.

1 Nikolai Rimsky-Korsakov, *My musical life.*
2 But see Introduction p 38 for Diaghilev's abortive attempt at presenting his company in Russia in 1912.
3 G. T. "Kniaz Igor" in *Rech*, St Petersburg 24 September (7 October) 1909, p 5.
4 In the St Petersburg production there were 17 Young Polovtsian Girls instead of 12, 19 Oriental Slaves instead of 17, 22 Warriors instead of 17. There were the same number, 6, of Young Polovtsian Men.
5 O-r. in *Rech*, St Petersburg 29 September (12 October) 1909, p 4.
6 Michel Fokine, *Memoirs of a ballet master*, p 148.
7 Cyril W. Beaumont, *Michel Fokine and his ballets*, pp 46, 49.
8 G. E. Fussell, "Notes on Décor" in *The Dancing Times*, London April 1930, p 57.
9 This date has been mistakenly thought by some historians to be the date of the first performance of this revival.
10 G. T. in *Rech*, St Petersburg 17 (30) December 1909, p 6.
11 O-r. in *Rech*, St Petersburg 29 September (12 October) 1909, p 4.
12 Michel Fokine, *Memoirs of a ballet master*, p 151.

Michel Larionov

Russian
born 1881 Tiraspol
died 1964 Fontenay-aux-Roses

Soleil de Nuit (The Midnight Sun)

Russian scenes and dances by Leonide Massine
Composer: Nikolai Rimsky-Korsakov (from the
    opera *The Snow Maiden*)
Conductor: Ernest Ansermet
Choreographer: Leonide Massine
Principal Dancers:
    The Sun: Leonide Massine
    Bobyl: Nicholas Zverev
Soprano solo: Mme Laute-Brun
Company: Diaghilev's Ballets Russes
First Performance: 20 December 1915, Grand
    Théâtre, Geneva

Synopsis

The ballet was inspired by an ancient Russian fairy tale and the traditional dances held in northern Russia in honor of the Midnight Sun.[1]

From the program: "At the time of year when the sun rises soon after midnight in the northern regions there are ceremonies and dances to hail the coming of Yarila, the ancient Sun-god.

The whole village takes part in the ritual, which includes dances by buffoons, and by the 'Innocent' (called Bobyl), always an important character in Russian folklore.

This is followed by the village watching the Snow Maiden dance. Finally the Midnight Sun is symbolised by a youth chosen from the village, who, at the end of the ritual, is lifted towards the dawn to propitiate the god and ensure the coming of the sun."

Larionov and Gontcharova had renewed their collaboration and friendship with Diaghilev in 1914 when they worked on *Le Coq d'Or* (*The Golden Cockerel*) in Paris.[2] Although they both painted the set, Gontcharova alone was credited with designing the set and costumes. They stayed in Paris for an exhibition of their paintings at the Galerie Paul Guillaume which opened on 17 June, and returned home when Germany declared war on Russia on 1 August. Larionov was called up into the Russian army, was wounded, spent three months in hospital, and was invalided out on 5 January 1915. In June Gontcharova received a telegram from Diaghilev and Stravinsky asking, or rather imploring, her and Larionov to leave Russia and join them in Ouchy in Switzerland where Diaghilev had rented the Villa Belle Rive.[3] They arrived on 16 July after a roundabout journey. Diaghilev made the villa his power house, but it was a lean time: his autumn European tour had collapsed because of the war. As Prince Lieven wrote: "The shells burst, the bullets whistled, and people were

killed in their hundreds of thousands. Nobody was interested in *pirouettes*, *entrechats*, and *fouettés*. Offers of contracts became rare."[4] Diaghilev had only a few dancers round him, as most had returned patriotically to Russia. He began to gather other dancers. He was hoping to convert his beautiful new favorite, Leonide Massine, who had appeared stunningly as a dancer the year before in the title role of *La Légende de Joseph*,[5] into a choreographer, for he badly needed to replace Fokine and Nijinsky. Stravinsky was living close by. Through him he met the conductor Ernest Ansermet. They made a new team.

The first project they all worked on was *Liturgie*, a silent ballet based on the Passion of Christ, inspired by the primitive Italian paintings and mosaics Diaghilev and Massine had seen together during their travels in Italy. Gontcharova designed sets and many costumes based on traditional Russian icon painting. Larionov helped Massine with the choreography. Diaghilev, realizing that silence was impossible on stage, had the idea of asking the Italian Futurists, Marinetti and Pratella, to compose suitable "sounds." But nothing came of this idea, nor of Diaghilev's attempts to get appropriate sacred music sent from Russia. Diaghilev then tried to persude Stravinsky to compose a suitable score, but the latter finally refused because he did not think sacred music should be performed on a stage and because he was not prepared to compose two works—*Liturgie* and *Noces*—for the same fee. He said he was just not interested, and *Liturgie* was abandoned.[6] The two projects intitiated at this time—Prokofiev's *Chout*, to be designed by Larionov, and Stravinsky's *Noces*, to be designed by Gontcharova—were both delayed because the music was not ready.[7] Diaghilev had to think of something else.

As usual, he began with a score. He asked Massine to consider making Rimsky-Korsakov's opera *Snegourochka* (see pp 56–58) into a ballet. Massine records: "As I did not know it, he played it through to me, and I was delighted with the rich melodious score and its superb delineation of Russian peasant character. It conjured up for me the singing-games of my childhood, and I told

Diaghilev that I could easily envisage it as a ballet."[8] Larionov, enthusiastic, was again asked to work with Massine, to supervize the choreography, and to design the sets and costumes. Larionov had not had any practical experience in choreography and therefore Diaghilev's request at first seems rather strange. However, it was not misplaced: he knew that Larionov's fascination with traditional Russian peasant folklore would inspire Massine in the right direction. Indeed, it was Larionov who suggested that the ballet should be focused on the figure of the sun-god. They both worked well together, as Massine recalled: "Larionov and I seemed to inspire each other as we discussed and tried out each scene. He felt strongly that the ballet must be done in authentic peasant style, and his costumes, in vivid shades of red, purple and green were based closely on Russian folk-art. For the dances I drew on my childhood memories of the *chorovod*[9] and of "Gori, gori jasno,"[10] which he helped me to embellish with suitably primitive earthy gestures. I think it was through Larionov that I first came to understand the true nature of these old ritual peasant dances."[11]

Larionov's designs were in his boldest Russian neo-primitive style in harsh, contrasting colors of red, blue, and yellow for the sets, and a wide range of complementary colors for the costumes. Unfortunately, in designing the costumes, he paid more attention to the requirements of peasant authenticity than the physical wellbeing of the dancers. So, while the total scenic effect was very striking, the dancers complained bitterly that the costumes were exceedingly uncomfortable. Lydia Sokolova remembered: "All our abandon and zest for dancing was nipped in the bud. We had horrible thick pads tied around our waists, then there were tight heavy costumes on top of them. The tall, mitre-shaped Russian headdresses, once they had slipped slightly to one side, just refused to stand up straight again. All this was a pity, because if our movements had been less hampered we could have danced with as much enthusiasm as we did in *Prince Igor*."[12] The discomfort affected the dancers, but was not perceived by the audience or the critics. The ballet was first produced in Geneva at a charity performance in aid of the Red Cross and repeated in Paris on 29 December 1915 in aid of the British Red Cross. The program in Geneva began with *Carnaval*. This was replaced in Paris by *Schéhérazade,* with new scenery and costumes by Léon Bakst. The rest of the program was *L'Oiseau de Feu* conducted by Igor Stravinsky, *Princesse Enchantée pas de deux, Soleil de Nuit, Mélodies Russes,* and *Polovtsian Dances* from *Prince Igor*. The new ballet was a success. Diaghilev was greatly encouraged by its reception, and relieved by the proof of his faith in Massine, as Grigoriev overheard him say: "You see: given the talent, one can make a choreographer in no time."[13] Diaghilev used these two performances as valuable dress rehearsals for his forthcoming tour of the United States. In the difficult and troubled times of the First World War, he had successfully and gratefully negotiated a lucrative contract which ensured the continuance of the Ballets Russes. The company set sail for America[14] from Bordeaux on 1 January 1916.

142   Costume design for Leonide Massine as the Sun (Yarila)

Graphite, tempera and/or watercolor, silver-gold
    leaf and red glaze on two sheets of paper
    mounted to board
12¾ x 7⅜ in: 32.4 x 20 cm
Signed, upper left in gouache over earlier pencil
    signature: "M. Larionov"
Inscribed top left "No 1" under white wash over
    whole background
(Reverse, unseen because of laying down, inscribed
    in Russian in pen: "костюм Мяс (costume
    Mias[sine])")
1933.491

Exhibitions: Paris 1918;[15] New York 1922;[15] Chicago
    1933, No 102;[15] Northampton 1934, No 102;
    Hartford 1934; New Haven 1935; San Francisco
    1935–6; New York 1937–8, No 70; Paris 1939,
    No 270; ? Los Angeles 1939–40; Poughkeepsie
    1940; Williamsburg 1940; Edinburgh 1954, No
    187; London 1954–5, No 212; Indianapolis
    1959, No 360; Rowayton 1960; Storrs 1963;
    New York 1965–6, No 112 (illustrated p 53);
    New York 1966–7; Princeton 1968; Strasbourg
    1969, No 239; Frankfurt-am-Main 1969, No 61;
    Hartford 1974; Hemsptead 1974, No 100;
    Chicago 1975; Hartford 1978–9; Worcester
    1989.
Illustrations: Bablet, p 160 No 293; Beaumont
    1946, p 80; Beaumont n.d., p 126 ; Parton, pl
    17 (color); Pozharskaya and Volodina, p 147;
    Propert 1921 (color); Williams 1981, No 43
    p 41 (color).

The main theme of the design for this ballet is, naturally enough, the sun: not a comforting or even warming sun, but a grinning, mocking sun. The set is a garland of grotesque, dark orange suns suspended above the dancers against a deep blue sky. The costumes, mostly in a dominant red, with contrasting blues and greens, are boldly extravagant interpretations of traditional Russian peasant designs, simplified and enlarged for theatrical effect.

The costume design for the Sun, while maintaining a peasant-like naivety, was inspired by Stefano della Bella's design for

Louis XIV as the Sun King in *Ballet de la nuit*.[16] Both costumes are constructed in essentially the same manner with enormous, radiating headdresses, and skirts *à la romaine*. The sun's face on the chest is the dominant design element in both costumes. The royal sun is classically discreet, but Larionov's sun is stylized in a scary child-like way in deliberate contrast to the placid, frank face of the character. An invention added by Larionov are the huge gold suns carried on the hands, which, like the head-dress, are in foil collage. Cyril W. Beaumont described the effect: "Finally, the Sun God appeared in a radiant costume of fire red and gold, his breast decorated with a giant sun and holding a resplendent red and gold sun in each hand, which scintillated as they were passed rapidly in front of each other or shot out at arm's length at various angles."[17]

There is a mystery about this painting. Both the illustrations, noted above as being in Beaumont, are identical and appear, in almost every respect, to be of this design. They include, however, the date "1917" after the signature and the inscription "Soleil de Nuit" below it. If they are reproductions of this design then Larionov washed the date and the inscription over with white, as he did an earlier signature in pencil, some time after Beaumont got the photograph but before Lifar got the design. On the other hand, the original design was done in 1915 and the fact that the date 1917 is visible on the illustrations may indicate simply that the illustrated design was a later copy. If so, then Larionov was a remarkable copyist of his own work.

143 Costume design for a Russian peasant

Graphite or charcoal, tempera and/or watercolor and red glaze on illustration board
23⁹⁄₁₆ x 16⅝ in: 59.8 x 42 cm
Signed in Russian with initials top: "М.Л.. (M.L.)"
Inscribed in Russian in blue watercolor top right: "Камаринс[кая] (Kamarins[kaia])," and in pencil below: "Милой и прекрасной / Марии Андреевне / на память о / русских балетах / и о Париже / 1918 март 15 / М Ларионов" ("To dear and beautiful Maria Andreevna in memory of the Ballets Russes and Paris 1918 March 15 M. Larionov"), in pencil under right arm: "Tagliata a punta alla voia" ("Cut to the tip as required")
1933.492
Provenance: Maria Andreevna ?[18]

Exhibitions: Chicago 1933, No 103; Northampton 1934, No 103; Hartford 1934; New Haven 1935; San Francisco 1935–6; ? Los Angeles 1939–40; Paris 1939, No 271; Williamsburg 1940; Edinburgh 1954, No 188; London 1954–5, No 213; New York 1965–6, No 113 (illustrated p 53); New York 1966–7; Princeton 1968; Hartford 1973; Hartford 1974; Hartford 1978–9; Columbus 1989; Worcester 1989.

Serge Lifar must have acquired this design after 1930, and, presumably on his authority, it has been exhibited as a costume design for *Soleil de Nuit* even though he may not necessarily have been correct. The doubt about the attribution arises because the inscription in the top right corner, "*kamarinskaya*," refers to a favorite Russian folk dance, and the American critic Louis Elson noted quite specifically in his review of the ballet: "The troupe were very interesting in some Russian national dances, in *Soleil de Nuit*, although the chief Russian dance, the Kamarinskaia, was notturally [sic] not among them, since this is danced by men only, in a great circle, all jumping and kicking for all they are worth."[19] On the other hand, either the dance may have originally been intended for one of the danced interludes of the ballet and was then cut, or it may have been introduced later.

If this design is not for *Soleil de Nuit*, it could be for *Contes Russes* or *Children's Tales* (see p 233), for which Larionov's costume designs were not dissimilar and which had interludes of Russian peasant dances between the episodes.

Notes

1 Diaghilev first called the ballet *Soleil de Minuit,* which explains the "Midnight" of the English title.

2 Opera by Nikolai Rimsky-Korsakov produced on 24 May 1914 at the Opéra, Paris.

3 Telegram dated 3 June 1915, "Leave immediately we are waiting impatiently for you Diaghilev Stravinsky" reproduced in Tatiana Loguine, *Gontcharova et Larionov*, fig 22 p 200 (see also Gontcharova, p 208).

4 Prince Peter Lieven, *The Birth of Ballets-Russes*, p 227.

5 Ballet by Count Harry Kessler and Hugo von Hofmannsthal with music by Richard Strauss, choreography by Michel Fokine, sets by José-Maria Sert, and costumes by Léon Bakst first performed by Diaghilev's Ballets Russes on 14 May 1914 at the Opéra, Paris.

6 The only ballet to have been rehearsed but not performed.

7 *Chout*, with sets and costumes by Michel Larionov and choreography by Thadée Slavinsky and Larionov, was first performed on 17 May 1921 at the Théâtre de la Gaîté-Lyrique, Paris; for *Noces* see pp 208–11.

8 Leonide Massine, *My Life in Ballet*, p 74.

9 A round dance.

10 "Burn, burn clearly."

11 Leonide Massine, *op cit*, p 75.

12 Lydia Sokolova, *Dancing for Diaghilev*, p 71.

13 Serge Grigoriev, *The Diaghilev Ballet*, p 118.

14 The first season in America was 17 January–29 April 1916.

15 In the catalogues for Paris 1918 Nos 177–194 were described as "Esquisses de Maquettes et de Costumes 'Soleil de Nuit'," for New York 1922 Nos 97–101 were described as "Costume designs 'Soleil de Minuit'," and for Chicago 1933 Nos 102–103 were described as "'Soleil de Minuit' costumes," but in no case was any of the designs individually identified.

16 Court ballet with libretto by Isaac de Benserade, music by Clément, performed at the Petit Bourbon, Paris in 1653. The design is illustrated in Beaumont 1946, p 6.

17 Cyril W. Beaumont, *The Diaghilev Ballet in London*, p 122.

18 "Andreevna" is the patronym, not the surname. She has not been identified. The Ballets Russes did not perform in Paris in 1918.

19 Louis C. Elson, "Dramatic Opening by Russian Ballet" in *The Boston Advertiser*, Boston 1 February 1916.

Kikimora

Choreographic miniature in one act based on
a Russian fairy story
Composer: Anatole Liadov
Conductor: Ernest Ansermet
Choreographer: Leonide Massine
Designer (set and costumes): Michel Larionov
Principal Dancers:
Kikimora: Maria Shabelska
The Cat: Stanislas Idzikowski[1]
Company: Diaghilev's Ballets Russes
First Performance: 25 August 1916, Teatro
Eugenia-Victoria, San Sebastian, Spain

Synopsis

Adapted from the program. Kikimora, embodiment
of wickedness, is guarded in her cradle by her
faithful servant, the Cat, the symbol of human
malice. When Kikimora begins to feel strong she
jumps about her house and forces her protector
to fight. She overpowers and kills the Cat and
escapes. Wickedness is let loose upon the world.

While the company was in Spain in
1916 (between their two tours of
America) rehearsing their first Spanish
ballet, *Las Meninas*,[2] Diaghilev suggested to
Massine, after the warm reception given to
Soleil de Nuit, that another ballet based on a
Russian folk tale should be added to the
repertory. Massine chose to choreograph the
story of the evil Kikimora and her cat to
music by Liadov.

Larionov was again asked to design the
set and costumes. As with his previous
designs for *Soleil de Nuit* he used very
bright, almost garishly bold colors, traditional in Russian folk art. The painted
backcloth is a jumbled fantasy of two
dragon heads like carved wooden spoon
handles, arching over suspended logs and a
brilliantly colored, decoratively tiled stove
painted in scale with the cat, not the
grotesque human form of Kikimora. The
decorative patterns and stylized flowers on
the false proscenium of the set and the stove
were derived from similar decorations on
liubki (plural of *liubok*, cheap Russian peasant prints on paper, wood, or glass) which
Larionov admired and collected. Roger Fry
summed up the impression of the set: "In
the Kikimora scene there is an almost crude
vehemence of colour which sets the right
key by its reminiscence of Russian peasant
art and children's toys. The colour here is
treated playfully and, as it were, half ironi-
cally."[3] Fry thought that the set and the
costumes merged into a unified whole, that
Larionov's designs underlined and supported the choreographic movements. This
exemplified Larionov's (and Gontcharova's)
theories about theatrical costume. On the
one hand they thought that a costume,

unlike dress, should symbolize and emphasize the character for whom it is designed,
and on the other hand they maintained that
"although a background can have an effect
on the visibility and expressive character of
a costume, every costume remains visible in
front of any background, even if they are
both of exactly the same tone and color. A
costume cannot disappear in front of a set,
whatever it is."[4] While true, I think this
underestimates the prime function of a
dance costume which is that the dancer
should be able comfortably to execute in it
the movements required by the choreographer, and that the spectators' attention
should not be distracted from them either
by the set or by a clumsy costume. Larionov
fortunately ignored his own principle in
Kikimora because the costumes are individual and contrast strongly with the set. The
costume for the cat was overall tights
painted like a tabby cat and a cat's mask,
and for Kikimora "one of Larionov's most
outlandishly repellent costumes—a stained,
patched blouse and skirt with gaudy red
stockings, and a wig of dark matted hair."[5]

Massine explained the ideas behind his
choreography: "In this highly-charged *pas
de deux* I had to maintain a constant interplay between the feline movements of the
animal desperately trying to defend itself
and the malicious fury of the witch. Fortunately both Sokolova[6] and Idzikovsky
understood the specifically Russian violence
inherent in the legend, which was further
emphasised by Liadov's music."[7] The violent movements were necessary in order to
ensure the essential "visibility" of the characters against the background. This short
ballet not only pleased the choreographer
but pleased audiences too. Michel Georges-
Michel, writing from Bilbao after the first
performance, thought that although Larionov's set was overpowering it was nevertheless "the first spark in an explosion of
Russian modernism which will probably
reach its full power when the Ballets Russes
return to Paris."[8]

Kikimora was only the first part of a
group of short ballets based on Russian folk
tales and legends which were later given
the collective title of *Contes Russes* in French
and *Children's Tales* in English. In 1917 *Bova
Korolevitch* and *Baba-Yaga* were added. The
definitive version was first performed in
1918 at the London Coliseum (see below).
The Times was delighted: "The Russian
Ballet presented *Children's Tales*, its contribution to the general Christmas gaiety at the

London Coliseum last night, and great fun
that contribution proved to be. M. Leonide
Massine has strung together three old Russian legends in a very ingenious way; the
grotesque setting is so quaint and unlike
anything that one usually associates with a
children's entertainment, the dancing of the
whole team is so exhilarating, that one
cannot wonder at the enthusiasm which
greeted it."[9] This was also the version which
Cyril W. Beaumont saw: "The most unusual
number was the Kikimora scene, an extraordinary presentation of venemous hate, most
forcibly rendered by Sokolova, whose
striped make-up gave her a fiendish appearance. Idzikovsky's remarkable *élévation* was
admirably suited to the Cat, and his miming
was excellent, especially his sorrow at the
death of the dragon. The whimsical manner
in which he despondently shook his head,
and dabbed his eyes with an orange handkerchief dangling from a trembling hand,
used to make Diaghilev shake with laugter."[10]

The credits for the first full version presented in
Paris were as follows:

Contes Russes (Russian Tales)

Three choreographic miniatures, with danced
interludes and an epilogue, on Russian themes
Composer: Anatole Liadov
Conductor: Ernest Ansermet
Choreographer: Leonide Massine
Designer (sets and costumes): Michel Larionov
Principal dancers:
La Princesse Cygne (the Swan Princess):
Lubov Tchernicheva
Bova Korolevitch: Leonide Massine
Kikimora: Lydia Sokolova
The Cat: Stanislas Idzikowski
? Leon Woizikovsky, Jean Jazvinsky
First Performance: 11 May 1917, Théâtre du
Châtelet, Paris

The credits for the definitive version presented in
London were as follows:

Children's Tales

People's Play by Leonide Massine
Composer: Anatole Liadov, with prelude and
lament orchestrated by Arnold Bax
Conductor: Henry Defosse
Choreographer: Leonide Massine
Designer (sets and costumes): Michel Larionov
Principal dancers:
Dance prelude: Leon Woizikovsky
Kikimora: Lydia Sokolova
The Cat: Stanislas Idzikowski
The Swan Princess: Lubov Tchernicheva
Bova Korolevitch: Leonide Massine
The Dragon's Funeral: Sophie Pavloff,
Leon Woizikovsky
Baba Yaga: Leonide Massine
The Little Girl: Helene Antonova
First Performance: 23 December 1918, London
Coliseum

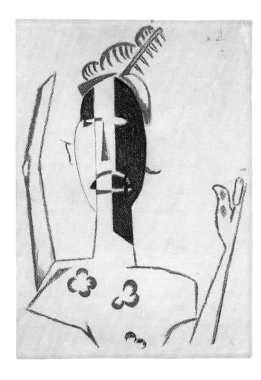

144   Design for Kikimora's make-up

Charcoal and crayon on paper
13³⁄₈ x 9⁷⁄₁₆ in: 33.4 x 24 cm
Signed top right in chalk: "M.L."
Reverse stamped: "Douane Centrale / Exportation /
   Paris"
1933.494

Exhibitions: Paris 1918 (Nos 195–197 described as
   being for "Kikimora" but not individually
   identified); Paris 1919 (Nos 207–216 described
   as being for "Kikimora" but not individually
   identified); New York 1922, No 108; New York
   1933, No 39; Chicago 1933, No 105;
   Northampton 1934, No 105; Hartford 1934;
   New Haven 1935; San Francisco 1935–6; Paris
   1939, No 277; Edinburgh 1954, No 194;
   London 1954–5, No 225; Michigan 1957;
   Indianapolis 1959, No 363; Storrs 1963; New
   York 1965–6, No 115 (illustrated p 55); New
   York 1966–7; Princeton 1968; Strasbourg 1969,
   No 263; Frankfurt-am-Main 1969, No 65;
   Amherst 1974; Hempstead 1974, No 98; Coral
   Gables 1982; Allentown 1986; Columbus 1989;
   Worcester 1989.
Illustrations: Beaumont, p 131 (another version);
   Parnack, pl 5 (color); Pozharskaya and Volodina,
   p 169 (lithograph).

Diaghilev's designers frequently paid careful attention to make-up, seeing it as an integral part of their design over which they should have control. Bakst was always particularly fussy, so was Picasso for *Le Tricorne*, and Derain made a whole series of drawings for the characters in *La Boutique Fantasque*.

Larionov's attitude to make-up was slightly different. He saw it as part of the process of painting, not merely as an aid to the definition of character. This design for Kikimora's make-up is, in effect, the practical application of his theory of painting on a human being, in this case a dancer, instead of on a canvas. Between 1912 and 1914 Larionov invented, defined, and elaborated the theory of *rayonnism*[11] which Parnack described as "painting which is not concerned with objects, but with the very meaning of painting, the color and movement of the lines which make up the shapes."[12] Make-up also replaces the mask. Lydia Sokolova wrote that she "loved dancing the ferocious and hideous witch, Kikimora, with her blue-striped face, who made her cat rock her in her cradle and then in a fury chopped off its head with an axe."[13] It was the band of white between the two bands of blue which made her look ferocious and hideous.

As this drawing was intended for reproduction, a light wash of white was applied at the top and round the head obliterating an inscription top left and right. The initials were written later.

Notes

1   "Idzikowski" was the spelling of his name in
    English upon which he finally settled.
2   *Las Meninas*, from the *Pavane* by Gabriel Fauré,
    set by Carlo Socrate, costumes by José-Maria
    Sert, was first performed at the Teatro Eugenia-
    Victoria, San Sebastián on 25 August 1916.
3   Roger Fry, "M. Larionow [sic] and the Russian
    Ballet" in *Burlington Magazine*, London March
    1919, p 117.
4   Nathalie Gontcharova and Michel Larionov, *Les
    Ballets Russes*, p 38.
5   Leonide Massine, *My Life in Ballet*, p 98.
6   Lydia Sokolova took over the part in 1917.
7   Leonide Massine, *op cit*, p 98–9.
8   M-G-M (Michel Georges-Michel) in unidentified
    cutting from Bilbao, Spain, dated 5 September
    1916.
9   Anon, *The Times* London 24 December 1918, p 9.
10 Cyril W. Beaumont, *The Diaghilev Ballet in
    London*, p 125.
11 *Rayonnisme* is the French translation of the
    Russian *luchism*. Anthony Parton prefers the
    English translation *rayism*.
12 Valentin Parnack, *Gontcharova Larionov: L'Art
    décoratif théâtral moderne*, p 15.
13 Lydia Sokolova, *Dancing for Diaghilev*, p 132.

Renard (The Fox)

A burlesque to be sung and played, adapted from
  a Russian story by Igor Stravinsky
Composer: Igor Stravinsky
Conductor: Igor Stravinsky
Choreographer: Serge Lifar
Set and costumes: Michel Larionov
Principal dancers:
  The Fox: Leon Woizikovsky
  The Cock: Nicolas Efimov and Louis Agustino
  The Ram: Boris Lissanevitch and
    Bernardo Agustino
  The Cat: Jean Hoyer and Adolph Hierlinger
Singers: Grégoire Raissoff, Michel Tkhorjewsky,
    Eugène Maltzeff, Jan Nedra
Company: Diaghilev's Ballets Russes
First performance of revival: 21 May 1929, Théâtre
  Sarah-Bernhardt, Paris

The first performance of the original production by
  Diaghilev's Ballets Russes was on 18 May 1922
  at the Théâtre national de l'Opéra, Paris when
  the credits were as follows:
Conductor: Ernest Ansermet
Choreographer: Bronislava Nijinska
Set and costumes: Michel Larionov
Principal Dancers:
  The Fox: Bronislava Nijinska
  The Cock: Stanislas Idzikowski
  The Ram: Jean Jasvinsky
  The Cat: Michel Federov
Singers: Fabert, Dubois, Narcon, Mahieux

Synopsis

Standing on his perch, the Cock gloomily describes his daily life. The Fox enters disguised as a nun. He begs the Cock to come down and confess his sins. The Cock says he has no need to confess. "Come, come," says the Fox, "you not only have far too many wives, but you also treat them badly." At this the Cock hops down from his perch, whereupon the Fox grabs him by the tail. The Cock screeches for help from his friends the Cat and the Goat. They come to rescue him, and all three dance triumphantly while the Fox escapes.

At the start of the second part, the Cock complacently regains his perch and resumes his melancholy song. The Fox enters again, this time not disguised. He tries again to entice the Cock to the ground by bribery and flattery. At first the Cock is not fooled, but eventually he is persuaded to jump down. The Fox immediately pounces on him, and this time the Cock's friends are slow in coming to the rescue. The Fox starts to pull out his feathers and the Cock begs for mercy. Realizing that all is lost, he prays for the welfare of his surviving relatives and passes out. The Cat and the Goat appear at last and, feigning friendship, insinuate to the Fox that his wife is being unfaithful. He is caught off his guard and they seize the opportunity to strangle him.

The Cat, the Goat, and the Cock dance with delight and beg for a token of gratitude from the audience if their tale has pleased them.

In 1915 Stravinsky was living precariously in Switzerland with his family, cut off by the war from any income from his estate in Russia. He was therefore glad to accept a commission from Princess Edmond de Polignac, who wanted to help him, to compose a work for performance in her private theater. This encouraged Stravinsky to finish a composition which he had already started and, moreover, it determined the scale of the work. He had chosen to adapt one of the several stories about a fox by Alexander Afanasiev, who had compiled a collection of Russian fables and fairy tales in the manner of Aesop. Stravinsky's original title was *The tale of the Cock, the Fox, the Cat, and the Ram*. He said that he "finished the libretto early in 1915, and the music by the end of the year," and that the score was "inspired by the *guzla*, an extraordinary instrument that is carried by the goat in the last part of the play, and imitated by the orchestra with good but imperfect success by the cimbalom. The *guzla* is a museum piece now . . . A kind of fine metal-stringed balalaika, it is strapped over the player's head like the tray of a cigarette girl in a night club."[1] Stravinsky composed *Renard* on the cimbalom, not the piano as usual. He finished the instrumentation on 1 August 1916, and dedicated the score to Princess Edmond de Polignac. But *Renard* was not performed in her house.

Even though Diaghilev could not pay Stravinsky during the early war years, and even though he knew that Princess de Polignac had no public theater, he was, according to Stravinsky "furious with jealousy,"[2] and refused even to mention *Renard*. Part of Diaghilev's anger was caused by his not having been consulted during its composition; so he talked only of *Les Noces* (see pp 208–11), which Stravinsky had begun at the same time.

At the beginning of 1922, after Bronislava Nijinska had pleased him with her additional choreography for parts of *The Sleeping Princess* (see pp 87–101), Diaghilev considered asking her to choreograph *Noces* for the forthcoming season at the Paris Opéra. But its production had to be delayed, as Stravinsky had not finished the orchestration. Princess de Polignac now gave Diaghilev permission to produce *Renard* instead, and even made it easy for him to overcome his previous anger by offering to sponsor the production. Diaghilev, still without a choreographer, then asked Nijinska to choreograph *Renard* as well as to direct Stravinsky's new short opera *Mavra* (see pp 318–22). Not being able to present *The Sleeping Princess* in Paris as originally planned because the scenery and costumes had been sequestered in London, Diaghilev also asked Nijinska to arrange a one-act ballet from the prologue and last act using the existing set and costumes from *Le Pavillon d'Armide* (see pp 108–16), and some new costumes designed by Gontcharova. Nijinska's new, highly successful, ballet was called *Le Mariage de la Belle au Bois Dormant* in Paris, and *Aurora's Wedding* in London.[3]

Renard was the first complete ballet choreographed by Bronislava Nijinska for the Ballets Russes. Her early experience of juggling and acrobatics in the circus inspired some of her choreography. "She introduced somersaults to further her artistic aim and to help develop a character's image, rather than as an acrobatic trick."[4] Diaghilev was so pleased with the result that he engaged her as the permanent choreographer. As well as arranging the choreography, Nijinska danced the leading role. Stravinsky exaggeratedly said that her choreography for *Renard* (and *Noces* a year later) "pleased me more than any other works of mine interpreted by the Diaghilev troupe."[5] Was he deliberately forgetting Fokine and Balanchine?

Diaghilev first approached Serge Soudeikine[6] to design the ballet, probably to take the sting out of an embarrassment. Soudeikine's wife Vera had recently left him—for Stravinsky. Soudeikine was the resident designer for Nikita Belieff's *Chauve-Souris* (*The Bat*) cabaret theater. He had a brash and vivid style which, while suited to revue sketches, was inappropriate to *Renard*. Diaghilev did not like Soudeikine's preliminary drawings, and was able to cancel the agreement without saying so because he could not accept Soudeikine's expressed condition: "That he had resolved to work in the theatre henceforth only if he were entrusted with the entire production."[7] Diaghilev could never have agreed to a single artist designing or even supervising all his new productions. He now turned to Larionov, who should have been his first choice, as the subject matter exactly matched his artistic interests. The basic idea for the set, however, was Diaghilev's; Larionov elaborated it in a series of similar paintings. He discarded the earlier vibrant color schemes of vivid reds, yellows, and blues which he had used in *Soleil de Nuit* and *Contes Russes* for more subdued tones of neutral browns and greens. Some writers have explained that Larionov's muted coloration was the result of his depressing war experiences. This is not so. The setting is clearly based on his painting *Winter*, one of the series of paintings of the four seasons which he made before the war in 1912–13. These paintings are all in monochrome, painted in his crude, neo-primitive style, divided into four unequal sections by lines, with a short text in one of the bottom corners, a skeleton tree in a top corner, a large, crude, flat stylized male or female figure in the other, and smaller figures or animals in the other bottom corner. Larionov made many versions of this composition. They all have similar characteristics—the animals, with the cock on his perch, the ladder, and the tree—and it is always winter. In spite of Stravinsky's feelings about this production it was not a success, and was not repeated after the first season at the Opéra.

It is therefore surprising that Diaghilev chose to revive *Renard* in 1929 as the first work to be choreographed by Serge Lifar. Diaghilev always desired to develop his favorite protégé dancers into choreographers: first Nijinsky, then Massine (Dolin had been too independent), now Lifar. Although his initial hopes of promoting Lifar as a choreographer had been thwarted over *Zéphire et Flore* (see pp 150–52), he planned to entrust him with the revival of *Renard*. In order to conceal any inadequacies Lifar might have, Diaghilev cleverly suggested that Larionov should help him, and had the brilliant idea that the dancers dancing the Cock, the Ram, and the Cat should be doubled up with acrobats engaged from a circus. Lifar himself describes how he became a choreographer quite differently: "During lunch Diaghilev, coldly confident of my approval, suggested that my name, as choreographer, should be included in the season's posters. 'No, not yet, Sergei Pavlovitch, let me think it over. When I've gone through the score I'll give you a definite answer. It will take only a few days now, and then I'll let you know definitely whether I feel able to accept your offer!' I took the score, studied it, and almost immediately conceived the idea of constructing the ballet round two parallel themes, one expressed in dancing, the other acrobatically. My idea was, so to build up the movements and develop them, as to create a sort of skyscraper of dancing in line with Stravinsky's music and Picasso's cubism. I told Diaghilev how I saw it, and he fully concurred."[8] There is enough evidence, however, to support the view that the idea

of the acrobats was not Lifar's but Diaghilev's, a view shared by Richard Buckle who wrote that Lifar "did not know how lucky he was. Diaghilev's 'gimmick' would give him the reputation of originality as a choreographer."[9] The complementary roles of the dancers and the "doubled" acrobats in the finished ballet were described by Grigoriev, the stage manager: "Parts of each [role] were performed by dancers and the rest by acrobats: what the dancer could not do being done by the acrobats and vice-versa. As the dancer and acrobat in each pair were of the same height (as near as might be) and wore similar costumes and masks (for they all represented animals), the public could scarcely tell the two apart."[10]

The rumour of a "new" style of dancing had got out. Diaghilev, the impresario,

Above: the scene for the revival in 1929, on stage at the Théâtre Sarah-Bernhardt, Paris.

naturally did not take any credit for it but loyally passed it all on to his choreographer, even though their relationship by this time had become rather strained. Before the first night of the London season, Diaghilev made one of his rare public gestures by writing to the press. Although the main purpose of his long letter was to bring his latest protégé, the sixteen-year-old composer Igor Markevitch to public attention, Diaghilev set out his ideas about the state of the art of ballet in an unequivocal way. The letter, printed under the title "Acrobatics and dancing," was translated from the Russian, which accounts for some of the idiosyncratic awkwardness:

The classical dance has never been and is not to-day the Russian Ballet. Its birthplace was France; it grew up in Italy, and has only been conserved in Russia. Side by side with the classical dance there always existed the national or character dance, which has given the evolution of the Russian Ballet. I do not know of a single classical

movement which was born of the Russian folk-dance. Why have we got to take our inspiration from the minuet of the French Court and not from the Russian village festival? That which apppears to you acrobatic is a dilettantic terminology for our national dance step. The mistake really, in fact, goes much deeper, because it is undoubtedly the Italian classical school which has introduced into the dance the acrobatic elements. The coarsest acrobatic tricks are the toe-dancing, the "Doubles tours en l'air," next to the classical "Pirouettes en dehors," and the hateful 32 "Fouettés," that is where acrobatics should be attacked. In the plastic efforts of Balanchine, in *The Prodigal Son*,[11] there are far less acrobatics than in the final classical *Pas de deux* of *Aurora's Wedding*. Monday next I am presenting to the public two new items. Lifar is, for the first time, in charge of the dances; he is the inventor of the choreography of the *Renard*, and it is there where really one has the first opportunity to talk of acrobatic ballet. It is not all Lifar's principle, but just because he could not see any other form to express the acrobatic music of Stravinsky. Stravinsky is, without doubt, the acrobat of sound, as Picasso is the acrobat of outline. Several constructive elements have introduced themselves into the field of acrobatics, and "Constructivisme" in painting, *décor*, music, and choreography is the craze of to-day. The forms change. In painting and in scenery this craze is finishing. But in music, where we were full of impressionism and neo-sentimentalism, and in choreography, where we paid reverence to the classical dance, "constructivisme" acquired an extraordinary strength . . . Lifar has the same sense of construction and the same dread of compromise [as Markevitch]. On the outside cover of the score of the *Renard* Stravinsky has written: "This *ballet* must be executed by buffoons, acrobats, or dancers." Lifar has taken dancers and real acrobats of the circus, and the task of the choreographist has been to combine the plastic of the circus and dance tricks, while Stravinsky compels the bass to sing with a female falsetto voice and expresses the sentimentality of the fox by the sounds of the cymballum of the restaurant. The public and the critics will probably be annoyed with my two young friends, but they are both "débutants," and they are not afraid of it.[12]

Diaghilev did not stifle the criticism, but rather fanned it, as the anonymous critic of *The Times* replied to the letter after seeing the performance: "To those who have said that his recent ballets have been acrobatic, not dancing, M. Diaghileff [sic] in his letter published in these columns on Saturday made the effective reply that classical dancing *en pointes* is itself acrobatic. Does not the word mean 'walking on tip-toe'? Last night at Covent Garden he carried the war into the enemy's camp. 'If you call my last novelties acrobatic,' he has said in effect, 'what will you call *Renard*?' The answer is 'a high-class circus.' There is no attempt to express an emotion or to weave a pattern of plastic beauty of line, and the story is consigned to four singers."[13] While this critic disapproved, another expressed the opposite point of view: "It is an action for clowns and acrobats and the present production is so successful because of the purely acrobatic treatment. The set is Larionow's [sic] and it leans strongly on the reality, if simplicity of its properties. The choreography is Lifar's and from the moment of the burlesque stalk of the cast across the stage, before the performance, to the finale which is a whirlwind of acrobatic tricks, the dancing expresses the very stuff of the music."[14] By common consent, though mostly, it must be said, by other members of the company who were jealous of Lifar's exalted position, the ballet was not a success. However, no one then expected that Diaghilev would be dead less than a month later. Lifar wrote his biography of Diaghilev ten years after his death; having begun his flight of fancy, it was easy for him to reach the conclusion that "the ballet proved an immense success and received a veritable ovation, to loud cries of Stravinsky, Stravinsky, Lifar. Stravinsky took the call with the artist and bowed. But the calls for Lifar went on increasing, drowning the applause."[15] It does not matter that he deceived himself. Stravinsky had the last word: "Nijinska's *Renard* was superior in every way to the 1929 revival, though the latter was ruined chiefly by some jugglers Diaghilev had borrowed from a circus—an idea of his that did not succeed at all."[16]

145   Sketch of the setting

Graphite and tempera and/or watercolor with black ink notations on paper mounted to board (sheet may be oiled or glazed)
20⅜ x 25⅞ in: 51 x 64.7 cm
Signed and inscribed in French and Russian lower left: "'Renard' / милому Серёже (молодому хореографу)/ на память от [illegible] / М. Аарионов / март 1929 / Иариж" ("To dear Seriozha (the young choreographer) as a souvenir from [illegible] M. Larionov, March 1929 Paris")
1933.493

Exhibitions: Paris 1929, No 32; London Claridge 1930, No 46; Paris 1930, No 68; London Tooth 1930, No 39; New York 1933, No 38; Chicago 1933, No 104; Northampton 1934, No 104; Hartford 1934; New Haven 1935; San Francisco 1935–6; Paris 1939, No 283; New York 1962; Eindhoven 1964, No 114; New York 1965–6, No 114 (illustrated p 54); New York 1966–7; Indianapolis 1969, No 359; Strasbourg 1969, No 359; Frankfurt-am-Main 1969, No 95; Amherst 1974; Chicago 1975, No 50; Hartford 1978–9; Coral Gables 1982; Basel 1984; Frankfurt-am-Main 1986, No 1803 (illustrated in color p 237); Columbus 1989; Worcester 1989.

This is not a design for the set, but rather an imaginative impression of part of the action at the beginning of the ballet, quite unrelated to the set as it was, as can be seen from the photograph. In technique, Larionov has kept to a child-like primitiveness and innocence, using the color of the paper as a monochrome background. Some might say this painting is just badly drawn and carelessly painted, but that would be ignoring its sophistication.

Notes

1 Igor Stravinsky, *Expositions and Developments*, pp 119–20.
2 Igor Stravinsky, *Conversations with Igor Stravinsky*, p 98.
3 *Le Mariage* was first performed at the Opéra, Paris on 18 May 1922, preceding the first performance of *Renard*.
4 *Bronislava Nijinska: a dancer's legacy*, exhibition catalogue, p 29.
5 Igor Stravinsky, *Memories and Commentaries*, p 40.
6 Soudeikine designed *La Tragédie de Salomé*. With music by Florent Schmitt, choreography by Boris Romanov, and Tamara Karsavina as Salomé, the ballet was first performed at the Théâtre des Champs-Elysées, Paris on 12 June 1913. He introduced Boris Kochno to Diaghilev.
7 Boris Kochno, *Diaghilev and the Ballets Russes*, p 179.
8 Serge Lifar, *Serge Diaghilev*, pp 493–4.
9 Richard Buckle, *Diaghilev*, p 518.
10 Serge Grigoriev *The Diaghilev Ballet*, p 260.
11 Produced at the same time (see pp 300–5).
12 Serge Diaghilev, "The Russian Ballet. Acrobatics and Dancing" in *The Times*, London 13 July 1929.
13 Anon, "Covent Garden: The Russian Ballet" in *The Times*, London, 16 July 1929, p 14.
14 Anon in *The Boulevardier* New York n.d., p 38.
15 Serge Lifar, *op cit*, p 501.
16 Igor Stravinsky, *Memories and Commentaries*, p 40.

Sur le Borysthène (On the Borysthène)

Choreographic poem in 2 scenes by Serge Lifar and
    Serge Prokofiev
Composer: Serge Prokofiev (Op. 57)
Conductor: Philippe Gaubert
Choreographer: Serge Lifar
Designer (sets): Michel Larionov
Designer (costumes): Nathalie Gontcharova
Principal Dancers:
    Serge: Serge Lifar
    Natacha: Camille Bos
    Olga: Suzanne Lorcia
    Olga's father: Férouelle
    Olga's fiancé: Nicolas Efimoff
First Performance: 16 December 1932, Théâtre
    national de l'Opéra, Paris

Synopsis

From the program, in which it was printed in both
English and French.

"I. The scene represents a plain near a village,
on the bank of the river Borysthene.

Natacha awaits the return of Serge whom she
loves and who comes back to the village after a
long absence.

Serge arrives and is welcomed by the young
villagers among whom is Olga. He falls in love with
Olga and she with him. Flirtation. Natacha has seen
Serge making love to Olga. Melancholy of Natacha.
Serge who becomes confused on seeing her tries to
comfort her. Return of Olga. Immediately Serge
rushes to meet her, leaving Natacha who goes
away sadly.

Display of affection between Olga and Serge
during which appear Olga's father and the fiancé
she is obliged to accept. The intrigue of the previous lovers is discovered and the friends of the new
fiancé swear to have their revenge.

Serge dances for Olga before his comrades,
and the girls of the village a dance of conquest.

Towards the end of the dance, in which the
onlookers join, Olga's father and fiancé together
with their friends arrive and they carry her off.

Natacha, hidden, has seen everything; she
announces to Serge the rape of Olga and promises
to help him find her.

II. The scene represents the courtyard of the
house of Olga's father.

The Fête.

The boys and girls of the village come to
celebrate Olga's engagement. They are welcomed
by Olga's father and fiancé and, according to
custom, Olga is surrounded by children. However,
her thoughts are far away; she is sad and thinks
only of Serge.

At the end of the ceremony, the men only, as is
customary, stay to feast the betrothed and Olga's
father.

They dance to give expression to their
jubilation.

The wine flows without stint.

Then Olga's father calls her to him and obliges
her to dance with her fiancé.

During the dance Serge, sullen and jealous,
watches his rival from a distance.

Half-hearted dance by Olga, during which the
guests, one by one, fall asleep. Olga laments.

Natacha, who has observed everything,
approaches, she calls Serge who comes forward
with his companions to deliver Olga.

There is a fight during which Olga's father and
the fiancé, helped by their friends, succeed in
overpowering Serge. They expel Serge's friends and
drive them away, leaving Serge who, they think, [is]
in a state of helplessness.

Natacha approaches Serge, tells him of her
sympathy and her disinterested affection and,
helped by her friends, she frees Serge.

Natacha then leads Serge to Olga, wishes them
happiness and urges them to flee. The two, much
affected, bid farewell to Natacha and go away
slowly. The poor Natacha watches them go away
slowly, remains alone, courageous, determined in
attitude, but weak and wounded in her feelings
and slowly she fades from sight in the darkness."

"Borysthene" is the classical name for the
Russian river Dnieper. *Sur le Borysthène*
was the fifth ballet choreographed by Serge
Lifar at the Paris Opéra where he was the
resident choreographer from 1930. After
Prométhée (see pp 306–10) in 1929, Lifar
choreographed, between February and May
1931, *Prélude dominical, L'Orchestre en Liberté*
(see pp 178–81), and *Bacchus et Ariane* (see
pp 172–75). He also claimed to revise some
of the choreography of *Giselle* (see pp
132–41), in which he performed the role of
Albrecht for the first time on 20 January
1932 with Olga Spessivtseva as Giselle.

Lifar, who had danced spectacularly in
Prokofiev's *Le Fils Prodigue* (see pp 300–5)
during the last season of the Ballets Russes
in 1929, commissioned Prokofiev in 1930 to
compose a new ballet—"a sort of autobio-
graphical choreography or a choreographical
autobiography entitled *Sur le Borysthène*."[1]

Serge Lifar has stated that the two main
female parts in *Sur le Borysthène* were
named Natacha and Olga after Nathalie
Paley[2] and Olga Spessivtseva while the
male part was called Serge to be played by
himself. Furthermore he wrote: "I was then
madly in love with Nathalie Paley and Olga
Spessivtseva did not fail to guess this."[3]
Lifar was writing in 1965 and so may be
forgiven this curious claim, more in the
nature of wish-fulfilment than a statement
of fact, as well as a reversal of the actual
plot line.

Rehearsals of the ballet began at the
beginning of 1932 in the Rotonde of the
Opéra. Lifar, describing a terrifying incident, continued: "Natacha was to be interpreted by Suzanne Lorcia. The drama
exploded during one of the rehearsals.
Spessivtseva realised with a dreadful shock
that in the ballet it was with Natacha that I
was to find happiness," and it was true that
in a moment of aberration during rehearsal

Spessivtseva "hurled herself towards the
open window. With one bound I also
reached the window, but she was already
on the other side. I just had time to clutch
her by the arms. My pianist Léonide
Gontcharov rushed up to join me . . . Olga
was hanging from our arms more than
thirty feet above the Place Garnier. With
enormous effort we managed to drag her in.
She struggled, she bit us, she did her best to
wriggle away from us. At one moment my
eyes met hers and I was appalled. We took
her home. She alternated between struggles
and delirious ramblings and then complete
apathy. The next day she did not turn up at
the rehearsal and sent word to Rouché[4] that
she was leaving the Opera for ever."[5] He
had clearly forgotten his own scenario.
Serge in fact deserts Natacha with her
selfless encouragement, while running away
with Olga. Lifar had also forgotten who was
playing whom: Spessivtseva was replaced
by Suzanne Lorcia, while Camille Bos was
Natacha.

Although the ballet took two years to
reach the stage Prokofiev composed it very
quickly, in a matter of weeks. He wrote:
"The music came easily to me and I enjoyed
writing it."[6] The score, similar in style to *The
Prodigal Son*, is written in a series of
episodic scenes invoking Russian folk and
popular melodies. To emphasize the Russianness of the production Lifar engaged
Larionov to design the sets and
Gontcharova the costumes. The intention
was to give the ballet a contemporary setting. The Russian collaborators were not yet
totally disenchanted with Soviet Russia, and
although Lifar, Larionov, and Gontcharova
would stay in France, Prokofiev was to
return. Lifar wrote that Larionov "made the
most of his modernism and his abstract
forms. But his conception was too advanced
for the public and . . . its real merit was not
appreciated."[7] Larionov designed two
stylized, "constructivist" settings within a
false proscenium, similar in style and color
to the one he had designed for *Renard*. But
instead of a setting for an historic fable,
Larionov designed a stylized setting with
an oil well and a farm for a contemporary
love story. After interviewing Larionov,
Frédéric Pottecher explained his intention:
"In his colors and decorative structures,
Larionov tries to combine human exertion
peculiar to the U.S.S.R. with the legendary
land of Russia, its sadness, its vastness, its
eternity. He has successfully evoked tradi-

tional Russia with a backcloth painted in graduated colors, and the Russia of Stalin with his constructions (the oil well and the peasant's house)."[8] He certainly succeeded. Furthermore, the costumes designed by Gontcharova were thought to be "both bold and classic."[9] The two designers were perfectly matched. This production had, as André Boll continued, "the most subtle and exceptional harmonies, and the most violent and least expected audacity, so that the whole, the set and costumes, was of the most appetizing originality."[10]

Lifar was right; André Boll was almost alone in giving great praise to the production. Most critics thought *Sur le Borysthène* merely dull. André Levinson, an astute and learned critic who had become a champion of Lifar, thought that the drama of the ballet

was "less in Natacha's sacrifice, Olga's thwarted loves, or Serge's tribulations than in the struggle between the composer of the dance and the composer of the music, because we see in this work the choreographer coming to grips with a recalcitrant score which is almost always contumacious to dance movement, even though it comes from the famous pen which put its name to *Le Pas d'Acier*[11] and *The Prodigal Son*."[12] Levinson hated the score, even though he approved of the fact that the composer, and indeed everyone concerned in the production, had avoided falling into a well of slavic folklore. Prokofiev, surprised by the reception, admitted a certain shortcoming but explained: "I attribute the cool reception given to *Sur le Borysthène* to the fact that I was too preoccupied with the subject matter

to pay sufficient attention to form. Originality of form is hardly less important for a composer than inner content. The great classics were also great innovators. True, the composer for whom originality of form takes precedence over content is working primarily against himself, for others will take his new ideas and clothe them with meaning and they, not he, will be writing for posterity. But equally unfortunate is the composer who is afraid of or incapable of originality, for whereas the creator of new harmonies is bound to be eventually acknowledged, the composer who has nothing new to offer will sooner or later be forgotten."[13]

The ballet was withdrawn from the repertory at the Opéra after a few performances, and was not repeated.

146 Design for the drop curtain (front cloth)

Charcoal, tempera and/or watercolor, white highlights and black ink notations on card stock
19¹¹/₁₆ x 24½ in: 49.2 x 61.3 cm
Signed lower right in watercolor: "M.L."
Signed and inscribed in Russian and French top
left: "Проэкт (project) Rideau pour Ballet de
Lifar / 'Au Bord du Borysthène' / M. Larionov 9-
XI-31 / Paris Opera"
1933.495

Exhibitions: New York 1933, No 40; Chicago 1933,
No 106; Northampton 1934, No 106; Hartford
1934; New Haven 1935; San Francisco 1935–6;
Williamsburg 1940; Elmira 1958, No 10;
Richmond 1959; Rowayton 1960; New York
1965–6, No 116 (illustrated p 55); New York
1966–7; Hartford 1978–9; Columbus 1989;
Worcester 1989.

As stated above, this ballet took two years to reach the stage from the time it was commissioned. The inscription on this design is dated more than a year before the production took place, and is called a "pro-ject" by the artist. It is therefore not the final version, but the yellow-green trees, the brown figures, and the pale blue sky are all in the color range Larionov used for his final overall design. Using as a basis certain familiar Russian folklore elements, Larionov has painted an almost abstract painting while still maintaining a recognizable land-scape: skeletal, disjointed trees, and dots for leaves. Only one female figure is discern-able. The two birds swooping are an origi-nal Larionov witticism adding fun to the painting.

147 Set design for scene 2: The courtyard

Graphite, tempera and/or watercolor, fabric, and
string on illustration board
False proscenium cut and painted on board (14⅜ x
25⅞ in: 36.5 x 64.7 cm), stuck on larger sheet
(28⅝ x 39 in: 72.6 x 99 cm) with painted edges
enlarged (to 17¹/₁₆ x 32¹³/₁₆ in: 45.2 x 82 cm),
and collage of cut canvas and loops of string
sewn on for roof, all laid over a sheet of
painted paper (21⅝ x 38³/₁₆ in: 54 x 98 cm)
The large (backcloth) sheet inscribed in ink bottom
right: "A Serge Lifar son ballet / 'Sur le Borysthène' à l'Opéra National / 16 Decembre 1932
Paris M. Larionov"
1933.496

Exhibitions: Chicago 1933, No 107; Northampton
1934, No 107; Hartford 1934; New Haven
1935; San Francisco 1935–6; Williamsburg
1940; New York 1965–6, No 117 (illustrated
p 55); New York 1966–7; Princeton 1968;
Hartford 1978–9.
Illustration: Parton, p 209 fig 206.
The different pieces of this design were originally
intended to be parts of a stage model. The
false proscenium and the backcloth were the
same for both scenes: the central frame was
changed and, as can be seen from the
photograph, other elements were used in
the actual set.

Right: scene 2, the courtyard,
on stage at the Opéra, Paris.

Notes

1 Serge Lifar, *Ma vie*, p 112.
2 The second daughter of Grand Duke Paul. The son of Alexander II had married for the second time morganatically Olga Valerianovna Karnovitch, who was given the title Princess Paley.
3 Serge Lifar, *op cit*, p 121.
4 Jacques Rouché (1862–1957) was Director of the Paris Opera 1914–44.
5 Serge Lifar, *op cit*, p 121. Lifar recounts the same incident in a slightly different and longer form in *Les Trois Grâces du XXᵉ Siècle*, pp 293–4. Spessivtseva continued to dance infrequently; she was finally put in an asylum in the United States in 1943. Astonishingly, in 1963 she recovered completely.
6 Serge Prokofiev, *Soviet Diary and other writings*, p 292.
7 Serge Lifar, "Les Magiciens du décor théâtral Russe" in Tatiana Loguine, *Gontcharova et Larionov*, p 126.
8 H.-Frédric Pottecher, "Dans un restaurant de la rive gauche avec Larionow [sic] fougueux décorateur et Mme Gontcharova" ("In a left bank restaurant with the impetuous designer Larionov and Mme Gontcharova") in *Comoedia*, Paris 17 December 1932.
9 André Boll, "Nouveau ballet à l'Opéra" in *La Volonté*, Paris 20 December 1932.
10 André Boll, *ibid*.
11 *Le Pas d'Acier*, ballet in two scenes by Serge Prokofiev and Georges Yakoulov, composed by Serge Prokofiev, with choreography by Leonide Massine, constructions and costumes by Georges Yakoulov, and principal dancers Lubov Tchernicheva, Alexandra Danilova, Leonide Massine, Serge Lifar, and Leon Woizikovsky was first performed on 7 June 1927 at the Théâtre Sarah-Bernhardt, Paris.
12 André Levinson, *Les Visages de la Danse*, p 149.
13 Serge Prokofiev, *op cit*, p 292.

Marie Laurencin

French
born 1885 Paris
died 1956 Paris

Les Biches (The House Party)

Ballet with songs in 1 act by Francis Poulenc
Composer: Francis Poulenc
Conductor: Edouard Flament
Designer (set and costumes): Marie Laurencin
Choreographer: Bronislava Nijinska
Principal Dancers:
    The Hostess: Bronislava Nijinska
    Girl in Blue: Vera Nemtchinova
    Girls in Grey: Lubov Tchernicheva,
       Lydia Sokolova
    Athletes: Anatole Wilzak, Leon Woizikovsky,
       Nicolas Zverev
Singers: Mme Romanitza, M Fouquet, M Cérésol
Company: Diaghilev's Ballets Russes
First Performance: 6 January 1924, Théâtre de
    Monte-Carlo

Synopsis

A plotless ballet, a suite of dances: *Rondeau,*
Chanson dansée, Adagietto, Jeu, Rag Mazurka,
Andantino, Chanson dansée, Final.

    The scenario as described by Poulenc: "This is
the theme: twelve women are attracted to three
men; but only one man responds, his choice falling
on a young person of equivocal appearance . . . A
lady no longer young but very wealthy and elegant
relies on her money to attach to herself the two
remaining young men, who seem to repel her
advances. A diversion is caused by two ladies,
outwardly as innocent as does, who appear on the
scene and altogether ignore the handsome males."

    Poulenc also stated: "*Les Biches* has no real
plot, for the good reason that if it had it might
have caused a scandal."[1]

"Diaghilev, the irreplaceable Diaghilev,
was a sorcerer, a magician. No sooner
had he achieved success than he would
burn what he had once worshipped (in
appearance at least) so as to keep pressing
ahead. So it was that from 1917 onwards,
smitten by everything to do with modern
art, he paired off painter and musician with
rare felicity. That's why he commissioned
me to do a ballet with Marie Laurencin."[2]
This is how Poulenc himself explained the
origin of *Les Biches*.[3] Apart from the misadventure of *The Sleeping Princess* (see pp
87–101), it is true that Diaghilev always
wanted to forge forwards, to be in advance
of fashion rather than set it. Furthermore, he
generally found that young artists were
more amenable to work with: being open-
minded, they too were eager to experiment.
Besides, everyone knew why Diaghilev so
liked young men, and the more cynical said
that they were also less expensive.

In May 1921 Poulenc was only twenty-
one when Diaghilev, no doubt at Cocteau's
invitation, heard the incidental music for *Le
Gendarme Incompris*, a play by Radiguet and
Cocteau, which prompted him to commission a ballet from the young composer.[4] In
fact, Poulenc had already begun a ballet
called *Les Demoiselles* (*The Girls*) to a scenario by Mme Germaine Bongard, sister of
Paul Poiret. But on 15 November 1921, just
before the first night of *The Sleeping Princess*,
Diaghilev, disconcerted, wrote to Poulenc:
"You tell me that I will be able to have the
piano score next October (?) and the orchestral score in December. As your letter was
written in November, I can only presume
that you are speaking of the year 1922;
consequently it will be a year before you are
ready, which is a long time and seems to be
in contradiction to the letter from Madame
Bongard in which she assures me that the
costumes are already partly finished."[5]
Poulenc worked slowly. The first title and
the original scenario were dropped. He later
explained: "Diaghilev having suggested
writing an atmospheric ballet for him, a sort
of modern *Les Sylphides*, he had had the idea
of a 1923 style 'fêtes galantes.'"[6] The deliberate connection with *Les Sylphides* was
superimposed after the event, but by July
1922 Poulenc had found a new title for his
ballet. As he was returning from the Bastille
in an open carriage he "suddenly yelled
'Why not *Les Biches*,' thus playing on the
animal nature of certain of Marie
Laurencin's women and also on the double
meaning of the word *biche* in the French
language."[7] At the same time, he wrote to
Stravinsky to say that he was "spending
long hours in the Bibliothèque nationale
looking for song texts,"[8] as he wanted his
score to incorporate seventeenth-century
French songs, set for an off-stage chorus.
Finding it very difficult to get in touch with
Diaghilev, Poulenc finally managed to track
him down and wrote to him on 24 September 1922: "I am hoping I can reach you
through Stravinsky to let you know that a
title for the ballet has been found: *Les Biches*.
It has so far met with general approval—
I hope it will have yours. It is absolutely
Marie Laurencin." He then described his
progress with the different numbers in the

ballet, ending his letter with "The *Rag-
Mazurka* (V) is terrifying. Tell la Nijinska
that she can start thinking of some frenetic
movements in triple time ."[9]

    So, by this time, it had been agreed that
Bronislava Nijinska would be responsible
for the choreography and Marie Laurencin
for the design. Boris Kochno states that
Diaghilev was at first rather dubious about
entrusting the choreography to Nijinska;
she had previously only choreographed
Russian works, and he "feared she might be
unresponsive to the Latin charm of the
Poulenc score."[10] Indeed, the first reports
Diaghilev received were not encouraging.
However, after he had seen some of the
work in progress Diaghilev wrote to
Kochno: "The choreography has delighted
and astonished me . . . Here and there her
choreography is perhaps a bit too ordinary,
a bit too *feminine*, but, *on the whole*, it is very
good. The dance for the three men has come
out extremely well, and they perform it
with bravura—weightily, like three cannon.
It doesn't at all resemble *Noces*, any more
than Tchaikovsky's *Eugene Onegin* resembles
his *Queen of Spades*."[11] Nijinska followed no
particular plot line, but invented a series of
scintillating dances to Poulenc's numbers,
episodes portraying the risqué and glamorous society of post-war Paris. Cyril Beaumont, refusing to be shocked, described the
action rather coyly: "The ballet was built up
on the reactions of the various groups—the
girls who flirted with the youths; the youth
who was attracted by the girl in blue velvet;
two young men who seemed to find their
own company sufficient; two young girls
who appeared to be very dear friends; and
the wiles of the enterprising hostess. This
artificial hothouse atmosphere provoked the
strangest emotions, although they were
masked by an affected and nervous air of
frivolous gaiety."[12] (According to Anton
Dolin, Nijinska always wanted to cut the
dance for the two young girls, but Poulenc
always refused.)

    Les Biches was a completely original
ballet which people, in their search for an
appropriate label, found difficult to classify.
It became known as one of the first "neo-
classical" ballets. But a few years after the
first performance Nijinska herself gave a

more accurate (and revealing) definition: "Some regarded *Les Biches* as a complete break with the old classicism. Others saw in that composition a return to it. As a matter of fact, *Les Biches* was the 'classical dance of our time.' *Les Biches* is Taglioni's *Sylphide* and *Giselle* of our own epoch of dancing. In its form and rhythm *Les Biches* reflected modern life. Yet *Les Biches*, like everything else created by me, has been raised on the basis of the classical dance. But the choreographic discovereies of this ballet in its design of movement, in the bodily forms and the new dancing rhythms, previously foreign to the classical ballet—have enriched the technique of the classical dance and have thereby created for the classical dance new expressions and forms."[13] Whatever definition of the choreographic style may be correct, the most seductive and provocative element of the ballet was its sexual ambiguity. Its charm successfully prevented it from being shocking. Jean Cocteau thought that, in *Les Biches,* "Madame Nijinska achieved greatness without intending to. She was protected by the absence of theme and by the apparent lightness of the musical style. The beauty and the melancholy of *Les Biches* is not in any way contrived."[14]

A large part of the charm and melancholy was due to Marie Laurencin's designs. By the beginning of the 1920s Laurencin had developed a new palette of colors—pale blues, pinks, and greens set against grays and blacks—which reflected her mood of lyrical pensiveness. The hint of sexual ambiguity in her fantasy world appealed to Diaghilev: dreamlike women staring with visionless eyes, standing in indeterminate landscapes among prancing hinds. He must have seen her exhibition in Paris at the Rosenberg Gallery in 1921 and, agreeing with Poulenc, thought that her refined feminine art would provide the right decoration for his ballet. But Laurencin caused endless problems for the scene painter, Prince Schervashidze, and the costume maker, Vera Soudeikine[15] because her drawings and instructions were impossibly imprecise. Boris Kochno, who was acting as go-between, described what happened: "When she saw the set that Schervashidze had executed in scrupulous accord with her design, Laurencin had him change it, but then, disappointed in the outcome, she went back to the original version. When Mme. Soudeikine shipped the costumes from Paris, she warned Diaghilev that they bore no relation to the sketches he had

approved because when they were being made, Laurencin, accompanied by Misia Sert, had constantly come to supervise the work and had completely altered them."[16] Schervashidze and Soudeikine must have had the patience of saints, especially as no one unconnected with the production knew of their frustrations, and Laurencin was in the end given all the praise. Her front cloth of horses, hinds, and ladies in blues and grays with a splash of pink was raised to reveal a simple set in pale pastel shades. Described by Beaumont: "It represented a lounge in an expensive ultra-modern seaside villa. There were pale grey walls, a large window draped with pinkish-blue curtain, and, beneath the window, a lavender-blue settee."[17] The costumes matched, complementing the gentle colors of the set.

Laurencin was not the only one to make changes to the original designs. When Vera Nemtchinova, as the Girl in Blue, appeared at a dress rehearsal in front of Diaghilev wearing a long blue velvet coat, he yelled for a pair of scissors. According to Richard Buckle: "He cut away the collar, to make a wide V-neck. He cut away the velvet, till it barely covered the buttocks. Nemtchinova had never shown so much leg before (what ballerina had?) and she protested. 'I feel naked!' 'Then go and buy yourself some white gloves!' said Diaghilev. The celebrated white gloves became almost part of the choreography."[18]

Although some "prudish shareholders in the Société [des Bains de Mer de Monaco] were scandalized by Nemtchinova's costume"[19] the ballet had an appreciative reception. Florence Grenfell wrote in her diary: "Sunday 6th January: We all went on afterwards to see the new Ballet *Les Biches* it had a grt: success. H.R.H. [the Duke of Connaught] was enthusiastic. Nijinska was a marvel in it, & the three men in it Leon, Zverev, & Wilzak danced too beautifully."[20] Poulenc was overjoyed and wrote to say so to Paul Collaer, a Belgian musicologist and pianist, and promoter of modern music: "Here at last is my news, and good news. The première of *Les Biches* was, if I may venture to say so, a triumph. There were eight curtain-calls which is *rarissime* [exceedingly rare] for Monte Carlo. One has to admit that Nijinska's choreography is of such beauty that even your old roulette-addicted English lady cannot resist it. It is the very essence of dance. And the *mise au point* is impeccable. Can you imagine, there were no less than 72 rehearsals—about 250 hours of work. That is the way to get

results. The sets, the curtain, the costumes, are a total success. I am really longing for you to see it. As for the music, although it is not exactly modest to say so, I won't hide the fact that I am very pleased with my orchestration. It has a brilliance and, I believe, a very personal range of colour."[21] He does not mention that Diaghilev had cut the off-stage chorus and used only three singers instead of the intended four, avowedly for artistic reasons but actually for economy's sake.

Objective critics had differing views of *Les Biches*. Some shared the public's enthusiasm, as for example the anonymous "Sitter Out:" "Of all the ultra-modern ballets there is not one which I enjoy so much. It always seems to me to be an extraordinarily clever satire on the sexual life of to-day in certain sets, and the dancing is brilliant in the extreme."[22] Victor Glover, on the other hand, wrote: "*Les Biches*, which is persistently given, is a ballet of very little merit. A little hopping about, some skirmishing and ungainly posing only bore one and make one wonder if the Russian craze is not more than a little passé."[23] One can take one's pick, and side with one or the other; but the lasting quality of *Les Biches* is undeniable.

148 Design for the cover of *Théâtre Serge de Diaghilew: Les Biches*

Graphite and tempera or watercolor on paper
10⅜ x 8⁵⁄₁₆ in: 26.4 x 21 cm
Signed in pencil lower right: "Marie Laurencin"
Inscribed in watercolor top: "Les Biches"
1933.497

Exhibitions: Paris 1930, No 74; ? New York 1933, No 41 (described as "Costumes for *Les Biches* 1924" but not identified); Chicago 1933, No 108; Northampton 1934, No 108; Hartford 1934; New Haven 1935; Paris 1939, No 292; Williamsburg 1940; New York 1941–2; Edinburgh 1954, No 342; London 1954–5, No 374; Elmira 1958, No 8 (?); Indianapolis 1959, No 369 (described as "Costume, Fox"); Hartford 1964; New York 1965–6, No 118 (illustrated p 56); New York 1966–7; Princeton 1968; Strasbourg 1969, No 397 (illustrated No 95); Frankfurt-am-Main 1969, No 112; Hartford 1974; Hempstead 1974, No 104; Chicago 1975, No 53; New York 1980; Coral Gables 1982; New York 1986, No 68; Columbus 1989; Worcester 1989.
Illustration: Rischbieter, p 124a.

This is not a costume design, as previously catalogued, but a project design for the cover of a limited edition, luxury souvenir portfolio in two volumes, which was published in Paris on 20 May 1924. Edited by Boris Kochno, volume I contains texts by Jean Cocteau and Darius Milhaud, a caricature of Nijinska by Cocteau, a portrait of Francis Poulenc by Marie Laurencin, and fourteen reproductions of her drawings and designs. Volume II contains photographs of the dancers in costume.[24]

This drawing is based on the actual costume for the Three Boys who were danced by Anatole Vilzak, Leon Woizikovsky, and Nicolas Zverev. Their costumes were tight blue shorts to the top of the thigh, and white and blue striped singlets with white sashes tied across the body over the right shoulder. Laurencin's costume design, on the other hand (illustrated as plate 10 in volume I of the portfolio), shows tight shorts to the top of the knee and the sash over the left shoulder.[25] Furthermore, the pose in this drawing is based exactly on a photograph of two of the dancers, Leon Woizikovsky and Nicolas Zverev, which could only have been taken shortly before or after the first night (illustrated in volume II of the portfolio).

Presumably Laurencin thought to give the dancer a deer-like mask and a doe-skin body in order to illustrate the title of the ballet. This suggested cover, however, was not used. Instead, the cover of the publication, more appropriately, is a reproduction of a watercolor of two girls in pastel colors holding hands, with a hind between them.

149 Costume design for a guest

Crayon and ink on translucent paper
10½ x 8³⁄₁₆ in: 26.6 x 20.9 cm
Signed in crayon bottom left: "M. L."
Inscribed in pencil lower left: "Narcisse"
Reverse inscribed in pencil: "11," "No 6," "382/690"
1933.498

Exhibitions: ? New York 1933, No 41 (described as "Costumes for *Les Biches* 1924" but not identified); Chicago 1933, No 109; Northampton 1934, No 109; Hartford 1934; New Haven 1935; San Francisco 1935–6; Paris 1939, No 293 ; Williamsburg 1940; Edinburgh 1954, No

343; London 1954–5, No 375; Indianapolis 1959, No 370; Storrs 1963; Hartford 1964; New York 1965–6, No 119 (illustrated p 56); New York 1966–7; Strasbourg 1969, No 398; Frankfurt-am-Main 1969, No 113; Hartford 1974; Hempstead 1974, No 103; Hartford 1978-9; Columbus 1989; Worcester 1989.
Illustration: Rischbieter, p 124c.

This is a first sketch design for one of the guests. It is not a good costume design; nor is it like any of the actual finished costumes for any of the guests, although it relates to a pencil and crayon drawing reproduced in volume I of the portfolio (see above) of a girl coming out of a gazebo. She is the same girl, but her arms are the other way round.

Laurencin must have had an accident with the ink, which she then tried to incorporate into the design as a long train, but the costume of the guests had neither a train nor a tutu striped in this crude fashion. The plain skirt fell below the knee, but there was a delicately striped sash tied round the waist. Peter Williams described the effect of seeing the costumes: "the first thing that hits you when the curtain rises is of ladies dressed in pink. But, and this is important, the pinks are not all the same— the difference is slight but it is enough to give the total effect a certain texture and lack of monotony."[26]

Although this drawing has a slight bearing on the costumes in *Les Biches,* the inscription "Narcisse" is inexplicable unless it refers to the color. Laurencin drew a similar figure with a similar inscription "Beige."

150 Two girls with a dog

Graphite and ink, tempera or watercolor on paper mounted to board
10⅞ x 10⅝ in: 27.5 x 26.5 cm
Signed in pencil bottom right: "Marie Laurencin"
1933.499

Exhibitions: Paris 1930, No 75; London Tooth 1930, No 40; ? New York 1933, No 41 (described as "Costumes for *Les Biches* 1924" but not identified); Chicago 1933, No 110; Northampton 1934, No 110; Hartford 1934; New Haven 1935; San Francisco 1935–6; Paris 1939, No 294; New York 1941–2; New York MoMA 1944; Minneapolis 1953; Edinburgh 1954, No 344; London 1954–5, No 376; Michigan 1957; Indianapolis 1959, No 371; Storrs 1963; Hartford 1964; New York 1965–6, No 120 (illustrated p 57); New York 1966–7; Princeton 1968; Strasbourg 1969, No 399; Frankfurt-am-Main 1969, No 114; Hartford 1973; Hartford 1974; Hartford 1978–9; Coral Gables 1982; Hartford 1988; Worcester 1989.

Illustrations: Buckle 1955, p 104 No 134; Haskell, p 94; Rischbieter, p 124c; Pozharskaya and Volodina, p 237.

The previous catalogue of this collection states: "According to Lifar this is for *Les Biches*." Did Lifar think that the dog was a doe? These two girls are not like any of the characters in the ballet. Their costumes and headdresses are different from anything worn by the dancers. The catalogue for Chicago 1933, however, describes this as "Esquisse de costume" without ascribing it to any production.

This painting is in a similar style to Laurencin's other work of the early 1920s, when she painted melancholy women accompanied by animals, the two worlds united in some sad but secret and peaceful bond.[27] Is this a young widow stretching out an arm to seek comfort from a friend? The only connection with *Les Biches* is that the souvenir portfolio referred to above (No 118) also contains several watercolor drawings which, being neither set nor costume designs, are dreamlike images expressing Laurencin's private symbolism.

1   "Francis Poulenc on his Ballets" in *Ballet* Vol 2 No 4, London September 1946, p 57.

2   Francis Poulenc, *My Friends and Myself*, p 43.

3   The title means literally "the does" or "the hinds," and in slang "the girls" or "the kept women." However, when the French title is not used, the usual (unsatisfactory) English title is "The House Party."

4   Poulenc had met Diaghilev at Misia Sert's in 1919. In a letter dated 28 April 1919 Poulenc thanks Diaghilev and agrees to work on a ballet with Massine, but nothing came of this project. Letter in I. S. Zilberstein and V. A. Samkov, *Sergei Diaghilev* Vol 2, p 129.

5   Serge Diaghilev, letter dated 15 November 1921 from Savoy Hotel, London, quoted in Francis Poulenc, *Correspondence*, p 43.

6   Francis Poulenc, *Entretiens avec Claude Rostand*, quoted in Nancy van Norman Baer, *Bronislava Nijinska: a dancer's legacy*, p 47.

7   Francis Poulenc to Claude Rostand, quoted in Francis Poulenc, *Correspondence*, p 334. See also note 1 for meanings of *biche*.

8   Francis Poulenc, *ibid*, p 52.

9   Francis Poulenc, *ibid*, p 55.

10 Boris Kochno, *Diaghilev and the Ballets Russes*, p 206.

11 Serge Diaghilev to Boris Kochno, quoted in Boris Kochno, *ibid*, p 206.

12 Cyril W. Beaumont, *The Diaghilev Ballet in London*, p 246. Anton Dolin, in "*Les Biches*: A misconception" in *The Dancing Times*, London February 1980, p 323, wrote that the hostess "could have been the late Dowager Lady St Just [Florence E. Grenfell]. In the days when *Les Biches* was made, in 1924, she was one of Diaghilev's closest English friends, chic, elegant and very *knowing*. It could have been the equally elegant, chic and alluring Daisy Fellowes, another great admirer of the great man Diaghilev."

13 Bronislava Nijinska, "Reflections about the production of *Les Biches* and *Hamlet* in Markova-Dolin Ballets" in *The Dancing Times*, London February 1937, pp 618–9.

14 Jean Cocteau, *Théâtre de Serge de Diaghilew: Les Biches*.

15 Later Stravinsky's second wife.

16 Boris Kochno, *op cit*, p 207.

17 Cyril W. Beaumont, *op cit*, p 245.

18 Richard Buckle, *Diaghilev*, p 420.

19 Boris Kochno, *op cit*, p 207.

20 Florence E. Grenfell, unpublished diaries, Monte Carlo 6 January 1924.

21 Francis Poulenc, *op cit* (from Monte Carlo, Tuesday [8 January 1924]), p 68.

22 "Sitter Out" in *The Dancing Times*, London August 1927, p 498.

23 Victor Glover in unidentified American newspaper, dateline Paris 27 May [1926].

24 See Bibliography under Jean Cocteau. A companion volume on *Les Fâcheux* was published at the same time.

25 The design became the property of Boris Kochno and is illustrated in color in his book *Diaghilev and the Ballets Russes*, 203. The design was also illustrated in *Dance and Dancers*, London August 1991, p 15.

26 Peter Williams, "Decor: *Les Biches*" in *Dance and Dancers*, London January 1965, p 17.

27 Such paintings as *La Chevauchée ou les Amazones* (1921), *La Visite* (1921), *Jeunes filles dans la forêt* (1922), *Deux femmes avec biche* (1923), and several called merely *Les Biches* (1923–4).

Fernand Léger

French
born 1881 Argentan (Orne)
died 1955 Gif-sur-Yvette (Essonne)

151   Two female nudes

Ink with graphite notation on paper
13 x 8¹/₁₆ in: 32.9 x 20.7 cm
Signed and dated very indistinctly in ink lower
    right: "F. Leger / 1912"
Reverse inscribed in pencil: "(2274)," "Leger
    dessin," stamped: "Douane Centrale Paris,"
    "CSLHLAVNICELNIURADITR PRAHA 4a"
1933.502

Exhibitions: London Tooth 1930, No 44; Chicago
    1933, No 113; Northampton 1934, No 113;
    Hartford 1934; New Haven 1935; San Francisco
    1935–6; Michigan 1957; Indianapolis 1959, No
    379; Vancouver 1964; New York 1965–6, No
    122 (illustrated p 58); New York 1966–7;
    Princeton 1968; Hartford 1973; Hartford 1974;
    Hempstead 1974, No 104; Hartford 1988;
    Worcester 1989.

Léger admitted that "Cézanne taught me
the love of shapes and volumes; he
made me concentrate on drawing. I realized
then that drawing should be rigid and not
at all sentimental."[1]

Léger was trained as an architect's
draughtsman, but before the First World
War he preferred to spend time drawing the
female nude in life classes at the Académie
Jullian in Paris and other private academies
rather than offical art schools. He gradually
developed his drawing style: from simple,
objective, life studies his nudes became
elaborate but stylized, geometric figures. As
Léger destroyed most of his drawings up to
1909, this must be considered as an early
work in his developing Cubist style. Unlike
Picasso and Braque, who broke up surfaces
into different facets, Léger maintained a
sense of volume and solidity in his Cubism.
The hatching is also a characteristic technique, and can be seen repeated in drawing
No 153.

152 The Trench Diggers

Ink, tempera and/or watercolor and red glaze on
    paper
12½ x 10¼ in: 31.8 x 26.2 cm (maximum)
Signed and inscribed in ink bottom right: "12–16 /
    Verdun / Le[s] foreurs (the trench diggers) /
    F. Leger"
Reverse signed in pencil: "L Vignoto"
1933.500

Exhibitions: London Tooth 1930, No 43; Chicago
    1933, No 111; Northampton 1934, No 111;
    Hartford 1934; New Haven 1935; San Francisco
    1935–6; Michigan 1957; Indianapolis 1959,
    ? No 377; Hartford 1965, No 27; New York
    1965–6, No 123 (illustrated p 58); New York
    1966–7; Princeton 1968; Hartford 1974; Frank-
    furt-am-Main 1986; Hartford 1988; Worcester
    1989.

Léger was called up into the army as a
sapper with the general mobilization on
1 August 1914. In 1915 he was sent to the
front at Argonne; in the autumn and winter
of 1916 he took part in the battle of Verdun;
in the spring of 1917 he was gassed on the
Aisne front, hospitalized at Villepinte near
Paris, and invalided out of the army in
January 1918. He felt that "it was during the
war that I put my feet on the ground,"[2] and
that he learnt more at the Front than in his
whole life. "It was the four years of war
which thrust me abruptly into a blinding
reality totally new to me . . . I discovered
the French people. At the same time, I was
dazzled by the open breech of a 75 mm gun
in full sunlight, the magic spell of light on
white metal. It needed nothing less than this
to make me forget the abstract art of
1912–13. It was a complete eye-opener for
me, both as a man and as a painter."[3]

From July 1915 to December 1916 Léger
made many drawings, quick sketches in
quiet moments, never detailed or finished
compositions, on any scrap of paper that
came to hand. They were usually done in
pencil, sometimes overlaid with pen and
ink, sometimes only in pen and ink, occasionally heightened with gouache, as in this
drawing. They are a unique record by a
French soldier at the Front during the First
World War. As Jean Leymarie has commented: "Other good painters have conjured up the atmosphere at a distance, at the
rear or even in the studio; but Léger's
drawings are records made on the spot,
with an intense immediacy."[4] The intensity
and the closeness, however, make them
sometimes obscure and difficult to "read."
The drawings fall into several groups of
subjects: sappers at work or playing cards,[5]
field kitchens, wagons. The human element

gradually gave way to the mechanical or,
rather, became absorbed in a pictorial synthesis in which neither element is immediately identifiable. As Léger wrote later:
"Perhaps my experiences at the Front and
the daily contact with machines led to the
change which marked my painting between
1914 and 1918."[6]

Between October and December 1916
Léger worked on a project called *Les Foreurs*
(the word literally means "drillers," but
here means "trench diggers" or possibly
"tunnelers"), for which he made at least six
drawings. Of the known drawings, apart
from this one, four are reproduced in Douglas Cooper's *Fernand Léger: Dessins de
Guerre*,[7] and one is in the collections of the
Museum of Modern Art, New York.[8] This
one, along with the MoMA drawing of the
same date, makes it one of the last in the
series when Léger had established the
composition, and had already defined the
volumes by his use of wash. These studies,
however, never led to a finished painting.

On 9 March 1917 Léger wrote to his
friend, Louis Poughon, from Champagne:
"I have just sold a pre-war painting and two
Verdun drawings to Diaghilev, the organiser
of the Ballets Russes. He is an important
collector and I am very happy to be in his
collection. When Diaghilev is in Paris with
his troupe, we can go and see them in the
director's box! That's always a pleasure.
Diaghilev is a kind of perfect European. He
likes my painting a lot and definitely wants
to get to know me. It could be a good
thing."[9]

Diaghilev got to know Léger through
Gontcharova and Larionov when they were
in Paris just before the war. He kept this
drawing, and it was acquired by Serge Lifar
after his death. He gave the other drawing,
La Rue Marzel, to Leonide Massine; it was
sold by Sotheby's on 1 March 1980 at the
sale of part of Massine's collection. The
whereabouts of the painting to which Léger
referred are not known.

Léger probably hoped to work for
Diaghilev, but in spite of his hopes he never
designed a ballet for him, no doubt because
he designed two productions for the Ballets
Suédois (see No 154), which Diaghilev
considered to be a rival company.

153 Two figures, c. 1920–21

Ink with graphite notation on paper with
    embossed canvas pattern
10⁹⁄₁₆ x 8¹⁄₄ in: 26.9 x 21 cm
Signed in ink lower right: "F. L."
Inscribed in pencil bottom right: "36"
Reverse inscribed in pencil: "Leger dessin," "No 5,"
    and stamped: "Douane Centrale. Paris," and
    "CSLHLAVNICELNIURADITR PRAHA 4a"
1933.501

Exhibitions: London Tooth 1930, No 45; Chicago
    1933, No 112; Northampton 1934, No 112;
    Hartford 1934; New Haven 1935; San Francisco
    1935–6; Detroit 1948; New York 1965–6, No
    121 (illustrated p 58); New York 1966–7;
    Hartford 1974; Amherst 1974; Columbus 1989;
    Worcester 1989.

From his war drawings, from about 1917,
Léger entered a mechanical period,
becoming inspired by industrial and
mechanical objects. In 1919 he wrote in a
letter: "I have used mechanical elements a
lot in my pictures these last two years; my
present method is adapting itself to this,
and I find in it an element of variety and
intensity. The modern way of life is full of
such elements for us; we must know how to
use them. Every age brings with it some
new elements which should serve us; the
great difficulty is to *translate* them into
plastic terms and avoid the error of Futurism."[10] But by 1919 Léger was again beginning to introduce the human form,
recognizable but diagrammatic and integrated with its surroundings. Technically,
these drawings are more precisely delin-
eated and shaded than the war drawings.
Léger expressed his attitude to the human
form in a statement he made in 1936: "For
me the human figure, the human body is no
more important than keys or bicycles. That's
true. For me they are objects valuable for
their artistic potentiality and disposable
according to my will. That is why in the
development of my work from 1905 to the
present day, the human figure has stayed
intentionally *inexpressive*."[11]

In this drawing, however, Léger seems
to belie his own statement. The conventional male figure on the left, holding the
(glass?) door open, has a definite expression
of wide-eyed curiosity, whereas the distorted, naked female figure, trying to prevent the other from seeing, has an
expression of nervous anxiety. Has someone
come to disturb the lovers? There are also
still life elements introduced here which
went on to form Léger's purist phase from
1923–26. The hatching technique has been

refined to essential lines, giving a sense of
volume to the shapes. Léger used the same
technique in a preparatory drawing for his
painting *Figures in a city*, so this too may
have been a preparatory drawing for a
projected painting.

Notes

1 Quoted by Jean Leymarie in Jean Cassou and
    Jean Leymarie, *Fernand Léger: Drawings and
    gouaches*, p 20.
2 Fernand Léger, quoted in Douglas Cooper,
    Fernand Léger: Dessins de Guerre (unpaginated).
3 Fernand Léger, *ibid*.
4 Jean Cassou and Jean Leymarie, *Fernand Léger:
    Drawings and gouaches*, p 34.
5 Léger later worked this up into the painting *The
    Card Game*, 1919.
6 Fernand Léger quoted in Douglas Cooper, *op cit*.
7 Douglas Cooper, *op cit*, plates 1, 18, 19, 20.
8 Museum of Modern Art No 142.44 (14⅛ x 10⅜
    in: 35.9 x 26.3 cm). The watercolor drawing has
    the same inscription and date.
9 Fernand Léger, *Une Correspandance de Guerre*,
    letter 33, p 77.
10 Fernand Léger in a letter to D. H. Kahnweiler
    dated 11 December 1919, quoted in Jean Cassou
    and Jean Leymarie, *Fernand Léger: Drawings and
    gouaches*, p 45.
11 Fernand Léger, quoted in René Jullian, *Fernand
    Léger*, p 36, from *La querelle du réalisme* (Paris
    1936).

La Création du Monde (The Creation of the World)

Ballet nègre[1] (negro ballet) in 1 act by Blaise
    Cendrars[2]
Composer: Darius Milhaud
Conductor: Désiré-Emile Inghelbrecht
Choreographer: Jean Börlin
Designer (set and costumes): Fernand Léger
Principal Dancers:
    Man: Jean Börlin
    Woman: Ebon Strandin
Company: Les Ballets Suédois
First Performance: 25 October 1923, Théâtre des
    Champs-Elysées, Paris

Synopsis

From the program:

"1. The curtain slowly rises on a dark stage. In the middle of the stage, we see a confused mass of intertwined bodies: chaos prior to creation. Three giant deities move slowly round the periphery. These are Nzame, Medere and N'kva, the masters of creation. They hold counsel together, circle round the formless mass, and utter magic incantations.

"2. There is movement in the central mass, a series of convulsions. A tree gradually begins to grow, gets taller and taller, rising up straight, and when one of its seeds falls to the ground, a new tree sprouts. When one of the tree's leaves touches the ground, it lengthens, swells, rocks back and forth, begins to walk, becomes an animal. An elephant hanging in mid-air, a creeping tortoise, a crab, monkeys sliding down from the ceiling. The stage has gradually become lighter in the course of creation, and with each new animal it is brilliantly illuminated.

"3. Each creature, with a dancer bursting from its center, evolves in its own individual way, takes a few steps, then gently begins to move in a circle, gradually gathering speed as it revolves round the three initial deities. An opening appears in the circle, the three deities utter fresh incantations, and we see the formless mass seething. Everything vibrates. A monstrous leg appears, backs quiver, a hairy head emerges, arms are extended. All of a sudden, two torsos straighten, cling together: this is man and woman, suddenly upright. They recognise one another; they come face to face.

"4. And while the couple perform the dance of desire, followed by the mating dance, all the formless beings that remained on the ground stealthily creep up and join in the round dance, leading it at a frenetic, dizzy pace. They are the N'guils, the invokers, the sorcerers and sorceresses, the fetishists.

"5. The round's frenzy abates; it checks and slows and fades right out. The figures disperse in little groups. The couple stand apart in an embrace which lifts them up in a wave. Spring has arrived."

The Ballets Suédois were founded in 1920 by Rolf de Maré, a rich Swedish aristocrat and inveterate traveller, who was passionately interested in modern art, folklore and dance. His collection included works by Picasso, Braque, and Léger. He created the company for Jean Börlin (1893–1930), dancer and choreographer, who had been taught by Fokine and chosen by him to be a soloist at the Swedish Royal Opera ballet. When de Maré failed to start his company in opposition to the Royal Opera in Stockholm, he chose Paris as his center instead.[3] He engaged Jacques Hébertot as his administrative director, who suggested calling the company Les Ballets Suédois in imitation of Diaghilev's Les Ballets Russes. It had two aims: to create contemporary, extremely avant-garde works, and to adapt and revise Swedish folklore to the twentieth century. The second aim was submerged by the first, with the company's repertory becoming "a sort of laboratory for aesthetic experiences." The ballets were all created at the Théâtre des Champs-Elysées[4] and then toured in France and abroad. The company lasted five years, during which time it created twenty-four ballets,[5] all with choreography by Jean Börlin, with a total of 2,678 performances. After the summer break in 1925, de Maré stopped the company.

The interest in black African art rapidly revived in France after the First World War, so much so that the Louvre held a serious enquiry as to whether it should collect it or not. The dealer Paul Guillaume was already asking and getting huge prices for African sculpture.[6] In 1919 he arranged the first exhibition of African and Oceanic art at the Devambez Gallery in Paris, and on 10 June, at the suggestion of Blaise Cendrars, he organised a *Fête nègre* at the Théâtre des Champs-Elysées. In March 1920 Jean Börlin performed a solo dance, *Sculpture nègre*, in a black African mask and costume in the form of a sculpture at the same theater in a setting by Paul Colin. In the same year Carl Einstein published his book *Negerplastik* illustrated with a hundred plates of African sculpture. In 1921 Blaise Cendrars published his *Anthologie Nègre* of African myths and legends based on his intensive studies.

In a letter dated 29 October 1921 Cendrars suggested to Léger, who was then designing *Skating Rink*[7] for the Ballets Suédois, that he approach de Maré with the idea of staging a "negro ballet" on the theme of the ancient African theory of the creation of the world. This was at variance with the Judaeo-Christian theory, while sharing some essential traits. The idea was accepted, but it was nearly a year later, on 12 September 1922, that Léger wrote to de Maré: "I should like to know what the position is with Börlin regarding the *negro ballet*. You know that we are thinking of creating an important and extremely *studied* work. It should be the only possible negro ballet in the whole world and one which will remain a model of its kind. This means a number of scrupulously careful meetings between Cendrars, Börlin and me. As for the composer (a very important choice), it is difficult to approach too young and inexperienced an artist. In the end we think that Milhaud is the only one among the present French composers capable of realizing this. We have thought of Satie, but he is working for Hébertot and I do not think it would be possible . . . When do you think of staging this ballet? You must understand that we need time (probably have to go to London, the British Museum, for documentation on masks)." In a further letter dated 1 October Léger wrote: "We see only Darius Milhaud as the composer . . . This ballet needs a *lot of care*, and we have to get on with it as soon as possible. When is it to be for? What does Börlin think of Cendrars' scenario? Do answer these questions so that we know where we stand."[8] The letters had the desired effect. Milhaud was commissioned to compose the score, and the three collaborators worked very closely together while keeping Börlin informed of their ideas and plans. In the end, Léger did not feel the need to visit the British Museum, but drew most of his inspiration for the costumes and masks from the plates in two books—Carl Einstein's *Negerplastik* and Marius de Zayas's *African Negro Art: Its influence on Modern Art*. He did not copy what he saw, but adapted the shapes and forms to his "mechanical" style. Milhaud explained that "Léger wanted to adapt primitive Negro art and paint the drop-curtain and the scenery with African divinities expressive of power and darkness. He was never satisfied that his sketches were terrifying enough. He showed me one for the curtain, black on a dark brown background, which he had rejected on the grounds that it was too bright and 'pretty-pretty.' He would have liked to use skins representing flowers, trees, and animals of all kinds, which would have been filled with gas and allowed to fly up into the air at the moment of creation, like so many balloons. This plan could not be adopted because it would have required a complicated apparatus for inflating them in each corner of the stage, and the sound of the gas would have drowned out the music. He had to be satisfied with drawing his inspiration from the animal costumes worn by African dancers during their religious rites."[9] At first, Léger wanted to confine his color range to the three traditional African colors of white, black, and red ochre, but he later increased the number of colors to include blue, yellow, and green. For practical reasons, he simplified the technicalities of the set and costumes while maintaining a complex structure which allowed a completely original relationship between set and costume. Léger described his intention: "When the curtain goes up, the three deities are on stage facing the audience. Behind them, as scenery, *mountains, clouds,* the *moon, stars* . . . The three deities—statues in high-relief and relief fragment—will be between five and six metres tall. Colour: ochre and black, and blue. Some white. These huge figures will have *mobile sections.* Same with the décor. Thus, throughout the ballet, continual slow movement of the scenic *Figure with four revolving faces* . . . Figures (dancers) heavily disguised, wearing carapaces, with the result that no dancers will have human proportions. By this means, we will achieve a *grandiose, dramatic* ballet, with, moreover, lighting effects which will allow for alterations of light and dark."[10] The differently proportioned elements of scenery and costumes (deities and animals), and the fact that the dancers were all expressionless within their costumes and masks, made *La Création du Monde* not so much a ballet as a complex mobile sculpture in several planes.

Milhaud's score provided a further dimension. Although he wrote that "at last in *La Création du monde* I had the opportunity I had been waiting for to use those elements of jazz to which I had devoted so much study. I adopted the same orchestra as used in Harlem, seventeen solo instruments, and I made wholesale use of the jazz style to convey a purely classical feeling,"[11] the choreography did not express the music in movement as usual, but followed its own rhythms, sometimes in deliberate antithesis to the music. Milhaud was generous in his praise of the designer, and justifiably ironic about the reception of his score: "Léger's contribution helped to make it an unforgettable spectacle. The critics decreed that my music was frivolous and more suitable for a restaurant or a dance hall than for a concert hall. Ten years later the selfsame critics were discussing the philosophy of jazz and learnedly demonstrating that *La Création* was the best of my works."[12] Madeleine Milhaud, the composer's widow, told Erik

Näslund that *La Création du Monde* was described as "décor in motion."[13]

Cyril W. Beaumont, in his description of the production, showed that Léger's scenic intentions had been fulfilled: "*La Création du Monde* is the story of Creation and the birth of man as an aboriginal might conceive it. There were several new elements in the choreography, for instance, the dancers who suggested herons moved on stilts, others who took the part of animals walked on all-fours. Again, the action took place in semi-darkness, with occasional dimming and lightening which produced an interesting play of light and shade."[14] Beaumont recognized that some of the choreography was "new," but he underestimated the genuine innovatory quality of the production. Léger's mobile scenery predated Calder's mobiles, and Börlin's abstract choreography of pure movement, unconnected to the music, predicted Alwin Nikolais' experiments. Very few critics were as open-minded as Beaumont, or as complimentary as Baird Hastings: "The feature of this primitive work was the fluid nature and interrelation of all aspects of the production. As the scene metamorphosed Léger's dark-hued and cubist inspired sets took on different forms in front of the spectators—much as occurred in baroque spectacles (yet with the advantage of modern machinery),"[15] and the critic of *The Times*: "M. Fernand Léger, the well-known cubist painter, has designed costumes, scenery and curtain of a really convincing cubism, and providing an admirable background for the evolutions of the strange creatures which are supposed to have peopled the earth when the Great Lords of Creation, Nzamé, Mébère, and N'Kwa, had just finished creating it."[16]

Most critics poured scorn on the production. André Levinson, a constant censurer of the Ballets Suédois (as he was of the Ballets Russes), was typical in his stricture. During a sustained ironic diatribe, he wrote: "What an aberration it is to engage living dancers to contort themselves in order to imitate the tenets of outlandish sculptors! One can never create a dance work by using dance movements to interpret conventions appropriate to the plastic arts. And so the universe contracts. After Spain and the Orient, and with the Congo and the gulf of Guinea annexed, there is only Greenland of the Nanouk Eskimos or the prairies of Sioux left for ballet to colonize."[17] Rigidly classical, blind to any experimentation, Levinson completely missed the point of *Le Création du Monde.*

154   Design for the set

Graphite, ink, tempera and/or watercolor with
    brown ink notations on paper
12⅜ x 15⁹⁄₁₆ in: 31.5 x 39.3 cm
Signed and inscribed in ink lower right: "2ᵉ état
    (2nd state) décor Création du / Monde / à
    Serge Lifar / 2me / amicalement F. Leger"
1933.503

Exhibitions: London Tooth 1930, No 43; New York
    1933, No 43; Chicago 1933, No 114;
    Northampton 1934, No 114; Hartford 1934;
    New Haven 1935; San Francisco 1935–6;
    Poughkeepsie 1940; Williamsburg 1940;
    Cambridge 1942; New York MoMA 1944;
    Michigan 1957; Sarasota 1958, No 51; Elmira
    1958, No 9; Indianapolis 1959, No 376; Storrs
    1963; Washington D.C. 1964; New York
    1965–6, No 124 (illustrated p 60); New York
    1966–7; Princeton 1968; Hartford 1973; Hart-
    ford 1974; Coral Gables 1982; Frankfurt-am-
    Main 1986, No 423 (illustrated p 365 bottom);
    Worcester 1989.
Illustration: Hartford Symphony 97/98 season
    prospectus, p 14 (color).

This is one of several preliminary
sketches for the design of the set which
Léger made with the three deities at the
beginning of the ballet. The masks of the
deities were inspired by illustrations in Carl
Einstein's book *Negerplastik*. The horned
mask on the right is based on plate 89 and
is closest to being a copy of an actual mask;
the central rectangular mask is based only
loosely on plates 85 and 86, and the circular
mask on the left has some similarities with
the masks in plates 8, 59, and 78. The
horned mask appears in the final design in
the same position, but in a more dehuman-
ized form; the other masks were developed
further, with Léger playing on geometrical
patterns. The final version of the design is
considerably more complex than this one
and includes the side wings.[18] In the production, the deities were enormous two-
dimensional flats which were moved from
behind by members of the company.

In his set design scheme, Léger used
three elements: first, a front cloth on which
he developed on a large scale in an even
more stylized form the geometric shapes he
saw in African masks; then a backcloth of
black and white clouds in a blue sky with a
yellow sun above an abstract design of
mountain peaks and crags, and, finally, the
ensemble as here, incorporating the deities,
with wings and borders of abstract patterns.
Bengt Häger described the effect of the
scenery: "Léger's pictures emerge through
the floor, float in from the wings, move
outside the stage, dance a ballet of abstract
patterns, a constantly changing picture. The
ballerinas had mixed feelings on the subject:
'We're not here to hump scenery,' they
pleaded."[19]

1 The ballet was so called because of the contemporary fascination with black African art.

2 Pseudonym of Frédéric Louis Sauser.

3 Another reason for de Maré choosing Paris was that his homosexual relationship with Börlin was likely to prove to be too scandalous for Stockholm.

4 After trying to rent several other theaters, Hébertot persuaded de Maré to take a lease on the Théâtre des Champs-Elysées which had become free.

5 25 October 1920: *Divertissement* (medley of Swedish music); *Jeux*, music by Claude Debussy, set by Pierre Bonnard, costumes by Jeanne Lanvin; *Iberia*, music by Isaac Albeniz orchestrated by D. E. Ingelbrecht, set and costumes by Theodore Steinlen; *Nuit de Saint Jean* by Jean Börlin, music by Hugo Alven, set and costumes by Nils Dardel; 8 November 1920: *Le Tombeau de Couperin*, music by Maurice Ravel, set and costumes by Pierre Laprade; *Maison des Fous* by Jean Börlin, music by Viking Dahl, set and costumes by Nils Dardel; 18 November 1920: *El Greco* by Jean Börlin, music by D. E. Ingelbrecht, set and costumes after El Greco; *Derviches* by Jean Börlin, music by Alexander Glazounov, set by Georges Mouveau, costumes by Jean Börlin; *Les Vierges Folles* by Kurt Atterberg, music by Kurt Atterberg after Swedish airs, set and costumes by Einar Nerman; *Chopiniana*, music by Frederic Chopin orchestrated by Ernest Bigot; 15 February 1921: *La Boîte à Joujoux* by André Hellé, music by Claude Debussy orchestrated by André Caplet, set and costumes by André Hellé; 6 June 1921: *L'Homme et son Désir* by Paul Claudel, music by Darius Milhaud, set and costumes by André Parr; 18 June 1921 *Les Mariés de la Tour Eiffel* by Jean Cocteau, music by Germaine Tailleferre, Georges Auric, Arthur Honegger, Darius Milhaud, Francis Poulenc, set by Irène Lagut, costumes by Jean Hugo; *Dansgille* music by Ernest Bigot on popular Swedish airs, set after a Swedish painting in the Museum of the North, Stockholm, national Swedish costumes; 20 January 1922: *Skating Rink* by Canudo, music by Arthur Honegger, set and costumes by Fernand Léger; 25 October 1923: *Marchand d'Oiseaux* by Hélène Perdriat, music by Germaine Tailleferre, set and costumes by Hélène Perdriat; *Offerlunden* by Jean Börlin, music by Algot Haquinius, set and costumes by Gunnar Hallstrom; *La Création du Monde* by Blaise Cenrdrars, music by Darius Milhaud, set and costumes by Fernand Léger; *Within the Quota* by Gerald Murphy, music by Cole Porter, set and costumes by Gerald Murphy; 19 November 1924: *Le Roseau* from a Persian story, music by Daniel Lazarus, set and costumes by Alexander Alexeieff after Persian miniatures; *Le Porcher* after a story by Hans Christian Andersen, music from old Swedish airs; *Le Tournoi Singulier* from a work by Louise Labé, music by Roland Manuel, set and costumes by Tsuguharu Foujita; *La Jarre* after Luigi Pirandello, music by Alfredo Casella, set and costumes by Giorgio de Chirico; 27 November 1924: *Relache*, instantaneous ballet in two acts and a cinematographic interval and the tail of a dog by Francis Picabia, music by Erik Satie, sets by Francis Picabia, cinematographic interval by René Clair.

6 He began his career as a dealer in African sculpture in 1914 at the Alfred Stieglitz Gallery in New York.

7 See note 5.

8 Both letters are quoted by Giovanni Lista, "Léger scénographe et cinéaste" in Brigitte Hédel-Samson, *Fernand Léger et le spectacle*, p 50.

9 Darius Milhaud, *Notes without music*, p 148.

10 Fernand Léger, quoted in Bengt Häger, *Ballets Suédois*, p 191.

11 Darius Milhaud, *op cit*, p 148.

12 Darius Milhaud, *ibid*, p 152.

13 Erik Näslund, *Les Ballets Suédois*, p 63.

14 Cyril W. Beaumont, *The Complete Book of Ballets*, p 830.

15 Baird Hastings, "Notes on Fernand Léger" in *Chrysalis* Vol 6 Nos 3–4 1953, p 17.

16 Anon, "La Création du monde" in *The Times*, London 30 October 1923, p 10. Léger's other works for the theater, apart from *Skating Rink* earlier for Ballets Suédois, were: *Match de Boxe*, a marionette play, in 1934 at the Théâtre de la Branche de Houx, Paris; *David Triomphant*, with choreography by Serge Lifar who also danced the title role, first performed on 15 December 1936 at the Théâtre de la Maison internationale des Etudiants universitaires, Paris, revived on 26 May 1937 at the Opéra, Paris; *Naissance d'une Cité* by Jean-Richard Bloch, first performed on 18 October 1937 at the Palais des Sports, Paris; *Le Pas d'Acier* by Georges Jaculov and Serge Prokofiev, with choreography by Serge Lifar, first performed on 28 May 1948 at the Théâtre des Champs-Elysées, Paris; *Bolivar* by Jules Supervielle, with music by Darius Milhaud and choreography by Serge Lifar, first performed on 12 May 1950 at the Opéra, Paris; *L'Homme qui Voulait Voler* by Maurice Cazeneuve, with music by Maurice Jarre and choreography by Janine Charrat, first performed on 13 July 1952 at the Château d'Amboise.

17 André Levinson, "Les Ballets Suédois" in *1929, Danse d'Aujourd'hui*, pp 98–9.

18 There was also a tapestry made of the set design.

19 Bengt Häger, *Modern Swedish Ballet*, p 7.

Louis Marcoussis
(Ludwig Casimir Ladislas Markous)

155   Serge Lifar

Graphite on translucent paper
21½ x 14⅝ in: 54.5 x 37 cm
Signed and inscribed in pencil bottom right: "au
    Dieu de la danse / offrande de (to the God of
    dance an offering by) / Marcoussis / Paris le
    28 Sept 1933"
On the reverse there is an erased sketch of a head
    in profile
1933.504

Exhibitions: New York 1933 (not in catalogue);
    Chicago 1933, No 115; Northampton 1934,
    No 115; Hartford 1934; New Haven 1935; Paris
    1939, No 296; Baltimore 1941, No 23; New
    York 1944; Edinburgh 1954, No 476; London
    1954–5, No 484; Michigan 1957; San Antonio
    1958; Richmond 1959; New York 1965–6, No
    125 (illustrated p 61); New York 1966–7;
    Princeton 1968; Strasbourg 1969, No 499;
    Hartford 1974; Hartford 1988; Columbus 1989;
    Worcester 1989.

Markous arrived in Paris from Poland in
1903. He joined, as many others, the
Académie Jullian, and painted, also as
many others, impressionist landscapes
influenced by Cézanne. In 1907 he abandoned painting for the more lucrative occupation of drawing caricatures until 1910
when he met Guillaume Apollinaire, who
suggested he took the name Marcoussis
from a small village just south of Paris. He
also met Braque, who introduced him to
Picasso, and so he was soon a member of
that astonishing variety act that was the
concentration of artists in Paris at the time,
frequenting the Café de l'Ermitage in the
boulevard de Clichy. Marcoussis fell under
the spell of Cubism. In 1912 he met Alice
Halicka, another painter, also Polish.[1] They
were married in 1913. During the First
World War he volunteered and served in the
13th regiment of the French artillery, and
was decorated in 1918 with the Croix de
Guerre.

After the war, Marcoussis began his
etchings with a portrait of Apollinaire and
his series of glass paintings
(*hinterglasmalerie*), a traditional Polish folk
art whose technique allows no maladroit-
ness.[2] Between 1919 and 1928 he made
about a hundred glass paintings. He also
continued his fascination with Cubism and

had his first one-man show at the Galerie Pierre in 1925, the same gallery that exhibited the paintings of Max Ernst and Joan Miró seen by Diaghilev before he commissioned them for *Romeo and Juliet* (see pp 193–97, 262–65). In 1927, Marcoussis renounced the formality of Cubism and moved toward a kind of tempered Surrealism.

In 1932 he began a series of portraits, drawings, and etchings, which he continued to make until the end of his life. Admitting to preferring the "company of duchesses to concierges," he concentrated on making portraits of society ladies, such as Lady Abdy, Comtesse de Maillé, and Vicomtesse Charles de Noailles; Misia Sert; musicians such as Henri Sauguet, Francis Poulenc, Darius Milhaud, and Igor Markevitch, and other artists, such as Picasso, Joan Miró, and Max Ernst. As all these were within the entourage of the Ballets Russes, Marcoussis must have known Diaghilev, but he never designed a ballet for him, or for anyone else.

Serge Lifar was the only dancer of whom Marcoussis made a portrait drawing. He also made portraits of writers such as e. e. cummings, Gertrude Stein, André Breton, Paul Eluard, and Marcel Jouhandeau who wrote that "Marcoussis had the gaze of a bird without eyelids, startling, bewitching."[3] This concentrated gaze was transmitted flawlessly to the hand guiding the pencil, in preparation for the same hand guiding the etcher's needle. Marcoussis's line is assured, defining the character of the sitter with the minimum of means and the greatest of ease. Through drawing the head alone, Marcoussis seems able to define the whole body. This is a proud, confidant, muscular, beautiful dancer. This is Serge Lifar.

The dedication deliberately flatters Lifar with a famous epithet. The first "God of the Dance" was the French dancer Louis Dupré (1697–1774) who enchanted audiences, mostly at the Opéra in Paris, for over thirty years. One of his pupils at the Académie, Gaetano Appolino Baldassare Vestris (1729–1808), succeeded him at the Opéra in 1751 and inherited the title when Gaetano's brother, during a performance, shouted out "C'est le Dieu de la Danse." The mantle subsequently passed unofficially to Nijinsky.[4] Lifar, who considered himself the natural successor of Nijinsky, would have thought the label perfectly legitimate.

The date of the inscription shows that this drawing was one of the last acquisitions Lifar made before going to the United States on his ill-fated tour which began in New York in November 1933 (see pp 306–8).

This portrait was made into an etching (facing, of course, the other way), confined approximately within the rectangle shown in the drawing;[5] a copy of the etching is in the Dance Collection of the New York Public Library. Helena Rubinstein, of whose portrait Marcoussis also made an etching, became his patron and organized exhibitions of his portraits at the Chicago Arts Club in October 1934 and at Knoedler's in New York in March 1935.[6]

Notes

1 In 1937 she would design Stravinsky's *The Fairy's Kiss* for George Balanchine's American Ballet.

2 Paint is applied behind the glass, so that the first layer is the foreground and the last layer the background (the reverse process of painting on canvas), with the glass itself acting like a layer of varnish. Traditional Polish folk paintings on glass are usually of religious subjects.

3 Marcel Jouhandeau, quoted in Jean Lafranchis, *Marcoussis*, p 158.

4 Referred to as such by M. Chavez, an Argentinian-French dressmaker, who introduced Nijinsky to his future wife Romola Pulszky, according to her in Romola Nijinsky, *Nijinsky*, p 230.

5 Etching and drypoint on buff paper 13⅛ x 9½ in: 32.8 x 24 cm. See Lafranchis, No D.112.

6 The etching of Serge Lifar was No 70 in Chicago, No 61 in New York.

Henri Matisse

French
born 1869 Le Cateau-Cambrésis (Nord)
died 1954 Nice

Le Chant du rossignol (The Song of the Nightingale)

Ballet in 1 act, adapted by Igor Stravinsky from his
opera *The Nightingale*,[1] after the story by Hans
Christian Andersen
Composer: Igor Stravinsky
Conductor: Ernest Ansermet
Choreographer: Leonide Massine
Designer (set and costumes): Henri Matisse
Principal Dancers:
   The Nightingale: Tamara Karsavina
   The Mechanical Nightingale:
      Stanislas Idzikowski
   The Emperor of China: Serge Grigoriev
   Death: Lydia Sokolova
Company: Diaghilev's Ballets Russes
First Performance: 2 February 1920, Théâtre
   national de l'Opéra, Paris

New production by Diaghilev's Ballets Russes on
   17 June 1925, Théâtre de la Gaîté-Lyrique, Paris
Conductor: Marc-César Scotto
Choreographer: George Balanchine
Designer (set and costumes): Henri Matisse
Principal Dancers:
   The Nightingale: Alicia Markova
   The Mechanical Nightingale:
      Stanislas Idzikowski
   The Emperor of China: Serge Grigoriev
   Death: Lydia Sokolova

Synopsis

From the program: "In the palace of the Emperor
of China everyone is busy preparing for the reception of the nightingale. All the doors are wide
open, and the draughts set myriads of bells a-
tinkling. In the distance can be heard the song of
the approaching nightingale. Hereupon the
Emperor's suite enters and the nightingale sings.
When her song is ended, enthusiasm breaks out.
Suddenly messengers from the Emperor of Japan
arrive bringing with them for their master a wonderful automatic nightingale which he is presenting
to his powerful neighbour.

"The Japanese Maestro makes this curious
automatic bird sing. The Emperor is taken ill, the
real nightingale has fled, and the newcomer is
driven out of the Palace. Distracted, the courtiers
improvise with their arms a throne upon which to
bear away the dying Monarch. They return to fetch
the throne, and the Chamberlains throw open the
curtains of the Emperor's room. Death is seen
watching near his bed. Then the nightingale arrives
and sings. She succeeds in enchanting Death, who,
about to drive her off, gives in, strangling and
carrying her away. The whole Court thinks the
Emperor is dead, and a train of mourners arrive.
These notice a movement of their master's hand,
upon which he rises, completely cured. Everyone
starts back enraptured by the miracle."

During the late autumn of 1916
Diaghilev, on his way back to Rome,
visited Stravinsky in Switzerland to renew
his suggestion of producing the opera *Le
Rossignol* (*The Nightingale*), which had not
met with much success, in ballet form. He
wanted to stage it as he had done Rimsky-
Korsakov's *The Golden Cockerel,* with the
action performed by dancers while the
singers remained invisible. Stravinsky
stated in his memoirs that he countered this
suggestion by agreeing that Diaghilev could
devise a ballet from the symphonic poem he
was thinking of making from the second
and third acts of *The Nightingale* which he
would call *Le Chant du rossignol*, and that
Diaghilev "warmly welcomed the suggestion."[2] It is therefore strange that only a few
pages later Stravinsky wrote: "I had des-
tined *Le Chant du rossignol* for the concert
platform, and a choreographic rendering
seemed to me quite unnecessary. Its subtle
and meticulous writing and its somewhat
static character would not have lent themselves to stage action and the movements of
dancing."[3] But by November 1916
Diaghilev, in a letter to Stravinsky, was
suggesting specific changes to the score, and
dictatorially: "Both of the Nightingale's
songs must be abbreviated and tedious
places eliminated. And there is no reason
for anyone to go off into a temper about
this! I am a man of the theatre and not,
thank God, a composer."[4] In spite of his
initial enthusiasm for the project several
years passed before its final production. Yet,
in some curious way, Diaghilev always
remained obsessed by *The Song of the
Nightingale*.

Diaghilev spent most of the winter and
the early part of 1917 in Rome where he had
set up his headquarters with Massine. Bakst
came to plan *Les Femmes de Bonne Humeur*
(see pp 82–84), Picasso and Cocteau came
for *Parade*. Fascinated as ever by new artistic
"isms," Diaghilev was intrigued by the
theatrical possibilities of futurism. He
engaged Giacomo Balla to stage Stravinsky's *Fireworks*[5] as a sound and light show,
and Fortunato Depero to design *Le Chant du
rossignol*.[6] Balla designed a set of various
multicolored shapes—cubes, cones, pyramids, polyhedrons etc.—which were lit up
internally or externally in time with the
music, according to a program devised by
Diaghilev. Depero, inspired by Balla, imagined a futurist garden of different multicolored shapes: cones, discs, huge flowers,
suspended suns, "a whole geometry of
cardboard with a marvelously decorative
effect,"[7] which he began to realize as a
model. For the costumes, he drew and made
paper collages of mandarins and court
ladies with "geometrical Chinese masks,
cylindrical sleeves, and heads in compart-
ments,"[8] which Diaghilev praised to
Stravinsky, writing that Depero "is doing
marvelous work; the decorations are splendid, and Massine is dreaming about presenting the ballet."[9] The production,
however, had to be postponed because
Stravinsky did not finish the score in time
for the ballet to be produced in Rome, and
Diaghilev had to leave in order to fulfill
engagements in Paris and London. Lynn
Garafola has stated that a "factor in dropping *Le Chant du rossignol* . . . may well have
been the unanticipated loss of revenue from
the American tour [of the Ballets Russes]."[10]
No one, however, has explained why
Depero's designs were ultimately not used,
given that Diaghilev—and, by all accounts,
Massine—were initially so satisfied with his
work. It may be that Depero's final designs
were impractical for ballet, or too expensive
to realize. In any case, Depero's landlady
"dismantled the set, selling the pieces for
the back rent the artist owed her."[11] Depero,
as designer of *Le Chant du rossignol*, is not
mentioned by Massine, nor by Serge Grigoriev, the company manager. Nor is he
mentioned by Alexandre Benois, the
designer of the opera *The Nightingale*, who
assumed that a new designer had to be
commissioned only because he was absent
in Russia and most of his original sets and
costumes had unfortunately perished in the
cellars of the Theatre Royal, Drury Lane, in
London where they were being stored
during the war. The most likely explanation
for Depero's disappearance is that
Diaghilev, in characteristically fickle mood,
decided, after Picasso's *Parade* and *Le Tricorne*, that it would prove to be more profitable to commission another painter of
comparable fame, Matisse. But this happened only in the autumn of 1919, when
Diaghilev again revived the idea of producing *Le Chant du rossignol*.

Diaghilev and Stravinsky visited Matisse while he was staying in Issy-les-Moulineaux near Paris, with a proposal, according to Alfred Barr, to "design new settings and costumes either for *Schéhérazade* or for the new ballet *Le rossignol*."[12] Diaghilev supposed that the "orientalism" of these ballets would appeal to Matisse. Apparently Stravinsky played him both on the piano, and Matisse decided in favor of *Le Chant du rossignol*. He had never expressed any particular interest in ballet or theater, but was seduced into working for Diaghilev not merely by his charm but by the fact that the Ballets Russes were manifestly in the center of the artistic limelight of Paris, and that the reputations of Picasso and Derain had recently been enhanced by their work for the company. Diaghilev and Matisse signed an agreement on 13 September 1919 whereby Matisse would be paid ten thousand francs for his work on *Le Chant du rossignol*. Alfred Barr states that once Matisse had "committed himself, he worked with his usual painstaking thoroughness."[13] Barr was right in some respects, but he does not go on to explain that, had Matisse known what he was doing, his work would have been easier. As the Ballets Russes were at the Empire Theatre in London from September to December 1919 Matisse went to work there.[14] The scene painter Vladimir Polunin described working with him: "Matisse, the designer of the scenery for *Le Chant du rossignol*, arrived from France without any sketches or definite plans. After having visited with me different museums, he set to work in the studio, scissors in hand, cutting out and piecing together a model. This work took a fortnight. His complete ignorance of the stage was surprising, so that the very alphabet of it had to be explained to him. Being a man of strong character, he often tried to discover his own America, only to return painfully and unwillingly to the one already known."[15] The model, which comprised the set, the furniture, and the props, as well as all the characters in costume, was constructed or, rather, slowly evolved out of pieces of colored paper cut by Matisse.

He was quite clear about one aspect of his designs: the color. He was opposed to Bakst's deliberate use of clashing colors. Instead, as he told Michel Georges-Michel: "I'm planning to have a curtain as white as porcelain . . . For it's to be a Chinese curtain, after all, isn't it? There will be as few lines as possible. As for the décors, those Russians expect something violent, don't they?

Well, they're not going to get it. I'm going to teach them the proper proportion of colour according to French tradition: pure white, pale pink, light blue. And they can take it or leave it."[16] Matisse also installed a small electric lamp in the top of his model to get a reasonably accurate impression of the effect of light on his three-dimensional colored paper picture. White is the most difficult color to use on stage because lighting white scenery creates the darkest shadows, but Matisse's inexperience in stage technique did not deter him from experimenting in this way. Polunin admired the result: "His model was of a very simple, almost austere character, and its concentrated tones, well combined and balanced, produced at once a soft and brilliant impression, free from any garish contrasts."[17] During the fortnight Matisse spent in London, he worked closely with Massine in developing the concept of the ballet and successfully discovered "his own America." As he admitted many years later: "Then I understood what a décor could be, that is to say that it could be thought of as a picture, with colors, that is the costumes, changing places. Colors changing their places should still leave the décor with the same expressiveness. A strong expressiveness should dominate the interplay of colors without destroying the harmony of the rest. I was greatly helped by the choreographer Massine who understood my idea perfectly."[18] This was not, of course, a new idea at all—Bakst's work for the theater was dominated by it—but a discovery for Matisse had to be his discovery. Massine thought that working closely with Matisse "to create a fusion of costumes, décor and choreography" was one of his "most successful efforts at collaboration with a designer."[19]

The other collaborators were impressed by both Matisse and Massine. Lydia Sokolova, who danced the part of Death, wrote of Matisse: "The décor, very simple and yet giving the impression of a fastidious Chinese splendour, was all conceived in black and white—but mostly white—with a little turquoise blue. Most of the costumes, too, were white, with designs sketched on them in little dashes and squiggles of black. As Death I was the only note of brilliant colour. I wore scarlet all-over tights, with a very uncomfortable brass waistcoat, suggesting the ribs of a skeleton. On my head was a black wig and a very painful headdress of brass supporting a china ball on which a skull was painted. Round my neck hung a necklace of *papier-mâché* skulls."[20]

And of Massine she wrote: "Massine, as ever, had been very thorough: whatever he did he worked at with the utmost seriousness, and he had crammed in some homework on Chinese art . . . There were some very fine and ingenious groupings of men in *Le Chant du rossignol*. They built themselves up into flat friezes, rather in the way that acrobats do, but their bodies were packed tight and knitted close together, some men on one leg, some upside down resting on a bent arm, some in a kind of hand-stand."[21]

Grigoriev, who played the part of the Emperor, was not quite right when he wrote that the ballet "turned out to be exactly what Paris liked,"[22] and misleading when he stated that it had to be given "at every performance up to the end of the season."[23] There were only five nights left of that (eleventh) season, and the ballet was given four more times.[24] In the following (twelfth) "season" in Paris from 8 May to 4 June 1920, *Le Chant du rossignol* was given only twice.[25] It was never repeated in Paris after that, and fared no better in London where it was not repeated after 1920.

The critics were not particularly enthusiastic, for the most part comparing the ballet unfavorably with their memories of the opera. Jean-Louis Vaudoyer was fairly dismissive: "As for *Le Chant du rossignol*, inspired by one of the most sensitive and human of Andersen's tales, it has been so elliptically reduced by M. Stravinsky that one should no longer try to find any meaning in it but be satisfied with the cheerful and sharp feast of colors offered to our eyes by M. Matisse's setting and costumes."[26] Louis Laloy wrote that the opera had been "a marvellous entertainment in which the emotional intensity reached ineffable heights," but that now it had been "abridged, condensed, concentrated and, with the singing and the spoken word eliminated, interpreted only by the movements, groupings and gestures of the characters. The two nightingales are no longer singing nightingales but dancing nightingales. The episodes follow one another without transition or explanation. The music has assumed the solidity of a symphony." On the other hand, Laloy was delighted by the choreography and the design: "The most remarkable thing here is the composition of the ensembles. M. Massine is not only a choreographer who arranges steps and dances, he is a painter who makes moving pictures in three-dimensional space. In a setting of refined simplicity, M. Matisse has provided him with sparklingly harmonious costumes which lend themselves to the most varied combinations."[27] W. A. Propert, the first historian and usually a great admirer of the Ballets Russes, thought that the opera, "a wonderful work of art, long planned and patiently wrought to perfection, had been deliberately spoilt" by everyone concerned—Diaghilev, Stravinsky, and Massine—and that "the fatal word Ballet was whispered, and away went the voices and on came the acrobats."[28] Propert is not so sure, however, about Matisse's contribution: "The great Matisse had undertaken to provide the décor for this astonishing performance. There was every prospect that the mounting would be as startling as the music and the dancing. He was as experienced in the treatment of large surfaces as he was scornful of precedent and tradition. But on this occasion I think he was puzzled and a little timid. The uniform paleness of colour was only decided on, I believe, after much searching of heart and trial of alternative schemes. It was misty, intangible, vague; the figures as they moved silently before the pale background were like spirits passing at dawn. One awaited impatiently the song of the birds and the coming of the sun."[29] And Alexandre Benois, the designer of the original opera, allowed himself the smug comment: "His costumes were enchanting in colour, but there was none of the sumptuous splendour of the first version, which in 1914, had made *Le Rossignol* a really Grand Spectacle."[30]

Neither the great name of Matisse nor the ingenious, but not altogether effective, choreography of Massine prevented the ballet from being quickly withdrawn from the repertory. And yet Diaghilev remained almost obstinately attached to the score, so much so that in 1925 he entrusted George Balanchine with reviving it with new choreography and a new nightingale—the thirteen-year-old Alicia Markova. The same set and costumes by Matisse were used, except for a new all-over white costume for Markova and some adjustments to the Mechanical Nightingale. This new version, Balanchine's first ballet for Diaghilev, was given two performances in Paris.

Stravinsky, who was never very enthusiastic about the ballet, later stated dismissively but without rancour: "The production, and especially Matisse's part in it, were failures. Diaghilev hoped Matisse would do something very Chinese and charming. All he did do, however, was to copy the China of the shops in the rue de la Boëtie."[31]

While the production of *Le Chant du rossignol* disappeared very quickly, Matisse later applied his experience of working in the theater to the design of the Chapel of the Rosary at Vence. He used the same technique, making a model for the architecture as he had for the set, and paper cutouts for the vestments as he had for the costumes.

156 Sketch design for the drop curtain (front cloth)

Graphite, ink, and white correction on paper mounted to board
12⅞ x 17¹⁵⁄₁₆ in: 32.8 x 45.3 cm (16¹¹⁄₁₆ x 21¼ in: 42.4 x 54 cm overall)
Inscribed in pencil center left: "noir [sic]," center right "n," and indicating flower "bl[eu]"
1933.505

Exhibitions: New York 1933, No 44; Chicago 1933, No 116; Northampton 1934, No 116; Hartford 1934; New Haven 1935; Paris 1939, No 298 (illustrated p 26); Williamsburg 1940; New York 1941-2; New London 1944; Minneapolis 1953; Edinburgh 1954, No 261; London 1954–5, No 301; Beloit 1956; Framingham 1956; San Antonio 1958; Elmira 1958, No 6; Indianapolis 1959; New York 1962–3; New York 1965–6, No 126 (illustrated p 62); New York 1966–7; Princeton 1968; Los Angeles 1969; Blommenholm 1971; Hartford 1973; Hartford 1974; Hempstead 1974, No 112; Hartford 1978–9; Coral Gables 1982; Oberlin 1985; Hartford 1988; Worcester 1989.

Illustrations: Amberg, pl 56; Baer 1988, fig 4 p 76; Barr, p 432; Barsky, p 11; Gontcharova, p 73; Oswald, No 1 p 20; Percival, p 105; Pozharskaya and Volodina, p 192; Propert 1921; Rischbieter, p 80.

After Matisse had spent a fortnight in London designing the set, Diaghilev asked him to paint a front cloth as well, considering it to be not only desirable but an essential part of the design of a production. It fulfilled several practical functions: it introduced the correct mood for the ballet about to be performed; it provided a visual break for the audience and a pictorial background for any overture or prelude; it allowed quite long scene changes to take place without irritating the audience by giving them something diverting to look at instead of a dull velvet house curtain, and, perhaps above all, it gave the artist-designer an opportunity to exhibit his two-dimensional artistry in spectacular fashion.[32]

Matisse, however, refused, saying he wanted to return to Paris to get on with his serious work, and was ready to give up his fee. But Diaghilev used his cunning and charm. Schneider, quoting Matisse, described what happened next: "Diaghilev asks him why. 'Because I don't want to,' replies the painter. Diaghilev takes a piece of paper and a pencil, draws out Matisse's idea asking him if that is it. 'Not at all!' he answers, and snatching the pencil, he draws his front cloth. 'A big frame. In the centre, a sort of large panel on which I put three

large theatrical masks, supported by griffons, which, in the set, were at least three metres high, large white Chinese griffons with green manes. Around these objects a sowing of pale blue flowers which could have five petals, vaguely like nasturtiums.' 'There you are,' Diaghilev told him, 'That's it. You've done it. There was no need to make such a fuss.' And Matisse decided that he was 'quite happy.'"[33]

Polunin, the scene painter, wrote a slightly different version of events: "The decision to have a drop-curtain necessitated Matisse's return to London, but again he brought no sketches, with the exception of one in pencil, so that the tones had to be composed on the canvas. Having begun with the lion on the left, he presently gave it up as he thought that the one on the right, painted by me, was more successful."[34]

The animals are neither dog nor lion, but mythical beasts called lion-dogs, or Dogs of Fo. They are usually to be found in pairs, as here, set in the grounds of Chinese temples to ward off demons.

158* Costume for a Mandarin

Short T-shaped robe and wide trousers, off-white satin with painted black scallop shapes, brass studs in center. Appliquéd gold lamé dragons with green glass eyes are enclosed in a circle of studs on front and back.
Cotton gauze lining inscribed in purple ink (partly in Russian) "Хор, А. Кост. ("Khor, A. Cost.) Koralle"
Pair of ivory satin broad trousers with draw-string waist
1996.7.8a–b

Below: the four Chamberlains in costume.

Provenance: Diaghilev and de Basil Ballets Foundation Ltd; Sotheby's, London, lot 76 (iii), 17 July 1968; Castle Howard Estate Ltd; Sotheby's, London, lot 43, 14 December 1995

In the original production, the Mandarins were Jazvinski, Statkevitch, Ribas, Pavlov, Stepanov, and Mascagno; in the revival in London they were Jazvinski, Fedorov, Pavlov, Kochanovsky, Vinter, and Hoyer.

159* Costume for a Lady of the Court

Short T-shaped robe (missing skirt), off-white satin with painted yellow roses accented with orange, outlined in black. Black velvet binding on neckline, sleeves, and hem, silver ball buttons and loops at front opening. Muslin label and cotton gauze lining inscribed "Evina." Pink satin skull cap appliquéd with matching rose motifs, with fringe of black beads.
Label inscribed "Zaleska"
1996.7.9a–b
Provenance: Diaghilev and de Basil Ballets Foundation Ltd; Sotheby's, London, lot 76 (iv), 17 July 1968; Castle Howard Estate Ltd; Sotheby's, London, lot 44, 14 December 1995

In the original production in 1920 the Court Ladies were Wassilewska, Nemtchinova, Klementovitch, Zaleska, Slavitska, Grabovska, Allanova, Pavlovska, Clark, Istomina, Forestier, Grantzera, Edinska, Evina, Mikulina, and Bewicke. In the revival in London in 1927 they were Petrova, Gevergeva, Branitska, Vadimova, Maikerska, Soumarokova, Chamie, Orlova, Zarina, Klemetska, Slavinska, Obidennaia, Kouchetovska, Miklachevska, Evina, Jasevitch, and Matveeva.

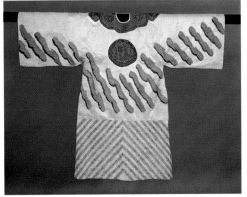

157* Costume for a Chamberlain

Full length T-shaped robe, off white satin with painted cloud patterns in orange outlined in black. Gold lamé roundels contain dragon figures on front and back, lamé collar yoke extends onto shoulders. Sea-wave pattern of gold braid extends from knee line to hem.
Cotton gauze lining inscribed "Slavinsky" and another illegible name.
Dark blue velvet hat with standing "pigtail" overlaid with gold braid.
1996.7.10a–b
Provenance: Diaghilev and de Basil Ballets Foundation Ltd; Sotheby's, London, lot 76 (ii), 17 July 1968; Castle Howard Estate Ltd; Sotheby's, London, lot 45, 14 December 1995

In the original production in 1920, the Chamberlains were Lukine, Kostezki, Bourman, and Ochimovski; in the revival they were Lissanevitch, Cleplinsky, Ignatov, and Strechnev.

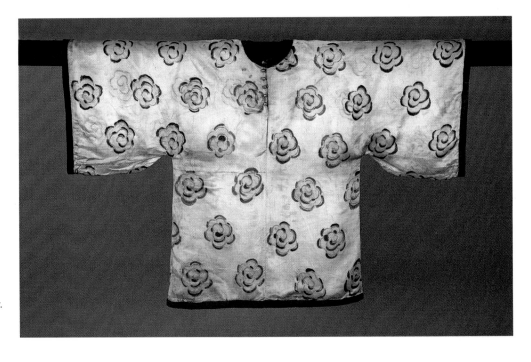

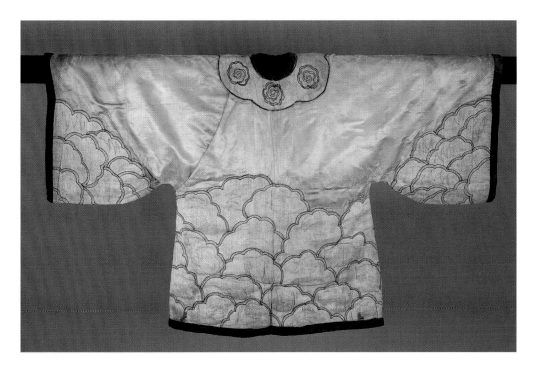

160* Costume for a Lady of the Court

Short T-shaped robe (missing skirt), pale green
    satin silver lamé neckline yoke and quilted
    cloud appliqués on sleeves and hemline. Black
    velvet binding on sleeves and hemline. Cotton
    muslin lining inscribed "Evina, Jazevitch."
Pink satin skull cap appliquéd with with matching
    rose motifs, with fringe of black beads.
Inscribed "Forestier, Kostrovska"
1996.7.11a–b
Provenance: Diaghilev and de Basil Ballets Founda-
    tion Ltd; Sotheby's, London, lot 79 (ii), 17 July
    1968; Castle Howard Estate Ltd; Sotheby's,
    London, lot 48, 14 December 1995

This again is not a single costume but a combination of two. Evina may have worn it also in
London in 1927 (see Pl 159). Forestier was one
of the original Court ladies; Kostrovska is
unidentified.

Notes

1 The ballet is a revision of acts 2 and 3 of the
    opera (see pp 128–31).
2 Igor Stravinsky, *Chronicle of my Life*, pp 110–1.
3 Igor Stravinsky, *ibid*, p 134. This autobiography,
    ghosted anonymously by Walter Nouvel, not
    only contains a number of inconsistencies and
    contradictions, but is often vague about dates.
4 Diaghilev from Rome to Stravinsky in Morges
    on 16 November 1916, quoted in *Stravinsky:
    Selected Correspondence*, p 29.
5 *Fireworks* was first performed on 12 April 1917 at
    the Teatro Costanzi, Rome, in the same program
    as the first performance of *Les Femmes de Bonne
    Humeur*.
6 Diaghilev wrote to Stravinsky at the end of
    November 1916 that he had "concluded a
    contract with Depero," quoted in *op cit*, p 30.

Depero was also commissioned to design the
knight's horse for the episode *Bova Koralevitch* in
Children's Tales, rehearsed in Rome, but first
performed on 11 May 1917 at the Châtelet
Theater, Paris. Massine described Diaghilev's
reaction to the horse: "As we walked into the
room the artist pointed proudly to his construction—a bulbous outsized elephant! We stood
staring at it silently for a few moments until
Diaghilev, in a sudden outburst of rage,
smashed the papier-mâché animal with his
walking stick." Leonide Massine, *My Life in
Ballet*, p 99.

7 Victor Beyer, *Les Ballets Russes de Serge de
    Diaghilev*, p 162.
8 From *Stravinsky: Selected Correspondence* ed.
    Robert Craft, vol 2, p 489, quoted by Vicente
    García-Márquez in *Massine*, p 88.
9 Diaghilev to Stravinsky in the letter cited in
    note 6.
10 Lynn Garafola, *Diaghilev's Ballets Russes*, p 208.
11 Selma Jeanne Cohen, "Le Chant du rossignol" in
    Genevieve Oswald, *Stravinsky and the Dance*,
    p 44. Ten costume designs by Depero were
    exhibited in New York 1962 and Strasbourg
    1969.
12 Alfred H. Barr, Jnr, *Matisse: His Art and His
    Public*, p 207. It seems improbable that Diaghilev
    proposed *Schéhérazade* as a design project to
    Matisse at this time. Although Bakst and
    Diaghilev had quarrelled over *La Boutique
    Fantasque* and were not then speaking to each
    other, Bakst had redesigned *Schéhérazade* in 1915
    for the American tour and so the sets and
    costumes would not yet have become dilapi-
    dated. Besides, asking someone else to design
    Schéhérazade would have stretched disloyalty
    beyond even Diaghilev's capacities. Boris
    Kochno in *Diaghilev and the Ballets Russes* (p 272)
    quotes a telegram which Diaghilev sent to
    Matisse on 31 August 1928 when he heard that
    Matisse liked Prokofiev's score for *Le Fils
    Prodigue* (see pp 300–5): "Delighted if you
    willing design the two ballets beginning with

Schéhérazade which intend to restage this win-
    ter." This makes sense, because Bakst was dead
    by this time. Matisse, in fact, designed neither
    ballet. It is unlikely that Diaghilev would have
    asked Matisse a second time to design
    Schéhérazade after his (supposed) first refusal.
    Schéhérazade was not performed in Paris after
    1922, nor in London after 1921.
13 Alfred H. Barr, Jnr, *op cit*, p 207.
14 A further agreement between Diaghilev and
    Matisse was signed on 5 November 1919, taking
    into account the work already done in London
    and confirming a further payment of two
    thousand francs to Matisse for expenses while in
    London. Reproduced in Charles Goerg, "Un
    manteau de Matisse," p 9.
15 Vladimir Polunin, *The Continental Method of
    Scene Painting*, p 61.
16 Michel Georges-Michel, *From Renoir to Picasso*,
    pp 31–2.
17 Vladimir Polunin, *op cit*, p 61.
18 Quoted by Pierre Schneider in *Matisse*, p 523–4,
    from a conversation with Pierre Courthion.
19 Leonide Massine, *My Life in Ballet*, p 148.
20 Lydia Sokolova, *Dancing for Diaghilev*, p 146.
21 Lydia Sokolova, *ibid*, p 147.
22 Serge Grigoriev, *The Diaghilev Ballet*, p 160.
23 Serge Grigoriev, *ibid*, p 160.
24 On 5, 7, 10, and 16 February 1920.
25 On 11 and 18 May 1920.
26 Jean-Louis Vaudoyer in *Le Gaulois*, Paris,
    11 February 1920.
27 Louis Laloy, "Le Chant du Rossignol" in
    Comoedia, Paris 4 February 1920, p 1.
28 W. A. Propert, *The Russian Ballet in Western
    Europe 1909–1920*, p 59.
29 W. A. Propert, *ibid*, p 60.
30 Alexandre Benois, *Reminiscences of the Russian
    Ballet*, p 362.
31 Igor Stravinsky and Robert Craft, *Conversations
    with Igor Stravinsky*, p 95.
32 It also gave Diaghilev, when short of money, an
    opportunity to sell it as a work of art, which he
    did with Picasso's front cloth for *Le Tricorne*.
33 Pierre Schneider, *Matisse*, p 625, quoting from a
    conversation with Pierre Courthion. Charles
    Goerg, in "Un manteau de Matisse pour 'Le
    Chant du Rossignol'" in *Revue mensuelle des
    muséees et collections de la ville de Genève*, p 8,
    described a slightly different version of the
    completed front cloth: "The curtain is made up
    of a broad white rectangle on a black back-
    ground with a yellow border, and three seated
    griffons three meters high in the center and two
    buddhistical lions with green manes and vermil-
    ion breasts." The nasturtiums recur later in
    Matisse's work in some of his preliminary
    drawings and the final ceramic wall of the
    "Vierge à l'Enfant" in the Chapel of the Rosary,
    Vence, 1950.
34 Vladimir Polunin, *The Continental Method of
    Scene Painting*, p 62. Matisse did return to the
    theater, nineteen years later, designing *L'Etrange
    farandole* (originally called *Rouge et Noir*), with
    music by Shostakovitch and choreography by
    Massine, for the Ballets de Monte-Carlo, first
    performed at Monte Carlo on 11 May 1939.

Joan Miró

Spanish
born 1893 Montroig (near Tarragona, Catalonia)
died 1983 Majorca

Romeo and Juliet

For production credits, synopsis, and general background note, see under Max Ernst, pp 193–99.[1]

Although Diaghilev described *Romeo and Juliet* as a "rehearsal without scenery" and justified his description by telling Grigoriev that "since Shakespeare used no scenery, neither shall we,"[2] he was not being literally exact. Even Diaghilev realized that sticking to Shakespearean practise or experimenting in staging techniques did not mean performing ballets on a completely bare stage. Having discarded Christopher Wood as designer, Diaghilev decided to use some of the paintings by Max Ernst and Joán Miró, which he had bought in Paris, as designs for drop curtains.[3] Prince Schervashidze, Diaghilev's regular scene painter at the time, enlarged the original oil paintings to the required measurements of the drop curtains. Miró was responsible for the front and back cloths for act one, Ernst for the cloths for act two. But that was not all. Miró provided some indications for such items of scenery and properties as were thought essential: it cannot be said that he "designed" any scenery or setting.[4] Grigoriev described the scenic effect of *Romeo and Juliet*: "This ballet had no décor in the accepted sense of the word. The curtain rose on an entirely bare stage—an effect that tended to embarrass the public, who imagined that it had been brought up by mistake . . . Such scenery as there was consisted of small flats, moved about by the dancers themselves, and representing, say, part of a hall, or a courtyard, or a balcony."[5] Miró also provided some rudimentary drawings for costumes, which Grigoriev stated "were all alike and nothing if not simple—yellow tunics for the ladies and practice clothes for the men. The only characters who wore period costumes were Romeo and Juliet themselves."[6] There are photographs of Serge Lifar as Romeo and Tamara Karsavina as Juliet, which show that their costumes were not exactly what is usually regarded as being period Shakespearean costume, nor was any attempt made to create any kind of historical authenticity or even period atmosphere. As the printed program did not distinguish between the two painters' work,

there was some confusion about who did what, as can be gauged from W. A. Propert: "The décor was so slight that it did not count much one way or the other. There was rather a happy patch of colour on the walls of the rehearsal room by one of the *sur-réalistes*, either Miro or Ernst, that compensated for a tiresome worm that the other had painted on the curtain."[7] Moreover, as noted previously when discussing Ernst's work, critics were not only singularly negligent about describing what they had seen, but were unable to remember accurately. The existing photographs are also totally inadequate for establishing what *Romeo and Juliet* looked like in either of its acts or any of its scenes. However, not all is guesswork.

161 Dream Painting (enlarged for the front cloth)

Oil on linen
50⅜ x 37¼ in: 100 x 96.5 cm
Signed and dated in oil paint lower right: "Miro / 1925"
1933.507

Exhibitions: Paris 1929, No 38; Paris 1930, No 79; New York 1933, No 45; Chicago 1933, No 118; Northampton 1934, No 118; Hartford 1934; New Haven 1935; San Francisco 1935; Williamsburg 1940; New York 1941–2; Springfield 1950, No 21; Minneapolis 1953; Edinburgh 1954, No 335; Indianapolis 1959, No 393; New York 1965–6, No 128 (illustrated p 64); Strasbourg 1969, No 420 (illustrated No 101); Frankfurt-am-Main 1969, No 127; Blommenholm 1971, No 128; New York 1972–3, No 20; Hartford 1974; Paris 1975, No 29; Hartford 1978–9; Coral Gables 1982; Hartford 1988; Worcester 1989; Barcelona 1994–5.
Illustrations: Bablet, No 303 p 161; Dupin, No 153 p 496; Gimferrer, No 284 p 347; Krauss, No 20 p 105.

This, presumably, is the "tiresome worm" described by W. A. Propert which he saw, without knowing who painted it, on the front cloth.[8] On the other hand, confusingly, Henry Malherbe, who attempted to describe the settings, seems not only to have seen something else but also to have combined two separate images in his description of the first front cloth when he wrote: "The first cloth is made of parallel lines,

circles, and a few clumsy, colored commas."[9] The first part of the description clearly refers to a painting by Ernst (see p 197), but the second part refers to this painting. A further confusion is that the proportions of this painting, being portrait instead of landscape, are unusual for a theatrical drop cloth. It is certainly possible that there were two cloths at the beginning of the ballet, a front cloth by Ernst followed by one by Miró. Diaghilev may well have wanted to begin *Romeo and Juliet* by showing off both his new-found artists, one after the other.

Malherbe then describes Miró's setting for act one, the rehearsal class for the dancers: "Standing out on the stage is a two-fold screen of which one wing is black and the other pale blue. On the back cloth a blue comet sails over a pink cloud."[10] This is an accurate description only of the left side of the back cloth (from the audience's point of view). The right side is of an abstract figure in a cloud, poised over a half-moon in a rectangular box. The left side detail and the right side detail were made from separate paintings which Miró made for the production. Miró gave the original for the right side detail to Schervashidze, the scene painter, with the inscription "who so admirably interpreted my painting and charmed my stay in Monte Carlo, May 1926." This was acquired by Serge Lifar in 1949, with another painting by Miró, and remained in his collection until it was sold in 1974.[11]

As both this painting and the following one are dated 1925, before Miró became involved in the production of *Romeo and Juliet*, they were not made specifically for it and may well have been exhibited at the first Surrealist exhibition at the Galerie Pierre, Paris, 14–25 November 1925, as well as at his first one-man show in the same gallery, 12–27 June 1925.

Both these paintings are in the open, loose style which Miró evolved during the late summer of 1924 when he became preoccupied with simplification. On 10 August 1924 he wrote to Michel Leiris: "There is no doubt that my canvases that are simply drawn, with a few dots of color, a rainbow, are more profoundly moving. These move

264 us in the elevated sense of the word, like the tears of a child."[12] His paintings at this time become quite childlike, with seemingly unpremeditated images painted haphazardly on unprimed and unprepared canvas as if during a hypnotic trance. Miró admitted to Leiris: "My latest canvases are conceived like a bolt from the blue, absolutely detached from the outer world,"[13] as if he had no control over what he was doing. This phase of Miró's painting lasted for three years from 1924 to 1927, a phase which Jacques Dupin called "dream painting," inspired by genuine hallucinations caused by hunger. Miró painted about a hundred of these "dream pictures." Most are monochrome but with well defined, irregular patches of pure, strong color floating among cloudlike undulations in a dreamlike atmosphere, animated occasionally by a meteor or a comet's tail. The frequently recurring images, lines, and colors suggest a disturbing, yet tranquil, private sexual symbolism. Rosalind Krauss suggests that the "circle or point with flame-like appendages is a sign for sexual excitement."[14] The red/black lozenge with the radiating spokes at the bottom of this painting is symbolic of the vagina. Therefore this painting, full of sexual innuendo, is certainly appropriate as a pictorial overture to the tragic love story of Romeo and Juliet, but it is unlikely that anyone either understood or appreciated the sexual symbolism. And they would have been very shocked if they had.

162   Dream Painting

Oil on linen
19⅝ x 25¾ in: 50 x 65.2 cm
Signed in oil paint lower right: "Miro / 1925"
Reverse signed on canvas: "Joan Miró / 1925,"
    inscribed on stretcher: "Projet de Mise en
    Scène," stamped on stretcher and canvas
    "Douane Centrale Exposition Paris"
Label on reverse: "Lucien Lefebvre-Foinet / 19 rue
    Vavin / 2 rue Bréa / Paris VI / couleurs et toiles
    fines," stamped "5229"
1933.508

Exhibitions: Chicago 1933, No 119; Northampton 1934, No 119; Hartford 1934; New York 1941–2; Edinburgh 1954, No 336; Elmira 1958. No 26; Indianapolis 1959, No 393; New York 1965–6, No 129 (illustrated p 64); Princeton 1968; Strasbourg 1969, No 421; Frankfurt-am-Main 1969, No 128; New York 1972, No 13; Hartford 1973; Hartford 1974; Hempstead 1974, No 113; Hartford 1978–9; Roslyn 1981; Coral Gables 1982; San Francisco 1986–7; Hartford 1988; Worcester 1989.
Illustrations: Bablet, No 304 p 164; Dupin, No 152 p 496.

Although this has been thought to be a project design for a curtain, it was not one of the paintings chosen by Diaghilev to be enlarged for *Romeo and Juliet*. It has no connection with either that production or any other. It is one of the "dream paintings" Miró was painting at the time (see above), and which Diaghilev bought at the same exhibition as the previous one.

The large white angled shape relates closely to a similar shape in *Head of a smoker*, also painted in 1925. If one accepts the idea of the sexual symbolism of these paintings, then the smoke billowing from the pipe and the form here are thought to be phallic, but to my mind this is reading something into the painting which is neither evident nor intended. More acceptable is the point of view of Jacques Lassaigne, who wrote that these paintings "often seem to have been made in a state of hypnosis or with the eyes shut, the artist's hand once it begins to move, following its own bent, tensing or relaxing automatically, guided by unconscious reflexes."[15]

Notes

1 The ballet was always known by its English title.
2 Serge Grigoriev, *The Diaghilev Ballet*, p 221.
3 Diaghilev almost certainly bought the paintings at the Galerie van Leer in Paris at an exhibition of Ernst's and Miró's work which he had encouraged Lifar and Kochno to visit (see p 195).
4 A drawing by Miró showing "how furniture was to be disposed on the undecorated stage" is reproduced in Richard Buckle, *In Search of Diaghilev*, p 108, along with two costume indications.
5 Serge Grigoriev, *op cit*, p 225.
6 Serge Grigoriev, *ibid*, p 225.
7 W. A. Propert, *The Russian Ballet 1921–1929*, p 44.
8 W. A. Propert, *ibid*.
9 Henry Malherbe in *Le Temps*, Paris, 2 June 1926, p 3.
10 Henry Malherbe, *ibid*.
11 *Collection Serge Lifar, Les Ballets Russes*, Hotel George V, Paris, 20 June 1974, by Commissaires-Priseurs Ader, Picard, Tajan, lot No 87.
12 Joan Miró, quoted in *Selected writings and interviews*, p 86.
13 Joan Miró, *ibid*, p 86.
14 Rosalind Krauss and Margit Rowell, *Joan Miró: Magnetic Fields*, p 14.
15 Jacques Lassaigne, *Miró*, p 46.

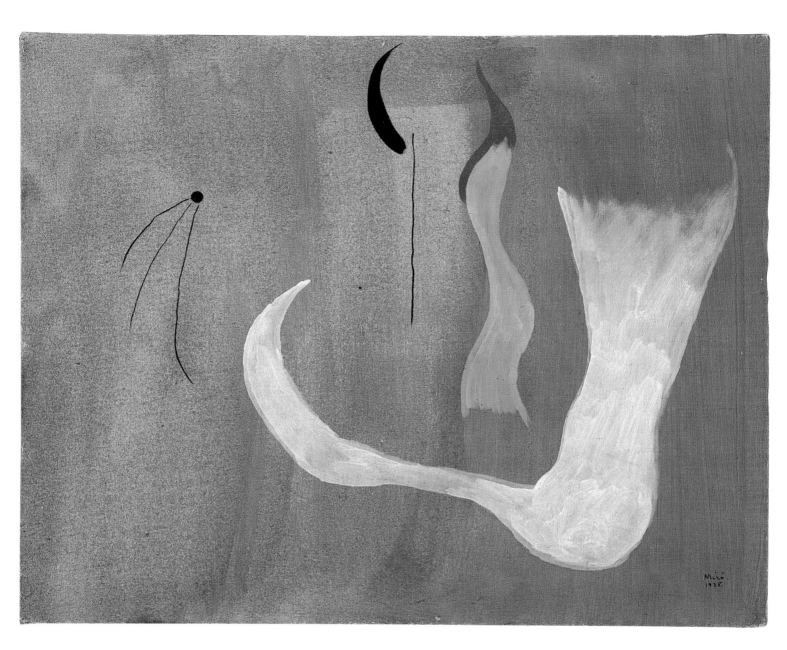

Amadeo Modigliani

Italian
born 1884 Livorno
died 1920 Paris

163   Léon Bakst

Graphite on paper
23 x 16⅞ in: 58.3 x 42.9 cm
Signed and dated in pencil lower right: "Modigliani
    / 17 janvier 1917"
1933.506

Exhibitions: Chicago 1933, No 117; Northampton
    1934, No 117; Hartford 1934; New Haven
    1935; San Francisco 1935-6; Paris 1939, No
    299; Baltimore 1941, No 20; New York 1944,
    No 255; New York MoMA 1944–5; Detroit
    1948; Cleveland 1951; Palm Beach 1954, No
    32; Chicago 1959, No 46; Milan 1960, No 138
    (illustrated p 91); New York 1963–4; New York
    1965-6, No 127 (illustrated p 63); New York
    1966–7; Chicago 1966, No 82; Princeton 1968;
    Hartford 1974; Storrs 1975; New York 1985–6;
    Hartford 1988; Worcester 1989.
Illustration: Schouvaloff 1987, p 250.

Modigliani had no direct connection with either Diaghilev or the Ballets Russes but, being acquainted as he was with Bakst, Picasso, Cocteau, and Derain, he found himself on the periphery of that circle. "Handsome, grave and Romantic,"[1] Modigliani was a familiar bohemian figure among the artists working and living in Paris during the First World War when Montparnasse was the center of the artistic universe. It was, wrote Cocteau, "our promenade, our haven and our kingdom."[2] La Rotonde and the Dôme, the two cafés opposite each other where the boulevard Raspail crosses the boulevard Montparnasse, were like two private artists' clubs.[3] Modigliani worked mainly in Kisling's studio in rue Joseph Bara, just round the corner. He had arrived in Paris in 1906 aged twenty-two. By 1914, when he was thirty, he had finally begun to find his true identity as a painter while continuing as a sculptor, carving caryatid heads, until about 1916. He also now began to sell his work.

1917 was a most prolific year, during which Modigliani is credited with having painted over a 120 paintings. Some of the accreditation is undoubtedly fanciful, based on dealers dating his work after he had become better known. Modigliani did not paint still lifes, and very rarely any landscapes. His paintings are of nudes and portraits. His subjects were his friends and acquaintances. They all posed for him like true models, usually sitting on a chair in front of an indeterminate background, quite relaxed, with hands resting on thighs, often crossed or, as here, with fingers interlocked, staring with vacant eyes directly at the painter. To say that Modigliani's portraits all resemble each other is as true as to say that all Mozart's compositions sound the same. The identity of the sitters is always mirrored, as it were, in the painter through the blank eyes, but their individual personalities are revealed through some minutely observed and carefully recorded detail. Bakst recognized this ability in Modigliani, and he seems not to have resented being given those tiny, piggy eyes.

As well as making this portrait drawing of Bakst early in the year he painted a portrait in oils during the summer.[4] Michel Georges-Michel, calling on Bakst at his apartment and studio at 112 boulevard des Malesherbes, was persuaded not to leave: "'Don't go just yet. I'm expecting somebody who really is "somebody"—the Italian painter and sculptor Modigliani, from Leghorn. He is doing my portrait. Here's a line-drawing he's done for it. Look at the care he has taken. All the features in my face are etched as if with a needle, and there's no retouching. I'm sure he must be poor; but he has the air of a *grand seigneur*. He really is "somebody," I assure you.' . . . Presently, into the studio walked a tall, upright young man, who had the lithe, springy gait of an Indian from the Andes. He was wearing espadrilles and a tight-fitting sweater. And in his pale face, which was shadowed by a shock of thick hair, his eyes burned beneath their sharp, rugged brows. I learned afterwards that the intensity of his gaze, which seemed to be fixed on some distant object, was unfortunately due to the use of drugs."[5]

This is the line drawing to which Bakst referred. Although quite finished, it served as a sketch for the later painting in which Modigliani exaggerated the particular characteristics he noticed as being peculiar to Bakst. The drawing catches Bakst's elegance, verging on dandyism, and his mischievous charm which concealed a certain unreliability.

Notes

1 Jean Cocteau, *My contemporaries*, p 70.
    Modigliani also painted his portrait in 1917.
2 Jean Cocteau, *ibid*, p 70.
3 Still there, they have not changed much, and
    remain favorite meeting places.
4 Now in the National Gallery of Art in Washington, D.C., Chester Dale Collection.
5 Michel Georges-Michel, *From Renoir to Picasso*,
    pp 142–3. He states, however, mistakenly, that
    the year was 1919.

Eugene Mollo

Russian
born 1905 Ufa
died 1985 Farnham, Surrey

Eugene Mollo left Russia after the Revolution and settled in England, where he attended the Royal College of Art from 1925 to 1928. He wanted to become a painter. Being Russian he naturally gravitated toward the Russian Ballet and, probably through Lifar, his exact contemporary, he met Diaghilev in London in 1928. Mollo was engaged as an assistant scene painter and worked intermittently for a year and a half for the Ballets Russes. He proposed a ballet based on Pushkin's poem *The Bronze Horseman* which appealed to Diaghilev. But the proposition did not result in a production; and Diaghilev died in 1929.

Mollo abandoned painting pictures for a living. Instead, in 1931, he founded Mollo and Egan Ltd, architectural decorators. The technique he had developed as a painter had taught him valuable lessons in the application of mixed media. With his partner, he introduced a modern conception of the cinema interior by inventing an entirely new way of applying paint and textured plastic paint to unevenly finished plaster surfaces. His method of surface treatment of the vast expanses of the interior walls of cinemas allowed architects to finish the buildings very quickly and economically. The early 1930s were years of rapid expansion in the building of cinemas in England as everywhere else: going to the movies was the booming leisure activity. In the first year his company decorated seven new cinemas, and by the fourth year more than thirty.

Mollo's paintings in this collection all date from the last year of the Ballets Russes and immediately afterwards. The size and technique of these paintings make it unlikely that any of them was done as a design for the theater. The six paintings divide into three distinguishable pairs.

Mollo himself apparently stated (according to the previous catalogue) that Nos 164 and 165 were made between 1928 and 1930 for a production by the Ballets Russes. If so, then the production remained unrealized; they were certainly not for the proposed *Bronze Horseman*. These two paintings, with the animal masked figures like foxes, have an affinity with, and may have been inspired by, the ballet *Renard (The Fox)* (see pp 235–38), the first ballet choreographed by Serge Lifar in 1929. In his production of

that ballet, Lifar used a dancer doubling with an acrobat for each of the characters, and there is certainly an acrobatic quality about the figures in these paintings.

According to Lifar, Nos 166, 167, and 168 were made in 1931. Nos 166 and 167 are like two studies for anthropomorphic pantomime costumes, amusing but impractical. Nos 168 and 169 were inspired by balletic movements and poses with which Mollo had become familiar through his observation of the Ballets Russes and especially Lifar. The central figure in No 168 is the same as the figure in No 169, and could be said to have a vague resemblance to Lifar. These paintings also show Mollo's experimentation with a variety of mixed media, with the addition, in No 169, of different collage materials.

All these paintings were either bought by Serge Lifar or given to him by the artist.

164 Grotesques (Two grotesque figures)

Graphite, oil paint or enamel, and tempera on paper
26⅞ x 33¹⁵⁄₁₆ in: 68.3 x 86.2 cm
Signed and dated in ink lower right: "E. Mollo / 1930"
1933.513

Exhibitions: New York 1933, No 46 (described as "Grotesques" but not identified); Chicago 1933, No 125 (described as "Deux personnages"); Northampton 1934, No 125; Hartford 1934; New Haven 1935; New York 1965–6, No 135 (illustrated p 66) (not shown in New York); New York 1966–7; Worcester 1989.

Eugene Mollo

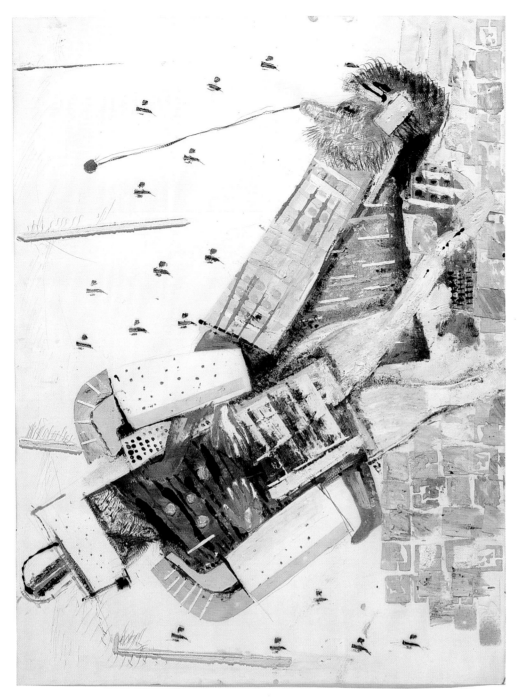

167 Two masked figures (Apes)

Graphite, glue, oil or enamel, tempera, silver paint
  on paper
22⁵⁄₁₆ x 15¼ in: 56.6 x 38.7 cm
Unsigned and undated
On reverse there is an incomplete sketch in watercolor and ink of a monkey in man's clothing
1933.511

Exhibitions: Chicago 1933, No 123 (described as
  "Deux perosnnages grotesques"); Northampton
  1934, No 123; Hartford 1934; Cambridge 1942;
  Elmira 1958, No 21; New York 1965-6, No 132
  (illustrated p 66); New York 1966-7; Princeton
  1968; Amherst 1974; Columbus 1989;
  Worcester 1989.

165 Grotesques (Two grotesque figures)

Graphite, ink, tempera and metallic paint on paper
18⁷⁄₈ x 24⁷⁄₈ in: 48 x 63.2 cm
Unsigned and undated
1933.514

Exhibitions: New York 1933, No 46 (described as
  "Grotesques" but not identified); Chicago
  1933, No 126 (described as "Deux personnages
  grotesques"); Northampton 1934, No 126;
  Hartford 1934; New Haven 1935; New York
  1965–6, No 130 (illustrated p 65); Princeton
  1968; Hartford 1974; Columbus 1989;
  Worcester 1989.

166 Masked figure (Ape)

Graphite, glue, oil or enamel paint, tempera and
  silver paint on paper
24⅛ x 13½ in: 61.1 x 34.3 cm
Unsigned and undated
1933.510

Exhibitions: Chicago 1933, No 122 (described as
  "Personnage"); Northampton 1934, No 122;
  Hartford 1934; Williamsburg 1940; New York
  1965–6, No 131 (illustrated p 66); New York
  1966–7; Princeton 1968; Hartford 1974; Coral
  Gables 1982; Allentown 1986; Columbus 1989;
  Worcester 1989.

168   Three Dancers

Graphite, glue, oil or enamel paint, tempera on
    paper
30⅞ x 22⅜ in: 78.6 x 57 cm
Unsigned and undated
1933.509

Exhibitions: New York 1933, No 47 (described as
    "Dancers"); Chicago 1933, No 121 (described
    as "Danseuses"); Northampton 1934, No 121;
    Hartford 1934; New Haven 1935; New York
    1965–6, No 133 (illustrated p 66) (not shown
    in New York); New York 1966–7; Worcester
    1989.

169   Dancer

Graphite, oil or enamel paint, plaster, and mixed
    media with collage of painted cloth woven
    with gold metal thread, talc, cut copper sheets,
    and plastic sewn to paper with black cotton
    thread
31 x 22½ in: 78.9 x 56.5 cm
Unsigned and undated
Reverse backing sheet inscribed in pencil: "Mollo /
    9403," "Danseuse," and stamped: "Douanes
    Exposition Paris"
Label on reverse: "Lucien Lefebvre-Foinet / 19 rue
    Vavin / 2 rue Bréa / Paris VI / couleurs et toiles
    fines," stamped "9403"
1933.512

Exhibitions: New York 1933, No 47 (described as
    "Dancers" but not identified); Chicago 1933,
    No 124 (described as "Danseuse"); Northamp-
    ton 1934, No 124; Hartford 1934; New Haven
    1935; New York 1965–6, No 134 (illustrated
    p 66; not shown in New York); Hartford 1974;
    Worcester 1989.

Pablo Picasso

Spanish
born 1881 Malaga
died 1973 Mougins (France)

170 Self portrait with two female nudes

Ink with lead white highlights and graphite
  signature on paper
7¹³⁄₁₆ x 4⁷⁄₁₆ in: 19.9 x 11.2 cm
Undated, signed in pencil upper right: "Picasso"
Reverse is a Barcelona advertisement: "Sastreria de
  B. Soler / Vidal / Plazcide Santa Ana 8 / Ramon
  Garcellas"
1933.519

Exhibitions: Chicago 1933, No 131; Northampton
  1934, No 131; Hartford 1934a; New Haven
  1935; Detroit 1948; Edinburgh 1954, No 510;
  London 1954–5, No 522 (illustrated p 65); New
  York 1965–6, No 136 (illustrated p 67); New
  York 1966–7; Princeton 1968; Hartford 1973;
  Hartford 1974; Columbus 1989; Worcester
  1989.
Illustrations: Buckle, *Dance and Dancers*, November
  1955, p 11; Buckle 1955, p 92 No 123; Eluard,
  p 19.

The date of the drawing, according to the
reproduction in Paul Eluard's *A Pablo
Picasso*, is 1902. The signature in pencil was
added later. Picasso made this drawing in

Barcelona. He was there from January until
October 1902 when he went to Paris; he
returned to Barcelona in January 1903 and
stayed until May. A very similar drawing of
himself (in overcoat, with scarf, beret, and
pipe) and his friend Sebastian Junyer arriving at the French frontier in 1903[1] suggests,
however, that this drawing may have been
made then.

   The drawing is on the back of an advertisement for Picasso's tailor and friend
Benet Soler, to whom Picasso gave paintings
in exchange for clothes. In 1903 Picasso
painted an oil painting of the Soler Family
picnicking on the grass,[2] reminiscent of
the *Déjeuner sur l'herbe* theme of the
Impressionists.

171 Woman's head

Ink on paper
8⅝ x 5⁵⁄₁₆ in: 21.2 x 13.5 cm
Signed in pencil top left: "Picasso"
1933.518

Exhibitions: Paris 1929 (illustrated on cover); New
  York 1933, No 52 (described as "Head of a
  Dancer"); Chicago 1933, No 130 (described as
  "Tête de danseur"); Northampton 1934, No
  130; Hartford 1934a; New Haven 1935; Michi-
  gan 1957; Richmond 1959; New York 1965–6,
  No 137 (illustrated p 67); New York 1966–7;
  Princeton 1968; Hartford 1973; Hartford 1974;
  Columbus 1989; Worcester 1989.

The date of this drawing is 1906. It relates
to the many drawings Picasso made
during the summer of 1906 when he stayed
in the Catalan village of Gósol, in the Pyre-
nees near Andorra, with his companion and
model Fernande Olivier. This was the time
when Picasso was moving away from the
picturesque, romantic Rose Period toward a
stark simplicity and the birth of Cubism
with *Les Demoiselles d'Avignon*, which he
painted at the beginning of 1907.

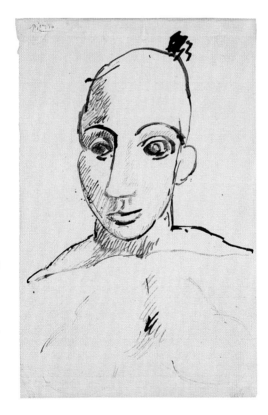

Notes

1 Reproduced in Jean Leymarie, *Picasso: the artist
   of the century*, p 208. But in the exhibition
   Picassso—The Early Years, 1892–1906 at the
   Museum of Fine Arts, Boston, 10 September
   1997–4 January 1998 this drawing, no. 2 from a
   series of 4, was dated April 1904.
2 Now in the Musée des Beaux-Arts, Liège.

Le Tricorne (The Three-Cornered Hat)

Ballet in 1 act by Gregorio Martínez Sierra, after
    the novel by Pedro Antonio de Alarcón
Composer: Manuel de Falla
Conductor: Ernest Ansermet
Choreographer: Leonide Massine
Principal Dancers:
    The Miller: Leonide Massine
    The Miller's wife: Tamara Karsavina
    The Corregidor: Leon Woizikovsky
    The Dandy: Stanislas Idzikowski
Company: Diaghilev's Ballets Russes
First Performance: 22 July 1919, Alhambra Theatre,
    London

Synopsis

The action takes place in the eighteenth century. A miller and his wife lead a peaceful life, teaching their pet bird to sing. Many people cross the bridge by the mill, including a young dandy who blows kisses at the miller's wife. The miller rushes onto the bridge and the dandy escapes. A march is heard and a procession approaches. It is the Corregidor in his three-cornered hat and his wife, surrounded by their suite of flunkies and policemen. The Corregidor leers at the miller's wife and drops his lacy handkerchief. She returns it with a curtsey, and the procession passes on. A young girl passes by and the Miller flirts with her. This upsets the Miller's wife. He apologizes and they dance together before he goes into the house. Left alone, the miller's wife dances while the Corregidor steals back to watch her. Then he approaches to dance with her, but she eludes him as he pursues her. The miller, who has watched the scene from the house, now arrives to help his wife. The Corregidor, exhausted, falls to the ground, and the Miller and his wife help him up. He realizes he has been made a fool of and departs threatening revenge. The miller and his wife continue their carefree dance, and the villagers join in the general festivities. The Miller gives them all wine and dances alone. Then, as they all begin to dance again, the police arrive and arrest the miller. The miller's wife is left alone. Then the Corregidor returns and again tries to catch her. As they cross the bridge, the miller's wife pushes him off and he falls into the mill stream. Frightened, the miller's wife helps to pull him out of the water. But the Corregidor again begins to chase her. She takes a musket from her house and, threatening him, runs away. The Corregidor at last gives up the chase, takes off his wet cloak and his three-cornered hat, lays them out to dry and goes into the house to sleep. When the miller returns he sees the Corregidor's clothes and the Corregidor himself in one of his nightshirts. Snatching up the cloak the miller baits him like a bull, and then decides to pursue the Corregidor's wife who is also young and beautiful. He scrawls a taunting message on the walls of his house and dashes away. Now the Corregidor is attacked by his own soldiers, who do not recognize him in the miller's nightshirt. The miller and his wife return and start attacking each other. Then they also attack the Corregidor. Then all the villagers join in. At last the policemen come and remove the Corregidor, while the miller, his wife, and the assembled group dance triumphantly, tossing an effigy of the Corregidor higher and higher into the air.

Between their two tours of the United States in 1916, the Ballets Russes performed in Spain with great success, and to the particular delight of King Alfonso XIII. After their first performance in Madrid on 26 May, according to Grigoriev: "Diaghilev was sent for by the King; and both he and the Queen warmly congratulated him. The King thereafter came to every one of our performances; and all the leading dancers were presented to him."[1] The King became a patron of the ballet.

Diaghilev, thrilled with Spain and in gratitude to the King, was inspired to produce a "Spanish" ballet. He suggested to Massine a ballet to the music of Fauré's *Pavane*. The result was *Las Meninas*.[2] To counterbalance it, Diaghilev thought that a "Russian" ballet was needed, and he and Massine chose *Kikimora* (see pp 233–34). The success of *Las Meninas* encouraged them to consider producing another Spanish ballet, but this time they wanted to create something completely Spanish, using traditional Spanish music and dancing.

Manuel de Falla—described by Massine as "a mild-mannered little man who, in his dark suit and felt hat, might easily have passed for a university professor"[3]—had been introduced to Diaghilev by Stravinsky, who had known him since 1910. Now in Spain, Falla became friends with Diaghilev and Massine and acted as their guide. They heard his *Noches en los jardines de España* (*Nights in the Gardens of Spain*) and at once wanted to use the score for a ballet. They also heard his work in progress, *El corregidor y la molinera*, incidental music for Gregorio Matínez Sierra's pantomime in two scenes based on the novel, *El sombrero de tres picos*, by Pedro Antonio de Alarcón,[4] which they felt would also make a ballet. Diaghilev wanted to sign a contract for both, but Falla refused to let his *Noches* be used for a ballet in a theater as he insisted it had been composed for the concert hall only; eventually he succeeded in making Diaghilev drop the idea. But on 15 September 1916, Falla signed a draft contract for a ballet of *El corregidor y la molinera*, now called *Le Tricorne*, with the stipulation that the piano score would be delivered by 15 November and the orchestral score by 15 December. Diaghilev, for his part, would produce the ballet in Rome in 1917. It was not to be.

Diaghilev and Massine went to Rome where they were joined by Picasso and Cocteau, and later by Bakst, Stravinsky, and Ansermet. But Falla did not not deliver on

time. Neither did Stravinsky with *Le Chant du Rossignol* (see pp 257–61). So Diaghilev had to change his plans (he was always having to change his plans). The new productions rehearsed in Rome were *Les Femmes de Bonne Humeur* (see pp 82–84) and *Parade*.

By the end of May 1917, Diaghilev and Massine were back in Spain and resumed their collaboration with Falla. He took them to a performance of *El corregidor y la molinera* at the Teatro Novedades in Barcelona, where they heard his music for the first time played by an orchestra. Massine wrote: "Falla's score, with its pulsating rhythms, played by eleven brass instruments, seemed to us very exciting, and in its blend of violence and passion was similar to much of the music of the local folk-dances."[5] Diaghilev was delighted, but suggested some alterations which Falla willingly made.

To make the ballet truly Spanish, as Lydia Sokolova rightly stated, "the essential was that Massine and the company should learn to perform Spanish steps in a Spanish way; and Massine in particular had to master the grammar of the Spanish dance before he could work out his choreography."[6] Merely watching the *flamenco* dancers was not enough; Diaghilev insisted that Massine had to be taught the authentic steps. They had found the right person in Seville in 1916 when they were first planning *Le Tricorne*, a discovery described by Massine: "One evening, at our favourite café, the Novedades, we noticed a small, dark young dancer whose elegant movements and compelling intensity singled him out from the rest of the group. When he had finished dancing Diaghilev invited him to join us at our table. He introduced himself as Felix Fernandez García, and as we talked to him I sensed that he was a nervous and highly-strung creature with a very original talent. He soon made it clear to us that he was not happy in his present life, and although it amused him to dance in the café, he did not find it very rewarding. We made a habit of going every night to see him dance, and were more and more impressed by his exquisite *flamenco* style, the precision and rhythm of his movements, and by his perfect control."[7] Felix Fernandez García was engaged to join the Ballets Russes and began to teach Massine the "fundamental grammar of the Spanish folk-dances."[8] When they returned to Spain at the end of May 1917, Massine and Diaghilev

274 renewed their contact with García. During July, Diaghilev organized a trip for himself and Massine round Spain visiting Saragossa, Toledo, Salamanca, Burgos, Seville, Cordoba, and Granada to absorb more Spanish culture and to study the variety of Spanish dancing. Falla and García went with them as their guides and were invaluable; wherever they went, García "was automatically accepted as a friend by the local dancers. He was able to arrange several special performances for us, and we spent many late nights listening to selected groups of singers, guitarists and dancers doing the *jota*, the *farruca*, or the *fandango*."[9]

Diaghilev and Massine initially thought that García would take the leading part, the Miller, in *Le Tricorne,* but it gradually became apparent that as his art was essentially improvizational he would be incapable of learning a clearly defined role, never mind repeating it exactly at every performance. Massine, on the other hand, from being taught by García, began to feel confident that he had sufficiently absorbed the intricacies of Spanish dancing to play the part himself. Furthermore, and tragically, it also became apparent that García had an unstable character. After several warning signs, a few weeks before the opening of *Le Tricorne* in London, García was found in the middle of the night dancing in a state of religious ecstasy in front of the altar of St Martin-in-the-Fields in Trafalgar Square. He was certified insane, taken to a mental institution in Epsom, Surrey, and stayed there until his death in 1941. Lydia Sokolova sadly commented by way of epitaph: "Felix's reason was the price fate demanded for the creation of a masterpiece."[10]

Sokolova was initially intended for the role of the Miller's Wife, and she and Massine spent hours rehearsing and developing their scenes. However, soon after the Ballets Russes season began at the Alhambra on 30 April 1919, Tamara Karsavina escaped from Russia and rejoined the company after an absence of five years. Diaghilev decided that she should create the role of the Miller's Wife. With generosity Sokolova wrote: "I had the pleasure of helping Massine to teach her the role."[11] But she had to admit that she could not teach her *all* the movements. Karsavina, in her turn, was generous about Massine: "I found him now no more a timid youth. Our first collaboration in the *Three-Cornered Hat* showed him to be a very exacting master. He now possessed accomplished skill as a dancer, and

his precocious ripeness and uncommon mastery of the stage singled him out, in my mind, as an exceptional ballet-master. It was his complete command of Spanish dancing that amazed me the most. On the Russian stage we had been used to a balletic stylisation of Spanish dancing, sugary at its best; but this was the very essence of Spanish folk-dancing."[12] His lessons had been well learnt.

Pablo Picasso, with his designs for the front cloth, décor, and costumes, provided the very essence of a Spanish setting. *Le Tricorne* was Picasso's second work for the theater. Diaghilev probably suggested the project to him when they were all working

on *Parade* in Rome in 1917.[13] Although Douglas Cooper wrote that Picasso was unaware of the plans to produce *Le Tricorne* when he returned to Paris from Barcelona in November 1917, it is more likely that García-Márquez is correct in his supposition when he states: "It seems safe to assume that Picasso, a member of Diaghilev's informal artistic council, would not be left out of any discussion of forthcoming productions, especially plans for a Spanish ballet."[14] In planning his Spanish ballet, Diaghilev wanted everything about it to be Spanish. As we have seen, there was a delay of more than year in putting the plan into effect and Diaghilev did not send a confirming con-

Below: Leonide Massine as the Miller on the set.

tract letter to Picasso until 15 April 1919.[15] The letter includes a reference to the front cloth suggested earlier by Picasso as a desirable addition in order to establish the right atmosphere. He had also suggested adding the human voice to some of the numbers for a more authentic Spanish sound. Diaghilev agreed, and wrote to Falla asking him to provide a short overture, perhaps orchestrations from the three piano pieces entitled *Andalusia*, and some vocalizations.

Surprisingly, Picasso found it difficult to reach the right scenic solution. Perhaps, being himself a native of Andalusia, he was spiritually too close to the setting to distil its essence immediately. It was only after making a great many sketches, with pencil or pen and ink, followed by watercolors, that he arrived at a solution which satisfied him by its simplicity. According to Douglas Cooper, all the drawings for *Le Tricorne* were made in London. For the front cloth, Picasso did not illustrate any particular moment in the ballet, but devised instead a typically recognizable Spanish scene of spectators at a bullfight, as a central panel between two borders. He painted this himself in Vladimir Polunin's scene-painting studio in Floral Street opposite the stage door of the Royal Opera House, Covent Garden.[16] Polunin described the making of the set: "Diaghileff came into the studio accompanied by a gentleman of medium height, southern complexion and wonderful eyes, whom he introduced to me as Pablo Picasso. After mutual greetings, Picasso showed me the booklet-*maquette* of his scene for a new ballet *Le Tricorne*, and we all began discussing the construction of the future setting. Having dealt so long with Bakst's complicated and ostentatious scenery, the austere simplicity of Picasso's drawing, with its total absence of unnecessary detail, the composition and unity of the colouring—in short, the synthetical character of the whole—was astounding. It was just as if one had spent a long time in a hot room and then passed into the fresh air . . . Picasso came to the studio daily, evinced a keen interest in everything, gave his instructions regarding the drawing and requested us to preserve its individuality and pay special attention to the colouring. The drawing, despite its deviation from the usual perspective, was set down with mathematical precision. The tones, of which there were four fundamental ones, were reproduced to a high degree of exactitude. All this care was of the utmost importance, for the entire scene was based on the very clever combination of the four fundamental tones and on a deeply meditated composition. The colours appeared remarkably quiet and required the addition of zinc white, a proceeding which, in scenes of the Bakst type, would have been considered a crime; but Picasso maintained that this led to a general unity of tone and effected a uniform opacity of colour . . . With him, there were never any doubts, alterations and variations so characteristic of 'designers' of inferior calibre, which react against the successful execution of a scene. Different proposals and variations were discussed while deciding on the colours, but, once everything had been settled, the given tone was not altered on the canvas by a hair's breadth."[17]

Picasso paid equal attention to the costumes, although some changes were forced on him by Diaghilev. One change, resulting in a compromise, was to Massine's costume, described by Grigoriev: "Picasso had given Massine knee-breeches. But the most important of all the dances was the Miller's *Farruca* for which dancers in Spain usually wear long, very tight trousers. Diaghilev therefore insisted that Massine should wear such trousers, maintaining that otherwise the true character of this dance would be obscured. Picasso, however, equally insisted on the knee-breeches; and it was only with some reluctance that he agreed to a compromise, whereby Massine should wear long trousers during the first half of the action and then change into knee-breeches for the rest."[18] Indeed, the costume design for the Miller shows a long trouser on the right leg and a knee-breech on the left. One can only imagine the fiery argument which Diaghilev and Picasso must have had, but which Grigoriev, tactfully, does not mention. There was no argument over Karsavina's costume, as she wrote: "The costume he finally evolved was a supreme masterpiece of pink silk and black lace of the simplest shape—a symbol more than an ethnographic reproduction of a national costume."[19]

All the participants concentrated on achieving a unity of expression, and the whole production became a symbol for Spain. Massine wrote: "*Le Tricorne* had begun as an attempt to synthesize Spanish folk-dances with classical techniques, but in the process of evolution it emerged as a choreographic interpretation of the Spanish temperament and way of life."[20]

Ansermet conducted at rehearsals. He wrote to Stravinsky on 18 July: "I am having great difficulty in setting Falla. The material is ignoble, full of faults, and illegible. The music is fresh, delightful, very beautiful in parts. But I am not mad about the orchestration. (Dare I say it's a bit 'pianistic'). A rehearsal on stage this morning: we're going to sweat from now till Tuesday. A white décor by Picasso, which is dazzling; wonderful costumes. And excellent choreography. Massine is a Spanish dancer. What he does is unforgettable. And they say that Karsavina doesn't dance as she used to, but I love her for her intelligent face and her poetic eyes."[21] Falla was to have conducted the first performance, but was unable to do so: only hours before, he heard that his mother was critically ill in Spain. A sympathetic Ansermet accompanied Falla to the station who, sadly, did not reach his mother in time to see her alive. Ansermet conducted the first performance instead.

Florence Grenfell, as was her custom, went to the first night and wrote in her diary: "Tuesday 22nd July. Teddy [Edward Grenfell] & I went to the Ballet in the evening. A new one was given called the 'Three Cornered Hat,' entirely a Spanish idea with Spanish music & scenery, it was most interesting & got a wonderful reception from a packed house."

The critic of *The Tatler*, neither very serious nor knowledgeable, wrote with flippant enthusiasm: "It is all very dainty and charming, and the dancing of Karsavina and M. Messine [sic] in the principle [sic] *roles* is more than sufficient in itself to fill the theatre whenever the little ballet is performed. Moreover, the convention-defying scenery and dresses by M. Picasso are an added attraction."[22] Cyril Beaumont, more serious, was most impressed by Massine: "Few of those who saw that first night will have forgotten the colour and bravura with which he invested his Farruca, the slow snap of the fingers followed by the pulsating thump of his feet, then the flickering movement of his hands held horizontally before him, palms facing and almost touching his breast. All at once this gave place to a new movement in which his feet chopped the ground faster and faster until he suddenly dropped to the ground on his hands, and as quickly leapt to his feet and stopped dead, his efforts greeted with thunderous applause."[23]

Le Tricorne remained Massine's own favorite ballet. It has been frequently revived, first by him (he danced in it until the 1950s), and subsequently by other companies.

172 Preliminary sketch for the setting

Iron gall ink with graphite signature on paper
6³/₁₆ x 8¹³/₁₆ in: 15.8 x 20 cm
Signed in pencil bottom right: "Picasso"
1933.515

Exhibitions: Paris 1929, No 54 (illustrated); Paris 1930, No 80; London Tooth 1930, No 47; New York 1933, No 49; Chicago 1933, No 127; Northampton 1934, No 127; Hartford 1934a; New Haven 1935; Middletown 1935; New York 1937–8, No 711; Paris 1939, No 304; Los Angeles 1939–40; Williamsburg 1940; Cambridge 1942; New York MoMA 1944a; New York 1946–7; Lawrence 1949; Edinburgh 1954, No 255; London 1954–5, No 294; Framingham 1956; Elmira 1958, No 4; Sarasota 1958; Indianapolis 1959, No 407; Hartford 1959, No 407; Eindhoven 1964; New York 1965–6, No 141 (illustrated p 69); Toulouse 1965, No 26; New York 1966–7; Princeton 1968; Strasbourg 1969, No 277 (illustrated No 120); Frankfurt-am-Main 1969, No 67; Blommenholm 1971; Hartford 1973; Hartford 1974; Hempstead 1974, No 115; Chicago 1975, No 48; Hartford 1978–9; New York 1980; Coral Gables 1982; Hartford 1988; Worcester 1989.
Illustrations: Buckle 1955, p 89 No 113; Clarke and Crisp 1978, pl 92 p 127; Cooper, No 167; Gontcharova, p 71; Haskell, p 85; Rischbeiter, p 77 No 77c.

This is one of the many preliminary drawings Picasso made for the setting. In his definitive book on Picasso's work for the theater, Douglas Cooper reproduced eighteen different versions as well as pages from a sketchbook showing other variations: "He seems to have tried out at least twenty different ways of setting the stage—some with the bridge in front of the arch, some with no arch at all, some with trees—as well as a number of colour combinations."[24] The bridge was an essential part of the set because it was essential to the action,

but it is always shown behind the arch, not in front of it. This sketch is the only one of its kind; the others are line drawings. In it Picasso was considering and trying out tonal values in black and white by shading some parts of the drawing, while ignoring the natural perspective and the shadows which would fall realistically. In the final drawing, the tonal values of the underside of the arch and the sky were reversed so that the sky was darker than the arch. The architecture was also simplified, and the ladder and millstone wheels were left out.

Picasso could not resist contributing to the painting of his set, as the scene painter Vladimir Polunin described: "Diaghileff laughingly transmitted to me Picasso's wish to paint the stars on the sky with his own hand, which he informed me he had granted on the strict condition that no blot should be made. Picasso, putting on slippers, then painted on the back-cloth seven stars and the silhouette of the distant town."[25]

Cyril Beaumont described the set as he saw it at the first night: "Picasso's scenery, a remarkably successful attempt to express the sun-scorched mountains of Spain in the simplest terms, was acclaimed by painters as a masterpiece. Brevity is the soul of wit, and, it might be added, of good stage decoration. In essence, the scene consisted of a white back-cloth with a patch of blue sky at the top and a few grey lines suggesting distant mountains; before the back-cloth was a white cut-cloth in the shape of a great arch, its edges shaded with grey, and, inset, a practicable semi-circular bridge stretching from one leg to the other."[26]

173   Seated dancer

Graphite and conté crayon on paper
12⁹⁄₁₆ x 9⅝ in: 31.9 x 24.5 cm
Unsigned and undated
Reverse inscribed in pencil in Picasso's hand: "4-1-23," and in another hand: "720 / le noir seulement / on fera le grattage / et restitution sur le zinc (only black / we will do the scratching and restoration on the zinc)," "No 2"
1933.517

Exhibitions: New York 1933, ? No 51 (described as "Dancer"); Chicago 1933, No 129; Northampton 1934, No 129; Hartford 1934a; New Haven 1935; San Francisco 1935–6; Chicago 1940; New York 1941; Michigan 1957; San Antonio 1958; Elmira 1958, No 55; Indianapolis 1959 (not in catalogue); Toronto 1964, No 64; Toulouse 1965, No 90; Hartford 1965, No 28; New York 1965–6, No 138 (illustrated p 69); New York 1966–7; Hartford 1973; Hartford 1974; Bielefeld 1988; Hartford 1988; Worcester 1989.
Illustration: Cooper, No 297.

The title is Douglas Cooper's, and he dates the drawing 1921. In the exhibition in Toulouse in 1965, *Picasso et le Théâtre*, with which Cooper was associated, this drawing was exhibited grouped with designs for *Cuadro Flamenco*, a suite of Andalusian dances with set and costumes by Picasso, first performed at the Théâtre de la Gaîté-Lyrique in Paris on 17 May 1921. The suggestion in the catalogue is that this drawing was made during rehearsals.

However, the attitude and the costume of the sitter relate closely to other drawings reproduced in Cooper's book, two called *Saltimbanque seated* dated 1922 (on pp 52, 53), and one called *The Sigh* (No 315) dated 1923. The latter drawing is ostensibly a portrait of Serge Lifar, according to Lifar, done in the basement rehearsal room of the theater in Monte Carlo during a break in rehearsals for *Noces*. This was when Picasso said to Diaghilev about Lifar, "He'll make a dancer." Picasso's date on the reverse, while possibly the date of the conversion of the drawing into a print rather than that of the drawing itself, suggests that the later date 1923 is the correct one. The costume in this drawing, less defined than in the others, is also reminiscent of a *saltimbanque*, or member of a traveling circus, a favorite recurring figure in Picasso's imagery.

174* Two dancers resting

Ink on paper
13¾ x 10 in: 35 x 25.4 cm
Signed and dated in ink bottom left: "Picasso / 25"
Gift of Felix Wildenstein
1934.2

Exhibitions: ? Connecticut Valley Schools Art 1937–8; New York 1939; Chicago 1940, No 196; Boston 1940; Detroit 1948; Hartford 1949, No 59; Stamford 1957; Milwaukee 1957, No 104; Hartford 1973, No 29; New York 1965–6, No 139 (illustrated p 68); New York 1966–7; Princeton 1968; Hartford 1973; Hartford 1974; Little Rock 1987–8; Worcester 1989.
Illustration: Cooper, No 356.

The title is Douglas Cooper's, and he dates the drawing 1925, adding that it was executed in Monte Carlo. It is one of a group of thirty drawings Picasso made of dancers resting or rehearsing in Monte Carlo during April 1925. Cooper wrote: "Picasso spent a short time with his wife [the Russian dancer Olga Khoklova] and young son at Monte Carlo, where the company was performing and rehearsing new works. Once again, Picasso resumed his close contacts with them all. Massine was

there, working as choreographer. The great ballet teacher Enrico Cecchetti had temporarily closed his school in Italy to help train Diaghilev's new young dancers, and on 29 April Picasso drew his portrait in a seated pose . . . But Picasso seems to have spent most of his time in the practice studio. For during this visit he produced one of his great series of ballet drawings: a man and woman in an abandoned pose, groups of female dancers, and especially a series showing *corps de ballet* boys exercising at the bar or elegantly relaxing. Of particular interest among these is a drawing of Serge Lifar."[27]

175   Two dancers

Ink on paper
24¹¹⁄₁₆ x 18¾ in: 62.8 x 47.9 cm
Signed and dated in ink top right: "Picasso /
    1ᵉʳ janvier 1926"
1933.516

Exhibitions: New York 1933, No 50; Chicago 1933,
    No 128; Northampton 1934, No 128; Hartford
    1934a; New Haven 1935; San Francsico
    1935–6; Paris 1939, No 314; Poughkeepsie
    1940; Baltimore 1941, No 21; Sarasota 1958,
    No 62; Richmond 1959 (illustrated fig 3);
    Hartford 1964; Toulouse 1965, No 101 (illus-
    trated); New York 1965–6, No 140 (illustrated
    p 69); New York 1966–7; Princeton 1968;
    Hartford 1973; Hartford 1974; Little Rock
    1987–8; Hartford 1988; Worcester 1989.
Illustration: Cooper, No 384; Schaikevitch, pl XIX
    (with a signature added later. titled "Move-
    ment").

According to Douglas Cooper this drawing, dated
January 1926, was made in Paris, yet it is part
of the same series as the previous drawing.

Notes

1   Serge Grigoriev, *The Diaghilev Ballet*, pp 122–3.
2   *Las Meninas*, with set by Carlo Socrate, costumes
    by José-Maria Sert, was first performed at the
    Teatro Eugenia-Victoria, San Sebastian on
    25 August 1916. Massine wrote: "In choreo-
    graphing the various *pas de deux* I made no
    attempt to re-create the grandeur of Spain's
    Golden Age. It was merely a personal
    interpretation of the formality and underlying
    sadness that I had glimpsed in Velazquez and in
    so many seventeenth-century Spanish paintings,
    counterbalanced by flowing movements which
    blended with the melancholy strains of Fauré's

evocative music." Leonide Massine, *My Life in
Ballet*, p 90. It was planned to enlarge *Las
Meninas* into *Les Jardins d'Aranjuez* in 1919. The
production was announced for the Alhambra
season, but never took place.
3   Leonide Massine, *op cit*, p 115.
4   *El corregidor y la molinera* is a traditional Spanish
    story based on an anonymous eighteenth-
    century romance *El molinero de arcos*, related as a
    novel by Alarcón in 1874.
5   Leonide Massine, *op cit*, p 115. Massine then
    wrongly telescopes events by stating that this
    was the first time that the ballet was suggested.
6   Lydia Sokolova, *Dancing for Diaghilev*, p 113.
7   Leonide Massine, *op cit*, p 114.
8   Leonide Massine, *ibid*, p 116.
9   Leonide Massine, *ibid*, p 117.
10 Lydia Sokolova, *op cit*, p 137.
11 Lydia Sokolova, *ibid*, p 136.
12 Tamara Karsavina, *Theatre Street*, pp 245–6.
13 In London *Le Tricorne* was produced before
    Parade.
14 Vicente García-Márquez, *Massine*, p 108.
15 "My dear Picasso. I ask you to undertake the
    design of the ballet *Three-Cornered Hat* with
    music by E. de Falla for my Ballets Russes
    productions. You will make the necessary
    sketches for the front-cloth, set, costumes, and
    properties for the said ballet and you will direct
    the execution of the work of making the scenery
    and costumes painting yourself certain parts of
    the canvas as you deem fit. For the said work I
    will pay you the sum of ten thousand francs.
    You will be in London from 20 May 1919 until
    the first night of the ballet in London. It is
    understood that the sketches remain your
    property and that the front-cloth, set and
    costumes become my property. Your devoted,
    Serge de Diaghilev." The Archives of the Musée
    Picasso, quoted in Brigitte Léal *Picasso: Le
    Tricorne*, p 25.
16 In 1926, Diaghilev, again short of money, cut the
    central panel out of the front cloth and sold it as
    a painting through the dealer Paul Rosenberg.
    The Swiss collector G. F. Reber bought it in 1928.
    After the Second World War, it was acquired by
    Seagram and is now displayed in "The Four
    Seasons" restaurant in the Seagram Building in
    New York City.
17 Vladimir Polunin, *The Continental Method of
    Scene Painting*, pp 53–4.
18 Serge Grigoriev, *op cit*, pp 156–7. But John
    Percival has stated that in later years Massine
    kept to his long trousers all through.
19 Tamara Karsavina, *op cit*, p 247.
20 Leonide Massine, *op cit*.
21 Ernest Ansermet to Igor Stravinsky, dated
    18 July 1919 in Claude Tappolet, *Correspondance
    Ernest Ansermet–Igor Stravinsky*.
22 Anon, in *The Tatler* London 22 July 1919.
23 Cyril W. Beaumont, *The Diaghilev Ballet in
    London*, p 145.
24 Douglas Cooper, *Picasso Theatre*, p 40.
25 Vladimir Polunin, *The Continental Method of
    Scene Painting*, p 55.
26 Cyril W. Beaumont, *The Diaghilev Ballet in
    London*, p 144.
27 Douglas Cooper, *Picasso Theatre*, p 61.

Pedro Pruna

Spanish
born 1904 Barcelona
died 1977 Barcelona

Les Matelots (The Sailors)

Ballet in 5 scenes by Boris Kochno
Composer: Georges Auric
Conductor: Marc-César Scotto
Choreographer: Leonide Massine
Principal Dancers:
The Young Girl: Vera Nemtchinova
    Her Friend: Lydia Sokolova
    First Sailor: Leon Woizikovsky
    Second (American) Sailor: Théodore Slavinsky
    Third Sailor: Serge Lifar
    Musician: George Dines
Company: Diaghilev's Ballets Russes
First Performance: 17 June 1925, Théâtre de la
    Gaîté-Lyrique, Paris

Synopsis
Adapted from two different programs.
    Scene 1: The Betrothal, and the Departure of
the Sailors.
    Scene 2: Solitude. The young girl awaits the
return of the first sailor, her fiancé.
    Scene 3: Return and Variations of the sailors.
The Test: unrecognizable under the disguise of false
beards, the first sailor and his two companions try
in vain to seduce the young girl.
    Scene 4: The Temptation in the bar. Her friend
tries to lure the young girl toward the bar where
she wants her to find the sailors, but the young girl
refuses to be lured.
    Scene 5: Finale. *Entrée* by the sailors who
remove their disguises. The young girl recognizes
her fiancé to whom she has remained faithful. The
sailors salute her.

In 1925 Massine returned to the Ballets Russes after some typical chicanery by Diaghilev to choreograph two ballets (for the circumstances, see *Zéphire et Flore*, pp 150–52, the first of the two ballets to be produced). The second was *Les Matelots*, described by Massine as "a lighthearted romp with practically no plot."[1]

Planning for the ballet, originally called *Les Marins*, began in 1924. The scenario, such as it is, was elaborated by Boris Kochno. It was his first original ballet.[2] A score was commissioned from Georges Auric. It was their second ballet together; they had collaborated on *Les Fâcheux* (see pp 147–49), first produced on 19 January 1924 in Monte Carlo. *Les Matelots* was also intended by Diaghilev to be another step on Lifar's ladder to stardom.

This youthful team was joined by another young man, Pedro Pruna, a Catalan artist, whom Jean Cocteau had met in Picasso's studio in 1924, and whose paintings he much admired. Cocteau spoke about his work to Kochno, who arranged a meeting: "Shortly thereafter, Pruna came to call on us—Diaghilev and me—at the Hôtel Savoy in Paris, and showed us photographs of his canvases. Inspired by Picasso's 'Ingres period,' they promised a limpid, poetic theatrical work."[3] Diaghilev immediately commissioned him to design *Les Matelots*.

Rehearsals took place in Monte Carlo where the Ballets Russes were now regularly based during the winter. At first Massine objected strongly to Kochno's idea that the ballet should have only five characters, and insisted on introducing a *corps de ballet*. But, as Kochno wrote: "After attending one rehearsal, however, Diaghilev disapproved of the 'overpopulated' version of the ballet, and on leaving the studio, he said to Massine, 'This ballet is written for five people and it will be danced by five people. Not one more!'"[4] Massine does not refer to his argument with Kochno, and modestly merely states that his choreography "consisted mainly of a series of dances by three sailors, the fiancée of one of them, and her girl-friend."[5] Lydia Sokolova, who danced the part of the girlfriend, was more revealing about the choreography: "In working out *Les Matelots* Massine really seemed to be back in his old form: it was one of the most successful of our light-hearted ballets . . . With the exception of Lifar, we were all old hands at Massine's choreography and he knew exactly what he could expect from each of us . . . Lifar looked about sixteen: he was slim, agile, flexible in movement and altogether delightful to watch. His variation was a waltz, with a number of slow turns in attitude or arabesque, which showed off the great advance of his technique. We all enjoyed dancing in this ballet, not only because of the amusing steps Massine had given us, but because Auric's music was danceable and easy to understand."[6] The visible enjoyment of the dancers was one of the main reasons for the ballet's success. Another reason was accidental. Massine had arranged a dance with chairs for the three sailors. On the first night in Paris, as described by Lifar, "the first to appear on the stage was Woizikowsky, the second Slavinsky, and the third myself. I was busy pasting a small moustache on to my lip in the wings, and was about to take hold of a chair, when that very moment Woizikowsky tries a chair, then quickly exchanges it with Slavinsky, who in turn takes my chair, handing me Woizikowsky's. I seize it, and, to my dismay, find it completely loose in the joints. We begin our dance with the chairs, and first the seat of my chair falls out, and then one of the legs goes . . . Nevertheless, I jump on my chair, but only to find a second leg drop off, leaving me with the back, the frame and two diagonal legs . . . With a more cheerful smile than possibly my part demands, I jump on my chair yet again, by some miracle preserving my balance, then drop on my seat as the last chord is struck; at which the whole thing collapses with a sound like the crack of a whip, and I fall to the stage amid the wild applause of the house."[7] The audience, of course, thought the collapse was deliberate, and the unintentional comic business was then retained.

In 1925 Diaghilev had arranged with Sir Oswald Stoll a long season at the London Coliseum from 18 May until 1 August, so it seemed that for the first time there would be no Paris season that year. However, Diaghilev managed to fit in six performances as his "Eighteenth Season" at the Gaîté-Lyrique between 15 and 20 June, during which *Les Matelots* was given for the first time. Although, on Diaghilev's instructions, *Les Matelots* was to be danced by only five dancers, he introduced a sixth character during final rehearsals. He had been so taken by a busker whom he had noticed entertaining the queues outside the theater waiting for gallery seats by playing on a pair of spoons like castanets, that he engaged him to perform on stage. Kochno writes that George Peter Dines appeared on stage only in London, but in fact he also appeared in Paris.[8] Although the critic of *The Times* praised Dines and wrote that he "added a touch of appropriate colour to the café scene, and was too like the real thing not to be true,"[9] Cyril Beaumont, a more sensitive ballet critic, was of the opinion that "notwithstanding his skill, he did not really fit into the scheme, because the essence of ballet is suggestion rather than photographic reproduction, and the two did not blend."[10]

Above, left to right: Leon Woizikovsky as the First Sailor, Vera Nemtchinova as the Young Girl, Théodore Slavinsky as the Second Sailor, Lydia Sokolova as the Young Girl's Friend, and Serge Lifar as the Third Sailor.

176 Cube design for the set for scenes 1, 2, 3, and 4: The Betrothal, Solitude, the Return, and the Temptation

Crayon or pastel, ink and glaze, chalk and graphic notations on paper mounted to board
23¾ x 19½ in: 65.5 x 49.5 cm (board 69.7 x 53.7 cm)
Signed and dated in ink lower right: "Pruna / 1925"
Inscribed at top in pencil: "pour le dé[cor]"; and in pen: "matelots"; at bottom in pencil: "à faire dé[cor]"
1933.523

Exhibitions: Paris 1929, No 60; Paris 1930, No 85; Chicago 1933, No 135; Northampton 1934, No 135; Hartford 1934b; New Haven 1935; San Francisco 1935–6; Paris 1939, No 318; Poughkeepsie 1940; Edinburgh 1954, No 306; London 1954–5, No 348; Indianapolis 1959, No 416; New York 1965–6, No 145 (illustrated p 71); New York 1966–7; Strasbourg 1969, No 404; Frankfurt-am-Main 1969, No 117; Hartford 1974; Hartford 1978–9; Columbus 1989; Worcester 1989.

An important part of the audience's enjoyment of *Les Matelots* was also the scenery by Pruna. According to Propert, "*Les Matelots* showed us the freshest, liveliest décor we had seen since *Le Tricorne*,"[11] an opinion shared by the critic of *The Times*.[12] They compared Pruna's talent to Picasso's, while maintaining that he retained his own individuality: "There was nothing whatever of the copyist in him. The language he spoke in may have been that of Picasso, but what he said came directly from his own brain. Whatever one thought of his drawings, they could not have been mistaken, or intended to be mistaken, for Picasso's."[13] André Levinson was not so impressed: "With M. Pruna we relapse into pastiche; it is chocolate box Picasso. M. Pruna wants to recast what that genius has done in the theater: but instead of genius all he has is taste, that quality of the feeble-minded."[14]

Florence Grenfell, in her diary, encapsulated the feeling at the time:

Saturday 13th June: The company are off to Paris tomorrow for one week & then come back here, they have been cruelly over-worked lately preparing for Paris & are fagged out in this grt: heat.

Friday 26th June: Vera [Nemtchinova] and I went shopping in the afternoon & also went to see Hilda Sokolova in her dressing room at the Coliseum. The week in Paris was not a grt: success, Dolin had an awful row with Diaghileff & has left the company, so Lifar is now left alone in his glory! They say Miassine's [sic] new Ballet "Les Trois Matlots" [sic] is a masterpiece.

Monday 29th June: We went to see the new Ballet "Les Trois Matlots", it is quite splendid. Miassine's choreography is delicious & has real humour, & is interpreted superbly by the dancers especially Slavinsky, Hilda & Leon, the music by Auric is charming & excellent scenery & costumes by a young Spanish painter Pruna by name. It received an ovation, & Miassine who was dragged onto the stage was quite overcome. It is the best Ballet Diaghileff has produced for a v. long time. I went on to a party at Sybil Colefax, there was music but such crowds & so much talking one could not enjoy it.

In London *Les Matelots* was repeated every season, but in Paris it was dropped from the repertoire after 1927.

Each of these designs was painted on one of the four sides of a large cube, positioned to the right of the stage as seen by the audience. The appropriate side was turned to face the audience to indicate the relevant episode in the story: thus the ship, top left, faced the audience to show the departure of the sailors and again to show the return; the cupid, top right, showed both the betrothal and the temptation; the figure bottom right showed solitude. The cube remained confusingly *in situ* while the backcloths were changed. It was removed for the finale.

The critic of *The Times*, describing the set in general, wrote: "It is also full of amusing invention—we liked especially the revolving cube which signified for us the departure of the sailors, the loneliness and fidelity of the maiden, and then by the return of the ship on its first surface, the homecoming—and there was some excellent draughtsmanship in the designs."[15] Levinson, on the other hand, wrote rather sourly: "M. Pruna's décor tries to create an atmosphere; it is split up into several backcloths one after the other and a cube which pivots with a different image on each vertical surface; I could not figure out what this cube was meant to do."[16]

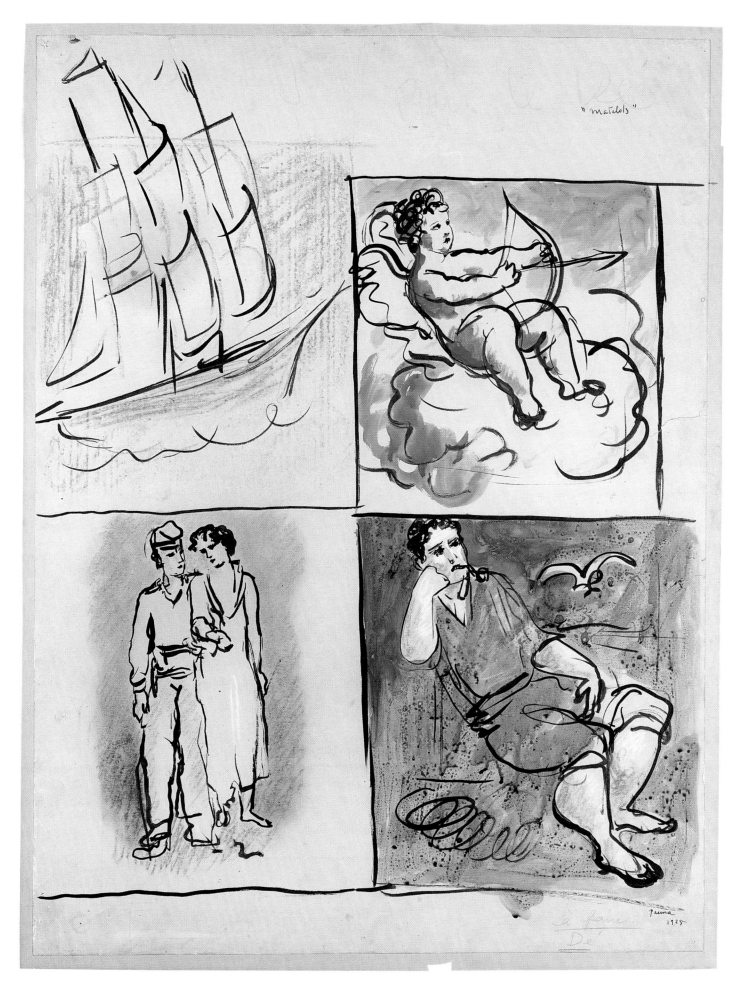

"Matelots"

Pruna
1925

177 Design for the back cloth for scene 4: A slum quarter at night

Graphite, pastel and ink, collage of paper mounted on board
18¹¹⁄₁₆ x 23½ in: 47.4 x 59.6 cm (board 55.4 x 70.8 cm)
Signed and dated in pencil lower right: "Pruna / 25"
1933.522

Exhibitions: London 1926, No 33; Paris 1929, No 59; London Tooth 1930, No 59; London Claridge 1930, No 82; Paris 1930, No 84; Chicago 1933, No 134; Northampton 1934, No 134; Hartford 1934b; New Haven 1935; San Francisco 1935–6; Paris 1939, No 317; Williamsburg 1940; Edinburgh 1954, No 298; London 1954–5, No 340; Elmira 1958, No 11; Indianapolis 1959, No 415; New York 1965–6, No 144 (illustrated p 70); New York 1966–7; Princeton 1968; Strasbourg 1969, No 403 (illustrated No 99); Frankfurt-am-Main 1969, No 116; Amherst 1974; Hempstead 1974, No 119; Chicago 1975; Hartford 1978–9; Columbus 1989; Worcester 1989.

Illustrations: Gadan and Maillard, p 226 (color); Gontcharova, p 87; Hansen, fig 54; Pozharskaya and Volodina, p 244; Souvenir Program, Théâtre de Monte-Carlo 1926.

The five scenes in the ballet had five different backcloths: all of them, except the finale, have a distant view of a port suggested by the tops of masts. All the backcloths, with the exception of this one, were painted in pale pastel colors. As this is the only scene which takes place at night, it is in darker colors with a subtle effect of moonlight beaming through the alley between the houses and through the open door. The painted cube was placed in front of the house in the right foreground.

Another design, the backcloth for scene 2, remained in the Lifar collection until it was sold at the Lifar sale in Paris in 1974, lot 90. It was acquired by the Bibliothèque-Musée de l'Opéra, Paris.

178 Design for the back cloth for scene 5: Finale

Graphite, ink, tempera and/or watercolor, yellow
glaze with white highlights on paper
14⁵/₁₆ x 16⁹/₁₆ in: 36.5 x 42 cm
Signed in pencil bottom right: "Pruna"
1933.521

Exhibitions: London 1926, No 32; Paris 1929, No
58; London Tooth 1930, No 58; Paris 1930, No
83; New York, No 53; Chicago 1933, No 133;
Northampton 1934, No 133; Hartford 1934b;
New Haven 1935; San Francisco 1935–6; Paris
1939, No 316 (illustrated p 38); Williamsburg
1940; New York MoMA 1944a; Edinburgh
1954, No 294; London 1954–5, No 336; Michigan 1957; Indianapolis 1959, No 414; Storrs
1963; New York 1965–6, No 143 (illustrated
p 70); Princeton 1968; Strasbourg 1969, No
406; Frankfurt-am-Main 1969, No 119; Hartford 1974; Hartford 1978–9; Worcester 1989.
Illustrations: Amberg, pl 49; Buckle, p 108 No 145;
Lynham, p 141; Percival, p 107; Pozharskaya
and Volodina, p 245b; Propert 1931, pl XIV;
The Studio London September 1933, p AD VI.

For his setting for the finale Pruna turned
away from the impressionistic realism of
the other scenes. The dancers were dwarfed
by the two huge figures leaning against a
pale brown rock painted in fine outline,
with large areas left as unpainted canvas, in
front of a pale blue sea merging into a sky
without an obvious horizon. The symbolism
of the girl with her fishing net and the sailor
with his sailing boat, with the anchor
between them, may be obvious, but was
perfect for the mood of the ballet. The
delicacy of the painting ensured that the
dancers were not overpowered.

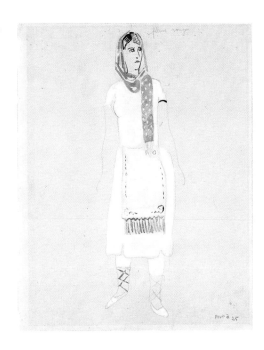

dark serge skirt with a grey top, a little white bolero jacket with criss-cross braid embroidery, and a fish-net snood with a tassel. Slavinsky, Woizikovsky and Lifar represented an American, a Spanish and a French sailor."[18] Sokolova refers to Nemtchinova's "red satin dress" but both the design and the photograph show a white dress. Perhaps Sokolova remembered wrongly, or perhaps the color of Nemtchinova's dress was changed later.

Two other costume designs (an earlier version for Sokolova's costume, and one for George Dines, the spoons player) remained in Lifar's collection and were sold at Sotheby's London, Lot 42, on 9 May 1984.

179 Costume design for Vera Nemtchinova as the Young Girl

Graphite, tempera and/or watercolor, ink with
    white highlights on paper
10⁹⁄₁₆ x 8¼ in: 26.7 x 21 cm
Signed and dated in crayon bottom right: "Pruna /
    25"
Inscribed in pencil top right: "fleurs rouges" ("red
    flowers"), bottom center right: "espadrilles"
Reverse inscribed in pencil (not in artist's hand) top
    right: "Nemtchinova"
1933.524

Exhibitions: Paris 1929;[17] London Tooth 1930;[17]
    Paris 1930;[17] New York 1933;[17] Chicago 1933,
    136–138;[17] Northampton 1934, No 136;
    Hartford 1934b; New Haven 1935; San Fran-
    cisco 1935–6; Paris 1939, No 320 ?; Williams-
    burg 1940; Washington D.C. 1950–1;
    Edinburgh 1954, No 305 ?; London 1954–5,
    No 347 ?; Michigan 1957; Indianapolis 1959,
    No 417; New York 1965–6, No 146 (illustrated
    p 72); New York 1966–7; Princeton 1968;
    Hartford 1978–9; Worcester 1989.

The costume designs are all drawn in the manner of straightforward, traditional costume designs without any ambiguity, so that they can be interpreted accurately and easily by a costumier. Indeed, a comparison between the designs and the photograph of the dancers demonstrates just how accurate the results were.

There is, however, a strange discrepancy. Lydia Sokolova wrote: "Vera Nemtchinova's role was that of a rather better-class girl than mine: she looked pretty in a short red satin dress with a spotted apron, and a neat scarf on her head. In keeping with my more oafish character, I was given an ugly and shapeless garment which consisted of a

180 Costume design for Lydia Sokolova as the Young Girl's Friend

Graphite, tempera and/or watercolor, ink with
    white highlights on paper
10⁹⁄₁₆ x 8¼ in: 26.9 x 21 cm
Signed in pencil lower right: "Pruna"
Inscribed in pencil bottom right: "espadrilles
    blanches" ("white espadrilles")
Reverse inscribed in pencil: "Sokolova"
1933.529

Exhibitions: Paris 1929;[17] London Tooth 1930;[17]
    Paris 1930;[17] New York 1933;[17] Chicago 1933,
    Nos 136–138;[17] Northampton 1934, No 141;
    Hartford 1934b; New Haven 1935; Paris 1939,
    No 320 ?; Poughkeepsie 1940; Williamsburg
    1940; Edinburgh 1954, ? No 305 ; London
    1954–5, ? No 347; Indianapolis 1959, No 424;
    New York 1965–6, No 147 (illustrated p 72; not
    shown in New York); New York 1966–7;
    Worcester 1989.

181 Costume design for Leon Woizikovsky as the First Sailor

Graphite, tempera and/or watercolor with crayon
    notations on paper
10⁹⁄₁₆ x 8³⁄₁₆ in: 26.7 x 20.9 cm
Signed and dated in crayon bottom right: "Pruna /
    25"
Inscribed in crayon top left: "à Serge Lifar / en
    attendant / le voir sur les / planches, pour le
    triomphal succès / à l'Opera" ("for Serge Lifar
    waiting to see him on the boards in a tri-
    umphal success at the Opera"); top right (not
    in Pruna's hand): "SK4"; lower center right:
    "espadrilles blanches"; lower center left: "sac
    marin" ("sailor's kit bag"); in pencil bottom left
    (not in Pruna's hand): "Leon / Woizikowsky"
1933.525

Exhibitions: ? Paris 1929;[17] ? London Tooth 1930;[17]
    ? Paris 1930;[17] New York 1933;[17] Chicago
    1933;[17] Northampton 1934, No 137; Hartford
    1934b; New Haven 1935; Washington D.C.
    1950–1; Edinburgh 1954, No 304; London
    1954–5, No 346; Michigan 1957; Elmira 1958,
    No 37; Indianapolis 1959, No 418; New York
    1965–6, No 148 (illustrated p 72); New York
    1966–7; Princeton 1968; Hempstead 1974, No
    118; Hartford 1978–9; Columbus 1989;
    Worcester 1989.

It is curious that Pruna gave to Lifar the costume design for Woizikovsky and not the one for him. It is also curious that Pruna, in his dedication, is waiting to see Lifar on the boards of the Opéra when *Les Matelots* was performed at the Gaîté-Lyrique. As Pruna could not have mistaken the theater, the only explanation is that he gave Lifar the design later. After 1925, the only times the Ballets Russes performed at the Opéra were on 27 and 29 December 1927, and for four performances between 20 December 1928 and 3 January 1929.

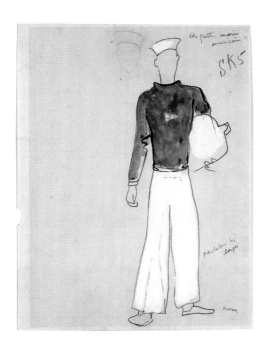

182 Costume design for Théodore Slavinsky as the Second (American) Sailor

Graphite, tempera and/or watercolor and ink with white highlights on paper
10⁹⁄₁₆ x 8½ in: 26.8 x 21.1 cm
Signed in pencil bottom right: "Pruna"
Inscribed in pencil top right: "casquette marin / americain" ("American sailor's cap"); lower center right: "pantalons très / larges" ("very wide trousers"); upper right (not in Pruna's hand): "SK5"
1933.526

Exhibitions: ? Paris 1929;[17] ? London Tooth 1930;[17] ? Paris 1930;[17] ? New York 1933;[17] Chicago 1933;[17] Northampton 1934, No 138; Hartford 1934b; New Haven 1935; San Francisco 1935–6; Williamsburg 1940; Washington D.C. 1950–1; Edinburgh 1954, No 303; London 1954–5, No 345; Michigan 1957; Elmira 1958, No 38; Indianapolis 1959, No 419; New York 1965–6, No 149 (illustrated p 72); New York 1966–7; Columbus 1989; Worcester 1989.

183 Design for the cover of the Souvenir Program of Diaghilev's Ballets Russes season in Paris, June 1925

Graphite, ink, tempera and/or watercolor, glaze with white highlights and red ink notations on paper
11⁹⁄₁₆ x 14¹⁄₁₆ in: 30.2 x 35.4 cm
Signed and dated in ink lower right: "Pruna / 25"
Inscribed in red ink bottom center: "fond noir si possible" ("black background if possible")
1933.520

Exhibitions: London Tooth 1930, No 64; Chicago 1933, No 132; Northampton 1934, No 132; Hartford 1934b; New Haven 1935; San Francisco 1935–6; Paris 1939, No 315; Washington

D.C. 1950–1; Edinburgh 1954, No 307; London 1954–5, No 349; Indianapolis 1959, No 421; New York 1965–6, No 142 (illustrated p 70); New York 1966–7; Strasbourg 1969, No 413; Frankfurt-am-Main 1969, No 120; Hartford 1974; Hartford 1978–9; Coral Gables 1982; Columbus 1989; Worcester 1989.
Illustration: Ballets Russes *Souvenir Program* 1925, cover.

Pruna's instruction was ignored. Instead of an overall black background, the illustrated cover of the souvenir program was an exact reproduction of this design which makes it look misconceived and incongruous.

There is a preliminary drawing for this design in the Dance Collection of the New York Public Library.

Notes

1 Leonide Massine, *My Life in Ballet*, p 164.
2 Previously he had adapted Pushkin for Stravinsky's *Mavra* (see pp 318–22), Molière for *Les Fâcheux* (see pp 147–49), and Didelot for *Zéphire et Flore* (see pp 150–52).
3 Boris Kochno, *Diaghilev and the Ballets Russes*, p 228.
4 Boris Kochno, *ibid*, p 229.
5 Leonide Massine, *op cit*, p 164.
6 Lydia Sokolova, *Dancing for Diaghilev*, pp 234–5.
7 Serge Lifar, *Serge Diaghilev*, pp 413–4.
8 There were three performances in Paris on 17, 18 and 20 June. The first performance in London was on 29 June 1925.
9 Anon, *The Times* London 30 June 1925, quoted by Nesta Macdonald in *Diaghilev Observed*, p 310.
10 Cyril W. Beaumont, *The Diaghilev Ballet in London*, p 250.
11 W. A. Propert, *The Russian Ballet 1921–1929*, p 33.
12 In his notice dated 30 June, see note 9.
13 W. A. Propert, *op cit*, p 34.
14 André Levinson, "Les Matelots" in *Comoedia* Paris 19 June 1925, p 2.
15 Anon, *The Times* London 30 June 1925, quoted by Nesta Macdonald in *Diaghilev Observed*, p 310.
16 André Levinson, "Les Matelots" in *Comoedia* Paris 19 June 1925, p 2.
17 The catalogue for the exhibition Paris 1929 includes No 63, described as "2 costumes pour le ballet *Les Matelots*"; for London 1930 includes Nos 60 and 61, described as "Two costumes for the ballet *Les Matelots*"; for Paris 1930 includes Nos 87 and 88, each described as "costume"; for New York 1933 includes No 54, described as "costumes"; for Chicago 1933 includes Nos 136–138, described as "'Les Matelots' costumes," but in each case it is not possible to identify the particular designs exhibited. This note therefore applies also to the following costume designs Nos 180–182. The catalogue for Chicago 1933 also includes No 141, described as "'Pastorale' costume." Since there is no costume design for *La Pastorale* in the collection, but four designs for *Les Matelots* in the collection, but four designs for *Les Matelots*, this would have been the unidentifiable fourth (only three were included in the catalogue as being for *Les Matelots*).
18 Lydia Sokolova, *Dancing for Diaghilev*, p 234.

Ballet in 12 scenes by Boris Kochno
Composer: Georges Auric
Conductor: Roger Desormière
Choreographer: George Balanchine
Principal Dancers:
    The Star: Felia Dubrovska
    The Telegraph Boy: Serge Lifar
    The Young Lady: Tamara Gevergeva
    The Director: Leon Woizikovsky
Company: Diaghilev's Ballets Russes
First Performance: 29 May 1926, Théâtre Sarah-
    Bernhardt, Paris

Synopsis

From the program:
    "1   Prelude.
    2   *Entrée* of the Telegraph Boy on a bicycle. He stops, sees a river, puts down his satchel of telegrams, and rushes off for a swim.
    3   *Entrée* and *divertissement* of the Young Girls. One of them discovers the bather and decides to play a trick on him. She runs off with her friends carrying his satchel of telegrams.
    4   The Telegraph Boy gets out of the water. Not noticing anything he falls asleep behind a rock in the middle of a field.
    5   *Entrée* of the members of a film company. Stars, actors, the director, camera crew and technicians. They do not see the sleeping Telegraph Boy.
    6   Dance of the Director. He indicates what he wants done.
    7   The scenery is erected. A cinematic town takes shape.
    8   Musical interval. The camera crew begin to turn the cameras, the technicians light the lamps.
    9   Filming. The Star and two actors. She receives a letter while the others sing. She dismisses the actors. Left alone, she tears up the letter.
    10 The Telegraph Boy wakes up. He is surprised to find himself in the middle of a set, near an unknown woman. His appearance interrupts the action.
    11 *Pas de deux*. The Star and the Telegraph Boy. Surprise, invitation, dance and exit of the couple.
    12 Scandal. The villagers, not having received their mail, advance on the Telegraph Boy. The camera crew, the actors, and the Director are furious and run in from all sides. The Young Girl who took away the satchel returns to see the result of her prank. The villagers snatch the satchel and distribute the mail among themselves. The Young Girl is distraught and sorry. The Star and the Telegraph Boy return. When he sees the scandal he has caused he runs away. The set is taken down to reveal the field and the river again, but under a night sky. The members of the film company go away, followed by the villagers. The Young Girl is left alone.
    13 The Telegraph Boy creeps on stealthily towards the bicycle he left behind, mounts it and crosses the stage. The Young Girl catches him up, jumps on behind him, and they ride off together."

Diaghilev was so encouraged by the success of *Les Matelots* in 1925 that he wanted to repeat the recipe in 1926. He tried to use the same ingredients: Kochno as librettist, Auric as composer, Massine as choreographer, Pruna as designer, and many of the same dancers including Lifar in a starring role.

Diaghilev wanted to engage Massine to revive *Mercure* as well as to create *La Pastorale* and *Jack-in-the-Box* (see pp 185–90). Massine, however, preferred to fulfill his commitment to C. B. Cochran and *Cochran's 1926 Revue*, and when Picasso withdrew from the revival of *Mercure* and the staging of *Jack-in-the-Box* he decided not to work for Diaghilev at all during 1926. Diaghilev was then forced to give the choreography of *La Pastorale* and *Jack-in-the-Box* to George Balanchine. The choreographer, therefore, was the only new ingredient, but what Diaghilev hoped to make into another lightweight soufflé turned out to be an indigestible pudding.

The fault lay primarily with the libretto. Kochno, who devised it, had the honesty to write: "The action was confused, and the plot, based on antic situations that arise between some screen actors and villagers acting as extras in a film being shot outdoors, was incomprehensible to the audience."[1] But the action, however much confused, gave Balanchine an opportunity for inventing a technically demanding and acrobatic choreography which showed off the athletic skills of the dancers. He borrowed certain movements from the circus which he adapted within a classical framework, thereby extending the vocabulary of dance. This choreography met with criticism from the purists. Cyril Beaumont, for example, dismissed it: "There was very little dancing in this production except for a solo rendered by Dubrovska, whose exotic features and abnormally long and supple arms and legs made her well suited to the role of a glamorous film star."[2]

Beaumont does not mention, or perhaps did not see, the result of an argument Diaghilev had with Lifar about his technical ability. Diaghilev had refused Lifar permission to sign a testimonial for a firm selling patent milk in return for a cheque for £50. When Lifar discovered that other dancers had signed he also signed, and a few days later showed his cheque to Diaghilev who, as Lifar remembered, "flew into a tearing rage, began shouting abuse, and finally slapped my face . . . Next day we were reconciled, but nevertheless it was clear that Diaghilev still bore me a grudge. A few

Below: scene 6, the dance of the Director.

days later we were about to give *La Pastorale* and I was pumping up my bicycle tyres in readiness for the show, when Sergei Pavlovitch approached me crossly: 'I say, have you changed your variation in the *Pastorale*?' (referring to his wish that I should do thirty-two *entrechat-six* instead of thirty-two *entrechat-quatre*, a suggestion we were considering for the future, but which had by no means been finally decided upon). 'No, I haven't, and anyhow I can't do anything without Balanchine.' Diaghilev said nothing and went out into the auditorium. *La Pastorale* began. Well in the middle of my variation, with horror, I heard the orchestra beginning a long *ritenuto* and thus, after all, I was forced to dance the thirty-two *entrechat-six* so that I almost scorched the soles off my feet . . . After which I attempted to rush to the orchestra, intending to thrash Desormière, the conductor, for executing Diaghilev's orders without giving me the least warning. The performance over, I found some flowers from Sergei Pavlovitch, with a card bearing but one word: 'Peace'."[3] This story clearly illustrates the fiery jealousy and tempestuous anger which Diaghilev was so easily capable of expressing, but it also shows how he liked to stretch his dancers beyond their own perceived ability.

The dancers may have fulfilled their roles, but another fault lay with Pruna's design. Grigoriev, the stage director, criticized it from a technical point of view when he stated that the ballet "was in no less than twelve scenes; and the dancing was much hampered by the employment of a large number of small rostrums and screens on wheels, which were moved about in the course of the action."[4] Propert was sad when he wrote: "That Pruna should have provided a décor so lacking in distinction was a disappointment, but it was obvious that, having no chance of introducing human figures into his background, his interest had flagged."[5] Beaumont was more dismissive: "The setting and costumes were undistinguished; few would have recognised the lively and inventive Pruna of *Les Matelots* in the decorator of *La Pastorale*."[6]

Nicolas Nabokov thought that *La Pastorale* was "probably the silliest ballet produced in the twenties by the Diaghilev ballet."[7] Richard Buckle thought that it "was perhaps too clever by half."[8] But whatever anyone thought, Diaghilev, for some reason, liked it enough to revive it, with some alteration, in Paris and London in 1929. It still did not convince Propert: "*La Pastorale*

was reconstructed and a good deal simplified before its revival in 1929, but its inherent weakness of design and its thin and tiring music were enough to keep it finally among the second-class ballets."[9]

184 Design for the drop curtain (front cloth)

Ink and pastel on paper originally blue-gray, now faded
19¾ x 24⅛ in: 50 x 61.2 cm
Unsigned and undated
On the reverse is a sketch of a girl's head
1933.527

Exhibitions: Paris 1929, No 62; London Tooth 1930, No 62; Paris 1930, No 89; Chicago 1933, No 139; Northampton 1934, No 139; Hartford 1934b; New Haven 1935; San Francisco 1935–6; Paris 1939, No 322; Williamsburgh 1940; Washington D.C. 1950–1; Edinburgh 1954, No 308; London 1954–5, No 350; Indianapolis 1959, No 422; New York 1965–6, No 150 (illustrated p 73; not shown in New York); Strasbourg 1969, No 422; Amherst 1974; Hartford 1978–9; Worcester 1989.

André Levinson described this front cloth as "fragile and insignificant: a cover for *Vogue*; Picasso at a garden party."[10]

Notes

1 Boris Kochno, *Diaghilev and the Ballets Russes*, p 238.
2 Cyril W. Beaumont, *The Diaghilev Ballet in London*, p 260.
3 Serge Lifar, *Serge Diaghilev*, pp 424–5.
4 Serge Grigoriev, *The Diaghilev Ballet*, p 227. Lifar had seven designs for these screens, which were in his collection until they were included in the Lifar sale at Sotheby's London (Lot 46) on 9 May 1984, when they remained unsold.
5 W. A Propert, *The Russian Ballet 1921–1929*, p 45.
6 Cyril W. Beaumont, *op cit*, p 259.
7 Nicolas Nabokov, *Old Friends and New Music*, p 69.
8 Richard Buckle, *Diaghilev*, p 482.
9 W. A. Propert, *op cit*, p 45.
10 André Levinson, "Pastorale" in *Comoedia* Paris 31 May 1926, p 1.
11 Boris Kochno, *Diaghilev and the Ballets Russes*, p 238.
12 André Levinson, *op cit*, p 1.

185   Design for the backcloth

Graphite, pastel, and ink on paper
18⁷⁄₁₆ x 21¼ in: 46.9 x 54 cm
Signed and dated in pencil bottom right: "Pruna / 1926"
1933.528

Exhibitions: Paris 1929, No 61; London Tooth 1930, No 63; Paris 1930, No 90; Chicago 1933, No 140; Northampton 1934, No 140; Hartford 1934b; New Haven 1935; San Francisco 1935–6; Paris 1939, No 323; Williamsburg 1940; Washington D.C. 1950–1; Michigan 1957; Elmira 1958, No 16; Indianapolis 1959, No 423; Rowayton 1960; New York 1965–6, No 151 (illustrated p 73; not shown in New York); New York 1966–7; Amherst 1974; Hartford 1978–9; Worcester 1989.

The fault in this design for the backcloth appears to lie both in the tone and the drawing. The colors of the background are too delicate and the drawing too imprecise to register firmly when seen from the stalls of a theater. Compare the drawing of this hilltop village with that of Picasso's for *Le Tricorne* (p 276). Picasso's, though merely a couple of bold lines, is infinitely more suggestive and defined.

This is the setting for the first scene when, according to Kochno, "Lifar's entrance on a bicycle was a sensation."[11] As noted above, painted screens were positioned by invisible stage hands in time with the music in front of this backcloth after the film crew arrived, which Levinson called the "mazurka of setting the scene."[12]

The time of the ballet was the present, while the film being shot during the action was set in the period of Henri III, who reigned in France from 1574–89.

Isaac Rabinovitch

Russian
born 1894 Kiev
died 1961 Moscow

Rastratchiki (The Embezzlers)

Satirical comedy in eight scenes by Valentin Kataev
adapted from his story of the same title
Director: Ilya Sudakov
Artistic Director: Constantin Stanislavsky
Designer (sets and costumes): Isaac Rabinovitch
Principal actors:
   Prokhorov, Philip Stepanovitch, an accountant:
      M. M. Tarkhanov
   Vanichka, a cashier: V. O. Toporkov
   Nikita, a courier: N. P. Batalov
   Yanina, Prokhorov's wife: M. P. Lilina[1]
   Zoia, Kolya, their children: S. N. Garrel,
      E. N. Moress
   Isabella, a lady: S. V. Khaliutina
   Kashkadamov, an agent: B. S. Maloletkov
   Scholte, Caesar Nikolaevitch, a bon-vivant:
      N. P. Khmelev
Company: Moscow Art Theater
First Performance: 20 April 1928, Moscow Art
   Academic Theater

The Moscow Art Theater was founded by Constantin Stanislavsky (1865–1938) and Vladimir Nemirovitch-Danchenko (1859–1943) in 1898. Although their greatest early successes were undoubtedly the productions of the plays by Anton Chekhov, their inaugural production was of Alexei Tolstoy's historical drama *Tsar Feodor Ioannovitch* (see pp 315–17). The company developed a particular naturalistic style of acting through a system of training developed by Stanislavsky which he described in his books. The system, much admired when the company undertook an extensive tour of Europe and America in the early 1920s, exerted a considerable influence on actors in both continents.

In the mid 1920s the company was required by the government to revive its repertory by introducing contemporary Soviet plays. Although this change in policy was not according to Stanislavsky's personal artistic taste, the adaptation of Mikhail Bulgakov's novel *The White Guard* into the play *The Days of the Turbins,* directed by Ilya Sudakov in 1926, was a great success, not exactly what the authorities either wanted or expected. By treating the White Guard officers with sympathy and showing characters who were hostile to the Revolution, this play created such a furore that it had to be withdrawn twice although it remained in the repertory until 1941. Forced to be more conformist, the company produced, a year later in 1927,

Vsevolod Ivanov's *Armored Train No 14–69*, also directed by Sudakov, which was chosen to celebrate the tenth anniversary of the Revolution.

The Moscow Art Theater then again tried to vary the repertory by introducing some comedies or, at least, more light-hearted works. In 1928 they produced first Leonid Leonov's *Untilovsk*, followed by *The Embezzlers* and *Squaring the Circle*, both by Kataev. Only the last was a success, with 650 performance over ten seasons. *Untilovsk* had twenty performances. But *The Embezzlers* was performed only eighteen times after a cool reception and after being almost universally condemned by the press. "The Moscow Art Theater's production of the play *The Embezzlers* from the story by Kataev only provokes bewilderment . . . There are, however, a few technical novelties of positive virtue."[2] Another critic wrote: "The social theme of the play is not deep. Its literary quality is no more than that of a newspaper article, and there is nothing to be said about its 'revolutionary enthusiasm.' We had read the entertaining and clever story by Kataev. But the same author has turned his entertaining and clever story into eight incidental, dramatically weak, and disjointed episodes . . . The design by I. Rabinovitch is in itself interesting and inventive but at odds with the style of the play."[3] In fact, Rabinovitch's designs were completely altered by the director who "consciously brought the artist's hyperbolic, expressive ideas 'down to earth' and instead of grotesque images the stage carried photographically exact reproductions of the contemporary milieu and contemporary types."[4]

Rabinovitch studied art in the studio of A. A. Murashko in Kiev from 1912 to 1915. He specialized in film and theater design, beginning his career at the Solovtzov Theater in Kiev in 1919 with Lope da Vega's *Fuenteovejuna*[5] which in Russia was considered to be the first proletarian play, and Oscar Wilde's *Salomé*. He moved to Moscow where he joined Alexis Granovski's State Jewish Theater after the ban on Yiddish theater was removed by the Revolution. He designed *The Sorceress* in 1922. In 1923 Rabinovitch had his first connexion with the

Moscow Art Theater, when he designed *Lysistrata* by Aristophanes for its Music Studio, directed by Nemirovitch-Danchenko. He then worked with Alexandra Exter on Yakov Protazanov's extraordinary film *Aelita* in 1924. His first production for the Bolshoi Theater in Moscow in 1928 was Prokofiev's *The Love for Three Oranges*.[6] Rabinovitch's sets were so ruinously complicated (the scene changes took longer than the scenes) that the production became known as *The Love for Three Intervals*.

Abram Efros, the theater historian, wrote in praise of the designer: "Watch Rabinovitch when he is at work on the stage, parcelling out the available space in three dimensions or when he is making a stage model. Here is a new race of stage designer. He has a strange receptivity, a different eye and unusual hands. He lives on the stage as if he were born on it. For him this is absolute atmosphere and absolute soil. Stanislavsky says: 'When an actor and a chance visitor walk side by side across the stage, their feet touch the floor differently: one merely walks on the boards, the other on "new ground."' For Rabinovitch the stage is ever such 'new reality.'"[7]

**186 Costume design for
M. M. Tarkhanov as Prokhorov**

Graphite and chalk or pastel on black paper
8¹³⁄₁₆ x 12³⁄₁₆ in: 47.7 x 31 cm
Signed and dated in pastel in Russian lower right:
  "Исаак Рабинович (Isaac Rabinovitch) / 1927"
1933.530

Exhibitions: Chicago 1933, No 142 (described as
  "Costume d'ivrogne pour un ballet donné à

Moscou" ("Costume for a drunkard for a ballet
in Moscow"); Northampton 1934, No 142;
Hartford 1934b; New Haven 1935; Williamsburg 1940; Elmira 1958, No 25; New York
1965–6, No 152 (illustrated p 73; not shown in
New York); New York 1966–7; Princeton 1968;
Amherst 1974; Coral Gables 1982; Columbus
1989; Worcester 1989.

The design shows the main character,
Prokhorov, comparing contemporary
Soviet life unfavorably with life in an earlier
age, by using a favorite music-hall or circus
routine of telling a story by exchanging hats
when changing characters. This explains the
two hats in the design, with the silk top hat
symbolizing a more refined and glorious
vanished past.

Rabinovitch often used colored paper for
his designs. The technique of using pastel
on black paper is an economical way of
making an effective costume design for the
theater.

This design is unique in this collection
for being the only example from the 1920s
post-revolutionary period of Russian experimental theater. It is not known how Serge
Lifar acquired it, nor did he know what the
design was for, as, presumably, the description in the 1933 catalogue, "Costume for a
drunkard for a ballet in Moscow," was
provided by him. It is curious, however,
that he could not identify it correctly. In the
catalogue for New York 1965–6, this design
was thought to be possibly for the Moscow
production of *The Love for Three Oranges*,
perhaps because of the link with Prokofiev
who may have given it to Lifar at the time
of *The Prodigal Son* (see pp 300–5), quite
ignoring the fact that all the designs for the
opera are in the style of Italian eighteenth-
century *commedia dell'arte*. Prokofiev was in
Moscow in 1928, but there is no evidence to
link this design with him in any way.

Notes

1 The stage name of Maria Petrovna
  Perevoshchikova, Stanislavsky's wife.
2 Yuri Sobaev in *Vechernei Moskve (Moscow
  Evening)*, 23 April 1928.
3 E. M. in *Pravda (Truth)*, 24 April 1928.
4 Konstantin Rudnitsky, *Russian and Soviet Theater
  1905–1932*, p 254.
5 Lope Felix da Vega Carpio (1562–1635), Spanish
  playwright, credited with over 2,000 plays,
  although only 725 titles are known and about
  470 have been identified.
6 His other productions for the Bolshoi included
  Turandot in 1931, *Eugene Onegin* in 1933, and *The
  Huguenots* in 1935.
7 Quoted in Oliver M Sayler, *Inside the Moscow
  Art Theatre*, p 101.

Nikolai Roerich

Russian
born 1874 St Petersburg
died 1947 Nagar, Kulu Valley, Punjab

Le Sacre du Printemps (The Rite of Spring)

Tableau of pagan Russia in two parts by Igor
    Stravinsky and Nikolai Roerich
Composer: Igor Stravinsky
Conductor: Pierre Monteux
Choreographer: Vaslav Nijinsky
Scenery and costumes: Nikolai Roerich
Principal dancers:
    A Wise Man (part 1): Konstantin Woronzov
    The Chosen Maiden (part 2): Maria Piltz
Company: Diaghilev's Ballets Russes
First performance: 29 May 1913, Théâtre des
    Champs-Elysées, Paris

Synopsis

Part 1: the Adoration of the Earth. Ritual dances
celebrating the return of Spring. Part 2: the Sacrifice. The victim is chosen and is sacrificed.

    The following was the synopsis in the program
for the performances in London:

    "This, the third and most recent of M. Stravin-
sky's ballets has for theme the ritual of primeval
mysticism and, for setting, the Muscovy of
dimmest antiquity. Its two scenes evoke the worship of Iarillo, God of Light, on the return of
spring, with ceremonies that include the sacrifice
of a young girl—who represents the mother of the
future's unborn springs—and divers rites symbolizing and exalting the benignant earth's fertility, the
majesty of the great forces of nature, and the
mystery of everlasting stars.

    It is a luminous spring evening in the first
scene, and an aged woman of the tribe is instruct-
ing the young men in the season's appropriate
incantations. Soon the young girls come up from
the river side, and there are dances and symbolic
games. Part of the rite is a simulated abduction.
Now approaches a procession of elders of the tribe
escorting the most venerable, the high priest of the
cult, who pronounces solemn blessing on the
earth's unfailing fruitfulness and seeks omens in
the enigmatic calm of nature's face. In the second
scene, that of the sacrifice, the maiden-victim is
chosen by hazard in the mazes of a dance of the
young girls. In a dance of heroic nature the rest of
the girls then do her honour, and there are pious
ceremonies by the elders in evocation of the spirit
of their ancestors and in preparation for the mystic
marriage. The bride meanwhile has lain rigid in a
kind of trance. On a sudden she stirs and begins a
dance of religious exaltation. The exaltation turns
to frenzy, the frenzy fades to exhaustion, and the
girl expires—the sacrifice accomplished."

"Once we have everything the way you
and I want it, I know that *Sacre du
Printemps* will be something astounding.
The ordinary spectator will be stunned, and
for the others, new and vast horizons,
flooded with different illuminations, will
open up. People will see new, diverse colors
and lines. Everything will be different, new,

and beautiful."[1] So wrote Nijinsky to
Stravinsky on 25 January 1913. "When *Le
Sacre du Printemps* was put on in Paris, the
first night was what Cecchetti calls a 'scan-
dale.' At the rehearsal M. Diaghilev asked
Cecchetti what he thought, and Cecchetti
did not mince matters. 'What do I think? I
think the whole thing has been made by
four idiots. First: M. Stravinsky, who wrote
the music. Second: M. Bakst [sic], who did
the *décor*. Third: M. Nijinsky, who is the
choreographist [sic]. Fourth: M. Diaghilev,
who has put so much money into it!'"[2]
Cecchetti's point of view, after correcting
the slip of the tongue about the designer,
was more in tune with popular feeling,
while Nijinsky's prediction was perceptively accurate.

    More controversy has surrounded the
production of *Le Sacre du Printemps* than any
other ballet staged by Diaghilev. It begins
with the composition of the scenario. The
idea for *Le Sacre du Printemps* apparently
came to Stravinsky while he was composing
The Firebird in 1910. He dreamed of a pagan
ritual in which a chosen sacrificial virgin
danced herself to death. But then he began a
Konzertstück for piano and orchestra which
was developed into *Petrushka* (see
pp 117–27). When he wrote his autobiography in 1935 (actually ghosted by Walter
Nouvel), he was writing in the safety of
solitude without fear of contradiction, since
Roerich had disappeared to India and
Nijinsky had gone mad: "Although I had
conceived the subject of the *Sacre du Printemps* without any plot, some plan had to be
designed for the sacrificial action. For this it
was necessary that I should see Roerich. He
was staying at the moment at Talachkino,
the estate of Princess Tenichev, a great
patroness of Russian art. I joined him, and it
was there that we settled the visual embodiment of the *Sacre* and the definite sequence
of its different episodes. I began the score
on returning to Oustiloug, and worked at it
through the winter at Clarens."[3] This abbreviated account omits the fact that it was
Diaghilev who suggested to Roerich, after
his success with the design of the *Polovtsian
Dances* from *Prince Igor* in 1909, that he
collaborate with Stravinsky on a new ballet
after *The Firebird*. Early in 1910 Roerich

suggested two alternative ideas: either *A
Game of Chess,* in which the action would
take place on a chess board with giant
hands directing the game, or *The Great
Sacrifice,* in which a chosen virgin would be
sacrificed to the sun god Yarila in order to
ensure the return of spring. Stravinsky was
more inspired by the second idea, and they
developed the scenario together. *The Firebird*
was first performed on 25 June 1910 at the
Opéra in Paris, and on 15 July this
announcement appeared in the Russian
newspaper *Russkoe slovo (Russian word)*:
"The Academician N. K. Roerich, the young
composer of *The Firebird* I. F. Stravinsky and
the ballet master M. M. Fokine are working
on a ballet called *The Great Sacrifice*, dedicated to ancient slavic religious customs.
The subject matter and the staging is by
Roerich."[4] Progress, however, on evolving
the ballet was slow to nonexistent. On
9 October 1910, Diaghilev wrote to Roerich
in a postscript to a letter: "P. S. What a
nuisance that Stravinsky will not be in time
by next spring with the ballet, but ce qui est
remis n'est pas perdu [what is put off is not
lost]."[5] Work on *The Great Sacrifice*, interrupted by finishing and staging *Petrushka*,
was put off until July 1911. (The ballet was
then given its different and final title, now
referred to as *Le Sacre du Printemps*.[6])
Stravinsky later again described in more
detail how he went to meet Roerich at
Princess Tenichev's estate. As well as being
a patron of the arts she was a collector of
ethnic Slav and Russian folk art: "In July
1911, after the first performance of
Petrushka, I travelled to Princess Tenichev's
country estate near Smolensk, to meet with
Nicolas Roerich and plan the scenario of *Le
Sacre du Printemps*; Roerich knew the
Princess well, and he was eager for me to
see her collections of Russian ethnic art . . .
I set to work with Roerich, and in a few
days the plan of action and the titles of the
dances were composed. Roerich also
sketched his famous Polovtsian-type backdrops while we were there, and designed
costumes after real costumes in the
Princess's collection."[7] Roerich's first design
for act 1 was a bare, green landscape of
rocky hills falling to a lake under a
threatening cloud-filled sky with a vast,

spiky, leafless tree in the center. In the final production, the tree became a huge boulder, the symbolic "sacred stone" which Roerich repeated in many of his paintings. The original design for act 2, called *The Great Sacrifice*, shows the silhouettes of four figures, with skins of antlered heads on their backs making them appear like elks, moving over a low horizon under a huge pale-blue sky toward a female figure waiting for them, while a hunter with a bow and arrow aims at them. This design became the drop curtain between the two acts. The final design for act 2 was the top of a rounded hill with sacred stones and a ring of poles hung with the votive skins and antlered heads. Stravinsky continued: "The composition of the whole of *Le Sacre* was completed, in a state of exaltation and exhaustion, at the beginning of 1912, and most of the instrumentation—a mechanical job, largely, as I always compose the instrumentation when I compose the music—was written in score form by the late spring. The final pages of the Danse sacrale were not completed until November 17th, however; I remember the day well, as I was suffering from a raging toothache, which I then went to treat in Vevey."[7] This explains why *Le Sacre du Printemps* was not produced in 1912 either, although Stravinsky does not mention that Diaghilev accepted the postponement because he was also then working on *Les Noces*.

By the end of the Paris season in 1912, a fundamental change had taken place with the Ballets Russes. Fokine, in a temper, had resigned as choreographer, partly because he considered himself to have been unfairly treated by Diaghilev over his production of *Daphnis and Chloë* (see pp 79–81), and partly because he realized that after *L'Après-midi d'un faune* (see pp 74–78) Nijinsky would be given more ballets to choreograph while he would be sidelined. It was true that Diaghilev wanted to cultivate Nijinsky as a choreographer, but he also thought that Fokine had run out of steam. Grigoriev, the company manager, remarked discerningly that Diaghilev "valued his collaborators only as long as, in his view, they had something new to contribute. Once they ceased to fulfil this role he felt no regret in parting with them. And so it was with Fokine."[8] For the 1913 season it had been planned that Nijinsky would choreograph Debussy's *Jeux*, in which he would also dance the male part. Now the postponement of *Le Sacre du Printemps* meant that Nijinsky became its controversial choreographer as well.

In February 1912, while the Ballets Russes were performing in Dresden, Diaghilev and Nijinsky first visited Emile Jaques-Dalcroze's school for "Eurythmics" at nearby Hellerau. Jaques-Dalcroze believed that "man instinctively feels rhythmic vibrations in all his conscious muscles; that is why it behoves a teacher of rhythm to train through and in rhythm the *whole* muscular system, so that every muscle may contribute its share in awakening, clarifying, moulding, and perfecting rhythmic consciousness."[9] Diaghilev, impressed by these doctrines, was sure that Nijinsky could benefit greatly by them when composing a ballet. Therefore, at the end of the year, when *Le Sacre du Printemps* was going into rehearsal, Diaghilev and Nijinsky visited Jaques-Dalcroze again. Diaghilev then asked him to send one of his pupils to help with the choreography as the music was "so inconceivably difficult, full of constantly changing rhythms; and even with Stravinsky's anxious assistance Nijinsky's composition progressed very slowly indeed."[10] Marie Ramberg (later known as Marie Rambert) was chosen to help the dancers disentangle the complicated rhythms. Bronislava Nijinska, originally cast as the sacrificial virgin but who had to be replaced, against her will, when she became pregnant, wondered: "What can Marie Rambert, who hardly knows how to dance, teach Nijinsky?"[11] The answer is that she taught Nijinsky a great deal, but in her own memoirs was most generous toward him: "As to his choreography, I would not hesitate to affirm that it was he, more than anyone else, who revolutionised the classical ballet and was fifty years ahead of his time. Fokine was a logical development of Petipa, but Nijinsky introduced completely new principles."[12] Revolutions are difficult to cope with; it was not surprising that the dancers not only had the greatest difficulty in executing the steps Nijinsky required, but also protested vehemently at having to attempt to execute them at all. According to Nijinska the choreography "was strange and unfamiliar to the artists brought up in the traditions of the old classical ballet, in which, though used to maintaining an even distance between the dancers, whether dancing in straight, parallel, diagonal, or circular line, they had always been allowed a certain freedom in the execution of the ballet. They resented and did not understand Nijinsky's demand for exactness."[13]

In his choreography, Nijinsky sought a way to complement the music by matching its extraordinary rhythms with extraordinary movements. His experiments were supported and encouraged by Roerich, who probably led him toward defining the basic "primitive" position adopted by the dancers: feet turned in, knees slightly bent, arms held in reverse, head on one side. This typical position is seen in some of Roerich's costume designs and the few existing photographs of the actual dancers. The circular movements, too, and the patterns formed by the dancers on stage were inspired by the geometric patterns on the costumes. However, in spite of the apparent difficulty the dancers had in interpreting Nijinsky's instructions, Rambert insisted that "the steps were very simple: walking smoothly or stamping, jumps mostly off both feet, landing heavily. There was only one a little more complicated dance for the maidens in the first scene. It was mostly done in groups, and each group has its own precise rhythm to follow. In the dance (if one can call it that) of the Wisest Elder, he walked two steps against every three steps of the ensemble. In the second scene the dance of the sacrifice of the Chosen Virgin was powerful and deeply moving. I watched Nijinsky again and again teaching it to Maria Piltz. Her reproduction was very pale by comparison with his ecstatic performance, which was the greatest tragic dance I have ever seen."[14] But Marie Rambert was in love with Nijinsky, while Bronislava was jealous both of her and of Maria Piltz.

By contrast, Stravinsky formed a different opinion of Nijinsky's choreography, based on a curiously mistaken refusal to believe that he knew anything about music: "My own disappointment with Nijinsky was due to the fact that he did not know the musical alphabet. He never understood musical metres and he had no very certain sense of tempo. You may imagine from this the rhythmic chaos that was *Le Sacre du Printemps*, and especially the chaos of the last dance where poor Mlle Piltz, the sacrificial maiden, was not even aware of the changing bars. Nor did Nijinsky make any attempt to understand my own choreographic ideas for *Le Sacre*. In the *Danses des Adolescents*, for example, I had imagined a row of almost motionless dancers. Nijinsky made of this piece a big jumping match."[15] Stravinsky was always ambivalent about Nijinsky's choreography—never very enthusiastic, but not always condemnatory. Contrary to Stravinsky's opinion, Nijinsky had certainly studied music, knew about it, played the piano,[16] and seems even to have understood it better than did the conductor Pierre Monteux when he heard it for the first time. Monteux described the occasion: "The room was small and the music was large, the sound of it completely dwarfing the poor piano on which the composer was pounding, completely dwarfing Diaghilev and his poor conductor listening in utter amazement, completely dwarfing Monte Carlo, I might say. The old upright piano quivered and shook as Stravinsky tried to give us an idea of his new work for ballet. I remember vividly his dynamism and his sort of ruthless impetuosity as he attacked the score. By the time he had reached the second tableau, his face was so completely covered with sweat that I thought, 'He will surely burst, or have a syncope.' My own head ached badly, and I decided then and there that the symphonies of Beethoven and Brahms were the only music for me, not the music of this crazy Russian! I must admit I did not understand one note of Le Sacre du Printemps. My one desire was to flee that room and find a quiet corner in which to rest my aching head. Then my Director [Diaghilev] turned to me and with a smile said, 'This is a masterpiece, Monteux, which will completely revolutionize music and make you famous, because you are going to conduct it.' And of course, I did."[17]

The first night of Le Sacre du Printemps is renowned or, rather, notorious for the sensation it caused. Diaghilev welcomed the controversy and may even have helped to engineer it; he knew what was good for publicity. Jean Cocteau, peering into the packed auditorium, sensed the inevitable: "For the experienced eye, all the material for a scandal is there: a fashionable audience, in décolleté, decked out in pearls, aigrettes and ostrich feathers; and side by side with the tails and tulle, the lounge suits, head bands, and conspicuous rags and tatters of the aesthetes who applaud anything new without rhyme or reason just because they hate those people in the boxes."[18]

Romola de Pulszky, who married Nijinsky at the end of the year, described what it was like to be in that smart auditorium: "The excitement, the shouting, was extreme. People whistled, insulted the performers and the composer, shouted, laughed. Monteux threw desperate glances towards Diaghileff, who sat in Astruc's box and made signs to him to keep on playing. Astruc in this indescribable noise ordered the lights turned on, and the fights and controversy did not remain in the domain

of sound but actually culminated in bodily conflict. One beautifully dressed lady in an orchestra box stood up and slapped the face of a young man who was hissing in the next box. Her escort rose, and cards were exchanged between the men. A duel followed next day. Another Society lady spat in the face of one of the demonstrators. La Princesse de P.[19] left her box, saying "I am sixty years old, but this is the first time anyone has dared to make a fool of me." At this moment Diaghileff, who was standing livid in his box, shouted "Je vous en prie, laissez achever le spectacle [I beg you, let the performance finish]." And a temporary quieting-down followed, but only temporary. As soon as the first tableau was finished the fight was resumed. I was deafened by this indescribable noise, and rushed back stage as fast as I could. There it was as bad as in the auditorium. The dancers were trembling, almost crying; they did not even return to their dressing-rooms."[20] Diaghilev, too, if various memoirs are accurate, also darted between the auditorium and the stage. He tried to calm the unnerved dancers, although it is clear that as the demonstration began with the first notes of the score being played it was directed against the music rather than the dancers. Stravinsky watched most of the performance from the wings: "As for the actual performance, I am not in a position to judge, as I left the auditorium at the first bars of the prelude, which had at once evoked derisive laughter. I was disgusted. These demonstrations, at first isolated, soon became general, provoking counter-demonstrations and very quickly developing into a terrific uproar. During the whole performance I was at Nijinsky's side in the wings. He was standing on a chair, screaming 'sixteen, seventeen, eighteeen'—they had their own method of counting to keep time. Naturally the poor dancers could hear nothing by reason of the row in the auditorium and the sound of their own dance-steps. I had to hold Nijinsky by his clothes, for he was furious, and ready to dash on to the stage at any moment and create a scandal. Diaghileff kept ordering the electricians to turn the lights on or off, hoping in that way to put a stop to the noise. That is all I can remember about the first performance."[21]

The second night, the remaining performances in Paris, and all the performances in London passed without any demonstration in an atmosphere of respectable calm. The final controversy is the disagreement among

historians about how many performances there were. The daily announcements in the newspapers show that there were only eight performances in all: 29 May, 2, 4, 6, and 13 June in Paris; and 11, 14, and 23 July in London. It was announced for 18 July also, but not performed.

Le Sacre du Printemps certainly bewildered audiences and critics alike. W. A. Propert sums up the general feeling and thoughts of both: "The Le Sacre du Printemps was an unlucky business. It was a headlong leap into the music of wilful, intentional, purposeful dissonance, and breaking away from traditional dancing every bit as revolutionary. The world was baffled by it, but the active hostility of the French was at least more intelligent than the polite indifference of the English audiences. Its difficulties from the point of view of the spectator were undoubtedly very great, but was there ever anything new and strange presented to our intelligence that did not demand time and experience for their comprehension? And I, for one, am sure that in the case of a musician so sincere and so able as Stravinsky his score would have yielded up its secrets and its power and beauty would have revealed themselves could we but have had time to absorb it. Roerich's scenery was pale in colour, his dresses of primary green and red in complete accord with the chilly atmosphere and crude violence of the action—it was learned, impressive and personal, another example of the archaeological spirit that informs without intruding."[22]

Le Sacre du Printemps was given a concert performance, conducted by Monteux, at the Casino de Paris in April 1914 when the score was finally properly appreciated. Diaghilev revived the ballet in 1920 with new choreography by Massine as no dancer who was still in the company could remember anything of Nijinsky's. Massine admitted: "Some critics found my version too mechanical and felt it lacked the warmth and pathos of the original."[23] Stravinsky could not decide between them: he liked the music best when unadulterated by choreographers. One point of view in 1960: "Massine did the choreography for the revival of Le Sacre du Printemps. I thought this excellent—incomparably clearer than Nijinsky's,"[24] or another in 1952: "The choreography (by Massine) was too gymnastic and Dalcrozian to please me. I realized then that I prefer Le Sacre as a concert piece."[25]

Le Sacre du Printemps was not, as Cecchetti thought, a production made by idiots, but was, as Ottoline Morrell observed, just too uncomfortable: "Nijinsky talked a good deal about his new ballet *Le Sacre du Printemps*, in which he expressed the idea of pagan worship, the religious instinct in primitive nature, fear, ecstasy, developing into frenzy and utter self-oblation. It was too intense and terrible, too much an expression of ideas to please the public who are accustomed to graceful toe-dancing or voluptuous eastern scenes."[26]

187* Seven figures in costume

Tempera and/or watercolor and chalk on paper
14¾ x 18½ in: 37.4 x 47 cm
Signed bottom left with monogram
Purchased through the gift of Henry and
    Walter Keney
1994.23.1
Provenance: Roerich Museum, New York; Parmenia
    Migel Ekstrom; Arne Ekstrom; Julian Barran Ltd

Exhibitions: New York 1974, No 2 (illustrated);
    Hempstead 1974, No 123; Chicago 1975, No
    37; Basel 1984.
Illustration: Nijinska 1982, No 100 facing p 452.

This is not in fact seven costume designs for *Le Sacre du Printemps,* but a study of figures in a landscape as a pictorial evocation of pagan Russia suggesting the intended mood of the ballet. It is one of several such drawings (some remain only as fragments) which Roerich made when he first began to discuss the ballet with Stravinsky in order to determine the scenario. The dresses of these figures reveal Roerich's pedantic attention to authentic ethnographic detail, based on his research into ancient Slav customs and folklore. The costumes which Roerich subsequently designed for the ballet were made lighter in weight for dancing in, and the decorative patterns, although based on similar designs and infinitely intricate, were both simplified and unified in color (see Nos 188–190).

In spite of the provenance, and in spite of the attribution by Mrs Ekstrom, an expert historian of the Diaghilev ballet, it has been suggested that this and other similar drawings are not connected with *Le Sacre du Printemps* but with some other production. I believe this suggestion to be wrong. While it is true that the actual costumes for *Le Sacre du Printemps* were different from those depicted here, this difference is explained above and, while there is some similarity between these costume drawings and the ones Roerich designed for *The Snow Maiden* for Chicago in 1922, the artist's style for the two productions is quite different. These figures are of an earlier date. Furthermore, and crucially, Roerich was in New York in 1920 and authenticated these earlier drawings himself.

188* Costume for Fedorov as one of the Elders of the Tribe in act 1

Cotton flannel robe with placket-front opening and beaten brass brooches at neckline. Painted orange and gold undulating bands highlighted with purple spots around neckline yoke, sleeves and hem. Red underarm godets. Label inscribed in Russian "Рис.[унок] No 13 Г. Федоров" ("Drawing No 13. Mr Fedorov"). Remains of blue "Diaghilev" stamp.
Narrow leather belt with double straps, adorned with embossed brass plaques.

Grey suede ballet slippers with pink stripes and long purple leg ties.
    1996.7.7a–d
Provenance: Diaghilev and de Basil Ballets Foundation Ltd; Sotheby's, London, lot 70 (iii), 19 December 1969; Castle Howard Estate Ltd; Sotheby's, London, lot 31, 14 December 1995

The Elders of the Tribe were Mssrs Fedorov, Froman, Sergueiev, Statkevitch, Kowalsky, Maligin, Kostecki, and Zelinski.
Fedorov was also an Ancestor in part 2.

The belt and slippers are not necessarily part of this costume. When these costumes were first sold in 1969, each lot consisted of several costumes. Those now in this collection were all part of Lot 70 which consisted altogether of six costumes. By the time the costumes came to be lotted the various caps, leggings, belts, and slippers

were for the most part no longer with the tunics to which they belonged. As they could not be positively identified, they were distributed between the tunics merely in order to make each costume complete without matching them to any single costume. This applies to all three costumes.

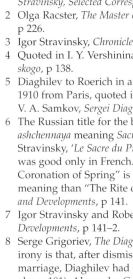

189* Costume for Ivanovsky as one of the Six Youths in act 1

Cotton flannel robe with placket-front opening. Painted geometric bands around neckline, sleeves, and hems with stencilled design on shoulder in orange. Orange underarm godets. Label inscribed in Russian "Рис.[унок] No 9 Г. Ивановскій" ("Drawing No 9 Mr Ivanovsky"), superimposed on "Унг." ("Ung.") and on lining "Hapy [illegible] Naru [illegible]".
Leather belt with brass embossed brass medallions.
Blue suede ballet slippers stencilled with brown rectangles, with peach and purple spotted leg ties.
1996.7.5a–d
Provenance: Diaghilev and de Basil Ballets Foundation Ltd; Sotheby's, London, lot 70 (ii), 19 December 1969; Castle Howard Estate Ltd; Sotheby's, London, lot 26, 14 December 1995

The Six Youths were Semenoff, Rachmanoff, Ivanovsky, Warzinsky, Romanov, and Oumansky.

190* Costume for Loboiko as one of the Five Young Men in act 1

Cotton flannel robe with placket-front opening. Painted geometric motifs on shoulders, neckline yoke, and hem in pink with purple spots and outlines. Bright yellow underarm godets. Label inscribed in Russian "Рис[унок] No 1 Г. Лобойко" ("Drawing No 1 Mr Loboiko"), superimposed on "Воров " ("Vorov") and "Ladoiko".
Narrow leather belt with pendant painted silver wooden dagger.
Domed painted cotton cap with rabbit trim, the peach ground painted with purple chevrons and toothed bands which follow the shape of the hat. Label inscribed "Loboiko" and "Drawing No 1" with "Diaghilev" stamp.
Pair of olive green-yellow suede ballet slippers bordered with pink and mauve stripes and bands on an ivory ground, purple and mauve ribbon leg ties.
1996.7.6a–e
Provenance: Diaghilev and de Basil Ballets Foundation Ltd; Sotheby's, London, lot 70 (iv), 19 December 1969; Castle Howard Estate Ltd; Sotheby's, London, lot 27, 14 December 1995

The Five Young Men in part 1 were Savitsky, Tarasov, Kegler, Loboiko, and Goudin.
As the only legible inscription is on the cap, the other parts of this costume may have been worn by other dancers (see No 189).

Notes

1 Vaslav Nijinsky to Igor Stravinsky on 25 January 1913 from Leipzig, quoted in Igor Stravinsky, *Stravinsky, Selected Correspondence vol II*, pp 46–7.
2 Olga Racster, *The Master of the Russian Ballet*, p 226.
3 Igor Stravinsky, *Chronicle of my Life*, p 63.
4 Quoted in I. Y. Vershinina, *Ranie Baleti Stravinskogo*, p 138.
5 Diaghilev to Roerich in a letter dated 9 October 1910 from Paris, quoted in I. S. Zilberstein and V. A. Samkov, *Sergei Diaghilev* vol 2, p 114.
6 The Russian title for the ballet is *Vesna Sviashchennaya* meaning *Sacred Spring*. According to Stravinsky, '*Le Sacre du Printemps*, Bakst's title, was good only in French. In English, "The Coronation of Spring" is closer to my original meaning than "The Rite of Spring."' *Expositions and Developments*, p 141.
7 Igor Stravinsky and Robert Craft, *Expositions and Developments*, p 141–2.
8 Serge Grigoriev, *The Diaghilev Ballet*, p 76. The irony is that, after dismissing Nijinsky on his marriage, Diaghilev had to recall Fokine (see also p 191). Alexander Gorsky had also been considered as a possible choreographer.
9 Emile Jaques-Dalcroze, *Rhythm, Music and Education*.
10 Serge Grigoriev, *op cit*, p 88.
11 Bronislava Nijinska, *Early Memoirs*, p 457.
12 Marie Rambert, *Quicksilver*, pp 60–1.
13 Bronislava Nijinska, *op cit*, p 460.
14 Marie Rambert, *op cit*, pp 63–4.
15 Igor Stravinsky and Robert Craft, *Memories and Commentaries*, p 37.
16 There is a well-known photograph showing Nijinsky and Ravel playing the piano together.
17 Doris G. Monteux, *It's all in the music*, pp 88–9.
18 Jean Cocteau, *Le Coq et l'Arlequin*, p 93.
19 Identified by Richard Buckle as Comtesse René de Pourtalès in *Nijinsky*, p 358.
20 Romola Nijinsky, *Nijinsky*, pp 202–3.
21 Igor Stravinsky, *op cit*, p 81.
22 W. A. Propert, *The Russian Ballet in Western Europe, 1909–1920*, p 31.
23 Leonide Massine, *My Life in Ballet*, p 153.
24 Igor Stravinsky and Robert Craft, *Memories and Commentaries*, p 42.
25 Igor Stravinsky and Robert Craft, *Expositions and Developments*, p 144.
26 Ottoline Morrell, *The Early Memoirs*, pp 239–40.

Sir Francis Rose

English
born 1909 Moor Park
died 1979 London

Gertrude Stein, in a line of her poetry, invented "A rose is a rose is a rose is a rose,"[1] which anticipated her delight at meeting Sir Francis Rose in 1931, then a young man of twenty-one, round whom she wound her garland phrase. She thought him to be a greater painter than Picasso, and began to buy his pictures. "Again just before leaving Paris at this same picture gallery [Galerie Bonjean] she saw a picture of a poet sitting by a waterfall. Who did that, she said. A young englishman, Francis Rose, was the reply. Oh yes I am not interested in his work. How much is that picture, she said. It cost very little. Gertrude Stein says a picture is either worth three hundred francs or three hundred thousand francs. She bought this picture for three hundred and we went away for the summer."[2] Picasso told her that she could have got something quite good for that amount. But she went on buying Rose's paintings and soon had over thirty. She did not confess to the fact that it was her brother Leo's good taste and perceptive eye which had encouraged her at first to buy Picasso and the other masters; after she quarrelled with him, she lapsed into collecting, on her own, merely the second rate.

Francis Rose inherited his father's title and his fortune at the age of five. He had no formal training as an artist but was given lessons by Count de Molina, José-Maria Sert, and Francis Picabia: three quite distinctive influences which are apparent in the diversity of his work.

As Cecil Beaton wrote: "Rose seems to have absorbed from all the big painters, yet with no slavish eclecticism. When I asked Miss Stein about him, she told her story with Steinian simplicity. 'Well, his mother was French, his father a baronet, he is about twenty-seven years old, with very pretty ways and gentle manners. He was brought up in Paris, came under the influence of Cocteau and that *galère*. He painted, painted, painted. It's the only thing that interested him.'"[3] Rose himself confirmed his attitude to painting: "I love paint, and all forms of making paint live, as much by its medium as by any idea expressed in a picture. I have painted either with violence or with softness, and generally there are no

tricks in my work for critics to hook their intelligence onto."[4] This accounts for the variable quality of his work, which Gertrude Stein seemed neither to notice nor care about.

191   Portrait of Isadora Duncan

Oil and wax on artist board
19¾ x 12¹⁄₁₆ in: 50.4 x 30.6 cm (frame 61 x 42.7 cm)
Signed in oil lower right: "Francis Rose"
Reverse inscribed in ink: "Isadora Duncan / Francis Rose / 1926," and in pencil: "for Diaghilev"
Reverse stamped "Douanes Exposition Paris"
Label on reverse: "Lucien Lefebvre-Foinet / 19 rue Vavin / 2 rue Bréa / Paris VI / couleurs et toiles fines," stamped "5150"
1933.534

Exhibitions: New York 1933, No 58; Chicago 1933, No 146; Northampton 1934, No 146; Hartford 1934b; New York 1965–6, No 156 (illustrated p 76; not shown in New York); Worcester 1989.

Francis Rose wrote: "I think that my real life began in the winter of 1925, when I left Italy to join my mother in Villefranche."[5] She had taken some rooms on the first floor of the Welcome Hotel, where Jean Cocteau also had a room. He fell under Cocteau's spell. Rose remembered: "In his corner room grouped all the talented people of the period: the great and the interesting, the foolish and the charming. All the artistic youth of France and America met there." With flamboyant exaggeration Rose continued by giving a roll-call of their names: Picasso, Faulkner, Scott Fitzgerald, Stravinsky, Honegger, Milhaud, Christian Dior, Mary Butts, Coco Chanel, Daisy Fellowes, and, "above all these in my mind was my beloved Isadora Duncan."[6] Rose spent the winters of 1925–27 with his mother at the Welcome Hotel. Cocteau stated: "It all began with Francis Rose. His mother was clairvoyant. In the dining-room she would get up from the table, approach some gentleman or lady and foretell their future. She wore linen dresses on which Francis used to paint flowers. He was nearly seventeen. Everything dates from the dinner party given for his seventeenth birthday. An armchair draped in red velvet had been prepared for me at the end of the table and a bust of Dante stood beside my plate. Lady Rose had only invited some English officers and their wives. About eight o'clock a strange procession appeared at the bottom of the slope which led from the town to the harbour. Crowned with roses Francis gave his arm to Madame Isadora Duncan in a

Greek tunic. She was very fat, a little drunk, escorted by an American woman, a pianist and a few people picked up *en route*. The stupefaction of Lady Rose's guests, her anger, the entry of the procession, the fishermen flattening their noses against the window panes, Isadora kissing me, Francis very proud of his crown, that is how this birthday dinner began."[7] Francis Rose was often seen walking arm-in-arm with Isadora Duncan.

Rose himself described painting his uncannily prophetic portrait: "I painted her in a studio that I had rented in the port of Villefranche. For this portrait she wore a large red shawl with a very long fringe that was later to be the instrument of her death. When I showed her the finished picture, in which I was experimenting with a form of cubism, she cried out: 'But Francis, you have cut my throat.' By a strange coincidence, it was the large fringe of the shawl that became entangled in the spokes of the wheel of the low sports car that had just been given to her, and almost decapitated her outside the Henri Plage, as the car was driven away."[8] The portrait is not a likeness, but is a painting of an anguished, strangled figure. Nor does it appear to be an experiment in "a form of cubism," but Rose wrote his autobiography more than thirty years after painting the picture.

Isadora Duncan was born in San Francisco in 1877. Not trained as a dancer, she evolved her own theories of dancing which were not based on classical ballet. Instead, she pioneered a new system of freely expressive movement supposedly inspired by ancient Greek dancing. She had a considerable influence on the development of modern dance, not least through her dancing in bare feet and discarding the tutu. She visited Russia in 1905. While Fokine was impressed by seeing her dance, it is questionable how much influence she had on him. Diaghilev, too, denied her influence. She became almost as famous for her lovers as for her dancing. She died in 1927, strangled by her trailing shawl.

According to a letter from Francis Rose, "Serge Lifar obtained the portrait of Isadora from Serge Diaghilev's will."[9] Rose was unaware that Diaghilev had not made a will; Lifar in fact acquired the portrait, along with all his other purchases, from Diaghilev's heirs.

The portrait is in its original gold frame which, after framing, was washed over with silver paint, some of which, left and right, went onto the painting.

192   Project for a ballet on Samson

Oil on canvas, wax-lined
25⁹⁄₁₆ x 21¹⁄₁₆ in: 65 x 54.5 cm
Signed in oil lower left: "Francis Rose / 2.2.29"
Inscribed in oil bottom right: "The Blind"
1933.531

Exhibitions: New York 1933, No 55; Chicago 1933, No 143; Northampton 1934, No 143; Hartford 1934b; New Haven 1935; New York 1965–6, No 157 (illustrated p 76; not shown in New York); New York 1966–7; Worcester 1989.

Although the title of this painting is apparently "The Blind," Rose himself suggested the present title in a letter of 4 November 1969 to Mrs Edwin T. Dean.[10] The story of Samson is told in Judges, chapters 13–16. Although it is possible that Diaghilev may have been thinking of a ballet on the theme of the Old Testament story, there is no evidence for such a project other than Rose's word. It is more likely that Rose, having met Lifar, himself suggested the theme to him with this painting. This is not a straightforward project in the manner of a set design: the seated, resting, blind figure, albeit inexpertly painted, slightly resembles Lifar, and the scene in the background, perceived symbolically in his mind's eye, is theatrical. The two pillars are in the Samson story, but the three costumed figures on the stage belong more to a play than a ballet, based on the Prodigal Son rather than Samson.

193   Dr Tarr's Dinner, project for a setting after a short story by Edgar Allan Poe

Ink, tempera and/or watercolor on paper
10³⁄₁₆ x 12¹⁄₁₆ in: 25.9 x 30.6 cm
Signed and dated in ink lower left: "Francis Rose 1.1932"
Inscribed in ink lower right: "Dr Tarr / Edgar Allen [sic] Poe (inscription "Paffen Gatken" crossed out)
1933.532

Exhibitions: New York 1933, No 56;[11] Chicago 1933, No 144;[11] Northampton 1934, No 144; Hartford 1934b; New Haven 1935; Williamsburg 1940; Michigan 1957; Elmira 1958, No 27;[11] New York 1965–6, No 153 (illustrated p 74); Princeton 1968; Hartford 1974; Columbus 1989; Worcester 1989.

Rose himself provided the title of this work in his previously quoted letter.[12] According to him this sketch, made for Serge Lifar when he was already the ballet director at the Paris Opéra, was to be used for a ballet called *La Maison de Fous,* based on a story by Edgar Allan Poe, *The System of Doctor Tarr and Professor Fether*. It was never produced, and Lifar does not mention this projected ballet. The title was changed to *Dr Tarr's Dinner* because of the ballet *Maison de Fous* by Jean Börlin, with music by Viking Dahl, sets and costumes by Nils Dardel, which had been produced by the Ballets Suédois at the Théâtre des Champs-Elysées in Paris in 1920 (see Léger, p 248).

The drawing illustrates Poe's description closely: "At six dinner was announced; and my host conducted me into a large *salle à manger*, where a very numerous company were assembled—twenty-five or thirty in all. They were, apparently, people of rank— certainly of high breeding—although their habiliments, I thought, were extravagantly rich, partaking somewhat too much of the ostentatious finery of the *vieille cour*. I noticed that at least two-thirds of these guests were ladies; and some of the latter were by no means accoutred in what a Parisian would consider good taste at the present day . . . The dining-room itself, although perhaps sufficiently comfortable and of good dimensions, had nothing too much of elegance about it . . . The table was superbly set out. It was loaded with plate, and more than loaded with delicacies. The profusion was absolutely barbaric. There were meats enough to have feasted the Anakim. Never in all my life had I witnessed so lavish, so wasteful an expenditure of the good things of life. There seemed very little taste, however, in the arrangements; and my eyes, accustomed to quiet lights, were sadly offended by the prodigious glare of a multitude of wax candles which, in silver *candelabra*, were deposited upon the table and all about the room, wherever it was possible to find a place."

A large dining table occupying most of the center of a stage, however, is not obviously an appropriate setting for a ballet. Rose later did design a ballet for Lifar which was produced: *La Péri* in 1946 for the Nouveau Ballet de Monte-Carlo.

194   Project for a setting for a ballet

Ink on paper
11³⁄₈ x 16⁷⁄₈ in: 28.8 x 43 cm
Signed and dated in ink lower right: "Francis Rose / 1932"
1933.533a

Exhibitions: New York 1933, ? No 57;[13] Chicago 1933, ? No 145;[14] Northampton 1934, ? No 145;[13] Hartford 1934b; New Haven 1935; New York 1965–6, No 154 (illustrated p 75); New York 1966–7; Princeton 1968; Columbus 1989; Worcester 1989.

The same paper, the same medium, and the same size of this and the following sketch presume that they were done at the same time, 1932, even though No 195 is undated. They are not for the same ballet, and they are for unknown ballets. Indeed, they are fluent and expressive visualizations of quite different themes: this sketch is on some rural middle-European fantasy with a woodman and a magic arborescent ballerina, and No 195 on some *commedia dell'arte* pantomime with Venetian symbols. Rose may or may not have discussed these projects with Lifar, but the fact that these drawings are in this collection explains the relationship.

1 First mentioned in *Geography and Plays* published in 1922 without the indefinite article, which was added in 1923 in *An elucidation*.
2 Gertrude Stein, *The Autobiography of Alice B. Toklas*, pp 248–9.
3 Cecil Beaton, *The Wandering Years*, p 282.
4 Francis Rose, *Saying Life*, p 180.
5 Francis Rose, *ibid*, p 49. Villefranche was then a small fishing port on the Côte d'Azur near Nice, already a fashionable winter resort.
6 Francis Rose, *ibid*, p 56.
7 Jean Cocteau, *The Difficulty of Being*, pp 73–4.
8 Francis Rose, *op cit*, p 73.
9 Letter from Francis Rose to Mrs Edwin T. Dean at the Wadsworth Atheneum, dated 4 November 1969.
10 In *ibid*.
11 Described, incomprehensibly, as "Le Banquet d'après Oscar Wilde."
12 See note 9.
13 Described as "Design for a Ballet," but not identified.
14 Described as "Projet de décor," but not identified.

195   Project for a setting for a ballet

Ink on paper
11³⁄₈ x 16⁷⁄₈ in: 28.8 x 43 cm
Unsigned and undated
1933.533b

Exhibitions: New York 1933, ? No 57;[13] Chicago 1933, ? No 145;[14] Northampton 1934, ? No 145;[13] Hartford 1934b; New Haven 1935; Michigan 1957; New York 1965–6, No 155 (illustrated p 75); New York 1966–7; Princeton 1968; Amherst 1974; Columbus 1989; Worcester 1989.

Georges Rouault

French
born 1871 Paris
died 1958 Paris

Le Fils Prodigue (Prodigal Son)

Ballet in 3 scenes by Boris Kochno, after the
  parable
Composer: Serge Prokofiev
Conductor: Serge Prokofiev
Choreographer: George Balanchine
Principal Dancers:
  The Prodigal Son: Serge Lifar
  The Siren: Felia Dubrovska
  The Father: Michel Fedorov
  Servants: Eleanora Marra, Natalie Branitska
  Confidants of the Prodigal Son:
    Leon Woizikovsky, Anton Dolin
  Friends of the Prodigal Son: Efimov, Tcherkas,
    Borovsky, Kochanovsky, Jazvinsky, Hoyer,
    Lissanevitch, Petrakevitch, Ladre,
    Matouchevsky, Ignatov, and Katchourovsky
Company: Diaghilev's Ballets Russes
First Performance: 21 May 1929, Théâtre Sarah-
  Bernhardt, Paris

Synopsis

Adapted from the program.

Scene 1—Home. Two confidants of the prodigal son arrange a store of wine jugs as if embarking on a journey. The prodigal son comes out of the tent followed by his two servants. They try to engage his attention but he is in high spirits and dances energetically, acting out the adventures he and his confidants will have when they leave home. His dance stops when he finds himself face to face with his stern father. The father beckons to him, but then the prodigal son backs away. Finally he ignores his father and the servants, summons up his two confidants and points to the open road. With a flourish they leave. The servants watch in dismay but the father raises his hand in an unacknowledged farewell.

Scene 2—In a far country. A scene of great revelry in a tent by a group of grotesquely bald men is interrupted by the entrance of the prodigal son and his confidants. The group is suspicious at first but when the prodigal son offers them his wine they all begin to dance exuberantly again. They are joined by the siren who voluptuously captivates the prodigal son until he is totally in her power. She then makes him drink and so completely intoxicates him that he collapses in a stupor. He is then robbed by his confidants and the other revellers, with the siren snatching the medallion round his neck. Slowly the prodigal son wakes. He realises what has happened and acknowledges the betrayal of his confidants and his own self-betrayal. He drags himself on his knees back towards his home. The others return and divide their loot.

Scene 3—Home. The prodigal son, exhausted, returns crawling and suddenly sees that he has reached his home. The servants see him, and, overjoyed, help him. The father comes out of the tent and remains motionless while the prodigal son struggles towards him. Finally the father shows his forgiveness and holds him in his arms like a child.

Prokofiev's score for the three scenes is in ten separate movements:

Scene 1
1. The Prodigal Son leaves the paternal home, accompanied by his two confidants.

Scene 2
2. The Prodigal Son meets his friends and takes part in their festivities.
3. Entry and dance of the Siren.
4. Confidants of the Prodigal Son entertain the guests.
5. The Prodigal Son dances with the Siren.
6. The Siren and Friends of the Prodigal Son force him to drink.
7. Confidants, Friends and the Siren strip the sleeping Prodigal Son and take flight.
8. Awakening and lamentations of the Prodigal Son.
9. Promenade of the Siren and Friends laden with spoils.

Scene 3
10. Return of the repentant Prodigal Son to the paternal home.

The Prodigal Son[1] was the last ballet produced by Diaghilev before his unexpected death on 19 August 1929.

After the success of Le Pas d'Acier,[2] Diaghilev immediately commissioned another ballet from Prokofiev and began looking round for a suitable scenario which would "be simple and easy to follow, unlike Prokofiev's earlier ballets, and not require a cumbersome set."[3] After some time, and with Prokofiev growing impatient, Boris Kochno suggested a ballet version of the parable of the prodigal son from St Luke's gospel,[4] which would be universally familiar to audiences. On 21 September 1928 Prokofiev wrote to Diaghilev: "I look on writing a new ballet for you, as always, with great interest, but quite bluntly I don't want to hang around, because there is hardly enough time left to compose it properly."[5] In preparing his scenario Kochno made some changes to the parable: he left out the envious elder son, and introduced the Siren as an irresistibly seductive character being the principal cause of the prodigal son's downfall. Balanchine, the choreographer, has stated that the end of the ballet was inspired by an image in Pushkin's story *The Stationmaster*: "In this story Pushkin described a wayside station at which travellers rested and changed horses. The walls of the waiting room were covered with litho-

graphs of the story of the prodigal son. The last print showed the boy returning on his knees."[6] While this acknowledgement is true, more of the ballet was inspired by Pushkin's story than he admitted.[7] Kochno neglects to mention Pushkin, so it is not clear whether the crib came from him or from Balanchine.

Diaghilev was pleased with Prokofiev's score and stated during an interview before the first performance in London[8] that he considered it to be "one of the greatest of modern Russian compositions," and that he was "happy to be its god-father. It is Prokofieff's [sic] third ballet,[9] and I do not hesitate to say that it is one of his finest. The composer has never before been more clear, more simple, more melodious, and more tender than in 'The Prodigal Son.' There are some beautiful moments in the three tableaux which Boris Kochno has arranged, such as the concentration of love and forgiveness when the son returns to his father. In these days, where there is so little sentiment, it is incredible that Prokofieff has been able to find such an expression in his music."[10] Diaghilev was not merely whipping up favorable advance publicity, he genuinely admired the score. He had written earlier to Serge Lifar: "Yesterday I listened to Prokofiev with Boris [Kochno]. The last scene (the return of the prodigal son) is excellent. Your variation—the awakening after the orgy is completely new for Prokofiev. It is a kind of profound and majestic nocturne. The tender theme of the sisters is good too; the robbing scene, for three clarinets is very good à la Prokofiev."[11] One of the reasons for doing the ballet at all was to create another starring vehicle for Serge Lifar. As Diaghilev said: "Serge Lifar has a magnificent opportunity. He is able to reveal himself in a style that has been neglected for many years, and the role shows him as a mimic tragedian such as we have never seen."[12]

Diaghilev knew that Matisse also admired Prokofiev. He therefore asked him to design the ballet, after first getting his conductor, Henri Defosse, to acquaint him with the music. Diaghilev sent Matisse a telegram on 31 August 1928: "Defosse informs me of your good impression of the music. Delighted if you willing design the two ballets beginning with *Schéhérazade* which intend to restage this winter."[13] Matisse refused both commissions. He had not much enjoyed working in the theater before (see *Le Chant du Rossignol,* pp 257–61), finding the work too time-consuming and unrewarding because he felt that he never had overall control. After Matisse's refusal, Kochno suggested to Diaghilev that he commission Georges Rouault. It was an inspired suggestion but a risk, because although his painting had the necessary biblical quality Rouault had not worked in the theater before.

Just how much of a risk became apparent when Rouault arrived in Monte Carlo without his promised designs. He casually informed Diaghilev that he had brought his painting materials with him and would quickly do the required drawings. He dutifully attended rehearsals but produced no designs, although he did teach Balanchine and the dancers how to balance a chair on their noses. After usually lunching with Diaghilev and others at the Café de Paris, he would return to his hotel, ostensibly to carry on with his work. After a while Diaghilev grew suspicious, so one day after lunch he persuaded Rouault to go off for a drive along the Grande Corniche. During his absence Diaghilev bribed the hotel management to let him into his room. Kochno described what happened next: "Diaghilev returned from this trespass empty-handed and wild-eyed. He had searched everywhere, turned the room upside down, and had discovered not one ballet sketch, indeed no trace whatever of any work. He had not even found sketching paper and had seen neither brushes nor colors. That evening, Diaghilev announced to Rouault that a reservation had been made for him on the Paris train for the next day. He said nothing whatever about *Le Fils Prodigue*. Although Rouault had arrived with a single piece of luggage, he now seemed anxious to go up to his room to pack his bags, and he disappeared for the entire evening. The following morning, before boarding the train, Rouault brought Diaghilev a stack of sketches for *Le Fils Prodigue*—admirable gouaches and pastels which he had executed in one night."[14] Kochno's version makes a good story, but Lifar gives a different, and for once more plausible, version of events: Diaghilev did enter Rouault's empty hotel room and "thus gained access to the painter's sketches, and from these was able to choose the sketch for the first scene of the ballet.[15] The second—the tent scene—he designed himself, and, managing to find Rouault, set him to work on it the same day. After which he busied himself with the costumes, and in developing such preliminary sketches as were ready."[16] The revealing point about this version, if true, is that it explains why the design for the second scene is in a different scale (see p 304). Lincoln Kirstein, later Balanchine's closest colleague, more or less confirmed Lifar's version (regarding the costume designs), saying that Diaghilev found in Rouault's empty hotel room "heaps of sketches in various stages of completion. Choosing a handful, he gave them to Vera Soudeikina (presently Madame Stravinsky), and she created Rouaultesque costumes."[17] Of the "heaps of sketches" for the sets only very few remain, and some of these are probably working drawings by Prince Schervashidze, the scene painter, who transformed the set designs into backcloths. Balanchine, praising Rouault's sets and costumes, thought that he "seemed to enjoy the whole experience of doing scenery for the ballet."[18]

Although it appears that the ballet was prepared over a long period, it was in fact devised very quickly. Balanchine's choreography was a mixture of stylized dramatic movements infused with formal classicism.

Pure dancing was left to the Siren, and her *pas de deux* with the Prodigal Son was described by John Taras as "a manual of erotic combinations."[19]

The essentially mimic quality of the choreography suited perfectly the theme of the ballet and Lifar's particular athletic virtuosity. But Balanchine admitted that he only had time to sketch in the movements: "if I am pressed for time I expect the soloists to perfect themselves. This was the case with the ballet *The Prodigal Son*, which I had to produce in a fortnight. It was only an hour before the dress-rehearsal that I conceived and arranged the scene where the table is used as a boat."[20]

Lifar subsequently claimed the credit for his interpretation of the title role. During rehearsals he was urged uncharacteristically by Diaghilev: "'Don't be afraid to put more feeling into the part of *Le Fils Prodigue*. And don't be afraid to dramatise it, either, if you see it that way,' and later: 'Seriozha, I beg of you, please save my twenty-second season in Paris. Never yet have I had a failure, but now I feel we might, if you will not consent to help me, if you go on refusing to treat *Le Fils Prodigue* more dramatically, as it should be treated, instead of in this cold academic manner. I am relying absolutely on you, Seriozha.'"[21] On the afternoon of the first performance, Lifar returned to his hotel

Below: Serge Lifar (center) as the Prodigal Son, with his friends, in scene 2.

after rehearsal and went to bed, saying: "'I can't go to the theatre to-day. I don't feel I am in sympathy with the part of the Prodigal Son, and so I'm afraid I may turn it into a failure. I can't understand what sort of way they want me to treat the part. Let them act it themselves. I can't, and I don't want to, and prefer to stay here at home. Even if it is a failure, they can't blame me.' . . . A terrific struggle was going on inside me. Sombrely, sadly, I thought of Sergei Pavlovitch, he who was my spiritual father, and of our relations together. I thought of the past, that life I had offered up as a sacrifice to him, uselessly and so unnecessarily. Why? To what end? Then visions out of the remote past came thronging round me . . . The love, tenderness and care Sergei Pavlovitch had lavished on me, the manner in which, through him, I had become an artist; all, all rose before me again, and a feeling of intolerable poignancy, of pity for the ailing, weary, aged old man—for suddenly he had begun to seem much older—sent a wave of endless commiseration pulsing through my being. Was it possible I could betray him? The memory of things past, my sudden vision of the old man, merged into one image of . . . The Prodigal Son. I *am* that prodigal son of his . . . In my ears there sounded Prokofiev's music. Suddenly I saw the light, I began to understand . . . I leapt out of bed. 'Let's be off to the theatre. I have created my Prodigal Son . . . It is myself.'"[22] Lifar wrote that he first performed *L'Après-midi d'un faune*, but this is not so. The evening began with *Les Fâcheux* (see pp 147–49). This was followed by the first performance of the revival of *Renard* (see pp 235–38) with Lifar's new choreography which, according to him, "proved an immense success and received a veritable ovation, to loud cries of Stravinsky, Stravinsky, Lifar. Stravinsky took the call with the artist [Larionov] and bowed. But the calls for Lifar went on increasing, drowning the applause."[23] Lifar refused to take a call in spite of Stravinsky and Grigoriev entreating him to do so. After the interval he gave his first performance as the Prodigal Son. "When the curtain went down, pandemonium broke loose. Numbers of people were crying, though no one had realised it was my self, my life, that had been enacted."[24] The performance ended with the *Polovtsian Dances* from *Prince Igor*. At a party afterwards at the Capucines restaurant, Lifar, sitting between Misia Sert and Coco Chanel, raised his glass of champagne and drank to Diaghilev and his

twenty-second season. Lifar wrote that Diaghilev raised his glass, gazed at him, and with tears in his eyes said: "Thank you, thank you Seriozha. You are a great, a true artist. There is nothing more I can teach you . . . I can only learn from you now . . ."[25]

The only one who was displeased with the production was Prokofiev. Although he had to admit that his ballet got a very good reception, he was dissatisfied with the choreography. In his opinion "it did not always follow the music."[26] This is a surprising opinion because Balanchine, more than most choreographers, was extremely musical. He explained Prokofiev's dissatisfaction differently: "He wanted a real garden and real wine and real mustaches and all that . . . You know Prokofiev was a great chess player, and that's how he thought—in straight mathematical lines. He wanted *The Prodigal Son* to look like *Rigoletto*. He complained so insistently that Diaghilev finally told him, 'look, this is how we're doing it. If you don't like it, you can just get out of here.'"[27] Diaghilev was not afraid to criticize his artists, but he always protected them when he thought that what they were doing was right. In this case Diaghilev let Balanchine continue with his choreographic interpretation. Prokofiev publicly (at least in a diary intended for publication) praised the design: "The sets by Rouault, one of France's leading artists, were excellent."[28] But Francis Poulenc probably expressed his private opinion more accurately when he said: "Prokofiev loathed Rouault's scenery. He would have liked something more Russian for *The Prodigal Son* . . . you understand . . . he preferred Gontcharova and Larionov who'd done *Chout*. And that side . . . what shall I say? That Palestinian side to Rouault's scenery, perhaps rather in the vein of 'twilight on the Bosphorus.' That scenery with its ochres and yellows and that moon up in the sky . . . He didn't like it."[29]

The opinions of the critics did not match those of Prokofiev. Cyril Beaumont, describing the choreography, was hesitant at first: "The dance movements were unusual. There were some elements of classical ballet technique in the dance for Dubrovska, but the men's movements had an element of acrobacy, as though inspired by gymnastics or the circus. In fact, they suggested tumblers rather than dancers."[30] Beaumont was pinpointing the controversy of the time about the developing fashion for "acrobatics" replacing "dancing," into which Diaghilev plunged himself with a letter to *The Times* justifying his stance.[31] But Beau-

mont was unequivocal about Lifar: "Lifar's role in this ballet was mime rather than dancing, and he revealed himself a fine exponent of that difficult art. His actions seemed to come straight from the heart, as though he felt the moving story in every fibre of his being. When the ballet ended I felt conscious of having witnessed one of those rare performances that constitute a landmark in one's memories, something to be treasured and relived."[32] Lifar's self-adulation had not been overdone. Florence Gilliam, in her review, encapsulated the *raison d'être* of the Ballets Russes when she wrote: "*Le Fils Prodigue* . . . is drama, danced of course, but above all acted to Prokofieff's music and its most striking value is in the recreation in ballet form of the whole temper and aspect of the painter Rouault. There is plenty of chance for argument as to whether this sort of thing is the real province of the Ballet, but it never seems to me to matter much what boundary lines are crossed if the thing is good enough in itself."[33] Unwittingly, perhaps, she described Diaghilev's successful artistic philosophy.

196 Design for the backcloth for Scenes 1 and 3: Home

Pastel or chalk, ink and tempera and/or watercolor on paper
20⁵⁄₁₆ x 28¹³⁄₁₆ in: 53 x 75 cm
Unsigned and undated
Backing board stamped: "Douane Centrale Exportation Paris"
(There is a tear at the bottom of this design with a missing piece replaced and repaired by the artist)
1933.536

Exhibitions: Paris 1929, No 64; London 1930, No 65; Paris 1930, No 91; New York 1933, No 59; Chicago 1933, No 147; Northampton 1934, No 147; Hartford 1934b; New Haven 1935; Paris 1939, No 332 (illustrated p 33); ? Los Angeles 1939–40; Williamsburg 1940; New York 1941–2; New York 1945, No 156 (illustrated p 75); Grand Rapids 1947; Syracuse 1949–50; Minneapolis 1953; Elmira 1958, No 23; Indianapolis 1959, No 430; Hartford 1964; New York 1965–6, No 158 (illustrated p 77); Edinburgh 1966, No 54; Spoleto 1966; Princeton 1968; Strasbourg 1969, No 460 (illustrated in color p 240); Frankfurt-am-Main 1969, No 159; Hartford 1973; Hartford 1974; Chicago 1975; New York 1980; Hartford 1988; Worcester 1989.

Illustrations: Amberg, pl 50; Bablet, p 161 No 298; Gontcharova, p 95; Hansen, Fig 69; Haskell, p 111 (bottom); Lynham, pl XXVIII p 134; Percival, p 111 (bottom); Rischbieter, p 112a; Pozharskaya and Volodina, p 260; Shead 1989, p 170 (color); Spencer 1974, p 130; Hartford Symphony 97/98 season prospectus, p 9 (color).

This strange, empty, glowing landscape, with its curious phallic lighthouse, may have taken Rouault a long time to devise, but it is entirely in the spirit of his work at this time. Similar images recur in other landscape paintings, but in the ballet the emptiness was filled by the movements of the dancers dressed in vivid costumes, contrasting with the somber tones of the backcloth. The expressionistic, stained-glass quality of this design creates the illusion of reality when it is integrated with Prokofiev's music and Balanchine's choreography, and becomes totally convincing. Rouault understood that his role as designer was to collaborate with and not dominate the others' work. He wrote: "I reiterate again in all simplicity that I am only a collaborator. M. Prokofiev is the musician. One has to listen to him without, however, closing the eyes too much in front of my imperfect attempts."[34] The resolution of the apparent puzzle in theater design appealed to Rouault, and, as he admitted to Michel

Georges-Michel, he wanted to experiment with his own painting methods: "'I agreed to do these décors,' he explained, 'because I felt that I should be painting immense stained-glass windows. The light would be caught in them instead of passing through. But that is the difference between stained-glass and stage-settings, and I had to give considerable study to the problem. And this time I'm going to have to work quickly, feverishly. It is something new for me, as I often take five years to paint a canvas, scraping it out, doing it over again . . .'"[35] The quality of stained glass is that it is translucent as well as being incandescent; therefore, when properly lit, it is almost insubstantial.

None of this quality was apparent at the first night in Paris. For once, Diaghilev may not have attended to the lighting as meticulously as he usually did. The critic of *The Times* was definitely not impressed by the setting: "The muddy colours which this painter affects are entirely unsuitable to

stage decoration. A backcloth, which seems to have been painted in colours mixed with coal-dust and mud, casts a gloom which the most vivid dresses are powerless to dispel."[36] Yet by the time the ballet opened in London on 1 July 1929 the critic of *The Times*[37] wrote: "The glowing colours of M. Rouault's décor, which are caught in the velvets of the costumes, provide a fine spectacle."[38] The lighting had been properly adjusted by then, so that the cloth was lit from behind as well as from in front, thereby giving it Rouault's intended glow. But the setting provided more than glow, it was perfectly apt in its apparent embracement. David Hays, who probably saw only the revival, wrote: "Thus the dancers seem to be performing within the drop and not in front of it. And as the story unfolds in the village we seem to have been inside Rouault's mind—to have seen for the first time the actual scene—the landscape with its mood—in front of which Rouault set his easel."[39]

Apart from the lighting, however, the set in performance was not as Rouault intended. The backcloth, painted by Prince Schervashidze from this design, remained in place throughout the ballet. The tent in the following design was meant to be lowered in front of this backcloth for the second scene. This explains the difference in scale between the two designs. In the production, however, the tent was also on stage throughout, beginning in the first scene on one side as the Prodigal Son's home, and then more central for the second scene. No one seems to have noticed the incongruity of having the same backcloth for both scenes. There were no vases of flowers in scene two, but there were jars. The long trellis table began upturned in scene one as a palisade, turned upside down for a table in scene two, and a stage for the Siren, upended as a screen and a slide, turned upside down again to become a fence, and, when the Siren and the Friends arrange themselves in it, a boat. Rouault complained to Diaghilev: "Certain conditions beyond my control were imposed: 1) By those awful stagehands. As I planned it, the tent was to be like a bird descending from heaven. As it is, it hides my setting for the greater part of the performance. They have made it look like a sentry box, only a bit squarer, fortunately! (I had to spend three nights repainting it so it would not be too frightful looking.) There is also the matter of the dancers' bar which was added. 2) Chirico (for *Le Bal*)[40] painted all his own settings in Monaco, where he had everything he needed within easy reach. Whereas when I came back to Paris, the set dresser and the choreographers went to Monte Carlo and worked on their own. And once they were back in Paris, nothing could be changed! All that within two or three days of the opening. In my opinion, the man who writes the libretto should be the choreographer and the set decorator as well."[41] This could have been an ideal toward which Diaghilev also strived.

197 Design for the banqueting tent for scene 2: In a far country

Pastel or chalk, ink and tempera and/or watercolor on paper
20¾ x 28⅞ in: 52.5 x 73.5 cm
Unsigned and undated
Backing board stamped: "Douane Centrale Exportation Paris"
Label on backing board: "Georges Rouault / Le Fils Prodigue / Décor / Coll. S. Lifar 1929"
1933.535

Exhibitions: Paris 1929, No 65; London 1930, No 66; Paris 1930, No 92; New York 1933, No 59; Chicago 1933, No 148; Northampton 1934, No 148; Hartford 1934b; New Haven 1935; New York 1937–8, No 712; Boston 1938; Paris 1939, No 332 ; ? Los Angeles 1939–40; Williamsburg 1940; New York 1941–2; New York 1945, No 157 (illustrated p 75); Grand Rapids 1947; Syracuse 1949–50; Cleveland 1953 (illustrated p 32); Sarasota 1958, No 68; Indianapolis 1959; Hartford 1964; New York 1965–6, No 159 (illustrated p 77); Edinburgh 1966, No 55; Spoleto 1966; Princeton 1968; Strasbourg 1969, No 462 (illustrated No 117); Frankfurt-am-Main 1969, No 161; Hartford 1973; Hempstead 1974, No 124 (illustrated); Hartford 1974; Chicago 1975, No 69; New York 1980; Hartford 1988; Worcester 1989.
Illustrations: Bablet, p 161 No 299; Kirstein, p 45 No 81; Rischbieter, p 112b; Pozharskaya and Volodina, p 262; Williams 1981, p 48 No 50 (color).
This has always previously been described, inaccurately, as the setting for scene 2 (see above under No 196).
The figures at the banqueting table have been painted out in green.

Notes

1 The definite article was dropped from the title when Balanchine revived the ballet in 1950 for the New York City Ballet. In the revival, Servants, who had originally been Sisters, returned to being Sisters; Confidants became Servants, and Friends became Drinking Companions.

2 Le Pas d'Acier, ballet in two scenes by Serge Prokofiev, Georges Yakoulov, and Leonide Massine, with choreography by Massine, set constructions and costumes by Yakoulov, was first performed on 7 June 1927 at the Théâtre Sarah-Bernhardt, Paris. (There has never been a satisfactory translation of the title. The Steel Way is sometimes used, but usually the French title is maintained.)

3 Boris Kochno, Diaghilev and the Ballets Russes, p 272.

4 St Luke, chapter 15, 11–24. Verses 25–32 continue the parable with the elder son who was omitted from the ballet.

5 Serge Prokofiev to Serge Diaghilev, quoted in I. S. Zilbertsein and V. A. Samkov, Sergei Diaghilev, Vol 2, p 142.

6 George Balanchine, Balanchine's New Complete Stories of the Great Ballets, p 322.

7 This is the full relevant extract from Pushkin's story: "I began to look at the pictures that adorned his humble but tidy abode. They portrayed the story of the Prodigal Son: in the first, a venerable old man in a night-cap and dressing gown was saying good-bye to a restless youth, who was hastily receiving his blessing and a purse of gold. Another vividly depicted the young man's depraved conduct: he was sitting at a table surrounded by false friends and shameless women. Further on, the young man, in ragged clothes, with a three-cornered hat, was herding pigs and sharing their food; there was an expression of profound sorrow and penitence on his face. The last picture illustrated his return to his father: the kind old man in the same dressing-gown and night-cap running to meet him; the prodigal son was on his knees; in the background the cook was killing the fatted calf, and the elder brother was asking the servants the reason for such rejoicing."

8 The first performance in London was on 1 July 1929 at the Royal Opera House, Covent Garden.

9 Apart from Le Pas d'Acier and Le Fils Prodigue, Prokofiev composed Chout which, with set and costumes by Michel Larionov and choreography by Thadée Slavinsky and Larionov, was first performed on 17 May 1921 at the Théâtre de la Gaîté-Lyrique, Paris.

10 Serge Diaghilev, quoted in "The Russian Ballet" in The Observer, London, 30 June 1929.

11 Serge Diaghilev to Serge Lifar in a letter dated 2 December 1928, quoted in I. S. Zilbertsein and V. A. Samkov, op cit, Vol 2, p 144.

12 Serge Diaghilev, quoted in "The Russian Ballet," op cit.

13 Telegram quoted in Boris Kochno, op cit, p 272. Diaghilev had also become disenchanted with Schéhérazade, thinking it had become merely ludicrous. However, it was not restaged. See also p 258.

14 Boris Kochno, op cit, p 275.

15 A preliminary sketch for scenes 1 and 3 in watercolor and crayon remained in Lifar's collection until it was included in the sale of the Lifar Collection at Sotheby's, London, in 1984 as lot 63 but it remained unsold.

16 Serge Lifar, Serge Diaghilev, p 499.

17 Lincoln Kirstein, "Balanchine Trio" in The Dancing Times, London January 1973, p 186 (reprinted from About the House, the magazine of the Friends of Covent Garden).

18 George Balanchine, op cit, p 322.

19 John Taras, quoted in Richard Buckle George Balanchine: Ballet Master, p 51.

20 George Balanchine in Dance Journal, August–October 1931, quoted in Cyril W. Beaumont, Complete Book of Ballets, p 969.

21 Serge Lifar, op cit, pp 498, 499.

22 Serge Lifar, ibid, p 501.

23 Serge Lifar, ibid, p 501.

24 Serge Lifar, ibid, p 502.

25 Serge Lifar, ibid, p 504.

26 Serge Prokofiev, Soviet Diary and other writings, p 287.

27 George Balanchine, quoted in Harlow Robinson, Serge Prokofiev, p 229.

28 Serge Prokofiev, op cit, p 229.

29 Francis Poulenc, My Friends and Myself, pp 117–8.

30 Cyril W. Beaumont, The Diaghilev Ballet in London, p 294.

31 The letter appeared on 13 July 1929. It is quoted extensively on p 234.

32 Cyril W. Beaumont, op cit, p 295.

33 Florence Gilliam, "And so to the theatre" in The Boulevardier, New York July 1929, pp 38, 41.

34 Georges Rouault, "En marge du 'Fils Prodigue'" in L'Intransigeant Paris 28 May 1929, p 6.

35 Quoted in Michel Georges-Michel, From Renoir to Picasso, pp 39–40.

36 "The Russian Ballet in Paris" in The Times London, 31 May 1929, p 10.

37 As criticisms then were anonymous it is not known whether the one in London was the same as the one in Paris or not; probably not.

38 "A new ballet by Prokofiev" in The Times London, 2 July 1929, p 14.

39 David Hays, "Painters in the theatre" in Chrysalis Vol 6 Nos 3–4, New York 1953, pp 5–8.

40 With Renard this was the other new ballet in 1929, see pp 155–71.

41 Georges Rouault to Serge Diaghilev, quoted in Pierre Courthion, Georges Rouault, pp 205–6.

Prince Alexandre Schervashidze

Russian
born 1867 Russia
died 1968 Monte Carlo

Prométhée (Prometheus)

Ballet in 1 act and 5 scenes by Serge Lifar (based
on *Les Créatures de Prométhée*, ballet in 2 acts
by Salvatore Vigano, revised by Maurice Lena
and Jean Chantavoine)
Composer: Ludwig van Beethoven
Conductor: not credited
Choreographer: Serge Lifar
Designer (costumes): Prince Alexandre
Schervashidze
Principal dancers:
Prometheus: Serge Lifar
The Man: L. Katchourovsky
The Woman: Alice Nikitina
Death: Felia Doubrovska
The Warriors: Théodore Slavinsky, V. Karnetzky
Apollo: not credited
Company: Ballets Serge Lifar
First performance: 3 July 1933, Savoy Theatre,
London

The remainder of the program was as follows:

Part Two
L'Après-midi d'un faune[1]
Composer: Claude Debussy
Choreographer: Serge Lifar inspired by
Vaslav Nijinsky
Dancer:
The Faun: Serge Lifar

Interlude: Overture *Rouslan and Ludmila* by Glinka

Le Spectre de la Rose
Composer: Weber orchestrated by Berlioz
Choreographer: Michel Fokine
Dancers:
The Girl: Alice Nikitina
The Rose: Serge Lifar

Part Three
Divertissement
Choreographers: Marius Petipa, Michel Fokine,
George Balanchine, Serge Lifar
1   Overture *La Belle au Bois Dormant* by
Peter Tchaikovsky
The Orchestra
2   *Valse* by Frederic Chopin
Alice Nikitina and Serge Lifar
3   *Mazurka* by Frederic Chopin
Serge Lifar
4   *Danse l'Elysée* by Jacques Offenbach
Felia Doiubrovska
5   *Badinerie* by Johann Sebastian Bach
Alice Nikitina
6   *Danse Guerrière* by Guy Ropartz
T. Slavinsky, V. Karnetzky, and L. Katchourovsky
7   *L'Oiseau Bleu* (from *La Belle au Bois Dormant*) by
Peter Tchaikovsky
a. *Adagio*: Felia Doubrovska and Serge Lifar
b. *Variation*: Serge Lifar
c. *Variation*: Felia Doubrovska
d. *Final*: Felia Doubrovska and Serge Lifar
8   *Danse des Bouffons* by Nicholas Tcherepnine
T. Slavinsky, V. Karnetzky, and L. Katchourovsky

9   *La Belle et le Prince Charmant* (from *La Belle au
Bois Dormant*) by Peter Tchaikovsky
Alice Nikitina and Serge Lifar

For the revival of *Prometheus* in New York on
5 November 1933, Forrest Theatre:
Conductor: Alexander Labinsky
Principal dancers:
Prometheus: Serge Lifar
The Man: Roman Jasinsky
The Woman: Olga Adabache
Death: Lycette Darsonval
The Warriors: Théodore Slavinsky, V. Karnetzky,
L. Matlinsky, S. Bousloff
Apollo: S. Kochanovsky
In New York, Olga Adabache replaced Alice Nikitina
in *Le Spectre de la Rose*, and *La Chatte* (see
pp 202–5) at first replaced *Divertissement*

Synopsis
From the program:
"Scene 1. Prometheus creates the Man and the
Woman.
Scene 2. The Road of Life toward Parnassus.
Scene 3. The Encounter with Death.
Scene 4. Prometheus Conquers Death.
Scene 5. Apollo takes under his protection the
Mortals created by Prometheus.

Prometheus has just stolen Fire from Heaven to
give life to the two statues he has made, but in
despair because he cannot awake a soul within
them, he must appeal to the gods and takes the
statues to Parnassus.

There Apollo receives Prometheus and the two
beings he has created, but tells him that they must
learn the lessons of suffering and death.
Prometheus defends them against the cruel God.

The two figures awake to feelings of love and
Prometheus reveals to them the meaning of
modesty.

When his task is accomplished, his triumph is
celebrated."

Diaghilev died in Venice on 19 August
1929. For a time everyone hoped that
the Ballets Russes company would continue, either under Boris Kochno,
Diaghilev's secretary and aide, or under
Serge Lifar, Diaghilev's protégé and last
star. These were Diaghilev's natural but
undeclared successors. Kochno's name,
however, was unknown to the public; the
company would not serve under Lifar, and,
moreover, the two did not much like each
other. They decided therefore to "abdicate"
together, and signed an open letter to the
company to that effect (see Appendix C).

To know what happened next is to
decide whose version of events is the more

reliable, George Balanchine's or Serge
Lifar's. According to Balanchine's biogra-
phers, Bernard Taper and Richard Buckle,
the director of the Paris Opera, Jacques
Rouché, approached Balanchine in October
1929 with a proposal to stage a new version
of Beethoven's *Les Créatures de Prométhée*[2] at
the Opéra to commemorate, two years late,
the centenary of the composer's death.
Rouché hoped at the same time to revive a
genuine interest in ballet with the regular
audience at the theater. Balanchine enthusiastically accepted the commission, but
refused the offer of becoming the resident
ballet master. After two weeks' rehearsal,
Balanchine fell ill with pneumonia which
developed into pleurisy followed by tuber-
culosis, and therefore had to relinquish the
choreography. He suggested to Rouché that
Lifar, who had the leading part, should
finish the ballet. Alexandra Danilova, who
was in love with Balanchine and took him
to a sanatorium near Mont Blanc, wrote:
"But before he left, he explained his plans
for the ballet to Lifar, so that Lifar could
finish it for him. 'Do you think I can do it?'
Lifar asked. *Renard* (see pp 235–38), the one
ballet he had made for Diaghilev, had been
a failure, and Diaghilev had given up on
him as a choreographer. But George was
reassuring—half the ballet was already
finished, and the rest he laid out according
to the music. Everything was ready: he had
the skeleton of the ballet and knew exactly
what he wanted it to be. Lifar finally
agreed."[3] They agreed also that Lifar would
take all the credit for the choreography, but
that Balanchine would keep all the fee,
10,000 francs, which he needed for his
medical expenses.

Lifar, predictably, has a different version
modestly favouring himself. According to
him, Rouché said: "Lifar, I'd very much like
to see you on the stage of the Opera. What
would you say if I suggested you should
produce a ballet and dance in it? Say, for
instance, the *Prométhée* of Beethoven . . ." To
which Lifar, after a few excuses, replied,
"'Very well, then, I'll try. Engage a choreographer, I'll learn the part and try to dance
it.' 'A choreographer! But I'm counting on
you; the author of *Renard* . . .'"[4] Lifar continued, however, that he persuaded Rouché to

engage Balanchine, who fell ill after one rehearsal and would be "out of action for a month." He quotes Rouché: "'Upon my word, Lifar, it is clearly fated that you must take on the choreography of *Prométhée*. You cannot refuse any more.' And I had not the slightest wish to refuse since the whole ballet was already sketched out in my mind."[5]

The first version has more veracity. *Les Créatures de Prométhée* was premiered at the Opéra on 30 December 1929.[6] Its reception, though favorable, was not quite as ecstatic as Lifar would have us believe: "Each of my *tours* with the sideways drop provoked applause. My *grand jetés* roused the whole audience . . . my own fever had communicated itself to the public. When the curtain fell it was a real triumph."[7] The success of the production was enough, however, for Rouché to appoint Lifar as the resident ballet master.[8] When Balanchine, cured of his illness, called on Lifar at the Opéra with Danilova, they were turned away by the stage doorman on Lifar's orders. Although they did work together again in Cochran's *1930 Revue*,[9] they now really went their separate ways.

In 1933 Edward James, "a young Englishman of taste, culture and wealth, but with absolutely no experience, and most certainly not born to command,"[10] agreed to finance a number of new ballets devised by Balanchine and Kochno provided that his wife, the Viennese dancer Tilly Losch, would be given some suitable parts. James presented the company which he formed, called "Les Ballets 1933," at the Théâtre des Champs-Elysées[11] in Paris and the Savoy Theatre in London. When James heard that Lifar was planning to present an *ad hoc* company in London at the same time, he bought him out of his engagement at the Aldwych Theatre, and arranged instead for him to perform at the Savoy during his "Les Ballets 1933" season. As Jane Pritchard comments, "This way James could have the cachet of presenting Lifar, Alice Nikitina and Felia Doubrovska (all former stars of Diaghilev's Ballets Russes) and audiences would flock to see them dance the old favourites, *Le Spectre de la Rose*, *The Bluebird pas-de-deux* and Lifar's solo version of *L'Après-midi d'un Faune*."[12] Although the ballets were not going to be staged on a lavish scale, and the costumes for the old Diaghilev ballets were made according to traditional Bakstian designs, Lifar commissioned new designs for *Prometheus* from Prince Schervashidze. Having worked in

the theater in Russia as a designer since 1909, Schervashidze emigrated to France in 1922 to become Diaghilev's most talented and regular scene painter. He was particularly adept at maintaining an artist's individual style on a large, scenic scale.

Lifar's "season" of three performances on 3, 7, and 10 July began with the first performance of the shortened version of *Les Créatures de Prométhée* with a small cast, called simply *Prométhée*, and he made sure that all the attention was centered on him. Lifar knew only too well that stardom had to be helped along, and so he arranged for a personal panegyric to be distributed in the theater.[13] André Levinson, the writer, though always critical of Diaghilev and his aesthetic, was seduced by Lifar: "That which makes Serge Lifar the foremost dancer of our time, is the blending in him of a striking personality and an impeccable mastery. His early triumphs, under the auspices of Serge de Diaghileff, and his earliest attempts at choreography, revealed him as a born creator and also as a rebel, breaking with the traditional forms of ballet . . . He was called upon to direct Beethoven's *Prométhée*—a lengthy suite of dances, in which the legend of the Titan serves only as the slight pretext for an allegorical show. The *Prométhée*, who comes into the performance, is the quintessence and the synthesis of that work, whose tragic and heroic features are thrown into relief by Serge Lifar. We see him, pursued by Jupiter's thunderbolts, hastening down steep Olympus, whence he has stolen the fire which shall breathe life into the beings he has created—and then, with his whole soul, defending his creatures against the furies of Death. To this superhuman contest, Serge Lifar brings an emphasis, a tension, as much physical as spiritual, which show him to be one of the greatest mimic actors of to-day . . . This twenty-eight years old dancer is now a master endowed with the most contradictory gifts: an imagination daring to the point of temerity, and the strictest self-discipline; perfect technique and an ever responsive sensitivity; a faultless purity of line and a peculiar—quite exotic—charm. And that is why we know of no one, among contemporary dancers, whose future seems to hold more radiant promise than that of Serge Lifar." This immodest burst of self-aggrandisement, for that is how it was seen even though it had been written by a renowned critic, upset the vanity of the other dancers, especially Alice Nikitina, who recalled: "On the first night of our

ballet a little booklet was distributed in the audience concerning Lifar alone. When I heard about it, I asked him why he had limited the booklet to himself, and he replied that anybody was at liberty to do so. The next day I saw to it that there were booklets about me as well. As we had a great success, we danced a second time at the request of Edward James. After this he asked Lifar to appear in his wife's company and it was then that the quarrel between them took place and acquired such an ugly shape. My maid told me one day, as she came to wake me, half crazy with excitement, that she had seen 'Mr James and Mr Lifar hitting one another in the Savoy lobby.'"[14] Nikitina does not say that James wanted Lifar to appear in *Le Spectre de la Rose*[15] during the program of "Les Ballets 1933," which went against every artistic purpose that Balanchine and Kochno had, and that the quarrel was first about Lifar refusing to dance because of a cut finger, and secondly about his refusing to dance *Le Spectre de la Rose* with Alicia Markova instead of Tamara Toumanova.[16] The whole season must have been fraught with backstage nervous tension verging on hysteria, but this did not apparently impinge on either the audience or the critics. "Last night Mr Serge Lifar ruled at the Savoy Theatre . . . His 'Prometheus' is a superb resetting of the ballet for which Beethoven wrote the music. From the moment when he steals the fire from Heaven there was not a moment's slackening of the tension which Mr Lifar imparts to every movement and every expression of his extraordinarily expressive features. He is ecstatic as the giver of life to the creatures whom he has created, strong and determined in leading them to Parnassus, fierce in his agonising contest with Death, who was beautifully impersonated by Mme Felia Doubrovska, and magnificent in his victory."[17] And Arnold Haskell was able to write of Lifar's performances: "It was his first visit as a great classical dancer, and he revelled in his virtuosity sometimes at the expense of the art, that he had so often proved. He danced like a god . . ."[18]

After London, Lifar planned to go on a tour of America, with engagements in New York, Providence, Buffalo, Toronto, Chicago, and Montreal. Barbara Hutton promised to sponsor him. He went with a small company but without Nikitina and Doubrovska. In spite of an impressive build-up of advance publicity—"Sensational Young Russian Dancer, Legitimate Successor of Nijinsky, Coming Here Direct from Paris

Opera, Where He is Director and Premier Danseur of Ballet"[19]—New York was much more severely critical than London, and did not think Lifar was at all like a god, nor even comparable to Nijinsky. "But only disappointment could come from the tendency to compare him with such dancers as Nijinsky, Fokine and Mordkin. He is of their type, but scarcely of their order." So wrote Oscar Thompson, who continued with his review of *Prometheus*: "The original ballet in the Vienna of the early eighteen-hundreds may have been pretty poor stuff, but we doubt if it had less point than the symbolic contortions of the Lifar 'scenario.'"[20] Marc Blitzstein was more scathing: "But Lifar got off to a very poor start in New York (Nov. 5). None of his best ballets appeared on his program. Instead, the audience was made to sit through his own dreadful interpretation

of Beethoven's *Prometheus*; he is, unluckily, no choreographer. Everything good and bad in it he learned from Balanchine (there were dismally inept imitations of Balanchine's telegraphic style, and use of knees and hands). There is nothing, too, so painful or funny as a chorus of bad male dancers; Lifar has picked a bevy of the clumsiest of them, all soubrettes and ingénues. They disported themselves in short drawers which hung and clung, vine-fashion; they ruined the chances of a ballet, already (in idea and general execution) very inferior to the local movie-house product."[21] The critic of the New York Times simply wrote: "*Prometheus* has nothing to recommend it."[22]

Lifar had the sense to take note of the critics. He withdrew *Prometheus* from the program for the rest of the tour. Barbara Hutton let him down. The box office

receipts did not pay for the costs. The orchestra was reduced to two pianos. To meet all his expenses and to be able to return with his company to Europe, he had to sell his collection of designs to the Wadsworth Atheneum.

198 Design for a backcloth

Pastel or chalk and tempera and/or watercolor on paper
18⅞ x 23⅞ in: 47.5 x 60.5 cm
Signed in Russian and inscribed in French in chalk lower left in chalk: "A mon cher Serge Lifar Schervashidze"
Inscribed on back of board in pencil: "Prince Schervashidze / maquette pour un / décor romantique / Paris 1931," and in red crayon: "Schervashidze"
Label on reverse: "Lucien Lefebvre-Foinet / 19 rue Vavin / 2 rue Bréa / Paris VI / couleurs et toiles fines," stamped "3035," and inscribed in pencil "Prometheus 1932"
1933.538

Exhibitions: New York 1933, No 60; Chicago 1933, No 149; Northampton 1934, No 149; Hartford 1934b; New Haven 1935; Elmira 1958, No 28; Indianapolis 1959, No 442; New York 1965–6, No 160 (illustrated p 78); New York 1966–7; Hartford 1974; Hartford 1978–9; Worcester 1989.

Although the label on the reverse of this design ascribes it to *Prometheus*, the inscription "Romantic decor," with its earlier date of 1931, is without doubt a more accurate indication of its originally intended use. In essence this is a perfect design for *Les Sylphides* which requires a dreamily mysterious, romantic, silvan landscape. Presumably, however, it was used as the setting for *Prometheus* during Lifar's tour, as well as for some of his other ballets in the program. The tour was not arranged with any great extravagance, and therefore a single backcloth or just black drapes were probably the only setting. This backcloth would also have been appropriate for Part Three of the program at the Savoy Theatre, *Divertissement*, which included two numbers from *Les Sylphides*: *Valse* danced by Nikitina and Lifar, which Edwin Evans described as "some of the best dancing" of the evening, and *Mazurka* danced as a solo by Lifar.

199 Costume design for [S. Kochanovsky] as Apollo

Graphite, ink and tempera and/or watercolor with white highlights on paper
12⅛ x 9¹¹⁄₁₆ in: 32 x 24.5 cm
Signed in pencil in Russian bottom right: "Шервашидзе (Schervashidze)"
Inscribed in pencil top left in pencil: "Promothée [sic]
1933.537a

Exhibitions: New York 1933, No 61;[23] Chicago 1933, No 150;[24] Northampton 1934, No 150;[23] Hartford 1934b; New Haven 1935; San Francisco 1936; Williamsburg 1940; Cambridge 1942; Indianapolis 1959, No 439; Hartford 1965, No 30; New York 1965–6, No 161 (illustrated p 78); New York 1966–7; Princeton 1968; Hartford 1974; Columbus 1989; Worcester 1989.
This design is a simplification of a traditional baroque dance costume, except that the skirt, so rightly criticized, not being stiff, must have looked ridiculous on the dancer.

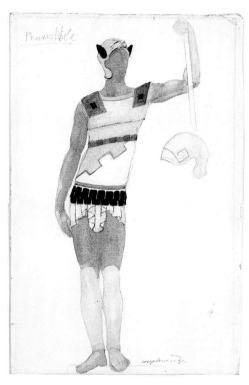

200 Costume design for the Warriors

Graphite and tempera and/or watercolor with white highlights, on paper mounted to heavy-weight paper
11¼ x 7⁷⁄₁₆ in: 28.4 x 18.7 cm
Signed in pencil in Russian bottom right: "Шервашидзе (Schervashidze)"
Inscribed in pencil top left: "Promethée," and inscribed in pencil (erased) upper left: "Mr Woitzikovsky [sic] / Mr Katcherowsky [sic]"
1933.537b

Exhibitions: New York 1933, No 61;[23] Chicago 1933, No No 150;[24] Northampton 1934, No 150;[23] Hartford 1934b; New Haven 1935; San Francisco 1935–6; Poughkeepsie 1940; Williamsburg 1940; Cambridge 1942; Michigan 1957; Indianapolis 1959, No 440; New York 1965–6, No 162 (illustrated p 78); New York 1966–7; Hartford 1974; Hartford 1978–9; Columbus 1989; Worcester 1989.

There were two Warriors in London, and four in New York. This design and the following one are for Warriors, but this one was for *Prometheus* while the following one was for *Danse Guerrière*, one of the numbers in *Divertissement* which formed part three of the program. In common with many designers Schervashidze has taken a shortcut by drawing essentially the same figure for both. The only difference, apart from the design of the actual costume, is in the angle of the head and the face. This design is faceless.

201 Costume design for T. Slavinsky, V. Karnetzky, and L. Katchourovsky as the Warriors in *Danse Guerrière* in *Divertissement*

Graphite and tempera and/or watercolor on paper
11³⁄₈ x 7½ in: 28.9 x 19.2 cm
Signed in pencil in Russian bottom right:
"Шервашидзе (Schervashidze)"
Inscribed in pencil top left: "Danse Guerrière," and inscribed in pencil (erased) upper left: "Mr Voitzokovsky [sic] / Jasinsky / Katcherowsky [sic]"

On the reverse is a pencil and watercolor sketch of figure in Greek chiton costume, crossed out with two pencil lines
1933.537c

Exhibitions: New York 1933, No 61;²³ Chicago 1933, No 150;²⁴ Northampton 1934, No 150;²³ Hartford 1934b; New Haven 1935; San Francisco 1935–6; Williamsburg 1940; Michigan 1957; Indianapolis 1959, No 441; Hartford 1965, No 31; New York 1965–6, No 163 (illustrated p 78); New York 1966–7; Princeton 1968; Hartford 1974; Hartford 1978–9; Columbus 1989; Worcester 1989.

The fact that there are three names on the design, even though they have been erased and even though two of them are different, means that the costumes were all of the same design. (See also entry for No 200.)

Notes

1 This version was danced as a solo.
2 The ballet is based on the German ballet *Die Geschöpfe des Prometheus* which Beethoven wrote for Salvatore Vigano (1769–1821) and which was first performed in Vienna in 1801.
3 Alexandra Danilova, *Choura*, p 108.
4 Serge Lifar, *Ma vie*, p 86.
5 Serge Lifar, *ibid*, p 91.
6 *Les Créatures de Prométhée* was conducted by J.-E. Szyfer, the sets and costumes were by Francis Quelvée, and the principal dancers were Olga Spessiwtzewa [sic], Serge Lifar, Serge Peretti, and Suzanne Lorcia.
7 Serge Lifar, *op cit*, p 95.
8 Lifar finally left the Paris Opéra only in 1958, after revolutionizing and dominating the ballet scene there for thirty years.
9 Lifar danced in *Luna Park* by Lord Berners with choreography by George Balanchine, set and costumes by Christopher Wood.
10 Arnold Haskell, *Balletomania*, pp 230–1.
11 The first performance was on 7 June.
12 Jane Pritchard, *Les Ballets 1933*, p 15.
13 "Homage to Serge Lifar" by André Levinson, dated Paris 24 June 1933, a folded sheet referred to by Alice Nikitina as a "booklet."
14 Alice Nikitina, *Nikitina by herself*, p 116.
15 *Le Spectre de la Rose*, danced by Lifar and Nikitina, had been included in Lifar's three-performance season.
16 Lifar refused to dance on 11 and 12 July. Edward James said that he was in breach of contract and sued him. Lifar was reported in the *Evening Standard* as saying: "I am Lifar. Contracts don't trouble me." In May 1934 the court awarded James damages of £600 with costs against Lifar
17 H. E. W., "Serge Lifar at the Savoy" in unidentified newspaper, London 4 July 1933.
18 Arnold Haskell, *op cit*, p 236.
19 Press release from Columbia Concerts Corporation, New York City, dated 4–5 November 1933, p 1.
20 Oscar Thompson, "Serge Lifar Makes Introductory Bow in Program of Ballets" in unidentified newspaper, New York 6 November 1933.
21 Marc Blitzstein in unidentified, undated journal, p 40.
22 John Martin, "The Dance: Lifar's Debut" in *The New York Times*, New York 12 November 1933.
23 This and the following note apply to all costume designs. Described as "Costumes: *Promethée* (Opéra) 1932" but not identified.
24 Described as "'Promethée' deux costumes" but not identified.

José-Maria Sert

*Spanish
born 1876 Barcelona
died 1945 Barcelona*

Le Astuzie Femminili (Woman's Wiles)

Comic opera/ballet in 3 scenes by Giuseppe
    Palomba
Composer: Domenico Cimarosa, re-orchestrated by
    Ottorino Respighi
Conductor: Ernest Ansermet
Director and Choreographer: Leonide Massine
Principal Singers:
    Bellina: Mafalda de Voltri
    Ersilia: Mme Romanitza
    Leonora: Zoia Rosovska
    Romualdo: Angelo Masini-Pieralli
    Filandro: Aurelio Anglada
    Giampaolo: Gino de Vecchi
Principal Dancers:
    Pas de trois: Lubov Tchernicheva,
        Vera Nemtchinova, Zygmund Novak
    Pas de six: Klementovitch, Wassilewska,
        Hilda Bewicke, Nicolas Kremnev,
        Nicolas Zverev, Anatole Bourman
    Tarantella: Lydia Sokolova, Leon Woizikovsky
    Contre-Danse: *Corps de ballet*
    Pas de deux: Tamara Karsavina,
        Stanislas Idzikowski
Company: Diaghilev's Ballets Russes
First Performance: 27 May 1920, Théâtre national
    de l'Opéra, Paris

Synopsis

From the program:

"Bellina is the richest heiress in Rome. By her
father's will, she is to marry Giampaolo, a merchant from Bergamo. Her tutor, Doctor Romualdo,
also wishes to marry her in spite of his vows to
Leonora, Bellina's governess. Bellina escapes from
these two ridiculous suitors and marries her cousin
Filandro.

Her friend Ersilia is her aid and abetter in her
woman's wiles.

Tableau I. *Romualdo's Apartment*. Entrance of
Giampaolo, the ridiculous fiancé. Bellina amuses
herself at his expense, feigns shyness and then
declares her intention of wedding successively an
officer, a ballet-master, a student. Giampaolo is
disconcerted. Leonora unfolds to him the dark
intentions of Romualdo. Filandro, who hears this
conversation, thinks he has been deceived, and
challenges the grave doctor to a duel.

Tableau II. *The Gardens of Romualdo's House*.
Ersilia and Leonora are making fun of Romualdo.
Giampaolo arrives and enters with him into a
juridicial argument as to the right he has of marry-
ing Bellina. Meanwhile Bellina has fled. No sooner
has the news spread, than a Cossack officer rushes
into the house in search of his perfidious fiancée,
who has abandoned him to follow a certain
Filandro. Immediately afterwards a Cossack woman
appears; who is pursuing a lover by whom she has
been betrayed for a certain Bellina. The two Cossacks meet, quarrel and laugh up their sleeves.
Complete reconciliation takes place, and they end
in getting engaged. The whole company is invited
to the wedding.

Tableau III. *A Terrace in Rome*. Nuptial feast
interrupted by the double revelation: 'I am Bellina!'
'I am Filandro!' Rage, spite, general reconciliation.
THE RUSSIAN BALLET"

Diaghilev, by his own admission, was
"head over heels in love with the
eighteenth century Italian music."[1] During
his search through a huge number of Italian
scores he became irresistibly attracted to *Le
Astuzie Femminili*,[2] probably because
Domenico Cimarosa had been Catherine the
Great's music master for three years in St
Petersburg from 1787, and had included a
Russian peasant dance, the *kamarinskaya*, in
the finale. Diaghilev was also still intrigued
by the problem of trying to combine successfully the different requirements of opera
and ballet in a single production. He again
engaged Respighi to arrange and re-orches-
trate the music, as he had Rossini's *La
Boutique Fantasque* (see pp 182–84).
Although *Le Astuzie Femminili* was planned
in 1918, work on the production was
delayed until February 1920, partly because
the extension of the London seasons
restricted the number of new works the
company could mount.

Massine was responsible for the whole
staging and, as he wrote, was "very glad to
have the chance of handling vocal and
choreographic problems at the same time.
Working on this comic opera was a refreshing change for me, and I enjoyed directing
the singers."[3] Diaghilev discussed the principles behind the staging of the opera with
Massine, which he later expressed in an
interview: "whilst every singer naturally
knows how to sing well, none in all their
experience ever learned to make good
movements. In order, in fact, to get really
beautiful movements it is necessary to
study them for about ten years, but as there
was no time for that they were instructed to
make as little movement as they could. If
the characters have to fight a duel they of
course fight it; if they have to make love
they make love; but all superfluous gesture
is cut out."[4] He hoped that Massine would
avoid any potential conflict between singers
and dancers in the staging, and achieve a
unified production. He never thought that
opera and ballet were necessarily such

distinct art forms that opera could not
include dancing, nor ballet singing. In *Le
Astuzie Femminili* the integration of singing
and dancing was taken further than it had
been, for example, in *Pulcinella*[5] which was
produced ten days earlier. The Paris program made the intention clear: "In this
piece, in fact, the singing is not relegated to
the background as in *Pulcinella*: the musical
part is not limited to singing off stage, to
distant choirs. The characters take part in
the action: they act a role. They are close to
our ears, under our eyes."[6] Diaghilev
always had a positive idea about what he
wanted but, as the responsible impresario,
he let Massine get on with it except when
he felt the need to interfere.

Taking Cimarosa's final instruction of a
"Ballo Russo" at its face value, Massine had
the idea of developing the whole end of the
opera into a choreographic *divertissement* of
a suite of dances instead of a single dance.
Diaghilev did not approve at all. According
to Massine: "When Diaghilev came to a
rehearsal and saw what I was doing, he
objected strongly. He said that the *divertissements* were entirely unnecessary and
wanted me to dispense with them. I, on the
other hand, insisted that a suite of dances
was entirely in keeping with the pervading
eighteenth-century style of the production.
This led to a heated argument, but I finally
persuaded Diaghilev to let me have my way
and the dances remained in."[7] One can only
imagine how heated the argument was but,
by all reports, Diaghilev was easily capable
of flying into the most frenzied and hysterical rages at the slightest pretext. This, however, was about a matter of artistic
judgment: that Massine won the argument
shows that his self-confidence was solid
enough to withstand any bullying from
Diaghilev. The victory was not without a
penalty, because Massine goes on to say:
"That was our first real disagreement, and
the beginning of a gradual decline in our
relationship and in our artistic collaboration."[8] On the other hand, Diaghilev was
not a fool and soon realized that Massine
had had a bright idea, although he did not
exactly give him the credit for it.

José-Maria Sert had already expressed
his desire to design the production when he

and Misia Sert had discussed it with Diaghilev and Massine on their return from Spain in 1918. Massine wrote: "He immediately began to discuss its scenic possibilities, pointed out that it would be essential to design a set in the baroque style, and by the time Diaghilev assured him that he would let him know as soon as the company was free to rehearse, he was obviously deep in gilded Italianate balconies with baroque details!"[9] When the production came to be realized, Diaghilev undoubtedly felt that he had already committed himself to engaging Sert to design the sets and costumes. Besides, he probably also felt that he owed it to him from a sense of loyalty to his devoted friend Misia. This was the third production Sert was involved in for Diaghilev, having designed the sets for *La Légende de Joseph* in 1914,[10] in which Massine had first appeared in the title role, and the Spanish costumes for *Las Meninas* in 1916.[11] Diaghilev described the design for *Le Astuzie* during his interview: "The first scene is an eighteenth century interior, influenced by the Chinese importations which one met with in palaces such as Aranjuez. The second is a colonnade in a garden. A tree in the centre looks like a tree of coral and has been much discussed. The third scene, in which the ballet takes place, is a broad terrace with a panoramic view of Rome. The costumes are a trifle ahead of the date, being those of the opening year of the nineteenth century."[12]

According to Grigoriev, the stage director, *Le Astuzie Femminili* "failed to produce the impression expected. Its reception was indeed favourable; but Paris was far from being carried away by it; and Diaghilev was disappointed."[13] The reason why the production was not entirely successful was simply because the enormous cavern of the stage of the Opéra swamped the delicate, witty, but lightweight opera. The critics did not blame the singers: "They did their best, under the adroit baton of M. Ansermet, to preserve the lively spontaneity of the sung dialogue and, as far as possible, to make allowances for the disproportionate size of the stage."[14] Other critics were more harsh, but all were agreed that the ballet was the most successful part of the production, and all praised Sert's sets and costumes. "To console us we have, it is true, the decors by Sert. His emerald front cloth with black and gold tiling is painted with warm-hearted ardour; his chinese style interior with a purple background is a delight even though the perspective is a little delusive; his amber

avenue leading to a radiantly decorative coral tree is like a mannered landscape; his vision of the architecture of Rome is bold and faultless. And what imagination he has put into the costumes! The movements with which the ballet ends are a fairyland of colors, like an ebb and flow of precious stones; and we must salute Sert, the magician."[15] Louis Handlern of *Comoedia*, after the dress rehearsal, put Sert's contribution into context: "Finally, let me add that M. J.-M. Sert's costumes are most forcefully imaginative, and his sets in vibrant colors evoke the splendour of Rome. Once again, M. de Diaghilew shows us that he does not owe his allegiance to any particular school and that his preferences are without bias, after the stylization of M. Henri Matisse, the irony of M. Derain and the conciseness of M. Picasso, he opens wide the stage space to the imagination which fills it to the edges with one of the most powerful master-builders of modern painting."[16]

The production enjoyed much greater success in London than in Paris. Ernest Newman, with rare enthusiasm, wrote that he had "enjoyed nothing so much for a long time in the theatre . . . This rippling, sparkling music should be the delight of the town. The new principles of gesture and movement that Massine has gone upon for the opera singers deserve more detailed

consideration than I can give them today: briefly, no gesture is made that is not necessary and pertinent. The acting thus wins a curious and paradoxical repose as well as an animation. Massine's ballet (that follows the opera) is one of the most beautiful creations of the extraordinary young genius."[17] In spite of such appreciation *Le Astuzie Femminili* was not repeated in subsequent seasons.

Although Diaghilev was disappointed by the general reception, and particularly by the fact that his notion of integrating opera with ballet more closely had not succeeded, he recognized that the last-act ballet had been well received and was therefore salvageable as an entity.

The production was first revived as a ballet only, with the title *Ballet de l'Astuzie Femminili* on 8 January 1924 at the Théâtre de Monte-Carlo with the following principal dancers:

Pas de trois: Lubov Tchernicheva, Felia Doubrovska, Anatole Wilzak
Tarantella: Lydia Sokolova, Leon Woizikovsky
Pas de deux: Vera Nemtchinova, Stanislas Idzikowski
Pas de six: Maikerska, Soumarokova, Joan Coxon, Nicolas Kremnev, Nicolas Zverev, Thadée Slavinsky

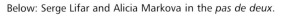

Below: Serge Lifar and Alicia Markova in the *pas de deux*.

The title *Cimarosiana* was first used on 24 April 1924 at the Teatro Liceo, Barcelona, when the *contre danse* was reintroduced. On 11 October 1924 a *pas de quatre* was added, with choreography by Bronislava Nijinska, danced by Alice Nikitina, Ninette de Valois, Constantin Tcherkas, and Serge Lifar. A *pas rustique*, danced by Alexandra Danilova, Leonide Massine, and Serge Lifar, was added on 7 January 1927. With its new title *Cimarosiana* it became a favorite piece in London, as noted by the critic of *The Times*: "In *Cimarosiana* the Russian Ballet do all the things that a London audience can never tire of seeing them do. They whirl and caper, balance and float in kaleidoscopic patterns of bright colours against a dark background. Every pattern is the counterpart of Cimarosa's symmetrical melodies."[18] It was repeated in London every season from 1924 to 1929, but in Paris the ballet was not performed after 1924. Then as now, Paris was more exigent of artistic endeavor and originality, especially on the part of the Russian Ballet.

202 Costume design for Tamara Karsavina as the Woman and Stanislas Idzikowski as the Man in the *pas de deux* in scene 3

Graphite and tempera with black ink notations on paper
13⅞ x 19⅝ in: 32.5 x 49.7 cm
Inscribed in gouache center right: "Pas de deux / No. II," and, not in Sert's hand, in ink under man: "K2," under woman: "K1," in pencil under woman: "Karsavina"
1933.539

Exhibitions: New York 1933, No 62 (described as "Costumes for *Cimarosiana* 1923"); Chicago 1933, No 151 (described as "'Cimarosiana' deux personnages"); Northampton 1934, No 151; Hartford 1934b; New Haven 1935; San Francisco 1935–6; New York 1937–8, No 713; Boston 1938; Paris 1939, No 335 (illustrated p 16); Poughkeepsie 1940; Williamsburg 1940; Edinburgh 1954, No 119 (described as being for *Cimarosiana*); London 1954–5, No 127 (described as being for *Cimarosiana*); New York 1958; Indianapolis 1958, No 445; Elmira 1958, No 42; Hartford 1965, No 32; New York 1965–6, No 164 (illustrated in color facing p 13); New York 1966–7; Princeton 1968; Strasbourg 1969, No 307 (illustrated No 82); Frank-furt-am-Main 1969, No 75; Hartford 1973; Hartford 1974; Hartford 1978–9; Worcester 1989.
Illustrations: Ballets Russes Souvenir Programme May–June 1920 cover (color); Beaumont, p 135; Detaille, p 92; Lynham, p 128; Pozharskaya and Volodina, p 196; Propert 1921.

This at first appears to be too sketchy a design from which to make a costume, but photographs of the dancers wearing the finished costumes show that it was interpreted with great accuracy. Sert designed two fanciful costumes in a quasi-chinese style but followed the classic rules of designing costumes suitable for dancing: close fitting all-over tights for the man, embellished with a decorative pattern of semi-precious stones and blue Wedgwood plaques, and a variation on the basic tutu for the woman with tassel decorations, and colored patchwork bodice. The trousers in the design were not so long in the final costume. Sert made the decorative details on the man's costume, the woman's headdress and the edge of her skirt by scratching out the wet paint. He had second thoughts about the headdress, changing it to make it smaller and therefore more practical for dancing.

Cyril Beaumont described the *pas de deux* and the costumes: "The *Pas de Deux* was classical in feeling and full of refined grace and charm. The woman's role was worked out by Massine on Vera Clark[19] who, however, was told that Karsavina would dance it. Here again the costumes were most original, a delightful confection of *chinoiserie*. Idzikovsky wore a circular hat with a spire—suggested perhaps by the *mokot* of Cambodian dancers—and pink fleshings decorated with wedgwood blue cameos, looped with tasselled cord. Karsavina's costume consisted of a cap like a fuschia flower, trousers with the ends slashed in points, and a close fitting bodice which at the waist jutted out to a ruff-like shape; the colours were pink, blue, black, and green."[20]

This dance was one of those singled out by the critic of *The Morning Post*: "The Tarantelle and the *pas de deux* between Mme Karsavina and M Idzikowski take their places as part in a whole that constitutes an artistic triumph."[21] In 1967 Karsavina herself wrote: "In our pagoda hats we looked like *bibelots* that any collector might have contentedly put on his mantlepiece. I wish this precious little masterpiece of Massine could be revived, and that Stass [Idzikowski] could be seen in it."[22]

As noted above, this design was used as the cover illustration for the souvenir program of the twelfth season of the Ballets Russes.

On the reverse of this drawing there are two incomplete sketches in charcoal of a woman's headdress.

Notes

1 Serge Diaghilev, quoted in the *Observer*, London 20 June 1920.
2 First performed in Florence in 1794.
3 Leonide Massine, *My Life in Ballet*, p 148.
4 See note 1.
5 *Pulcinella*, music by Igor Stravinsky after Giambattista Pergolesi, choreography by Leonide Massine, sets and costumes by Pablo Picasso, was first performed on 15 May 1920 at the Opéra, Paris.
6 From "Gazette de l'Opéra" in the program "La Semaine à l'Opéra," Paris 21–26 May 1920.
7 Leonide Massine, *op cit*, pp 148–9.
8 Leonide Massine, *op cit*, p 149.
9 Leonide Massine, *op cit*, p 128.
10 *La Légende de Joseph*, with music by Richard Strauss, choreography by Michel Fokine, costumes by Léon Bakst was first performed on 14 May 1914 at the Opéra, Paris.
11 *Las Meninas*, with music by Gabriel Fauré, choreography by Leonide Massine, set by Carlo Socrate, was first performed on 25 August 1916 at the Teatro Eugenia-Victoria, San Sebastian.
12 See note 1.
13 Serge Grigoriev, *The Diaghilev Ballet*, p 165.
14 Gustave Samazeuilh in *République Française*, Paris 29 May 1920.
15 Nozière in *L'Avenir*, Paris 29 May 1920.
16 Louis Handlern, "Avant Astuce Féminine" in *Comoedia*, Paris 27 May 1920, p 1.
17 Ernest Newman, *The Sunday Times*, London 27 June 1920.
18 Anon, "The Russian Ballet" in *The Times*, London 26 June 1928.
19 As Vera Savina she became Massine's wife.
20 Cyril W. Beaumont, *The Diaghilev Ballet in London*, p 162.
21 *The Morning Post*, London 23 June 1920, quoted in Nesta Macdonald, *Diaghilev Observed*, p 250.
22 Tamara Karsavina, *The Dancing Times*, London February 1967.

Dimitri Stelletsky
Russian
born 1875 Brest-Litovsk
died 1947 Ste Geneviève des Bois (near Paris)

Tsar Feodor Ioannovitch

Tragedy in 5 acts and 11 scenes by Alexei Tolstoy
Director: N. V. Smolich
Designer (sets, props and costumes):
    Dimitri Stelletsky
Composer: Y. A. Shaporin
Principal characters:
    Tsar Feodor Ioannovitch: N. V. Smolich
    Tsaritsa Irina Feodorovna: M. I. Danilova
    Boris Feodorovitch Godunov: U. M. Yuriev
    Prince Ivan Petrovitch Shuisky: Y. O. Maliutin
    Prince Vasili Ivanovitch Shuisky: V. A. Borozdin
    Andrei Petrovitch Lup-Kleshnin: K. N. Yakovlev
    Princess Mstislavskaya: M. P. Domasheva
    Vasilisa Volokhova: E. P. Korchagina-
        Aleksandrovskaya
Company: State Academic Dramatic Theater
First performance of this production: 28 September
    1923, State Dramatic Theater (previously
    Alexandrinsky Theater, St Petersburg)

Synopsis

The action takes place in Moscow at the end of the sixteenth century. Two parties struggle for power within the state: the representative of the old order, Prince Shuisky, and the representative of reform and the new, Boris Godunov. Both parties strive to capture the support of the well-intentioned, pious weakling Tsar Feodor. Instead of supporting one party in favor of the other, or subduing both, the Tsar vacillates between them and, through his irresolution, causes the rebellion of Shuisky and his violent death, and the murder of his heir the Tsarevitch Dimitri and the consequent extinction of his dynasty.

This historical play in verse by Alexei Tolstoy (1817–75), a cousin of the more famous Leo, is the central part of a trilogy of which the other two parts are *The Death of Ivan the Terrible* and *Boris Godunov*. The trilogy covers a turbulent twenty-one-year period of Russian history from the 1580s to the death of Boris Godunov in 1605. *Tsar Feodor Ioannovitch*, written in 1868, is a separate self-contained drama as well as being the link between the other two. The real hero of the trilogy is Boris Godunov, and Tolstoy's conception of his character followed the one accepted by historians at the time of writing (which has since been disproved by historical research)—that Boris had risen to the Regency through intrigue and cunning, and from the Regency to the throne through the murder of the rightful heir, which he had inspired if not directly organized. After he had written his play, Tolstoy expressed his doubts about whether it would be performed or not;

indeed, it was not allowed to be performed by the censor until 1898, long after the writer's death. Even then, it was performed only with considerable alterations: members of the clergy were not allowed to be represented on stage, so their speeches were cut.

The strong rivalry between Moscow and St Petersburg ensured that both cities planned productions as soon as they could. St Petersburg was first, with Paul Orlenev as Tsar Feodor, at the Maly Theater of the Literary-artistic circle. Almost at the same time, Constantin Stanislavsky chose the play as the inaugural production of the Moscow Art Theater. Their first performance was at the Hermitage Theater on 14 October 1898. In 1924 Stanislavsky wrote in his autobiography: "The curtain of our theater rose first on the tragedy *Tsar Feodor*, written in a somewhat cinematographic manner. The author illustrates with great logicalness every passing moment of the plot. At the time the play was written this was considered to be necessary on the stage. Modern taste considers too much detail bad in the theatre, and at present we play *Tsar Feodor* in shortened form."[1] It was a surprising choice of play in view of Stanislavsky's theories about introducing greater realism into the theater, although the historical panorama in a succession of short scenes in different exterior and interior settings must have appealed to him. The production, however, was not entirely successful. It was seen by Sophia Tolstoy, wife of Leo, who commented in her diary: "It was well acted, although caricatured, and they overdid the desire for realism with a lot of shouting and bustling about on stage."[2]

Dimitri Stelletsky began as a sculptor, but turned to painting as a preference when he began to develop an interest in ancient Russian art. Unlike Roerich (see pp 291–95) whose work is steeped in the ancient pagan and primitive culture of Russia, Stelletsky was inspired by early Russian Orthodox Christian imagery and Byzantine church symbolism. His art is based on traditional religious, rather than peasant, forms and images. Stelletsky developed such a deep understanding of early Russian art that his own painting style became in no way imitative or interpretative, but could itself be accepted as authentically primitive. He was

therefore a natural artist to choose to design the historical drama *Tsar Feodor Ioannovitch*. He made all the designs for the sets, front cloth, props, costumes, and make-up in 1908 for a proposed production at the Alexandrinsky Theater that year. This production, however, did not take place then, and Stelletsky's designs were finally realized only in 1923, as is evident from the credits noted above, by which time he had left Russia and was living in Paris.

Although the designs were not used when they were done, a number of them were published in 1911 in the fine art magazine *Apollon* illustrating an article by Alexandre Benois,[3] including the front cloth; the set designs for act 1 scene 1 "Shuisky's room"; act 1 scene 2 "Royal apartments"; act 3 scene 2 "Tsar Feodor's room"; act 4 scene 4 "The Bank of the Yaüza river"; act 5 scene 2 "An open space in front of the Cathedral of the Archangel"; three costume designs, and six make-up designs painted like icons. Benois, after commiserating with Stelletsky, praised his work: "It fell to Stelletsky's lot to design the production of Alexei Tolstoy's dull, old-fashioned, 'Paul Delaroche-like' tragedy *Tsar Feodor Ioannovitch*. But once again he composed, no, he amassed, something completely unexpected, absolutely his own, absolutely enthralling, by supplanting the drama and putting himself in its place."[4]

Stelletsky also designed the costumes for Rimsky-Korsakov's *Ivan the Terrible* which Diaghilev presented as *La Pskovitaine (The Maid of Pskov)* in 1909, his only work for Diaghilev. It has been mistakenly thought that the designs in this collection are for that production and for a later production of the opera in St Petersburg: a confusion between "Ivan" and "Ioannovitch." He also designed the sets and costumes for Rimsky-Korsakov's *The Snow Maiden* for the Mariinsky Theater in 1910. In Paris, during the 1920s, Stelletsky worked occasionally for Nikita Balieff's cabaret *La Chauve-souris (The Bat)*, designing sets and costumes for sketches and burlesques with a particularly distinctive old Russian background. Stelletsky's most lasting memorial is in the decorations he made in antique style for the painted walls of the Russian Orthodox church in the rue de Crimée, Paris.

203 Set design for act 4 scene 3, the Tsaritsa's room, and false proscenium

Graphite, ink and tempera and/or watercolor on brown cardboard

Proscenium 17⅞ x 24½ in: 45.2 x 62.1 cm; set design 14⅞ x 23 in: 37.5 x 58.5 cm

Signed and dated in pencil in Russian on set design lower right: "22 Марта (March) / 1915 / Д. Стеллецкий (D. Stelletsky)"

Inscribed in pencil in Russian on set design across bottom: "Комната Царици Ирине жена Царя Федора [?] В Аргутинскому в денЬ взятия [illegible]" ("Room of Tsaritsa Irina, wife of Tsar Feodor, to V Argutinsky on the day of capture [illegible]")

Inscribed in pencil in Russian on proscenium: "3 порт" ("portals")

1933.540

Provenance: Prince Vladimir Argutinsky-Dolgorukov, given by the artist

Exhibitions: New York 1933, No 63 (described as "Ivan the Terrible (Marinsky Theater, St Petersburg) 1914"); Chicago 1933, No 152 (described as "'Ivan le Terrible' décor Théâtre Impérial St Petersburg"); Northampton 1934, No 152; Hartford 1934b; New Haven 1935; Williamsburg 1940; Storrs 1963; New York 1965–6, No 165 (illustrated p 79); New York 1966–7; Columbus 1989; Worcester 1989.

The date of the inscription is not the date of composition, but the date of dedication. This design, as noted above, is in two parts. One of the problems a theater designer has to resolve when tackling a production with a large number of different interior and exterior scenes, varying in scale, is to fit them all into the same stage space while maintaining the same illusion of reality or authenticity. In this scene, Stelletsky has deliberately introduced a false proscenium which, by enclosing and concentrating the space, gives a private room or boudoir the required intimate atmosphere. But not too intimate, because it is, after all, the tsaritsa's room: the touch of necessary grandeur is evoked by the symmetry of the design in the classical manner, modified by the bold folkloric decorative details.

Since, by the time the play came to be produced, this set design, the following two costume designs and other designs were no longer in the theater company's possession, they must have had copies from which to work.

*

The dedicatee was Prince Vladimir Argutinsky-Dolgorukov (1874–1941), whose name was often familiarly shortened to "Argutinsky" and sometimes abbreviated to "Arguton." He was a diplomat and an impassioned art collector on friendly terms with the *World of Art* group. In 1909 he was the first secretary at the Russian Embassy in Paris, and one of the members of the unofficial committee who, with Alexandre Benois, Léon Bakst, Nicholas Tcherepnine (the conductor and composer of *Le Pavillon d'Armide*; see pp 108–16), Valerian Svetlov the ballet critic, General Bezobrazov, and Serge Diaghilev himself, planned the inaugural season of what became the Ballets Russes. When Diaghilev lost his imperial subsidy, Prince Argutinsky-Dolgorukov agreed to be the guarantor for a large loan from a bank, to be repaid from box-office receipts, which made it possible for the season to take place. Prince Lieven records about the meetings that: "Prince Argoutinsky [sic], an old and true friend, who often acted a peacemaker among the friends, was always there. Although his praise or condemnation was never expressed in more than monosyllables, the friends relied upon his judgment."[5] In 1910 he guaranteed a further sum to Diaghilev against express instructions from the Tsar. He remained a faithful friend and supporter of the Ballets Russes. In 1920 he escaped from Russia. Arriving in Paris he found Bakst in a terrible state of depression; after comforting him, he tried unsuccessfully to act as peacemaker between Bakst and Diaghilev who had quarrelled irrevocably.

205 Costume design for a young man

Graphite, ink and tempera and/or watercolor on paper
13¹⁵/₁₆ x 6⅞ in: 35.4 x 17.6 cm
Signed in pencil in Russian with initials lower right: "Д. С." (D. S.)"
Inscribed (right side of paper has been cut) in pencil in Russian top right: "корж . . . (korzh . . .) / меш (mesh . . .)"
Reverse inscribed in pencil in Russian: "Для Царя Федора / костюм" ("for Tsar Feodor costume"), in ink: "N 27 / D. S. Stelletzky / £7.7.0"
1933.542

Exhibitions: Chicago 1933, No 154 (described as "'Ivan le Terrible' costumes"); Northampton 1934, No 154; Hartford 1934b; New Haven 1935; New York 19656, No 167 (illustrated p 79); New York 19667; Columbus 1989; Worcester 1989.

B oth these costume designs are for minor, unnamed characters. They are painted, as all the costume designs, in the style of primitive Russian art.

The inscriptions on the reverse show prices in English guineas (a guinea was equivalent to 1 pound and 1 shilling), which were often used for pricing works of art. The price indicates that these designs were exhibited for sale in England some time before 1933. Serge Lifar may well have bought them.

Seven costume designs, mistakenly attributed to *Boris Godunov*, and two set designs, mistakenly attributed to *Ivan the Terrible*, remained in Lifar's collection until they were included in the sale at the Hotel George V, Paris on 20 June 1974 as Lots 95–99. One design (Lot 95), unsold, was later sold at Sotheby's London on 9 May 1984 as Lot 6 (still attributed to *Boris Godunov*). A set design, again mistakenly attributed to *Boris Godunov* and also dedicated by the artist to Prince Argutinsky-Dolgorukov on the same day as No 203, 22 March 1915, was included in the same Sotheby's sale, but remained unsold.

204 Costume design for a nun

Graphite, ink and tempera and/or watercolor on paper
14 x 6³/₁₆ in: 35.4 x 15.8 cm
Signed in pencil in Russian with initials lower right: "Д. С. (D. S.)"
Inscribed (incomplete words as the paper has been cut) in pencil in Russian top right: "чер . . ." ("чер . . . black"), "Цар . . ." ("Tsar"), upper left: ". . . по 30 / . . . по 20 / . . . 10 арш (arshins)"[6]
Reverse inscribed in pencil in Russian: "Для Царя Федора / костюм монашки / Д. С." ("for Tsar Feodor costume of a nun D. S."), in pencil: "LLF 9466," in ink: "No 29 [crossed out] 30 / £7.7.0
1933.541

Exhibitions: Chicago 1933, No 153 (described as "'Ivan le Terrible' costumes"); Northampton 1934, No 153; Hartford 1934b; New Haven 1935; New York 1965–6, No 166 (illustrated p 79); New York 1966–7; Columbus 1989; Worcester 1989.

Notes

1 Constantin Stanislavsky, *My Life in Art*, p 335.
2 Sophia Tolstoy, *The Diaries of Sophia Tolstoy*, the entry for 10 November 1898, p 352.
3 Alexandre Benois, "Iskusstvo Stelletskago [Stelletsky's art]" in *Apollon* No 4, St Petersburg 1911, pp 5–21.
4 Alexandre Benois, *ibid*, p 7.
5 Prince Peter Lieven, *The Birth of Ballets-Russes*, p 79.
6 An "arshin" is an old Russian measurement equivalent to 28 in: 70 cm.

Léopold Survage
(pseudonym for Sturzwage)

Russian
born 1879 Moscow
died 1968 Paris

Mavra

Comic opera in 1 act by Boris Kochno, after
Alexander Pushkin's poem *The Little House in
Kolomna*
Composer: Igor Stravinsky
Conductor: Gregor Fitelberg
Choreographer/Director: Bronislava Nijinska
Designer (set and costumes): Léopold Survage
Principal Singers:
Parasha: Oda Slobodska
The Neighbour: Hélène Sadovène
The Mother: Zoïa Rosovska
Vassili, the Hussar: Stephan Belina
(Stepan Bélina-Skoupevski)
Company: Diaghilev's Ballets Russes
First Performance: 3 June 1922, Théâtre national de
l'Opéra, Paris

Synopsis

Parasha has not seen her love for a whole week.
Her love, Vassili, the Hussar, returns. They arrange
to meet again the following evening. The mother
comes in and laments the cook's death. Parasha
asks if she can help. The mother sends her out to
look for a new cook. The mother again sings the
praises of her dead cook, Thecla. A neighbor calls.
They sing about the weather, the cost of living, and
clothes. Parasha returns with a new cook whose
name is Mavra. Actually, it is Vassili in disguise. The
mother is delighted and asks Parasha to give
instructions to the new cook while she gets ready
to go out. Parasha and the cook, Vassili, rejoice
that they are together. Parasha and her mother go
out. The cook, left alone, feels it is time to shave.
He takes off his disguise. The mother returns,
thinks he is a burglar, and faints. Parasha revives
her mother. The neighbor comes in. The cook,
Mavra, escapes. Parasha calls after him.

While working on some orchestrations
for the production of *The Sleeping
Princess* in 1921 (see pp 87–101), Stravinsky
had the idea of composing a short comic
opera based on a poem by Pushkin which
he would dedicate to the memory of
Tchaikovsky, Glinka, and Pushkin. He chose
the poem, *The Little House in Kolomna,* and
asked Boris Kochno, Diaghilev's young
secretary who was also a poet, to write the
lyrics. They first changed the title to *La
Cuisinière* (*The Cook*) and then settled on
Mavra. Originally planned as a curtain-
raiser to *The Sleeping Princess*, Diaghilev
postponed the production when he realized
that the Tchaikovsky ballet was going to
take a whole evening. As Stravinsky later
said: "He [Kochno] had a gift for versifica-
tion, however, and his *Mavra* is at least, and
in the best sense, musical (in Russian, any-

way). The scheme of action with the
sequence of numbers was worked out by
the two of us together, in London, after
which I retired to Anglet [a district of Biar-
ritz] to await the libretto and compose the
music."[1]

As Diaghilev was still without a permanent choreographer, he asked Bronislava
Nijinska, who was arranging some of the
dances in the last act of *The Sleeping
Princess*, to direct the opera as well. The
appointment of the designer caused serious
problems. Diaghilev, having failed to entice
Alexandre Benois out of Russia to design
The Sleeping Princess, had turned instead to
Léon Bakst. Diaghilev made the right
choice: Bakst alone was capable of providing the blazingly colorful sumptuousness
required. Bakst, however, tried to be canny;
not wanting to be known only as a designer
of Louis XIV and Louis XV grandeur, he
agreed to work on *The Sleeping Princess* only
on condition that he would be given *Mavra*
as well. Diaghilev reluctantly had to acqui-
esce in order to be sure of getting the
designs for *The Sleeping Princess* in time.
They were both playing games with each
other—and, in a sense, they both lost.
Although Bakst designed a set for *Mavra*,[2]
Diaghilev broke his agreement; on Larionov's recommendation, he engaged
Léopold Survage instead. This action
caused the final rift between Diaghilev and
Bakst. They never spoke to each other
again.

Survage had become friends with Larionov and Gontcharova in 1902 at the School
of Fine Art in Moscow. Survage was so
enthused after visiting Shchukine's house—
where he saw his amazing collection of
Impressionists, and met Matisse—that he
decided to quit the school and go and paint
in Paris. Diaghilev became interested in his
work in 1916; he made vague suggestions
about designing ballets but, in that difficult
time during the First World War, they did
not lead then to any commission.

Survage has described how, six years
later, Larionov re-introduced him to
Diaghilev: "In 1922, one evening at eleven
o'clock he came into my room. 'Come
quickly,' he said, 'Diaghilev is waiting for
you. He wants to talk to you.' We went to

the Hotel Meurice. In an attic room, on the
sixth floor, we found Diaghilev between a
bed, a table and a chair. Diaghilev sat down
on the bed, I sat on the chair. Larionov
remained standing. Diaghilev explained
that it was a question of making some
sketches for the set of the opera *Mavra*
composed by Stravinsky. But he wanted to
see them the next morning. I thanked Larionov, made two drawings during the night.
Diaghilev chose one of them. For a long
time I never heard any more and didn't see
Larionov again. Suddenly he reappeared.
He came to fetch me to go to Belleville, to
an enormous scene-painting studio.
Diaghilev was there, furious, screaming that
the production of *Mavra* was going to take
place in three days' time at the Opéra and
that he had to have the set at any price.
Larionov had not kept me informed. I told
Diaghilev: 'You shall have it!' I left him to
start work at once. And Larionov, who was
working with an American I knew, Gerald
Murphy,[3] came to help me stretch the canvas which measured 27 by 16 meters, the
dimensions of the proscenium opening.
There were also the costumes. I went to
work, as did Larionov. We spent three days
and three nights on it. Larionov was there
all day and some of the night. On the third
night he had to give me sugar as I was
having cold sweats. But on the morning
after this third night everything was ready.
Larionov and I rolled up the canvas and put
it on a truck. I kissed my friend who had
helped me so much, and left. I remember I
had on a navy blue overall covered with
blobs of paint, and near 'Printemps' I met
Diaghilev . . . He was furious to see me
'dressed like that in the heart of Paris' and
ordered me 'to go at once and hide myself
at home.'"[4]

Before the first staged performance at
the Opéra, Diaghilev organized a special
preview performance for a few friends and
guests at the Hotel Continental on 29 May
1922, with Igor Stravinsky accompanying
the singers at the piano. Before the performance, Stravinsky confided in a telegram:
"We begin in fifteen minutes and we are all
terribly nervous."[5] On the one hand he was
right to be nervous, because after the performance he could see that his "deliberately

démodé music horrified Diaghilev,"[6] but on the other hand he was wrong because Kochno called the evening "a triumphant success."[7] Kochno was probably right, but evenings for sycophants are not notorious for providing an objective response.

Stravinsky, catching Diaghilev's look, foresaw the public reception of *Mavra* more accurately. When it was performed between *Le Sacre du Printemps* and *Petrushka* on the huge stage of the Opéra it failed, almost passing unnoticed. Stravinsky refused, however, to accept all the blame for the failure of his opera: "I was deeply disappointed by the disastrous surroundings in which my poor *Mavra* and little *Renard* found themselves. Being a part of a *Ballets Russes* programme, my two intimate acts were dwarfed when sandwiched between spectacular pieces which formed the repertory of Diaghileff's season and were the special attraction for the general public. This crushing environment, the enormous framework of the Opera House, and also the mentality of the audience, composed

mainly of the famous *abonnés*, all combined to make my two little pieces, especially *Mavra*, seem out of place."[8] Stravinsky also blamed Diaghilev for insisting on Nijinska as director: "From the staging point of view, the real trouble was that the singers were unable to execute Mlle Nijinska's choreographic ideas."[9] The real fault, however, was that *Mavra* was a quite unsuitable work to be presented in such a large theater. Kochno described the reaction of the audience: "At the premiere of *Mavra*, the first duet, which had been received with an ovation at the Continental, met with no response at all from the Opéra audience; one might have supposed that the theatre was empty. After a moment of attentive silence, people began to stir and speak to one another; if the house lights had not been turned up and the curtain lowered to signal the intermission, one would scarcely have noticed that the performance was over.'[10]

The opera was given seven performances during the season, but was never revived by Diaghilev.

206   Set design

Tempera on paper
18¾ x 27¾ in: 47.5 x 70.4 cm
Signed in red gouache lower right over earlier signature in pencil: "Survage"
Inscribed in pencil lower left: "Decor pour 'Mavra' / de Stravinski"
Reverse stamped: "Douane Centrale Exportation Paris"
Label on reverse: "Lucien Lefebvre-Foinet / 19 rue Vavin / 2 rue Bréa / Paris VI / couleurs et toiles fines," stamped "8451"
1933.543

Exhibitions: Paris 1930, No 96; Paris 1933; Chicago 1933, No 155; Northampton 1934, No 155; Hartford 1934b; New Haven 1935; San Francisco 1935-6; Paris 1939, No 341 (illustrated p 34); Williamsburg 1940; New York 1941–2; Edinburgh 1954, No 288; London 1954–5, No 330; Elmira 1958, No 17; Richmond 1959; Rowayton 1960; New York 1962; New York 1965–6, No 168 (illustrated p 80); Spoleto 1966; New York 1966–7; Princeton 1968; Strasbourg 1969, No 368; Frankfurt-am-Main 1969, No 103; Hartford 1974; Hartford 1978–9; Basel 1984; Hartford 1988; Worcester 1989.
Illustrations: Ballets Russes, Souvenir Program 1922 (color); Cogniat 1930, pl 42.

This is one of two very similar designs made by Survage overnight (see p 318), and is the one which Diaghilev kept and used for the set. The opera was meant to be intimate but it was being produced on a potentially overpowering stage. In theory, Survage's solution of creating small exterior and interior units within a single setting for what was essentially a chamber opera, and keeping them downstage, was ingenious. It was also a practical solution as *Mavra* was followed on 3 and 12 June 1922 by *Petrushka*, on 6 June by *Renard*, on 7 and 9 June by *Schéhérazade*, and on 13 June by *Le Mariage de la Belle au Bois Dormant,* which were all big productions with complicated sets.

Guillaume Apollinaire, in his preface to Survage's first exhibition in 1917, had written: "No one, before Survage, has known how to put a whole town with the interior of its houses on to a single canvas."[11] *Mavra* was Survage's first work for the theater,[12] and in this set he applied the principles of his two-dimensional painting in a three-dimensional way. The third dimension, however, was supplied by the performers, as the set was constructed in a series of flat folding screens with the furniture along the walls of the drawing room painted in *trompe l'oeil*. In the actual set, but not in the design, there was also a cat which, motionless from the first note of the opera to the last, the audience eventually realized was also in *trompe l'oeil*. Survage had taken to Cubism, and this was a Cubist solution, but in his own manner. The preferred subject matter of the Cubists was still life, but Survage found that expressing space solely on the basis of volume was too restricting, that "the basis of our vision is certainly not volume (the domain of still life), but space (landscape)."[13] However, this was not an entirely successful solution. The Paris Opéra became a devouring mammoth.

The other almost identical design made overnight originally belonged to Boris Kochno and is now in the collection of the Bibliothèque-Musée de l'Opéra.[14] The only real difference is in the furniture and the oval painting in the drawing room, and the view out of the window.

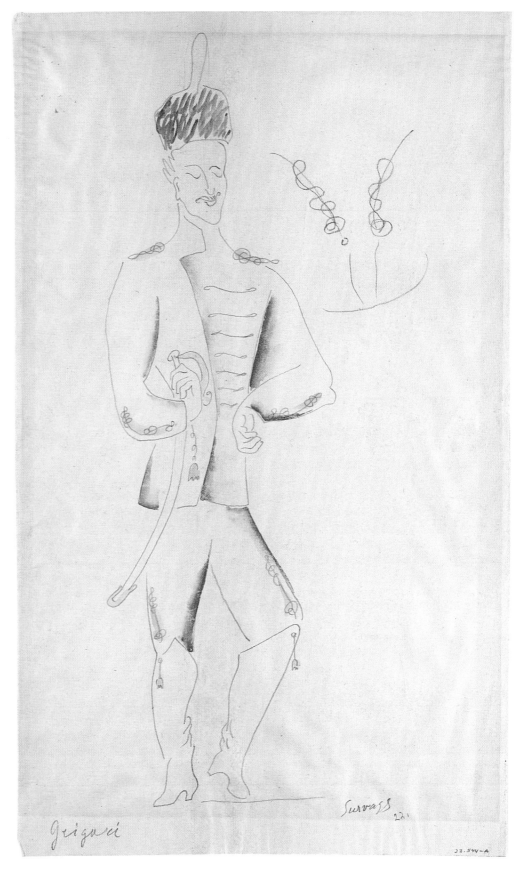

207 Costume design for Stephan Belina as Vassili the Hussar

Graphite and tempera and/or watercolor on paper
16⅝ x 10¹⁄₁₆ in: 42.2 x 25.2 cm
Signed and dated in pencil bottom right: "Survage / 22"
Inscribed in pencil bottom left: "Grigori"
1933.544a

Exhibitions: New York 1933, No 64;[15] Chicago 1933, No 156-8;[16] Northampton 1934, No 156-8;[16] Hartford 1934b; New Haven 1935; San Francisco 1935–6; Paris 1939, No 345; Williamsburg 1940; Washington D.C. 1950–1; Edinburgh 1954, No 293; London 1954–5, No 335; New York 1962; New York 1965–6, No 169 (illustrated p 80); Spoleto 1966; New York 1966–7; Hartford 1974; Hartford 1978–9; Columbus 1989; Worcester 1989.
Illustration: Ballets Russes, Souvenir Program 1922 (color).
The name of the character is not Grigori as on the inscription, but Vassili (see also the following design, No 208).

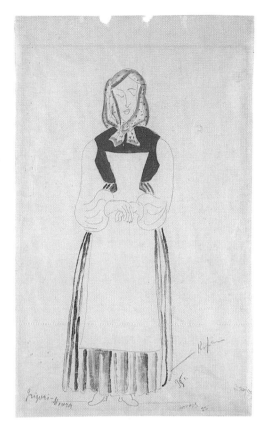

While other productions by the Ballets Russes, such as *Apollon Musagètes*, *Le Bal*, *Jack-in-the-Box*, *Les Matelots*, and *Le Fils Prodigue* are well represented by their designs, *Mavra* is the only production for which all the designs, both set and costumes, are in the Lifar Collection.[17]

In designing *Mavra*, Survage used two different styles. He turned to a classically traditional style for the costume designs. Although the drawing is boldly economical and the line sure, the character is clear and the instruction precise. (The figures in the set design, by comparison, are surprisingly weak.) In view of the confident manner in which these drawings have been made, it is curious that Survage did no more work for the theater. He preferred, like Matisse, to work in isolation. "The eye of the artist is an eye of man, that is to say it is not merely a registering organ but one of the instruments of the mind."[18]

208 Costume design for Stephan Belina disguised as Mavra

Graphite and tempera or watercolor on paper
16⁹⁄₁₆ x 10⅛ in: 42 x 25.5 cm
Signed and dated in pencil bottom right: "Survage / 22"
Inscribed in pencil lower left: "Grigori-Mavra," lower right: "Kopa . . ."
1933.545b

Exhibitions: Paris 1930; New York 1933, No 64;[15] Chicago 1933, No 156–8;[16] Northampton 1934, No 156–8;[16] Hartford 1934b; New Haven 1935; San Francisco 1935; Paris 1939, No 344; Williamsburg 1940; Washington D.C. 1950–1; Edinburgh 1954, No 290; London 1954–5, No 332; New York 1962; New York 1965–6, No 171 (illustrated p 80); Spoleto 1966; New York 1966–7; Hartford 1978–9; Columbus 1989; Worcester 1989.
Illustration: Cogniat 1930, pl 41.

209 Costume design for Oda Slobodska as Parasha

Graphite and tempera or watercolor on paper
16⁹⁄₁₆ x 10 in: 41.9 x 21 cm
Signed and dated in pencil lower right: "Survage / 22"
1933.544b

Exhibitions: New York 1933, No 64;[15] Chicago 1933, No 156–8;[16] Northampton 1934, No 156–8;[16] Hartford 1934b; New Haven 1935; San Francisco 1935–6; Paris 1939, No 344; Washington D.C. 1950–1; Edinburgh 1954, No 292; London 1954–5, No 334; Elmira 1958, No 17; New York 1962; New York 1965–6, No 170 (illustrated p 80); Spoleto 1966; New York 1966–7; Hartford 1978–9; Columbus 1989; Worcester 1989.
Illustrations: Ballets Russes, Souvenir Program 1922 (color); Oswald, No 2 p 26.

210 Costume design for Zoïa Rosovska as Parasha's mother

Graphite and tempera and/or watercolor on paper
16⁹⁄₁₆ x 10⅛ in: 42 x 25.3 cm
Signed and dated in pencil bottom right in pencil:
   "Survage / 22"
Inscribed in pencil bottom left: "La mere [sic]"
On reverse is a sketch in pencil of pattern of leaves
   and flowers
1933.545a

Exhibitions: Paris 1930; New York 1933, No 64;[15]
   Chicago 1933, No 156–8;[16] Northampton 1934,
   No 156–8;[16] Hartford 1934b; New Haven 1935;
   Paris 1939, No 343; Cambridge 1942; Washing-
   ton D.C. 1950–1; Edinburgh 1954, No 291;
   London 1954–5, No 333; Richmond 1959; New
   York 1962; New York 1965–6, No 172 (illus-
   trated p 80); Spoleto 1966; New York 1966–7;
   Princeton 1968; Amherst 1974; Hartford
   1978–9; Columbus 1989; Worcester 1989.
Illustration: Cogniat 1930, pl 40.

211 Costume design for Hélène Sadovène as the Neighbour

Graphite and tempera and/or watercolor on paper
16⁹⁄₁₆ x 10 in: 42.0 x 25.5 cm (pasted on larger
   sheet 17 1/4 x 10 3/8 in: 45.1 x 27.8 cm)
Signed and dated in pencil bottom right: "Survage
   / 22"
Inscribed in pencil lower left: "La Voisine" ("The
   Neighbor"), and clockwise from top right "9
   cms," "2.80," "3if," "3.50"
Reverse inscribed in pencil on larger sheet: "passe
   partout No 59 M / Survage / 'Mavra' / de
   Stravinski / pour les Ballets Russes de / Diagileff
   [sic]"
Stamped twice "Douane Centrale Exportation Paris"
Label on reverse: "Lucien Lefebvre-Foinet / 19 rue
   Vavin / 2 rue Bréa / Paris VI / couleurs et toiles
   fines," stamped "7897"
Part label on reverse with typed inscription: "Mavra
   / Costume / (La Voisine)" ("The neighbor")
1933.546

Exhibitions: New York 1933, No 64;[15] Chicago
   1933, No 156–8;[16] Northampton 1934, No
   156–8;[16] Hartford 1934b; New Haven 1935;
   San Francisco 1935–6; Paris 1939, No 342;
   Cambridge 1942; Washington D.C. 1950–1;
   Edinburgh 1954, No 289 (described as "La
   Voiture"); London 1954–5, No 331; New York
   1962; New York 1965–6, No 173 (illustrated
   p 80); Spoleto 1966; New York 1966–7; Princeton 1968; Amherst 1974; Hartford 1978–9;
   Columbus 1989; Worcester 1989.

Notes

1 Igor Stravinsky and Robert Craft, *Expositions and
   Developments*, p 82. Most of the opera was
   written in Biarritz while rehearsals for *The
   Sleeping Princess* were taking place in London.
   Boris Kochno had been introduced to Diaghilev
   by Serge Soudeikine, one of the main designers
   of Nikita Balieff's *Chauve-Souris (Bat)* cabaret
   theater from Moscow. Now Kochno, in London,
   acted as a secret go-between for Stravinsky who
   was sending love letters to Soudeikine's wife
   Vera. She became Stravinsky's second wife in
   1940. Richard Taruskin, in *Stravinsky and the
   Russian Traditions* (vol 2 pp 1538–49) suggests
   that *Mavra* could not have been intended as a
   curtain-raiser to *The Sleeping Princess*, but was
   perhaps inspired by the kind of nostalgic
   Russian act which Stravinsky saw at the *Chauve-
   Souris* when they were on tour in Paris in 1921.
2 In the collections of the Victoria and Albert
   Museum, London.
3 Gerald Murphy (1888–1964) wrote the libretto
   and designed the set and costumes for *Within
   the Quota*, music by Cole Porter, choreography
   by Jean Börlin, produced by Ballets Suédois on
   25 October 1923 at the Théâtre des Champs-
   Elysées, Paris (see Léger, p 248).
4 Léopold Survage, "Larionov, homme actif—
   Gontcharova, femme douce et discrète" in
   Tatiana Loguine, *Gontcharova et Larionov*, p 134.
5 In a private collection.
6 Igor Stravinsky, *op cit*, p 82.
7 Boris Kochno, *Diaghilev and the Ballets Russes*,
   p 184.
8 Igor Stravinsky, *Chronicle of my Life*, pp 169–70.
   Stravinsky implies that *Mavra* and *Renard* were
   first performed together on the same evening. In
   fact *Renard* was first performed on 18 May. The
   first performance of *Mavra* was preceded by *Le
   Sacre du Printemps* and followed by *Petrushka*.
   Mavra and *Renard* were only performed in the
   same program on 6 June, when they were
   preceded by *Contes Russes* and followed by the
   Dances from *Prince Igor*.
9 Igor Stravinsky, *op cit*, p 82.
10 Boris Kochno, *op cit*, p 185.
11 Guillaume Apollinaire, quoted in Maximilien
   Gauthier, *Survage*, p 37.
12 His only other work for the theater was designing sets and costumes for the opera *La Petite
   Marchande d'Allumettes* by Antonio Veretti
   (1900–78) in 1925 for the Théâtre de Cagliari,
   Paris.
13 Léopold Survage, quoted in Maximilien Gauthier, *op cit*, p 16.
14 This was exhibited in Edinburgh as No 287, in
   London as No 329, and is illustrated in color in
   his book *Diaghilev and the Ballets Russes*, p.184,
   and in Martine Kahane, *Les Ballets Russes à
   l'Opéra*, p 137.
15 This and the following note apply to all the
   costume designs. Described as "Costumes for
   Mavra 1922," but not identified.
16 Described as "'Mavra' costumes," but not
   identified.
17 Excluding the variations which were in Boris
   Kochno's collection, now in the Musée de
   l'Opéra, Paris; and two costume design variations which are in Nikita and Nina Lobanov-
   Rostovsky's collection.
18 Léopold Survage, quoted in Maximilien
   Gauthier, *op cit*, p 9.

Pavel Tchelitchew

Russian
born 1898 Moscow
died 1957 Rome

Ode

An evening meditation on the Majesty of God on the occurrence of the great northern lights[1]
Spectacle in 3 scenes by Boris Kochno, words by Mikhail Lomonosov[2]
Composer: Nicolas Nabokov
Conductor: Roger Desormière
Choreographer: Leonide Massine
Choirmaster: Dimitri Aristov
Designer (set and costumes): Pavel Tchelitchew
Lighting (projections): Pierre Charbonnier
Principal Dancers:
    Nature: Ira Belianina[3]
    The Pupil: Serge Lifar
    Felia Dubrovska, Alice Nikitina,
       Leonide Massine, Nicholas Efimov,
       Constantin Tcherkas
Solo singers:
    Sandra Yakovleva, Georges Lanskoi
Company: Diaghilev's Ballets Russes
First Performance: 6 June 1928, Théâtre Sarah-Bernhardt, Paris

Synopsis
From the program:
    "Scene 1. Nature descends from her pedestal, answers her pupil's questions and shows him the Constellations (nine male dancers), the River (eight female and six male dancers), Flowers and Mankind (projections).
    Scene 2. Not satisfied with what he has seen, the pupil begs Nature to show him her Festival.
    Scene 3. Captivated by the beauty of the Festival, the pupil darts forward, enters it and destroys by his presence the vision of the Aurora Borealis. Nature becomes again a Statue."

The young Nicolas Nabokov, aged twenty-three, first played some excerpts of his cantata to Diaghilev during the winter of 1926–7, and, encouraged, finished the piano score by the midsummer of 1927. The subject was taken from an ode by the eighteenth-century court poet Mikhail Lomonosov. According to Nabokov the ode "represents a thinly veiled allegory on the enthronement of Empress Elizabeth,"[4] but this is not quite so. Lomonosov, a physicist as well as a poet who had been born in Archangel within the latitude of the northern lights, was quite simply deeply affected by this strange natural phenomenon, and the allegory is more to do with Nature showing the Student its miracles of the Universe: water, the planets, and the reflection of light. The final miracle is the northern lights, which do indeed symbolize the Empress. This allegorical interpretation suited the composer very well: Diaghilev

was rumored to be a great-great-grandson of one of the Empress's natural children, and so was very taken with Nabokov's idea. Besides, Diaghilev became enthusiastic about producing a Russian period piece and asked Boris Kochno to devise a suitable libretto for the ballet. Nabokov describes how Diaghilev later intelligently criticized some of the score: "I had written a short introduction to the second act; Diaghilev wanted a longer and more 'ample' one. He objected to my introduction and called it a 'meagre pot of Conservatory porridge.' I felt hurt, and defended myself by saying that the way I had written it was right, that it was good fugato in the style of the eighteenth-century French overtures. Diaghilev smiled mockingly and replied, 'Maybe, *mon cher*, it *is* a fugato, maybe even a fugue, but it certainly isn't any good. You know I don't really care whether you write a fugue or a fugato, a French or a Brazilian overture; what matters is that you write good music.'" He concluded, "This goes equally for Richard Strauss and the waltz-Strauss, for Bach and Offenbach. It is a simple but a very golden rule."[5] Nabokov made all the changes Diaghilev required by October 1927, but it was only Stravinsky who, liking the music when it was played to him, persuaded Diaghilev to commit himself to producing *Ode*. Nabokov thought that his meeting Stravinsky was arranged by Diaghilev and "was part of a carefully planned and slightly feudal ritual."[6]

By the late 1920s Diaghilev did not interfere in the productions of his ballets unless he felt the need to do so, but he felt the need rather more frequently than Kochno and others have cared to admit. He was a persistent stickler for detail which his colleagues often found irritating and exhausting, but which ultimately won their respect. Diaghilev had to interfere a lot on *Ode*.

Kochno wanted Balanchine as choreographer, a desire seconded by Nabokov, but as Balanchine had been engaged for Stravinsky's *Apollon Musagète* (see pp 103–7), Diaghilev engaged Massine for *Ode* against Kochno's wishes. Diaghilev also wanted the ballet to be set in the eighteenth century, with the sets and costumes based "on engravings of Court balls and the corona-

tion festivities of the Empress Elizabeth."[7] Kochno persuaded Diaghilev to commission the set and costumes from Pavel Tchelitchew whom they had first met in Berlin in 1923.

Tchelitchew took hold of the production and made it completely his own. Like a great whale, he swallowed everyone else's contribution and spewed up something entirely different and new. He ignored Diaghilev's request for a realistic set as being too obvious. Realism, he thought, only constrained the imagination, whereas the theater was the realm of fantasy. He saw *Ode* as his opportunity for expressing his individual ideas of theater by evolving a revolutionary stage technique using all manner of light and lighting equipment, cinematic projections, and a variety of new materials never before used on stage. He knew that to impose his own ideas was risky, particularly as Diaghilev had the reputation for being a tyrant, but it was a risk he was prepared to take even though it meant that he did not see eye to eye with his collaborators. The fact that his ideas all worked in the end and that the production was a success was justification enough. But it was touch and go most of the time; and, reading between the lines of the various recollections, one can see how fraught with danger the whole project was until Diaghilev rescued it.

Kochno comes nearest to being direct, while not being dispassionate. He wrote: "Tchelitchew was extremely high-strung and quite incompetent in the matter of film techniques, so that the atmosphere of our collaboration was dramatic."[8] "High-strung" and "dramatic" are obvious euphemisms for "extremely bad-tempered and impossible, with endless shouting matches." Kochno was right about Tchelitchew's ignorance about film techniques—which is why Pierre Charbonnier, who had worked in films, was engaged to assist him. But Kochno also had some reason to complain about their collaboration. Although he is credited with the libretto of the ballet, there is a complete script dictated by Tchelitchew to Charbonnier which describes every moment of the action.[9] Without having Kochno's scenario, it is impossible to say how closely Tchelitchew followed it, if at all. His script divides the action into eight scenes instead of Kochno's three and, because it is meant primarily for Charbonnier, concentrates on the required lighting effects. In fact, as A. V. Coton wrote: "The story ceased to matter—in so far as any relevant story could be presented through this complication of beautiful mechanisms and dancing—about ten seconds after the first gigantic light-bursts clearly indicated that attention could be completely occupied in grasping and assimilating the visual images created, without reference to any other factor in the startling picture."[10]

Massine also suffered from Tchelitchew's temperament, describing him as "a nervous, highly-strung and compulsive talker, so carried away by his own ideas that one could almost see his imagination creating new shapes and patterns as he talked." But in the next sentence he also makes it clear that Tchelitchew's ideas dictated the choreography: "He decided that as a background for the ballet we should have a row of puppets in period costume hung on a string. He also created an irregular framework of white cords which we used to enclose the action, and in visual contrast to the puppets I dressed the dancers in tight-fitting costumes and created a succession of shifting geometrical patterns to express the theme of Lomonosov's poem."[11] While giving Tchelitchew the credit for the striking image of the puppets, Massine redresses the balance in ideas by claiming the design of the other costumes.

Nabokov, in hindsight, was the most objective in his assessment of the situation: "But all these pictorial experiments of Tchelitchev [sic] and all his new ideas about stage design had little in common with the whole project of the ballet *Ode*, with my music, and with the didactic-allegorical ballet story cooked up by Boris Kochno. Tchelitchev seemed to like my music, but not the story . . . He thought the story had nothing to do with what my music was 'really' expressing and that the whole piece should be treated as a surrealist vision of a mysterious phenomenon of nature, the Aurora Borealis. Thus from the outset there were three different and in a way irreconcilable points of view involved in the *Ode* project. First there was Diaghilev's notion about a great Elizabethan period piece, a tribute to the epoch of the great Russian court-poet Lomonosov; second there was Tchelitchev's view of *Ode* as a modern surrealist experiment; and third there was

my music, which did not fit into either of the first two categories. The music of *Ode* was essentially tender, gentle, and lyrical . . ."[12]

Diaghilev realized that the ballet was in trouble because when Nabokov arrived in Monte Carlo to work on the production with Massine he told him: "If all of you finally decide to start working, don't pull the cart in three different directions. It will get stuck and *I'm* not going to help you pull it out of *your* mud!"[13] The production did get stuck in the mud: everyone's highly strung nervousness was only producing inertia. Diaghilev was forced to act.

Nabokov, in a marvelously evocative and almost unique description of Diaghilev at work, wrote how, four days before the first night, on 2 June 1928, he was suddenly woken up by him shouting down the telephone: "'Get up and get dressed right away and come to the theatre. This mess can't go on any longer. I have ordered a full stage rehearsal at ten, a full orchestra rehearsal at two, a full chorus rehearsal at five, and all evening we will rehearse the lights.' . . . From that moment on and for the next three days, until the last curtain had fallen on a highly successful performance of *Ode*, I lived in a state of frenzy. Like everyone else connected with the production, I worked day and night, in an agony of sleeplessness and exhilaration the like of which I never experienced before or since. Diaghilev had taken over in the fullest sense. From then on *he* gave the orders, *he* made the decisions and assumed the responsibilities. He was everywhere, his energy was limitless. He ran to the prefect of police to have him overrule the fire department's decision forbidding the use of neon lights on stage [they were thought to be unsafe] . . . He supervised the dyeing, cutting, and sewing of the costumes. He was present at every orchestra and choral rehearsal and made the conductor, Desormière, the soloists, and the chorus repeat sections of the music over and over again until they blended well with the choreographic motions and the light-play of Tchelitchev's scenery. He encouraged the leisurely and sluggish stagehands of the Théâtre Sarah-Bernhardt by bribes and flattery. He helped all of us paint the props and the scenery. But above all else he spent two whole nights directing the complicated lighting rehearsals, shouting at Tchelitchew and at his technical aids when the delicate lighting machinery went wrong, at me when my piano playing slackened and became uneven, and at Lifar when his steps

ceased following the rhythm of the music and change of lighting. On June 6th, the day of the opening, I was exhausted, stunned and shaking with the kind of precarious excitement which comes after long exertion and sleepless travel. But when, fifteen minutes before the curtain went up, I saw Diaghilev come in through the backstage door, in full dress, bemonocled, his famous rose pearl shining on a snow-white shirt front, I knew that it had been only thanks to this man's incredible drive and energy that *Ode* had been pieced together and the curtain would be able to rise at all."[14]

Serge Lifar put a different complexion on the production, claiming for himself, as was often the case, more credit for it than was truly his due: "The *Ode* frankly bewildered Diaghilev, both in its music and choreography, and he could hardly decide to allow us to put it on. Nevertheless, later in Paris, I was able to persuade him to allow us to include it, which he did for my sake, though it did not interest him at all. He spent the night before the première at the theatre, and helped to get the production into shape, but he never, in fact, got to the ballet himself."[15] *Ode* may indeed not have turned out as Diaghilev had originally intended, but Nabokov's account is more believable. It gives the lie to the view so often expressed that Diaghilev took little or no interest in his later productions. Of course Diaghilev saw the ballet: it was simply not in his character not to see anything staged by his company.[16] He took his responsibilities seriously. It is therefore strange that Lifar wrote what he did, especially as Diaghilev was always generous toward his artists and collaborators, and never claimed credit for himself. His enthusiasm for his own productions was not entirely in pursuit of favorable publicity, but always genuinely felt. *Ode* may not even have been to Diaghilev's taste, but he respected it. In an interview for a Russian newspaper in Paris, he enthused: "This production takes me back to my first seasons abroad. As then, young artists are appearing for the first time, full of creative fire. It reminds me of the time when Fokine, Nijinsky, Bakst and the beginner Stravinsky were working with me."[17] Nostalgic, perhaps, but still attracted by the young and the new.

The critic of *The Times*, reporting on the first performance in Paris, appreciated the revolutionary quality of the production: "*Ode* is a definite break with the past. An effort is made here to increase the scope and significance of the ballet by the introduction

of new elements and the use of mechanical devices. Thus we see M. Lifar—described upon the programme as the Pupil of Nature—struggling with a rope which attaches him to the earth, and making with it, as he struggles, vast geometrical figures, like the 'cat's cradle' made by a giant. Abstract designs are thrown upon the back cloth by means of a cinema projector, and these are alternated with nebulous human figures slowly girating and changing in size. A man and a woman in flesh-coloured tights execute a slow dance behind blue fish-netting, and other strange and sometimes beautiful things happen with disconcerting inconsequence . . . The choreography by M. Massine contains some fine invention, particularly in M. Lifar's dances, and the whole production is undeniably interesting even if it is not very successful."[18]

The sting in the tail of this critic's comments was endorsed by others, except that everyone seems to have thought that the ballet was "beautiful" without necessarily understanding any of it. For A. V. Coton, the "strongest remaining impression is of the unearthly beauty created in most of the scenes by a revolutionary use of light never before seen in any form of Theatre—floods, spots, panoramic effects, projections against a screen and great bursts of light suggesting the sudden animation of pyrotechnical set-pieces, as the groups of dancers and static figures were bathed in pools of glowing illumination, swiftly dimmed and flooded again, almost imperceptibly changing colours . . . never before were the senses so delightfully assaulted with unrelated and unrelatable forms of movement, music, lighting, and colour."[19] Florence Grenfell has

the last word. After seeing the first performance in London she wrote in her diary: "Monday 9th July. I dined with Puffin Asquith & went to the Ballet. 'Ode' was interesting & exceedingly beautiful in parts, especially the music & stage effects."

212 Set design with figures for scene 3

Graphite and ink or tempera on blue paper, now faded
7⁷/₁₆ x 9⁹/₁₆ in: 19 x 24.2 cm (on 19.8 x 24.8 cm)
Signed in gouache bottom right: "P. Tchelitchew"
1933.549

Exhibitions: New York 1933, No 66; Chicago 1933, No 161; Northampton 1934, No 161; Hartford 1934b; New Haven 1935; Paris 1939, No 349 (illustrated p 38); Poughkeepsie 1940; Williamsburg 1940; Minneapolis 1953; Edinburgh 1954,

Above: scene 3.

Diaghilev explained Tchelitchew's method of working to a Russian journalist during an interview before the first night of *Ode*: "Tchelitchew created the sets which are neither painted nor constructed, consisting entirely of light, cinematographic film, and of course completely unrealistic. Every possible kind of lighting effect: electric light, phosphorescent light, transparent surfaces, gauzes . . . During the coronation everyone is dressed in an identical costume, or rather, not even a costume but a sort of 'container', mid-eighteenth century, but again of course un-naturalistic, only evoking a period. All the decorative part is by Tchelitchew, and the purely technical, mechanical part is by the French artist Charbonnier. It is worth remarking that Tchelitchew did not draw any designs beforehand. He created the costumes directly on the 'performers.' A French journalist asked him for a design to reproduce in his newspaper and Tchelitchew had to draw one after the costume had already been made."[20] If Diaghilev is to be believed, and there is no reason to doubt his word, then this design was made after the event, as were the following drawings; except that it is also more than likely that Tchelitchew, being a visual artist, made some preliminary sketches to illustrate and explain his scenic intentions.

This design illustrates the third scene according to Kochno, or the sixth scene of Tchelitchew's scenario: "Lifar asks Nature who these dancers are. Nature binds his hands and draws the curtain open. We see the round podium. In front, steps go up into the wings on both sides. A large triangle creates a luminous perspective on the backcloth. In the foreground there are female dancers in dresses with crinoline skirts of bluish satin and pearl grey and male dancers in costumes of the same color. The group of dancers is continued against the backcloth by a line of marionettes which get smaller and smaller to create a perspective. Projected above are bright dots which get smaller and smaller and closer together delineating heavenly vaults. The dancers on the steps sit down and we see the dancers on the podium. There are 4 or 5 of them in white leotards. Each dancer is followed in his dance by a light which he uses as a (projected) costume. Simultaneously with this dance the lights of the vaults above the triangle go out and we see projected a scene of pagan festivity, naked men and women in the middle of flames. The dance on the podium combines with that of the projection. The dance and the projections disappear. The vaults light up, then go out, form cascades, then the light jumps from one vault to another etc. The overall light trembles. Fixed signs begin to appear on the (transparent) backcloth. Everyone looks at them. The fixed signs come to life, multiply, and increase in intensity. These are the stars, flashes of lightning, balls of fire, turning rods, and spirals. The general light becomes blue, greenish, yellow, orange, red. Abruptly flickering white, then steady red, flickering white, steady red, two or 3 times. Finally a prolonged very violent red like fire coming from everywhere. At this moment all the lights in the background are dimmed and become only glittering (silvery) reflections which move in different directions (on a roller system)."[21]

The drawing does not begin to illustrate the complexity of the technical effects or the magic of the scene on stage. Donald Windham was obviously deeply affected by seeing the ballet, because he gives a graphic evocation of what this drawing is meant to show: "Mannequins, indistinguishable from the dancers and hung in space to create a false perspective, aided the light in creating an illusion of endless space in which the action was seen ideally from all sides at once as the acrobats in the ring are seen by the circle of spectators. Film projected chalk drawings swirled like lightning in the firmament, and on the pale mirror of the sky stars and planets grew from pinpoints of light like the handwriting on the wall at Belshazzar's feast but made of life rather than fire and death. The acrobats, building in space and supported only by light, begin to phosphorescently create the earth. The stage caught the light as the fog over a bright metropolis catches the city's illumination at dusk and perspective gave emphasis to all the details. The acrobats had created the world, and the apotheosis was the sunburst of the Aurora Borealis, a pyrotechnical explosion created behind the screens with neon and a blinding klieg light turned on into the faces of the audience."[22]

The blue paper on which the drawing was originally made has faded completely to green.

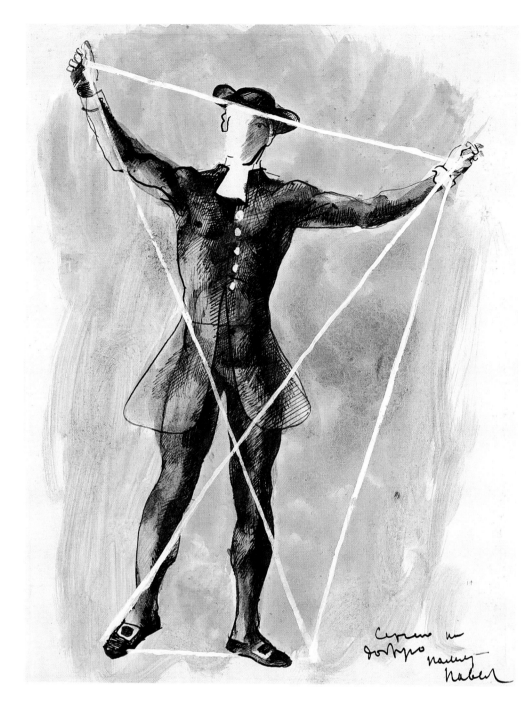

emphasising his limbs."[23] Parker Tyler places the action of this drawing, which was made after the production of the ballet, in scene seven of Tchelitchew's scenario: "The Student unbinds his hands somehow for he performs a solo, in which he stands with one foot on the rope while making various geometric designs with it; that is, he is demonstrating the wonders of nature's hidden geometry, prophesying the Celestial Physiognomies and echoing the net which is already a fulcrum of the artist's plastique."[24]

214 Costume design for a female dancer in a crinoline skirt

Ink and tempera on card stock
12⅝ x 9⅝ in: 32 x 24.5 cm
Signed and inscribed in ink lower left: "'Ode' / à Serge [Lifar] / P. Tchelitchew"
1933.550

Exhibitions: Paris 1929, No 69 (described as "2 dessins pour costumes"); Paris 1930, No 98 (described as "costumes"); New York 1933 (unidentified, described as "costume for *Ode*"); Chicago 1933, No 162–4 (not identified); Northampton 1934, No 162–4 (not identified); Hartford 1934b; New Haven 1935; Paris 1939, No 350; Williamsburg 1940; New York MoMA 1942, No 195; Edinburgh 1954, No 357; London 1954–5, No 391; Ottawa 1956, No 11; Michigan 1957; Elmira 1958, No 33; Indianapolis 1959, No 473; New York 1965–6, No 180 (illustrated p 83) ; New York 1966–7; Strasbourg 1969, No 440; Frankfurt-am-Main 1969, No 143; Hartford 1974; Hempstead 1974, No 131; Hartford 1978–9; Boston 1982–3; Columbus 1989; Worcester 1989.

213 Costume design for Serge Lifar as the Pupil

Ink and tempera on card stock
12⅝ x 9⅝ in: 32 x 24.4 cm
Inscribed in ink in Russian lower right: "Сергею на добрую память Павел" ("To Sergei in fond memory Pavel")
1933.551

Exhibitions: London 1930, No 76; New York 1933, No 67 (described as "Costumes"); Chicago 1933, No 162–4 (not identified); Northampton 1934, Nos 162–4 (not identified); Hartford 1934b; New Haven 1935; Paris 1939, No 351; Poughkeepsie 1940; New York MoMA 1942, No 196–7; Edinburgh 1954, No 356; London 1954–5, No 390; Ottawa 1956, No 12; Michigan 1957; Indianapolis 1959, No 474 (described as "Costume, Priest"); New York

1964, No 42 (described as "Priest's Costume"); Hartford 1965, No 35; New York 1965–6, No 181 (illustrated p 83); New York 1966–7; Princeton 1968; Strasbourg 1969, No 439; Frankfurt-am-Main 1969, 142; Hartford 1973; Hartford 1974; Hartford 1978–9; London 1981; Boston 1982–3; Columbus 1989; Worcester 1989.
Illustrations: Amberg, pl 107; Buckle, No 150 p 117; Komisarjevsky, p 51; Propert 1931, pl IV right facing p 73; Windham, p 11.

Tchelitchew, ignoring Diaghilev's intention to set the ballet in eighteenth-century Russia, dressed the Student or Pupil in a "costume imitating that of a French cleric of the time of Louis XV [eighteenth-century France], tight and semi-transparent,

Illustrations: Buckle 1955, No 151 p 117; Propert
    1931, pl IV left facing p 73; Windham, p 11.
Note: Nos 98 and 99 in the catalogue of Billiet-
    Pierre Vorms, Paris 1930, Nos 68 and 69 in
    Arthur Tooth, London 1930, and No 67 in
    Julien Levy, New York, are described as
    "Costumes for *Ode*" but none is identified.

215 Costume design for the men with phosphorescent markings

Ink on two sheets of paper
13¼ x 8¼ in: 35.7 x 20.9 cm
Unsigned and undated
1933.552

Exhibitions: Chicago 1933, No 162–4 (not identi-
    fied); Northampton 1934, No 162–4 (not
    identified); Hartford 1934b; New Haven 1935;
    San Francisco 1936; Paris 1939, No 352;
    Edinburgh 1954, No 359; London 1954–5, No
    393; New York 1964, No 33; Hartford 1965, No
    36 (described as "Black silhouette of man's
    figure"); New York 1965–6, No 182 (illustrated
    p 83); Strasbourg 1969, No 441; Frankfurt-am-
    Main 1969, No 144; Hempstead 1974, No 129
    (illustrated); Hartford 1974; London 1981;
    Columbus 1989; Worcester 1989.
Illustrations: Amberg, pl 106; Buckle, No 154
    p 117; Windham, p 11.
Of all the drawings for this ballet, this one looks as
    if it has been made before the production.

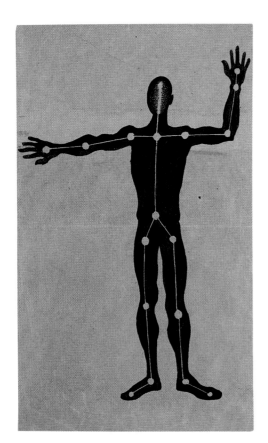

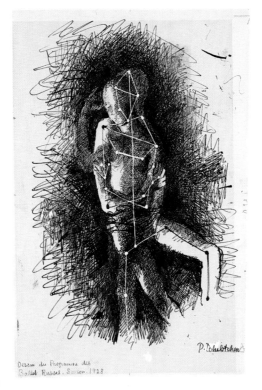

216 Project design for the cover of the Souvenir Program for Diaghilev's Ballets Russes 1928 Season

Ink and graphite notations on paper mounted to
    blue paper
14⁹⁄₁₆ x 9⅝ in: 36.9 x 24.1 cm
Signed in ink lower right: "P. Tchelitchew"
Inscribed in charcoal lower left: "Dessin du Pro-
    gramme des / Ballets Russes. Saison. 1928"
Label on reverse: "Lucien Lefebvre-Foinet / 19 rue
    Vavin / 2 rue Bréa / Paris VI / couleurs et toiles
    fines," stamped "9422"
1933.547

Exhibitions: New York 1933, No 65; Chicago 1933,
    No 159; Northampton 1934, No 159; Hartford
    1934b; New Haven 1935; Paris 1939, No 347;
    New York MoMA 1942, No 194; Edinburgh
    1954, No 353; London 1954–5, No 388;
    Ottawa 1956, No 8; Michigan 1957; Indiana-
    polis 1959, No 470; New York 1964, No 27;
    Hartford 1965, No 33; New York 1965–6, No
    177 (illustrated p 81); New York 1966–7;
    Princeton 1968; Strasbourg 1969, No 437;
    Frankfurt-am-Main 1969, No 140; Hartford
    1973; Amherst 1974; Hartford 1974; Coral
    Gables 1982; Columbus 1989; Worcester 1989.
Illustration: Buckle 1955, No 152 p 117.

In 1926 Tchelitchew began to experiment
with a theory of simultaneity by drawing
the human figure in several positions at
once. His technique consisted of drawing
interconnected torsos, with limbs and heads
not necessarily attached to the same torso,
nor being of the right number, and a lighter
figure often emerging from a darker one, or

merging with it, in order to give a three-
dimensional effect to a two-dimensional
object. He called this system "laconic"
composition. Tchelitchew's preliminary idea
for the program was to use such a "laconic"
composition. The two figures are merged by
being connected through the dots and lines
copied from the idea of the phosphorescent
markings in the previous design. This
design was not used for the program.

217 Preliminary design for the cover of the Souvenir Program for Diaghilev's Ballets Russes 1928 Season

Ink on paper
18¹⁵⁄₁₆ x 12½ in: 47.7 x 31.3 cm
Signed and inscribed in ink lower left: "à mon [sic]
    mouche (to my fly) / de Pavlik"
1933.548

Exhibitions: London Tooth 1930, No 67; Paris 1930,
    No 97; Chicago 1933, No 160; Northampton
    1934, No 160; Hartford 1934b; New Haven
    1935; Paris 1939, No 348; Poughkeepsie 1940;
    New York MoMA 1942, No 195; Edinburgh
    1954, No 358; London 1954–5, No 392;
    Ottawa 1956, No 9; Elmira 1958, No 2; Indi-
    anapolis 1959; New York 1964, No 28; Hartford
    1965, No 35; New York 1965–6, No 178 (illus-
    trated p 82); New York 1966–7; Princeton
    1968; Strasbourg 1969, No 438; Frankfurt-am-
    Main 1969, No 141; Hartford 1974; Storrs
    1975, No G5; Hartford 1978–9; Toledo 1983;
    Allentown 1986; Hartford 1988; Worcester
    1989.
Illustrations: Bremser, vol II p 1397; Windham, p 11.

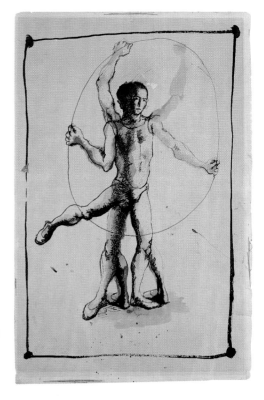

Tchelitchew has developed his "laconic" composition further by drawing a single torso for two figures facing each other and adding an extra leg. Moreover, the figures are obviously dancers. He was clearly also inspired by Leonardo da Vinci's drawing, *The Proportions of the human body according to Vetruvius*, an appropriate image to be influenced by for the theme of *Ode*.

There are several versions of this drawing. This is very similar to the one used for the program. In the final design, the features are less defined and the rectangle round the figures is smaller and is drawn through the legs and arms. Devoted followers of the Ballets Russes were not daunted by the task of piercing the cover of the printed program by hand with many pinpricks through the figures.

218   Serge Lifar, 1928

Tempera and/or watercolor on paper
22⅜ x 17⅜ in: 56.7 x 44.4 cm
Signed in ink lower right: "P. Tchelitchew"
1933.554

Exhibitions: ? New York 1933, No 68 (described as "Portrait of Serge Lifar," but see also entry for Pl 219); Chicago 1933, No 166; Northampton 1934, No 166; Hartford 1934b; New Haven 1935; New York MoMA 1942, No 85; Edinburgh 1954, No 471 (illustrated); London 1954–5, No 480; Sarasota 1958, No 81; New York 1964, No 38; New York 1965–6, No 175 (illustrated facing title page; not shown in New York) ; New York 1966–7; Princeton 1968; Strasbourg 1969, No 514a (addenda to catalogue); Frankfurt-am-Main 1969, No 179; Hartford 1974; Worcester 1989.
Illustration: Ballets Russes, Souvenir Program 1928.

In this portrait, Tchelitchew has discovered the character of his subject and so is able to stylize, as well as romanticize, his painting. Diaghilev obviously liked it because he chose it to be reproduced in the season's program.

219   Serge Lifar, 1929

Ink, tempera and/or watercolor and sand on
  cardboard
21¼ x 17¼ in: 55 x 46.3 cm
Signed in watercolor lower right: "P. Tchelitchew"
Reverse inscribed in pencil: "Portrait Serge Lifar,"
  and stamped: "Douane Centrale Exportation
  Paris" (twice), and "Douanes Exportation Paris"
1933.553

Exhibitions: London 1930, No 75; ? New York 1933,
  No 68 (described as "Portrait of Serge Lifar,"
  but see also entry for No 218); Chicago 1933,
  No 165; Northampton 1934, No 165; Hartford
  1934b; New Haven 1935; Paris 1939, No 354;
  Washington D.C. 1950–1; Michigan 1957; New
  York 1964, No 39; New York 1965–6, No 174
  (illustrated p 6; not shown in New York); New
  York 1966–7; Hartford 1974; Columbus 1989;
  Worcester 1989.

This is a confident portrait, but in the
manner of an exercise. Tchelitchew was
still experimenting with his new-found
medium and color range. He used his
gouache–sand–coffee technique for many of
his paintings of 1927–29, in "laconic" compositions, nudes, and portraits. He often
piled up the texture so that "the surface of
my painting looked like maps of earth in
low relief."[25] He also painted a portrait of
Boris Kochno at about the same time.

220   Serge Lifar as Albrecht in *Giselle*, 1932

Graphite and ink on paper
17⅝ x 14¼ in: 44.7 x 36.6 cm
Signed in watercolor lower right: "P. Tchelitchew"
1933.555

Exhibitions: Chicago 1933, No 167; Northampton
  1934, No 167; Hartford 1934b; New Haven
  1935; Paris 1939, No 356; New York MoMA
  1942, No 84; Edinburgh 1954, No 472; London
  1954–5, No 481; New York 1965–6, No 176
  (illustrated p 4); New York 1966–7; Princeton
  1968; Strasbourg 1969, No 79 (illustrated No
  123); Frankfurt-am-Main 1969, No 22; Hartford
  1974; Columbus 1989; Worcester 1989.
Illustrations: Clarke and Crisp, No 156 p 125;
  Buckle, p 121 No 168.

Serge Lifar first performed Albrecht on
20 January 1932 at the Opéra, Paris. As
ever, there is no false modesty (and even
inaccuracy) in Lifar's account of his production: "Owing to an accident I had during
rehearsal, the first performance of *Giselle*
had to be put off and the ballet was not
given until February [sic] 1932. That
evening all the choreographic notabilities of
Paris turned up—I might say on a war
footing. This was to be the most searching
test of any I had undergone and one that
would determine, maybe decisively, all my
career. I must say that I had taken the greatest possible care in the preparation of that
ballet. I changed the color of the costume—
violet instead of white—and I added a
romantic cape. With his complete agreement, I also modified entirely Benois' stage-
setting. So as to lend more dramatic relief to
Albert–Hamlet, in the second act I put a
great bunch of flowers in his arms so that he
might, with melancholy, pose them on the
tomb of his beloved. I insisted that these
flowers, arums and lilies, must be real,
because as living things they seemed to me
to add, as it were, a human presence to this
romantic drama which, for my part, I
wanted to see transformed into a Shakespearean tragedy. This success of *Giselle*
made ballet history. Spessivtseva's interpretation of the part of Giselle was, in my
opinion, the absolute perfection of a choreographic art. In this role she was the greatest,
the most sublime, dancer of the 20th century. I myself endeavoured in this ballet,
which I danced over a period of twenty-five
years all over the world, to ennoble the role
of Prince Albrecht by enhancing it with an
ideal of which death through love is the
symbol."[26]

Tchelitchew's interpretation lives up to
Lifar's account. It is the essence of romanti-

cism, as is the ballet; but the artist has also
been careful to get the balletic details right.

Lifar was not alone in thinking himself
to be the greatest living dancer. André
Levinson, in his review, wrote: "I would go
so far as to say that the 1932 version is equal
to, and at times surpasses, the one produced
by the Ballets Russes in [1910][27] on the same
stage, and that the couple Spessivtseva–
Lifar, admirably matched, have no need to
envy the duo Karsavina–Nijinsky."[28]

Notes

1   "Вечернее размышление о божием величестве
    при случае великаго севернаго сияния."
2   Mikhail Lomonosov (1711–65), a scientist as well
    as a poet, wrote two series of odes, ten called
    "Spiritual Odes," of which this was No 10
    written in 1743, and another series called
    "Celebratory and Laudatory Odes," mostly in
    praise of Empress Elizabeth.
3   Stravinsky's niece, whose real name was Irina
    Beliankina.
4   Nicolas Nabokov, *Old Friends and New Music*,
    p 66.
5   Nicolas Nabokov, *ibid*, p 67.
6   Nicolas Nabokov, *ibid*, p 75.
7   Boris Kochno, *Diaghilev and the Ballets Russes*,
    p 260.
8   Boris Kochno, *ibid*, p 260.
9   In the Museum of Modern Art, New York,
    Spec. Coll. * 94.3 033 T244.
10 A. V. Coton, *A Prejudice for Ballet*, p 87.
11 Leonide Massine, *My Life in Ballet*, p 174.
12 Nicolas Nabokov, *op cit*, p 77.
13 Nicolas Nabokov, *ibid*, p 85.
14 Nicolas Nabokov, *ibid*, pp 98–9.
15 Serge Lifar, *Serge Diaghilev*, p 466.
16 The only one of his productions which
    Diaghilev never saw was *Til Eulenspiegel*,
    choreographed by Nijinsky, as it was performed
    only in America in 1917 during the second tour
    when the company went without him.
17 Diaghilev interview in Возрождение [*Renais-
    sance*], Paris, 3 June 1928 by Lev Liubimov,
    quoted in I. S. Zilberstein and V. A. Samkov,
    Sergei Diaghilev Vol 1, p 250.
18 Anon [the Paris correspondent], "The Russian
    Ballet" in *The Times*.
19 A. V. Coton, *op cit*, pp 86, 87.
20 Diaghilev interview in Возрождение [*Renais-
    sance*], Paris, 3 June 1928, by Lev Liubimov,
    quoted in I. S. Zilberstein and V. A. Samkov,
    Sergei Diaghilev Vol 1, p 249.
21 Tchelitchew's scenario in the Museum of Mod-
    ern Art, New York, Spec. Coll * 94.3 033 T24.
22 Donald Windham, "The Stage and Ballet
    Designs of Pavel Tchelitchew" in *Dance Index*
    vol III No 1, 2, New York Jan.–Feb. 1944, p 10.
23 Tchelitchew's scenario in the Museum of Mod-
    ern Art, New York, Spec. Coll * 94.3 033 T24.
24 Parker Tyler, *The Divine Comedy of Pavel
    Tchelitchew*, p 333–4.
25 Quoted in James Thrall Soby, *Tchelitchew*, p 17.
26 Serge Lifar, *Ma vie*, pp 115–6.
27 Levinson wrote 1911 by mistake.
28 André Levinson in *Comeodia*, Paris 23 January
    1932.

Tchelitchew

Appendix A

Chronological (first performances) list of stage works represented in the Lifar Collection

Date	Title	Company	Page
7 February 1903	*Feya Kukol (The Fairy Doll)*	Imp Th	59
7 February 1907	*The Legend of the Invisible City of Kitezh*	Imp Th	221
19 May 1909	*Le Pavillon d'Armide*	DBR	108
14 December 1909	*Knyaz Igor (Prince Igor)*	Imp Th	223
4 June 1910	*Schéhérazade*	DBR	62
19 April 1911	*Le Spectre de la rose*	DBR	67
13 June 1911	*Petrushka*	DBR	117
13 May 1912	*Le Dieu Bleu*	DBR	71
29 May 1912	*L'Après-midi d'un faune*	DBR	74
8 June 1912	*Daphnis and Chloë*	DBR	79
29 May 1913	*Le Sacre du Printemps*	DBR	289
5 June 1913	*Khovanshchina (The Khovansky Affair)*	DBR	198
16 April 1914	*Papillons*	DBR	189
26 May 1914	*Le Rossignol*	DBR	126
20 December 1915	*Soleil de Nuit*	DBR	228
25 August 1916	*Kikimora*	DBR	231
12 April 1917	*Les Femmes de Bonne Humeur*	DBR	82
20 May 1919	*Aladin ou la Lampe Merveilleuse*	Marigny	85
5 June 1919	*La Boutique Fantasque*	DBR	180
22 July 1919	*Le Tricorne*	DBR	271
2 February 1920	*Le Chant du Rossignol*	DBR	255
27 May 1920	*Le Astuzie Femminili (Woman's Wiles)*	DBR	309
2 November 1921	*The Sleeping Princess*	DBR	87
23 January 1922	*Snegourotchka*	Met	56
3 June 1922	*Mavra*	DBR	316
13 June 1923	*Les Noces*	DBR	206
28 September 1923	*Tsar Feodor Ioannovitch*	State	313
25 October 1923	*La Création du Monde*	B Suéd	249
3 January 1924	*Les Tentations de la Bergère*	DBR	215
6 January 1924	*Les Biches*	DBR	240
19 June 1924	*Les Fâcheux*	DBR	145
13 November 1924	*Giselle*	Opéra	130
28 April 1925	*Zéphire et Flore*	DBR	148
17 June 1925	*Les Matelots*	DBR	277
21 January 1926	*Les Sylphides* (new setting)	DBR	151
4 May 1926	*Romeo and Juliet*	DBR	191, 260
29 May 1926	*La Pastorale*	DBR	284
3 June 1926	*Jack-in-the-Box*	DBR	183
25 November 1926	*L'Oiseau de Feu* (revival)	DBR	210
30 April 1927	*La Chatte*	DBR	202
20 April 1928	*Rastratchiki (The Embezzlers)*	MXT	287
6 June 1928	*Ode*	DBR	321
12 June 1928	*Apollon Musagète*	DBR	103
9 May 1929	*Le Bal*	DBR	153
21 May 1929	*Renard* (revival)	DBR	233
21 May 1929	*Le Fils Prodigue*	DBR	298
4 March 1930	*Night*	Cochran	140
16 February 1931	*L'Orchestre en Liberté*	Opéra	176
22 May 1931	*Bacchus et Ariane*	Opéra	170
16 December 1932	*Sur le Borysthène*	Opéra	237
3 July 1933	*Prométhée*	Lifar	304

Abbreviations

Imp Th	Russian Imperial Theaters, St Petersburg
DBR	Diaghilev's Ballets Russes
Marigny	Marigny Theater, Paris
Met	Metropolitan Opera, New York
State	State Dramatic Theater, Leningrad
B Suéd	Ballets Suédois
Opéra	Opéra, Paris
MXT	Moscow Art Theater
Cochran	Charles B. Cochran's Revue
Lifar	Lifar Ballets Tour

Appendix B

Works exhibited in the first three exhibitions of the Serge Lifar Collection in London and Paris

The descriptions and numbers are those given in the original catalogues. The works marked with * are in the Wadsworth Atheneum. In some cases, it is no longer possible to identify the works, e.g. Miró.

**The New Chenil Galleries
London, July 1926**
Serge Lifar's Collection of Modern Paintings

André Derain
Jack in the Box – Ballet 1926
1   Stage setting *
2–3   Groups *
4–9   Costumes *
10   Cloud *

Max Ernst
11   Panneau (1926)
12   The Night (1926) *
13   Curtain (1926)
14–15 The Sea (1925) *
16   The Sun (1925) *
17   Projet (1926)
18   The Wood (1926)

Joan Miró
19–24 (1924–1926)

Pablo Picasso
25   Aquarelle (March 1925)
26   Colour print (1922)

Pedro Pruna
27   Portrait of Serge Lifar (1925)
28   Drawing (1925) A. Nikitina
29   Drawing (1925) W. Dukelsky
30   Drawing (1925) B. Kochno
31   Drawing (1925) Serge Lifar
      (illustrated on the cover)
32–33 Stage settings "Les Matelots"
      (Ballet 1925) *
34   Stage setting "Pastorale" (Ballet 1926) *
35   Composition (May 1926)

**Galerie Vignon, Paris
16–31 December 1929**
*Collection de Peintures de nos jours appartenant
à Serge Lifar*

Bauchant
1   Fleurs des champs
2   Les pêcheurs
3   Les mufliers
4   Persée *
5   Retour des Moissoneurs
6   Fleurs
7   Inondation
8   Champs-Elysées * ⎫
9   Ciel d'Apollon * ⎬ décors

Bombois
10   Pavillon du Brig Forestier (1928)

Giorgio de Chirico
11   Construction
12   Idéal
13   Construction
14   Rideau pour le Bal *
15   Décor pour le Bal *
16   Détail du décor pour le Bal *
17   19 costumes pour le Bal *

Derain, Jack in the Box
18   Décor *
19 ⎫
20 ⎬ Groupes *
21   6 costumes *

Max Ernst
22   Panneau 1926
23   La Nuit 1926 *
24   Rideau pour le ballet Romeo and
      Juliet *
25 ⎫
26 ⎬ La Mer 1925 *
27 ⎫
28 ⎬ Le Soleil 1925 *
29   Nature morte
30   Nature morte (dessin)

Nathalie Gontcharova
31   2 costumes pour Oiseau de Feu *

Michel Larionov
32   Esquisse du décor pour Renard 1929 *
33   Costume pour Renard
34   Dessin Hommage

Marie Laurencin
35   Demoiselles *
36   Portrait du poète

Henri Laurens
37   Bas relief

Joan Miró
38   Rideau pour Romeo & Juliet * ⎫
39–44 Panneaux   ⎬ 1924–6

Picasso
45   Peinture 1914
46   Aquarelle mars 1925
47   Les fruits gouache
48   Autoportrait aquarelle
49   Une tête (dessin) *
50   Une fenêtre
51   Guitare
52   Guéridon
53   Un verre
54   Dessin pour le Tricorne *
55   Une loge   ⎫
56   Fleurs   ⎬ Cuadro Flamenco

Pruna
57   Portrait de Serge Lifar
58 ⎫
59 ⎬ Décors pour Matelots *
60 ⎭
61   Décor pour Pastorale *
62   Rideau pour Pastorale *
63   2 costumes pour Matelots *

Georges Rouault
64 ⎫
65 ⎬ Décors pur le Fils Prodique *

Pavel Tchelitchew
66   Portrait. Serge Lifar 1929 *
67   L'homme au clou
68   Les acrobates
69   2 dessins pour costumes Ode *
70   Le raisin aquarelle
71   Tête et oeuf
72   Portrait de Boris Kochno
73   Esquisse pour un portrait
74   Les oeufs
75   Tête renversée

Vivain [sic]
76   A Paris

No 49 was illustrated on the cover; nos 36, 52, 54 were illustrated in the text; no 14 was illustrated as plate no II; no 18 as plate no III; nos 64, 65 as plate nos VII, VIII.

Arthur Tooth & Sons Ltd
16–27 September 1930
La Collection de Peintures de nos jours
Appartenant à Serge Lifar

André Bauchant
1   Champs-Elysées (décor for the ballet d'Apollon) 1928 *
2   Sky (décor for the ballet d'Apollon) 1928 *
3   Flowers
4   Perseus *
5   The Reapers
6   Flowers
7   Fishermen

Christian Bérard
8   Décor *
9   Study

Bombois
10   Gameskeeper's [sic] Cottage

Georges Braque
11   Décor for the Ballet "Les Sylphides" (1925) *
12   Curtain for the Ballet "Les Facheux" (1924) *
13   Curtain for the Ballet "Zéphyr and Flora" (1925) *
14   Costume for the Ballet "Zéphyr and Flora" *

Giorgio di Chirico
15   Curtain *
16   Décor *
17–24 Eight Costumes *
the three above for the Ballet "Le Bal" 1929
25   Watercolour Design for the last programme of the Diaghileff Ballet *
26   Construction
27   Gladiators

André Derain
28   Décor *
29   Groups *
30   Groups *
31–33 Three Costumes *
all for the Ballet "Jack in the Box" 1926

Gabo
34   Costume for the Ballet "La Chatte" 1927 *

Nathalie Gontcharova
35–36 Two costumes for the Ballet "L'Oiseau de Feu" 1926 *

Juan Gris
37   Drawing for the Ballet "La Tentation de la Bergère" [sic] 1923 *
38   Watercolour

Michel Larionow
39   Décor for the Ballet "Renard" 1929 *

Marie Laurencin
40   Drawing for the costumes for the Ballet "Les Biches" 1924 *
41   Young Ladies *
42   Portrait of a poet

Fernand Léger
43   Watercolour *
44   Drawing *
45   Drawing *

Joan Miró
46   Painting ?*

Pablo Picasso
47   Sketch for the décor of the Ballet "Tricorne" *
48   Flowers from the Ballet "Quadro Flamenco"

49   Watercolour
50   Fruit
51   Head
52   A Window
53   Guitar
54   Still Life
55   A Glass
56   Painting
57   A Dancer ?*

Pedro Pruna
58   Décor *
59   Décor *
60–61 Two Costumes *
the three above for the Ballet *Les Matelots* 1925
62   Décor *
63   Sketch *
the two above for the Ballet *"La Pastorale"* 1926
64   Design for the Programme of the Russian Ballet 1925 *

Georges Rouault
65, 66 Décor for the Ballet "Le Fils Prodigue" 1929 *

Paul Tchelitcheff
67   Motif for the Ballet "Ode" 1928 *
68, 69 Two costumes for the Ballet "Ode" 1928 *
70   Acrobats
71   Sketch for a Portrait
72   Head
73   Portrait of Serge Lifar, 1929 *

All the designs for décor and costumes were created for use in the Ballets produced by the late M. Serge de Diaghileff.

Appendix C

A literal translation of the text of the "abdication" written and signed by Boris Kochno and Serge Lifar. It is erroneously dated 5 August 1929 instead of 5 September 1929.

There are two known copies of this text which was originally in Russian, hand written by Kochno in his most florid calligraphy. One copy belonged to Kochno and was included in the sale of his collection at Sotheby's, Monte Carlo, on 11–12 October 1991; the other copy belonged to Serge Lifar. The text was published in French, in Lifar's translation, in the catalogue of the exhibition *Serge Lifar: Une vie pour la danse*, Musée Historique de l'Ancien-Evêché, Lausanne, 1986, as item 58, p 50.

Dear Friends and Colleagues,

We come before you at this time to say good-bye to you who have been for so many years participants and colleagues in the Ballets Russes of Sergei Pavlovitch Diaghilev, the significance and importance of which critics have pronounced upon and historians will no doubt further pronounce upon.

Diaghilev died suddenly. He did not live his whole life and did not complete his work. But one cannot complete this work just as one cannot go on living for him. We do not want to take on the responsibility of carrying on Diaghilev's work. Diaghilev was a creator of artists, who in their turn created works. One can "collaborate with a creator," help him by word and deed, but one cannot paint for Picasso or compose for Stravinsky.

In order to continue to carry the name which Diaghilev gave his work, his own name, we his disciples would always have had to remember his words, his thoughts, his desires, in other words we would either stagnate or retrace our steps, and that would be the death of living work.

Now, our reason, feeling and taste compel us to continue to progress. Whatever trust the Master bestowed upon his disciples when he was alive, we would be in danger of substituting our own work for his, and the name of Diaghilev would merely serve as a guarantee for something which was alien to him.

We therefore say goodbye to you and to our work together, but just as we believe you do, we will never forget everything he taught us.

(signed) Boris Kochno. Serge Lifar

Appendix D

Bibliography of works, in French and English, by Serge Lifar concerning ballet

Note: Russian editions of those works which were first published in Russian, such as Lifar's biography of Diaghilev, have been excluded from this list. Also excluded are the many articles in specialist dance and ballet periodicals or in newspapers, program notes, lectures, and prefaces to other works.

Le manifeste du chorégraphe (Paris, 1935)

Du temps que j'avais faim (Paris, 1935)

La danse: les grands courants de la danse académique (Paris, 1938)

Ballet: Traditional to Modern, trans. Cyril W. Beaumont (London, 1938)

Serge Diaghilev: His life, his work, his legend, trans. unacknowledged (London, 1940)

Carlotta Grisi (Paris, 1941)

Giselle, apothéose du ballet romantique (Paris, 1942)

Terpsichore dans le cortège des muses (Paris, 1943)

Pensées sur la danse, preface by Paul Valéry, illustrations by Aristide Maillol (Paris, 1946)

Traité de danse académique, drawings by Monique Lancelot (Paris, 1949)

A l'aube de mon destin: chez Diaghilev, sept ans aux Ballets Russes (Paris, 1949)

Histoire du ballet russe depuis les origines jusqu'à nos jours (Paris, 1950)

Adages et pas de deux, lithographs by Monique Lancelot (Paris, 1956)

Auguste Vestris: le dieu de la danse (Paris, 1950)

Traité de chorégraphie, drawings and lithographs by Monique Lancelot (Paris, 1952)

Serge de Diaghilev: sa vie—son œuvre—sa légende (Monaco, 1954)

Le livre de la danse, with 70 illustrations by Serge Lifar, Aristide Maillol, Pablo Picasso, Yves Brayer, Jean Cocteau, Christian Bérard, Léon Leyritz and Jean-Denis Malcles (Paris, 1954)

La musique par la danse: de Lulli à Prokofiev (Paris, 1955)

Les trois Grâces du XXe siècle: légendes et vérité (Paris, 1957)

The Three Graces: Anna Pavlova, Tamara Karsavina, Olga Spessivtzeva, the legends and the truth (London, 1959)

Au service de la danse: à la recherche d'une science: chorélogie (Paris, 1958)

Ma vie (Paris, 1965)

La danse académique et l'art chorégraphique (Geneva, 1965)

Histoire du ballet (Milan, 1966)

Les voies du ballet mondial: bilan chorégraphique (1960–1970) (Paris, 1969)

Ma Vie: from Kiev to Kiev, trans. James Holman Mason (London, 1970)

Les mémoires d'Icare (Lausanne, 1993)

The exhibition history of each item in the notes to the plates is given by using the abbreviation below.

Cynthia Roman, Curatorial Assistant at the Wadsworth Atheneum, was almost entirely responsible for compiling this exhibition list from the available records in the Museum, and I am indebted to her for her painstaking and meticulous industry in its preparation.

All the works have been exhibited frequently both before and since their acquisition by the Wadsworth Atheneum, sometimes as a collection, sometimes as individual items. The list below includes every known exhibition, although the details available, such as the title or precise dates, occasionally remain elusive. The relevant catalogues have been consulted wherever possible, but often they are too vague—as, for example, when describing an object merely as "costume." In many cases, however, no catalogue or list was published, and consequently it has not always been possible to include the number of the work in the relevant exhibition.

Paris 1911
Musée des Arts Décoratifs, Palais du Louvre, Pavillon de Marsan, Paris, *Oeuvres de L. Bakst*, 6 July–15 October 1911

London 1912
Fine Art Society, London, *Léon Bakst*, June 1912

London 1917
Fine Art Society, London, *Designs for the Ballet "La Belle au Bois Dormant"*, June 1917

Paris 1918
Galerie Sauvage, Paris, *Exposition des Oeuvres de Gontcharova et de Larionow: L'Art Décoratif Théâtral Moderne*, 16 April–7 May 1918

Paris 1919
Galerie Barbazange, Paris, *Les Oeuvres de Larionov et Gontcharova*, 11–28 June 1919

London 1921
Whitechapel Art Gallery, London, *First Russian Exhibition of Arts and Crafts*, 1921

New York 1922
The Kingore Gallery, New York, *The Goncharova–Larionov Exhibition*, 1922

Paris 1925
Musée des Arts Décoratifs, Paris, *Léon Bakst*, 5–19 November 1925

London 1926
The New Chenil Galleries, London, *Serge Lifar's Collection of Modern Paintings*, July 1926 (35 items; see Appendix B)

London 1927
Fine Art Society, London, *Memorial Exhibition of the work of Léon Bakst*, May 1927

Paris 1927–8
Galerie Jeanne Bucher, Paris, *Fleurs et Paysages d'André Bauchant*, 21 December 1927–6 January 1928

Paris 1928
Galerie Jeanne Bucher, Salle Magellan, Paris, *Bauchant*, 5–30 June 1928 (paintings for *Apollon Musagète* only exhibited from 13 June)

London 1928
Alex Reid & Lefevre, London, *André Bauchant*, 11–28 July 1928

Paris 1929
Galerie Vignon, Paris, *Collection de Peintures de nos jours appartenant à Serge Lifar*, 16–31 December 1929 (76 items; see Appendix B)

London Claridge 1930
Claridge Gallery, London, *Memorial Exhibition of Russian Ballet Art*, March 1930

London Tooth 1930
Arthur Tooth & Sons Ltd, London, *La Collection de Peintures de nos jours appartenant à M. Serge Lifar*, 16–27 September 1930 (73 items; see Appendix B)

Paris 1930
Galerie Billiet-Pierre Vorms, Paris, *Exposition Rétrospective de Maquettes, Décors & Costumes exécutés pour la Compagnie des Ballets Russes de Serge de Diaghilew*, 14–28 October 1930 (100 items)

Munich 1931–2
Theatre Museum, Munich, *Modernes Theater in Frankreich*

Paris 1933
Musée Galliera, Paris, *L'Art décoratif au Théâtre et dans la Musique*, June 1933

New York 1933
Julien Levy Gallery, New York, *Twenty-five years of Russian Ballet from the collection of Serge Lifar*, 2–18 November 1933

Chicago 1933
The Arts Club, Chicago, *Twenty Five Years of Russian Ballet from the collection of Serge Lifar*, 28 November–23 December 1933

Northampton 1934
Smith College Museum of Art, Northampton, Massachusetts, *Quelques artistes contemporains: Les Ballets Russes de Serge de Diaghilew, décors et costumes*, 7–22 January 1934.
Also shown at Museum of Art, Cleveland, Ohio, 14 March–11 April 1934; Art Museum, Cincinnati, Ohio, 22 April–20 May 1934. Arranged before the collection had been acquired by the Wadsworth Atheneum, but shown on the poster to have been loaned by it. The catalogue list is unnumbered but follows the same order as the list for Cincinnati (see above). Therefore these numbers have been given under the relevant item.

Hartford 1934a
Wadsworth Atheneum, Hartford, Connecticut, *Pablo Picasso*, 6 February–1 March 1934

Hartford 1934b
Wadsworth Atheneum, Hartford, Connecticut, 12 November 1934

Chicago 1934
Arts Club, Chicago, *Leonide Massine Collection of Modern Paintings*, 4–31 December 1934.
Also shown at Toledo, Ohio, Marie Harriman Gallery, 18 February–9 March 1935, and Wadsworth Atheneum, May–2 October 1935

New Haven 1935
Yale University, New Haven, Connecticut, 2 January 1935–25 February 1936

Pittsfield 1935
Berkshire Museum, Pittsfield, Massachusetts, traveling exhibition, 31 January–26 July 1935

Poughkeepsie 1935
Vassar College, Poughkeepsie, New York, 25 April–14 June 1935

Middletown 1935
Wesleyan University, Middletown, Connecticut, 8 November–3 December 1935

New York 1935
Pierre Matisse Gallery, New York, 21 November 1935

San Francisco 1935–6
San Francisco Museum of Art, San Francisco, California, 21 November–29 January 1936

New York 1936
Julien Levy Gallery, New York, 20 October–28 November 1936

New York 1937–8
Rockefeller Center, New York, *Dance International 1900–1937*, 29 November 1937–1 January 1938

Boston 1938
Boston Museum of Modern Art, Boston, Massachusetts, *Ballet Show*, 12 January 1938

Paris 1939
Musée des Arts Décoratifs, Palais du Louvre, Pavillon de Marsan, Paris, *Ballets Russes de Diaghilew 1909–1929*, April–1 July 1939

New York 1939
Museum of Modern Art, New York, 27 October 1939

Chicago 1939
Arts Club of Chicago, Chicago, Illinois, *Braque Retrospective*, November 1939
Also shown at Phillips Memorial Gallery, Washington D.C., 1 December 1939–7 January 1940; San Francisco Museum of Art, San Francisco, California, February 1940

Los Angeles 1939–40
Los Angeles Museum of History, Science and Art, Exposition Park, Los Angeles, California, *Exhibition of the Dance*, 2 December 1939–8 January 1940

Chicago 1940a
Art Institute of Chicago, Chicago, Illinois, *Picasso: Forty Years of His Art*, 1 February–3 March 1940
Also shown at Institute of Modern Art, Boston, Massachusetts, 27 April–26 May 1940

Williamsburg 1940
College of William and Mary, Williamsburg, Virginia, mid-February–mid-March 1940

Poughkeepsie 1940
Vassar College, Poughkeepsie, New York, 9 October–4 November 1940

Chicago 1940b
Civic Opera Company Ballet Theatre, Chicago, Illinois, 1 November–15 December 1940
8 items also shown at John Hopkins University, Baltimore, *Divertissements*, January 1941

New York 1941
Junior League Clubhouse, New York, *Exhibition of Ballet Art*, 6–18 January 1941

New York 1941–2
Museum of Modern Art, New York, *Painters as Ballet Designers*. An exhibition circulated by

MoMA shown at City Art Museum, St Louis, Missouri, 8 December 1941–7 January 1942; California Palace of the Legion of Honor, San Francisco, California, 19 January–16 February 1942; Henry Gallery, University of Washington, Seattle, Washington, 24 February–17 March 1942

New York 1942
Ballet Theatre, New York, March 1942

New York MoMA 1942
Museum of Modern Art, New York, *Tchelitchew*, October 1942

Cambridge 1942
Fogg Museum of Art, Cambridge, Massachusetts, 1 May 1942

San Francisco 1942
M. H. De Young Museum, San Francisco, California, September 1942

Massillon 1943
Massillon Museum, Massillon, Ohio, *Thirty Pictures from the Lifar Collection*, March–April 1943

New York 1944
Wildenstein Gallery, New York, *Five Centuries of Ballet*, 10 April–13 May 1944

New York MoMA 1944
Museum of Modern Art, New York, *Art in Progress*, 27 May–17 September 1944

New York MoMA 1944–5
Museum of Modern Art, New York, *Modern Drawings*, 16 February–10 May 1944
     Also shown at Carnegie Institute, Pittsburgh, Pennsylvania, 20 June–18 July 1944; California Palace of Honor, San Francisco, California, 1–29 August 1944; Washington County Museum of Fine Arts, Hagerstown, Washington, 1–29 October 1944; The St Paul Gallery and School of Art, St Paul, Minnesota, 12 November–10 December 1944; Walker Art Center, Minneapolis, Minnesota, 3–31 January 1945; Milwaukee Art Institute, Milwaukee, Wisconsin, 14 February–14 March 1945; Worcester Art Museum, Worcester, Massachusetts, 28 March–25 April 1945; J. P. Speed Art Museum, Louisville, Kentucky, 9 March–7 June 1945

New London 1944
Connecticut College for Women, New London, Connecticut, *Five Arts Weekend*, 28–29 April 1944

New York 1945
Museum of Modern Art, New York, *Georges Rouault*, 27 March–3 June 1945

New York 1946–7
Museum of Modern Art, New York, *Ballet Designs*, 12 November 1946–12 January 1947

Grand Rapids 1947
Grand Rapids Art Gallery, Grand Rapids, Missouri, *The Paintings and Prints of Georges Rouault*, 11 April–2 May 1947

Chapel Hill 1948
University of North Carolina, Chapel Hill, Carolina, 1948

Detroit 1948
Detroit Institute of Arts, Detroit, Michigan, *Paul J. Sachs, 70th Birthday Celebration: Sixty Drawings from the Wadsworth Atheneum, Hartford*, 20 November–31 December 1948

Lawrence 1949
University of Kansas Museum of Art, Lawrence, Kansas, *Art in the Theatre*, 21 March–21 April 1949

Hartford 1949
Wadsworth Atheneum, Hartford, Connecticut, *In Retrospect—Twenty–one Years of Museum Collecting*, 2 April–29 May 1949

Sarasota 1949
The John and Mable Ringling Museum of Art, Sarasota, Florida, *Art Carnival and the Circus*, 1949

Farmington 1949
Miss Porter's School, Farmington, Connecticut, 4 October 1949

Syracuse 1949–50
Syracuse University School of Art, College of Fine Arts, Syracuse, New York, *Exhibition of Rouault's Prints and Paintings*, 6 December 1949–6 January 1950

Springfield 1950
Museum of Fine Arts, Springfield, Massachusetts, *In Freedom's Search*, 15 January–19 February 1950

Washington D.C. 1950–1
American Federation of Arts, Washington, D.C., Circulating Exhibition: Baltimore, Maryland, 1–22 May 1950; Charleston, Virginia, 1–22 October 1950; Sarasota, Florida, The John and Mable Ringling Museum of Art, 5–26 November 1950; Louisville, Kentucky, The J. B. Speed Art Museum, 10–31 December 1950; Chicago, Illinois, University of Illinois, 1–22 April 1951; Ann Arbor, Michigan, University of Michigan, 6–27 May 1951

Sarasota 1950
The John and Mable Ringling Museum of Art, Sarasota, Florida, *Lifar Collection of Ballet Designs by Great Modern Artists*, 5 November 1950

Cleveland 1951
Cleveland Museum of Art, Cleveland, Ohio, *Modigliani Retrospective*, 30 January–18 March 1951
     Also shown at Museum of Modern Art, New York, 10 April–24 June 1951

Hartford 1952
Wadsworth Atheneum, Hartford, Connecticut, 27 February–1 March 1952

Minneapolis 1953
Walker Art Center, Minneapolis, Minnesota, 1 March–5 April 1953

Cleveland 1953
Cleveland Museum of Art, Cleveland, Ohio, *Rouault Retrospective*, 1953
     Also shown at Museum of Modern Art, New York, 1953

Palm Beach 1954
Society of Four Arts, Palm Beach, Florida, *Modigliani*, 8–31 January 1954
     Also shown at Lowe Gallery, Coral Gables, Florida, 11–28 February 1954; Houston, Texas, 15 April–23 May 1954

Minneapolis 1954
Walker Art Center, Minneapolis, Minnesota, *Reality and Fantasy 1900–1954*, 23 May–2 July 1954

Edinburgh 1954
College of Art, Edinburgh, *The Diaghilev Exhibition*, 22 August–11 September 1954

London 1954–5
Forbes House, London, *The Diaghilev Exhibition*, 3 November 1954–16 January 1955
     Enlarged and transferred from Edinburgh

Beloit 1956
Beloit College, Beloit, Wisconsin, 20 January 1956

Framingham 1956
Shopper's World, Framingham, Massachusetts, *Shoppers' World Art Festival*, 20 June–14 July 1956

Ottawa 1956
National Museum of Canada, Ottawa, Canada, *Paintings, Theatre and Ballet Designs by Pavel Tchelitchew and Leslie Hurry* (for Stratford Shakespeare Festival), 1956

Stamford 1957
The Stamford Museum and Nature Center, Stamford, Connecticut, *Modern Watercolors and Drawings*, 11 January–15 March 1957

East Lansing 1957
College of Communication Arts, Michigan State University, East Lansing, Michigan, 15 April–15 May 1957

Milwaukee 1957
Milwaukee Art Institute, Milwaukee, Wisconsin, *Six Great Painters: El Greco, Rembrandt, Goya, van Gogh, Cézanne and Picasso*, 12 September–20 October 1957

Hartford 1957
G. Fox and Co., Hartford, Connecticut, 28 October 1957

New York 1958
Knoedler Galleries, New York, *Masterpieces from the Wadsworth Atheneum, Hartford*, 21 January–15 February 1958

San Antonio 1958
Marion Koogler McNay Art Institute, San Antonio, Texas, 21 February 1958

Sarasota 1958
The John and Mable Ringling Museum of Art, Sarasota, Florida, *A. Everett Austin Jr.: A Director's Taste and Achievement*, 23 February–30 March 1958
     Also shown at Wadsworth Atheneum, Hartford, Connecticut, 23 April–1 June 1958

Elmira 1958
Elmira College Art Gallery, Elmira, New York, 23 September–10 October 1958

Chicago 1959
Arts Club of Chicago, Chicago, Illinois, *Amadeo Modigliani*, 30 January–28 February 1959
     Also shown at Milwaukee Art Institute, Milwaukee, Wisconsin, 3 March–1 April 1959; Cincinnati Art Museum, Contemporary Art Center, Ohio, 10 April–20 May 1959

Richmond 1959
Virginia Museum of Fine Arts, Richmond, Virginia, *Sketches for the Ballet*, 20 February–29 March 1959 (catalogue is *Bulletin of the Virginia Museum of Fine Arts*, XIX No.6, February 1959)

London 1959
Victoria and Albert Museum, London, *Mstislav V. Dobujinsky Memorial Exhibition*, March–June 1959

Indianapolis 1959
John Herron Art Institute, Indinapolis, Indiana, *Fifty Years of Ballet Designs*, 22 March–29 April 1959

Also shown at Wadsworth Atheneum, Hartford, Connecticut, 5 May–7 June 1959; California Palace of the Legion of Honor, San Francisco, California, 11–16 August 1959

The exhibition was then divided into two sections and circulated by the American Federation of Arts, New York, as follows: Section 1: Corning Museum of Glass, Corning, New York, 24 August–7 September 1959; Atlanta Public Library, Atlanta, Georgia, 2–22 October 1959; Pensacola Art Center, Pensacola, Florida, 4–24 November 1959; The J. B. Speed Art Museum, Louisville Kentucky, 8–28 December 1959; Everson Museum, Syracuse, New York, 16 January–28 February 1960; Denison University, Granville, Ohio, 12 March–2 April 1960; Newcomb College, New Orleans, Louisiana, 14 April–5 May 1960; Cornell University, Ithaca, New York, 1 July–30 August

Section 2: Art Gallery of Greater Victoria, Victoria, British Columbia, Canada, 6–25 October 1959; Kansas State Teachers College, Emporia, Kansas, 8–28 November 1959; Santa Monica Art Gallery, Santa Monica, California, 8–28 December 1959; Phoenix Art Museum, Phoenix, Arizona, 12 January–2 February 1960; Charles and Emma Frye Museum, Seattle, Washington, 14 February–7 March 1960; Public Library of Winston–Salem, Winston–Salem, North Carolina, 3–23 April 1960; Fort Lauderdale Art Center, Fort Lauderdale, Florida, 5–20 May 1960; "Chetewode" Astor House, Newport, Rhode Island, 1 August–7 September 1960

Atlanta 1960
Atlanta Art Association, Atlanta, Georgia, *The Art of Modigliani*, 31 March–17 April 1960

Milan 1960
Palazzo Reale, Milan, Italy, *Arte Italiana del XXmo Secolo da Collezioni Americani*, 30 April–26 June 1960

Also shown at Galleria Nazionale d'Arte Moderna, Rome, 15 July–18 September 1960

Rowayton 1960
Five Mile River Gallery, Rowayton, Connecticut, 14 October–10 November 1960

Hartford 1961
Wadsworth Atheneum, Hartford, Connecticut, *Salute to Italy: 100 Years of Italian Art*, 20 April–28 May 1961

New York 1961
World House Galleries Corp., New York, *Max Ernst*, 7 March–1 April 1961

Hartford 1962
Wadsworth Atheneum, Hartford, Connecticut

Lisbon 1962
Fundacoa Calouste Gulbenkian, Lisbon, Portugal, *Claude Debussy*

New York 1962
Wildenstein Gallery, New York, *Stravinsky and the Dance*, 2 May–2 June 1962

Also shown at Museum of Modern Art, New York, 4 June–15 September 1962; Museum of New Mexico, Santa Fe, New Mexico 1–22 August 1962; The Virginia Museum of Fine Arts, Richmond, Virginia, 16 September–14 October 1962; The Arts Club of Chicago, Chicago, Illinois, 13 December 1962–10 January 1963;

Isaac Delgado Museum of Art, New Orleans, Louisiana, 23 January–13 February 1963; Philbrook Art Center, Tulsa, Oklahoma, 1–24 March 1963; Portland Art Association, Portland, Oregon, 3–24 April 1963; Walker Art Center, Minneapolis, Minnesota, 6–28 May 1963; Allentown Art Museum, Allentown, Pennsylvania, 7–28 June 1963; The Corning Museum of Glass, Corning, New York, 10–31 July 1963; Montreal Museum of Fine Arts, Montreal, Canada, 10 August–1 September 1963

Storrs 1963
University of Connecticut, Storrs, Connecticut, *The Painter in the Theater*, 18 March–4 April 1963

Westport 1963
Westport Community Art Association, Westport, Connecticut, *Music in Art*, 25 March–13 April 1963

New London 1963
Lyman Allyn Museum, New London, Connecticut, *Art Nouveau*, 9 February–10 March 1963

New York 1963–4
The Solomon R. Guggenheim Museum, New York, *Twentieth Century Master Drawings*, 6 November 1963–5 January 1964

Also shown at University of Minnesota Gallery, Minneapolis, Minnesota, 1 February–15 March 1964; Fogg Art Museum, Cambridge, Massachusetts, 6 April–24 May 1964

Toronto 1964
The Art Gallery of Toronto, Toronto, Canada, *Picasso and Man*, 11 January–16 February 1964

Also shown at Montreal Museum of Fine Arts, Canada, 28 February–31 March 1964

New York 1964
Gallery of Modern Art, New York, *Pavel Tchelitchew*, 16 March–19 April 1964

Hartford 1964
Hartford National Bank, Exhibit Hall, Hartford, Connecticut, *Diaghilev–Lifar Collection of Ballet Designs* ("Plaza 7" Arts Festival), 29 September–4 October 1964

Eindhoven 1964
Stedelijk Van Abbe Museum, Eindhoven, Netherlands, *Beeldend Experiment op de Planken* (*Fine Arts and the Theatre*), 9 October–22 November 1964

Vancouver 1964
Vancouver Art Gallery, Vancouver, British Colombia, *The Nude in Art*, 3–29 November 1964

Hartford 1965
Austin Arts Center, Trinity College, Hartford, Connecticut, *Opening Exhibition: "Selections from the Ella Gallup Sumner and Mary Catlin Sumner Collection,"* 14 May–13 June 1965

Toulouse 1965
Musée des Augustins, Toulouse, *Picasso et le Théâtre*, 22 June–15 September 1965

Houston 1965
Museum of Fine Arts, Houston, Texas, *The Heroic Years: Paris 1908–1915*, 20 October–8 December 1965

Washington D.C. 1965
Museum of African Art, Frederick Douglas Townhouse, Washington, D.C., October–December 1965

New York 1965–6
Harkness House for Ballet Arts, New York, *The Serge Lifar Collection of Ballet Set and Costume*

Designs, 18 November–18 February 1966

Also shown at Wadsworth Atheneum, Hartford, Connecticut, 25 February–10 April 1966

Chicago 1966
Arts Club of Chicago, Chicago, Illinois, *Drawings 1916–1966*, 28 February–11 April 1966

Spoleto 1966
Festival of Two Worlds, Spoleto, Italy, 25 June–17 July 1966

Edinburgh 1966
Edinburgh International Festival, Edinburgh, *Rouault*, 20 August–18 September 1966

Also shown at Tate Gallery, London, 8 October–13 November 1966

New York 1966–7
New York State Council on the Arts, New York, *The Serge Lifar Collection of Ballet Set and Costume Designs*, a circulating exhibition shown at:
Charles A. Dana Creative Arts Center, Colgate University, Hamilton, New York, 5–28 October 1966
Rochester Memorial Art Gallery, Rochester, New York, 4–27 November 1966
Albany Institute of History and Art, Albany, New York, 5 December 1966–1 January 1967
Albright Knox Gallery, Buffalo, New York, 10–27 January 1967
Vassar College Art Gallery, Poughkeepsie, New York, 3–20 February 1967
Munson–Williams Proctor Institute, Utica, New York, 27 February–27 March 1967
Roberson Memorial Center, Binghampton, New York, 2–30 April 1967
Everson Museum of Art, Syracuse, New York, 5 May–21 June 1967

Princeton 1968
Art Museum, Princeton University, Princeton, New Jersey, *Designs from the Lifar Collection* (during the North Eastern Regional Ballet Festival), 30 April–26 May 1968

Los Angeles 1969
L.A. County Museum of Art, Los Angeles, California, *Ballet Costumes from Les Ballets Serge Diaghilev*, 24 February–13 April 1969

Strasbourg 1969
L'Ancienne Douane, Strasbourg, *Les Ballets Russes de Serge de Diaghilev 1909–1929*, 15 May–15 September 1969

Frankfurt-am-Main 1969
Farbwerke Hoechst Co., Frankfurt-am-Main, *Les Ballets Russes et Serge de Diaghilev* (to open ballet season in Century Hall), 28 September–17 October 1969

Philadelphia 1970
Institute of Contemporary Art, University of Pennsylvania, Philadelphia, Pennsylvania, *Against Order: Chance and Art*, 14 November–22 December 1970

Blommenholm 1971
Sonja Henie-Niels Onstad Foundations, Blommenholm, Norway, *Scenography in the Twentieth Century*, April–May 1971

Washington 1971
National Portrait Gallery, Smithsonian Institution, Washington, D.C., *Portraits of the American Stage 1771–1971*, 11 September–21 November 1971

Wellesley 1972
Wellesley College Art Museum, Wellesley, Massachusetts, *The Finished Study and its Object*, 10 September–10 October 1972

New York 1972
Acquavella Galleries Inc., New York, *Joan Miró*, 18 October–18 November 1972

New York 1972–3
The Solomon R. Guggenheim Museum, New York, *Miró: Magnetic Fields*, 26 October 1972–21 January 1973

Hartford 1973
Austin Arts Center, Trinity College, Hartford, Connecticut, (exhibition under the direction of the Department of Fine Arts), 2–30 April 1973

Hartford W.A. 1973
Wadsworth Atheneum, Hartford, Connecticut, *Picasso Memorial Exhibition*, 10 April–[?] 1973

Hartford 1974
Wadsworth Atheneum, Hartford, Connecticut, *Selections from the Serge Lifar Collection*, 11 January–10 April 1974

Amherst 1974
Amherst College, Department of Fine Arts, Mead Art Center, Amherst, Massachusetts, *Selections from the Lifar Ballet Collection*, 1 March–1 April 1974

Hempstead 1974
Emily Lowe Gallery, Hofstra University, Hempstead, Long Island, New York, *Diaghilev/Cunningham*, 16 April–26 May 1974

Paris 1975
Grand Palais, Paris, France, 17 May–13 October 1975
Also shown at Louisiana Museum, Humelbaek, Denmark, 9 November 1975–12 January 1976

Storrs 1975
William Benton Museum of Art, University of Connecticut, Storrs, Connecticut, *Drawings: Techniques and Types*, 8 February–9 March 1975

Chicago 1975
University of Chicago, Regenstein Library, Chicago, Illinois, *The Diaghilev Ballets Russes, 1909–29, An Exhibition of Original Designs and Documents*, 8 July–31 October 1975

Houston 1976
Museum of Fine Arts, Houston, Texas, *Russian Art & Culture, Selected Objects*,14 January–21 March 1976

New York 1976
Ballet Theater Foundation Inc., New York, *American Ballet Theater*, 1 March–24 July 1976

Fresno 1977
California State University, Fresno, California, *The Spirit of Isadora Duncan, the Vision of Serge de Diaghilev*, 17 April–8 May 1977

Hartford 1978–9
Wadsworth Atheneum, Hartford, Connecticut, *Designs for the Ballets Russes: Selections from the Serge Lifar Collection*, 22 December 1978–18 March 1979

Munich 1979
Haus der Kunst, Munich, Germany, *Max Ernst*, 17 February–29 April 1979
Also shown at National Gallery, Berlin, Germany, 10 May–15 July 1979

New York 1979
CBS Inc., New York, *Dancer's Choice/Vera Zorine*, 1979

New York 1980
New York Public Library and Museum of the Performing Arts, New York, *Diaghilev*, 16 January–10 May 1980

Roslyn 1981
Nassau County Museum of Fine Art, Roslyn, New York, *The Abstract Expressionists and their Precursors*, 17 January–22 March 1981

London 1981
Victoria and Albert Museum, London, England, *Spotlight: Four centuries of Ballet Costume, a Tribute to The Royal Ballet*, 8 April–26 July 1981

Coral Gables 1982
Lowe Art Museum, Coral Gables, Florida, *Artists and the Theater* 4 June–22 August 1982

Boston 1982–3
Institute of Contemporary Art, Boston, Massachusetts, *Art and Dance*, 9 November 1982–8 January 1983
Also shown at I.C.A., Toledo Museum of Art, Toledo; Neuberger Museum, Purchase, New York

Basel 1984
Kunstmuseum, Basel, Switzerland, *Stravinsky: Sein Nachlass Sein Bild*, 6 June–9 September 1984

Oberlin 1985
Allen Memorial Art Museum, Oberlin College, Oberlin, Ohio, *Costumes from Castle Howard, England*, 25 March–14 April 1985

Indianapolis 1985
Indiana State Museum and Memorials, Indianapolis, Indiana, *Setting the State for Dance* (in conjunction with the opening performance of the Indiana Ballet Theater), 15 August–11 October 1985

Madrid 1985
Salas Pablo Ruiz Picasso, Paseo de Recoletos, Madrid, *Juan Gris (1887–1927)*, 29 September–24 November 1985

New York 1985–6
The Jewish Museum, New York, *The Circle of Montparnasse Jewish Artists in Paris 1910–1945*, 22 October 1985–2 February 1986

Frankfurt–am–Main 1986
Schirn Kunsthalle, Frankfurt–am–Main, *Die Maler und das Theater in 20, Jahrhundert*, 1 March–26 May 1986
Also shown at Palais de Papes and Maison Jean Vilar, Avignon, France, summer 1986

Allentown 1986
Muhlenberg College, Allentown, Pennsylvania, *Avant–garde Alchemy: Russian Stage Design 1898–1932*, 1–25 April 1986

New York 1986
Cooper Hewitt Museum, New York, *Bronislava Nijinska: A Dancer's Legacy*, 18 March–20 July 1986
Also shown at The Fine Arts Museums of San Francisco, San Francisco, California, 30 August 1986–5 January 1987

New York 1987–8
Fashion Institute of Technology, New York, *Fashion and Surrealism*, 5 October 1987–31 January 1988

Little Rock 1987–8
Arkansas Art Center, Little Rock, Arkansas, *Picasso: Drawings of the Classical Period*, 4 December 1987–31 January 1988

Bielefeld 1988
Kunsthalle, Bielefeld, Germany, *Picassos Klassizismus*, 17 April–31 July 1988

Hartford 1988
Wadsworth Atheneum, Hartford, Connecticut, *Diaghilev's Designers: The Serge Lifar Collection of Ballet Set and Costume Designs*, 2 July–25 September 1988

San Francisco 1988–9
The Fine Art Museums of San Francisco, M. H. de Young Memorial Museum, *The Art of Enchantment: Diaghilev's Ballets Russes 1909–1929*, 3 December–26 February 1989

Columbus 1989
Columbus Museum of Art, Columbus, Ohio, *The Serge Lifar Collection of Ballet Set and Costume Designs*, 29 January–5 March 1989

Worcester 1989
Worcester Art Museum, Worcester, Massachusetts, *The Serge Lifar Collection of Ballet Set and Costume Designs*, 26 September–26 November 1989

Barcelona 1994–5
Fundacio Joan Miró, Centre d'estudes d'art contemporari, Barcelona, Spain, *Joan Miró and the Theatre*, 1 December 1994–12 February 1995

This bibliography excludes references to contemporary notices and reviews in newspapers and periodicals of the productions discussed. For these, refer to the newspapers and periodicals published in the relevant cities on or about the date of the first performances, which are given with the detailed credits for each production.

Publication dates given are those of the editions consulted.

Alexandre, Arsène, *The Decorative Art of Léon Bakst (with notes on the ballets by Jean Cocteau)* (London, 1913)

Amberg, George, *Art in Modern Ballet* (London, 1947)

Anderson, Jack, "The Fabulous Career of Bronislava Nijinska" in *Dance Magazine* (New York, August 1963) pp 40–46

André Bauchant (exhibition catalogue), Musée International d'Art Naïf Anatole Jakovsky (Nice, 1987). *See* Devroye–Stilz, Anne

André Bauchant (exhibition catalogue), Musée des Beaux–Arts de Tours (Tours, 1991). *See* Schaettel, Charles

Annenkov, George P., *Russian Painters and the Rebirth of Theatre Arts*, introduction to catalogue *Russian Stage & Costume Designs* (New York, 1967)

Ansermet, Ernest, *see* Tappolet, Claude

Archer, Kenneth, "Nicolas Roerich et la genèse du *Sacre*" and "Un festin visuel d'une violence absolue" in *Le Sacre du Printemps: Carnets du Théâtre des Champs–Elysées* (Paris, 1990)

Aschengreen, Erik, *Jean Cocteau and the Dance*, trans. Patricia McAndrew and Per Avsum (Copenhagen, 1986)

Assouline, Pierre, *An artful life: a biography of D. H. Kahnweiler*, trans. Charles Ruas (New York, 1990)

Astruc, Gabriel, *Le Pavillon des fantômes* (Paris, 1929)

Augsburg, Georges, *La vie en images de Serge Lifar* (Paris, 1937)

Bablet, Denis, *Esthéthique générale du décor de théâtre de 1870 à 1914* (Paris, 1965)

—, *The Revolutions of Stage Design* (Paris/New York, 1977)

—, "Les Peintres et le Théâtre" in *Théâtre en Europe* No 11 (Paris, July 1986) pp 5–22

Bablet, Denis et al., *Die Maler und das Theater im 20. Jahrhundert* (Frankfurt–am–Main, 1986)

Baer, Nancy van Norman et al., *Bronislava Nijinska: a dancer's legacy* (exhibition catalogue) (San Francisco, 1986)

—, *The Art of Enchantment: Diaghilev's Ballets Russes, 1909–1929* (exhibition catalogue) (San Francisco, 1988)

—, *Paris Modern: The Swedish Ballet 1920–1925* (exhibition catalogue) (San Francisco, 1995)

Bakshy, A., *The path of the Modern Russian Stage and other essays* (London, 1913)

Bakst, Léon, "Chorégraphie et Décors des nouveaux Ballets Russes" in *Souvenir program Diaghilev's Ballets Russes* (Paris, 1917 season)

—, "Tchaikovsky at the Russian Ballet" in Alhambra Theatre *Souvenir program The Sleeping Princess* (London, 1921)

—, "Tchaikowsky aux Ballets Russes" in *Comoedia* (Paris, 9 October 1921)

—, "L'Evolution du décor – opinion de M. Léon Bakst. Réponse à l'enquête de Raymond Cogniat" in *Comoedia* (Paris, 3 September 1923)

—, *and see* Svetlov, Valerian

Balance, John (pseudonym of Edward Gordon Craig), "Kleptomania, or the Russian Theatre" in *The Mask* vol 4 (Florence 1911–12) pp 97–101

Balanchine George, *Balanchine's Complete Stories of the Great Ballets*, ed. Francis Mason (New York, 1954)

—, *Balanchine's New Complete Stories of the Great Ballets* (New York, 1968)

Baldwin, Frances, "Critical Response in England to the work of Designers for Diaghilev's Russian Ballet 1911–1929," unpublished M.A. thesis, Courtauld Institute (London, 1980)

Banes, Sally, "An introduction to the Ballets Suédois" in *Ballet Review* vol 7 nos 2–3 (New York, 1978–9)

Barbey, Valdo, "Les Peintres Modernes et le Théâtre" in *Art et Décoration* Vol XXXVII (Paris, 1920) pp 97–108, 155–160

Barnes, Clive, "Daphnis and Chloë" in *Dance and Dancers* (London, July 1958) pp 16–17

—, "The Sleeping Beauty" in *Dance and Dancers* (London, May 1961) pp 5–14, 23

—, "The Good Humoured Ladies" in *Dance and Dancers* (London, July 1962) pp 27–9

—, "The Firebird" Parts 1 & 2 in *Dance and Dancers* (London, April–May 1963) pp 28–30, 23–8

Barr, Alfred H., Jr, *Matisse: His Art and His Public* (London, 1975)

—, *Picasso: Fifty Years of his Art* (London, 1975)

Barsky, Vivianne, *Matisse at the Ballet: Le Chant du Rossignol* (exhibition catalogue) (Jerusalem, 1991)

Bauchant, André, *see André Bauchant*

Beaton, Cecil, *Ballet* (London, 1951)

—, *The Wandering Years: Diaries 1922–1939* (London, 1961)

Beaumont, Cyril W., *Impressions of the Russian Ballet 1918 No 2, The Good Humoured Ladies* (London, 1918)

—, *Impressions of the Russian Ballet 1919, Schéhérazade* (London, 1919)

—, *Impressions of the Russian Ballet 1919, L'Oiseau de Feu* (London, 1919)

—, *Impressions of the Russian Ballet 1921. The Sleeping Princess* (in 2 parts) (London, 1921)

—, *Serge Diaghilev* (London, 1933)

—, *Michael Fokine and his Ballets* (London, 1935)

—, *The Diaghilev Ballet in London* (London, 1940)

—, *Vaslav Nijinsky* (London, 1933 and 1943)

—, *The Ballet Called Giselle* (London, 1944)

—, *Five centuries of ballet design* (London, n.d.)

—, *Design for ballet* (London, n.d.)

—, *Ballet design past and present* (London, 1946) (a combination and extension of the same author's *Five centuries of ballet design* and *Design for ballet*)

—, *Complete book of ballets* (London, 1951)

—, "Christian Bérard" in *The Studio* (London, October 1959) pp 75–80

—, "Cyril W. Beaumont answers" in *Dance and Dancers* (London, March 1962) pp 20–1

—, *Bookseller at the ballet* (London, 1975)

Beecham, Sir Thomas, *A Mingled Chime* (London, 1944)

Benois, Alexandre, "Uchastie khudozhnikov v teatre" ("Artists' participation in the theatre") in *Rech* (*Speech*) (St Petersburg, 25 February 1909)

—, "Russkie spectakli v Parizhe" ("Russian performances in Paris") in *Rech* (St Petersburg, 19 June 1909)

—, "Russkie spectakli v Parizhe" in *Rech* (St Petersburg, 25 June 1909)

—, "Russkie spectakli v Parizhe" in *Rech* (St Petersburg, 12 July 1910)

—, "Russkie spectakli v Parizhe" in *Rech* (St Petersburg, 18 July 1910)

—, "Diaghilevskie spectakli" ("Diaghilev's performances") in *Rech* (St Petersburg, 25 June 1911)

—, *Reminiscences of the Russian Ballet*, trans. Mary Britnieva (London, 1941)

—, *Memoirs*, trans. Moura Budberg (London, 1964, 2 vols)

Berezkin, V. I., *Khudozhniki Bolshogo Teatra* (*Artists of the Bolshoi Theater*) (Moscow, 1976)

Beyer, Victor et al., *Les Ballets Russes de Serge de Diaghilev* (exhibition catalogue) (Strasbourg, 1969)

Birnbaum, Martin, *Léon Bakst* (introduction to exhibition catalogue, Berlin Photographic Company) (New York, 1913). The same introduction was reprinted, unattributed, in the *Catalogue of a Memorial Exhibition of the Works of Léon Bakst* at the Fine Art Society, London, 1927

Blanche, Jacques–Emile, *Portraits of a Lifetime*, trans. and ed. Walter Clement (London, 1937)

Boissel, Jessica et al., *Natalie Gontcharova/Michel Larionov* (exhibition catalogue) (Paris, 1995)

Boll, André, "Léon Bakst" in *Revue Musicale* (Paris, June 1925) pp 225–31

—, "L'Oiseau de Feu et ses décorateurs," unpublished lecture (Paris, April 1954)

Bowlt, John E., *The Silver Age: Russian art of the early twentieth century and the "World of Art" group* (Newtonville, Massachusetts, 1982)

—, *Russian Stage Design, Scenic Innovation, 1900–1930, from the Collection of Mr and Mrs Nikita D. Lobanov-Rostovsky* (Jackson MS, 1982)

—, *Sobranie Nikiti i Nini Lobanovikh Rostovaskikh "Khudozhniki Russkogo Teatra 1880–1930" Katalog-Razone (Nikita and Nina Lobanov-Rostovsky Collection "Artists of the Russian Theatre 1880–1930" catalogue raisonné)* (Moscow, 1994)

Brahms, Caryl (ed.), *Footnotes to the Ballet* (London, 1936)

Bremser, Martha (ed.), *International Dictionary of Ballet* vols I & II (Detroit, 1993)

Breton, André, "Le Surréalisme et la peinture" in *La Révolution surréaliste* (Paris, 1925)

Brinton, Christian, *The Nicolas Roerich Exhibition* (New York, 1922)

Brown, Frederick, *An impersonation of Angels: A biography of Jean Cocteau* (London, 1969)

Brown, Ismene, "Ballet row over bodyline" in *The Daily Telegraph* (London, 3 February 1996) p A11

Buckle, Richard, *In search of Diaghilev* (London, 1955)

—, *Nijinsky* (London, 1971)

—, *Diaghilev* (London, 1979)

— (ed.), *The Diaghilev Exhibition* (exhibition catalogue) (Edinburgh, 1954). The exhibition was subsequently enlarged and transferred to London for which a new catalogue was published

— in collaboration with John Taras, *George Balanchine: Ballet Master* (London, 1988)

—, *see also* Sokolova, Lydia; Sotheby & Co

Calvocoressi, M. D., *Musicians Gallery* (London, 1933)

Cassou, Jean and Leymarie, Jean, *Fernand Léger: Drawings and Gouaches* (London, 1973)

Cendrars, Blaise, *Anthologie nègre* (Paris, 1921)

—, *The African Saga*, trans. Marjery Bianco (New York, 1927)

Chabert, Philippe (ed.), *André Derain* (exhibition catalogue) (Paris, 1994)

Chadd, David and Gage, John, *The Diaghilev Ballet in England* (exhibition catalogue) (Norwich, 1979)

Chalput, René, *Ravel au miroir de ses lettres* (Paris, 1956)

Chamot, Mary, *Goncharova: Stage Designs and Paintings* (London, 1979)

Cheney, Sheldon, *Stage Decoration* (London, 1928)

Ciranna, Alfonso, *Giorgio de Chirico catalogo delle opere grafiche* (Milan, 1969)

Clarke, Mary and Crisp, Clement, *Ballet in Art* (London, 1978)

—, *Ballet: an illustrated history* (London, 1992)

Cochran, C. B., *I had almost forgotten . . .* (London, 1932)

Cocteau, Jean, *Vaslav Nijinsky: six vers de Jean Cocteau, six dessins de Paul Iribe* (Paris, 1910)

—, *Théâtre Serge de Diaghilew: Les Fâcheux*, with Georges Braque, Jean Cocteau, Louis Laloy, Georges Auric (Paris, 1924)

—, *Théâtre Serge de Diaghilew: Les Biches*, with Darius Milhaud (Paris, 1924)

—, *Le Coq et l'Arlequin*, preface by Georges Auric (Paris, reissued 1993)

—, *La difficulté d'être* (Paris, 1947); *The Difficulty of Being*, trans. Elizabeth Sprigge, introduction by Ned Rorem (New York, 1967)

—, *Modigliani* (London, 1950)

—, *The journals of Jean Cocteau*, ed. and trans. with introduction by Wallace Fowlie (London, 1957)

—, *My Contemporaries*, ed. Margaret Crosland (London, 1967)

—, Valéry, Paul and Lifar, Serge, *Serge Lifar à l'Opéra* (Paris, 1943)

see also Valéry, Paul

Cogniat, Raymond, *Décors de théâtre* (exhibition catalogue) Galerie de France (Paris, 1930)

—, *Ballets russes: Bakst et Larionow—Décors du Théâtre* (Paris, 1930)

—, *Les Décorateurs de Théâtre* (Paris, 1955)

—, *Braque* (Paris, 1970)

see also *Evolution du Décor, L'*, etc.

Cohen, S. J., *Apollon Musagète* in *Stravinsky and the Dance: A survey of ballet production 1910–1960* (New York, 1962)

Collection des plus beaux numéros de "Comoedia Illustré" et des programmes consacrés aux Ballets et Galas Russes depuis le début à Paris 1909–1921 (Paris, 1922)

Conlan, Barnett D., *Roerich* (Riga, 1939)

—, *Nicholas Roerich: A Master of the Mountains* (Libert, Indiana, n.d., similar to above)

Cooper, Douglas, *Juan Gris, letters 1913–1927* (London, 1956)

—, *Fernand Léger: Dessins de guerre 1915–1916* (Paris, 1956)

—, *Picasso Theatre* (London, 1968)

Coton, A. V., *A Prejudice for Ballet* (London, 1977)

Courthion, Pierre, *Georges Rouault* (London, 1962)

Craig, Edward Gordon, *Gordon Craig on Movement and Dance*, ed. Arnold Rood (London, 1977)

and see Balance, John; Smith, C. G.

Crisp, Clement, *see* Clarke, Mary

Croce, Arlene, "Bronislava Nijinska" in *Ballet Review* vol 4 no 2 (New York, 1972)

Crosland, Margaret, *Jean Cocteau* (London, 1955)

Daix, Pierre, *Picasso: life and art*, trans. Olivia Emmet (London, 1994)

Danilova, Alexandra, *Choura* (London, 1987)

Davidova, M. V., *Ocherki istorii russkogo teatralno–dekoratsionnogo iskusstva XVII–nachala XX veka* (*Essays on the history of Russian theatre design from the eighteenth to the beginning of the twentieth centuries*) (Moscow, 1974)

Debussy, Claude, *Lettres de Claude Debussy à son éditeur* (Paris, 1927)

Decter, Jacqueline, *Nicholas Roerich* (New York and London, 1989)

de Francia, Peter, *Fernand Léger* (Newhaven and London, 1983)

de Maré, Rolf et al., *Les Ballets Suédois* (Paris, 1931)

de Marly, Diana, *Costume on the stage 1600–1940* (London, 1982)

de Mille, Agnes, *The Book of the Dance* (New York, 1963)

Depaulis, Jacques, *Ida Rubinstein* (Paris, 1995)

Derouet, Christian and Lehni, Nadine, *Jeanne Bucher: Une galerie d'avant–garde 1925–1946. De Max Ernst à de Staël* (exhibition catalogue) (Strasbourg and Geneva, 1994)

De Saint–Georges, Théophile Gautier et Coraly [sic], *Giselle ou les Wilis* (Paris, 1841)

Detaille, Georges and Mulys, Gérard, *Les Ballets de Monte–Carlo 1911–1944* (Paris, 1954)

de Valois, Ninette, *Invitation to the ballet* (London, 1937)

—, *Come Dance with Me: a memoir 1898–1956* (London, 1957)

Devroye–Stilz, Anne, *André Bauchant* (exhibition catalogue) Musée International d'Art Naif Anatole Jakovsky (Nice, 1987)

Diaghilev, Serge, *see* Zilberstein, I. S. and Samkov, V. A.

Dobuzhinsky, Mstislav, "O Bakste (iz moikh vospominanii)" ("About Bakst [from my reminiscences]") in *Segodnya* (*Today*) (Riga, 6 January 1925)

—, *Vospominaniya* (*Reminiscences*) (New York, 1976)

Docherty, Peter (ed.), *Design for Performance: From Diaghilev to the Pet Shop Boys* (London, 1996)

Dolin, Anton, *Divertissement* (London, 1931)

—, *Autobiography* (London, 1960)

—, *The Sleeping Ballerina: The story of Olga Spessivtseva* (London, 1966)

—, "*Les Biches*: a misconception" in *The Dancing Times* (London, February 1980) p 323

—, *Last Words* (London, 1985)

Drummond, John, *Speaking of Daighilev* (London, 1997)

Duke, Vernon [Dukelsky, Vladimir], *Passport to Paris* (Boston, 1955)

Dukelsky, Vladimir, *Poslaniya* (*Epistles*) (Munich, 1962)

Dupin, Jacques, *Joán Miró* (Paris, 1961)

Durand, Jacques, *Quelques Souvenirs d'un Editeur de Musique* (Paris, 1928)

Durey, Jacques, *see* Léal, Brigitte

E. O. H., "The Art of the Theatre: The Russian Ballet" in *The Studio* Vol 77 No 317 (London, 15 August 1919) pp 107–11

Edelstein, Hermine, "Influence of Modern Stage Setting on Music of Future" in *Musical America* (New York, 9 September 1916)

Ekstrom, Parmenia Migel, *Nicholas Roerich* (exhibition catalogue) (New York, 1974)

see also Migel, Parmenia

Eluard, Paul, *A Pablo Picasso* (Paris, 1947)

Select Bibliography

Ernst, Max, *Beyond Painting and other writings by the Artist and his friends* (New York, 1948)

—, "An informal life of M. E." in *Max Ernst* (exhibition catalogue) (London, 1961)

Ernst, Sergei, *N. K. Rerikh* (Petrograd, 1918)

Etkind, Mark, *A. N. Benua i russkaya khudozhestvennaya kultura* (*A. N. Benois and Russian artistic culture*) (Leningrad, 1989)

"Evolution du décor, L'opinion de M. Léon Bakst. Réponse à l'énquête de Raymond Cogniat" in *Comoedia Illustré* (Paris, 3 September 1923)

Fernand Léger et le Spectacle (exhibition catalogue), *see* Hédel–Samson, Brigitte

Flam, Jack D., *Matisse on Art* (Oxford, 1978)

Flint, Janet Altic, *Boris Anisfeldt: Twenty Years of Designs for the Theater* (exhibition catalogue) (Washington D.C., 1971)

Fokine, Michel, *Memoirs of a ballet master*, trans. Vitale Fokine (London, 1961)

—, *Protiv techeniya. Vospominaniya baletmeistera. Stati, pisma* (*Against the tide. Memoirs of a ballet master. Articles, letters*) (Leningrad and Moscow, 1962). A fuller version of above

Fuerst, Walter René and Hume, Samuel J., *XX century stage decoration* (New York, 1929, reissued 1967)

Fülöp–Miller, René and Gregor, Joseph, *The Russian Theatre* (London, 1930, reissued New York, 1968)

Gabo, Naum, *see* Nash, Steven A. and Markert, Jörn

Gadan, Francis and Maillard, Robert (gen. eds.), *A Dictionary of Modern Ballet* (London, 1959)

Garafola, Lynn, *Diaghilev's Ballets Russes* (New York, 1989)

Garaudy, Roger, *Pour un réalisme du XXᵉ siècle. Dialogue posthume avec Fernand Léger* (Paris, 1968)

García–Márquez, Vicente, *The Ballets Russes: Colonel de Basil's Ballets Russes de Monte Carlo, 1932–1952* (London, 1992)

—, *Massine* (London, 1996)

Gauthier, Maximilien, *André Bauchant* (Paris, 1943)

—, *Survage* (Paris, 1953)

Gautier, Théophile, "Omphale" in *Journal des gens du monde* (Paris, 1834)

—, *and see* De Saint-Georges

Gelmersen, Ludwig A. (ed.), *Ezhegodnik Imperatorskikh Teatrov, vipusk XIII sezon 1902–1903* (*Imperial Theaters Annual, issue XIII season 1902–1903*) (St Petersburg, 1903)

George, Waldemar, "Les Ballets de 1933" in *Formes* No 33 (Paris, 1933), pp 377–9

Georges–Michel, Michel, "Ballets Russes" in *Les Oeuvres Libres* No 13 (Paris, July 1922)

—, *Ballets Russes: histoire anecdotique* (Paris, 1923)

—, "Diaghilev et les peintres" in *L'Art Vivant* (Paris, May 1930) pp 718–21

—, *From Renoir to Picasso* (London, 1957)

Gilyarovskaya, N., *F. F. Fedorovsky* (Moscow and Leningrad, 1946)

Gimferrer, Pere, *The roots of Miró* (Barcelona, 1993)

Goerg, Charles, "Un manteau de Matisse pour 'Le Chant du Rossignol'" in *Revue mensuelle des musées et collections de la ville de Genève* no 264 (Geneva, April 1986)

Gold, Arthur and Fizdale, Robert, *Misia* (New York, 1980)

Goncharova, Natalia, "The Metamorphosis of the the ballet *Les Noces*" in *Leonardo* Vol 12 (London, 1979) pp 137–143

Gontcharova, Nathalie; Larionov, Michel and Vorms, Pierre, *Les Ballets Russes de Serge de Diaghilev et la décoration théâtrale* (Paris, 1955)

Goode, Gerald, *The Book of Ballets*, New York 1939

Goodman, G. E., "Stage Designs at the Russian Exhibition: Notes on Decor" in *The Dancing Times* (London, July 1935) pp 402–3

—, "Notes on Decor: Colonel de Basil's Ballets Russes" in *The Dancing Times* (London, August 1935) pp. 527–8

—, "Twenty–five years of Decor" in *The Dancing Times* (London, October 1935) pp 45–8

—, "Notes on Decor: The Return of Leon Bakst" in *The Dancing Times* (London, July 1936) pp 412–3

Grabar, I. E. (ed.), *Istoria Russkogo Iskusstvo* (*History of Russian Art*) vol. X book 2 (section by Davidova, M. V. on theatre design) (Moscow, 1969)

Gray, Camilla, *The great experiment: Russian art 1863–1922* (London, 1962)

Green, Christopher, *Cubism and its enemies* (Newhaven and London, 1987)

—, with von Maur, Karin and Perouet, Christian, *Juan Gris* (exhibition catalogue) (London, 1992)

Grigoriev, S. L., *The Diaghilev Ballet 1909–1929*, trans. Vera Bowen (London, 1953)

Guest, Ann Hutchinson and Jeschke, Claudia, *Nijinsky's Faune Restored* (Philadelphia, 1990)

Gusarova, A., *Mir Iskusstva* (*The World of Art*) (Leningrad, 1972)

Häger, Bengt, *Modern Swedish Ballet* (exhibition catalogue) Victoria and Albert Museum (London, 1970)

—, *Ballets Suédois*, trans. Ruth Sherman (London, 1990)

Halicka, Alice, *Hier: Souvenirs* (Paris, 1946)

Hansen, Robert C., *Scenic and costume design for the Ballets Russes* (Ann Arbor, 1985)

Hanson, Lawrence and Elizabeth, *Prokofiev: The Prodigal Son* (London, 1964)

Harewood, The Earl of, *Kobbé's Complete Opera Book* (London, 1987)

Harvey, John W., *The Eurythmics of Jaques–Dalcroze* (London, 1917)

Haskell, Arnold, *Balletomania* (London, 1934)

—, *Ballet* (Harmondsworth, 1954)

—, *Ballet Russe* (London, 1968)

—, in collaboration with Walter Nouvel, *Diaghileff: His artistic and private life* (London, 1935, reprinted 1955)

Hédel–Samson, Brigitte et al., *Fernand Léger et le spectacle* (exhibition catalogue) (Paris, 1995)

Howard, Deborah, "A sumptuous revival" in *Apollo* (London, April 1970) pp 301–8

Hyland, Douglas K. S. and McPherson, Heather, *Marie Laurencin: artist and muse* (exhibition catalogue) (Birmingham, Alabama, 1989)

Ingleby, Richard, *Christopher Wood* (London, 1995)

Jaques–Dalcroze, Emile, *Rhythm, Music and Education* (London, 1921)

Jarintzov, N., "Un peintre russe: Nicolas K. Roerich" in *Le Studio* Vol 79 No 325 (London, April 1920) pp 60–9

Jullian, René, *Fernand Léger 1881–1955* (Basel, 1970)

Kahane, Martine, *Les Ballets Russes à l'Opéra* (Paris, 1992)

Kahnweiler, Daniel–Henry, *Juan Gris: his life and work*, trans. Douglas Cooper (London, 1947)

Karsavina, Tamara, *Theatre Street* (London, 1954)

Kean, Beverly Whitney, *French Painters, Russian Collectors* (London, rev. 1994)

Kirby, Michael, *Futurist Performance* (New York, 1971)

Kirstein, Lincoln, *Fokine* (London, 1934)

—, "Balanchine Trio" in *The Dancing Times* (London, January 1973) pp 186–7

—, *Four Centuries of Ballet: Fifty Masterworks* (New York, 1984)

Kochno, Boris, *Le Ballet* (Paris, 1954)

—, *Diaghilev and the Ballets Russes* (New York, 1970)

—, *Diaghilev et les Ballets Russes* (Paris, 1973)

—, *Christian Bérard* (Paris, 1987 / London, 1988)

Kodicek, Ann (ed.), *Diaghilev: creator of the Ballets Russes* (exhibition catalogue) (London, 1996)

Koegler, Horst, *The Concise Oxford Dictionary of Ballet* (Oxford, 1987)

Kogan, D., *Konstantin Korovin* (Moscow, 1964)

Kolodin, Irving, *The Metropolitan Opera* (New York, 1936)

Koltai, Ralph, "Theatre design – the exploration of space" in *Royal Society of Arts Journal* No 5368 Vol CXXXV (London, March 1987) pp 298–309

Komisarjevsky, Theodore and Simonson, Lee, *Settings and costumes for the modern stage*, Studio winter number (London, 1933)

Kostilev, N., "Nash balet v Parizhe" ("Our ballet in Paris") in *Apollon* No 9 (St Petersburg, 1913–14)

Krasovskaya, Vera, *Russkii baletnii teatr nachalo xx veka* (*Russian ballet at the beginning of the 20th century*): vol 1 *Khoreografi* (*Choreographers*) (Leningrad, 1971); vol 2 *Tanzovchiki* (*Dancers*) (Leningrad, 1972)

—, *Nijinsky* (published in Russian, Leningrad, 1974), trans. John E. Bowlt (New York, 1979)

Krauss, Rosalind and Rowell, Margit, *Joan Miró: Magnetic fields* (exhibition catalogue) Solomon Guggenheim Foundation (New York, 1972)

Labrusse, Rémi, "Matisse's second visit to London and his collaboration with the 'Ballets Russes'," *The Burlington Magazine*, Vol CXXXIX No 1134 (London, September 1997), pp 588–99

Lafranchis, Jean, *Marcoussis, sa vie, son oeuvre* (Paris, 1961)

La Jeunesse, Ernst, *Des soirs, des gens, des choses . . . (1909–1911)* (Paris, n.d.)

Lanchner, Carolyn, *Joan Miró* (New York, 1993)

Lapshina, N., *Mir Iskusstva* (Moscow, 1977)

Larson, Orville K., *Scene Design in the American Theatre from 1915–1960* (Fayetteville, London, Arkansas, 1989)

Lassaigne, Jacques, *Miró* (Lausanne, 1963)

Laurent, Jean and Sazonova, Julie, *Serge Lifar: Rénovateur du ballet français* (Paris, 1960)

Laver, James, "The Russian Ballet: a retrospect" in *The Studio* I: Vol 93 No 41 (London, May 1927) pp 307–11; II: Vol 94 No 413 (London, August 1927) pp 100–8

—, *Taste and Fashion* (London, 1937)

Léal, Brigitte et al., *Picasso: Le Tricorne* (exhibition catalogue) (Lyon, 1992)

Lederman, Minna (ed.), *Stravinsky in the Theatre* (New York, 1975)

Legat, Nicolas, *Ballet Russe*, trans. with a foreword by Sir Paul Dukes (London, 1939)

Léger, Fernand, *Une correspondance de Guerre à Louis Poughon, 1914–1918*, ed. Christian Derouet (Cahiers du Musée National d'Art Moderne) (Paris, 1990)

Léon–Martin, Louis, "Georges Rouault" in *Art et Décoration* (Paris, April 1930) pp 111 4

Lesure, François, *see* Stravinsky, Igor

Levinson, André, *Bakst: the story of the artist's life* (London, 1923)

—, *L'Oeuvre de Léon Bakst pour La Belle au Bois Dormant* (Paris, 1922) (English edition, London, 1923)

—, "Stravinsky and the Dance" in *Theatre Arts Monthly* vol 8 (New York, November 1924) pp 741–54

—, *1929, Danse d'Aujourd'hui* (Paris, 1990)

—, *Les visages de la danse* (Paris 1933)

—, *Serge Lifar: Destin d'un danseur* (Paris 1934)

Levy, Julien, *Memoir of an Art Gallery* (New York, 1977)

Leymarie, Jean, *Picasso: The Artist of the Century*, trans. James Emmons (New York, 1973)

—, *and see* Cassou, Jean

Lieven, Prince Peter, *The Birth of Ballets–Russes* (London, 1936)

Lifar, Serge, *Du temps que j'avais faim* (Paris, 1935)

—, *Ballet: Traditional to Modern* (London, 1938)

—, *Serge Diaghilev: His life, his work, his legend* (London, 1940)

—, *A l'aube de mon destin: chez Diaghilev, sept ans aux Ballets Russes* (Paris, 1949)

—, *The Three Graces: Anna Pavlova, Tamara Karsavina, Olga Spessivtzeva, the legends and the truth* (London, 1959)

—, *Ma Vie: from Kiev to Kiev*, trans. James Holman Mason (London, 1970)

see also Sotheby & Co; Valéry, Paul

for a complete bibliography, *see* Appendix D

Lissim, Simon, "Léon Bakst, ses décors et costumes de théâtre" in *L'Oeuvre* No 2 (Paris, March 1924) pp 38–9

—, "Bakst as I remember him" *see* Lister, Raymond, *The Muscovite Peacock*

Lister, Raymond, "Bakst" in *Apollo*, vol 52 No 307 (London, September 1950) pp 90–2

—, *The Muscovite Peacock: a study of the art of Léon Bakst* (Cambridge, England, 1954)

Lobet, Marcel, *Le Ballet Français d'Aujourd'hui* (Brussels, n.d.)

Lockspeiser, Edward, *Debussy: His life and mind* (London, 1965)

Loguine, Tatiana (ed.), *Gontcharova et Larionov* (Paris, 1971)

Lomonosov, M. V., *Polnoe sobranie sochinenii* (*Complete works*, Vol 8, poetry, oratorical prose, epitaphs 1732–1764) (Moscow, 1959)

Lynham, Deryck, *Ballet, Then and Now* (London, 1947)

Macdonald, Nesta, *Diaghilev observed* (New York/London, 1975)

Magriel, Paul (ed.), *Nijinsky: An Illustrated Monograph* (New York, 1946)

Mannin, Ethel, *Confessions and Impressions* (London, 1938)

Marcoussis, Louis, "La gravure à l'eau–forte" in *Les artistes à Paris* (Paris 1937), reprinted in Lafranchis, Jean, *Marcoussis*

Markert, Jöru, *see* Nash, Steven A.

Markova, Alicia, *Markova Remembers* (London, 1986)

Martin, Paul-René et al, *Serge Lifar: Une vie pour la danse* (exhibition catalogue) (Lausanne, 1986)

Mason, Francis, *see* Balanchine, George

—, "Bronislava Nijinska: Dancers Speak" in *Ballet Review* (New York, Spring 1990)

Massine, Leonide, *My life in ballet* (London, 1968)

Mauclair, Camille, "Les Ballets Russes, Russie (Art Moderne)" in *L'Art et les Artistes* (Paris, November 1917) pp 43–7

Max Ernst, see Ernst, Max

Mayer, Charles S., *Bakst* (introduction to exhibition catalogue) Fine Art Society (London, 1976)

Michaut, P. and Kuhlmann, A. E., "Les Ballets Russes de M. Serge de Diaghilev" in *L'Art Vivant* (Paris, 15 December 1929) pp 718–21

Migel, Parmenia, "The Artistic Genius Behind *Les Biches*: Bronislava Nijinska" in *Dance Magazine* (New York, December 1982) pp 98–106

—, *see also* Ekstrom, Parmenia Migel

Milhau, Denis, *Picasso et le Théâtre* (exhibition catalogue) (Toulouse, 1965)

Milhaud, Darius, *Notes without music* (New York, 1953)

Miró, Joan, *Selected writings and interviews*, ed. Margrit Rowell (London, 1987)

Moderwell, Hiram Kelly, "Music of the Russian Ballet" in *The New Republic* (New York, 22 January 1916)

Monteux, Doris G., *It's all in the music* (New York, 1965)

Morrell, Ottoline, *Ottoline: The Early Memoirs of Ottoline Morrell*, ed. Robert Gathorne–Hardy (London, 1963)

Morton, Andrew, *The Lamberts* (London, 1986)

Moussinac, Léon, *La Décoration Théâtrale* (Paris, 1922)

Murray, Alden, "A Problematical Pavilion: Alexandre Benois' First Ballet" in *Russian History/Histoire Russe* 8, pts 1–2 (1981) (Tempe, Arizona, 1981) pp 23–52

Myers, Rollo H., *Ravel: life and works* (London, 1960)

Nabokov, Nicolas, *Old Friends and New Music* (London, 1951)

Nash, Steven A. and Markert, Jörn (eds.), *Naum Gabo: sixty years of constructivism* (exhibition catalogue) (Munich, 1985)

Näslund, Erik, *Les Ballets Suédois* (Paris, 1994)

—, *Överdådets Konst* (*The Art of Extravagance*) (exhibition catalogue) (Stockholm, 1996)

Nectoux, Jean–Michel, *L'Après–midi d'un faune* (exhibition catalogue) Les Dossiers du Musée d'Orsay 29 (Paris, 1989)

Nijinska, Bronislava, "Reflections about the production of *Les Biches* and *Hamlet* in Markova–Dolin Ballets," trans. Lydia Lopokova, in *The Dancing Times* (London, February 1937) pp 617–20

—, "Creation of 'Les Noces:' Bronislava Nijinska," trans. and introduced by Jean M. Serafetinides and Irina Nijinska, in *Dance Magazine* (New York, December 1974) pp 58–61

—, *Early Memoirs*, trans. Irina Nijinska and Jean Rawlinson (London, 1982)

Nijinsky, Romola, *Nijinsky and The Last Years of Nijinsky* (London, 1980)

Nijinsky, Tamara, *Nijinsky and Romola* (London, 1991)

Nikitina, Alice, *Nikitina*, transl. Moura Budberg (London, 1959)

Olson, Ruth and Chanin, Abraham, *Naum Gabo/Antoine Pevsner* (catalogue of the Museum of Modern Art) (New York, 1948)

Oswald, Genevieve et al., *Stravinsky and the Dance* (exhibition catalogue) (New York, 1962); *see Stravinsky and the Dance*

Ostwald, Peter, *Vaslav Nijinsky* (London, 1991)

Palmer, Mary Carpenter, "Théophile Gautier and Diaghilev's Russian Ballets" in *Wadsworth Atheneum Bulletin*, Winter 1966 (Hartford, 1966) pp 9–24

Pankratova, E. A., *Russkoe teatralno–dekoratzionnoe iskusstvo kontsa XIX nachala XX veka* (*Russian theatre design at the end of the nineteenth and beginning of the twentieth centuries*) (Leningrad, 1983)

Pann, E., "Russkii sezon v Parizhe" ("The Russian season in Paris") in *Maski* No 7–8 (St Petersburg, 1912–13) pp 58–75

Select Bibliography

Parnack, Valentin, *Gontcharova Larionov: L'Art décoratif théâtral moderne* (Paris, 1919)

Parton, Anthony, *Mikhail Larionov and the Russian Avant–Garde* (London 1993)

Pasi, Mario, *Le Ballet* (Paris, 1989)

Péladan, Joséphin, "Les Arts du Théâtre: Un Maître du Costume et du Décor: Léon Bakst" in *L'Art Décoratif* vol 25 (Paris, 1911)

Penrose, Roland, *Picasso: his life and work* (London, 1981)

Percival, John, *The World of Diaghilev* (New York, 1971, revised London, 1979)

—, "Dance to the music of time" in *The Times Saturday Review* (London, 25 August 1990)

—, "The forgotten company" in *Dance and Dancers* (London, April 1991) pp 32–3

Peters, Arthur King et al., *Jean Cocteau and the French scene* (New York, 1984)

Pétry, Claude et al., *Paul Colin et les spectacles* (exhibition catalogue) (Nancy, 1994)

Pevsner, Alexei, *A biographical sketch of my brothers Naum Gabo and Antoine Pevsner* (Amsterdam, 1964)

Picasso: Le Tricorne, see Léal, Brigitte

Platonov, Y., *Fedor Fedorovitch Fedorovsky* (Moscow and Leningrad, 1948)

Poe, Edgar Allan, *Tales of Mystery, Imagination and Humour* (London, n.d.)

Polunin, Vladimir, *The Continental Method of Scene Painting*, ed. Cyril W. Beaumont (London, 1927, repr. 1980)

Poulenc, Francis, "Francis Poulenc on his ballets" in *Ballet* vol 2 no 4 (London, September 1946)

—, *My friends and myself* (conversations assembled by Stéphane Audel), trans. James Harding (London, 1978)

—, *"Echo and Source" Selected correspondence 1915–1963*, trans. and ed. Sidney Buckland (London, 1991)

Pozharskaya, M. N., *Russkoe teatralno–dekoratsionnoe iskusstvo kontsa XIX–nachala XX veka* (*Russian theatre design at the end of the nineteenth and beginning of the twentieth centuries*) (Moscow, 1970)

—, *The Russian Seasons in Paris: Sketches of the Scenery and Costumes, 1908–1929* (Moscow, 1988), dual text Russian and English. Also published in a reduced format as Pozharskaya, Militza and Volodina, Tatiana, *The Art of the Ballets Russes: the Russian Seasons in Paris 1908–1929* (London 1990); this is the version referred to in the catalogue entries

Pritchard, Frances, *Diaghilev's Russian Ballet in Manchester* (exhibition leaflet) (Manchester, 1994)

Pritchard, Jane et al., *Les Ballets 1933* (exhibition catalogue) (Brighton, 1987)

Prokofiev, Sergei, *Soviet Diary 1927 and other writings*, trans. and ed. Oleg Prokofiev (London, 1991)

Propert, W. A., *The Russian Ballet in Western Europe 1909–1920* (London, 1921)

—, *The Russian Ballet 1921–1929* (London, 1931)

Proujan, Irina, *Léon Bakst. Set and costume designs, book illustrations, paintings and graphic works* (Harmondsworth, 1987)

Pruzhan, Irina N., *Lev Samoilovitch Bakst* (Leningrad, 1975)

Racster, Olga, *The Master of the Russian Ballet (The Memoirs of Cav. Enrico Cecchetti)* (London, 1923)

Rambert, Marie, *Quicksilver* (London, 1972)

Reade, Brian, *Ballet Designs and Illustrations, 1581–1940* (London, 1967)

Renault–Bauchant, Francoise (in collaboration with Geneviève Ritzenthaler), *André Bauchant* (Tours, 1994)

Ricketts, Charles, *Self Portrait taken from the letters and journals,* ed. Cecil Lewis (London, 1939)

Rimsky–Korsakov, Nikolai, *My musical life* (London, 1974)

Rischbieter, Henning (ed.), *Art and the Stage in the 20th century* (Greenwich, Connecticut, 1969)

Roberts, Mary Fanton, "The New Russian Stage, a Blaze of Colour: What the genius of Léon Bakst has done to vivify productions which Combine Ballet, Music and Drama" in *Craftsman* vol 29 (New York, 1915) pp 257–69, 322

Robinson, Harlow, *Serge Prokofiev* (London, 1987)

Roland–Manuel, *Maurice Ravel et son oeuvre dramatique* (Paris, 1928)

Rood, Arnold, *see* Craig, Edward Gordon

Rose, Sir Francis, *Saying Life* (London, 1961)

—, *Gertrude Stein and Painting* (London, 1968)

see also *Sir Francis Rose*

Rose, June, *Modigliani: the pure bohemian* (New York, 1991)

Rosse, Herman, *Theatre Arts Monthly* (New York, 1924)

Russell, John, *Max Ernst: Life and Work* (London, 1967)

Sacks, Lois, "Fernand Léger and the Ballets Suédois" in *Apollo* (London, 1970) pp 463–8

Salmina–Haskell, Larissa, *Russian Drawings in the Ashmolean Museum* (Oxford, 1970)

—, *Russian drawings in the Victoria and Albert Museum* (London, 1972)

Sazonova, Julie, *see* Laurent, Jean

Schaettel, Charles, *André Bauchant* (exhibition catalogue) Musée des Beaux–Arts de Tours (Tours, 1991)

Schaikevitch, André, *Serge Lifar et le Destin du Ballet de l'Opéra* (Paris, 1971)

Schneider, Marcel, *Henri Sauguet* (Paris, 1959)

Schneider, Pierre, *Matisse* (Paris, 1984)

Schouvaloff, Alexander, *The Thyssen–Bornemisza Collection: Set and costume designs for ballet and theatre* (London, 1987)

—, *Theatre on Paper* (London, 1990)

—, *Léon Bakst: The Theatre Art* (London, 1991)

—, and Borovsky, Victor, *Stravinsky on stage* (London, 1982)

Sert, Misia, *Two or Three Muses*, trans. Moura Budberg (London, 1953)

Shead, Richard, *Music in 1920s* (London, 1976)

—, *Constant Lambert* (London, 1973 rev. c. 1986)

—, *Ballets Russes* (Seacaucus, New Jersey, 1989)

Simmonds, Harvey (ed.), *Choreography by George Balanchine: A catalogue of works* (New York, 1983)

Simonson, Lee, *The Stage is Set* (New York, 1932)

—, *The designer in the theatre* (introduction to exhibition catalogue) Museum of Modern Art (New York, 1934)

see also Komisarjevsky, Théodore

Siordet, Gerard C., "Léon Bakst's Designs for Scenery and Costume" in *The Studio* Vol 60 No 247 (London, 15 October 1913) pp 3–6

Sir Francis Rose 1909–1979 A retrospective (exhibition catalogue) England and Co (London, 1988)

Slonimsky, Yuri, "Balanchine: The Early Years" in *Ballet Review* vol 5 no 3 (New York, 1975–6)

Smith, C. G. (pseudonym of Edward Gordon Craig), "This Little Theatre: Bakst" in *The Mask* no 11 (Florence, 1925) pp 68–70

Soby, James Thrall, *Tchelitchew* (exhibition catalogue) Museum of Modern Art (New York, 1942)

—, *Georges Rouault* (exhibition catalogue) Museum of Modern Art (New York, 1945)

Sokolova, Lydia, *Dancing for Diaghilev,* ed. Richard Buckle (London, 1960)

Solodovnikov, A., *F. F. Fedorovsky* (Moscow, 1956)

Sotheby and Co., *Costumes and Curtains from Diaghilev and de Basil Ballets* (sales catalogues) (London, 17 July 1968 and 19 December 1969). Reissued as a single volume under the same title with a new introduction by Richard Buckle (London, 1972)

—, *Costumes and Curtains from The Diaghilev and de Basil Ballets* (sale catalogue) (London, 3 March 1973)

—, *Ballet Material and Manuscripts from the Serge Lifar Collection* (London, 9 May 1984)

—, *Collection Boris Kochno* (Monaco, 11–12 October 1991)

—, *The Diaghilev and Ballets Russes Costumes from Castle Howard* (London, 14 December 1995)

Souhami, Diana, *Gertrude and Alice* (London, 1991)

Souriau, Etienne et al., *Le Sacre du Printemps de Nijinsky* (Paris, 1990)

Spencer, Charles, *Léon Bakst* (London, 1973)

—, with contributions by Philip Dyer and Martin Battersby, *The World of Serge Diaghilev* (London, 1974)

Spies, Werner, *Max Ernst: Frottages* (London, 1969)

—, *Max Ernst Oeuvre–Katalog Werke 1925–1929* (Cologne, 1976)

Stanciu–Reiss, Françoise et al., *Nijinsky* (exhibition catalogue) (Paris, 1989)

Stanislavsky, Constantin, *My Life in Art,* trans. J. J. Robbins (New York, 1956)

Steegmuller, Francis, *Cocteau: A biography* (London, 1986)

Stein, Gertrude, *The autobiography of Alice B. Toklas* (London, 1966)

Stravinsky and the Dance: A survey of Ballet Productions, 1910–1962 (published in conjunction with exhibition *New York 1962*) (New York, 1962)

Stravinsky and the Theatre: A catalogue of Decor and Costume Designs for Stage Productions of his works, 1910–1962 (published in conjunction with exhibition *New York 1962*) (New York, 1962)

Stravinsky, Igor, *Chroniques de ma vie* (Paris, 1935, 2 vols); *Chronicle of my life* (London, 1936)

—, *Selected Correspondence* vol II (ed. and with commentaries by Robert Craft) (London, 1984)

—, *"Le Sacre du Printemps" Dossier de Presse/Press book,* compiled by Francois Lesure (Geneva, 1988)

—, and Craft, Robert, *Conversations with Stravinsky* (London, 1959)

—, *Memories and Commentaries* (London, 1960)

—, *Expositions and Developments* (London, 1962)

and see Tappolet, Claude

Stravinsky, Vera and Craft, Robert, *Stravinsky in Pictures and Documents* (New York, 1978)

Svetlov, Valerian, *Sovremennii balet: izdano pri neposredsvennom uchastii L. S. Baksta (The contemporary ballet: edited with the direct participation of L. S. Bakst)* (St Petersburg, 1911); *Le ballet contemporain; ouvrage édité avec la collaboration de L. Bakst* (St Petersburg, 1912)

—, "Favn" ("The Faun") in *Peterburgskaya Gazeta* (St Petersburg, 27 May 1912)

—, "Les peintres décorateurs Russes" in *Comoedia Illustré* (Paris, 5 June 1913)

Taper, Bernard, *Balanchine* (London, 1964)

Tappolet, Claude (ed.), *Correspondance Ernest Ansermet–Igor Stravinsky* (Geneva, 1990)

Taruskin, Richard, *Stravinsky and the Russian Traditions* (Berkeley and Los Angeles, 1996, 2 vols)

Teliakovsky, Vladimnir, *Vospominaniya (Reminiscences)* (Leningrad, Moscow, 1965)

Terry, Ellen, *The Russian Ballet* (London, 1913)

Tolstoy, Sophia, *The Diaries of Sophia Tolstoy* trans. Cathy Porter (New York, 1985)

Tugendhold, J., "Russkii sezon v Parizhe" ("The Russian season in Paris") in *Apollon* No 10 (St Petersburg, September 1910) pp 5–23

Tyler, Parker, *The Divine Comedy of Pavel Tchelitchew* (London, 1967)

Vaillat, Léandre, "Les décors russes" in *L'Art et les Artistes* (Paris, August 1910)

—, "Nouveaux propos sur les décors" in *L'Art et les Artistes* no 13 (Paris, September 1911) pp 479–88

Valéry, Paul, Cocteau, Jean and Lifar, Serge, *Serge Lifar à l'Opéra* (Paris, 1943)

van den Toorn, Pieter C., *Stravinsky and "The Rite of Spring"* (Oxford, 1987)

Vaudoyer, Jean–Louis, *Léon Bakst* (introduction to exhibition catalogue) Musée des Arts Décoratifs (Paris, 1911)

—, "Léon Bakst" in *Art et Décoration* vol 29 (Paris, 1911) pp 33–46

—, "Léon Bakst et les Ballets Russes" in *Nouvelles Littéraires* (Paris, 3 January 1923)

—, "Impressions et souvenirs" in *L'Art Vivant* (Paris, 15 December 1929) pp 709–10

Vershinin, I. Y., *Ranie Baleti Stravinskogo (The Early Ballets of Stravinsky)* (Moscow, 1967)

Vlassova, R. I., *Russkoe teatralno–dekoratzionnoe iskusstvo nachala XX veka (Russian theatre design at the beginning of the twentieth century)* (Leningrad, 1984)

Volta, Ornella, *Satie et la danse* (Paris, 1992)

von Maur, Karin, "Music and Theatre in the Work of Juan Gris," *see* Green, Christopher, *Juan Gris*

Walker, Kathrine Sorley, *De Basil's Ballets Russes* (London, 1982)

Wallace, Jo–Ann, *see* Elliott, Bridget

Walsh, Stephen, *The Music of Stravinsky* (London, 1988)

Warnod, André, "Les peintres et les ballets russes" in *La Revue Musicale* (Paris, 1 December 1930) pp 78–89

White, Eric Walter, *Stravinsky: The composer and his works* (Berkeley, 1979)

Whitworth, Geoffrey, *The Art of Nijinsky* (London, 1913)

Williams, Peter, "Les Biches" in *Dance and Dancers* (London, January 1965) pp 11–17

—, *Masterpieces of Ballet Design* (Oxford, 1981)

Wilson, G. B. L., *A Dictionary of Ballet* (Harmondsworth, 1957)

Windham, Donald, "The Stage and Ballet Designs of Pavel Tchelitchev" in *Dance Index* Vol III No 1–2 (New York, January–February 1944)

Wright, Sir Peter et al., *The Designers: Pushing the boundaries—Advancing the Dance* (exhibition catalogue) (London, 1995)

Yakovleva, Elena, *Teatralno-Dekoratsionnoe Iskusstvo N. K. Rerikha (The Theater Art of N. K. Roerich)* (St Petersburg, 1996)

Zilberstein, I. S. and Samkov, V. A. (eds.), *Sergei Diaghilev i Russkoe Iskusstvo (Serge Diaghilev and Russian Art)* 2 vols (Moscow, 1982)

Photographic Credits

The author and publishers would like to thank the following for their kind permission to reproduce photographs.

Color

All set and costume designs photographed by David Stansbury

All costumes photographed by Cathy Carver, except those with inventory numbers beginning 1968, photographed by Joseph Szaszfai

Black-and-white

The Art Institute of Chicago, Gift of Patricia and Frank Kolodny in memory of Julien Levy

p 13

Bibliothèque nationale, Paris

pp 28, 29, 39, 41 (both), 45, 48 (both), 52, 75, 106, 109, 149, 173, 182, 187, 193, 234, 239, 272, 278, 284, 299, 324

British Library

p 216

Collection on the Russian Ballets of Serge Pavlovitch Diaghilev formed by Howard D. Rothschild, The Harvard Theatre Collection, The Houghton Library

pp 18, 258, 310

Dance Collection, The New York Public Library for the Performing Arts: Astor, Lenox and Tilden Foundation

pp 33, 40, 44, 50, 68, 120, 122, 124, 135, 158, 176

SBM Monte Carlo, Département Coordination et Préservation du Patrimoine Historique

pp 51, 154, 157, 204

Courtesy of the Victoria and Albert Museum Picture Library

p 19

Wadsworth Atheneum Archives

p 16